Teacher's Wraparound Edition

Glencoe
Computer Applications and Keyboarding

Glencoe McGraw-Hill

New York, New York   Columbus, Ohio   Woodland Hills, California   Peoria, Illinois

ABOUT THE AUTHOR

Arlene Rice is a professor at Los Angeles City College, where she teaches a broad list of office administration courses. She is a co-author of the eighth edition of the best-selling postsecondary keyboarding text in the U.S.—*College Keyboarding and Document Processing.*

In addition to teaching Windows, Word, WordPerfect, Skillbuilding and Keyboarding, and Concepts in Information Systems, your author has developed the curricula for many of the courses taught in her department at the college. Her past teaching experience included positions at other community colleges, California State University—Los Angeles, Sawyer College of Business, Moon Valley High School, and Albuquerque Technical Vocational Institute.

As vice chairperson of the office administration department at her current school, which has been recognized as a model program for innovative curriculum, she staffed 33 office administration courses and supervised five computer labs. The department's curriculum includes telecommunications, desktop publishing, and individualized keyboarding.

Active in both state and national professional education associations, Ms. Rice is a noted speaker on the topics of keyboarding and office systems and technology.

Glencoe/McGraw-Hill
A Division of The **McGraw·Hill** Companies

Glencoe Computer Applications and Keyboarding

Copyright © 1998 by The McGraw-Hill Companies, Inc. Printed in the United States of America. All rights reserved. Except as permitted under the United States Copyright Act of 1976, no part of this publication may be reproduced or distributed in any form or by any means, or stored in a database or retrieval system, without prior written permission of the publisher.

Send all inquiries to:
Glencoe/McGraw-Hill
21600 Oxnard St., Suite 500
Woodland Hills, CA 91367-4906

ISBN 0-02-813777-9 (Student Edition)
ISBN 0-02-803397-3 (Teacher's Edition)

5 6 7 8 9   071   05 04 03 02 01

CONTRIBUTING WRITERS

Jean Geiger
Educational Consultant
Collegeville, PA

Diane Hogan
Writer and Education Consultant
Charlotte, North Carolina

Barbara Oakley
AnB Graphics
San Diego, CA

Kent Swick
Wm. S. Hart Union HS District
Santa Clarita, CA

William Zimmerman
Santa Monica College
Santa Monica, CA

REVIEWERS

Sandra Clark
Carl Stewart MS
Conway, AR

Linda Wilson
Sycamore JHS
Anaheim, CA

Sue Smialek
N. Quincy, MA

Richard Murrell
Concord MS
Concord, NC

Cheryl Green
Mentor Shore JHS
Mentor, OH

Gary E. Smith
Union MS
San Jose, CA

Linda Lee
Henry MS
Denver, CO

Mary Ann Patterson
Lakeview JH
Kansas City, MA

Jimmy Smith
State Dept.
Raleigh, NC

Harriet Rogers
U of Wis. Whitewater
Whitewater, WI

John Weneta
Serrano Intermediate
San Clemente, CA

Darlene Platter
Kathleen MS
Lakeland, FL

Edna Jackson
Wiley MS
Winston Salem, NC

Margaret Peterson
Clark County MS
Las Vegas, NV

Contents
Teacher's Wraparound Edition

Course Overview	**T5**
Teacher's Wraparound Edition Features	**T8**
Program Resources	**T11**
Student Guides	**T11**
Teacher's Resource Binder	**T11**
Lesson Plans	T11
Tests and Solutions	T11
Grading and Evaluation	T12
Multicultural Timings	T12
Supplemental Projects and Solutions	T12
Reteaching, Reinforcement, and Enrichment	T12
Transparency Masters	T12
Textbook Project Solutions for ClarisWorks 4.0 for Macintosh	T12
Electronic Textbook Project Solutions	T12
Teacher's Electronic Classroom Resources	**T13**
Transparency Binder	**T13**
Windows/Macintosh Student Multimedia CD-ROM	**T13**
Windows/Macintosh Teacher's CD-ROM Package	**T13**
Site License Software (Windows and Macintosh)	**T13**
Professional Notes	**T14**
Teacher Responsibilities	**T14**
Student Responsibilities	**T14**
Integrated Curriculum	**T14**
Types of Assessment	**T15**
Objective Tests	T15
Performance Tests	T15
Student Portfolio Projects	T15
Observation and Questioning	T15
Self-Evaluation	T15
SCANS Foundations and Competencies	**T15**
Block Scheduling	**T15**
Planning Grid	**T18**

Course Overview

Many of today's students have lived with computers from the time they were born—probably several generations of computers in many homes. Their parents work with computers on a day-to-day basis and use various computer programs to manage their personal finances as well as home businesses. Mailing lists, budgets, checking accounts, tax records, recipes—all these and more are ways the computer is used in homes.

In addition, many people are using computers to do research about which products to buy and reading newspapers and magazines via computer. They can download income tax forms rather than picking them up from the library or other physical locations and can actually do their shopping without leaving home because of computers.

Students both in their homes and at school have been using computers to learn. The learning can take place in gamelike fashion or through more serious programs that actually test the concepts learned. Students likewise are fascinated with computer games, which have in many homes displaced television watching.

Some of your students no doubt may know more about computers than you or perhaps some of your colleagues. While some adults fear the computer, it is second nature to many students.

Course Goals

While the multimedia program, about which you will learn later, contains several educational games, the intent of this course is to give the students keyboarding and computer skills that will serve them throughout their school years and adult working years. Although computers will continue to improve and software programs will continue to do tasks more easily, your students will learn the basics. They will be able to use the computer keyboard much more efficiently than they would with the "hunt and peck" system often used by people who have never taken a keyboarding course.

Your students will be able to use various software applications that will enable them to create documents, create and maintain data, use the Internet and e-mail, and apply their computer skills in many aspects of their lives. While they are learning these skills, your students will be working with documents, data files, calculations, and communications that connect with other curricular areas. This course provides tools to help students in their other courses.

Standards

The level of achievement in this course will depend upon the amount of time you have in the course and the number of units you are able to include in your course. In the Student Edition of the text, other parts of the Teacher's Wraparound Edition, timings both in the multimedia/software and the Teacher's Resource Binder, and the performance and objective tests, you will have ways to evaluate your students. Suggested standards are provided for you to adopt or modify.

Not only should your students be able to perform at the standards established for the course, but they should acquire other valuable skills for their personal, academic, and occupational endeavors. They will learn to think more critically and creatively, evaluate the quality of their own work, recognize acceptable document formats, appreciate the relationships among the subjects they study, enjoy differences between themselves and their classmates, and communicate more effectively with the computer-literate population.

Course Overview

CD-ROM Guide

Glencoe Computer Applications and Keyboarding provides an exciting, pedagogically sound introductory course and instructional system for middle school keyboarding. The CD-ROM component of the program contains most elements of the student textbook plus videos, animations, photographs, illustrations, and games to enhance students' keyboarding skills and motivate them to learn to use computer software applications. With this flexible, interactive system, you can introduce, reinforce, or remediate any part of the keyboarding or computer applications curriculum at any time.

A teacher management system enables teachers to set up classes; add, delete, or transfer students; choose paths to link the program with student software; and set preferences such as editing capability or music selections. The teacher is also able to view student records.

CONTENTS

The *Glencoe Computer Applications and Keyboarding* CD-ROM is designed around the thematic metaphor of a television newsroom run by young people—KEYS, the Typing Channel. Inside the newsroom, students are greeted by video agents, who describe the three newsroom environments that contain various components of the program.

1. The Assignment Desk

The Assignment Desk environment has a number of components that lead students to interactive lessons.

On the Assignment Board students are presented with the keyboarding lessons contained in Unit 2 of the student text in an interactive format that includes immediate feedback for scored timings and keeping a record of the lessons students complete. When students complete the lessons listed on the board, new lessons display. Each new key reach is introduced with an animated demonstration.

The Computer Monitor enables students to access a list of all the lessons in the program and to select lessons from that list.

When the Computer Keyboard is clicked, a menu of animated demonstrations of all the key reaches is displayed. Students may choose a demonstration to review.

Students may view their reports as well as their scored text when the fax machine is clicked.

Clicking the Clock accesses a menu of More Timings—12-second, 30-second, 1-minute, 2-minute, and 3- or 5-minute. Students may use these timings to help build speed and accuracy.

Clicking the Language Links book allows students to access an open typing screen on which they may complete their Language Links lessons or practice their typing skills.

Clicking the Inbox displays a menu from which students may select from several options:

- An interactive Computer Basics lesson that introduces computer hardware components and software applications. (Students are even given a look inside the computer. When they become familiar with the various software applications, they can take a quiz in which they decide which one to use in different scenarios.)
- Format guides on which students may base their computer applications projects and link with their software—Word Processing, Desktop Publishing, Spreadsheet, Database, and Communications.

T6

Course Overview

- A reference guide that presents a listing of terms used in the format guides.(When students click a term, they are linked with the format guide in which the term is defined.)

2. The Research File Drawers

The Research File drawers contain cross-curricular typing selections. The cross-curricular areas are literature, mathematics, technology, social studies, and science. Students may choose to practice their typing skills in context or to take a 1-minute, 2-minute, 3-minute, or 5-minute timing. They may also choose from a selection of slow, medium, and fast music of various styles to listen to as they type.

3. The Studio

Careers in Technology contains ten videos that illustrate for students the importance of computers and keyboarding skills in today's world. The videos include law enforcement, meteorologist, book author, TV newswriter, power plant control operator, nurse, audio engineer, software engineer, interior designer, and inventory tracker.

The All About Typing slide show humorously shows students examples of correct and incorrect keyboarding techniques, including hints to help students avoid repetitive stress syndrome.

The Get the Scoop and Uncover the Story games provide an excellent way for students to build their keyboarding skills. In Get the Scoop, students strive for both speed and accuracy. They set their speed and skill level and then type their way to the scene of a late-breaking news story. Uncover the Story focuses on accuracy. Students select a skill level and type for points to uncover puzzle pieces that reveal a news event from the past, such as D-Day, the completion of the first transcontinental railway, or the tearing down of the Berlin Wall.

Students learn interesting facts about the history of typing and computers by selecting Computer and Typing Trivia. Through graphics and text, students understand the inventions and ideas that have advanced computer technology to where it is today.

Teacher's Wraparound Edition Features

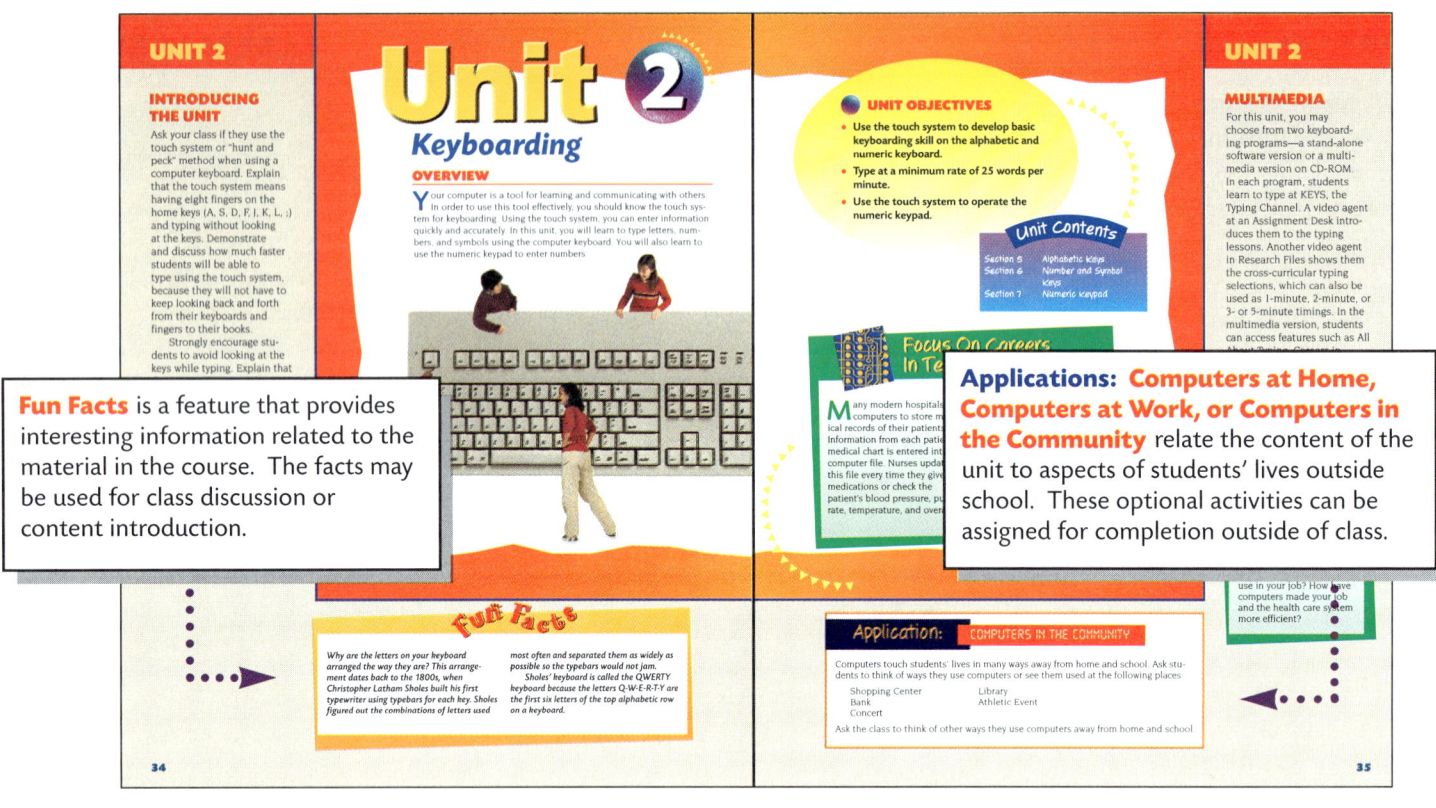

Fun Facts is a feature that provides interesting information related to the material in the course. The facts may be used for class discussion or content introduction.

Applications: Computers at Home, Computers at Work, or Computers in the Community relate the content of the unit to aspects of students' lives outside school. These optional activities can be assigned for completion outside of class.

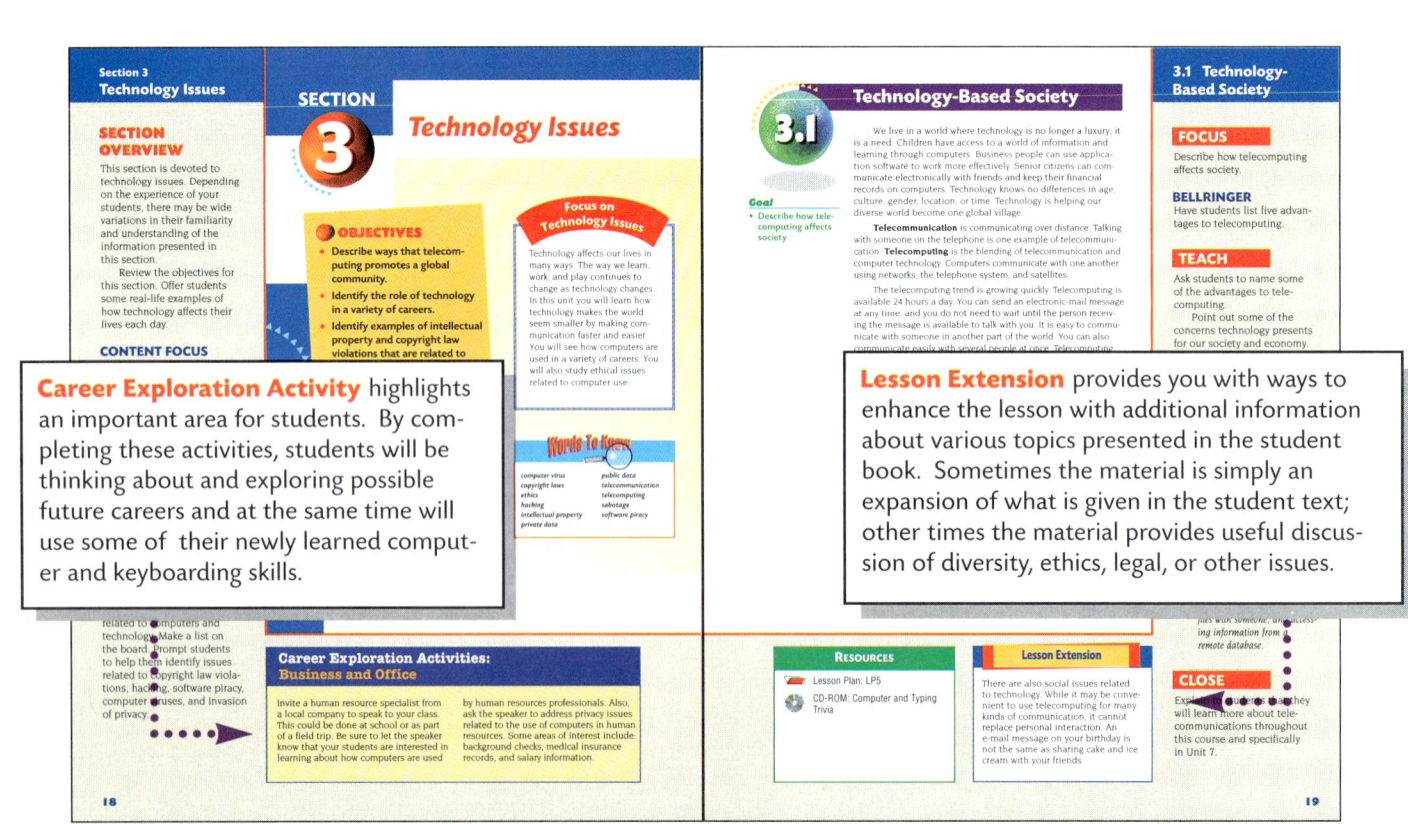

Career Exploration Activity highlights an important area for students. By completing these activities, students will be thinking about and exploring possible future careers and at the same time will use some of their newly learned computer and keyboarding skills.

Lesson Extension provides you with ways to enhance the lesson with additional information about various topics presented in the student book. Sometimes the material is simply an expansion of what is given in the student text; other times the material provides useful discussion of diversity, ethics, legal, or other issues.

T8

Teacher's Wraparound Edition Features

The Unit Organizer at the beginning of each unit lists the sections and subsections of the unit. For each of these subdivisions, you are given the listing of special features, such as Bits and Bytes, Do This, and Did You Know. The organizer also gives you a list of the projects, their focus, and their level of difficulty. Assessment instruments are also listed.

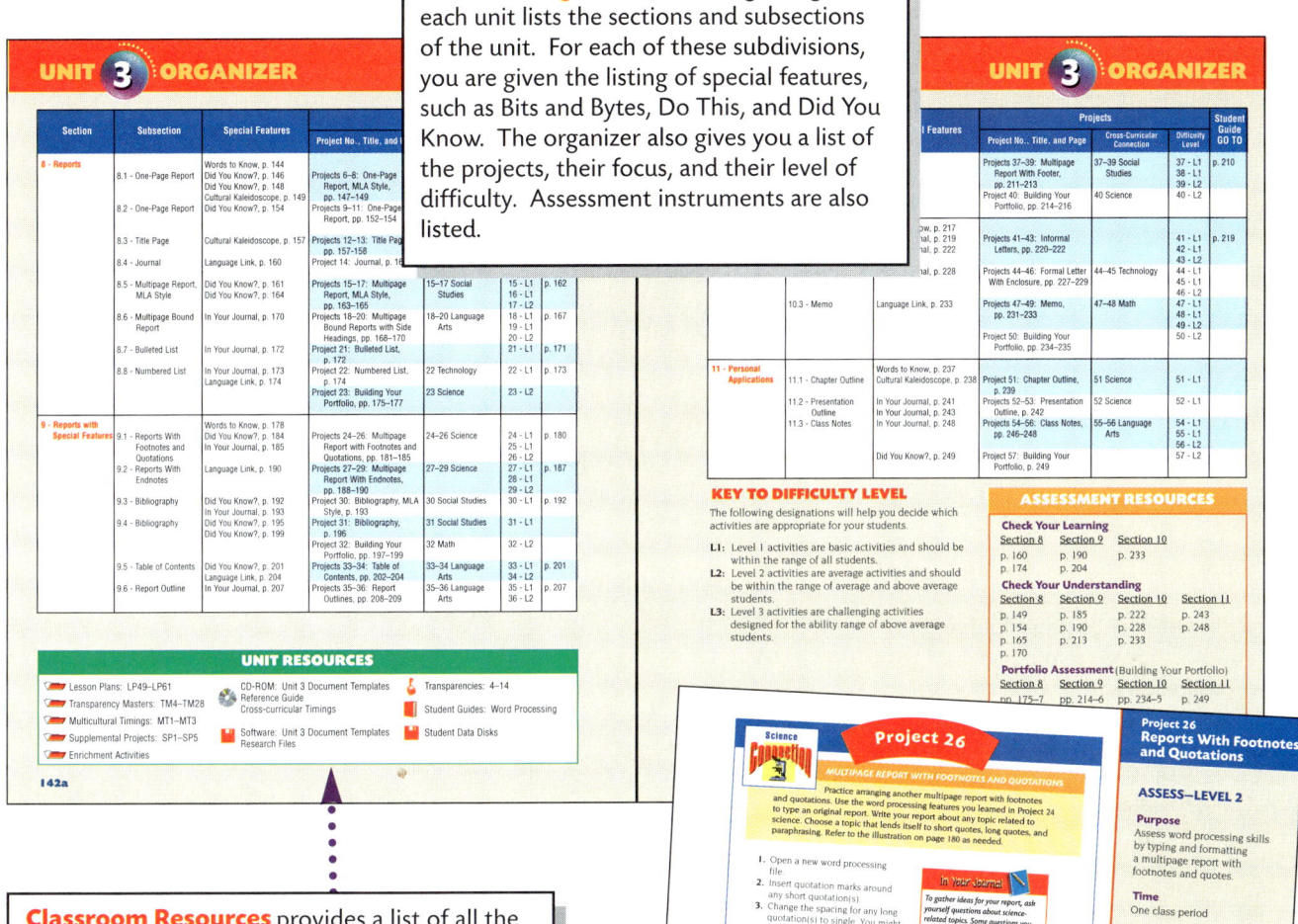

Classroom Resources provides a list of all the resources available to you for teaching the lesson, including materials in the *Teacher's Resource Binder* or the *Electronic Teacher's Classroom Resources*. In addition to specific resources to be used with each lesson, you may want to select some of the optional multicultural timings or supplementary projects to use as a challenge to students who complete their work early or simply need or want more practice.

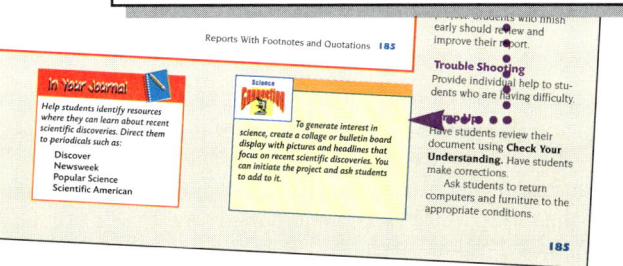

Cross-Curricular Connections are used throughout to enable students to see that the skills they are learning can be used for reports, communication, calculations, data maintenance, and other purposes related to any of their other studies.

T9

Teacher's Wraparound Edition Features

Four-Step Instructional Plan

The four-step instructional plan presents sound teaching strategies for each lesson, including these four essential steps: Focus, Teach, Assess, Close.

Focus, the first step, includes a statement of the objectives, the unit overview, and section focus. The focus portion of the teaching suggestions in the Teacher's Wraparound Edition includes a Bellringer activity that you can use to get students involved in the lesson while you take care of classroom management activities.

Teach, the second step, involves the presentation and examination of new material. The suggestions in the margins of the Teacher's Wraparound Edition give you questions to facilitate class discussion and strategies that assist students in understanding the content, software use, and document preparation. Practice activities are provided that will help the students put their new knowledge into practice under your supervision. In the side and bottom margins you will also find suggestions for using the special features as well as answers to *Check Your Learning.*

Assess is the third step. You may choose to administer reproducible tests from the Teacher's Resource Binder—either test projects or objective tests, create your own tests, or evaluate the students on their abilities demonstrated in the Building Your Portfolio projects. In addition, many of the projects include a Check Your Understanding feature. Students should be encouraged to use this self-assessment strategy—an extremely valuable technique for them to master when it comes to producing attractive, accurate, usable documents.

Close, the final step of the instructional plan, provides you with ideas for closing each class session. You might have students look back over what they have learned for the day, do a quick final review of any problem topics, view the relevance of the new material to their own lives, assure that they take care of their work stations and equipment, and develop an appreciation for computers and use of software in all their school subjects.

Program Resources

Student Guides

Four versions of the Student Guide for use with *Glencoe Computer Applications and Keyboarding* provide illustrations to make learning a feature easy and fun. The versions are based upon the following computer software platforms:

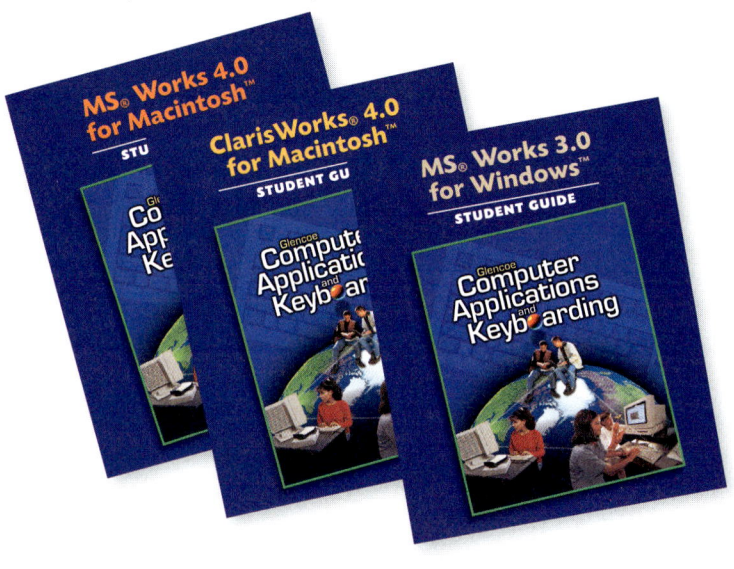

- ClarisWorks® 4.0 for Macintosh™
- MS® Works 4.0 for Macintosh™
- MS® Works 3.0 for Windows™
- MS® Works 4.0 for Windows™

Each Student Guide lists in alphabetical order by units the software features and functions that the students will be using to complete the projects in the Student Edition. The "Go To" feature in the Student Edition directs the students to specific features and functions that should be studied and used for a project. The directions for use of the software feature, of course, vary from one Student Guide to another. You will have students use the version that corresponds to the software package you currently have in your classroom or lab.

If you are using software other than these three versions, your students may need to refer to the software manual you received when the software was purchased. You may also need to modify the names assigned to those functions to correlate to the names used in the specific software.

Teacher's Resource Binder

The Teacher's Resource Binder provides you with resources that will assist you with teaching from *Glencoe Computer Applications and Keyboarding*. The components included for you in this binder are as follows:

LESSON PLANS

A complete set of abbreviated teaching plans are provided to serve as a convenient preparation aid. The one-page overview is organized according to the four-step instructional plan, with headings for Focus, Teach, Assess, and Close. Under each heading, you will find a complete listing of the resources available for use with the lesson, including contents and features within the Student Edition, the Teacher's Wraparound Edition, the Student Guide, and this Resource Binder.

Space is provided for marking the day or date on which you plan to work with each part of the unit and for noting features you particularly want to highlight. There is also room on each lesson plan page for writing brief notes or for recording homework assignments.

Unit and section opener material is presented separately to provide the flexibility of using it at the end of your current unit or section or at the beginning of the new instruction.

TESTS AND SOLUTIONS

Objective test questions have been provided for each of the seven units within the student text. In addition, performance tests have been provided for Units 3 through 6 covering the software applications, giving the students the opportunity to demonstrate their ability to complete projects using the unit instruction. One test project is provided at the end of each section of these units. Answers to the objective questions as well as suggested solutions for the performance test projects are provided at the end of this section in the Resource Binder.

Program Resources

GRADING AND EVALUATION
This section provides suggestions for grading the supplemental multicultural timings as well as the projects. Several checklists will facilitate your evaluating the students' keyboarding techniques learned in Unit 2, Keyboarding.

MULTICULTURAL TIMINGS
In addition to the timings in the Student Edition and in the cross-curricular timings in the multimedia and software programs, 29 essays dealing with multicultural topics are provided for use as timings. Word count for manual scoring is provided; explanation of this manual scoring is provided in the Grading and Evaluation portion of this Teacher's Resource Binder.

SUPPLEMENTAL PROJECTS AND SOLUTIONS
Five additional projects are provided for each of Units 3 through 7 to reinforce the students' skills, software use, and document knowledge. In addition, the final five projects represent situations in which the use of all software applications packages has been integrated. This integration demonstrates workplace applications. Reference is made to the formatting and design tips within the Student Edition for the purpose of evaluation.

RETEACHING, REINFORCEMENT, AND ENRICHMENT
This section of your Teacher's Resource Binder provides you with some ideas for using a different approach to presenting the Student Edition material in all seven units. These ideas will assist you in giving students who need more instruction an alternative way of looking at the material.

Level 3 enrichment projects are provided to be used following each of the "Building Your Portfolio" projects in the Student Edition as well as at the end of Unit 2, Keyboarding. These projects are open-ended and give the students an opportunity to make decisions, use their creativity, and apply what they have learned from completing the textbook projects.

TRANSPARENCY MASTERS
Blackline masters of the models of each document are provided for use in reteaching and reinforcing students' learning. By making transparencies of these models, you will be able to project them and talk in more detail about the design tips, formatting techniques, parts of the document, and evaluation of projects completed by the students.

TEXTBOOK PROJECT SOLUTIONS
Printed solutions for all the projects in the student edition are provided for ClarisWorks® 4.0 for Macintosh™. These are intended as models and in some cases suggested examples of how the students' final work should look, following design and formatting tips given them in the instruction for each type of document.

ELECTRONIC TEXTBOOK PROJECT SOLUTIONS
Solutions are provided on 3.5" diskettes for each of the software platforms: ClarisWorks® 4.0 for Macintosh™, MS® Works 4.0 for Macintosh™, and MS® Works 3.0 for Windows™. From these diskettes you may print out solutions for the platform your students are using or you may pull the project solutions up on your computer to compare with the students' work. Diskettes containing Performance Test templates and solutions are included for each software platform.

Electronic Teacher's Classroom Resources
This CD-ROM includes an electronic version of all the resources printed in the Teacher's Resource Binder as well as the textbook project solutions and Performance Test templates and solutions for each software platform.

Program Resources

Transparency Binder (Includes Wallcharts)

This binder includes a set of 32 transparency acetates that show various illustrations from the student textbook as well as examples of solutions of desktop publishing projects. Also included are wallcharts of IBM and Macintosh™ keyboards. You may want to post them in your classroom for reference by the students.

Windows/Macintosh Student Multimedia CD-ROM

The student CD-ROM contains all the computer software needed for both the Windows and Macintosh formats. A detailed overview of the content of the CD-ROM is given on pp. T6-T7.

Windows/Macintosh Teacher's CD-ROM Package

The teacher's CD-ROM package contains the same disk as the student's multimedia CD-ROM; however, the teacher's package includes a User's Guide that gives more detailed instructions for managing the classroom, maintaining student records, and using the various features and content within the program.

Site License Software

Software packages for either Windows™ or Macintosh™ are available to be networked within your school's computer lab or classroom. These packages contain the templates that students will need for completing the textbook projects. The templates, when downloaded to a blank disk for each student, become the Student Data Disk.

Student Data Disk

The Student Data Disk, created from a blank disk for each student by downloading the templates for the specific applications software format, will be used for most of the projects in the student textbook. The student is directed to open an existing document, add and/or change the document, then save the document back to the disk. In some instances the student will create new documents on the Student Data Disk, using the project instructions.

If individual students are using the CD-ROM version of the program, each student will open a document from the CD-ROM but will be instructed to save the revised or newly created document to a Student Data Disk.

PROFESSIONAL NOTES

Teacher Responsibilities

In a Computer Applications and Keyboarding course, students are involved in learning skills that will be valuable to them for the rest of their lives. As their teacher, you have responsibilities that will make the difference in how well students learn these skills. Your responsibilities include:

- Observe students' keyboarding techniques to assure efficient operation of the keys.
- Be available to the students to clarify the instructions for software functions.
- Facilitate the student's self-evaluation of documents prepared.
- Encourage students to strive for increased speed and accuracy.
- Provide opportunities for students to work together whenever possible.
- Provide appropriate materials, software, and equipment.
- Evaluate student outcomes.

Student Responsibilities

Students also have responsibilities if they are going to develop skills that will serve them well throughout the rest of their lives. Students must:

- Use correct techniques to insure efficient operation of the keyboard and to avoid fatigue or wrist problems.
- Have their textbook, appropriate student guide, and student data disk at all times during the course.
- When working with other students on desktop publishing or other types of projects, draw upon their own creativity and on the strengths of their teammates.
- Evaluate the appearance and accuracy of the documents they produce.
- Communicate with their teacher whenever they are having difficulties in order to avoid wasted time.

Integrated Curriculum

Integrating academic education refers to applying what is learned in one course to that learned in another. Seeing this relationship emphasizes to the students that the concepts presented have meaning outside that particular course. *Glencoe Computer Applications and Keyboarding* provides many ways to integrate the academic subjects with skills learned in the seven units.

Most of the 150+ projects in the student text are related to other courses the students take. Students are asked to prepare reports, letters, databases, and spreadsheets that represent topics studied in other courses. The skills learned may help reinforce concepts in other courses, prove useful in their personal lives, or help to get their first jobs. In fact, many of the projects are identified as having connection with one of the following subjects: language arts, math, science, social studies, or technology.

In addition to the projects in the textbook, the Teacher's Resource Binder provides supplemental projects. If the student is asked to research a topic and write a two-page report for some other course, the topic selected may well be one that could be a topic appropriate for a report or project that would apply in another course. An outline to be prepared might be the outline of a chapter in a social studies text; the outline may be used for review or for an oral presentation in the other course. A desktop published flyer might be an announcement of the meeting or another function for a science or math club, or a newsletter might consist of summaries of current events for a social studies course. A letter may be composed and properly formatted to request information about an environmental issue for a science course.

PROFESSIONAL NOTES

Types of Assessment

Your students have many different learning styles and different means of expressing their knowledge and skills. The combination of learning styles and the need to evaluate the students' skills calls for alternative methods of assessment.

OBJECTIVE TESTS

If you wish to test the students on their understanding and recall of content, objective questions are provided for each of the seven units. All units have at least 25 multiple-choice questions; some tests also have a number of true-false questions. In the true-false questions a word or phrase is underscored. If the student selects false as the correct answer, a substitute word or phrase is to be provided by the student that will make the statement true.

PERFORMANCE TESTS

In this course, students spend most of their time doing; thus, the best measure of their learning and skill acquisition is the performance test. In the Teacher's Resource Binder or on the Teacher's Electronic Resources CD-ROM, test projects are given for all units except Unit 1, Computer Basics, and Unit 2, Keyboarding. Suggested solutions are also provided in the Teacher's Resources (binder or electronic).

STUDENT PORTFOLIO PROJECTS

Following each set of three projects dealing with the same document, spreadsheet, or database, a "Building Your Portfolio" project is provided. These portfolio projects incorporate all the instruction and content from the previous projects. These projects, when completed, may easily be used as evidence that the student has acquired the skills and knowledge needed to perform well.

"Building Your Portfolio" projects will serve as model documents to follow in the student's other courses, as evidence of the quality of computer work the student is capable of doing. Each student should have a three-ring notebook with a set of tabbed dividers that can be labeled according to the type of project or by the unit titles of the student text. In addition to the portfolio projects, Level 3 Enrichment projects (see the Reteaching, Reinforcement, and Enrichment section of your Teacher's Resource Binder or Electronic Teacher's Resources CD-ROM) may become part of the student's portfolio. You may also suggest that the student insert some of the completed "In Your Journal" documents into the binder to keep for future reference.

OBSERVATION AND QUESTIONING

Observation of keyboarding techniques, operation of the computer, ability to follow instructions, use the Student Guide and study the software functions, and the ability to work as part of a team or within a whole-class setting will enable you to assess the student's progress. In the "Grading and Evaluation" section of your Teacher's Resource Binder, several checklists are provided as tools for you to use in checking the student's keyboarding techniques.

SELF-EVALUATION

A student's ability to evaluate performance in a course like computer applications and keyboarding is invaluable. Such a skill will enable the student to be a better student and later a better worker than someone who must rely on others to say "Job well done" or "You could do better." Several features are provided in the student text to facilitate self-evaluation. With a new document or computer application, a model is presented with callouts identifying its essential parts of the document. Formatting and design tips, given in bulleted lists, enable the student to check the outcome of the project. In addition, most projects include a "Check Your Understanding" section that gives the student a list of self-evaluation questions to answer.

PROFESSIONAL NOTES

SCANS Foundations and Competencies

In 1991, the U.S. Department of Labor released a report entitled *What Work Requires of Schools: A SCANS Report for America 2000.* SCANS stands for the Secretary's Commission on the Acquisition of Necessary Skills. The report identified five competencies which, in conjunction with a three-part foundation of skills and personal qualities, lie at the heart of job performance and are needed by all workers in order to prosper in the emerging workplace. *Glencoe Computer Applications and Keyboarding* integrates these skills throughout and will provide your students an outstanding basis for future development of these skills and competencies in other aspects of their schooling.

THE FOUNDATION	COMPUTER APPLICATIONS AND KEYBOARDING
Basic Skills—reading, writing, mathematics, speaking, and listening.	The following units deal with writing: Units 3, 4, and 7 In the following units, students improve reading and writing through completion of Language Link activities: Units 2, 3, and 6 Research of topics for reports (Unit 3) "In Your Journal" activities (Units 3-7) Unit 5, Spreadsheets, deals with math skills.
Thinking Skills—creative thinking, decision making, problem solving, knowing how to learn, and reasoning.	The following units deal with creative thinking: Units 3, 4, and 7 All seven chapters involve decision making and problem solving as students complete the projects, design documents, and prepare spreadsheets and databases.
Personal Qualities—individual responsibility, self-esteem, self-management, sociability, and integrity.	Students are responsible for self-evaluation in all chapters in the "Check Your Understanding" boxes. Students demonstrate competency in completion of the "Building Your Portfolio" projects. The students demonstrate responsibility by following the instructions in the "Go To" boxes, which appear in all units except Unit 2 and direct them to information about the software functions. Through timings, students strive to reach higher levels of skill throughout the course. Through working in teams on some of the projects, especially Units 4 and 5, the students demonstrate the ability to work with others.

PROFESSIONAL NOTES

SCANS COMPETENCIES	COMPUTER APPLICATIONS AND KEYBOARDING
Resources—allocate time, money, materials, space, staff.	Throughout the course, particularly in Units 2-7, the students deal specifically with resources: time for completion of drills and projects, maintenance of their workstations, care of their computers and their software.

Interpersonal Skills—work in teams, teach others, serve customers, lead, negotiate, and work with people from culturally diverse backgrounds.	The following units deal with interpersonal skills:
	    Units 3, 4, and 7
	In the following activities, students demonstrate competency in interpersonal skills:
	    Cultural Kaleidoscope, Units 1-7
	    Word Processing projects, Unit 3
	    Desktop Publishing projects, Unit 4
	    Communication projects, Unit 7
	    Internet Connection, Unit 7
	    In Your Journal
	    E-mail netiquette, Unit 7

Information—acquire and evaluate data, organize and maintain files, interpret and communicate information, use computers to process information.	The following units deal with information: Units 1-7.
	In the following activities, students demonstrate competency information:
	    Focus on Careers in Technology (Units 1-7)
	    Did You Know? (Units 1-7)
	    Bits and Bytes (Unit 2)
	    Reports, letters, and memos (Unit 3)
	    Projects in Desktop Publishing (Unit 4)
	    Spreadsheet projects (Unit 5)
	    Database projects (Unit 6)
	    Internet Connection and e-mail (Unit 7)
	    Cross-curricular connections—Language Arts, Math, Science, Social Studies, and Technology—in Units 3-7.

Systems—understand social, organizational, and technological systems; monitor and correct performance; design and improve systems.	The following units deal specifically with systems:
	    Units 1, 3-7
	In the following activities, students demonstrate competency in designing and improving systems:
	    Focus on Careers in Technology (Units 1-7)
	    Internet Connection (Unit 7)
	    Building Your Portfolio (Units 3-7)

Technology—select equipment and tools, apply technology to specific tasks, and maintain and troubleshoot technologies.	The following units deal specifically with technology:
	    Units 1, 3-7
	In the following activities, students demonstrate competency in technology:
	    Unit 1 on Computer Basics
	    Projects (Units 1, 3-7)
	    Internet Connection (Unit 7)

PROFESSIONAL NOTES

Block Scheduling

If your school has adopted—or is in the process of considering—block scheduling, you will find that the material in *Glencoe Computer Applications and Keyboarding* is easily adapted to your scheduling needs. With block scheduling, fewer class sessions are offered for longer blocks of time over fewer days. Some of the advantages of block scheduling reported by teachers are these:

- The longer class periods offer teachers more instructional flexibility and more time to incorporate different teaching methods.
- The longer class periods also provide opportunities for team projects.
- Time spent on introducing and closing classes is cut in half.

Students benefit from block scheduling by learning and retaining more. They can enjoy more cooperative learning activities and develop stronger team skills for later workplace experience and problem-solving skills. With block scheduling, students appear to have a more positive attitude about both school and life in general.

Planning Grid

Whether you are teaching in a block scheduling environment or a traditional setting, the Planning Grid provided suggests the structure for your course depending upon the length of your class period, its frequency, and the number of class periods allotted to your course. Whether you have a 30-, 45-, 50-, or 90-minute class period, the Planning Grid will assist you in determining the potential amount of coverage of each topic. The grid provides a suggested amount of coverage; however, you may choose to spend more time on some of the units, or not cover some of the units at all.

The Single Class column indicates the approximate amount of time for each section and subsection. For example, you might spend nine 45-minute class periods on Unit 1, Computer Basics. The Grid suggests two classes on Hardware, two on Software, two on Technology Issues, and three on Software Basics. If you were teaching in a 90-minute block class period, the total number of class periods for Unit 1 would be 4.5—one on Hardware, one on Software, one on Technology Issues, and one and a half on Software Basics.

Unit 2, Keyboarding, would perhaps require 28 class periods with each lasting 45 minutes or 14 ninety-minute periods. The amount of time spent on learning the basic keyboarding skills, however, may depend upon the levels of speed and accuracy you wish your students to reach.

Planning Grid

UNIT	CHAPTER/SECTION	SINGLE CLASS	BLOCK
UNIT 1	**COMPUTER BASICS**	**9**	**4.5**
1	**Hardware**	2	1
	1.1 Types of Computers	1	0.5
	1.2 Input, Output, and Storage Devices	1	0.5
2	**Software**	2	1
	2.1 Operating System Software	1	0.5
	2.2 Application Software	1	0.5
3	**Technology Issues**	2	1
	3.1 Technology-Based Society	0.5	0.25
	3.2 Computing and Careers	0.5	0.25
	3.3 Ethical Use of Computers	1	0.5
4	**Software Basics**	3	1.5
	4.1 Introduction to Software	1	0.5
	4.2 Navigating and Changing Text	0.5	0.25
	4.3 Previewing and Printing Documents	0.5	0.25
	4.4 Editing and Saving Files	0.5	0.25
	4.5 Help	0.5	0.25
UNIT 2	**KEYBOARDING**	**28**	**14**
5	**Alphabetic Keys**	19	9.5
6	**Number and Symbol Keys**	7	3.5
7	**Numeric Keypad**	2	1
UNIT 3	**WORD PROCESSING**	**22**	**11**
8	**Reports**	7	3.5
	8.1 One-Page Report	2	1
	8.2 One-Page Report	1	0.5
	8.3 Title Page	0.5	0.25
	8.4 Journal	0.5	0.25
	8.5 Multipage Report, MLA Style	1	0.5
	8.6 Multipage Bound Report	1	0.5
	8.7 Bulleted List	0.5	0.25
	8.8 Numbered List	0.5	0.25
9	**Reports With Special Features**	6	3
	9.1 Reports With Footnotes and Quotations	1	0.5
	9.2 Reports With Endnotes	1	0.5
	9.3 Bibliography	0.5	0.25
	9.4 Bibliography	0.5	0.25
	9.5 Table of Contents	1	0.5
	9.6 Report Outline	1	0.5
	9.7 Multipage Report	1	0.5

Planning Grid

UNIT	CHAPTER/SECTION	SINGLE CLASS	BLOCK
UNIT 3	**WORD PROCESSING (continued)**		
10	**Letters and Memos**	**4**	**2**
	10.1 Informal Letter	1	0.5
	10.2 Formal Letter	1	0.5
	10.3 Memo	2	1
11	**Personal Applications**	**5**	**2.5**
	11.1 Chapter Outline	1	0.5
	11.2 Presentation Outline	1	0.5
	11.3 Class Notes	3	1.5
UNIT 4	**DESKTOP PUBLISHING**	**17**	**9.5**
12	**Document Enhancement**	**7**	**3.5**
	12.1 Title Page With Borders	3	1.5
	12.2 Cover Page	2	1
	12.3 Flyer	2	1
13	**Graphics**	**6**	**3**
	13.1 Flyer With Clip Art	3	1.5
	13.2 Personal Stationery	3	1.5
14	**Templates**	**4**	**2**
	14.1 Invitation, Greeting Card, or Letterhead	1	0.5
	14.2 Certificate	1	0.5
	14.3 Newsletter	2	1
UNIT 5	**SPREADSHEET**	**28**	**14**
15	**Spreadsheet Basics**	**15**	**7.5**
	15.1 Explore a Spreadsheet	1	0.5
	15.2 Enter, Format, and Edit Data	1	0.5
	15.3 Create a Spreadsheet	2	1
	15.4 Formulas and Print Range	4	2
	15.5 Functions, Copy, and Move	3	1.5
	15.6 Fill Right, Fill Down, and Fill Series	1	0.5
	15.7 Spreadsheet Structure	3	1.5
16	**Enhanced Spreadsheets and Charts**	**8**	**4**
	16.1 Borders, Gridlines, and Pictures	3	1.5
	16.2 Styles	1	0.5
	16.3 Bar and Line Charts	2	1
	16.4 Pie Charts	2	1
17	**Analysis and Integration**	**5**	**2.5**
	17.1 What If Analysis	2	1
	17.2 Integration	3	1.5

Planning Grid

UNIT	CHAPTER/SECTION	SINGLE CLASS	BLOCK
UNIT 6	**DATABASE**	**33**	**16.5**
18	**Database Basics**	**11**	**6.5**
	18.1 Use a Database	2	1
	18.2 Update a Database	2	1
	18.3 Create a New Database	1	0.5
	18.4 Design a Database	2	1
	18.5 Sort Records	1	0.5
	18.6 Find Records	3	1.5
19	**Enhanced Databases and Reports**	**22**	**11**
	19.1 Database Structure	2	1
	19.2 Formula Field	2	1
	19.3 Search a Database	4	2
	19.4 Enhance a Form	4	2
	19.5 Create a Report	2	1
	19.6 Database Template	3	1.5
	19.7 Database Integration	5	2.5
UNIT 7	**COMMUNICATIONS**	**13**	**6.5**
20	**Communications Basics**	**2**	**1**
	20.1 Network Connections	1	0.5
	20.2 Communications Software	1	0.5
21	**E-Mail Basics**	**5**	**2.5**
	21.1 Introduction to E-Mail	1	0.5
	21.2 E-Mail Messages	1	0.5
	21.3 Communicate Using E-Mail	3	1.5
22	**Internet Basics**	**6**	**3**
	22.1 Newsgroups	1	0.5
	22.2 Internet Sites	1	0.5
	22.3 Browser	2	1
	22.4 Integration	2	1
		150	**76**

Contents

About Your Book ..... viii–xi

Unit 1 — Computer Basics

SECTION 1	Hardware	2
1.1	Types of Computers	3–5
1.2	Input, Output, and Storage Devices	6–10

SECTION 2	Software	11
2.1	Operating System Software	12
2.2	Application Software	13–17

SECTION 3	Technology Issues	18
3.1	Technology-Based Society	19
3.2	Computing and Careers	20
3.3	Ethical Use of Computers	21–24

SECTION 4	Software Basics	25
4.1	Introduction to Software	26
4.2	Navigating and Changing Text	27–28
4.3	Previewing and Printing Documents	29–30
4.4	Editing and Saving Files	31–32
4.5	Help	33

Unit 2 — Keyboarding

SECTION 5	Alphabetic Keys	36–106
SECTION 6	Number and Symbol Keys	107–132
SECTION 7	Numeric Keypad	133–141

iv   Table of Contents

Unit 3

Word Processing

SECTION 8   Reports — 144

8.1	One-Page Report, MLA Style	145–149
8.2	One-Page Report	150–154
8.3	Title Page	155–158
8.4	Journal	159–160
8.5	Multipage Report, MLA Style	161–165
8.6	Multipage Bound Report	166–170
8.7	Bulleted List	171–172
8.8	Numbered List	173–174
Building Your Portfolio		175–177

SECTION 9   Reports With Special Features — 178

9.1	Reports With Footnotes and Quotations	179–185
9.2	Reports With Endnotes	186–190
9.3	Bibliography, MLA Style	191–193
9.4	Bibliography	194–196
Building Your Portfolio		197–199
9.5	Table of Contents	200–204
9.6	Report Outline	205–209
9.7	Multipage Report	210–213
Building Your Portfolio		214–216

SECTION 10   Letters and Memos — 217

10.1	Informal Letter	218–222
10.2	Formal Letter	223–228
10.3	Memo	229–233
Building Your Portfolio		234–235

SECTION 11   Personal Applications — 236

11.1	Chapter Outline	237–239
11.2	Presentation Outline	240–243
11.3	Class Notes	244–248
Building Your Portfolio		249

Unit 4 — Desktop Publishing

SECTION 12 Document Enhancement — 252

12.1	Title Page With Borders	253–256
12.2	Cover Page	257–262
12.3	Flyer	263–267
Building Your Portfolio		268–269

SECTION 13 Graphics — 270

13.1	Flyer With Clip Art	271–275
13.2	Personal Stationery	276–280
Building Your Portfolio		281–282

SECTION 14 Templates — 283

14.1	Invitation, Greeting Card, or Letterhead	284–286
14.2	Certificate	287–289
14.3	Newsletter	290–292
Building Your Portfolio		293

Unit 5 — Spreadsheet

SECTION 15 Spreadsheet Basics — 296

15.1	Explore a Spreadsheet	297–299
15.2	Enter, Format, and Edit Data	300–302
15.3	Create a Spreadsheet	303–306
15.4	Formulas and Print Range	307–315
Building Your Portfolio		316
15.5	Functions, Copy, and Move	317–322
15.6	Fill Right, Fill Down, and Fill Series	323–327
15.7	Spreadsheet Structure	328–332
Building Your Portfolio		333

SECTION 16 Enhanced Spreadsheets and Charts — 334

16.1	Borders, Gridlines, and Pictures	335–339
16.2	Styles	340–342
16.3	Bar and Line Charts	343–348
16.4	Pie Charts	349–352
Building Your Portfolio		353–354

SECTION 17 Analysis and Integration — 355

17.1	What If Analysis	356–359
17.2	Integration	360–364
Building Your Portfolio		365

vi Table of Contents

Unit 6

Database

SECTION 18 Database Basics — 368

18.1	Use a Database	369–371
18.2	Update a Database	372–374
18.3	Create a New Database	375–376
18.4	Design a Database	377–380
18.5	Sort Records	381–383
18.6	Find Records	384–387
Building Your Portfolio		388

SECTION 19 Enhanced Databases and Reports — 389

19.1	Database Structure	390–391
19.2	Formula Field	392–394
19.3	Search a Database	395–398
Building Your Portfolio		399
19.4	Enhance a Form	400–404
19.5	Create a Report	405–408
19.6	Database Template	409–412
Building Your Portfolio		413
19.7	Database Integration	414–420
Building Your Portfolio		421

Unit 7

Communications

SECTION 20 Communications Basics — 424

| 20.1 | Network Connections | 425–426 |
| 20.2 | Communications Software | 427–428 |

SECTION 21 E-Mail Basics — 429

21.1	Introduction To E-Mail	430–432
21.2	E-Mail Messages	433–434
21.3	Communicate Using E-Mail	435–438
Building Your Portfolio		439

SECTION 22 Internet Basics — 440

22.1	Newsgroups	441–442
22.2	Internet Sites	443–445
22.3	Browser	446–448
Building Your Portfolio		449
22.4	Integration	450–453

Glossary — 454
Index — 462

Table of Contents **vii**

About Your Book

Structure of Your Book. *Glencoe Computer Applications and Keyboarding* contains seven units. Each unit is divided into sections made up of information about computers, keyboarding, and various software applications. You will learn to operate the computer keyboard by touch and with speed and accuracy that will enable you to use the computer efficiently. By studying the information in your book and applying it to projects, you will learn valuable skills you can use both at school and at home.

Each **Unit Opener** in your book provides an Overview of the unit as well as a list of the objectives and sections within the unit. A **Focus on Careers in Technology** box for each unit explains ways in which people you and your classmates may know use the skills you are learning to earn a living for themselves and their families. As you begin each new unit, you may want to consider whether the career featured is something you would like to do when you get out of school.

Each **Section Opener** gives a list of objectives and a Focus box that tells you the purpose of the section. The **Words to Know** lists new words you will be learning in the section. The definitions of these words shown in boldface appear in the **Glossary** at the end of your text.

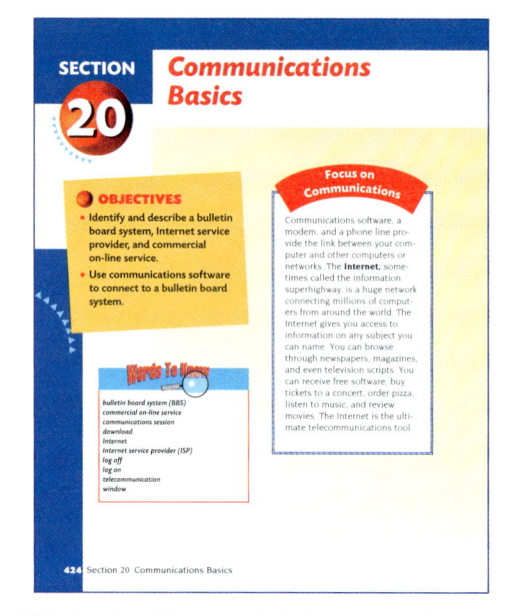

This book will not only help you reach a good level of keyboarding skill, but will show you how to format letters, reports, and other documents attractively. You will be able to design your own personal stationery, solve math problems using a spreadsheet, and use an automatic database to keep track of your favorite CDs or sports cards.

You will be challenged to combine your new software application skills to do things like research a report topic on the Internet and type and enhance the report using word processing and desktop publishing. You can even integrate a table from a spreadsheet into your report or sort information in your report using a database! Let's get started and learn these valuable skills that will carry you well into the twenty-first century!

The special features in your book are identified and explained on the sample pages that follow.

viii   About Your Book

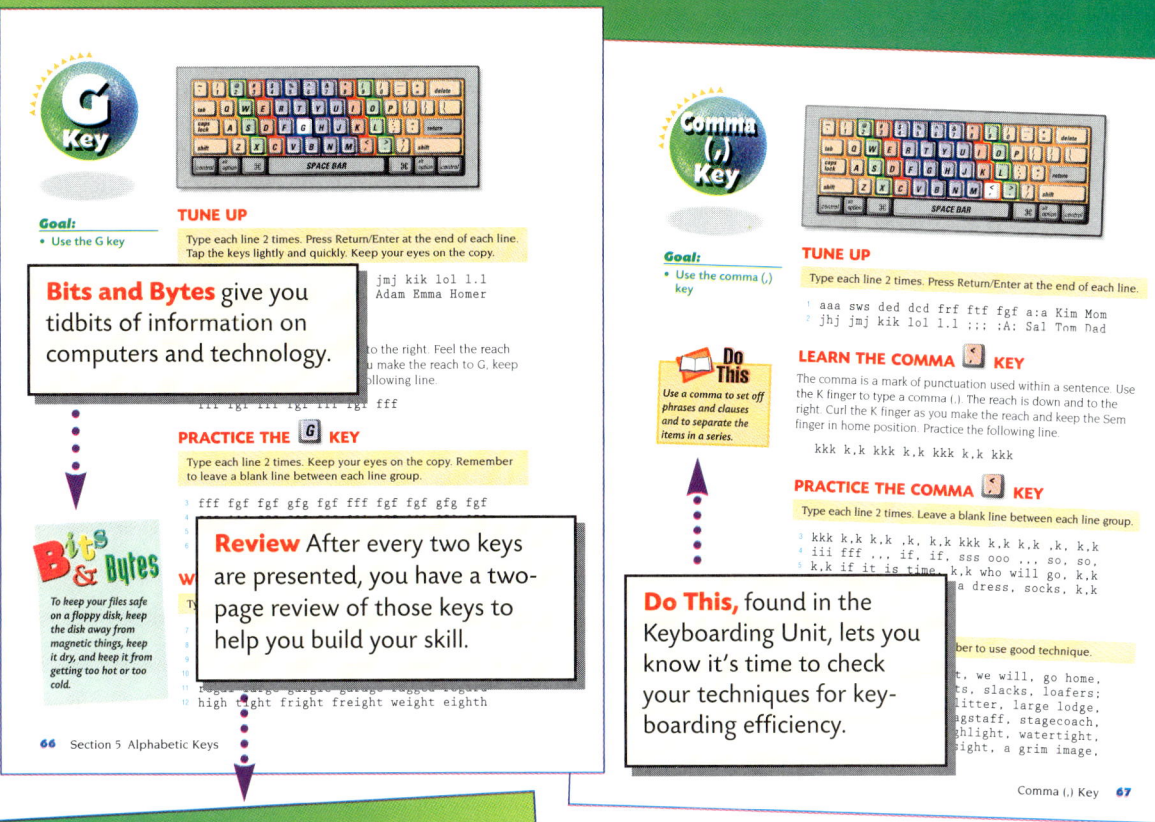

Bits and Bytes give you tidbits of information on computers and technology.

Review After every two keys are presented, you have a two-page review of those keys to help you build your skill.

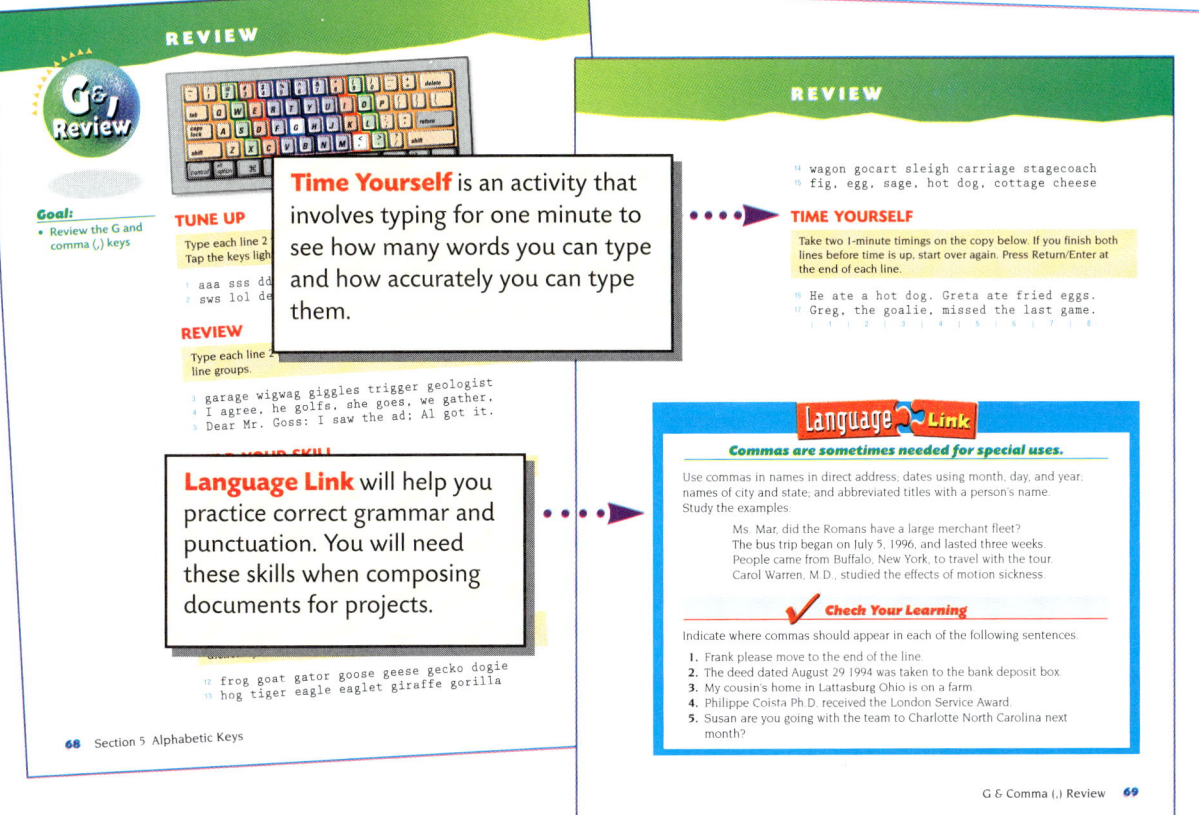

Do This, found in the Keyboarding Unit, lets you know it's time to check your techniques for keyboarding efficiency.

Time Yourself is an activity that involves typing for one minute to see how many words you can type and how accurately you can type them.

Language Link will help you practice correct grammar and punctuation. You will need these skills when composing documents for projects.

About Your Book   ix

Internet Connection will give you great ideas for interesting places to visit when you are 'surfing the Net.'

Design Tips In the desktop publishing projects, design tips give guidelines for creating attractive pages.

Building Your Portfolio, the final project in a series, gives you the chance to demonstrate that you have mastered the concepts and skills as they apply to this application. You may want to keep the documents as examples of your work.

Check Your Understanding will help you find out if you have learned the main ideas or if you need to go back and review.

Projects give you an opportunity to practice the new software features and your keyboarding skills. Other projects will then help you reinforce what you have learned.

Did You Know? boxes provide interesting facts related to the unit.

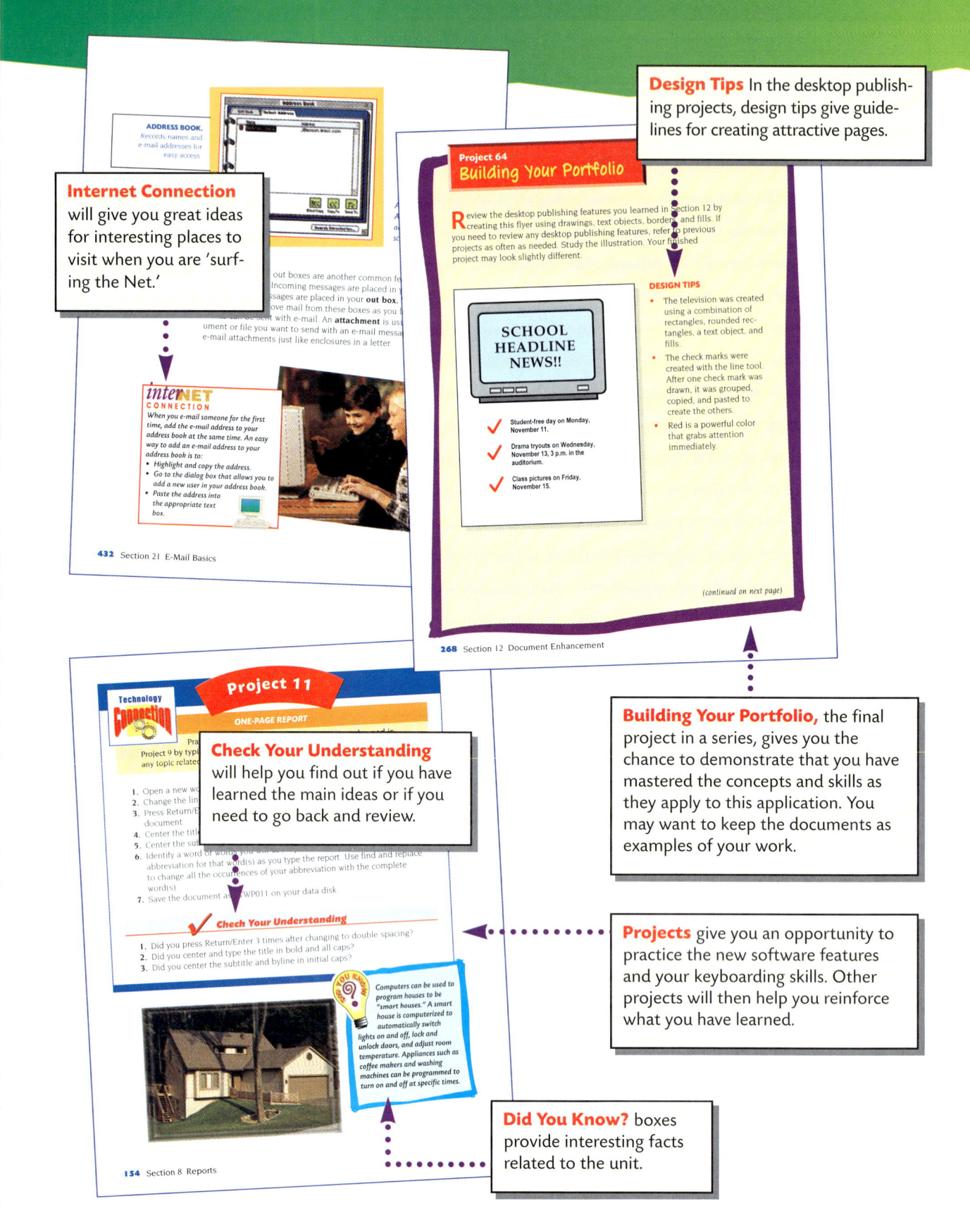

x   About Your Book

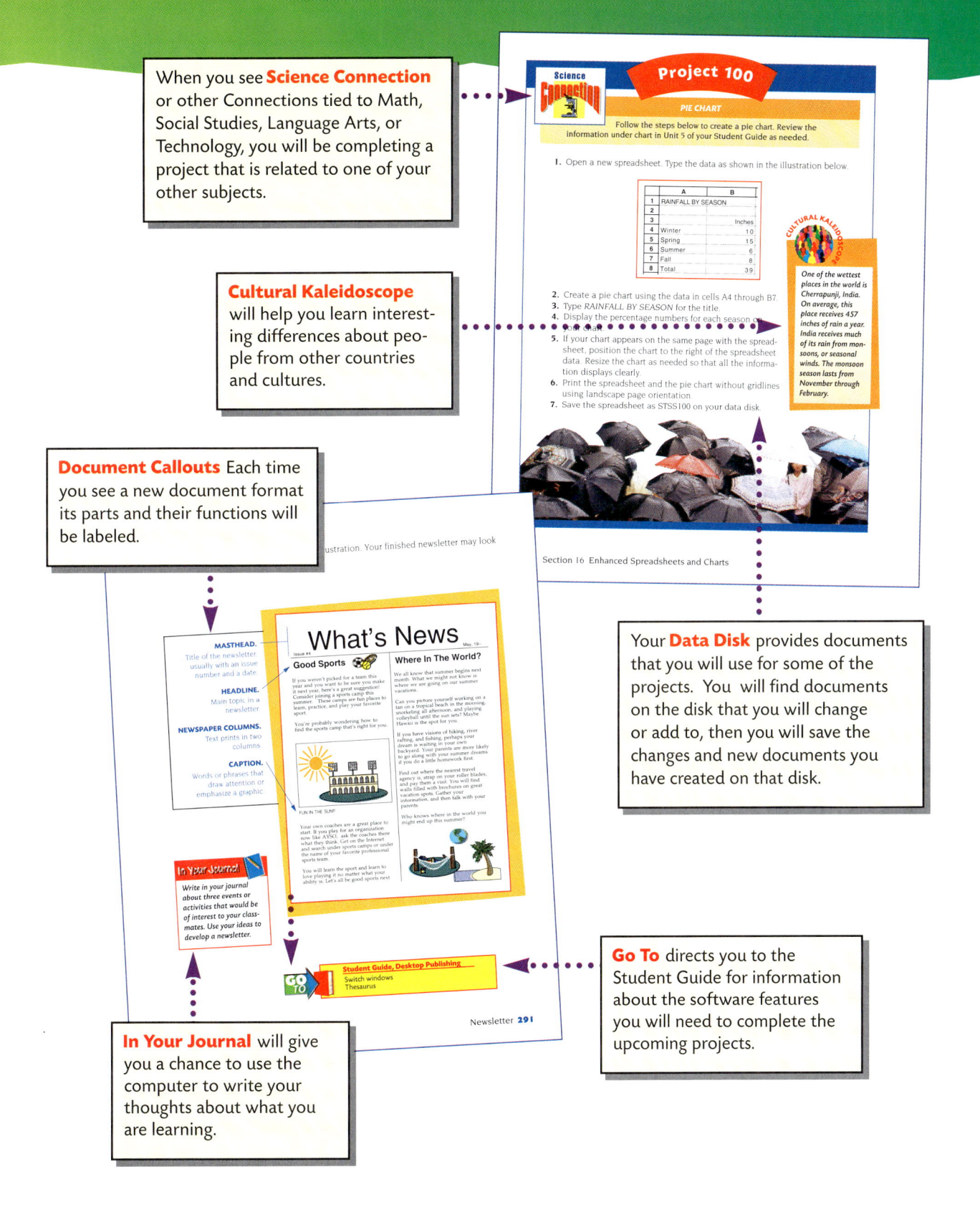

When you see **Science Connection** or other Connections tied to Math, Social Studies, Language Arts, or Technology, you will be completing a project that is related to one of your other subjects.

Cultural Kaleidoscope will help you learn interesting differences about people from other countries and cultures.

Document Callouts Each time you see a new document format its parts and their functions will be labeled.

Your **Data Disk** provides documents that you will use for some of the projects. You will find documents on the disk that you will change or add to, then you will save the changes and new documents you have created on that disk.

Go To directs you to the Student Guide for information about the software features you will need to complete the upcoming projects.

In Your Journal will give you a chance to use the computer to write your thoughts about what you are learning.

About Your Book   xi

UNIT 1 ORGANIZER

Section	Subsection	Special Features	Projects: Project No., Title, and Page	Cross-Curricular Connection	Difficulty Level	Student Guide GO TO
1 - Hardware	1.1 - Types of Computers 1.2 - Input, Output, Storage	Words To Know, p. 2				
2 - Software	2.1 - Operating System Software 2.2 - Applications Software	Words To Know, p. 11 Did You Know?, p. 16 Cultural Kaleidoscope, p. 17				
3 - Technology Issues	3.1 - Technology-Based Society 3.2 - Computing and Careers 3.3 - Ethical Use of Computers	Words To Know, p. 18 Did You Know?, p. 22 Cultural Kaleidoscope, p. 24				
4 - Software Basics	4.1 - Introduction to Software 4.2 - Navigating and Changing Text 4.3 - Previewing and Printing Documents 4.4 - Editing and Saving Files 4.5 - Help	Words To Know, p. 25 Cultural Kaleidoscope, p. 28 Did You Know?, p. 30 Cultural Kaleidoscope, p. 32	Project 1: Introduction to Software, p. 26 Project 2: Navigating and Changing Text, p. 28 Project 3: Previewing and Printing Documents, p. 30 Project 4: Editing and Saving Files, p. 32 Project 5: Help, p. 33		1 - L1 2 - L1 3 - L1 4 - L1 5 - L1	p. 26 p. 28 p. 30 p. 31 p. 33

UNIT RESOURCES

- Lesson Plans: LP1–LP9
- Enrichment Activities
- CD-ROM: Unit 1 Document Templates, Computer and Typing Trivia, Computer Basics
- Software: Unit 1 Document Templates
- Student Guides: Introduction
- Student Data Disks

UNIT 1 ORGANIZER

KEY TO DIFFICULTY LEVEL

The following designations will help you decide which activities are appropriate for your students.

L1: Level 1 activities are basic activities and should be within the range of all students.

L2: Level 2 activities are average activities and should be within the range of average and above average students.

L3: Level 3 activities are challenging activities designed for the ability range of above average students.

ASSESSMENT RESOURCES

Check Your Understanding

Section 1	Section 2	Section 3	Section 4
p. 5	p. 13	p. 19	none
	p. 14	p. 20	
	p. 15	p. 21	
	p. 16	p. 22	
	p. 17	p. 23	
		p. 24	

Unit Test
(Teacher's Resource Binder)
Objective Test

UNIT 1

INTRODUCING THE UNIT

Ask your students if they have used computers. Ask how many have used computers at home, at a friend's house, or at the library. Ask how they used the computer. Did they use it to play a game, send or receive an e-mail message, or do some research for a school project? Make a list on the board.

Ask how other members of their families use computers at home and at work. Ask students to think of other ways that computers affect their lives. Examples might include the computer used to generate report cards, control heating and air conditioning systems, keep track of library books, and control traffic lights. Ask students to think about computers other than personal computers. Examples might include grocery store scanners, weather forecasting equipment, video games, and scoreboards.

Unit 1
Computer Basics

OVERVIEW

Computers make using and sharing information easier. Like a textbook, your computer is another tool for learning. In this unit you will learn the basics about computer hardware and software. You will also explore and discuss various technology issues that are related to computers.

Fun Facts

In 1983 there were about 2 million personal computers in use in the United States. By 1993 there were more than 90 million.

While this increase appears dramatic, the computer is not nearly as prevalent in U.S. homes as telephones and televisions.

Only 37 percent of U.S. households have a computer while more than 95 percent have telephones. Televisions can be found in 98 percent of homes and 81 percent have VCRs. In addition, more than 65 percent of households subscribe to cable TV.

UNIT 1

UNIT OBJECTIVES

- Identify and use computer hardware.
- Identify and use basic software features.
- Identify and discuss issues related to a technology-based society.

Unit Contents

Section 1	Hardware
Section 2	Software
Section 3	Technology Issues
Section 4	Software Basics

MULTIMEDIA

To enhance Unit 1, view the interactive lesson "Computer Basics." This lesson includes a look at hardware—outside and inside—and software. Students are introduced to various input and output devices, as well as the components inside the computer. The lesson also explains software applications. During the course of the interaction, students take a quiz in which they decide what kind of software application to use in a particular scenario.

At any time, you may refer students to "Computer and Typing Trivia." In this feature, students will learn interesting facts about computers.

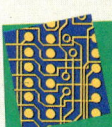

Focus On Careers In Technology

Computer games are created by software engineers. A software engineer uses the keyboard to input the programming code. This programming code is like an engine that runs the game. The games included in this computer applications course were written by software engineers in a language called Lingo™. If you don't understand this kind of language, you might think it looks like a foreign language. This is an example of a code that tells the computer to read a text file from a certain location:

```
on openTextFile
set fileObj = new(xtra "FileIO")
openFile(fileObj, "practic2.txt", 1)
set theFile = readFile(fileObj)
closeFile(fileObj)
set fileObj = 0
end
```

Software engineers take programming courses to learn the vocabulary and "grammar" rules of programming languages. They also learn how to use the programming language.

Focus On Careers In Technology

Have students share information about their favorite video games with the class. Have them describe what they like about the games. Specific features they might identify include graphics, animation, and sound. Have students compare and contrast computer games to other games such as board games and sports games.

Application: COMPUTERS AT WORK

Divide the class into small groups and assign an occupational area to each group. Ask each group to make a list of ways a computer might be used in their assigned area. As time permits, ask each group to select a spokesperson. Have the spokesperson for each group share the group's list with others in the class.

Occupational areas to consider include:

Agriculture	Health Care
Architecture	Maintenance
Construction	Manufacturing
Education	Marketing
Entertainment	Sales
Food Service	Transportation

Section 1
Hardware

SECTION OVERVIEW

In this section, students will learn about computer hardware. Take students on a "tour" of the hardware they will be using in this course. Identify the basic parts of the personal computer. Tell students about the personal computers they will be using.

Use the photographs and illustrations in the textbook as a reference as you explain hardware. Consider using a catalog or advertisement to illustrate the wide array of computers available.

CONTENT FOCUS

- Types of computers
- Input devices
- Output devices
- Storage devices

OPENING ACTIVITY

Have students write the names of the basic hardware components of a personal computer system on index cards. Include the following parts: computer case, keyboard, monitor, printer, mouse, and speakers. Emphasize the correct spelling of these words.

One at a time, ask students to tape a card on the appropriate part of the computer system. Continue until all parts you have designated are correctly tagged.

SECTION 1
Hardware

OBJECTIVES

- Identify the types of computers.
- Identify computer input devices.
- Identify computer output devices.
- Describe computer storage devices.

Focus on Hardware

In order to use a computer effectively, you must be able to identify basic computer hardware. Hardware is any part of your computer that you can see or touch. Look at your computer as you read about computers. Then, you will use your computer and software to open, edit, and print a document.

Words To Know

bar code reader	magnetic tape	personal computer
computer case	mainframe	pointing stick
desktop computer	memory	printer
disk drive	microphone	scanner
fax	minicomputer	speaker
floppy disk	modem	storage device
hard disk	monitor	supercomputer
hardware	mouse	touch screen
input device	network	touchpad
keyboard	notebook computer	trackball
laptop computer	optical disc	workstation
light pen	output device	

2   Section I Hardware

Career Exploration Activities:
Marketing and Distribution

There are many career opportunities related to the marketing of computer hardware. Ask students to think of examples of jobs related to the manufacturing, sales, and servicing of computers and peripherals. Have them research and report on a specific job using references such as the *Occupational Outlook Handbook*, the *Occupational Outlook Quarterly*, and the *Dictionary of Occupational Titles*. All of these books are published by the Bureau of Labor Statistics. Reports should include the job title, educational requirements, and average salary for the position.

Types of Computers

1.1

Goals
- Identify types of computers
- List examples of basic hardware for personal computers

Computers help people process (calculate, sort, summarize, arrange) and share information. The **supercomputer** is the most powerful computer of all. Supercomputers are used to do things like predict hurricanes and navigate satellites through distant outer space. **Mainframes** and **minicomputers** are used by business and government to process large amounts of information. For example, they might generate payroll checks for thousands of employees or maintain records for millions of citizens. **Personal computers** are smaller and less powerful than the other types of computers. However, they can still perform many of the same tasks but on a smaller scale.

Supercomputers, minicomputers, and personal computers help people process and share information.

RESOURCES
- Lesson Plan: LP2
- CD-ROM: Computer and Typing Trivia

1.1 Types of Computers

FOCUS
Identify types of computers. List examples of basic hardware for personal computers.

BELLRINGER
When students enter the room, direct their attention to the assignment on the board:
Review the list of basic computer hardware that appears on page 4.

TEACH
Use the photograph on this page to illustrate different kinds of computers. Emphasize that personal computers are only one kind of computer.

Types of Computers

TEACH

Guide your students through the list of basic hardware shown on this page. Using a personal computer, point to or describe each item listed. If available, show the students a memory chip. Consider having the computer turned on so that students can see how a monitor is similar to a television screen. Demonstrate inserting and removing a diskette. Demonstrate the use of the speakers.

A workstation is equipped with basic hardware.

Personal computers come in a variety of sizes, and most of them have the same basic **hardware:**

Computer Case	Contains the major components of the computer such as the CPU
	CPU stands for central processing unit; the "brains" of the computer where work is done
Monitor	Screen similar to a TV screen for viewing information
Keyboard and Mouse	For entering information into the computer and giving instructions called commands
Memory	For storing or "remembering" instructions and information
Disk drive	For reading or storing information on computer disks
Speakers	For generating voice, music, and other sounds

The **desktop computer** is designed to be used on a desktop. The desktop computer might have the monitor and computer case as individual parts or built as one unit.

4   Section I   Hardware

Lesson Extension

Consider removing the case of a computer and showing students the internal hardware. Point out how the internal workings match up with the outside of the computer. Show students where the keyboard, mouse, and monitor hook into the outside of the case. Then show them how these items are connected to the internal workings of the computer. Be sure to unplug the power supply before you open the CPU case. Use the reference material supplied by the manufacturer to locate key items to show students.

The **notebook computer** is designed to be used on a desktop but still be small enough to be portable. Typically, it is the size of an 8½- × 11-inch notebook. The screen, computer case, and keyboard are designed to unfold like an open notebook when in use.

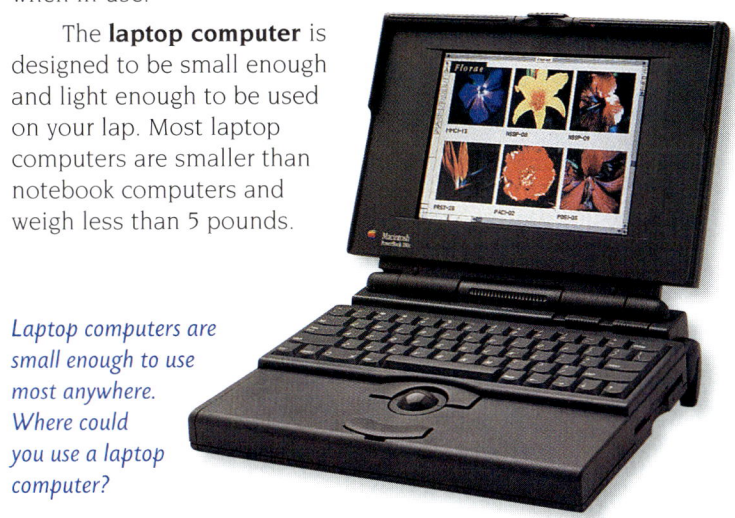

The **laptop computer** is designed to be small enough and light enough to be used on your lap. Most laptop computers are smaller than notebook computers and weigh less than 5 pounds.

Laptop computers are small enough to use most anywhere. Where could you use a laptop computer?

A computer **workstation** is a place where a computer is used. The computer at your workstation may be connected to other computers in a **network**. Computers that are networked can share information and can sometimes share hardware such as printers.

You might have cables that link computers in your classroom in a local network. Perhaps your computers are linked using the telephone system in a wide-area network. The Internet is a huge network that connects smaller computer networks. If you use the Internet in your classroom, you are indeed networked to computers around the world. You will learn more about the Internet in the Communications unit.

✓ Check Your Understanding

1. Name three types of personal computers.
2. Describe how your classroom computer might be linked to other computers.

Types of Computers

interNET CONNECTION

Introduce students to the Internet. Go to the Web page for an organization or company that is located in another city. Demonstrate using a projection system or capture screens from the site to show off line.

Types of Computers

TEACH

If you have access to a laptop or notebook computer, consider showing students how these computers are similar to the personal computers they will use in this class. Emphasize the portability of laptops and notebooks. Ask students to identify reasons why some people want to have a portable computer. Responses might include taking the computer to class, taking the computer on a business trip, and using the computer to make a presentation.

ASSESS

Use **Check Your Understanding** to assess students' understanding of the information presented in this lesson.

Possible Responses:

1. *Three types of personal computers include desktop, laptop, and notebook computers.*
2. *Classroom computers might be linked to other computers through a network.*

CLOSE

Explain to students that the basic information in this lesson is the foundation for learning to actually use a computer.

1.2 Input, Output, and Storage Devices

FOCUS
Identify input devices, output devices, and storage devices.

BELLRINGER
When students enter the room, direct their attention to the assignment on the board:

Look at the photographs on pages 4 and 6. Make sure you can identify the keyboard, mouse, and trackball.

TEACH
Help students understand the key terms in this section by providing as many visual cues as possible. Use the computer equipment that is readily available to you. Consider a "mini" field trip to another location within the school if different equipment is available in another classroom or the administrative offices.

1.2 Input, Output, and Storage Devices

Goal
- Identify input, output, and storage devices

In addition to the basic parts of a computer described earlier, several other types of hardware can be connected to your computer. An **input device** is hardware that allows you to communicate with your computer. A keyboard, for example, allows you to enter information and issue commands. An **output device** is hardware that allows your computer to communicate with you. For example, the monitor that displays information or the printer that prints letters are both devices that give you information from the computer. A **storage device** allows you to store or retrieve information.

Examples of input and output devices and computer storage devices are described below. As you read each description, see if you can find these devices on a computer system in your classroom or home.

COMPUTER INPUT DEVICES

The **keyboard** of the computer is similar to the keyboard of a typewriter. It contains a collection of letters, numbers, and special symbols you can use to enter information.

The **mouse** and the **trackball** are hand-held devices. You can use them to select and move information around the computer screen and to give commands. It may take a little practice to be able to "point, click, and move" with the mouse or the trackball.

The keyboard, mouse, and trackball are computer input devices.

6   Section I Hardware

RESOURCES
- Lesson Plan: LP2
- CD-ROM: Computer Basics

A **light pen** is used with the computer screen to move around or give commands. You simply hold the pen to the computer screen. Next, highlight the area you wish to select or move to. Then, click and draw with the pen or type the information.

A **pointing stick** is often used on portable computers. It is a small device that looks much like a pencil eraser. The pointing stick is used in place of a mouse to move around the screen.

A **touchpad** is a pressure-sensitive and motion-sensitive device that is used in place of a mouse to move around the screen and give commands.

A **touch screen** allows you to use your fingers to make selections on the computer screen. Touch screens are often used for younger children who may not be able to operate a keyboard or a mouse. By touching a selection on the monitor, you can input the information you want by following on-screen instructions.

You can make selections by touching the computer screen.

A **bar code reader** is a wand or screen that uses a light source to read the bar code characters. Bar codes, such as the one on the back of your textbook, store pieces of information about a product. Bar code readers are used by businesses to input price and product information quickly.

A **scanner** allows you to place a picture (graphic image) into the computer. By using a light source, the scanner turns the picture into groups of dots (called pixel codes) that the computer can understand. You can place the scanned picture into documents, such as letters or greeting cards, you create with your computer.

A **microphone** allows you to record sounds as input to your computer. These sounds can be used to give the computer instructions or to answer a telephone connected to the computer.

Input, Output, and Storage Devices   **7**

Input, Output, and Storage Devices

TEACH

Ask students where they might have seen or used a touch screen or a bar code reader. Responses might include touch screen cash registers at a convenience store or restaurant; touch screens as part of an exhibit at a zoo, museum, or amusement park; bar code readers in department or general merchandise stores, and grocery store scanners. Ask students where they might have seen or used any of the other devices discussed on this page.

Lesson Extension

Most grocery, department, and general merchandise stores use bar code readers to scan prices of purchases. The scanning process can also track inventory and purchasing trends. Data generated during the purchase process can be used by managers as they purchase merchandise from suppliers.

Input, Output, and Storage Devices

TEACH

Demonstrate the monitors you have readily accessible. Point out the quality and size of the image on different monitors.

Demonstrate all the printers you have readily accessible. Consider creating a document and printing it on several different kinds of printers—dot matrix, inkjet, and laser printers. Point out the difference in the quality of the different printers.

If you do not have access to more than one kind of printer in your classroom, consider creating the printouts using printers in other parts of the school or at home. Some copy shops have self-serve computers and printers that you could use for this project. You can also ask a computer dealer to help you prepare the printouts.

You might want to use some color in your document if you have access to a color printer.

COMPUTER OUTPUT DEVICES

The computer **monitor** is a screen that displays information such as text, numbers, and pictures. Monitors come in different sizes and with different degrees of sharpness and clarity. Depending on the type of monitor you have, you may see the information in only a few colors or in a dazzling array of colors.

A **printer** gives you information from the computer in printed form. There are three common types of printers.

- A *dot matrix printer* gives a printed image in a pattern (matrix) of tiny ink dots. These printers are generally less expensive than other types of printers and the image is not as clear as that of other printers.

- An *inkjet printer* gives a better quality of printed document because the machine uses an ink cartridge and a printing element to print a finer image on the paper. Color inkjet printers are popular for creating newsletters, greeting cards, and other documents where colored text or pictures are appropriate.

- A *laser printer* gives the best quality of printed documents. A laser beam and an ink toner cartridge are used to produce the images. Laser printers can print an entire page of words and pictures quickly. These printers are generally more expensive than other types of printers.

A laser printer produces the best quality of printed documents very quickly.

8 Section 1 Hardware

Lesson Extension

In addition to the printers that are used with personal computers, there are high-speed, high-capacity printers that are used by businesses. Examples of the output from these printers include addresses on catalogs and magazines, utility and credit card bills, and personalized direct mail pieces.

A **speaker** allows you to hear voice, music, and other sounds from your computer. The speakers may be built into the computer case or monitor unit of your computer, or they might be separate pieces of equipment.

A **modem** allows you to use your computer to communicate with other computers. Using a modem you can:

- send or receive electronic-mail messages,
- transfer computer files to or from another computer located nearby or far away, and
- access the Internet.

The modem may be built into the computer case. A modem may also be in its own case connected to the computer by a cable.

Some modems allow you to send and receive a **fax.** Fax is short for *facsimile* which means *copy* or *duplicate*. Using a fax machine or a fax/modem is like making a copy of a document by long distance. You can send information directly from your computer to a fax machine or receive information directly from a fax machine. Once the information is received, you can print the document using a printer connected to your computer.

STORAGE DEVICES

A **hard disk** is a magnetic platter that holds a large amount of information in a form the computer can understand. Hard disks are usually inside the computer, but can be a separate connected unit. The computer can store information on and read information from a hard disk very quickly. The programs you will use to complete the projects in this book are probably stored on the hard disk in your computer.

A **floppy disk** is a flat disk made of plastic. Inside the diskette casing is a magnetic surface that can store information in a form the computer can understand. Once information has been saved on the disk, it can be removed from the computer disk drive and stored for later use.

Input, Output, and Storage Devices

Input, Output, and Storage Devices

TEACH

Demonstrate the use of speakers by playing a sound clip. Point out that many programs have audio cues. Examples include the sounds that are heard when programs or operating systems are started or closed.

Demonstrate the use of the modem by sending a fax or accessing the Internet. (See Internet Connection below.)

Demonstrate the use of the hard drive by saving a document. Point out how the indicator light on the drive is activated during the storage process.

Bring a collection of disks to class and pass them around for students to examine. Consider opening a diskette so students can see what is inside. Remind students that opening the diskette case damages the data stored on the disk. Try to locate magnetic tape reels or cassettes used to store data for large computer systems. Create a bulletin board display of the various storage media.

interNET CONNECTION

Demonstrate using a modem to access the Internet. Select a Web site or e-mail address for a company that has ties to your community. Examples of some World Wide Web directory services include:

Info Seek Net Search:
   http://www.infoseek.com
Webcrawler: http://www.webcrawler.com
Yahoo:
   http://www.yahoo.com

Input, Output, and Storage Devices

TEACH

Demonstrate how you can use a CD-ROM with a personal computer. Show students how CD-ROMs are packaged, how to handle them, and how to insert them.

In addition to demonstrating a CD-ROM containing reference information, clip art, or a software program, play a music CD in the computer. Point out that the same medium is used for data and music.

ASSESS

To assess students' understanding, ask them to categorize the items listed below as input devices, output devices, or storage devices. The correct responses appear in parentheses.

    CD-ROM (storage)
    Disk (storage)
    Keyboard (input)
    Magnetic tape (storage)
    Microphone (input)
    Printer (output)
    Speakers (output)
    Touch screen (input)
    Trackball (input)

CLOSE

Introduce students to the input, output, and storage devices that they will be using in this course. Let them know when they can expect to actually start using the computer.

When needed, the computer can read the information from the disk. Information can be erased from a floppy disk and more, new information recorded in its place.

You will probably use a floppy disk to store and retrieve information as you complete the projects in this book. Treat the floppy disk with care to avoid losing the information stored there. Keep the disk in a cool, dry place when not in use. Protect the disk from moisture, magnetic fields, and extreme heat or cold. Do not bend the disk or remove it from its hard plastic covering.

Magnetic tape allows you to store information on reels, cartridges, or cassettes that look similar to video or audio tapes. Magnetic tape is used by companies that need to store information for long periods of time. Magnetic tape is also used to store computer files that are too large to fit on a floppy disk.

Optical discs, sometimes called laser discs or compact discs (CDs), can hold a very large amount of computer information. These discs look similar to a music CD and are commonly called CDs. Computer programs that include music, animation, and video often come on CDs because these programs are very large and require a lot of storage space.

Information is recorded on an optical disc using a laser. Unlike floppy disks described above, most optical discs can have information recorded on them only once. Most computers do not have a disc drive for recording information on optical discs. However, many computers do have a drive for reading information from a CD. When handling a CD, carefully avoid scratching the surface of the underside of the disc.

Section 1 Hardware

Software

SECTION 2

Focus on Software

Computer software provides instructions that tell the computer how to operate. You will learn about two types of computer software—operating system software and application software. Both types of software are necessary for a computer to work correctly and to be useful to you.

OBJECTIVES

- Identify computer operating systems.
- Give examples of application software and its uses.

Words To Know

application software
clip art
database
desktop publishing
graphics
GUI
IBM-compatible
icon
interactive
Macintosh
operating system software
software
spreadsheet
word processing

Section 2 Software 11

Career Exploration Activities: Communications and Media

There are many career opportunities in the communications industry. Discuss the kinds of skills needed for careers in advertising, broadcasting, journalism, photography, and publishing.

Plan a field trip to an advertising agency. Ad agencies use a variety of software programs. Examples include:

Accounting	Layout and design
Animation	Research
Drawing	Word Processing

Section 2 Software

SECTION OVERVIEW

This section is devoted to computer software—operating systems and application software. Emphasize the difference between Macintosh and IBM-compatible systems.

Tell students about the personal computers they will be using in this course. If you have both Macintosh and IBM-compatible systems in your classroom or school, consider a demonstration of how each system works.

Provide a brief explanation and demonstration of the kinds of software that will be used in this course. Include word processing, desktop publishing, spreadsheet, database, and communications software.

CONTENT FOCUS

Operating system software
Business software
Communications software
Graphics software
Educational and reference software
Entertainment and leisure software
Integrated software programs

OPENING ACTIVITY

Ask students what kinds of tasks they have completed using a computer. Make a list of the tasks on the board. If students do not have personal experience using a computer, ask them to tell you how they have seen others use computers including characters in movies and on television.

2.1 Operating System Software

FOCUS
Define operating system software.

BELLRINGER
When students enter the room, direct their attention to the assignment on the board:

Read page 12 of your textbook. Then list the most common types of operating systems in use for both IBM-compatible and Macintosh computers.

TEACH
Show students the basics about the computer operating system they will be using in this course. Explain that it is important that you know what operating system you are using in order to know what application software you can use.

Discuss the differences and similarities between Macintosh, DOS, and Windows systems. Emphasize that DOS and Windows systems are both used on IBM-compatible computers. Note the use of the mouse and icons when using Macintosh and Windows systems.

ASSESS
To assess understanding, have students explain an operating system in their own words.

CLOSE
Let students know what operating system they will be using during this course.

Operating System Software

2.1

Goal
- Define operating system software

Computers must have a series of **software** programs that tell the computer what to do. The **operating system** software is a type of program that acts like a conductor in an orchestra. It directs all the activities and sets all the rules for how the hardware and software work together.

Different types of computers, such as the **Macintosh** and **IBM-compatible** computers, use different operating systems. Currently, these operating systems cannot talk to one another very well. For this reason, you cannot usually use Macintosh software on an IBM-compatible computer, and vice versa. Technology is coming closer and closer to bridging the gap between the different types of computers and operating systems. One day the same software may work on all types of computers.

IBM-compatible computers use various operating systems. The most commonly used types are DOS (Disk Operating System) and/or Windows software. For Macintosh computers, the operating system software is referred to by number, such as System 6 or System 7.

Both Macintosh and Windows system software use a **GUI** design. GUI stands for *graphical user interface*. In a GUI program, pictures and symbols called **icons** are used to represent files and commands. It is usually easier to click on an icon or click on a button with a picture than it is to type a command.

Students practice using computers in a lab environment.

12   Section 2 Software

RESOURCES
- Lesson Plan: LP3
- CD-ROM: Computer and Typing Trivia

Lesson Extension
Macintosh computers and the operating system used to run them are products of Apple Computer, Inc. The company was founded by Steven Jobs and Stephen Wozniak. They built the first Apple computer in a garage.

2.2 Application Software

Goal
- Give examples of application software for
  - business
  - communications
  - graphics
  - education and reference
  - entertainment and leisure
  - integrated programs

Application software programs work with the operating system software to help you use your computer to do specific types of work. For example, you may use word processing software to write a letter or graphics software to draw a picture. There are many types of application software. For our discussion, we will group these programs into these categories:

- business
- communications
- graphics
- education and reference
- entertainment and leisure
- integrated programs

BUSINESS SOFTWARE

Business software includes word processing, spreadsheet, and database programs. A **word processing** program allows you to create, edit, and print text documents like a report or a flyer.

Data in a **spreadsheet** program appear in numbered rows and lettered columns in a grid pattern. You can enter data into cells on the grid. The spreadsheet helps you process financial or mathematical information. For example, you might use a spreadsheet to figure out how much money your school club needs to raise to take a field trip.

A **database** program lets you set up an electronic filing system. By entering text and numbers, you can find, search, and print information in many different ways. You can sort information and design a report to show the data as needed. You might use a database to keep an inventory of your videos or CDs.

✓ Check Your Understanding
1. How can you use a word processing program?
2. Describe a spreadsheet program. How is it used?
3. What are some ways to use a database program?

RESOURCES
- Lesson Plan: LP4
- CD-ROM: Computer Basics

Lesson Extension
MS-DOS and Windows are products of the Microsoft Corporation. Bill Gates and Paul Allen founded Microsoft in 1975. Microsoft introduced MS-DOS in 1981 and Windows in 1985.

2.2 Application Software

FOCUS
Give examples of application software for business, communications, graphics, education and reference, entertainment and leisure, and integrated programs.

BELLRINGER
Direct students to review the list of software categories on page 13.

TEACH
Demonstrate some of the key features of word processing, spreadsheet, and database software. If available, use a projection unit or large monitor for the demonstration.

Use **Check Your Understanding** to assess students' understanding of the information presented on this page.

Possible Responses:
1. A word processing program can be used to create, edit, and print text documents like a report or flyer.
2. A spreadsheet program includes numbered rows and lettered columns in a grid pattern. You can enter data in the cells. You can use a spreadsheet to help process financial or mathematical information.
3. Responses will vary.

Application Software

TEACH

Demonstrate communications software. Send an e-mail message to someone you know and ask them to send a message back to your class. You and your students can view the returned e-mail the next day.

Use **Check Your Understanding** to assess students' understanding of the information presented on this page.

Possible Responses:

1. *Examples of how communications software is used include to send and receive electronic mail (e-mail), to access the Internet, to exchange computer files, to send and receive fax messages, and to make a computer act as a speakerphone or an answering machine.*
2. *Computers communicate with other computers by using software that works with a modem or network.*

Scientists often input data to help them process information. What type of application software would a scientist use?

COMMUNICATIONS SOFTWARE

Communications software works with your modem or network hardware and allows your computer to communicate with other computers. You need communications software to send electronic-mail messages or access the Internet. Using communications software, you may be able to exchange computer files with someone in another location. You can choose from a variety of settings on the communications software for your fax/modem. For example, you might want the computer to send fax messages automatically at a later time. You can set some computers to act as a speakerphone and answering machine. Communications software and hardware make this possible.

✓ Check Your Understanding

1. Give an example of how communications software is used.
2. How can your computer communicate with other computers?

14   Section 2 Software

---

interNET CONNECTION

Access a Web page. Find an advertisement in a magazine or newspaper that includes the Internet address for a company's Web site. Show the students the ad and point out how the address is written. Examples of Web page addresses found in magazines include:

U.S. Space Camp: http://www.spacecamp.com
Sports Illustrated for Kids: http://www.sikids.com
Quaker Oatmeal: http://www.quakeroatmeal.com

GRAPHICS SOFTWARE

Graphics software uses pictures or images to help communicate messages. You can choose from a variety of graphics programs, depending on what you want to create. Graphics software that allows you to draw and paint gives you the chance to become your own artist. Using a mouse or light pen, you can select different lines, designs, and colors to create images. **Clip art** consists of graphic images that you can add to documents. For example, you might include a picture of a cake with candles on a birthday card. You can size, move, and color clip art pictures to suit your needs. **Desktop publishing** software uses both pictures and words to give you the ability to create documents such as newsletters and brochures.

✓ Check Your Understanding

1. Name an example of a desktop publishing program. How is it used?
2. Name an example of a piece of clip art. How is it used?

EDUCATION AND REFERENCE SOFTWARE

Education and reference software programs are available on many topics. Do you want to learn a new language, improve your math skills, or study astronomy? Educational programs can help. Educational games and software "books" are popular with young people. Some reference programs, such as a dictionary, thesaurus, and writing style manual, make your job of writing and editing easier. Encyclopedia programs include all the volumes of an encyclopedia on one CD. Most reference materials traditionally found in print are now available as software programs.

✓ Check Your Understanding

1. Give an example of an educational software program. How is it used?
2. Give an example of a reference software program. How is it used?

Desktop publishing software allows you to create exciting newsletters.

Application Software 15

Application Software

TEACH

Demonstrate graphics software. Create a simple flyer for a book sale. Include the date and times. Add clip art depicting books. If available as a graphic file, consider inserting the school logo in your document.

Use **Check Your Understanding** to assess students' understanding of the information presented on this page.

Possible Responses:

1. Answers will vary. Desktop publishing programs are used to create documents such as newsletters and brochures.
2. Answers will vary. Clip art consists of graphic images that can be added to documents.

Demonstrate reference software. Use an encyclopedia on CD-ROM to demonstrate one way to do research using a personal computer. In advance, select a topic that showcases some of the features of the program, such as sound and video clips. For example, the entry for Martin Luther King, Jr., might include a biography, a picture, and a sound clip of a speech; the entry for dance might include a description of dances and a video clip; and the entry for a specific country might include a population chart, a picture of the country's flag, and a sound clip of the national anthem.

Use **Check Your Understanding** to assess students' understanding of the information presented on this page. Answers will vary.

Lesson Extension

Provide a list of reference software that is available for student use in your classroom or in the school library. Review the list and give examples of the kinds of information contained in each reference.

Application Software

TEACH

Demonstrate entertainment software. Many students have used the computer for playing games and other entertainment. Perform a quick demonstration using entertainment or leisure software with which you are familiar. If your computer came with games installed, you might want to use one of them for your demo.

Use **Check Your Understanding** to assess students' understanding of the information presented on this page. Answers will vary.

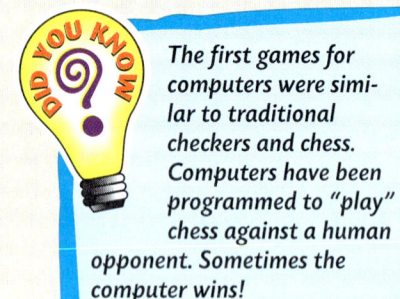

DID YOU KNOW?
The first games for computers were similar to traditional checkers and chess. Computers have been programmed to "play" chess against a human opponent. Sometimes the computer wins!

ENTERTAINMENT AND LEISURE SOFTWARE

Entertainment and leisure software is one of the most widely used types of software. From games and simulations to electronic sporting events, you can test your skills. Many children's stories have been turned into **interactive** books. These books show text and images on screen. Some programs read the story to you and give you an opportunity to make choices that affect the story. Programs on gardening, home repair, crafts, collecting, music, art, and other leisure activities are all available.

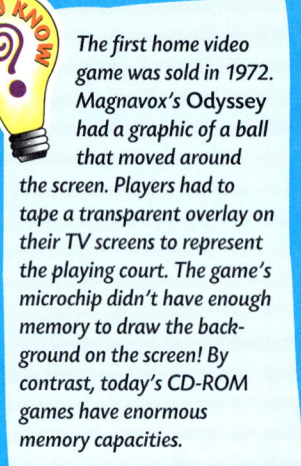

DID YOU KNOW?
The first home video game was sold in 1972. Magnavox's Odyssey had a graphic of a ball that moved around the screen. Players had to tape a transparent overlay on their TV screens to represent the playing court. The game's microchip didn't have enough memory to draw the background on the screen! By contrast, today's CD-ROM games have enormous memory capacities.

Many students enjoy testing their skills playing computer games.

✓ Check Your Understanding

1. Give an example of an interactive book or other entertainment program.
2. Which types of entertainment software have you used, or would like to use?

16 Section 2 Software

INTEGRATED SOFTWARE

Integrated software packages combine several software applications into one program. They are sometimes called software suites. Most integrated packages include word processing, spreadsheet, database, and communications applications. You will use one of these integrated programs to complete the projects in this book.

✓ Check Your Understanding

1. Give an example of an integrated software package.
2. Why are software suites helpful?

CULTURAL KALEIDOSCOPE

A company in Japan has developed a computer that can translate spoken language. This computer understands about fifteen hundred spoken words in Japanese, English, and German. It took 7 years to develop this computer.

Application Software **17**

Application Software

TEACH

Tell students about the integrated software programs that are available in your classroom or lab. The package or the reference material that accompanies the software might provide a list of features of the integrated software.

ASSESS

Use **Check Your Understanding** to assess students' understanding of the information presented on this page.

Possible Responses:

   1. Answers will vary.
   2. Software suites are helpful because they contain multiple applications in one program.

CLOSE

Introduce students to the specific software they will be using for Unit 2. Explain that good keyboarding skills are the foundation of good computer skills. Point out that students will learn more about word processing, spreadsheet, and database software programs in Units 3, 5, and 6, respectively.

CULTURAL KALEIDOSCOPE

When a computer is first set up you must indicate your country, the layout of your keyboard, and the language and measurements you intend to use. In most cases the setup choices are made for you when you buy a computer or load software. If you live in the United States and you plan to communicate in English, your setup will be as follows:

   Country: United States
   Language: English (American)
   Keyboard layout: US
   Measurements: English

17

Section 3
Technology Issues

SECTION OVERVIEW

This section is devoted to technology issues. Depending on the experience of your students, there may be wide variations in their familiarity and understanding of the information presented in this section.

Review the objectives for this section. Offer students some real-life examples of how technology affects their lives each day.

CONTENT FOCUS

Technology-based society
Computing and careers
Ethical use of computers

OPENING ACTIVITY

Discuss the pros and cons of computers in our society. Ask students to explain how computers and technology enhance people's lives. Make a list on the board. Encourage students to give examples from their own lives. Ask them to expand the list with examples they have read about or heard about.

Ask students to think about the negatives or cons related to computers and technology. Make a list on the board. Prompt students to help them identify issues related to copyright law violations, hacking, software piracy, computer viruses, and invasion of privacy.

SECTION 3
Technology Issues

OBJECTIVES

- Describe ways that telecomputing promotes a global community.
- Identify the role of technology in a variety of careers.
- Identify examples of intellectual property and copyright law violations that are related to computer use.
- Identify examples of unethical use of computers such as hacking and software piracy.
- Define the term *computer virus*, and list ways to protect software and hardware from computer viruses.
- Contrast public data and private data.

Focus on Technology Issues

Technology affects our lives in many ways. The way we learn, work, and play continues to change as technology changes. In this unit you will learn how technology makes the world seem smaller by making communication faster and easier. You will see how computers are used in a variety of careers. You will also study ethical issues related to computer use.

Words To Know

computer virus
copyright laws
ethics
hacking
intellectual property
private data
public data
telecommunication
telecomputing
sabotage
software piracy

18   Section 3 Technology Issues

Career Exploration Activities:
Business and Office

Invite a human resource specialist from a local company to speak to your class. This could be done at school or as part of a field trip. Be sure to let the speaker know that your students are interested in learning about how computers are used by human resources professionals. Also, ask the speaker to address privacy issues related to the use of computers in human resources. Some areas of interest include background checks, medical insurance records, and salary information.

18

3.1 Technology-Based Society

Goal
- Describe how telecomputing affects society

We live in a world where technology is no longer a luxury; it is a need. Children have access to a world of information and learning through computers. Business people can use application software to work more effectively. Senior citizens can communicate electronically with friends and keep their financial records on computers. Technology knows no differences in age, culture, gender, location, or time. Technology is helping our diverse world become one global village.

Telecommunication is communicating over distance. Talking with someone on the telephone is one example of telecommunication. **Telecomputing** is the blending of telecommunication and computer technology. Computers communicate with one another using networks, the telephone system, and satellites.

The telecomputing trend is growing quickly. Telecomputing is available 24 hours a day. You can send an electronic-mail message at any time, and you do not need to wait until the person receiving the message is available to talk with you. It is easy to communicate with someone in another part of the world. You can also communicate easily with several people at once. Telecomputing allows you to make friends with people around the world, exchange information, and solve problems more quickly and efficiently.

What are some advantages and disadvantages of telecomputing from a home office?

✓ Check Your Understanding

1. Name a use of telecomputing in your personal life.
2. Name a use of telecomputing on the job.

Technology-Based Society **19**

RESOURCES
- Lesson Plan: LP5
- CD-ROM: Computer and Typing Trivia

Lesson Extension

There are also social issues related to technology. While it may be convenient to use telecomputing for many kinds of communication, it cannot replace personal interaction. An e-mail message on your birthday is not the same as sharing cake and ice cream with your friends.

3.1 Technology-Based Society

FOCUS
Describe how telecomputing affects society.

BELLRINGER
Have students list five advantages to telecomputing.

TEACH
Ask students to name some of the advantages to telecomputing.

Point out some of the concerns technology presents for our society and economy. For example, the technology exists for home computers and access to the Internet, but not every family can afford a home computer or the monthly access charge for the Internet.

ASSESS
Use **Check Your Understanding** to assess students' understanding of the information presented in this lesson.

Possible Responses:
1. Sending or receiving electronic mail, surfing the Internet, and visiting an on-line chat room.
2. Sending or receiving electronic mail, exchanging computer files with someone, and accessing information from a remote database.

CLOSE
Explain to students that they will learn more about telecommunications throughout this course and specifically in Unit 7.

19

3.2 Computing and Careers

FOCUS

Describe how technology is used in careers.

BELLRINGER

Have students list the occupations of five people they know personally.

TEACH

Make a list of occupational areas that are of interest to your students. Ask students what occupational fields they might consider for careers. Ask students about the occupational fields of friends and family members.

Ask students to give examples of how technology is used in the careers on your list.

ASSESS

Use **Check Your Understanding** to assess students' understanding of the information presented in this lesson.

Possible Responses:

1. *Any career that requires technology skills is acceptable.*
2. *In addition to job-specific skills, most careers require basic computing skills including word processing, database, spreadsheet, and telecommunications skills.*

CLOSE

Explain that students will be exploring careers all through this course.

Computing and Careers

3.2

Goal
- Describe how technology is used in careers

Computing skills are necessary in many careers. Doctors, pilots, musicians, and artists may use computers often as they work to make their jobs more productive. For example, medical diagnoses are more accurate if kept on electronic databases. Computer recordings allow a musician to simulate an entire orchestra using a software program. An artist can use the computer to redesign or animate pictures. An airline pilot can program the flight destination to help pinpoint the route the airplane is to travel. Jobs related more directly to computers include computer programming, troubleshooting and maintenance, computer applications, and data entry.

Whatever career you choose, you will need a wide range of computing skills. Your knowledge of how to use and create documents through word processing, databases, spreadsheets, and telecommunications will help you now during your school years and also in your future career.

✓ Check Your Understanding

1. Name a career that uses technology skills.
2. What preparation do you need for that job?

20   Section 3 Technology Issues

RESOURCES

- Lesson Plan: LP5
- CD-ROM: Careers in Technology

Ethical Use of Computers

3.3

Ethics are the standards of honesty, morality, and fairness. These standards relate to using computers. You have a responsibility to respect the property, rights, and privacy of others in the way you use computers at home and at school. You should find out about your school's rules for using computers.

Goals
- Identify intellectual property and copyrights
- Discuss unethical uses of computers
- Identify the difference between public and private data

✓ Check Your Understanding

1. Does your school have policy statements or rules concerning the ethical use of computers?
2. Give an example of a rule that might be included in a computer use policy.

INTELLECTUAL PROPERTY AND COPYRIGHTS

Intellectual property is a product someone creates based upon his or her thoughts or ideas. Examples of intellectual property include the following:

- a picture or a clip art collection
- music
- computer games
- computer animations
- software programs

Copyright laws exist to protect those who create an idea or product. The U.S. Copyright Act of 1978 protects software companies and creators from illegal use of their products. This symbol © on a product tells you the material carries a copyright.

Most copyrighted materials, such as computer software, may not be copied without consent of the owner. Some software programs have built-in security codes to help protect against illegal use. If you do copy the material without permission, you are breaking the law. You are also taking advantage of someone's intellectual property. The unauthorized use or duplication of a software program is called *software piracy*.

Ethical Use of Computers **21**

RESOURCES
- Lesson Plan: LP6
- CD-ROM: Computer Basics

3.3 Ethical Use of Computers

FOCUS
Identify intellectual property and copyrights. Discuss unethical uses of computers. Identify the difference between public and private data.

BELLRINGER
When students enter the room direct their attention to the assignment on the board:
Read the copyright notice that appears in the front of this textbook.

TEACH
Use visual aids to show students where copyright and trademark notices can be found. Books and magazines usually include a copyright notice on one of the first few pages of the publication. Videos, CDs, tapes, and software programs generally include copyright notices on both the package and label. Movies, television shows, and software programs include on-screen copyright notices.

Explain your school's policies and rules for the ethical use of computers. Make sure that students understand the difference between rules that relate to ethics and general rules for using school computers. An example of a rule related to ethics: Copying commercial software programs is forbidden. An example of a general rule: Eating and drinking are not permitted in the computer lab.

Use **Check Your Understanding** to assess students' understanding of the information presented about ethics. Answers will vary.

21

Ethical Use of Computers

TEACH

Shareware software is available for the user to try before paying for it. You can use the software and decide if you like it before you buy it.

Use **Check Your Understanding** to assess students' understanding of the information presented about intellectual property and copyrights. Answers will vary.

Explain that computer hacking is wrong regardless of the motivation. Some hackers break into systems just to prove they can do it. They usually do not intend to use or alter data. Other hackers deliberately damage systems, alter data, or use data to their own benefit. For example, a hacker might try to access bank records in order to steal money.

Use **Check Your Understanding** to assess students' understanding of the information presented about hacking.

Possible Responses:

1. Answers will vary.
2. Computer hacking is serious because hackers violate the rights of others. This includes the owners of the computer program and persons whose private information is stored in the program.

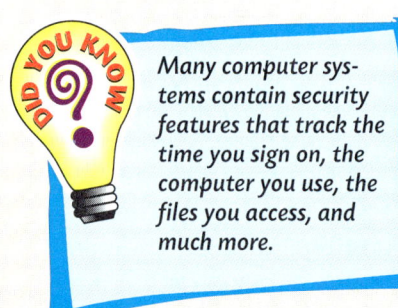

Many computer systems contain security features that track the time you sign on, the computer you use, the files you access, and much more.

Sometimes you may borrow or use someone else's computer program. Even if you have the program owner's permission, if the software license does not allow for many users, then you could be guilty of software piracy. If you are found illegally using software that is copyrighted, you may be sued and be required to pay a heavy fine.

Some software, called *freeware* or *shareware*, is not usually copyrighted. This software may be sampled and may often be copied freely.

✓ Check Your Understanding

1. Check a copy of a software license. How many legal copies of the software may you make?
2. Give an example of something you have created that may be considered your "intellectual property."

HACKING

You may hear the term **hacking** associated with computer ethics. Hacking is the unauthorized use of a computer system or program. Computer hackers may be breaking into a system just for fun. Other hackers may have a more serious reason for trying to unlawfully access a computer program. They may want to change or steal data. Computer hacking is a violation of the law and is punishable.

One way to protect information on computers is to encode it. This process "scrambles" information so that unauthorized users cannot read it.

✓ Check Your Understanding

1. Give an example of computer hacking.
2. Why is computer hacking a serious violation?

22 Section 3 Technology Issues

Lesson Extension

Shareware that is available through on-line services contains a message about the cost and where to send the payment if you decide to use the software. If you order shareware from a dealer, you will probably have to pay for the shipping at the time you order. If you decide to use the software, you must send an additional payment to the dealer. Shareware includes games, antivirus programs, and screen savers.

Freeware does not require any payment. It is the consumer's responsibility to read the program label or documentation and use the shareware or freeware appropriately.

COMPUTER VIRUSES

A **computer virus** is any software program that destroys information or makes it difficult to use the contents of a computer disk. Some viruses damage the computer hardware, software, or stored information. Others are simply practical jokes someone wants to play on the computer user. In either case, a computer virus is a form of **sabotage.** Sabotage, as it relates to computers, is a deliberate act that causes the damage or destruction of computer hardware or software as a virus does.

A computer virus can copy itself onto your system when you use a floppy disk that has a virus on it. You may also copy infected files onto your system from outside sources such as the Internet. A good way to protect your computer from becoming infected with a virus is to use write-protect tabs on your original software. When you use a write-protect tab, nothing can be saved to the protected disk.

As a result of the number of computer viruses that have been created, virus-protection software products are available to help protect your computer from viruses. You should purchase a virus-protection software program for your computer and update it frequently. As our use of telecomputing grows, the risk for infection from computer viruses will also grow.

✓ Check Your Understanding

1. Describe a problem that could occur as a result of a computer virus.
2. Why should you protect your computer from computer viruses?

PUBLIC AND PRIVATE DATA

With the wide use of computers comes the ability to gather a lot of data about people. Just by using a Social Security number, someone may be able to get both public and private data about others. **Public data** is information that is either not personal or that carries your permission for use. Your name and your phone number are examples of public data. **Private data** includes information such as credit card numbers and security passwords. You should be careful about giving out your private data.

Ethical Use of Computers

Ethical Use of Computers

TEACH

Demonstrate the use of antivirus software. Make sure students know how to scan disks they have used at home before they use them in the computers at school. Ask students if they know about any specific viruses.

Some computer viruses infect your computer as soon as you use an infected file. Others are programmed to activate on a certain date. If your hard drive is infected, the virus will activate when you turn on your computer on the target date.

Discuss with students the importance of standards of honesty, ethics, and fairness with regard to the use of computers.

Use **Check Your Understanding** to assess students' understanding of the information presented about computer viruses.

Possible Responses:

1. *A virus might damage computer hardware, software or data.*
2. *It is time-consuming and expensive to repair the damage done by a virus. You should protect your computer against computer viruses as insurance against damage to hardware, software, and data.*

---

interNET CONNECTION

Arrange for your students to communicate via e-mail with someone in a different country. Try to establish a link with school children who are the same age as your students. Use the Internet or a commercial on-line service to find a site related to pen pals.
Examples might include the following sites:
Africa Online Kids Only: http://www.africaonline.com/AfricaOnlinekidsonly.html
Kids' Place: http://www.islandnet.com/~bedford/kids.html
Kids' Space: http://www.interport.net/kids_space

Ethical Use of Computers

ASSESS

Use **Check Your Understanding** to assess students' understanding of the information presented on public and private data.

Possible Responses:

1. Responses will vary. Examples of private information include medical records, a PIN for a bank teller machine, and a computer password.
2. Responses will vary. Examples of public information include information on a birth certificate and property tax records.

CLOSE

Review the key points of your school's policy for the ethical use of computers.

Most of the information associated with Social Security numbers is collected by the federal government. This information is stored by the government in computer files. Other institutions, such as banks, schools, and hospitals, store private data about people. The Privacy Act of 1974 protects people from the unauthorized collection and distribution of information contained in computer files. This law gives you the right to know what information about you is being collected, to correct it if it is wrong, and to be informed about how the information will be used.

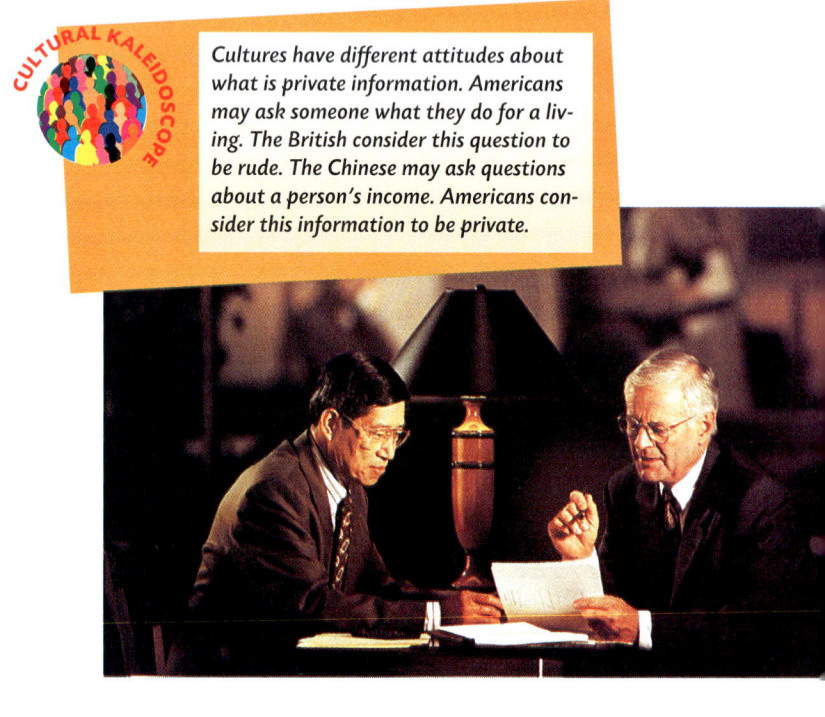

CULTURAL KALEIDOSCOPE

Cultures have different attitudes about what is private information. Americans may ask someone what they do for a living. The British consider this question to be rude. The Chinese may ask questions about a person's income. Americans consider this information to be private.

✓ Check Your Understanding

1. What information about you would you consider private?
2. What information about you would you consider public?

Section 3 Technology Issues

CULTURAL KALEIDOSCOPE

In Latin and South American countries one's family is often a source of pride. It is generally acceptable to ask about the health and well-being of the family of a business acquaintance. In most Arab countries family matters are considered private.

interNET CONNECTION

Select a notable person who lives in your community. Choose someone who holds an elected office or owns a business. See what kinds of public information are available about this person on the Internet.

Software Basics

SECTION 4

Focus on Software Basics

Before you begin creating documents, you need to know some basic information about using your software. In this section you will learn how to start and quit the software, navigate through a document, and give commands. You will also learn about some software features, such as printing a document and using a speller, that are the same no matter which part of the software you use. Follow the steps in the projects in this unit and in the Student Guide carefully. Projects in other units will build upon the skills and information you learn here in Software Basics.

OBJECTIVES

- Start a software program and open a document.
- Choose software commands.
- Navigate through a document.
- Select text and perform simple edits.
- Preview and print a document.
- Access the software help feature.
- Save a document.
- Quit the software program.

Words To Know

choose commands	open	selecting
close	preview	speller
font	print	start
editing	quit	view
help	save	window
navigating	save as	

Section 4 Software Basics 25

Section 4 Software Basics

SECTION OVERVIEW

This section is devoted to software basics. Depending on the experience of your students, there may be wide variations in their familiarity and understanding of the information presented in this section.

Review the objectives for this section. Remind students that this is an introduction to using software. Details about using various software programs are presented in Units 2 through 7.

CONTENT FOCUS

Introduction to software
Navigating and changing text
Previewing and printing documents
Editing and saving files
Help

OPENING ACTIVITY

Review the basic rules for using computers in your classroom or lab. Demonstrate the procedures you expect students to perform at the beginning and end of each project.

Career Exploration Activities: Business and Office

Ask students to review the employment advertisements in the Sunday newspaper. Instruct them to look for ads related to business and office administration. After selecting and mounting an ad, make a list of the computer skills required for the selected position. Have students discuss their findings. Ask them to determine which computer skills were required most.

25

4.1 Introduction to Software

FOCUS
Start software. Open a new document. Choose commands. Quit software.

BELLRINGER
Have students read page 26 and list the four steps in creating documents.

TEACH
Explain that the first five projects will help students become familiar with the software and hardware used throughout the course.

GO TO *Refer students to the appropriate section of the Student Guide.*

PRACTICE—LEVEL 1

Purpose
To introduce software.

Time
One class period.

Preparation
Review guidelines and procedures for classroom or lab.

Teaching Tip
Be sure students are becoming familiar with the document window and practicing choosing commands.

Trouble Shooting
If students need additional help, work with them to complete instructions in the Student Guide.

Introduction to Software
4.1

Are you ready to begin creating documents using your computer? Many different steps are involved. First, you must start your software program. Then you will open a blank, new document screen for either word processing, spreadsheet, database, or one of the other choices. Next, you will choose commands by using menus, toolbars, buttons, or keystrokes. Finally, you will quit your software program. In Project 1, you will learn how to perform all of these steps.

Goals
- Start software
- Open a new document
- Choose commands
- Quit software

GO TO
Student Guide, Introduction	
Start software	Choosing commands
New document	View
Window	Quit

Project 1

INTRODUCTION TO SOFTWARE

1. In your Student Guide, read and follow the steps for Unit 1, **start software**, to learn how to launch your software.
2. Open a **new document** for word processing.
3. In your Student Guide, read and follow the steps for Unit 1, **window**, to familiarize yourself with the basic parts of a document window.
4. Practice **choosing commands** using the keyboard, menus, and buttons by displaying or hiding the items discussed under **view** in the Student Guide.
5. **Quit** your software program without saving the document.

Section 4 Software Basics

RESOURCES
- Lesson Plan: LP7
- CD-ROM: Computer Basics—Software

4.2 Navigating and Changing Text

You can change the style of text in a document by applying bold, italic, or underline to a word. In order to change text, you must learn to navigate or move the insertion point to the text to be changed.

Goals
- Navigate through a document
- Change style

NORMAL. Plain text without any special style.
> This is normal text.

BOLD. Darkened text.
> **This is bold text.**

ITALIC. Slanted, slightly lightened text.
> *This is italicized text.*

UNDERLINED. Line drawn under text.
> <u>This is underlined text</u>.

In Project 2, you will practice opening an existing document, navigating through the document, changing the appearance of text, and saving the changed file under a new name.

Resources
- Lesson Plan: LP7
- CD-ROM: Inbox—Word Processing

4.2 Navigating and Changing Text

FOCUS
Navigate through a document. Change fonts.

BELLRINGER
Have students read page 27 in the textbook and find examples of normal text, bold text, and italic text.

TEACH
Changing the text style in a document can add interest to a page and draw attention to important information. It is important that the text styles you use complement the written message and do not confuse the reader.

Ask students to give examples of documents that should be kept simple. Responses might include business letters, book reports, and term papers. Also ask for examples of documents where varied type styles are appropriate. Responses might include newsletters, flyers, and announcements.

ASSESS
To assess understanding have students turn to page 193 and identify normal, bold, italicized, and underlined text.

CLOSE
Explain to students that they are now ready to navigate through a document and change fonts. Refer to Project 2.

Project 2
Navigating and Changing Text

GO TO — *Refer students to the appropriate section of the Student Guide.*

PRACTICE—LEVEL 1

Purpose
To navigate through a document and to change text styles.

Time
Fifteen minutes.

Preparation
Make sure the appropriate data disks are available.

Teaching Tip
Observe students carefully to make sure they are using the arrow keys and scroll bar to move around the document. Make sure they are practicing with different text styles. Students who finish early should repeat the project.

Trouble Shooting
Make sure students are saving their work to their data disks.

Wrap Up
Have students return workstations to the appropriate condition.

GO TO — **Student Guide, Introduction**
Open — Save as
Navigating — Close
Font

Project 2
NAVIGATING AND CHANGING TEXT

1. Start your software and choose a word processing document type.
2. **Open** the file CB002 on your data disk.
3. Practice **navigating** through the document using the arrow keys and scroll bar.
4. Practice choosing commands by clicking inside the title and changing the **font** style to bold.
5. Use the **save as** command to save the document as STCB002 on your data disk.
6. **Close** the document.

Note: In the file name STCB002, **ST** stands for student, **CB** stands for the computer basics unit, and **002** (zero, zero, two) stands for Project 2. Be sure to press the zero key and not the letter O when typing zeros.

CULTURAL KALEIDOSCOPE
Some cultures consider being on time important. Other cultures are more flexible about time. For example, in Central and South America it is common to arrive 30 minutes late for an appointment.

Section 4 Software Basics

CULTURAL KALEIDOSCOPE
When conducting business in another country, it is always a good idea to be punctual. While your client or supplier might arrive late or keep you waiting, you should be on time for business appointments and social events.

4.3 Previewing and Printing Documents

Goals
- Preview a document
- Print a document

As you work on a document, you normally see only a part of the document on the screen. You usually cannot see things like margins and page numbers clearly or easily.

When you finish creating a document, you can preview the entire document on one screen to get a good idea of how the finished document will look when it is printed. You can make changes until you are satisfied, and then print the document. In this project, you will open an existing document and learn to preview and print.

PREVIEW. A view of the entire document, including margins and page numbers.

> SUMMER OLYMPICS 1996
>
> My summer vacation was the perfect trip for a swimmer. I was able to get tickets to the Summer Olympic games in Atlanta, Georgia. What a wonderful trip! The tickets were compliments of my grandparents. This was a vacation I will never forget.
>
> I have been a competitive swimmer since the age of 8 and am hoping to receive a college scholarship for swimming. I am now in my junior year of high school and plan to compete for my high school swim team and my club team.
>
> Competitive swimming may seem strange to some people, but I really like the individual as well as the team competitions. People who are dedicated to top level swimming are called elite athletes. Every swimmer at the Olympics is definitely an elite athlete. My skill is certainly not of their caliber, but I am a nationally ranked swimmer. This ranking should help get colleges to offer me an athletic scholarship.

Previewing and Printing Documents

Resources
- Lesson Plan: LP8
- CD-ROM: Inbox—Word Processing

4.3 Previewing and Printing Documents

FOCUS
Preview a document. Print a document.

BELLRINGER
When students enter the room, direct their attention to the assignment on the board:

Read the text and look at the illustration on page 29.

TEACH
Emphasize key elements to check when previewing a document, including margins, space between lines and paragraphs, and page number position.

Point out that using the preview feature saves paper and printer supplies.

Explain that a printer can be connected directly to a single computer. A printer can also be directly connected to more than one computer with a switchbox. Often in school and business settings, multiple computers share one or more printers through a network connection. Explain how printers are set up in your classroom or lab.

ASSESS
To assess understanding have students explain the purpose of previewing a document.

CLOSE
Explain to students that they are now ready to preview and print a document. Refer to Project 3.

Project 3
Previewing and Printing Documents

GO TO — *Refer students to the appropriate section of the Student Guide.*

PRACTICE—LEVEL 1

Purpose
To preview a document and to print a document.

Time
Fifteen minutes.

Preparation
Make sure printers are ready including full paper trays.

Teaching Tip
Students who finish early should repeat the project.

Trouble Shooting
Provide individual help to students who are having difficulty.

Wrap Up
Have students return computers and furniture to the appropriate conditions.

DID YOU KNOW? *In 1642, Blaise Pascal invented a mechanical calculator. Pascal, a French mathematician constructed the device using gears and pulleys. (Pascal has a powerful computer language named for him.)*

GO TO — Student Guide, Introduction
Preview
Print

Project 3
PREVIEWING AND PRINTING DOCUMENTS

1. Open the file CB003 on your data disk.
2. Use the **preview** feature of your software to view the entire page.
3. **Print** the document.
4. Quit your software without saving the document.

DID YOU KNOW? *The modern computer is a descendant of the abacus—one of the world's first calculators. Thousands of years ago, people in the Middle East, China, and Greece used abacuses to add and subtract large numbers. The abacus used units of ones, tens, hundreds, and thousands. Today, we still use the base 10, or decimal, number system.*

30   Section 4 Software Basics

4.4 Editing and Saving Files

Goals
- Save a document
- Select and edit text
- Use the speller

Suppose you are writing a paper. You may think of a better way to say something, or you may want to change the order of the sentences in your paper. You may need to edit or change your document several times before you decide on the final content and format. You don't have to start over to make these changes. Basic editing includes cutting or deleting text, copying and pasting text, moving text, and learning to undo and redo any of these changes.

SELECTED TEXT. Text that is highlighted by a colored or shaded box. Select text before applying any formatting changes.

> My summer vacation was the **perfect** trip for a competitive swimmer. I was given tickets to the Summer Olympics held in Atlanta, Georgia. What a wonderful trip! The tickets were compliments of my grandparents. This was a vacation I will never forget.

You should save your documents frequently as you edit. If your computer should lose power or the system freezes, any work that has not been saved to a disk may be lost. In this project, you will learn to save a document, select and edit text, and use the speller to help find spelling errors.

GO TO
Student Guide, Introduction
Selecting   Save
Editing   Speller

Editing and Saving Files **31**

RESOURCES
- Lesson Plan: LP8
- CD-ROM: Inbox—Word Processing

4.4 Editing and Saving Files

FOCUS
Save a document. Select and edit text. Use the speller.

BELLRINGER
When students enter the room, direct their attention to the assignment on the board:
Read the text and look at the illustration on page 31.

TEACH
Remind students of the importance of saving documents frequently. In addition to editing and saving a file, Project 4 introduces the speller. Remind students that the speller is no substitute for accurate typing and careful proofreading. Write a sentence that has errors on the board. Point out the errors the spell check will not detect. An example you might use: Ash the children if they are to tired to eat there I scream.

ASSESS
To assess understanding have students give examples of basic editing.

CLOSE
Explain to students that they are now ready to save a document, select and edit text, and use the speller. Refer to Project 4.

GO TO Refer students to the appropriate section of the Student Guide.

31

Project 4
Editing and Saving Files

PRACTICE—LEVEL 1

Purpose
To edit a file and to save a file.

Time
Fifteen minutes.

Preparation
Make sure appropriate data disks are available.

Teaching Tip
Students who finish early should repeat the project.

Trouble Shooting
Provide individual help to students who are having difficulty selecting text. For some individuals it is easier to highlight from right to left.

Wrap Up
Have students proofread their documents and mark any corrections. If they have time, they should open STCB004, make the corrections, and print the document.

Project 4
EDITING AND SAVING FILES

1. Open the file CB004 on your data disk.
2. Save the document as STCB004 on your data disk.
3. Practice navigating, **selecting,** and **editing** the document. Select and cut *being in the stands and* in the first sentence. Undo the cut. Redo the cut.
4. **Save** the document again.
5. Copy *Jilen Siroky* and paste the name to the beginning of the first line of the paragraph.
6. Insert one blank line between the name and the first line of the paragraph.
7. Use the **speller,** and proofread to check for other errors. Preview the document. Make corrections as needed.
8. Save again. Preview and print the document.
9. Quit your software.

CULTURAL KALEIDOSCOPE
Over 10,000 athletes competed in the 1996 Summer Olympic Games in Atlanta, Georgia. These athletes represented 197 nations and territories. This was the largest group of athletes ever for an Olympics.

32 Section 4 Software Basics

CULTURAL KALEIDOSCOPE
During the 1996 Summer Olympics, athletes were invited to use the Internet to communicate with fans, family, and friends around the world. The Internet helped to bring people from around the world closer together.

4.5 Help

Most software today comes with on-screen help. Because your teacher will not always be available to answer your questions, it is a good idea to learn to use the help feature. On-screen help is like having an electronic reference manual at your fingertips. If you have a question about your software, you can go to the help feature, look up a keyword, and read any number of topics related to your question. Sometimes, you will even find animated help that will guide you step-by-step through a software feature. You can also print any help topics that you might want to save for reference. In this lesson you will practice finding and printing help topics.

Goals
- Find help topics
- Print help topics

GO TO: Student Guide, Introduction — Help

Project 5

HELP

1. Open a new word processing document.
2. In your Student Guide, read Unit 1, **Help.**
3. Find the help topics in your software that are listed in the help section of the Student Guide.
4. Print a help topic of your choice.
5. Quit the software.

RESOURCES
- Lesson Plan: LP9
- CD-ROM: Inbox—Reference Guide

4.5 Help

FOCUS
Find help topics. Print help topics.

BELLRINGER
Have students read the paragraph on page 33.

TEACH
Explain that on-screen help is a convenient way of getting help. Point out that additional reference material is often available in your classroom, lab, and library.

GO TO: Refer students to the appropriate section of the Student Guide.

PRACTICE—LEVEL 1

Purpose
To find a specific help topic and to print a help topic.

Time
Fifteen minutes.

Preparation
Make sure printers are ready with full paper trays.

Teaching Tip
Students who finish early should choose and print another help topic.

Trouble Shooting
Provide individual help to students having difficulty.

UNIT 2 ORGANIZER

Section	Key Presentation	Special Features
5 - Alphabetic Keys		
	Home Keys	Words to Know, p. 36
	Home Keys Review	Do This, p. 38
	E Key	Did You Know?; Language Link, p. 41
	H Key	Bits & Bytes, p. 42
	E & H Review	
	O Key	Language Link, p. 45
	C Key	Bits & Bytes, p. 46
	O & C Review	
	R Key	Did You Know?, p. 49
	I Key	Bits & Bytes, p. 50
	R & I Review	
	W Key	Cultural Kaleidoscope, p. 53
	Right Shift Key	Bits & Bytes, p. 54
	W & Right Shift Key Review	
	T Key	Language Link, p. 57
	Period (.) Key	Bits & Bytes, p. 58
	T & . Review	Do This, p. 59
	M Key	Cultural Kaleidoscope, p. 61
	Left Shift Key	Bits & Bytes, p. 62
	M & Left Shift Key Review	Do This, p. 63
	G Key	Language Link, p. 65
	Comma (,) Key	Bits & Bytes, p. 66
	G & , Review	Do This, p. 67
	X Key	Language Link, p. 69
	U Key	
	X & U Review	Cultural Kaleidoscope, p. 73
	Q Key	Bits & Bytes, p. 74
	N Key	
	Q & N Review	Language Link, p. 77
	V Key	Bits & Bytes, p. 78
	P Key	
	V & P Review	Language Link, p. 81
	B Key	Bits & Bytes, p. 82
	Slash (/) Key	Do This, p. 83
	B & / Review	Cultural Kaleidoscope, p. 85
	Z Key	Bits & Bytes, p. 86
	Y Key	
	Z & Y Review	Language Link, p. 89
	Hyphen (-) Key	Bits & Bytes, p. 90
	Caps Lock Key	
	- & Caps Lock Review	Language Link, p. 93
	Apostrophe (') Key	Bits & Bytes, p. 94

UNIT RESOURCES

- Lesson Plans: LP9–LP48
- Enrichment Activity
- CD-ROM: Unit 2 Learn the Keys All About Typing
- Software: Unit 2 Learn the Keys
- Transparencies: 1, 2

34a

UNIT 2 ORGANIZER

Section	Key Presentation	Special Features
	Tab Key (') & Tab Review A–F Review G–L Review M–S Review T–Z Review	Language Link, p. 97 Cultural Kaleidoscope, p. 99 Language Link, p. 101 Cultural Kaleidoscope, p. 103 Cultural Kaleidoscope, p. 105
6 - Number and Symbol Keys	4$ Key 7& Key 4$ & 7& Review 1! Key 0) Key 1! & 0) Review 3# Key 8* Key 3# & 8* Review 2@ Key 9(Key 2@ & 9(Review 5% Key 6^ Key 5% & 6^ Review =+ Key <>\ Keys =+ & <>\ Review	Words to Know, p. 107 Language Link, p. 111 Do This, p. 112 Do This, p. 113 Language Link, p. 115 Cultural Kaleidoscope, p. 119 Language Link, p. 123 Did You Know?, p. 127 Did You Know?, p. 131
7 - Numeric Keypad	Keypad 4-5-6 and Enter Keys Keypad 7-8-9 Keys Keypad 4-5-6-7-8-9 Review Keypad 1-2-3 Keys Keypad 0 and Decimal (.) Keys Keypad 1-2-3-0-. Review	Words to Know, p. 133 Language Link, p. 137 Cultural Kaleidoscope, p. 141

ASSESSMENT RESOURCES

Check Your Learning

Section 5

pp. 41, 45, 57, 65, 69, 77, 81, 89, 93, 97, 101

Section 6

pp. 111, 115, 123

Section 7

p. 137

Unit Test

(Teacher's Resource Binder)
Objective Test

Time Yourself

Section 5

pp. 45, 49, 53, 57, 61, 65, 69, 73, 77, 81, 85, 89, 93, 97, 99, 101, 103, 105

Section 6

pp. 111, 115, 119, 123, 127, 131

Section 7

pp. 137, 141

UNIT 2

INTRODUCING THE UNIT

Ask your class if they use the touch system or "hunt and peck" method when using a computer keyboard. Explain that the touch system means having eight fingers on the home keys (A, S, D, F, J, K, L, ;) and typing without looking at the keys. Demonstrate and discuss how much faster students will be able to type using the touch system, because they will not have to keep looking back and forth from their keyboards and fingers to their books.

Strongly encourage students to avoid looking at the keys while typing. Explain that doing so will prevent them from increasing their typing speed. Assure them how easy and efficient it is to type using the touch system.

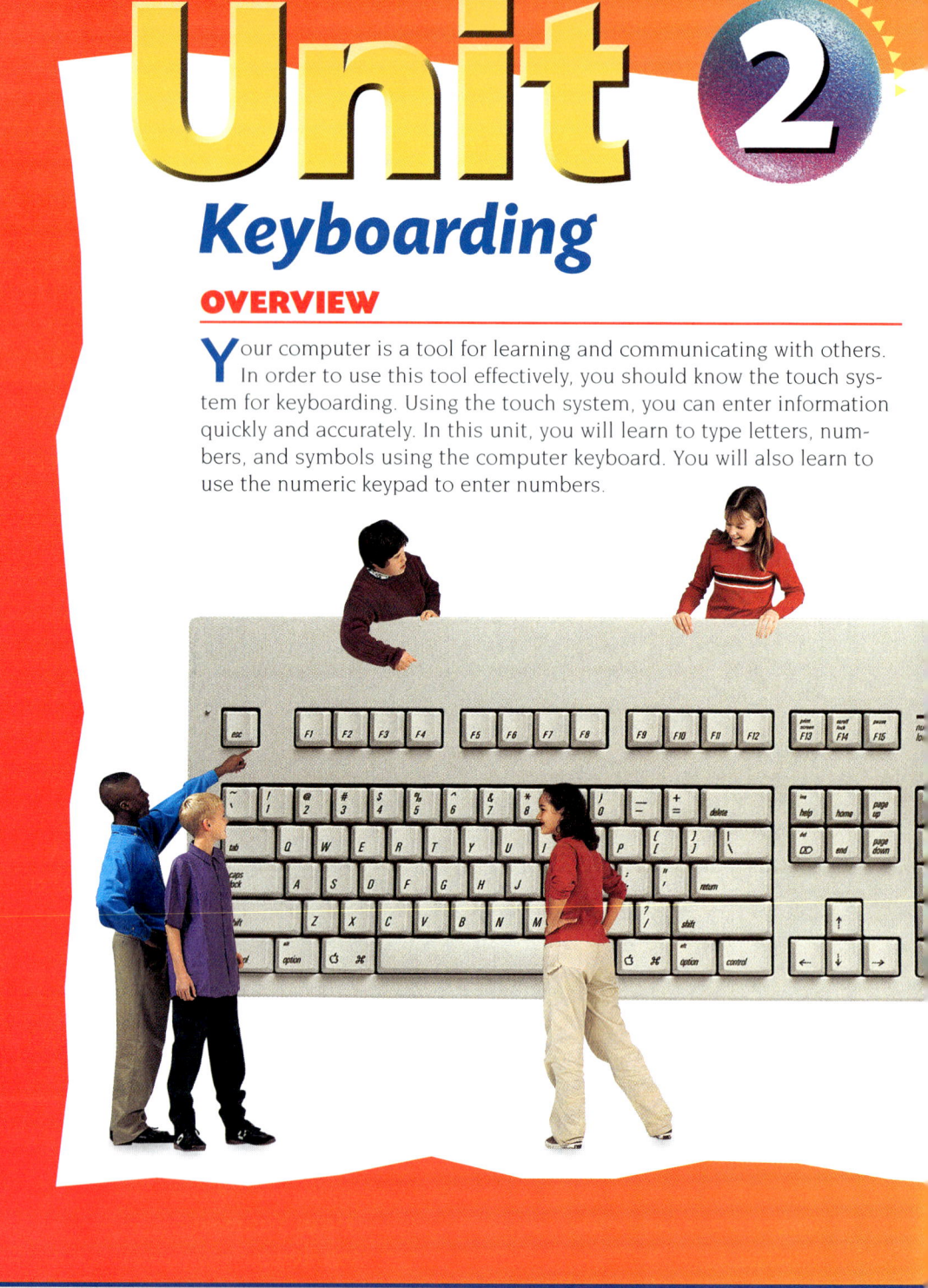

Unit 2
Keyboarding

OVERVIEW

Your computer is a tool for learning and communicating with others. In order to use this tool effectively, you should know the touch system for keyboarding. Using the touch system, you can enter information quickly and accurately. In this unit, you will learn to type letters, numbers, and symbols using the computer keyboard. You will also learn to use the numeric keypad to enter numbers.

Fun Facts

Why are the letters on your keyboard arranged the way they are? This arrangement dates back to the 1800s, when Christopher Latham Sholes built his first typewriter using typebars for each key. Sholes figured out the combinations of letters used most often and separated them as widely as possible so the typebars would not jam.

Sholes' keyboard is called the QWERTY keyboard because the letters Q-W-E-R-T-Y are the first six letters of the top alphabetic row on a keyboard.

UNIT 2

UNIT OBJECTIVES

- Use the touch system to develop basic keyboarding skill on the alphabetic and numeric keyboard.
- Type at a minimum rate of 25 words per minute.
- Use the touch system to operate the numeric keypad.

Unit Contents

Section 5	Alphabetic Keys
Section 6	Number and Symbol Keys
Section 7	Numeric Keypad

Focus On Careers In Technology

Many modern hospitals use computers to store medical records of their patients. Information from each patient's medical chart is entered into a computer file. Nurses update this file every time they give medications or check the patient's blood pressure, pulse rate, temperature, and overall progress. When nurses change shifts, a quick briefing is all that is necessary because the essential information about the patient's care is already on the computer. Doctors and other members of the health-care team can easily access a patient's records from their own computers.

MULTIMEDIA

For this unit, you may choose from two keyboarding programs—a stand-alone software version or a multimedia version on CD-ROM. In each program, students learn to type at KEYS, the Typing Channel.

In the multimedia version, a researcher at an Assignment Desk introduces them to the typing lessons. Another researcher in Research Files shows them the cross-curricular typing selections, which can also be used as 1-minute, 2-minute, or 3- or 5-minute timings. In the multimedia version, students can access features such as All About Typing, Careers in Technology, and Computer and Typing Trivia. Two games—Get the Scoop and Uncover the Story—focus on improving speed and accuracy.

Focus On Careers In Technology

Have students interview someone they know who works in the health care field. Questions that might be asked in the interview include How do you use the computer in your job? What types of data do you use in your job? How have computers made your job and the health care system more efficient?

Application: COMPUTERS IN THE COMMUNITY

Computers touch students' lives in many ways away from home and school. Ask students to think of ways they use computers or see them used at the following places:

- Shopping Center
- Bank
- Concert
- Library
- Athletic Event

Ask the class to think of other ways they use computers away from home and school.

35

Section 5
Alphabetic Keys

SECTION OVERVIEW

In this section, students will learn the alphabetic keyboard. The first lesson teaches the home keys and is followed by a review lesson. Each subsequent lesson introduces one new letter. Review lessons follow every two lessons (or letters). In a 40–50 minute class, you may wish to cover two keys or lessons.

OPENING ACTIVITY

Have your students prepare their workstations and themselves to get ready to type. Computers should be turned on with the correct software loaded. Discuss the importance of proper posture, emphasizing how it eliminates fatigue as well as eye and wrist strain. Demonstrate the correct body position for keyboarding—feet flat on the floor and hands slightly curved over the keyboard.

SECTION 5
Alphabetic Keys

OBJECTIVES

- Operate the alphabetic keys by touch.
- Type at a minimum rate of 20 words per minute.
- Develop language arts skills.

Focus on Alphabetic Keys

Entering information into the computer without knowing the touch typing system can be slow and frustrating. In this unit, you will learn the touch system for typing letters and punctuation keys. To help track your progress toward typing quickly and accurately, you will learn to identify your typing errors and measure your typing speed.

Words To Know

arrow keys	scrolling
caps lock	shift key
home keys	space bar
insertion point	tab
return/enter key	word wrap

Career Exploration Activities: Manufacturing

Plan a trip to a high-tech manufacturing facility in your area. Many manufacturers schedule educational tours routinely. Let the tour guide(s) know in advance that you are interested in showing students the many ways in which people interact with computer technology at the facility.

If you are unable to visit a facility, have students contact different manufacturing companies in the area and inquire about the types of jobs available. They should find out what aspects of computer technology each job involves.

Home Keys

Goals:
- Discuss features of the computer screen
- Use the home keys, space bar, and return/enter key

GETTING READY

Before you can begin to type, you need to know a few things about your computer screen.

Insertion point. The insertion point is a mark that blinks on the screen. It may be a line (| or _), a caret (^), or a rectangle (▮). The insertion point appears where text will be entered. As you type, the insertion point moves to the right on the screen.

Word wrap. When you reach the end of the line you are typing, the next words will move down to the next line. This is called word wrap—the words wrap to the next line.

Scrolling. Your computer screen is not very big. As you type text that is wider than the screen, the text moves up so you can see it. This is called scrolling.

Arrow keys. After text has been entered, the insertion point can be moved around the text—up, down, left, and right. You move the insertion point by using the arrow keys.

LEARN THE HOME KEYS

The eight keys where you keep your fingertips—A S D F J K L ; (semicolon)—are called the **home keys.** Each finger is used for several keys, as shown by the keyboard drawing. When any finger is not busy typing a key, it returns home. The home keys are always typed using the fingers as shown in the illustration.

Home Keys

FOCUS

Learn the computer screen features. Learn the home keys, space bar, and Return/Enter key.

BELLRINGER

As soon as students are seated, have them look over the parts of the computer keyboard. They should identify the (1) alphabetic keys, (2) punctuation keys, and (3) number and symbol keys.

TEACH

Discuss the insertion point, word wrap, scrolling, and arrow keys. (Students may be more familiar with the term "cursor" than insertion point.) Explain that these features help make the computer a more useful tool than the traditional typewriter.

Demonstrate the proper position of hands on the home keys. Emphasize the importance of proper hand placement and proper typing position.

Home Keys

TEACH

Show students the location of the space bar. Demonstrate how the thumb of the hand you write with taps the space bar between words and after periods. Dictate the line shown under **Learn the Space Bar,** and then have the students type it as you observe.

Next show students the location of the Return/Enter key. Demonstrate that the Sem finger stretches to the right to the Return/Enter key. Explain that the Return/Enter key is used to begin a new line. Dictate the line shown under **Learn the Return Key,** and then have the students type it as you observe.

Do This — Curl your fingers for keyboard position.

Do This — Put your fingers on the home keys.

Do This — Put your thumbs in correct typing position.

1. Put the fingertips of your left hand on the A S D F keys on the second row. From now on, your fingers are named for the home keys on which you have placed them.
2. Put the fingertips of your right hand on the J K L ; (semicolon) keys on the second row. From now on, your fingers are named for the home keys on which you have placed them.

As you type, tap the keys lightly and quickly. Practice tapping the home keys by copying the following line:

```
asdf;lkjasdf;lkjasdf;lkj
```

LEARN THE SPACE BAR

Locate the space bar. It is used to put spaces between words and letters. You will use the thumb of the hand you write with to tap the space bar.

1. Place the thumb of your writing hand over the space bar, about ½ inch above it.
2. Keep the other thumb close to the first finger of that hand. You will not use this thumb when you are typing.

Practice typing the home keys again, this time putting a space between each letter. Tap the space bar quickly.

```
a s d f ; l k j a s d f ; l k j
 ^ ^ ^ ^ ^ ^ ^ ^ ^ ^ ^ ^ ^ ^
```

LEARN THE return KEY

You can begin a new line even when the line you are working on is not filled up. To begin a new line, use the Enter or Return key (depending upon how your keyboard is labeled).

Use the Sem (semicolon) finger to press the Return/Enter key. Try to keep the J finger on its home key when you press the Return/Enter key.

Practice typing the home keys again. Press Return/Enter at the end of each line.

```
asdf ;lkj ↵
asdf ;lkj ↵
fdsa jkl; ↵
fdsa jkl; ↵
```

38 Section 5 Alphabetic Keys

RESOURCES

- Lesson Plan: LP10
- Wallchart: Point out the home keys
- Transparencies 1 and 2
- CD-ROM: Getting Ready Lesson
- Software: Getting Ready Lesson

Lesson Extension

Demonstrate correct sitting posture for students, including:
- Both feet on the floor
- Lower back supported against chair
- Upper back leaning slightly forward
- Elbows close to sides in relaxed position

Discuss the importance of practicing good posture while at the keyboard.

PRACTICE THE HOME KEYS

Type each line 2 times as shown. Press Return/Enter at the end of each line. After you finish each drill 2 times, press Return/Enter twice.

1 fff fff jjj jjj fff jjj ff jj ff jj f j ↵
   fff fff jjj jjj fff jjj ff jj ff jj f j ↵
   ↵

2 ddd ddd kkk kkk ddd kkk dd kk dd kk d k ↵
   ddd ddd kkk kkk ddd kkk dd kk dd kk d k ↵
   ↵

3 sss sss lll lll sss lll ss ll ss ll s l ↵
   sss sss lll lll sss lll ss ll ss ll s l ↵
   ↵

4 aaa aaa ;;; ;;; aaa ;;; aa ;; aa ;; a ; ↵
   aaa aaa ;;; ;;; aaa ;;; aa ;; aa ;; a ; ↵
   ↵

5 fff jjj ddd kkk sss lll aaa ;;; fff jjj ↵
   fff jjj ddd kkk sss lll aaa ;;; fff jjj ↵
   ↵

6 asdf ;lkj asdf ;lkj asdf ;lkj asdf ;lkj ↵
   asdf ;lkj asdf ;lkj asdf ;lkj asdf ;lkj ↵
   ↵

7 fdsa jkl; fdsa jkl; fdsa jkl; fdsa jkl; ↵
   fdsa jkl; fdsa jkl; fdsa jkl; fdsa jkl; ↵
   ↵

Home Keys **39**

Home Keys

PRACTICE THE HOME KEYS

Have students complete drills 1–7 as instructed. Remind them to press Return/Enter once after each line and twice between each drill. Explain that pressing Return/Enter twice will leave a blank line between drills.

ASSESS

While students are practicing the home keys, space bar, and Return/Enter key, walk around the room and help each student assume proper hand position.

CLOSE

Instruct students to properly close their workstations, taking their own supplies but leaving those that need to stay.

Encourage students to practice the home keys before the next class. Explain that keyboarding is a skill that must be practiced, much like playing a sport or musical instrument.

39

Home Keys Review

FOCUS
Review the home keys, space bar, and Return/Enter key.

BELLRINGER
After students have properly set up their workstations, they should begin typing the **Tune Up,** which will review the keys learned in the previous lesson.

TEACH
Review the importance of proper posture and hand position when typing.

REVIEW HOME KEYS
Dictate lines 3 and 4 to students as they type, referring to the keyboarding chart on the wall. This will help students to set a good rhythm and speed they can use to continue typing lines 5–7. It also will assure them that they can type without looking at their hands.

BUILD YOUR SKILL
Have students type lines 8–11, typing each line twice. Walk around the room and observe typing technique. Help students achieve the goal of proper hand placement and typing without looking at their hands.

In **Special Word Groups,** have students type lines 12 and 13. As students type the lines twice, encourage them to concentrate on proper technique. Suggest that they practice tapping keys quickly, curving fingers properly, and keeping eyes on the book.

REVIEW

Home Keys Review

Goal:
- Review the home keys

TUNE UP
Type each line 2 times, as shown. Type the lines slowly and evenly. Do not look at the keys.

```
1  a ; s l d k f j d k s l a ; s l d k f j
   a ; s l d k f j d k s l a ; s l d k f j

2  asdf ;lkj asdf ;lkj asdf ;lkj asdf ;lkj
   asdf ;lkj asdf ;lkj asdf ;lkj asdf ;lkj
```

REVIEW
Type each line once, as shown. Type the lines slowly and evenly. Press Return/Enter once at the end of each line. Press Return/Enter twice after the last line.

```
3  ddd aaa ddd dad dad aaa lll lll all all
4  sss aaa ddd sad sad aaa sss kkk ask ask
5  lll aaa ddd lad lad aaa ddd ;;; ad; ad;
6  aaa ddd ddd add add aaa ddd sss ads ads
7  fff aaa ddd fad fad aaa sss ;;; as; as;
```

BUILD YOUR SKILL
Type each line 2 times. The lines are shown one time. Be sure to type each line 2 times before beginning the next line. Remember to put a blank line between each group of lines.

```
8   dad dad ads ads fad fad ask ask ad; ad;   [repeat]
9   add add sad sad as; as; lad lad all all   [repeat]
10  fall fall lass lass asks asks alas alas   [repeat]
11  salad salad salsa salsa alfalfa alfalfa   [repeat]
```

Section 5 Alphabetic Keys

RESOURCES
- Lesson Plan: LP11
- Wallchart: Point out the home keys
- Transparencies 1 and 2
- CD-ROM: All About Typing

REVIEW

SPECIAL WORD GROUPS

Type each line 2 times.

```
12  a sad lad; a salsa salad; a lass falls;    [repeat]
13  a dad asks; a fall fad; alfalfa salads;    [repeat]
```

DID YOU KNOW

The word *salsa* comes from the Spanish word for sauce. Salsa is a spicy sauce made with tomatoes, onions, and hot peppers. Salsa is also the name of a popular type of music in Latin America.

Language Link

A noun is a word that names a person, place, thing, or idea. A pronoun is used in place of a noun.

Study the examples:

Noun	Pronoun
mother	she, hers
Alex	he, his
friends	they, their
freedom	it, its
group	our

✓ Check Your Learning

Identify the nouns and pronouns in each sentence.

1. The girls and boys went to the game after they finished their classes.
2. The gardener said the plant would keep its blooms for a long time.
3. Tom went with his dad to choose a ball for the game.
4. Betsy and I are planning a fun theme for our party.
5. The students worked very hard to master their assignments.

Home Keys Review   41

Home Keys Review

ASSESS

At this point, assess students only for proper typing technique, hand placement and posture. You may also assess them on the **Language Link**.

Language Link

ANSWERS

1. girls, boys, game, they their, classes
2. gardener, plant, blooms, its, time
3. Tom, his, dad, ball, game
4. Betsy, I, theme, our, party
5. students, their, assignments

CLOSE

Language Link is a language arts skill section. It can be used to enhance the keyboarding lesson. With your class, discuss the purpose of **Language Link** and then have them complete **Check Your Learning**.

DID YOU KNOW

Many words we use in our everyday speech have their origins in other languages. Students will encounter words derived from other languages throughout the keyboarding exercises. In most cases your margin notes will provide definitions.

Teacher's Notes

E Key

FOCUS
Review the home keys. Learn the E key.

BELLRINGER
As soon as their workstations are properly set up, students should begin typing **Tune Up,** which reviews the home keys.

TEACH
Show the class the location of the E key. Demonstrate the proper reach, showing them how the D finger reaches up to the E key. Dictate the line shown under **Learn the E Key;** then have students type it as you observe.

PRACTICE THE E KEY
Have students type lines 3–6. Remind them to leave a blank line between each group of lines.

ASSESS
While students are typing each line in **Word Practice** twice, walk around the room observing and commenting on proper hand position and technique in reaching for the E key.

CLOSE
Review proper technique at the keyboard and the reach for the E key.

Goal:
- Use the E key

TUNE UP
Type each line 2 times. Tap the keys lightly and quickly. Keep your eyes on the copy.

1. `asdf jkl; asdf jkl; asdf jkl; asdf jkl;`
2. `all sad lads fads asks lass alas salad;`

LEARN THE E KEY
Use the D finger to type E. The reach is up and a little to the left. Feel the reach from D to E and back to D. When you make the reach to E, keep the A finger at home. Practice the following line.

`ddd ded ddd ded ddd ded ddd`

PRACTICE THE E KEY
Type each line 2 times. Keep your eyes on the copy. Remember to leave a blank line between each group of lines.

3. `ddd ded ded ede ded ddd ded ded ede ded`
4. `eee eee lll eel eel lll eee ddd led led`
5. `aaa ddd eee ade ade eee lll fff elf elf`
6. `eee lll kkk elk elk sss eee aaa sea sea`

WORD PRACTICE
Type each line 2 times. Remember to use good technique.

7. `sea see fee lee eel ell elk elf fed led`
8. `jade fade fake lake sake sale dale kale`
9. `deed seed feed feel fell sell jell dell`
10. `seas ease easel lease leaks leeks sleek`
11. `lea flea leaf lead dead deal seal seals`
12. `ade deaf desk lakes ladle saddle jelled`

Bits & Bytes

To make it easy to find your files, save them to a folder or directory that you create on your hard drive. For example, you could create a folder titled **Reports** for any reports you must write for your classes.

Section 5 Alphabetic Keys

RESOURCES
- Lesson Plan: LP11
- Wallchart: Point out reach to the E key
- Transparency 1
- CD-ROM: E Key; All About Typing
- Software: E Key

H Key

Goal:
- Use the H key

TUNE UP

Type each line 2 times. Press Return/Enter at the end of each line. Tap the keys lightly and quickly. Keep your eyes on the copy.

1 asdf jkl; asdf jkl; asdf jkl; asdf jkl;
2 ded ades desk ease fade jell keel sleek

LEARN THE H KEY

Use the J finger to type H. The reach is on the same row to the left. Feel the reach from J to H and back to J. When you make the reach to H, keep the Sem finger at home. Practice the following line.

jjj jhj jjj jhj jjj jhj jjj

PRACTICE THE H KEY

Type each line 2 times. Keep your eyes on the copy. Remember to leave a blank line between each line group.

3 jjj jhj jhj hjh jhj jjj jhj jhj hjh jhj
4 aaa sss hhh ash ash hhh aaa ddd had had
5 hhh aaa sss has has aaa hhh aaa aha aha
6 hh she she hh half half hh shed shed hh

WORD PRACTICE

Type each line 2 times. Remember to use good technique.

7   has ash sash hash dash lash flash slash
8   half hall hale heal heel heed held head
9   shed shad shade shake shale shall shell
10 ash ashes dashes lashes slashes hassles
11 she shell heals leash sheaf shelf flesh
12 heads ahead headed healed heeled heeded

H Key

FOCUS

Review the home keys and E key. Learn the H key.

BELLRINGER

As soon as their workstations are properly set up, students should begin typing the **Tune Up,** which reviews the home keys and the E key.

TEACH

Show the class the location of the H key. Demonstrate the proper reach, showing them how the J finger reaches to the left to the H key. Dictate the line shown; then have students type it as you observe.

PRACTICE THE H KEY

Have students type lines 3–6. Remind them to leave a blank line between each group of lines.

ASSESS

While students are typing each line in **Word Practice** twice, walk around the room; observe and comment on proper position and technique in reaching for the H key.

CLOSE

Review proper keyboarding technique and the reach for the H key. Remind students that typing is a skill and must be practiced.

RESOURCES

- Lesson Plan: LP12
- Wallchart: Point out reach to the H key
- Transparency 1
- CD-ROM: H Key; All About Typing
- Software: H Key

E & H Review

FOCUS
Review the home keys. Review the E and H keys.

BELLRINGER
As soon as their workstations are set up, have students type each **Tune Up** line twice. This reviews the home keys plus the E and H keys.

TEACH
Review the importance of proper posture and keying technique. Demonstrate the correct reaches from the home keys to the E and H keys.

REVIEW E AND H KEYS
Have students type lines 3–5. Remind them to leave a blank line between each line group. Make sure students are using the proper fingers when typing.

BUILD YOUR SKILL
Have students type lines 6–11 twice. Instruct them to keep their eyes on the text. Students may not be familiar with some of the words they will be typing: Explain that *hadal* is the ocean below 6000 meters and *heddle* is part of a loom.

In **Special Word Groups,** have students type lines 12–15. As students type the lines twice, encourage them to concentrate on proper technique. Suggest that they practice tapping keys quickly, curving fingers properly, and keeping eyes on the book.

E & H Review

Goal:
- Review the E and H keys

TUNE UP

Type each line 2 times. Press Return/Enter at the end of each line. Tap the keys lightly and quickly. Keep your eyes on the copy.

1 aaa sss ddd fff jjj kkk lll ;;; ded jhj
2 ease dash jell shed desk half flee lash

REVIEW

Type each line 2 times. Remember to leave a blank line between line groups.

3 sad lad; ask dad; a lass falls; a salad
4 ade desk else flea jade keel sled ladle
5 he ash dash half lash shed ahead hassle

BUILD YOUR SKILL

Type each line 2 times.

6 ade had eke she fee aha leek heel sleek
7 jade jell ahead addle easel flesh flake
8 flash hadal hassle keeled shaded lessee
9 false lease jelled lashed leaked shakes
10 he desk shelf jaded ladle heddle saddle
11 ash has shall lakes shell leased dashed

SPECIAL WORD GROUPS

If you do not know the meanings of the words, look them up in a dictionary. Then type each line 2 times.

12 eel elk kea flea hake seal
13 leek hash kasha salad salsa shake

Section 5 Alphabetic Keys

RESOURCES

- Lesson Plan: LP12
- Wallchart: Point out reaches to the E and H keys
- Transparency 1
- CD-ROM: Build Skill on the E and H Keys; Uncover the Story
- Software: Build Skill on the E and H Keys

REVIEW

```
14  fee lee see deed feed feel flee heed
15  heel keel leek seed sleek lessee
```

TIME YOURSELF

Take two 1-minute timings on the copy below. If you finish both lines before time is up, start over again. Press Return/Enter at the end of each line.

```
16  sell a shed; a lake ahead; fake a deal;
17  lease a hall; feed a seal; had a flash;
    | 1 | 2 | 3 | 4 | 5 | 6 | 7 | 8
```

Language Link

A sentence expresses a complete thought.

A sentence must have a subject and a predicate. A group of words that does not have both a subject and predicate is not a sentence. It is a sentence fragment. Study the examples:

The truck, an old red one.	(lacks a predicate)
Slowly climbed the steep hill.	(lacks a subject)
On the country road outside of town.	(lacks a subject and a predicate)

✓ Check Your Learning

Determine whether each of the following items is a sentence or a sentence fragment. Add words to each sentence fragment to make a sentence.

1. The hot summer months.
2. Attacked animals and people without warning.
3. Most stinging incidents occur during the swarming season.
4. Allowed 26 queen bees and their swarms to escape.
5. The African bees readily nested in the wilds of Brazil.

E & H Review 45

Teacher's Notes

E & H Review

The first line of the **Special Word Groups** contains animal names; the second, food; the third and fourth, double letters. *Kea* is a parrot; *hake* is a fish; and *kasha* is barley.

ASSESS

Using lines 16 and 17, have students take two 1-minute timings or three 12-second timings. Your software program automatically records speed and accuracy. The students' goal should be to increase the number of words or decrease the number of errors on each attempt.

Language Link
ANSWERS

1. fragment
2. fragment
3. sentence
4. fragment
5. sentence

(Students' sentences will vary.)

CLOSE

Review the **Language Link** section with your class. Have students team up to complete **Check Your Learning.** Close the class with having each team report and discuss the correct answers.

45

O Key

FOCUS
Review learned keys. Learn the O key.

BELLRINGER
As soon as their workstations are properly set up, have students type **Tune Up,** which reviews the home keys and E and H keys.

TEACH
Point out the location of the O key. Emphasize that this key is only used for the letter O—not for the number zero (0). Demonstrate the proper reach, showing how the L finger reaches up and slightly to the left to the O key. Dictate the line shown; then have students type it as you observe.

PRACTICE THE O KEY
Have students type lines 3–6. Remind them to leave a blank line between each group of lines.

ASSESS
While students are typing each line in **Word Practice** twice, walk around the room observing and commenting on proper hand position and technique in reaching for the O key.

Speed: lines 7 and 8
Accuracy: lines 9 and 10
Speed and Accuracy: lines 11 and 12

CLOSE
Review proper keyboarding technique and the reach for the O key.

Goal:
- Use the O key

TUNE UP
Press Return/Enter at the end of each line. Tap the key lightly and quickly. Keep your eyes on the copy.

1 aaa sss ddd fff jjj kkk lll ;;; ded jhj
2 dash ease flea half jell keel hash shed

LEARN THE O KEY
Use the L finger to type O. The reach is up and slightly to the left. Feel the reach from L to O and back to L. When you make the reach to O, keep the J finger at home. Practice the following line.

lll lol lll lol lll lol lll

PRACTICE THE O KEY
Type each line 2 times. Keep your eyes on the copy. Remember to leave a blank line between each line group.

3 lll lol lol olo lol lll lol lol olo lol
4 ooo ddd ddd odd odd ooo lll ddd old old
5 ooo aaa kkk oak oak ddd ooo eee doe doe
6 oo off off oo sofa sofa oo hood hood oo

WORD PRACTICE
Type each line 2 times. Remember to use good technique.

7   off odd old ode doe hoe foe oaf oak ado
8   lose sole hole hold hood food fool fold
9   so shoe hose dose soda sofa floss lasso
10 oak joke folk kola soak also solo loose
11 doe dole doll loll look hook shook shoo
12 loss slosh shoal loads holds hoods hoof

Section 5 Alphabetic Keys

Bits & Bytes
It is a good idea to turn on your monitor or other equipment first and your computer last. A power surge caused by the other devices while the computer is booting could damage the computer circuitry.

RESOURCES
- Lesson Plan: LP13
- Wallchart: Point out reach to the O key
- Transparency 1
- CD-ROM: O Key; All About Typing
- Software: O Key

C Key

Goal:
- Use the C key

TUNE UP

Type each line 2 times. Press Return/Enter at the end of each line. Tap the keys lightly and quickly. Keep your eyes on the copy.

1. ded jhj lol a s d f j k l ; ded jhj lol
2. lol also doll fold halo joke loaf shook

LEARN THE C KEY

Use the D finger to type C. The reach is down and to the right. Feel the reach from D to C and back to D. When you make the reach to C, keep the A finger at home. Practice the following line.

ddd dcd ddd dcd ddd dcd ddd

PRACTICE THE C KEY

Type each line 2 times. Keep your eyes on the copy. Remember to leave a blank line between each line group.

3. ddd dcd dcd cdc dcd ddd dcd dcd cdc dcd
4. ccc aaa ddd cad cad ccc ooo ddd cod cod
5. cc ace ace cc cell cell cc lace lace cc
6. cc coo coo cc sock sock cc cold cold cc

WORD PRACTICE

Type each line 2 times. Remember to use good technique.

7. call calf cafe face lace lack calk cask
8. sock dock lock clock choke chose choose
9. coal cold scold scald scale slack clack
10. flock shock shocks shacks chalks cackle
11. ache each laces chaos chase chafe chaff
12. jack hack heck check cheek cheese chess

C Key 47

RESOURCES

- Lesson Plan: LP13
- Wallchart: Point out reach to the C key
- Transparency 1
- CD-ROM: C Key; All About Typing
- Software: C Key

C Key

FOCUS

Review the O key. Learn the C key.

BELLRINGER

As soon as their workstations are properly set up, students should begin typing the **Tune Up,** which reviews the home keys and the E, H and O keys.

TEACH

Point out the location of the C key. Demonstrate the proper reach, showing how the D finger reaches down and to the right to the C key. Dictate the line shown, and then have the students type it as you observe.

PRACTICE THE C KEY

Have students type lines 3–6. Remind them to leave a blank line between each group of lines.

ASSESS

While students are typing each line in **Word Practice** twice, walk around the room observing and commenting on proper position and technique in reaching for the C key.

Speed: lines 7 and 8
Accuracy: lines 9 and 10
Speed and Accuracy: lines 11 and 12

CLOSE

Review proper keyboarding technique and the reach for the C key. Remind students that typing is a skill and must be practiced.

47

O & C Review

FOCUS

Review the O and C keys.

BELLRINGER

As soon as their workstations are set up, have students type each **Tune Up** line twice. This reviews learned keys plus the O and C keys.

TEACH

Review the importance of proper posture and keying technique. Demonstrate the correct reaches from the home keys to the O and C keys.

REVIEW O AND C KEYS

Have students complete lines 3–5. Remind them to leave a blank line between each line group. Make sure students are using the proper fingers when typing.

While students are typing each line twice, they should take two 30-second timings on each line. The goal is to increase the speed and/or to decrease the number of errors.

BUILD YOUR SKILL

Have students type lines 6–11 twice. Instruct them to keep their eyes on the text.

In **Special Word Groups,** have students type lines 12–15. If more than 5 errors are made on the 4 lines, they should retype them.

O & C Review

Goal:
- Review the O and C keys

TUNE UP

Type each line 2 times. Press Return/Enter at the end of each line. Tap the keys lightly and quickly. Keep your eyes on the copy.

```
1  aaa sss ded dcd fff jjj jhj kkk lol ;;;
2  ace jack sod keel doe lack elf hole cod
```

REVIEW

Type each line 2 times. Remember to leave a blank line between line groups.

```
3  old jokes; holds a doll; loads of food;
4  chase a flock; class coach; cooks cake;
5  echo cool cooks clock choke cocoa local
```

BUILD YOUR SKILL

Type each line 2 times.

```
6   oaf oak soak sock dock lock clock flock
7   ace ache hack hock sock sack lack slack
8   food flood folded fooled flooded doodle
9   jack jackal hackle cackle shackle shack
10  ode odd old cold sold scold scald scale
11  oaf loaf calf cafe case cash clash lash
```

SPECIAL WORD GROUPS

If you do not know the meaning of the words, look them up in a dictionary. Then type each line 2 times.

```
12  cake cola kola oleo sloe soda cocoa
13  cheese coffee haddock hoecake heckle
```

48   Section 5 Alphabetic Keys

RESOURCES

- Lesson Plan: LP14
- Wallchart: Point out reaches to the O and C keys
- Transparency 1
- CD-ROM: Build Skill on the O and C Keys; Uncover the Story
- Software: Build Skill on the O and C Keys

REVIEW

```
14  ole casa aloha haole koala dolce facade
15  hood food fool cool loose choose school
```

TIME YOURSELF

Take two 1-minute timings on the copy below. If you finish both lines before time is up, start over again. Press Return/Enter at the end of each line.

```
16  local school; shake a cola; cocoa cake;
17  half a cheese; odd joke; chose a cloak;
    | 1 | 2 | 3 | 4 | 5 | 6 | 7 | 8
```

DID YOU KNOW

The koala is native only to Australia. Koalas are marsupials—mammals whose young grow and mature inside a pouch on the mother's belly. Koalas live in the eucalyptus trees of southeastern Australia. These animals spend at least 20 hours a day sleeping. The only food koalas eat is eucalyptus leaves. They eat about 2.5 pounds of these leaves a day.

O & C Review

Students may encounter words unfamiliar to them in lines 12–15: *oleo* is the short form of oleomargarine; *sloe* is a plum-like fruit; *hoecake* is cornbread; *seckle* is a type of pear; *ole* is a Spanish cheer; *casa* means house in Spanish; *aloha* is hello and/or goodbye in Hawaiian; *haole* means not native; *koala* is a small bearlike animal; *dolce* means sweet in Italian; *facade* is the front of a building in French.

ASSESS

Using lines 16 and 17, have students take two 1-minute timings or three 12-second timings. The students' goal should be to increase speed or accuracy on each attempt.

While students are typing each line twice, walk around the class observing and commenting on techniques.

CLOSE

Review proper typing technique. Remind students that improving their typing skill will require practice.

DID YOU KNOW

Ask the class if they can think of any other mammals in the order Marsupialia. Answers might include kangaroos, opossums, wombats, and bandicoots.

Teacher's Notes

R Key

FOCUS
Review learned keys. Learn the R key.

BELLRINGER
As soon as their workstations are properly set up, students should begin typing **Tune Up,** which reviews learned keys.

TEACH
Show the class the location of the R key. Demonstrate the proper reach, showing them how the F finger reaches up and slightly to the left to the R key. Dictate the line shown under **Learn the R Key;** then have students type it as you observe.

PRACTICE THE R KEY
Have students type lines 3–6. Remind them to leave a blank line between each group of lines.

ASSESS
While students are typing each line in **Word Practice** twice, walk around the room observing and commenting on proper hand position and technique in reaching for the R key.

Speed: lines 7 and 8
Accuracy: lines 9 and 10
Speed and Accuracy: lines 11 and 12

CLOSE
Review proper technique at the keyboard and the reach for the R key.

Goal:
- Use the R key

TUNE UP

Type each line 2 times. Press Return/Enter at the end of each line. Tap the keys lightly and quickly. Keep your eyes on the copy.

1 ded ease else deeds jhj half head ashes
2 lol oleo hood floss dcd cash coal cocoa

LEARN THE R KEY

Use the F finger to type R. The reach is up and slightly to the left. Feel the reach from F to R and back to F. When you make the reach to R, keep the A finger at home. Practice the following line.

   fff frf fff frf fff frf fff

PRACTICE THE R KEY

Type each line 2 times. Keep your eyes on the copy. Remember to leave a blank line between each line group.

3 fff frf frf rfr frf fff frf frf rfr frf
4 fff aaa rrr far far hhh eee rrr her her
5 eee aaa rrr ear ear jjj aaa rrr jar jar
6 rr for for rr free free rr rare rare rr

WORD PRACTICE

Type each line 2 times. Remember to use good technique.

7 car jar far for ore oar ear are ark arc
8 area acre care fare fear hear rear real
9 red reed read dear dread feared federal
10 hack shack rack crackle cracked cracker
11 ark lark dark hark shark fork cork jerk
12 her hero roses horse shore share shaker

Bits & Bytes

It is a good practice to name your file immediately after starting a new document and then to save it every few minutes.

Section 5 Alphabetic Keys

RESOURCES

- Lesson Plan: LP14
- Wallchart: Point out reach to the R key
- Transparency 1
- CD-ROM: R Key
- Software: R Key

I Key

Goal:
- Use the I key

TUNE UP

Type each line 2 times. Press Return/Enter at the end of each line. Tap the keys lightly and quickly. Keep your eyes on the copy.

1. ddd ded jjj jhj ddd ded lll lol fff frf
2. frf or ore ear fear free reef refer frf

LEARN THE I KEY

Use the K finger to type I. The reach is up and to the left. Feel the reach from K to I and back to K. When you make the reach to I, keep the Sem finger at home. Practice the following line.

kkk kik kkk kik kkk kik kkk

PRACTICE THE I KEY

Type each line 2 times. Keep your eyes on the copy. Remember to leave a blank line between each line group.

3. kkk kik kik iki kik kkk kik kik iki kik
4. sss kkk iii ski ski aaa iii rrr air air
5. rrr iii ddd rid rid sss iii rrr sir sir
6. ii ice ice ii kick kick ii like like ii

WORD PRACTICE

Type each line 2 times. Remember to use good technique.

7. kid rid ride hide hire fire fired filed
8. dial dill fill hill sill silk sick lick
9. child chide chisel riches relish shield
10. ideal idler riddle fiddle filler fliers
11. arch char chair choir crier cried fried
12. jail sail aisle slice slide aside raise

RESOURCES

- Lesson Plan: LP15
- Wallchart: Point out reach to the I key
- Transparency 1
- CD-ROM: I Key
- Software: I Key

I Key

FOCUS

Review learned keys and the R key. Learn the I key.

BELLRINGER

As soon as their workstations are properly set up, have students type the **Tune Up**.

TEACH

Point out the location of the I key. Demonstrate the proper reach, showing how the K finger reaches up and to the left to the I key. Dictate the line shown, and then have the students type it as you observe.

Point out that students are learning one letter using their left hand, then one using their right hand. This allows them to have a balanced hand movement in practicing the drills.

PRACTICE THE I KEY

Have students type lines 3–6, leaving a blank line between each group of lines.

ASSESS

While students are typing each line in **Word Practice** twice, walk around the room observing and commenting on proper technique.

Speed: lines 7 and 8
Accuracy: lines 9 and 10
Speed and Accuracy: lines 11 and 12

CLOSE

Review proper keyboarding technique and the reach for the I key. Remind students that typing is a skill and must be practiced.

R & I Review

FOCUS

Review the R and I keys.

BELLRINGER

As soon as their workstations are set up, have students type each **Tune Up** line twice. This reviews learned keys plus the R and I keys.

TEACH

Review the importance of proper posture and keying technique. Demonstrate the correct reaches from the home keys to the R and I keys.

REVIEW R AND I KEYS

Have students complete lines 3–5, typing each line twice. Dictate each line once to get an even pace going. Then have students take three 12-second timings on each line in this section so that they can increase their speed and/or decrease their errors. Remind them to leave a blank line between each line group. Make sure students are using the proper fingers when typing.

BUILD YOUR SKILL

Have students type lines 6–11 twice. Instruct them to keep their eyes on the text.

In **Special Word Groups,** have students type lines 12–16. If more than 5 errors are made on the 5 lines, they should retype them.

R & I Review

Goal:
- Review the R and I keys

TUNE UP

Type each line 2 times. Press Return/Enter at the end of each line. Tap the keys lightly and quickly. Keep your eyes on the copy.

```
1  ded ade deed frf far free dcd cad cocoa
2  jhj had hack kik kid kick lol old flood
```

REVIEW

Type each line 2 times. Remember to leave a blank line between line groups.

```
3  rare race acre clear reach shear cereal
4  ail file life chief chisel chaise raise
5  fierce fire; chair cracks; rich sailor;
```

BUILD YOUR SKILL

Type each line 2 times.

```
6   if fir fire hire hare share shore sheer
7   lice lick flick click crack creak creek
8   floor color coral choral chorale collar
9   hers horse coarse choice heroic rejoice
10  reed reef refer freer frier fried cried
11  lace lack lilac chill hills skill slick
```

SPECIAL WORD GROUPS

If you do not know the meanings of the words, look them up in a dictionary. Then type each line 2 times.

```
12  dill fish okra chili cider shark cereal
13  cookie farfel cracker radish relish
```

52 Section 5 Alphabetic Keys

RESOURCES

- Lesson Plan: LP15
- Wallchart: Point out reaches to the R and I keys
- Transparency 1
- CD-ROM: Build Skill on the R and I Keys; Uncover the Story
- Software: Build Skill on the R and I Keys

REVIEW

14 rio lei adios khaki raja chaise eclair
15 chassis charade dossier frijoles
16 deer drake eider horse shrike chickadee

TIME YOURSELF

Take two 1-minute timings on the copy below. If you finish both lines before time is up, start over again. Press Return/Enter at the end of each line.

17 a khaki kerchief; he saddled his horse;
18 her locker is here; a soldier rejoiced;
    | 1 | 2 | 3 | 4 | 5 | 6 | 7 | 8

CULTURAL KALEIDOSCOPE

Many cultures have certain foods that are staples of their diet. Tortillas, a thin, flat cornmeal bread, are an important food in Mexico. Tortillas filled with frijoles, or beans, are called tacos. Sushi, raw fish served with rice and vinegar, is a popular dish in Japan. If vegetables are added to sushi, the dish is called norimaki.

CULTURAL KALEIDOSCOPE

The United States is referred to as a "melting pot" culture because many people have relatives who came here from other countries. Because of this, many foods we eat have their origins in different cultures.

R & I Review

Students may not recognize some of the words they will be typing in **Special Word Groups:** Explain that *okra* is a vegetable; *farfel* is a type of pasta; *si* means yes in Spanish; *rio* is river in Spanish; *lei* is a Hawaiian word for flower necklace; *adios* is Spanish for goodbye; *khaki* means light brown, or dust-colored, in Hindi; *raja* is a Hindi king, prince, or chief; *chaise* means chair in French; *eclair* is a French custard-filled dessert; *chassis* is an automobile frame; *charade* is a pretense; *dossier* is a file of detailed information; *frijoles* is beans in Spanish; *eider* is duck; and *shrike* is a songbird.

ASSESS

Using lines 16 and 17, have students take two 1-minute timings or three 12-second timings.

While students are typing each line twice, walk around the class observing and commenting on techniques.

CLOSE

Discuss with students their various heritages. On the board, make a list of foods they have tried that originated from other cultures.

W Key

FOCUS

Review learned keys. Learn the W key.

BELLRINGER

As soon as their workstations are properly set up, students should begin typing **Tune Up,** which reviews learned keys.

TEACH

Point out the location of the W key. Demonstrate the proper reach, showing how the S finger reaches up and slightly to the left to the W key. Dictate the line shown under **Learn the W Key;** and then have students type it as you observe.

PRACTICE THE W KEY

Have students type lines 3–6. Remind them to leave a blank line between each group of lines.

ASSESS

While students are typing each line in **Word Practice** twice, walk around the room observing and commenting on proper hand position and technique in reaching for the W key.

Speed: lines 7 and 8
Accuracy: lines 9 and 10
Speed and Accuracy: lines 11 and 12

CLOSE

Review proper technique at the keyboard and the reach for the W key.

Goal:
- Use the W key

TUNE UP

Type each line 2 times. Press Return/Enter at the end of each line. Tap the keys lightly and quickly. Keep your eyes on the copy.

1. area sore dish fare jail kick like earl
2. hire oleo cake raid idea ear; ice; hoe;

LEARN THE W KEY

Use the S finger to type W. The reach is up and slightly to the left. Feel the reach from S to W and back to S. When you make the reach to W, keep the F finger at home. Practice the following line.

sss sws sss sws sss sws sss

PRACTICE THE W KEY

Type each line 2 times. Keep your eyes on the copy. Remember to leave a blank line between each line group.

3. sss sws sws wsw sws sss sws sws wsw sws
4. sss aaa www saw saw www hhh ooo who who
5. www aaa sss was was rrr ooo www row row
6. ww sew sew ww walk walk ww wish wish ww

WORD PRACTICE

Type each line 2 times. Remember to use good technique.

7. saw sew sow cow row raw war was wad wed
8. show slow slaw wash wish wise wire ware
9. low slow allow arrow rower sower sorrow
10. awake walker sidewalk sideshow showcase
11. flow flower slower lowers shower washer
12. draw drawer reward reword rework worker

Bits & Bytes

Your password is important, so keep it secret. It keeps others from reading your files or from changing or stealing your information.

54 Section 5 Alphabetic Keys

RESOURCES

- Lesson Plan: LP16
- Wallchart: Point out reach to the W key
- Transparency 1
- CD-ROM: W Key; Uncover the Story
- Software: W Key

54

Right Shift Key

Goal:
- Use the right shift key

TUNE UP

Type each line 2 times. Press Return/Enter at the end of each line.

1. sws frf kik ded dcd jhj lol sws frf kik
2. dash draw flaw flew flow slow show whoa

LEARN THE RIGHT shift KEY

The right shift key is used to capitalize letters typed with the left hand. Use the Sem finger to press and hold down the right shift key. Type the left-hand letter that is to be capitalized. Release the shift key. Practice the following line.

;;; ;A; ;;; ;A; ;;; ;A; ;;;

PRACTICE THE RIGHT shift KEY

Type each line 2 times. Leave a blank line between each line group.

3. ;;; ;S; ;S; ;;; ;D; ;D; ;;; ;F; ;F; ;;;
4. ;;; Sal Sal ;;; Cal Cal ;;; Wes Wes ;;;
5. ;; Ada Ada ;; Wade Wade ;; Rose Rose ;;
6. Eric Cleo Carl Dale Dora Ward Will Ella

WORD PRACTICE

Type each line 2 times. Remember to use good technique.

7. Drew draws; Rose arose; Rollo followed;
8. Carol; Eloise; Felicia; Rachel; Sheila;
9. Clark; Derek; Edward; Richard; Woodrow;
10. Carl led Cole; Rachel raced; Ella fell;
11. Willa will walk; Reid reads; Sal shall;

Right Shift Key

FOCUS

Review learned keys and the W key. Learn the right shift key.

BELLRINGER

As soon as their workstations are properly set up, have students type the **Tune Up**.

TEACH

Point out the location of the right shift key. Emphasize that the right shift key is used to capitalize letters typed with the left hand.

Demonstrate the proper use of the shift key, showing how the Sem finger reaches down and slightly to the right. Show students how they can still keep at least one finger on the home row. Dictate the line shown, then have students type it as you observe.

PRACTICE THE RIGHT shift KEY

As students are typing lines 3–6, make sure they are using a fluid motion when using the shift key. Make sure that they are using only the right shift key to capitalize letters with the left hand and keeping at least one finger on the home row of keys.

ASSESS

While students are typing each line in **Word Practice**, observe and comment on proper position and technique.

CLOSE

Review proper keyboarding technique and the reach for the right shift key.

RESOURCES

- Lesson Plan: LP16
- Wallchart: Point out reach to the right shift key
- Transparency 1
- CD-ROM: Right Shift Key
- Software: Right Shift Key

W & Right Shift Review

FOCUS

Review learned keys. Review the W and right shift keys.

BELLRINGER

As soon as their workstations are set up, have students type each **Tune Up** line twice. This reviews learned keys plus the W and right shift keys.

TEACH

Review the importance of proper posture and keying technique. Demonstrate the correct reaches from the home keys to the W and right shift keys.

REVIEW W AND RIGHT shift KEYS

Have students complete lines 3–5. They should take three 12-second timings on each line in this section. Have them begin to keep a chart for their speed and errors. Remind them to leave a blank line between each line group. Make sure students are using the proper fingers when typing.

BUILD YOUR SKILL

Have students type lines 6–11 twice. Instruct them to keep their eyes on the text.

Have students build accuracy by typing lines 12–15 in the **Special Word Groups** section. If more than 5 errors are made on the 4 lines, they should retype the lines.

REVIEW

W & Right Shift Review

Goal:
- Review the W and right shift keys

TUNE UP

Type each line 2 times. Press Return/Enter at the end of each line. Tap the keys lightly and quickly. Keep your eyes on the copy.

1 aaa sss ddd fff jjj kkk lll ;;; add all
2 aaa sws ded dcd frf jhj kik lol ;;; ;A;

REVIEW

Type each line 2 times. Remember to leave a blank line between line groups.

3 few sew saw jaw raw row low cow how who
4 Al Ed Sal Rod Cleo Dick Elsa Ross Sarah
5 Ward Wade Will Willa Wilda Wolfe Walker

BUILD YOUR SKILL

Type each line 2 times.

6   flow flower fellow follow hollow holler
7   car Carl war Ward she Sheri will Willis
8   show whose shower washer whaler welfare
9   Carla Errol Rhoda Carlos Sallie Wallace
10 ewe jewel sewer where wheel while whole
11 Ward washes; Della dials; Edward wades;

SPECIAL WORD GROUPS

If you do not know the location of any of the places, look them up in a dictionary. Then type each line 2 times.

12 Alaska Colorado Delaware Florida
13 Asia Fiji Wales Chile Rhodesia

Section 5 Alphabetic Keys

RESOURCES

- Lesson Plan: LP17
- Wallchart: Point out reaches to the W and right shift keys
- Transparency 1
- CD-ROM: Build Skill on the W and Right Shift Keys
- Software: Build Skill on the W and Right Shift Keys

REVIEW

14 Rio Erie Cairo Delhi Dallas Warwick
15 Weser Sahara Wallis Cascade Wallowa

TIME YOURSELF

Take two 1-minute timings on the copy below. If you finish both lines before time is up, start over again. Press Return/Enter at the end of each line.

16 chew a wafer; award a wish; work a row;
17 Dolores drew a cow; where Errol walked;
    | 1 | 2 | 3 | 4 | 5 | 6 | 7 | 8

Language Link

Capitalize the first word of every sentence. Capitalize the first word of a direct quotation (someone's exact words) that is a complete sentence.

Study the examples:

Pioneers pushed the American frontier westward.
"They left their homes," said Lee, "so that they could improve their lives."

✓ Check Your Learning

In each sentence, indicate the word(s) that should be capitalized.

1. we realized the pioneers had to be self-sufficient.
2. ann said, "some pioneers were trappers."
3. "the railroad," stated Carlos, "opened new lands to be settled."
4. "most families traveled in groups," noted Joan.
5. "the pioneers acted very bravely," exclaimed Trish, "and endured a lot."

W & Right Shift Review **57**

Teacher's Notes

W & Right Shift Review

Line 12 contains U.S. states; line 13 contains foreign lands; line 14 contains cities; and line 15 contains other geographic names. *Weser* is a river in Germany; *Wallis* is islands in the SW Pacific; *Cascade* is a mountain chain in the northwest U.S.; *Wallowa* is a mountain chain in Oregon.

ASSESS

Using lines 16 and 17, have students take two 1-minute timings or three 12-second timings. The goal should be to type each line with no more than two errors per line.

While students are typing each line twice, observe and comment on techniques.

Language Link

ANSWERS

1. We
2. Ann, Some
3. The
4. Most
5. The

CLOSE

Review the **Language Link** section with your class. Have students team up to complete **Check Your Learning.** Have each team report and discuss the answers.

57

T Key

FOCUS

Review learned keys. Learn the T key.

BELLRINGER

As soon as their workstations are properly set up, students should begin typing **Tune Up,** which reviews learned keys.

TEACH

Show the class the location of the T key. Demonstrate the proper reach, showing them how the F finger reaches up and to the right to the T key. Dictate the line shown under **Learn the T Key** and then have the students type it as you observe.

PRACTICE THE T KEY

Have students type lines 3–6. Remind them to leave a blank line between each group of lines.

ASSESS

While students are typing each line in **Word Practice** twice, observe and comment on proper hand position and technique in reaching for the T key.

Speed: lines 7 and 8
Accuracy: lines 9 and 10
Speed and Accuracy: lines 11 and 12

CLOSE

Review proper technique at the keyboard and the reach for the T key.

Goal:
- Use the T key

TUNE UP

Type each line 2 times. Press Return/Enter at the end of each line. Tap the keys lightly and quickly. Keep your eyes on the copy.

1 aa ss dd ff sws ded dcd frf ff dd ss aa
2 jj kk ll ;; jhj kik lol ;A; ;; ll kk jj

LEARN THE T KEY

Use the F finger to type T. The reach is up and to the right. Feel the reach from F to T and back to F. When you make the reach to T, keep the A finger at home. Practice the following line.

   fff ftf fff ftf fff ftf fff

PRACTICE THE T KEY

Type each line 2 times. Keep your eyes on the copy. Remember to leave a blank line between each line group.

3 fff ftf ftf tft ftf fff ftf ftf tft ftf
4 fff aaa ttt fat fat jjj eee ttt jet jet
5 ttt aaa rrr tar tar ttt hhh eee the the
6 tt two two tt cast cast tt talk talk tt

WORD PRACTICE

Type each line 2 times. Remember to use good technique.

7   jet set let lot jot hot rot cot dot tot
8   coat cost lost last east seat feat feet
9   cart carrot correct collect elect cleat
10 tack track tackle talker lather latched
11 hats chats chart heart cheat wheat what
12 rot roast toast taste tease steak skate

Bits & Bytes

Before you remove a disk from your computer, be sure the disk light is off. Removing the disk before the light goes off can corrupt your disk.

Section 5 Alphabetic Keys

RESOURCES

- Lesson Plan: LP17
- Wallchart: Point out reach to the T key
- Transparency 1
- CD-ROM: T Key
- Software: T Key

Period (.) Key

Goal:
- Use the period (.) key

Do This

*Space once after a period ending an abbreviation. Do not space after a period **within** an abbreviation. Space once after a period at the end of a sentence.*

TUNE UP

Type each line 2 times. Press Return/Enter at the end of each line. Tap the keys lightly and quickly. Keep your eyes on the copy.

```
1  aaa sss ddd fff jjj kkk lll ;;; sws lol
2  ded kik frf jhj dcd ;A; ftf Todd Teresa
```

LEARN THE PERIOD KEY

The period is a mark of punctuation used at the end of a sentence or with an abbreviation. Use the L finger to type the period. The reach is down and to the right. When you make the reach to the period, keep the J finger at home. Practice the following line.

```
   lll 1.1 lll 1.1 lll 1.1 lll
```

PRACTICE THE PERIOD KEY

Type each line 2 times. Leave a blank line between each line group.

```
3  lll 1.1 1.1 .1. 1.1 lll 1.1 1.1 .1. 1.1
4  SSS ttt ... St. St. RRR ddd ... Rd. Rd.
5  DDD rrr ... Dr. Dr. CCC ooo ... Co. Co.
6  .. Fla. Fla. Del. Del. c.o.d. c.o.d. ..
```

WORD PRACTICE

Type each line 2 times. Remember to use good technique.

```
7   Close the door. That draft is too cold.
8   Ted took the tests. Tess tasted a taco.
9   Ed collects the c.o.d. fee for Dr. Soo.
10  Thos. Trota has a D.D.S. with Cal Tech.
11  Rita talks to Art. Dot waited for Walt.
12  Ashe Rd. is ahead. Fifth St. is closed.
```

Period (.) Key **59**

Period (.) Key

FOCUS

Review learned keys and the T key. Learn the period (.) key.

BELLRINGER

As soon as their workstations are properly set up, students should begin typing the **Tune Up,** which reviews learned keys and the T key.

TEACH

Show the class the location of the period (.) key. Demonstrate the proper reach, showing them how the L finger reaches down and to the right to the period (.) key. Dictate the line shown, and then have the students type it as you observe.

PRACTICE THE KEY

Have students type lines 3–6. Remind them to leave a blank line between each group of lines.

ASSESS

While students are typing each line in **Word Practice** twice, walk around the room observing and commenting on proper position and technique in reaching for the period (.) key.

Speed: lines 7 and 8
Accuracy: lines 9 and 10
Speed and Accuracy: lines 11 and 12

CLOSE

Review proper keyboarding technique and the reach for the period (.) key. Remind students that typing is a skill and must be practiced.

RESOURCES

- Lesson Plan: LP18
- Wallchart: Point out reach to the period (.) key
- Transparency 1
- CD-ROM: Period Key
- Software: Period Key

T & Period Review

FOCUS

Review learned keys. Review the T and period (.) keys.

BELLRINGER

As soon as their workstations are set up, have students type each **Tune Up** line twice. This reviews learned keys plus the T and period (.) keys.

TEACH

Review the importance of proper posture and keying technique. Demonstrate the correct reaches from the home keys to the T and period (.) keys.

REVIEW T AND ? KEYS

Have students complete lines 3–5. Remind them to leave a blank line between each line group. Make sure students are using the proper fingers when typing.

BUILD YOUR SKILL

Have students type lines 6–11 twice. Instruct them to keep their eyes on the text.

Have students build accuracy by typing lines 12–15 in the **Special Word Groups** section. If more than 5 errors are made on the 4 lines, they should retype the lines.

T & . Review

Goal:
- Review the T and period (.) keys

TUNE UP

Type each line 2 times. Press Return/Enter at the end of each line. Tap the keys lightly and quickly. Keep your eyes on the copy.

```
1  sws ded dcd frf ftf jhj kik lol l.l ;A;
2  ade sew cad far tar jar has kit lot St.
```

REVIEW

Type each line 2 times. Remember to leave a blank line between line groups

```
3  tail tall tale stale store short shorts
4  st. Co. rd. Ala. Edw. i.e. D.D.S. c.o.d.
5  were tree tire trio tore wore wire write
```

BUILD YOUR SKILL

Type each line 2 times.

```
6   art earth wreath threw throw wrath thaw
7   Stella threw the whistle to the sitter.
8   district tickets tickle trickle whistle
9   Stewart assisted Dr. Theodora last Wed.
10  Edw. had tickets to a West St. theater.
11  Does it. Sit there. Eat crow. Catch it.
```

SPECIAL WORD GROUPS

If you do not know the meanings of the words, look them up in a dictionary. Then type each line 2 times.

```
12  stew roast toast carrot cashew fritter
13  owl cat hawk toad wolf catfish ostrich
```

60 Section 5 Alphabetic Keys

RESOURCES

Lesson Plan: LP18

Wallchart: Point out reaches to the T and period keys

CD ROM: Build Skill on the T and Period Keys; Uncover the Story

Transparency 1

Software: Build Skill on the T and Period Keys

REVIEW

```
14  rattler cockatoo tortoise swordfish
15  frito fiesta siesta torero solitaire
```

TIME YOURSELF

Take two 1-minute timings on the copy below. If you finish both lines before time is up, start over again. Press Return/Enter at the end of each line.

```
16  Theresa took a short ride to the store.
17  Walt wrote a c.o.d. order for Dr. Tate.
   |   1   |   2   |   3   |   4   |   5   |   6   |   7   |   8
```

CULTURAL KALEIDOSCOPE

Throughout the year Mexicans hold special celebrations called fiestas. *Fiesta* means "feast day" in Spanish. Fiestas are festivals that include parades, fireworks, music, and dancing. Some examples of celebrations are Cinco de Mayo (May 5) and Independence Day (September 15–16).

T & Period (.) Review **61**

CULTURAL KALEIDOSCOPE

Most Mexican fiestas begin before daylight with fireworks and bell ringing. Every Mexican town holds an annual fiesta honoring its patron saint. During these celebrations people pray and light candles. The churches are decorated with flowers and brightly colored tissue paper.

T & Period Review

Line 12 contains food words; lines 13 and 14, animal words; line 15, common foreign words. *Fritter* is a fried cake; *frito* means fried (Spanish); *fiesta* is a festival or party (Spanish); *solitaire* means lone or solitary (French).

ASSESS

Using lines 16 and 17, have students take two 1-minute timings or three 12-second timings. Students should type each line with no more than 2 errors in each line. Repeat until completed within the error limit.

While students are typing each line twice, observe and comment on techniques.

CLOSE

Have students type a list of festivals and holidays they enjoy celebrating each year.

61

M Key

FOCUS

Review learned keys. Learn the M key.

BELLRINGER

As soon as their workstations are properly set up, students should begin typing **Tune Up,** which reviews learned keys.

TEACH

Show the class the location of the M key. Demonstrate the proper reach, showing them how the J finger reaches down and to the right to the M key. Dictate the line shown under **Learn the M Key** and then have the students type it as you observe.

PRACTICE THE M KEY

Have students type lines 3–6 twice. Remind them to leave a blank line between each group of lines.

ASSESS

While students are typing each line in **Word Practice** twice, walk around the room observing and commenting on proper hand position and technique in reaching for the M key.

Speed: lines 7 and 8
Accuracy: lines 9 and 10
Speed and Accuracy: lines 11 and 12

CLOSE

Review proper technique at the keyboard and the reach for the M key. Encourage students to practice keyboarding on a daily basis.

Goal:
- Use the M key

TUNE UP

Type each line 2 times. Press Return/Enter at the end of each line. Tap the keys lightly and quickly. Keep your eyes on the copy.

1. sws ded dcd frf ftf jhj kik lol 1.1 ;A;
2. That towel is wet. Tad threw the stick.

LEARN THE M KEY

Use the J finger to type M. The reach is down and to the right. Feel the reach from J to M and back to J. When you make the reach to J, keep the Sem finger at home. Practice the following line.

jjj jmj jjj jmj jjj jmj jjj

PRACTICE THE M KEY

Type each line 2 times. Keep your eyes on the copy. Remember to leave a blank line between each line group.

3. jjj jmj jmj mjm jmj jjj jmj jmj mjm jmj
4. jjj aaa mmm jam jam aaa rrr mmm arm arm
5. hhh iii mmm him him mmm eee ttt met met
6. mm mar mar mm mark mark mm milk milk mm

WORD PRACTICE

Type each line 2 times. Remember to use good technique.

7. jam ham lam ram rim him dim mid mad mar
8. mark mask mast malt melt meet meat meal
9. calm camel camera macrame hammer jammed
10. more morale mortal tomato atomic comics
11. home some most moist storm forms formal
12. farm harm alarm flame shame theme chime

Bits & Bytes

If you take files on disks from home to a computer at school, you should install an antivirus software program on your home computer. Many disks that are put into school computers are at high risks for being infected and passing viruses.

62 Section 5 Alphabetic Keys

RESOURCES

- Lesson Plan: LP19
- Wallchart: Point out reach to the M key
- Transparency 1
- CD-ROM: M Key
- Software: M Key

Left Shift Key

Goal:
- Use the left shift key

TUNE UP

Type each line 2 times. Press Return/Enter at the end of each line.

```
1  sws ded dcd frf ftf jhj kik lol 1.1 ;A;
2  jmj jam ram rim dim dime time lime mime
```

LEARN THE LEFT [shift] KEY

The left shift key is used to capitalize letters typed with the right hand. Extend the A finger to press and hold down the left shift key. Type the right-hand letter that is to be capitalized. Release the shift key. Practice the following line.

```
   aaa aJa aaa aJa aaa aJa aaa
```

Do This: Space once after a colon at the end of a word.

PRACTICE THE LEFT [shift] KEY

The shift of the semicolon (;) is the colon (:). Type each line 2 times.

```
3  aaa aKa aKa aaa aLa aLa aaa a:a a:a aaa
4  aaa Kim Kim aaa Joe Joe aaa Lil Lil aaa
5  aa Lee Lee aa Kate Kate aa Jake Jake aa
6  Hal: Les: Jill: Otis: Iris: Mark: Kris:
```

WORD PRACTICE

Type each line 2 times. Remember to use good technique.

```
7   Lois likes; Jeff talked; Marsha marked;
8   Hilda: Jesse: Mildred: Jerome: Michael:
9   Ilka Karl Leila Homer Marie Oscar Jodie
10  Irma missed home. Mark filmed a farmer.
11  Leslie made jam. Joel met Mr. J. Odell.
```

Left Shift Key **63**

RESOURCES

- Lesson Plan: LP19
- Wallchart: Point out reach to the left shift key
- Transparency 1
- CD-ROM: Left Shift Key
- Software: Left Shift Key

Left Shift Key

FOCUS

Review learned keys and the M key. Learn the left shift key.

BELLRINGER

As soon as their workstations are properly set up, have students type the **Tune Up**.

TEACH

Point out the location of the left shift key. Review the difference between a capital letter and a lower case letter. Emphasize that the left shift key is used to capitalize letters typed with the right hand.

Review the proper use of the shift key, showing students how the A finger reaches down and to the left to the left shift key. Show students how they keep at least one finger on home row. Dictate the line shown; have students type it as you observe.

PRACTICE THE LEFT [shift] KEY

Have students type lines 3–6 twice.

ASSESS

While students are typing each line in **Word Practice** twice, observe and comment on proper position and technique in reaching for the left shift key.

CLOSE

Review proper keyboarding technique and the reach for the left shift key. Encourage students to spend some extra time working with the shift keys.

63

M & Left Shift Review

FOCUS

Review learned keys. Review the M and left shift keys.

BELLRINGER

As soon as their workstations are set up, have students type each **Tune Up** line twice. This reviews learned keys plus the M and left shift keys.

TEACH

Review the importance of proper posture and keying technique. Demonstrate the correct reaches from the home keys to the M and left shift keys.

REVIEW M AND LEFT shift KEYS

Have students complete lines 3–5. Students should take two 30-second timings on each line in this section. The goal is to increase the number of words or decrease the number of errors on each attempt.

Remind them to leave a blank line between each line group. Make sure students are using the proper fingers when typing.

BUILD YOUR SKILL

Have students type lines 6–11 twice. Instruct them to keep their eyes on the text.

Have students build accuracy by typing lines 12–15 in the **Special Word Groups** section. If more than 5 errors are made on the 4 lines, they should retype the lines. Make sure your students are recording their progress on their charts.

REVIEW

Goal:
- Review the M and left shift keys

TUNE UP

Type each line 2 times. Press Return/Enter at the end of each line. Tap the keys lightly and quickly. Keep your eyes on the copy.

1 sws ded dcd frf ftf jhj jmj kik lol l.l
2 ;A; Adam Dora Chase a:a Lisa Jake Karla

REVIEW

Type each line 2 times. Remember to leave a blank line between line groups.

3 malt male mare mark mask mash sham slam
4 Ida Hal Kim Lars Jill Keith Hilda Ollie
5 Mr. Ms. Mrs. Mars Marsh Marsha Marshall

BUILD YOUR SKILL

Type each line 2 times.

6   dome home some come came lame same tame
7   lot Lotta jam James mar Marie how Howie
8   dimmer hammer hammock homework shamrock
9   Ilka Jose Leila Michael Loretta Malcolm
10 Hello Jackie. Matt came home from Rome.
11 Dear Kim: I will write Miami or Moscow.

SPECIAL WORD GROUPS

If you do not know the meanings of the words, look them up in a dictionary. Then type each line 2 times.

12 Iowa Ohio Idaho Hawaii America Oklahoma
13 Mali Rome Haiti Korea Jamaica Morocco

Section 5 Alphabetic Keys

RESOURCES

- Lesson Plan: LP20
- Wallchart: Point out reaches to the M and left shift keys
- Transparency 1
- CD-ROM: Build Skill on the M and Left Shift Keys
- Software: Build Skill on the M and Left Shift Keys

REVIEW

14 ham jam lime milk malted tomato tamale
15 oatmeal mackerel molasses marmalade

TIME YOURSELF

Take two 1-minute timings on the copy below. If you finish both lines before time is up, start over again. Press Return/Enter at the end of each line.

16 Dear Joe: I met Tess. She is a chemist.
17 Miles will meet the swim team tomorrow.
  | 1 | 2 | 3 | 4 | 5 | 6 | 7 | 8

Language Link

Capitalize days of the week, months, and holidays.

Study the examples:

Our final track meet is next **Tuesday.**
My birthday is **August** 26.
The library will be closed for **Labor Day.**

✓ Check Your Learning

In each sentence, indicate each word that should be capitalized.

1. We celebrate the fourth of july with a picnic.
2. Arlene and Joe will finish the job in february.
3. Next friday is memorial day.
4. I plan to ride my bike every saturday in may.
5. My brother graduates from college in june.

M & Left Shift Review

Lines 12 and 13 are geographic words; lines 14 and 15 are food words.

ASSESS

Using lines 16 and 17, have students take two 1-minute timings or three 12-second timings. The students' goal should be to increase the number of words or decrease the number of errors on each attempt.

While students are typing each line twice, walk around the class observing and commenting on techniques.

Language Link

ANSWERS

1. Fourth of July
2. February
3. Friday, Memorial Day
4. Saturday, May
5. June

CLOSE

Review the **Language Link** section with your class. Have students type each sentence in **Check Your Learning** using proper capitalization.

After students have typed the answers, discuss them in class.

Teacher's Notes

G Key

FOCUS

Review learned keys. Learn the G key.

BELLRINGER

As soon as their workstations are properly set up, students should begin typing **Tune Up,** which reviews learned keys.

TEACH

Show the class the location of the G key. Demonstrate the proper reach, showing them how the F finger reaches to the right to the G key. Dictate the line shown under **Learn the G Key;** then have the students type it as you observe.

PRACTICE THE G KEY

Have students type lines 3–6. Remind them to leave a blank line between each group of lines.

ASSESS

While students are typing each line in **Word Practice** twice, walk around the room observing and commenting on proper hand position and technique in reaching for the G key.

Speed: lines 7 and 8
Accuracy: lines 9 and 10
Speed and Accuracy: lines 11 and 12

CLOSE

Review proper technique at the keyboard and the reach for the G key. Encourage students to practice keyboarding on a daily basis.

Goal:
- Use the G key

TUNE UP

Type each line 2 times. Press Return/Enter at the end of each line. Tap the keys lightly and quickly. Keep your eyes on the copy.

1. sws ded dcd frf ftf jhj jmj kik lol 1.1
2. a:a Mike Irma Merle ;A; Adam Emma Homer

LEARN THE G KEY

Use the F finger on G. The reach is to the right. Feel the reach from F to G and back to F. When you make the reach to G, keep the A finger at home. Practice the following line.

fff fgf fff fgf fff fgf fff

PRACTICE THE G KEY

Type each line 2 times. Keep your eyes on the copy. Remember to leave a blank line between each line group.

3. fff fgf fgf gfg fgf fff fgf fgf gfg fgf
4. ggg aaa ggg gag gag aaa ggg eee age age
5. eee ggg ggg egg egg rrr aaa ggg rag rag
6. gg got got gg game game gg glad glad gg

WORD PRACTICE

Type each line 2 times. Remember to use good technique.

7. gag rag sag lag wag wig fig dig dog hog
8. rage cage wage gage gate game gale gall
9. greed degree disagree daggers staggered
10. grid girl grill gorilla griddle wriggle
11. regal large gargle garage ragged regard
12. high tight fright freight weight eighth

Bits & Bytes

To keep your files safe on a floppy disk, keep the disk away from magnetic things, keep it dry, and keep it from getting too hot or too cold.

Section 5 Alphabetic Keys

RESOURCES

- Lesson Plan: LP20
- Wallchart: Point out reach to the G key
- Transparency 1
- CD-ROM: G Key
- Software: G Key

Comma (,) Key

Goal:
- Use the comma (,) key

Do This
Use a comma to set off phrases and clauses and to separate the items in a series.

TUNE UP

Type each line 2 times. Press Return/Enter at the end of each line.

1. aaa sws ded dcd frf ftf fgf a:a Kim Mom
2. jhj jmj kik lol 1.1 ;;; ;A; Sal Tom Dad

LEARN THE COMMA KEY

The comma is a mark of punctuation used within a sentence. Use the K finger to type a comma (,). The reach is down and to the right. Curl the K finger as you make the reach and keep the Sem finger in home position. Practice the following line.

   kkk k,k kkk k,k kkk k,k kkk

PRACTICE THE COMMA KEY

Type each line 2 times. Leave a blank line between each line group.

3. kkk k,k k,k ,k, k,k kkk k,k k,k ,k, k,k
4. iii fff ,,, if, if, sss ooo ,,, so, so,
5. k,k if it is time, k,k who will go, k,k
6. k,k a shirt, a tie, a dress, socks, k,k

WORD PRACTICE

Type each line 2 times. Remember to use good technique.

7. if it, he has, hit it, we will, go home,
8. dogs, cats, fish; hats, slacks, loafers;
9. college dorm, gold glitter, large lodge,
10. garage, mortgage, flagstaff, stagecoach,
11. fright, gaslight, highlight, watertight,
12. a good egg, a magic sight, a grim image,

RESOURCES
- Lesson Plan: LP21
- Wallchart: Point out reach to the comma key
- Transparency 1
- CD-ROM: Comma Key
- Software: Comma Key

Comma (,) Key

FOCUS
Review learned keys. Learn the comma (,) key.

BELLRINGER
As soon as their workstations are properly set up, have students type the **Tune Up.**

TEACH
Show the class the location of the comma (,) key. Demonstrate the proper reach, showing them how the K finger reaches down and slightly to the right to the comma (,) key.

Discuss the use of the comma, emphasizing proper spacing: one space after a comma. Dictate the line shown, and then have the students type it as you observe.

PRACTICE THE KEY
Have students type lines 3–6. Remind them to leave a blank line between each group of lines.

ASSESS
While students are typing each line in **Word Practice** twice, observe and comment on proper position and technique.

Speed: lines 7 and 8
Accuracy: lines 9 and 10
Speed and Accuracy: lines 11 and 12

CLOSE
Review proper keyboarding technique and the reach for the comma (,) key.

G & Comma Review

FOCUS

Review learned keys. Review the G and comma (,) keys. Review the proper spacing for the comma and the period.

BELLRINGER

As soon as their workstations are set up, have students type each **Tune Up** line twice. This reviews learned keys plus the G and comma (,) keys.

TEACH

Review the importance of proper posture and keying technique. Demonstrate the correct reaches from the home keys to the G and comma (,) keys.

REVIEW G AND , KEYS

Have students complete lines 3–5 twice. The goal is to increase speed and accuracy. Remind them to leave a blank line between each line group. Make sure students are using the proper fingers.

BUILD YOUR SKILL

Have students type lines 6–11 twice. Instruct them to keep their eyes on the text.

Have students build accuracy by typing lines 12–15 in the **Special Word Groups** section. If more than 5 errors are made on the 4 lines, they should retype the lines.

REVIEW

G & , Review

Goal:
- Review the G and comma (,) keys

TUNE UP

Type each line 2 times. Press Return/Enter at the end of each line. Tap the keys lightly and quickly. Keep your eyes on the copy.

1 aaa sss ddd fff jjj kkk lll ;;; fgf jhj
2 sws lol ded kik dcd k,k frf l.l ftf A:A

REVIEW

Type each line 2 times. Remember to leave a blank line between line groups.

3 garage wigwag giggles trigger geologist
4 I agree, he golfs, she goes, we gather,
5 Dear Mr. Goss: I saw the ad; Al got it.

BUILD YOUR SKILL

Type each line 2 times.

6 drag grad goad goat goal golf flog frog
7 gas grass glass gloss gross goose geese
8 Meg, Reg, Grace, Roger, Gloria, George,
9 glamor grammar massage wattage carriage
10 dig digit digest fidget freight fragile
11 Sell me a goldfish, a goose, or a frog.

SPECIAL WORD GROUPS

If you do not know the meanings of the words, look them up in a dictionary. Then type each line 2 times.

12 frog goat gator goose geese gecko dogie
13 hog tiger eagle eaglet giraffe gorilla

Section 5 Alphabetic Keys

RESOURCES

- Lesson Plan: LP21
- Wallchart: Point out reaches to the G and comma keys
- Transparency 1
- CD-ROM: Build Skill on the G and Comma Keys
- Software: Build Skill on the G and Comma Keys

REVIEW

G & Comma Review

```
14  great gocart sleigh carriage stagecoach
15  fig, egg, sage, hot dog, cottage cheese
```

Lines 12 and 13 contain animal words; line 14, transportation words; line 15, food words.

TIME YOURSELF

Take two 1-minute timings on the copy below. If you finish both lines before time is up, start over again. Press Return/Enter at the end of each line.

```
16  He ate a hot dog. Greta ate fried eggs.
17  Greg, the goalie, missed the last game.
    | 1 | 2 | 3 | 4 | 5 | 6 | 7 | 8
```

ASSESS

Using lines 16 and 17, have students take two 1-minute timings or three 12-second timings. Students should type each line with no more than 2 errors in each line. Repeat the exercise until it is completed within the goal.

While students are typing each line twice, walk around the class observing and commenting on techniques.

Language Link

Commas are sometimes needed for special uses.

Use commas in names in direct address; dates using month, day, and year; names of city and state; and abbreviated titles with a person's name. Study the examples:

> Ms. Mar, did the Romans have a large merchant fleet?
> The bus trip began on July 5, 1996, and lasted three weeks.
> People came from Buffalo, New York, to travel with the tour.
> Carol Warren, M.D., studied the effects of motion sickness.

✓ **Check Your Learning**

Indicate where commas should appear in each of the following sentences.

1. Frank please move to the end of the line.
2. The deed dated August 29 1994 was taken to the bank deposit box.
3. My cousin's home in Lattasburg Ohio is on a farm.
4. Philippe Coista Ph.D. received the London Service Award.
5. Susan are you going with the team to Charlotte North Carolina next month?

Language Link ANSWERS

1. Frank
2. August, 29, 1994
3. Lattasburg, Ohio,
4. Coista, Ph.D.,
5. Susan, Charlotte, North Carolina

CLOSE

Review **Language Link** with students. Have them type the sentences in **Check Your Learning**, inserting commas where appropriate. Then have them exchange papers and check each other's answers.

G & Comma (,) Review

Teacher's Notes

X Key

FOCUS
Review learned keys. Learn the X key.

BELLRINGER
As soon as their workstations are properly set up, students should begin typing **Tune Up**.

TEACH
Show the class the location of the X key. Demonstrate the proper reach, showing them how the S finger reaches down and slightly to the right to the X key. Dictate the line shown under **Learn the X Key** and then have the students type it as you observe.

PRACTICE THE X KEY
Have students type lines 3–6. Remind them to leave a blank line between each group of lines.

ASSESS
While students are typing each line in **Word Practice** twice, observe and comment on proper hand position and technique in reaching for the X key.

In line 7, *lox* means both smoked salmon and liquid oxygen.

Speed: lines 7 and 8
Accuracy: lines 9 and 10
Speed and Accuracy: lines 11 and 12

CLOSE
Review proper technique at the keyboard and the reach for the X key.

70

Goal:
- Use the X key

TUNE UP
Type each line 2 times. Press Return/Enter at the end of each line.

1 ask she dog fee jet kid lot ear hot owe
2 car red ice toe wig met gas A1; La. k,k

LEARN THE X KEY
Use the S finger to type X. The reach is down and a little to the right. Feel the reach from S to X and back to S. When you make the reach to X, curl the S finger into your palm. Keep either the A finger or the F finger at home. Practice the following line.

   sss sxs sss sxs sss sxs sss

PRACTICE THE X KEY
Type each line 2 times. Leave a blank line between each line group.

3 sss sxs sxs xsx sxs sss sxs sxs xsx sxs
4 aaa xxx eee axe axe fff iii xxx fix fix
5 lll aaa xxx lax lax ttt aaa xxx tax tax
6 xx fox fox xx axle axle xx coax coax xx

WORD PRACTICE
Type each line 2 times. Remember to use good technique.

7   wax max tax fax fix mix six sox fox lox
8   lax axe axle flax flex text taxes axles
9   fix affix exist exert exercise exterior
10 hoax coax climax matrix exclaim extreme
11 tax taxi exit exist exile excite exotic
12 flexed reflex relax extra latex textile

70   Section 5 Alphabetic Keys

RESOURCES
- Lesson Plan: LP22
- Wallchart: Point out reach to the X key
- Transparency 1
- CD-ROM: X Key
- Software: X Key

U Key

Goal:
- Use the U key

TUNE UP

Type each line 2 times. Press Return/Enter at the end of each line. Tap the keys lightly and quickly. Keep your eyes on the copy.

1. ax coax Dexter exit fox garage hex idea
2. jell kit lax mix ox relax six Texas wax

LEARN THE U KEY

Use the J finger to type U. The reach is up and to the left. Feel the reach from J to U and back to J. When you make the reach to U, keep the Sem finger at home. Practice the following line.

jjj juj jjj juj jjj juj jjj

PRACTICE THE U KEY

Type each line 2 times. Keep your eyes on the copy. Remember to leave a blank line between each line group.

3. jjj juj juj uju juj jjj juj juj uju juj
4. jjj uuu ggg jug jug uuu sss eee use use
5. ccc uuu ttt cut cut mmm uuu ddd mud mud
6. uu hut hut uu rude rude uu used used uu

WORD PRACTICE

Type each line 2 times. Remember to use good technique.

7. dug hug jug lug rug tug mug mud cud cut
8. duel duet dust rust must mush rush hush
9. cuddle huddles shuffle shudder struggle
10. could would should shoulder house mouse
11. couch cough dough rough through thought
12. curl cure cute acute accuse rescue clue

U Key

FOCUS

Review learned keys and the X key. Learn the U key.

BELLRINGER

As soon as their workstations are properly set up, have students type the **Tune Up.**

TEACH

Show the class the location of the U key. Demonstrate the proper reach, showing them how the J finger reaches up and to the left to the U key. Dictate the line shown, and then have the students type it as you observe.

PRACTICE THE U KEY

Have students type lines 3–6. Dictate the lines as you walk around the room observing technique and posture. Increase your speed of dictation with each line, but make sure to keep your tempo even.

ASSESS

While students are typing each line in **Word Practice** twice, observe and comment on proper position and technique.

Speed: lines 7 and 8
Accuracy: lines 9 and 10
Speed and Accuracy: lines 11 and 12

CLOSE

Review proper keyboarding technique and the reach for the U key.

RESOURCES

- Lesson Plan: LP22
- Wallchart: Point out reach to the U key
- Transparency 1
- CD-ROM: U Key
- Software: U Key

X & U Review

FOCUS
Review learned keys. Review the X and U keys.

BELLRINGER
As soon as their workstations are set up, have students type each **Tune Up** line twice.

TEACH
Review the importance of proper posture and keying technique. Demonstrate the correct reaches from the home keys to the X and U keys. Remind students to keep their hands on the home keys.

REVIEW X AND U KEYS
Have students complete lines 3–5 twice. Their goal is to increase speed and accuracy.

BUILD YOUR SKILL
Have students type lines 6–11 twice. Instruct them to keep their eyes on the text.

Have students build accuracy by typing lines 12–15 in **Special Word Groups.** If more than 5 errors are made on the 4 lines, they should retype the lines.

Line 12 focuses on proper names and nicknames; line 13, on U.S. geographic names; line 14, on foreign geographic names; and line 15, on food words.

REVIEW

Goal:
- Review the X and U keys

TUNE UP
Type each line 2 times. Press Return/Enter at the end of each line.

1. aaa sws ded frf ftf fgf jhj juj kik lol
2. sxs dcd jmj k,k l.l ;;; aJa Jud ;R; Rex

REVIEW
Type each line 2 times. Leave a blank line between line groups.

3. axis coax exams fixed latex relax toxic
4. dusk gulf house issue juice laugh mouth
5. excuse suffix tuxedos texture exhausted

BUILD YOUR SKILL
Type each line 2 times.

6. fox fur mix mug six sum tax tux hex hum
7. rut rust strut trust thrust thrush rush
8. toxic affix excess matrix reflex sextet
9. humour detour textual execute courteous
10. Lou must exit through the rusted gates.
10. Alexis laughed aloud at the Texas taxi.

SPECIAL WORD GROUPS
If you are not familiar with the words, look the words up in a dictionary. Then type each line 2 times.

12. Gus Alex Roxie Dutch Trixi Felix Ursula
13. Guam Utah Maui Kauai U.S.A. Excelsior
14. Austria Exeter Mexico Oxford Guatemala
15. fruit fudge juice mustard cauliflower

72 Section 5 Alphabetic Keys

RESOURCES
- Lesson Plan: LP23
- Wallchart: Point out reaches to the X and U keys
- Transparency 1
- CD-ROM: Build Skill on the X and U Keys; Uncover the Story
- Software: Build Skill on the X and U Keys

REVIEW

TIME YOURSELF

Take two 1-minute timings on the copy below. If you finish both lines before time is up, start over again. Press Return/Enter at the end of each line.

```
16  The exterior statue has rusted; fix it.
17  Roxie, Doug, or Max used the extra wax.
    |  1  |  2  |  3  |  4  |  5  |  6  |  7  |  8
```

CULTURAL KALEIDOSCOPE

If invited to someone's home, Austrians may bring flowers for the host. They always give an odd number of flowers because an even number is considered unlucky. They avoid giving roses, which symbolize romantic interest.

X & U Review

X & U Review

ASSESS

Using lines 16 and 17, have students take two 1-minute timings or three 12-second timings. The students' goal should be to increase the number of words or decrease the number of errors on each attempt.

While students are typing each line twice, walk around the class observing and commenting on techniques.

CLOSE

Review the **Cultural Kaleidoscope** with your class. Discuss the custom of bringing gifts when visiting someone's home. Ask them what types of gifts would be appropriate when visiting the home of a friend in the United States. Write their answers on the board; then have them type the list.

CULTURAL KALEIDOSCOPE

If invited to a home in Chile, guests should send flowers in advance. When visiting a home in Singapore, guests should not arrive with a gift of food—this may imply that the host cannot provide adequate food for the meal. Rather, the guest should send food afterward as a thank-you gift.

Q Key

FOCUS

Review learned keys. Learn the Q key.

BELLRINGER

As soon as their workstations are properly set up, have students type **Tune Up**.

Kudu is an African antelope.

TEACH

Show the class the location of the Q key. Demonstrate the proper reach, showing them how the A finger reaches up and slightly to the left to the Q key. Dictate the line shown under **Learn the Q Key** and then have the students type it as you observe.

PRACTICE THE Q KEY

Have students type lines 3–6. Have them type at an even speed. To achieve this, dictate the lines. Remind students to leave a blank line between each group of lines.

ASSESS

While students are typing each line in **Word Practice** twice, observe and comment on proper hand position and technique.

Speed: lines 7 and 8
Accuracy: lines 9 and 10
Speed and Accuracy: lines 11 and 12

CLOSE

Review proper technique at the keyboard and the reach for the Q key.

Goal:
- Use the Q key

TUNE UP

Type each line 2 times. Press Return/Enter at the end of each line. Tap the keys lightly and quickly. Keep your eyes on the copy.

1 axe six due fox gum hex jut lax use tux
2 out wax mix cut kudu Ruth Xerox maximum

LEARN THE Q KEY

Use the A finger to type Q. The reach is up and to the left. Feel the reach from A to Q and back to A. When you make the reach to Q, keep the F finger at home. Practice the following line.

   aaa aqa aaa aqa aaa aqa aaa

PRACTICE THE Q KEY

Type each line 2 times. Keep your eyes on the copy. Remember to leave a blank line between each line group.

3 aaa aqa aqa qaq aqa aaa aqa aqa qaq aqa
4 qqq uuu aaa qua qua qqq uuu eee que que
5 qq quo quo qq aqua aqua qq quit quit qq
6 qq quote qq quake qq quart qq squall qq

WORD PRACTICE

Type each line 2 times. Remember to use good technique.

7   aqua equal quail quill quilt quiet quit
8   quad squad squid squirt squirm squirrel
9   quail qualified required quarrel squall
10 request equator adequate lacquer liquid
11 acquit acquire aquarium squarish square
12 quart quarter quartet squatter quitters

Bits & Bytes

With some computer programs, you can activate the Help balloons to help you learn applications and commands more quickly and easily.

74   Section 5 Alphabetic Keys

RESOURCES

- Lesson Plan: LP23
- Wallchart: Point out reach to the Q key
- Transparency 1
- CD-ROM: Q Key
- Software: Q Key

Goal:
- Use the N key

TUNE UP

Type each line 2 times. Press Return/Enter at the end of each line. Tap the keys lightly and quickly. Keep your eyes on the copy.

1. aqa sws ded frf ftf fgf jhj juj kik lol
2. sxs dcd jmj k,k l.l ;;; qua quo qui que

LEARN THE N KEY

Use the J finger to type N. The reach is down and to the left. Feel the reach from J to N and back to J. When you make the reach to N, keep the Sem finger at home. Practice the following line.

   jjj jnj jjj jnj jjj jnj jjj

PRACTICE THE N KEY

Type each line 2 times. Keep your eyes on the copy. Remember to leave a blank line between each line group.

3. jjj jnj jnj njn jnj jjj jnj jnj njn jnj
4. aaa nnn ttt ant ant ttt aaa nnn tan tan
5. nnn ooo www now now ooo www nnn own own
6. nn new new nn noun noun nn next next nn

WORD PRACTICE

Type each line 2 times. Remember to use good technique.

7. can fan man ran run fun sun son sin din
8. hand hang sang rang ring sing song gong
9. jinx hexagon unequal antiques exchanged
10. wrinkle kitchen nesting janitor frantic
11. grants granite radiant ancient contains
12. rain gain again regain resign signature

N Key

FOCUS

Review learned keys and the Q key. Learn the N key.

BELLRINGER

As soon as their workstations are properly set up, have students type the **Tune Up**.

TEACH

Point out the location of the N key. Demonstrate the proper reach, showing how the J finger reaches down and to the left to the N key. Dictate the line shown; then have students type it as you observe.

PRACTICE THE N KEY

Have students type lines 3–6. Remind them to leave a blank line between each group of lines. Try playing some music as the students practice, making sure to use something with a lively rhythm.

ASSESS

While students are typing each line in **Word Practice** twice, observe and comment on proper position and technique.

Speed: lines 7 and 8
Accuracy: lines 9 and 10
Speed and Accuracy: lines 11 and 12

CLOSE

Review proper keyboarding technique and the reach for the N key. Encourage students to practice keyboarding daily.

RESOURCES

- Lesson Plan: LP24
- Wallchart: Point out reach to the N key
- Transparency 1
- CD-ROM: N Key
- Software: N Key

Q & N Review

FOCUS
Review learned keys. Review the Q and N keys.

BELLRINGER
As soon as their workstations are set up, have students type each **Tune Up** line twice. The first time they should push for speed, the second time, for accuracy. This reviews learned keys plus the Q and N keys.

TEACH
Review the importance of proper posture and keying technique. Demonstrate the correct reaches from the home keys to the Q and N keys.

REVIEW Q AND N KEYS
Have students complete lines 3–5. Remind them to leave a blank line between each line group.

Students should take two 30-second timings on each line in this section, again to increase their speed and/or accuracy.

BUILD YOUR SKILL
Have students type lines 6–11 twice. Instruct them to keep their eyes on the text.

Have students build accuracy by typing lines 12–15 in the **Special Word Groups** section. If more than 5 errors are made on the 4 lines, they should retype the lines.

Q & N Review

Goal:
- Review the Q and N keys

TUNE UP

Type each line 2 times. Press Return/Enter at the end of each line. Tap the keys lightly and quickly. Keep your eyes on the copy.

1 fox jinx quit make dock stew luck right
2 Now is the time for all good men to go.

REVIEW

Type each line 2 times. Remember to leave a blank line between line groups.

3 quilts liquid quitter squirrel squatter
4 hunger jungle journal adjourns doughnut
5 quint inquire quicken question frequent

BUILD YOUR SKILL

Type each line 2 times.

6 quit quiet quilt quart squat squad quad
7 Jane cane sane lane land sand wand hand
8 quack equator request lacquer aquariums
9 squint inquire hexagon antique frequent
10 The new squad wanted another quick win.
11 A quiet newsman quoted nine techniques.

SPECIAL WORD GROUPS

If you do not know the meanings of the words in Line 12, look them up in a dictionary. Then type each line 2 times.

12 franc cologne fiancee lingerie hacienda
13 Kansas Oregon Illinois Indiana Arkansas

76   Section 5 Alphabetic Keys

RESOURCES

- Lesson Plan: LP24
- Wallchart: Point out reaches to the Q and N keys
- Transparency 1
- CD-ROM: Build Skill on the Q and N Keys
- Software: Build Skill on the Q and N Keys

REVIEW

14 Maine Louisiana California Connecticut
15 Michigan Minnesota Tennessee Washington

TIME YOURSELF

Take two 1-minute timings on the copy below. If you finish all three lines before time is up, start over again. Press Return/Enter at the end of each line.

16 Andrew and Jan want to go to Wisconsin.
17 The squealing twins need another quilt.
18 In Montana, the aqua laquer was unseen.
| 1 | 2 | 3 | 4 | 5 | 6 | 7 | 8

Language Link

Commas are used to separate three or more words, phrases, or clauses in a series.

Study the examples:

> Red, orange, and blue are my favorite colors.
> I looked for the missing book in the room, under the bed, and in the closet.

✓ Check Your Learning

Indicate where commas should be inserted in the following sentences.

1. Draft write edit and rewrite each paragraph.
2. The race begins on Main Street crosses Clover Boulevard and finishes at Mill Lane.
3. Each group went to the pond collected samples and recorded the data.
4. The show was enjoyed by Cassandra Kirsten Scott and Brice.
5. Bring your lunch and a pair of dry shoes for the trip.

Q & N Review   77

Q & N Review

Line 12 contains foreign words; lines 13–15, U.S. states.

ASSESS

Using lines 16–18, have students take two 1-minute timings or three 12-second timings. The students' goal should be to increase the number of words or decrease the number of errors on each attempt.

While students are typing each line twice, walk around the class observing and commenting on techniques.

Language Link

ANSWERS

1. Draft, write, edit,
2. Street, ... Boulevard,
3. pond, ... samples,
4. Cassandra, Kirsten, Scott,
5. no commas

CLOSE

Have students type each of the sentences in **Check Your Learning,** inserting commas where appropriate. Discuss the correct answers with the class.

Teacher's Notes

V Key

FOCUS
Review learned keys. Learn the V key.

BELLRINGER
As soon as their workstations are properly set up, have students type **Tune Up.**

TEACH
Show the class the location of the V key. Demonstrate the proper reach, showing them how the F finger reaches down and slightly to the right to the V key. Dictate the line shown under **Learn the V Key** and then have the students type it as you observe.

PRACTICE THE V KEY
Have students type lines 3–6, leaving a blank line between each group of lines.

ASSESS
While students are typing each line in **Word Practice** twice, observe and comment on proper hand position and technique in reaching for the V key.

Speed: lines 7 and 8
Accuracy: lines 9 and 10
Speed and Accuracy: lines 11 and 12

CLOSE
Review proper technique at the keyboard and the reach for the V key.

Goal:
- Use the V key

TUNE UP
Type each line 2 times. Press Return/Enter at the end of each line. Tap the keys lightly and quickly. Keep your eyes on the copy.

```
1  aqa sws ded frf ftf juj kik lol ;A; ;Q;
2  sxs dcd fgf jhj jnj jmj k,k l.l a:a aNa
```

LEARN THE V KEY
Use the F finger to type V. The reach is down and a little to the right. Feel the reach from F to V and back to F. When you make the reach to V, keep the A finger at home. Practice the following line.

```
   fff fvf fff fvf fff fvf fff
```

PRACTICE THE V KEY
Type each line 2 times. Keep your eyes on the copy. Remember to leave a blank line between each line group.

```
3  fff fvf fvf vfv fvf fff fvf fvf vfv fvf
4  vvv aaa nnn van van vvv ooo www vow vow
5  eee vvv eee eve eve vvv iii aaa via via
6  vv vet vet vv dove dove vv five five vv
```

WORD PRACTICE
Type each line 2 times. Remember to use good technique.

```
7  rave save have cave cove love dove rove
8  hive five dive drive driven liven alive
9  chive grieve achieve receive convenient
10 quiver quaver overture convert vertical
11 eve veer ever even event invent venture
12 have halve lavish visual vision version
```

Bits & Bytes
If you are working on the computer for long periods of time, you should periodically rest your eyes to prevent eye strain and headaches. You can do this by first focusing on a distant object and then returning to a closer object.

78 Section 5 Alphabetic Keys

RESOURCES
- Lesson Plan: LP25
- Wallchart: Point out reach to the V key
- Transparency 1
- CD-ROM: V Key
- Software: V Key

P Key

Goal:
- Use the P key

TUNE UP

Type each line 2 times. Press Return/Enter at the end of each line. Tap the keys lightly and quickly. Keep your eyes on the copy.

1 ask saw doe far gum hot jug kit lot qua was
2 egg rim tan use irk old cow vat new mud axe

LEARN THE P KEY

Use the Sem finger to type P. The reach is up and to the left. Feel the reach from Sem to P and back to Sem. When you make the reach to P, keep the J finger at home. Practice the following line.

;;; ;p; ;;; ;p; ;;; ;p; ;;;

PRACTICE THE P KEY

Type each line 2 times. Keep your eyes on the copy. Remember to leave a blank line between each line group.

3 ;;; ;p; ;p; p;p ;p; ;;; ;p; ;p; p;p ;p;
4 aaa ppp eee ape ape ppp eee nnn pen pen
5 nnn aaa ppp nap nap sss iii ppp sip sip
6 pp pat pat pp pear pear pp jump jump pp

WORD PRACTICE

Type each line 2 times. Remember to use good technique.

7   pea pen pet pat pan pin pig pit pot pop
8   loop hoop hope dope rope ripe wipe pipe
9   expect expert expire explores explosive
10 nephew people whopper premium unpopular
11 pump plump pamper prompt proper propose
12 plaid plain plane plant planet platinum

P Key

FOCUS

Review learned keys and the V key. Learn the P key.

BELLRINGER

As soon as their workstations are properly set up, have students type the **Tune Up.** You may want to play music to establish a good tempo.

TEACH

Show the class the location of the P key. Demonstrate the proper reach, showing them how the Sem finger reaches up and slightly to the left to the P key. Dictate the line shown, and then have the students type it as you observe.

PRACTICE THE P KEY

Have students type lines 3–6, leaving a blank line between each group of lines.

Dictate line 3 to set the proper pace for your students. Then have them focus on proper technique.

ASSESS

While students are typing each line in **Word Practice** twice, observe and comment on proper position and technique in reaching for the P key.

Speed: lines 7 and 8
Accuracy: lines 9 and 10
Speed and Accuracy: lines 11 and 12

CLOSE

Review proper keyboarding technique and the reach for the P key.

RESOURCES

- Lesson Plan: LP25
- Wallchart: Point out reach to the P key
- Transparency 1
- CD-ROM: P Key
- Software: P Key

V & P Review

FOCUS
Review learned keys. Review the V and P keys.

BELLRINGER
Have students type each **Tune Up** line twice to review learned keys including the V and P keys.

TEACH
Review the importance of proper posture and keying technique. Demonstrate the correct reaches from the home keys to the V and P keys.

REVIEW V AND P KEYS
Have students complete lines 3–5. Remind them to leave a blank line between each line group.

Students should take three 12-minute timings on each line in this section. Remind students that their goal is to increase speed and accuracy.

BUILD YOUR SKILL
Have students type lines 6–11 twice. Instruct them to keep their eyes on the text.

Now have students take two 30-second timings on each line in this section. Again their goal is to increase speed and accuracy.

Have students build accuracy by typing lines 12–15 in **Special Word Groups.** If more than 5 errors are made on the 4 lines, they should retype them.

V & P Review

Goal:
- Review the V and P keys

TUNE UP

Type each line 2 times. Press Return/Enter at the end of each line.

1. as do if go he to we no me so up on van
2. The quick fox jumps over the white dog.

REVIEW

Type each line 2 times. Leave a blank line between line groups.

3. jive drive revolt cavern flavor elevate
4. flip gripe pickax sphinx upside complex
5. vapor preview approve deprive primitive

BUILD YOUR SKILL

Type each line 2 times.

6. shave slave solve evolve revolve devour
7. weep sweep spree press impress pressure
8. volume violate vitamin volcano vertical
9. puppet partial premium pageant pamphlet
10. Vince never visited the native village.
11. Patti put purple petunias on the patio.

SPECIAL WORD GROUPS

If you do not know the meanings of the words, look them up in a dictionary. Then type each line 2 times.

12. olive apricot ketchup avocado flapjack
13. pickle peanut ravioli venison spaghetti
14. veal cupcake tapioca pudding pineapple
15. peso villa coupe padre lanai chapeaux

Section 5 Alphabetic Keys

RESOURCES
- Lesson Plan: LP25
- Wallchart: Point out reaches to the V and P keys
- Transparency 1
- CD-ROM: Build Skill on the V and P Keys
- Software: Build Skill on the V and P Keys

REVIEW

TIME YOURSELF

Take two 1-minute timings on the copy below. If you finish all three lines before time is up, start over again. Press Return/Enter at the end of each line.

```
16  Vera chopped up five to seven pancakes.
17  The Viking jumped over the triple trap.
18  Peter and Paula visited Japan in April.
    | 1 | 2 | 3 | 4 | 5 | 6 | 7 | 8
```

Language Link

Use a comma after an introductory clause beginning with conjunctions such as if, as, when, although, since, and because.

Study the examples:

> If we leave now, we will see the last half of the game.
> As we boarded the plane, the flight attendant greeted us.
> When the statue was unveiled, most of the guests cheered.

✓ Check Your Learning

Indicate where commas should appear in each of the following sentences.

1. Because of Richard's quick thinking we were able to win the race.
2. When the applications are received they will be processed immediately.
3. Since I must finish my report I will be unable to go skating.
4. While my parents were at the meeting Roger and I planned their party.
5. If the pie cools quickly enough we can eat it for dessert.

V & P Review   81

Teacher's Notes

V & P Review

Lines 12–14 are food words; line 15 contains common foreign words. *Peso* is money (Spanish); *villa* is a house (French); *coupe* is a small car (French); *padre* is father (Spanish); *lanai* is a balcony (Hawaiian); *chapeaux* is hat (French).

ASSESS

Using lines 16–18, have students take two 1-minute timings or three 12-second timings. The students' goal should be to increase the number of words or decrease the number of errors on each attempt.

While students are typing each line twice, walk around the class observing and commenting on techniques.

Language Link

ANSWERS

1. thinking,
2. received,
3. report,
4. meeting,
5. enough,

CLOSE

Review the **Language Link** section with your class. Have each student type each of the sentences in **Check Your Learning,** inserting commas as appropriate. Then have them proofread each other's papers.

B Key

FOCUS

Review learned keys. Learn the B key.

BELLRINGER

Have students type **Tune Up.** Play peppy music and see if your students can keep pace.

TEACH

Show the class the location of the B key. Demonstrate the proper reach, showing them how the F finger stretches down and to the right, over the V key, to the B key. Dictate the line shown under **Learn the B Key;** then have students type it as you observe.

PRACTICE THE B KEY

Have students type lines 3–6. Emphasize proper technique. This is crucial now, as students will soon know every key and will be pushing for speed.

ASSESS

While students are typing each line in **Word Practice** twice, observe and comment on proper hand position and technique in reaching for the B key.

Speed: lines 7 and 8
Accuracy: lines 9 and 10
Speed and Accuracy: lines 11 and 12

CLOSE

Review proper technique at the keyboard and the reach for the B key.

Goal:
- Use the B key

TUNE UP

Type each line 2 times. Press Return/Enter at the end of each line.

```
1  aqa sws ded frf ftf fgf jhj juj kik lol
2  ;p; sxs dcd fvf jnj jmj k,k l.l ;A; a:a
```

LEARN THE B KEY

Use the F finger to type B. The reach is down and far to the right. You will have to stretch over the V key to reach the B. Feel the reach from F to B and back to F. When you make the reach to B, keep the A finger at home. Practice the following line.

```
   fff fbf fff fbf fff fbf fff
```

PRACTICE THE B KEY

Type each line 2 times. Leave a blank line between each line group.

```
3  fff fvf fbf bfb fbf fff fvf fbf bfb fbf
4  rrr iii bbb rib rib bbb aaa nnn ban ban
5  www eee bbb web web jjj aaa bbb jab jab
6  bb bit bit bb base base bb bill bill bb
```

WORD PRACTICE

Type each line 2 times. Remember to use good technique.

```
7   bed bid bit bin ban bat bad dab gab lab
8   base bare barn burn bran brat brag grab
9   ball baseball football fireball balloon
10  bubble gobble ribbon barbaric blackbird
11  birth broth bother brother border broad
12  beak break breath breathe beneath bench
```

Bits & Bytes

To prevent neckaches and the chance of neck injury, adjust your computer monitor so that it is at eye level or slightly higher.

82 Section 5 Alphabetic Keys

RESOURCES

- Lesson Plan: LP26
- Wallchart: Point out reach to the B key
- Transparency 1
- CD-ROM: B Key
- Software: B Key

Slash (/) Key

Goal:
- Learn the slash (/) key

Do This
Use the slash to construct fractions or to show alternates. Do not space before or after a slash.

Do This
Use a question mark at the end of a sentence that asks a question.

TUNE UP

Type each line 2 times. Press Return/Enter at the end of each line.

```
1  sxs dcd fvf fbf jnj jmj k,k l.l aqa ;p;
2  album elbow icebox object unable forbid
```

LEARN THE SLASH [?/] KEY

The slash is also called the diagonal. The shift of the slash is the question mark (?). Use the Sem finger to type a slash (/). The reach is down and to the right. When you type the slash, keep the J finger at home. Practice the following line.

```
   ;;; ;/; ;;; ;/; ;;; ;/; ;;;
```

PRACTICE THE SLASH [?/] KEY

Type each line 2 times. Leave a blank line between each line group.

```
3  ;;; ;/; ;/; /;/ ;/; ;;; ;/; ;/; /;/ ;/;
4  ;;; ;?; ;?; ?;? ;?; ;;; ;?; ;?; ?;? ;?;
5  ;/; true/false // and/or // his/her ;/;
6  /?/ Who? ?? What? ?? Where? ?? How? /?/
```

WORD PRACTICE

Type each line 2 times. Remember to use good technique.

```
7  his/hers, us/them, up/down, here/there,
8  Who is it? Is it Bette? Did Bill leave?
9  Will he take the true/false test? When?
10 Did we win/lose/tie? Will it rain/snow?
11 Was there a charge? Mark the bills n/c.
12 Is the web address http://www.abbi.com?
```

Slash (/) Key **83**

RESOURCES

- Lesson Plan: LP27
- Wallchart: Point out reach to the slash key
- Transparency 1
- CD-ROM: Slash Key
- Software: Slash Key

Slash (/) Key

FOCUS

Review learned keys and the B key. Learn the slash (/) key.

BELLRINGER

Have students type the **Tune Up.** Try working with the music again to capture and keep students' interest.

TEACH

Show the class the location of the slash (/) key. Review the use of the slash versus the question mark. Remind students not to space before or after a slash—this holds true for Internet addresses!

Demonstrate the proper reach, showing them how the Sem finger reaches down and to the right to the slash (/) key. Dictate the line shown, and then have the students type it as you observe.

PRACTICE THE [?] KEY

Have students type lines 3–6. Remind them to leave a blank line between each group of lines.

ASSESS

While students are typing each line in **Word Practice** twice, observe and comment on proper position and technique in reaching for the slash (/) key.

CLOSE

Review proper keyboarding technique and the reach for the slash (/) key.

B & Slash (/) Review

FOCUS

Review learned keys. Review the B and slash (/) keys.

BELLRINGER

As soon as their workstations are set up, have students type each **Tune Up** line twice. Continue using music to warm up.

TEACH

Review the importance of proper posture and keying technique. Demonstrate the correct reaches from the home keys to the B and slash (/) keys.

REVIEW B AND / KEYS

Have students complete lines 3–5. Remind them to leave a blank line between each line group. Students should take three 12-second timings on each line in this section. The goal is to increase speed and accuracy.

BUILD YOUR SKILL

Have students type lines 6–11 twice. Instruct them to keep their eyes on the text.

Students should take two 30-second timings on each line in this section, aiming for increased speed and accuracy.

Have students build accuracy by typing lines 12–15 in the **Special Word Groups** section. If more than 5 errors are made on the 4 lines, they should retype the lines.

REVIEW

Goal:
- Review the B and slash (/) keys

TUNE UP

Type each line 2 times. Press Return/Enter at the end of each line. Tap the keys lightly and quickly. Keep your eyes on the copy.

1 aqa ;p; sws lol ded kik frf juj ftf jhj
2 fgf ;/; sxs l.l dcd k,k fvf jmj fbf jnj

REVIEW

Type each line 2 times. Remember to leave a blank line between line groups.

3 Bob Ben Beth Barb Bruce Blanche Bernard
4 a/c who/whom either/or Who? What? When?
5 Will Mabel borrow the d/c TV now/later?

BUILD YOUR SKILL

Type each line 2 times.

6   bead bean been bent bend band bald balk
7   he/she good/bad start/stop When? Where?
8   bud bulldog bullfrog bulletin bumblebee
9   ?? on/off open/closed brother/sister ??
10 Can he/she pick the right/wrong answer?
11 Butch brought a big beagle for Barbara.

SPECIAL WORD GROUPS

If you do not know the meanings of the words, look them up in a dictionary. Then type each line 2 times.

12 bacon banana bologna broccoli brownie
13 cabbage cobbler lobster rhubarb sherbet

84 Section 5 Alphabetic Keys

RESOURCES

- Lesson Plan: LP27
- Wallchart: Point out reaches to the B and slash (/) keys
- Transparency 1
- CD-ROM: Build Skill on the B and Slash Keys
- Software: Build Skill on the B and Slash Keys

REVIEW

14 cobra robin baboon bluebird bobolink
15 adobe pueblo kabuki bonjour bouillon

TIME YOURSELF

Take two 1-minute timings on the copy below. If you finish all lines before time is up, start over again. Press Return/Enter at the end of each line.

16 Rob has a TV that works on a/c and d/c.
17 Deb had bread and butter for breakfast.
18 Did Bart go back? Will Bev broil bacon?
   | 1 | 2 | 3 | 4 | 5 | 6 | 7 | 8

CULTURAL KALEIDOSCOPE

Greetings take different forms in different countries. In Chile, friends and relatives commonly greet each other with an *abrazo*. An *abrazo* consists of a handshake and a hug, sometimes followed by a kiss to the right cheek. In Hungary, people usually greet each other by shaking hands. If their hands are dirty, they offer their elbows.

B & Slash (/) Review **85**

CULTURAL KALEIDOSCOPE

In Malaysia, the traditional greeting between members of the same sex is called the **salaam**. In this gesture, both people touch each other's outstretched hand lightly, then bring the hand to rest over their heart.

B & Slash (/) Review

Lines 12 and 13 contain food words; line 14, animal words; line 15, common foreign words. *Adobe* is building material (Spanish); *pueblo* is a town or village (Spanish); *kabuki* is a Japanese drama; *bonjour* is good-bye in French; *bouillon* is clear soup (French).

ASSESS

Using lines 16–18, have students take two 1-minute timings or three 12-second timings. The students' goal should be to increase the number of words or decrease the number of errors on each attempt.

While students are typing each line twice, walk around the class observing and commenting on techniques.

CLOSE

Review the **Cultural Kaleidoscope** with students. Discuss the kinds of greetings they use in different situations—those they use when meeting adults and those they use when meeting their friends.

Remind them to practice typing at least 20 minutes a day to improve their speed and accuracy.

85

Z Key

FOCUS

Review learned keys. Learn the Z key.

BELLRINGER

As soon as their workstations are properly set up, students should begin typing **Tune Up**, which reviews learned keys. Keep up the music, moving to a faster pace.

TEACH

Show the class the location of the Z key. Demonstrate the proper reach, showing them how the A finger reaches down and slightly to the right to the Z key. Dictate the line shown under **Learn the Z Key** and then have students type it.

PRACTICE THE Z KEY

Have students type lines 3–6. Remind them to leave a blank line between each group of lines.

ASSESS

While students are typing each line in **Word Practice** twice, observe and comment on proper hand position and technique in reaching for the Z key.

Speed: lines 7 and 8
Accuracy: lines 9 and 10
Speed and Accuracy: lines 11 and 12

CLOSE

Review proper technique at the keyboard and the reach for the Z key.

Goal:
- Use the Z key

TUNE UP

Type each line 2 times. Press Return/Enter at the end of each line.

```
1  quit roof user bake idea exit jump clam
2  mask gave vein Who? Nov. on/off ;:; k,k
```

LEARN THE Z KEY

Use the A finger to type Z. The reach is down and to the right. Feel the reach from A to Z and back to A. When you make the reach to Z, keep the F finger at home. Practice the following line.

```
   aaa aza aaa aza aaa aza aaa
```

PRACTICE THE Z KEY

Type each line 2 times. Leave a blank line between each line group.

```
3  aaa aza aza zaz aza aaa aza aza zaz aza
4  zzz ooo ooo zoo zoo zzz iii ppp zip zip
5  zzz aaa ggg zag zag bbb iii zzz biz biz
6  zz zap zap zz fuzz fuzz zz zone zone zz
```

WORD PRACTICE

Type each line 2 times. Remember to use good technique.

```
7   whiz quiz ritz size zinc zone zoom zero
8   haze gaze graze glaze blaze blitz waltz
9   czar zebra plaza amaze lizard criticize
10  razz pizza puzzle muzzle buzzer buzzard
11  seize seizure realize civilize colonize
12  breeze sneeze squeeze tweezers freezers
```

Bits & Bytes

One 3½-inch, high-density floppy disk will hold about 1,440 pages of double-spaced text.

Section 5 Alphabetic Keys

RESOURCES

- Lesson Plan: LP28
- Wallchart: Point out reach to the Z key
- Transparency 1
- CD-ROM: Z Key
- Software: Z Key

Y Key

Goal:
- Use the Y key

TUNE UP

Type each line 2 times. Press Return/Enter at the end of each line.

1. over zero rose rise ride race crab brag
2. exit quit twin mist ship skin join foil

LEARN THE Y KEY

Use the J finger to type Y. The reach is up and far to the left. You will have to stretch over the U key to reach the Y. Feel the reach from J to Y and back to J. When you make the reach to Y, keep the Sem finger at home. Practice the following line.

   jjj jyj jjj jyj jjj jyj jjj

PRACTICE THE Y KEY

Type each line 2 times. Leave a blank line between each line group.

3. jjj jyj jyj yjy jyj jjj jyj jyj yjy jyj
4. eee yyy eee eye eye yyy eee sss yes yes
5. yyy ooo uuu you you www hhh yyy why why
6. yy toy toy yy easy easy yy clay clay yy

WORD PRACTICE

Type each line 2 times. Remember to use good technique.

7. any aye eye yet yes say pay pry try cry
8. year yarn yard yawn away sway stay tray
9. foxy luxury sympathy equality geography
10. rhythm monkey company symphony monopoly
11. day daily daisy dairy diary dirty derby
12. twenty thirty forty fifty sixty seventy

Y Key

FOCUS

Review learned keys and the Z key. Learn the Y key.

BELLRINGER

Have students type the **Tune Up**.

TEACH

Show students the location of the Y key. Demonstrate the proper reach, showing them how the J finger stretches up and over the U key to reach the Y key. Dictate the line shown, and then have the students type it as you observe.

PRACTICE THE Y KEY

Have students type lines 3–6, leaving a blank line between each group of lines.

ASSESS

While students are typing each line in **Word Practice** twice, observe and comment on proper position and technique in reaching for the Y key.

Speed: lines 7 and 8
Accuracy: lines 9 and 10
Speed and Accuracy: lines 11 and 12

CLOSE

Review proper keyboarding technique and the reach for the Y key. Again, remind your class that daily practice will increase both their speed and accuracy, which will help them in other classes as well.

RESOURCES

- Lesson Plan: LP28
- Wallchart: Point out reach to the Y key
- Transparency 1
- CD-ROM: Y Key
- Software: Y Key

Z & Y Review

FOCUS
Review learned keys. Review the Z and Y keys.

BELLRINGER
As soon as their workstations are set up, have students type each **Tune Up** line twice. This reviews learned keys including the Z and Y keys. Have students type to peppy music, if available.

TEACH
Review the importance of proper posture and keying technique. Demonstrate the correct reaches from the home keys to the Z and Y keys.

REVIEW Z AND Y KEYS
Have students complete lines 3–5. Remind them to leave a blank line between each line group.

Make sure that your students are using the proper reaches for all learned keys. Emphasize the need to look at the book, not the keyboard or the screen.

BUILD YOUR SKILL
Have students type lines 6–11 twice. Instruct them to keep their eyes on the text.

Have students build accuracy by typing lines 12–15 in **Special Word Groups**. If more than 5 errors are made on the 4 lines, they should retype them.

Line 12 deals with science words; line 13, with sports words; and lines 14 and 15, with animal words.

REVIEW

Z & Y Review

Goal:
- Review the Z and Y keys

TUNE UP

Type each line 2 times. Press Return/Enter at the end of each line. Tap the keys lightly and quickly. Keep your eyes on the copy.

1. aqa aza juj jyj fvf fbf jmj jnj ;p; ;?;
2. Now is the time to come to their party.

REVIEW

Type each line 2 times. Remember to leave a blank line between line groups.

3. quiz hazel zebra hazard bazaar vaporize
4. heavily crystal gymnast anxiety mystery
5. lazy hazy zany cozy crazy woozy analyze

BUILD YOUR SKILL

Type each line 2 times.

6. gaze gauze zip zipper doze dozen dozing
7. grey gray gravy gravity activity vanity
8. razz prize hygiene typically rendezvous
9. zany breezy lazily hypnotize sympathize
10. Zeke will fly to Zanzibar next January.
11. In July, Lizzy buys zinnias in Yonkers.

SPECIAL WORD GROUPS

If you do not know the meanings of the words, look them up in a dictionary. Then type each line 2 times.

12. galaxy physics anatomy geology zoology
13. relay hockey varsity gymnast Olympics

88 Section 5 Alphabetic Keys

RESOURCES

- Lesson Plan: LP29
- Wallchart: Point out reaches to the Z and Y keys
- Transparency 1
- CD-ROM: Build Skill on the Z and Y Keys
- Software: Build Skill on the Z and Y Keys

REVIEW

14 coyote monkey buzzard bluejay butterfly
15 pony zebra hyena donkey python gazelle

TIME YOURSELF

Take two 1-minute timings on the copy below. If you finish all three lines before time is up, start over again. Press Return/Enter at the end of each line.

16 The gymnast won prizes at the Olympics.
17 The citizens colonized a new territory.
18 A yellow yacht amazed the Zurich youth.
   | 1 | 2 | 3 | 4 | 5 | 6 | 7 | 8

Language Link

An adjective is a word that describes or tells more about a noun or a pronoun.

An adjective answers the question *how many*, *what kind*, or *which one*. Study the examples:

    adj   adj noun   adj   noun
The quiet, large crowd toured the new building.
    adj noun   adj   adj   noun
My brother is a skillful, creative architect.

✓ Check Your Learning

For each sentence, identify each adjective and the noun or pronoun it describes.

1. The big city of Chicago has a circular building.
2. They arrange many different materials into beautiful shapes.
3. Jeanine studied for her final exam.
4. Famous old cathedrals have tall, graceful towers.
5. The two friends went to see the scary movie.

Z & Y Review **89**

Z & Y Review

ASSESS

Using lines 16–18, have students take two 1-minute timings or three 12-second timings. The goal should be to increase the number of words or decrease the number of errors on each attempt.

While students are typing each line twice, walk around the class observing and commenting on techniques.

Language Link

ANSWERS

1. adj n   adj n
   big city, circular building
2. adj   n
   different materials
   adj   n
   beautiful shapes
3. adj n
   final exam
4. adj   n
   famous cathedrals,
   adj   n
   old cathedrals;
   adj n
   tall towers,
   adj   n
   graceful towers
5. adj   n   adj n
   two friends, scary movie

CLOSE

Review the **Language Link** section with your class. Have students write their answers to **Check Your Learning** on a sheet of paper. Then have five students come up to the board and write an answer to one of the questions. Sentence 4 is tricky because each noun has two adjectives describing it.

Teacher's Notes

Hyphen (-) Key

FOCUS

Review learned keys. Learn the hyphen (-) key.

BELLRINGER

Have students type **Tune Up.**

TEACH

Explain the use of the hyphen by giving examples. Remind students that when using a word processor, they will not have to hyphenate a word at the end of a line because word wrap will automatically move text to the next line.

Point out the location of the hyphen (-) key. Demonstrate the proper reach, showing how the Sem finger stretches up and over the P key to the hyphen (-) key. Dictate the line shown; then have students type it.

PRACTICE THE (-) KEY

Have students type lines 3–6, leaving a blank line between each group of lines.

Check to make sure they understand the difference between the hyphen and the underline, and when each should be used.

ASSESS

While students are typing **Word Practice,** observe and comment on proper hand position and technique.

CLOSE

Review proper techniques at the keyboard and the reach for the hyphen (-) key.

Goal:
- Use the hyphen (-) key

TUNE UP

Type each line 2 times. Press Return/Enter at the end of each line.

1. abc def ghi jkl mno pqr stu vwx yza bcd
2. The quick fox jumps over a lazy badger.

LEARN THE HYPHEN (-) KEY

The hyphen is used in compound words. Do not space before or after a hyphen. The shift of the hyphen is the underline. Use the Sem finger to type a hyphen. Reach up and to the right. Keep the J finger at home. Practice the following line.

   ;;; ;p; ;p-; ;-; ;;; ;-; ;;;

PRACTICE THE HYPHEN (-) KEY

Type each line 2 times. Leave a blank line between each line group.

3. ;;; ;p- ;-; -;- ;-; ;;; ;p- ;-; -;- ;-;
4. ;;; ;-_ ;_; _;_ ;_; ;;; ;-_ ;_; _;_ ;_;
5. -- mix-up -- hush-hush -- well-known --
6. __ T-shirt __ drip-dry __ high-grade __

WORD PRACTICE

Type each line 2 times. Remember to use good technique.

7. self-destruct rock-bottom old-fashioned
8. old-time tip-off no-hitter ill-tempered
9. red-hot jai-alai two-by-four well-to-do
10. T-bone mix-up hari-kari daughter-in-law
11. My mother-in-law re-covered that chair.
12. Type a line seven spaces long: _____.

Bits & Bytes

Keeping your computer equipment clean is very important. Turn the system off before cleaning. Spray cleaner on a cloth and then clean the keyboard and monitor.

RESOURCES

- Lesson Plan: LP29
- Wallchart: Point out reach to the hyphen (-) key
- Transparency 1
- CD-ROM: Hyphen Key
- Software: Hyphen Key

Caps Lock Key

Goal:
- Use the caps lock key

TUNE UP

Type each line 2 times. Press Return/Enter at the end of each line.

1. and ham for pal bug jam wig let row nap
2. quiz axis play jump weed pool crew milk

LEARN THE [caps lock] KEY

The caps lock key enables you to type words in ALL-CAPITAL letters without having to shift for every letter. Use the A finger for the caps lock key. Feel the reach from A to the caps lock. Practice the following line.

   aaa ARM aaa AIM aaa ALL aaa

PRACTICE THE [caps lock] KEY

Type each line 2 times. Leave a blank line between each line group.

3. aaa ASK aa APPLE aaa ALLOW aa ANGRY aaa
4. aaa ANDY aaa AUNT aaa SAND aaa DART aaa
5. aa QUIT aa ZEBRA aa WALTER aa FAMILY aa

WORD PRACTICE

Type each line 2 times. Remember to use good technique.

6. AL wants a BLACK DOG with a RED COLLAR.
7. I broke an ARM and a LEG last THURSDAY.
8. Ask DAD. HELP me. Go AWAY. PLEASE stop.
9. This START/STOP safety LEVER was STUCK.
10. COMPUTERS scanned the FIRST-CLASS mail.
11. Did you see KARLA? SHE FELL in the GYM.

Caps Lock Key **91**

RESOURCES

- Lesson Plan: LP30
- Wallchart: Point out reach to the caps lock key
- Transparency 1
- CD-ROM: Caps Lock Key
- Software: Caps Lock Key

Caps Lock Key

FOCUS

Review learned keys. Learn the caps lock key.

BELLRINGER

As soon as their workstations are properly set up, have students type the **Tune Up.** Have students type as quickly as they can. Then have them slow down for accuracy.

TEACH

Point out the location of the caps lock key. Explain that this key is used only when typing several words that need to be capitalized.

Demonstrate the proper reach, showing them how the A finger reaches left to the caps lock key. Dictate the line shown, and then have the students type it as you observe.

PRACTICE THE [caps lock] KEY

Have students type lines 3–5, leaving a blank line between each group of lines.

ASSESS

While students are typing **Word Practice,** observe and comment on proper position and technique.

Speed: lines 6 and 7
Accuracy: lines 8 and 9
Speed and Accuracy: lines 10 and 11

CLOSE

Review proper keyboarding technique and the reach for the caps lock key.

91

Hyphen (-) & Caps Lock Review

FOCUS

Review learned keys, hyphen (-), and caps lock keys.

BELLRINGER

As soon as their workstations are set up, have students type each **Tune Up** line twice. This reviews learned keys plus the hyphen (-) and caps lock keys. Have students push for speed and accuracy on this exercise.

TEACH

Review the importance of proper posture and keying technique. Demonstrate the correct reaches from the home keys to the hyphen (-) and caps lock keys.

REVIEW `-` AND `caps lock` KEYS

Have students complete lines 3–5, leaving a blank line between each line group.

Students should take three 12-second timings on each line in this section. Remind students that their goal is to increase the number of words or decrease the number of errors.

BUILD YOUR SKILL

Have students type lines 6–11 twice. Instruct them to keep their eyes on the text.

Have students build accuracy by typing lines 12–14 in **Special Word Groups.** If more than 5 errors are made on the 3 lines, they should retype the lines.

REVIEW

Goal:
- Review the hyphen (-) and caps lock keys

TUNE UP

Type each line 2 times. Press Return/Enter at the end of each line.

1. when they also glen wilt slam clan roam
2. exam dear ploy join jump plum wade quad

REVIEW

Type each line 2 times. Leave a blank line between line groups.

3. self-help well-done pinch-hit by-and-by
4. STAY here; go AWAY; be QUIET; do it NOW
5. RED-HOT fifty-fifty NO-HITTER half-mast

BUILD YOUR SKILL

Type each line 2 times.

6. She hired the well-dressed baby-sitter.
7. SHOUT the news; CHEER the team; we WON.
8. get-up-and-go fly-by-night hi-fi say-so
9. HOW? You WAIT. Did she GO? WHEN? NEVER.
10. Fifty-one part-time students have jobs.
11. Do NOT go to the door IF you are ALONE.

SPECIAL WORD GROUPS

If you do not know where the cities are located, look them up in an atlas or an encyclopedia. Then type each line 2 times.

12. Opa-Locka Bel-Ridge Hastings-on-Hudson
13. Winston-Salem Wilkes-Barre Fleming-Neon
14. Mont-Royal Baden-Baden Port-au-Prince

92 Section 5 Alphabetic Keys

RESOURCES

- Lesson Plan: LP30
- Wallchart: Point out reaches to the hyphen (-) and caps lock keys
- Transparency 1
- CD-ROM: Build Skill on the Hyphen and Caps Lock Keys
- Software: Build Skill on the Hyphen and Caps Lock Keys

REVIEW

PUNCTUATION

You can make a dash by typing two hyphens. Do not space before or after a dash. Practice typing the lines below.

15 He may go or stay--I am not sure which.
16 My new dog--the spotted one--has fleas.

TIME YOURSELF

Take two 1-minute timings on the copy below. If you finish the lines before time is up, start over again. Press Return/Enter at the end of each line.

17 My mother-in-law is very old-fashioned.
18 Did Wanda finish reading WAR AND PEACE?
19 Jasper SAILED to Port-au-Prince, HAITI.
    | 1 | 2 | 3 | 4 | 5 | 6 | 7 | 8

Language Link

An adverb describes a verb, an adjective, or another adverb.

An adverb answers *how*, *when*, or *where* the action was done. An adverb may go before or after the word it describes or modifies.

　　　　　　　　　verb　　　　adv
The Incas worked carefully on the buildings.
　　　　　　　　　　　　　adv　　adj
Machu Picchu is a very large ruin in Peru.
　　　　adv　　verb
They slowly crossed rushing rivers.

✓ Check Your Learning

Identify each adverb and the verb, adjective, or adverb it describes.

1. The mist lifted briefly over the walled city.
2. The irrigation system used by the Incas carried water efficiently.
3. Several explorers walked quickly along the path.
4. Bill was pleased with the very recent discovery.
5. Machu Picchu sits silently in the Andes.

Hyphen (-) and Caps Lock Review   93

Teacher's Notes

Hyphen (-) & Caps Lock Review

Lines 12 and 13 contain names of U.S. cities; line 14 contains names of foreign cities. *Opa-Locka* is in FL; *Bel-Ridge* is in NJ; *Hastings-on-Hudson* is in NY. *Winston-Salem* is in NC; *Wilkes-Barre* is in PA; *Fleming-Neon* is in KY. *Mont-Royal* is in Quebec; *Baden-Baden* is in Germany; *Port-au-Prince* is in Haiti.

ASSESS

Using lines 17–19, have students take two 1-minute timings or three 12-second timings. Students should type these lines with no more than three errors. Repeat until the goal is reached.

While students are typing each line twice, walk around the class observing and commenting on techniques.

Language Link

ANSWERS

1. adv   v
    briefly lifted
2. adv   v
    efficiently carried
3. adv   v
    quickly walked
4. adv   adj
    very recent
5. adv   v
    silently sits

CLOSE

Review **Language Link** with your class. Have five students come up to the board and write an answer to one of the questions in **Check Your Learning**. Discuss the answers with the class.

93

Apostrophe (') Key

FOCUS

Review learned keys. Learn the apostrophe (') key.

BELLRINGER

Have students type **Tune Up.**

TEACH

Show students the location of the apostrophe key (') and the quotation mark. Explain that the apostrophe is used for possessives, contractions, and single quotes. The quotation mark (") is used for quotes.

Demonstrate the proper reach, showing them how the Sem finger reaches to the right to the apostrophe (') key. Dictate the line shown and then have the students type it as you observe.

PRACTICE THE ' KEY

Have students type lines 3–6, leaving a blank line between each group of lines.

ASSESS

While students are typing each line in **Word Practice** twice, observe and comment on proper hand position and technique in reaching for the apostrophe (') key.

Speed: lines 7 and 8
Accuracy: lines 9 and 10
Speed and Accuracy: lines 11 and 12

CLOSE

Review proper technique at the keyboard and the reach for the apostrophe (') key.

Goal:
- Use the apostrophe (') key

TUNE UP

Type each line 2 times. Press Return/Enter at the end of each line.

1 lend nape handy firms prowl gland kayak
2 I saw black liquid vanish from the jug.

LEARN THE APOSTROPHE ' KEY

The apostrophe is used in contractions and possessives. The shift of the apostrophe is the quotation mark. Use the Sem finger on the apostrophe ('). Reach from Sem to apostrophe, keeping the J finger at home. Practice the following line.

;;; ;'; ;;; ;'; ;;; ;'; ;;;

PRACTICE THE APOSTROPHE ' KEY

Type each line 2 times. Leave a blank line between each line group.

3 ;;; ;'; ;'; ';' ;'; ;;; ;'; ;'; ';' ;';
4 ;;; ;'" ;"; ";" ;"; ;;; ;'" ;"; ";" ;";
5 '' don't '' can't '' we're '' you've ''
6 "I won't." "We'll stop." "You'll stay?"

WORD PRACTICE

Type each line 2 times. Remember to use good technique.

7   ten o'clock, they're here, Andy's books
8   Fay wants to read Twain's "Tom Sawyer."
9   I'd let's we've doesn't could've Tony's
10 "Yes." "Wow." "Stop." "Help." "Please?"
11 Tom said, "I won't go if you can't go."
12 Ann said, "I'll leave by five o'clock."

Section 5 Alphabetic Keys

Bits & Bytes

Remember that making unlicensed copies of a program is illegal and similar to stealing someone's work.

RESOURCES

- Lesson Plan: LP31
- Wallchart: Point out reach to the apostrophe key
- Transparency 1
- CD-ROM: Apostrophe Key
- Software: Apostrophe Key

Tab Key

Goal:
- Use the tab key

TUNE UP

Type each line 2 times. Press Return/Enter at the end of each line.

```
1  come pane wish form work male alto soap
2  Web made quick jet flights over Paxton.
```

LEARN THE `tab` KEY

The tab key moves the insertion point to a tab stop where you will type text. Use the A finger for the tab key. Reach up and to the left, keeping your F finger at home. Practice the following line.

```
aaa [tab]    aaa [tab]    aaa [tab]    aaa
```

PRACTICE THE `tab` KEY

Type each line 2 times. Press the tab key between words. Do not space before or after pressing the tab key.

```
3  aaa      aaa      aaa      aaa      aaa
4  arm      boy      cat      dog      egg
5  face     glad     hope     idea     joke
6  ketch    likes    muddy    never    opera
```

WORD PRACTICE

Type each line 2 times. Press the tab key between words. Remember to use good technique.

```
7   bet      wet      met      set      jet
8   wink     link     pink     rink     mink
9   poppy    quart    racer    stare    treat
10  uncle    valve    waxed    youth    zebra
11  firm     lapse    dig      elfin    airy
12  and      them     slant    wish     fork
```

RESOURCES

- Lesson Plan: LP31
- Wallchart: Point out reach to the tab key
- Transparency 1
- CD-ROM: Tab Key
- Software: Tab Key

Tab Key

FOCUS

Review learned keys. Learn the tab key.

BELLRINGER

Have students type the **Tune Up.** Have students type as quickly as they can. Then have them slow down for accuracy.

TEACH

Point out the location of the tab key. Demonstrate the proper reach, showing how the A finger reaches up and to the left to the tab key. Emphasize to students that they need to reach above the caps lock key. Dictate the line shown; then have students type it as you observe.

PRACTICE THE `tab` KEY

Have students type lines 3–6. Encourage them not to look at the tab key. Have them do some exercises with the tab key versus the caps lock key and the shift key to get the proper feel. Remind them to leave a blank line between each group of lines.

ASSESS

While students are typing each line in **Word Practice** twice, observe and comment on proper position and technique in reaching for the tab key.

CLOSE

Review proper keyboarding technique and the reach for the tab key.

Apostrophe (') and Tab Review

FOCUS
Review learned keys, the apostrophe ('), and tab keys.

BELLRINGER
As soon as their workstations are set up, have students type each **Tune Up** line twice. This reviews learned keys plus the apostrophe (') and tab key. Have students push for speed and accuracy on this exercise.

TEACH
Review the importance of proper posture and keying technique. Demonstrate the correct reaches from the home keys to the apostrophe (') and tab keys.

REVIEW ' AND tab KEYS
Have students complete lines 3–5. Remind them to leave a blank line between each line group.

BUILD YOUR SKILL
Have students type lines 6–11 twice. Instruct them to keep their eyes on the text.

Students should take three 12-second timings on each line in this section. The goal is to increase speed and/or accuracy.

' & Tab Review

Goal:
- Review the apostrophe (') and tab keys

REVIEW

TUNE UP

Type each line 2 times. Press Return/Enter at the end of each line.

1. jinx zinc quad gawk czar manx quip onyx
2. We do not want to be late for the game.

REVIEW

Type each line 2 times. Leave a blank line between line groups.

3. he'd what's you've doesn't Jack's Bev's
4. I said, "Hello." You answered, "Aloha."
5. Alice   Brian   Carol   David   Edith

BUILD YOUR SKILL

Type each line 2 times. Use the tab key to indent lines 10 and 11.

6. I can't go; we've done it; ten o'clock;
7. you're not working; you aren't working;
8. Frank's   Patty's   Joseph's   Sandra's
9. "Ouch"   "Stop"   "Don't"   "Please"
10.   I read Twain's "Huckleberry Finn."
11.   The jewel was a "fake," wasn't it?

LEARN ABOUT WORD WRAP

When you type a paragraph on a computer, press Return/Enter at the end of the paragraph. When the insertion point reaches the end of the line, it will move down to the next line. This is called "word wrap." Practice using word wrap as you type the paragraphs that follow 2 times.

Section 5 Alphabetic Keys

RESOURCES

- Lesson Plan: LP32
- Wallchart: Point out reaches to the apostrophe and tab keys
- Transparency 1
- CD-ROM: Build Skill on the Apostrophe and Tab Keys; Uncover the Story
- Software: Build Skill on the Apostrophe and Tab Keys

REVIEW

```
12        Nan told Jake and Louise that she
13   would get some rye bread for our lunch.
14        Rachel wanted to go to the shore,
15   but Bob said it would be much too cold.
```

TIME YOURSELF

Take two 1-minute timings on the copy below. If you finish all three lines before time is up, start over again. Press Return/Enter only at the end of the paragraph.

```
16        Some students begin to excel just
17   by having peace and quiet as they work.
18   Analyze your study habits for success.
     | 1 | 2 | 3 | 4 | 5 | 6 | 7 | 8
```

Language Link

Use an apostrophe to show possession.

Use an *apostrophe* and *s* to form the possessive of a singular noun. Use an *apostrophe* and *s* to form the possessive of a plural noun that does not end in *s*. Use an *apostrophe* to form the possessive of a plural noun ending in *s*. Study the examples:

James + 's = James's   nation + 's = nation's
men + 's = men's   geese + 's = geese's
boys + ' = boys'   Thompsons + ' = Thompsons'

✓ Check Your Learning

Indicate the possessive form of each word.

1. teacher
2. teachers
3. Cynthia
4. deer
5. heroes
6. people
7. mice
8. teeth
9. dog
10. country

Apostrophe (') and Tab Review   **97**

Teacher's Notes

Apostrophe (') and Tab Review

Have students build accuracy by typing lines 12–15. If more than 5 errors are made on the 4 lines, they should retype the lines.

Students should take two 30-second timings on each line in this section. Again, the goal is to increase speed and accuracy.

Word Wrap—Tell your class how much easier it is to type using word wrap. On a typewriter, you have to worry about when to return the carriage; on the computer, you don't have to think about it—and it saves you another stroke!

ASSESS

Using lines 16–18, have students take two 1-minute timings or three 12-second timings. The students should type the paragraph with no more than three errors as the goal. Repeat this exercise until that goal has been met.

While students are typing each line twice, walk around the class observing and commenting on techniques.

Language Link

ANSWERS

1. teacher's
2. teachers'
3. Cynthia's
4. deer's
5. heroes'
6. people's
7. mice's
8. teeth's
9. dog's
10. country's

CLOSE

Review the **Language Link** feature with your class.

97

A–F Review

FOCUS
Review learned keys. Review keys A–F.

BELLRINGER
As soon as their workstations are set up, have students type each **Tune Up** line twice. This reviews the learned keys.

TEACH
Review the importance of proper posture and keying technique. Remind students of the proper position of the hands over the home keys.

REVIEW KEYS A – F
Have students complete lines 3–8. Remind your students to use proper typing technique: sitting up straight, eyes on the book, feet flat on the floor. Remind them to leave a blank line between each line group

BUILD YOUR SKILL
Have students type lines 9–14 twice. Instruct them to keep their eyes on the text.

Have students build accuracy by typing lines 15–18 in **Special Word Groups.** If more than 5 errors are made on the 4 lines, they should retype the lines. Because this is a review, students should feel comfortable with the keys and should push for speed and accuracy.

REVIEW

Goal:
- Review keys A–F

TUNE UP

Type each line 2 times. Press Return/Enter at the end of each line. Tap the keys lightly and quickly. Keep your eyes on the copy.

1. Glue those pictures on the cover sheet.
2. Quick brown foxes jump over a lazy dog.

REVIEW

Type each line 2 times. Remember to leave a blank line between line groups.

3. asks glad salads lizard animal airplane
4. bear able barn bring bread break absent
5. car cake sick scare cried chief correct
6. deed idea wide dandy guide slides ended
7. ever feel need seed enter level fifteen
8. fall fell feed first front offer frames

BUILD YOUR SKILL

Type each line 2 times.

9. Aaron was awakened again by the alarms.
10. Barbie has blue ribbons and a blue bag.
11. Can Cecilia call the children to class?
12. Duane drew a dog, a deer, and a donkey.
13. Emmett eagerly ate eleven ears of corn.
14. Faye found fifty jars of figs and fish.

SPECIAL WORD GROUPS

Locate each country listed in lines 15 and 16 in an atlas or an encyclopedia. Then type each line 2 times.

98 Section 5 Alphabetic Keys

RESOURCES
- Lesson Plan: LP32
- Wallchart: Point out reaches to the keys A, B, C, D, E, F
- Transparency 1
- CD-ROM: Build Skill on the A–F Keys; Uncover the Story
- Software: Build Skill on the A–F Keys

REVIEW

15 Angola Argentina Belgium Brazil Canada
16 China Denmark Djibouti Egypt Finland
17 apple artichoke banana broccoli chicken
18 duck doughnut eclair eggplant frijoles

TIME YOURSELF

Take two 1-minute timings on the copy below. If you finish all three lines before time is up, start over again. Press Return/Enter at the end of the paragraph only.

19   If Bobby and Deidre find the film,
20 they will bring a camera. Cyd can't be
21 here for Felice's birthday celebration.
    | 1 | 2 | 3 | 4 | 5 | 6 | 7 | 8

CULTURAL KALEIDOSCOPE

Canada has two official languages—English and French. The majority of French-speaking Canadians live in the province of Quebec. Most of the rest of Canada is largely English-speaking. Roughly 80 percent of the Canadian population lives within 100 miles of the United States border.

A–F Review   99

A–F Review

Angola is in Africa; *Argentina*, in South America; *Belgium*, in Europe; *Brazil*, in South America; *Canada*, in North America; *China*, in Asia; *Denmark*, in Europe; *Djibouti*, in Africa; *Egypt*, in Africa; *Finland*, in Europe.

ASSESS

Using lines 19–21, have students take two 1-minute timings or three 12-second timings. The goal should be to increase the number of words or decrease the number of errors on each attempt.

CLOSE

Discuss the **Cultural Kaleidoscope** with your class. Discuss the fact that Canada has two official languages, English and French.

CULTURAL KALEIDOSCOPE

A conflict exists in Canada between French-speaking Canadians (called "Francophiles") and English-speaking Canadians (called "Anglophiles") as to which language should be used. The province of Quebec recently attempted to pass a law that would require all outdoor signs for businesses to be in French.

99

G–L Review

FOCUS
Review learned keys. Review keys G–L.

BELLRINGER
As soon as their workstations are set up, have students type each **Tune Up** line twice. This reviews the learned keys plus keys G–L.

TEACH
Review the importance of proper posture and keying technique. Review the proper position of the hands over the home keys.

REVIEW KEYS G – L
Have students complete lines 3–8. Remind them to leave a blank line between each line group.

BUILD YOUR SKILL
Have students type lines 9–14 twice. Instruct them to keep their eyes on the text.

G–L Review

Goal:
- Review keys G–L

TUNE UP

Type each line 2 times. Press Return/Enter at the end of each line. Tap the keys lightly and quickly. Keep your eyes on the copy.

1. apple banks clothe driver earthy finger
2. Alice Bruce Connie Dennis Esther Foster

REVIEW

Type each line 2 times. Remember to leave a blank line between line groups.

3. gain game largely geography gingerbread
4. high head home hatchet highway headache
5. inch iced idea igloo ignition imaginary
6. joke jive just judge jolly jelly jungle
7. king know kick knife kneed kayak knocks
8. long look likely little lovely legalize

BUILD YOUR SKILL

Type each line 2 times.

9. Gary gets great gifts; I get gifts too.
10. Has Heloise helped hang holiday lights?
11. Is Irving kicking the final field goal?
12. Jack Jones enjoyed a huge jug of juice.
13. Karen knows how to be kind to the kids.
14. Larry will lift the large load of logs.

SPECIAL WORD GROUPS

Locate the countries listed in lines 15 and 16 in an atlas or an encyclopedia. Then type each line 2 times.

100 Section 5 Alphabetic Keys

RESOURCES

- Lesson Plan: LP33
- Wallchart: Point out reaches to the keys G, H, I, J, K, L
- Transparency 1
- CD-ROM: Build Skill on the G–L Keys; Uncover the Story
- Software: Build Skill on the G–L Keys

REVIEW

15 Germany Guyana Haiti Hungary Indonesia
16 Ireland Japan Jordan Kenya Latvia Libya
17 giblets hazelnut hamburger ice cream
18 juice jelly knockwurst licorice lobster

TIME YOURSELF

Take two 1-minute timings on the copy below. If you finish the lines before time is up, start over again. Press Return/Enter at the end of the paragraph.

19 　　　Dear Dave: Will you go to our next
20 jazz concert? As you work in the music
21 shop, it should be quite a bit of fun.
　| 1 | 2 | 3 | 4 | 5 | 6 | 7 | 8

Language Link

Use an apostrophe in contractions.

A *contraction* is a word formed by combining two words into one and leaving out a letter or letters. The apostrophe replaces the missing letter or letters. Study the examples:

is not = isn't	it is = it's
can not = can't	are not = aren't
I will = I'll	was not = wasn't
will not = won't	do not = don't
she is = she's	you are = you're

✓ Check Your Learning

Make contractions from the words in parentheses.

1. The space shuttle (was not) scheduled to land until next week.
2. (It is) possible that (you are) the newest member of the team.
3. (She is) able to complete the project on time.
4. Greg (has not) missed a practice since August.
5. Our puppy (is not) housebroken yet.

G–L Review **101**

Teacher's Notes

G–L Review

Have students build accuracy by typing lines 15–18. If more than 5 errors are made on the 4 lines, they should retype them. Because this is a review, students should feel comfortable with the keys and should push for speed and accuracy.

Germany is in Europe; *Guyana*, in South America; *Haiti*, in the West Indies; *Hungary*, in Europe; *India* and *Indonesia*, in Asia; *Ireland*, in Europe; *Japan*, on the Pacific coast off Asia; *Jordan*, in Asia; *Kenya*, in Africa; *Latvia*, in Europe; *Libya*, in Africa.

ASSESS

Using lines 19–21, have students take two 1-minute timings or three 12-second timings. Students should type the paragraph with no more than three errors.

Language Link
ANSWERS
1. wasn't
2. It's, you're
3. She's
4. hasn't
5. isn't

CLOSE

Review the **Language Link** section with your class. Have them type the sentences in **Check Your Learning,** inserting contractions as directed. Have students exchange and evaluate each other's work.

101

M–S Review

FOCUS
Review learned keys. Review keys M–S.

BELLRINGER
As soon as their workstations are set up, have students type each **Tune Up** line twice. This reviews learned keys plus keys M–S. Direct students to type this as quickly as possible.

TEACH
Review the importance of proper posture and keying technique.

REVIEW KEYS M – S
Have students complete lines 3–9. Remind them to press Return/Enter twice to leave a space between each group of lines.

BUILD YOUR SKILL
Have students type lines 10–16 twice. Each line is a complete sentence. Instruct them to keep their eyes on the text. Have students take two 30-second timings on each line in this section. The goal is to increase speed and/or accuracy.

REVIEW

Goal:
- Review keys M–S

TUNE UP
Type each line 2 times. Press Return/Enter at the end of each line. Tap the keys lightly and quickly. Keep your eyes on the copy.

1. games hurry inject juggle kindly length
2. Gilda Henry Isobel Joseph Kristi Lionel

REVIEW
Type each line 2 times. Remember to leave a blank line between line groups.

3. mind mill milk memo mimic moment summer
4. name need next nine nylon ninety napkin
5. oven once close onion outdoors overcoat
6. pink pint part pump paper pepper puppet
7. quit quick quake quarts quarter quarrel
8. race rich roll roar rider report rarely
9. same stage state switch savings sausage

BUILD YOUR SKILL
Type each line 2 times.

10. Meg remembered the money for the movie.
11. Ned needs nine nickels for new pencils.
12. Otto will be only one on October first.
13. Paula patted the perky puppy named Pug.
14. Quinn quickly quit the squeaky quartet.
15. Roderick ran races faster than Richard.
16. Susan sleeps every Sunday after supper.

Section 5 Alphabetic Keys

RESOURCES
- Lesson Plan: LP33
- Wallchart: Point out reaches to the keys M, N, O, P, Q, R, S
- Transparency 1
- CD-ROM: Build Skill on the M–S Keys; Uncover the Story
- Software: Build Skill on the M–S Keys

REVIEW

SPECIAL WORD GROUPS

If you do not know where the countries are located, look them up in an atlas or an encyclopedia. Then type each line 2 times.

```
17  Malaysia Mexico Nicaragua Nigeria Oman
18  Pakistan Peru Qatar Rwanda Switzerland
19  mushroom marmalade noodles onion olive
20  pumpkin quail rhubarb raspberry sausage
```

TIME YOURSELF

Take two 1-minute timings on the copy below. If you finish all three lines before time is up, start over again. Press Return/Enter at the end of the paragraph only.

```
21         Sammy and Phil ran past many of
22  the other runners. Our quick team took
23  first place on a quite "super" Sunday.
    |  1  |  2  |  3  |  4  |  5  |  6  |  7  |  8
```

CULTURAL KALEIDOSCOPE

The people of Nigeria belong to more than 250 ethnic groups, each with its own language. English is the official language of business and government. However, fewer than half of all Nigerians speak English fluently.

M–S Review **103**

CULTURAL KALEIDOSCOPE

The four largest ethnic groups in Nigeria include the Hausa in the north, the Yoruba in the southwest, the Ibo in the southeast, and the Fulani in the north. In Nigeria about half the population is Moslem and one-fourth is Christian. The others practice local religions.

M–S Review

Have students build accuracy by typing lines 17–20. If more than 5 errors are made on the 4 lines, they should retype them. Because this is a review, students should feel comfortable with the keys and should push for speed and accuracy.

Malaysia is in Asia; *Mexico*, in North America; *Nicaragua*, in Central America; *Nigeria*, in Africa; *Oman*, in the Arabian Peninsula; *Peru*, in South America; *Qatar*, in the Arabian Peninsula; *Rwanda*, in Africa; *Switzerland*, in Europe.

ASSESS

Students should type the paragraph with no more than three errors. Repeat the paragraph until this goal is reached.

While students are typing, observe and comment on techniques.

CLOSE

Remind students that they should be practicing the alphabetic keys daily to build accuracy and speed.

T–Z Review

FOCUS
Review learned keys. Review keys T–Z.

BELLRINGER
As soon as their workstations are set up, have students type each **Tune Up** line twice. This reviews the learned keys plus keys T–Z.

TEACH
Review the importance of proper posture and keying technique.

REVIEW KEYS T – Z
Have students complete lines 3–9. Students should take three 12-second timings on each line in this section. The goal is to increase speed and/or accuracy.

BUILD YOUR SKILL
Have students type lines 10–16 twice. Instruct them to keep their eyes on the text.

Students should take two 30-second timings on each line in this section. The goal is to increase speed and/or accuracy.

REVIEW

T–Z Review

Goal:
- Review keys T–Z

TUNE UP
Type each line 2 times. Press Return/Enter at the end of each line.

1. many next odors place quart radio shelf
2. Mark Nina Oscar Peggy Quinn Rhoda Scott

REVIEW
Type each line 2 times. Leave a blank line between line groups.

3. tree tire trim taste trade title taught
4. unit ugly under uncle union upset usual
5. view vast verse value velvet vegetables
6. wild what wear where would widow window
7. exit exam sixty exceed textile exercise
8. yard your yolk yoyo youth yellow yearly
9. zebra pizza blaze muzzle lizard buzzard

BUILD YOUR SKILL
Type each line 2 times.

10. Tina typed ten letters to the teachers.
11. Uncle Julius used an old blue umbrella.
12. Valerie never visited Vienna or Venice.
13. Will Woodrow wear a wool sweater? Why?
14. Xavier sent Alex sixty-six extra boxes.
15. Young Yolanda slowly ate a yellow yolk.
16. Zeke won a dozen fuzzy prizes at a zoo.

SPECIAL WORD GROUPS
Locate the countries listed in lines 17 and 18 in an atlas or an encyclopedia. Then type each line 2 times.

Section 5 Alphabetic Keys

RESOURCES
- Lesson Plan: LP34
- Wallchart: Point out reaches to the keys T, U, V, W, X, Y, Z
- Transparency 1
- CD-ROM: Build Skill on the T–Z Keys; Uncover the Story
- Software: Build Skill on the T–Z Keys

REVIEW

```
17  Tonga Thailand Ukraine Uganda Venezuela
18  Vietnam Wales Yemen Yugoslavia Zimbabwe
19  tomato tangerine cucumber vichyssoise
20  waffle walnut yams yeast zucchini
```

TIME YOURSELF

Take two 1-minute timings on the copy below. If you finish all three lines before time is up, start over again. Press Return/Enter at the end of the paragraph only.

```
21        We voted for Vaughn and Wendy as
22  varsity captains this year. Will Avery
23  and Zoe be excluded from our next team?
    |   1   |   2   |   3   |   4   |   5   |   6   |   7   |   8
```

CULTURAL KALEIDOSCOPE

Ukraine, once a part of the Soviet Union, became an independent republic in 1991. The rich, fertile soil and plentiful rainfall in Ukraine are ideal for farming. Farmers grow a variety of grains as well as potatoes and sugar beets. Because of the abundant grain harvests, Ukraine is known as the breadbasket of Europe.

T–Z Review

T–Z Review

Have students build accuracy by typing lines 17–20. Because this is a review, students should feel comfortable with the keys and should push for speed and accuracy.

Tonga is in the South Pacific; *Thailand*, in Asia; *Ukraine*, in Europe; *Uganda*, in Africa; *Venezuela*, in South America; *Vietnam*, in Asia; *Wales*, in Europe; *Yemen*, in the Arabian Peninsula; *Yugoslavia*, in Europe; *Zimbabwe*, in Africa. *Vichyssoise* is a cold cream soup.

ASSESS

Students should type the paragraph (lines 21–23) with no more than three errors. Repeat the paragraph until this goal is reached.

While students are typing, walk around the class observing and commenting on techniques.

CLOSE

Congratulate the class on completing the entire alphabetic section of the keyboarding material. Tell them that they will continue practicing alphabetic keys as they learn the remaining keys of the keyboard.

CULTURAL KALEIDOSCOPE

The word "Ukraine" means borderland because it has served as the border for several empires. Despite its reputation as "the breadbasket of Europe," Ukraine imports more goods from other countries than it exports.

TEACH

Ask the class what types of documents they will type rather than hand write—now that they have learned the touch method for alphabetic keys. Documents they may mention include homework, letters and notes to friends, flyers for school bake sales or car washes, party invitations, and more. Make a list on the board of these answers. Discuss the advantages of typing these documents rather than hand writing them.

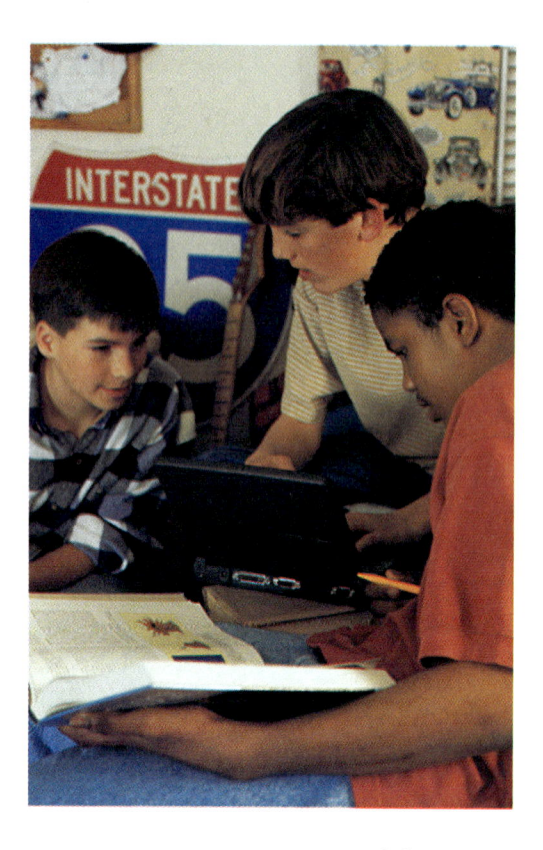

Composing a letter or report while you are at the keyboard will save you lots of time. You can create your document in your own words without writing your thoughts on paper. As you compose, you can add text easily as you think of new ideas.

Before you begin to compose, you will want to organize your thoughts in your head. For example, if you were composing a report about a country, you might ask yourself questions such as:

- Where in the world would I like to visit?
- Why would I like to visit there?
- What would I do there?
- What kind of food would I eat?

As you compose, you don't have to worry about correcting errors. You can check your document for errors in typing and grammar later. You can also change your text easily to make your report read the way you want.

While at your computer, use the questions listed above to compose a short paragraph that tells about a country. When you have finished typing your paragraph, review what you have typed.

- Check your document to see that you have spelled all the words correctly.
- Correct any errors you may have made in grammar in your report.
- Read your report to make sure that it makes sense and that it reads the way you want it to read.

106 Section 5 Alphabetic Keys

Lesson Extension

A common way to organize one's thoughts for writing is to prepare an outline for the document. The points in an outline should be arranged in a logical order. This will be the order of the topics in the document. Major topics should always be listed first; then each major topic should be divided into subtopics.

When composing at the keyboard, students may want to start by composing an outline first. After preparing their outline on screen, they can use the major points as headings in their document.

Number and Symbol Keys

SECTION 6

Focus on Number and Symbol Keys

Many of the reports or other class assignments you prepare include numbers and symbols. These numbers and symbols are located on the top row of the keyboard. Using the touch system, you will learn to operate these keys quickly and accurately. Continued practice on the alphabetic keys will help you build typing skill.

OBJECTIVES

- Operate the number and symbol keys by touch.
- Type at a minimum rate of 25 words per minute.
- Develop language arts skills.

Words To Know

ampersand
asterisk
at symbol
caret
exclamation point
parenthesis

Section 6 Number and Symbol Keys

SECTION OVERVIEW

Section 2 is devoted to the number and symbol keys. One letter and one symbol are taught in each lesson, using the same key (the number using lower case; the symbol using the shift key). After every two lessons, there is a review lesson.

OPENING ACTIVITY

List all of the symbols in this section on the board or on a transparency. Have students form teams to discuss the name and use of each symbol that will be learned in this section.

Career Exploration Activities: Consumer and Homemaking

Have students find a full-page advertisement in a newspaper or magazine for a grocery store. On a separate sheet of paper, have them list all the symbols they find on the page. They should group the symbols into categories, e.g., those used with numbers ($, @, %) and those used with words (!, &, ?).

4$ Key

FOCUS

Review learned keys. Learn the 4$ key.

BELLRINGER

Have students type **Tune Up.**

TEACH

Point out the location of the 4$ key. Explain that the dollar sign ($) is the shift of the 4 key. Demonstrate the proper reach, showing them how the F finger reaches up and to the left to the 4 key. Add the shift key to type a $ sign. When using the $ sign, there is no space between the $ and number that follows.

Dictate the line shown under **Learn the 4$ Key;** then have students type it.

PRACTICE THE 4$ KEY

Have students type lines 3–6. Remind them to leave a blank line between each group of lines. Encourage students to keep their eyes on the text, not the keyboard.

ASSESS

While students are typing each line in **Number and Symbol Practice** twice, observe and comment on proper technique.

Speed: lines 7 and 8
Accuracy: lines 9 and 10
Speed and Accuracy: lines 11 and 12

CLOSE

Review proper technique at the keyboard and the reach for the 4$ key.

Goal:
- Use the 4$ key

TUNE UP

Type each line 2 times. Press Return/Enter at the end of each line.

1. aqa aza sws sxs ded dcd frf fvf fgf jhj
2. juj jmj kik k,k lol l.l ;p; ;/; ;-; ;';

LEARN THE $4 KEY

The dollar sign ($) is the shift of the 4. Do not space between the $ and the number that follows it. Use the F finger to type a 4 or a $. The reach is up and to the left. Reach from F to 4, keeping your A finger at home. Practice the following line.

    fff frf fr4f f4f fff f4f fff

PRACTICE THE $4 KEY

Type each line 2 times. Leave a blank line between each line group.

3. frf fr4f f4f 444 f4f 4/44 f4f 4.44 fr4f
4. frf fr4f f4f f4$f f$f f4$f f$f f4$f f$f
5. 44 foes, 44 films, 44 fines, 44 folders
6. $4 fish, $44 fans, $44 flags, $444 furs

NUMBER AND SYMBOL PRACTICE

Type each line 2 times. Remember to use good technique.

7. I see 4 swans and 44 ducks on the lake.
8. I paid $4 for pears and $4 for oranges.
9. 44 yachts, 444 automobiles, 4,444 tires
10. $4 pencils, $44 textbooks, $444 tuition
11. Pam sang all 4 songs for the 44 people.
12. The school bought 44 books for $4 each.

Section 6 Number and Symbol Keys

RESOURCES

- Lesson Plan: LP35
- Wallchart: Point out reach to the 4$ key
- Transparency 1
- CD-ROM: 4$ Key; Get the Scoop
- Software: 4$ Key

7& Key

Goal:
- Use the 7& key

TUNE UP

Type each line 2 times. Press Return/Enter at the end of each line.

1. axle just sale kind lost fort hail good
2. quit your west used east inky real oven

LEARN THE 7& KEY

The ampersand ("and sign" &) is the shift of the 7. Space before and after the ampersand. Use the J finger to type a 7 or an ampersand (&). The reach is up and to the right. Reach from J to 7, keeping your Sem finger at home. Practice the following line.

    jjj juj ju7j j7j jjj j7j jjj

PRACTICE THE 7& KEY

Type each line 2 times. Leave a blank line between each line group.

3. juj ju7j j7j 777 j7j 7/77 j7j 7.77 ju7j
4. juj ju7j j7j j7&j j&j j7&j j&j j7&j j&j
5. 77 jobs, 77 jokes, 77 juries, 77 judges
6. && in & out && up & down && on & off &&

NUMBER AND SYMBOL PRACTICE

Type each line 2 times. Remember to use good technique.

7. Janice will perform June 7, not July 7.
8. Write Bashir & Sons and Katz & Company.
9. 77 junipers, 777 azaleas, 7,777 flowers
10. M&M, A&P, AT&T, Hall & Co., Hess & Hess
11. Those 7 people wanted 77 bags of chips.
12. Rupert & Frank are Tam & Sons' lawyers.

7& Key

FOCUS

Review learned keys and the 4$ key. Learn the 7& key.

BELLRINGER

Have students type **Tune Up.**

TEACH

Show the class the location of the 7& key. Demonstrate the proper reach, showing them how the J finger reaches up and to the right to the 7& key. Add the shift key to type the ampersand (&) sign. Explain that & is used to replace the word "and". Dictate the line shown, and then have the students type it as you observe.

PRACTICE THE 7& KEY

Have students type lines 3–6. Remind them to leave a blank line between each group of lines.

ASSESS

While students are typing each line in **Number and Symbol Practice** twice, observe and comment on proper position and technique in reaching for the 7& key.

Speed: lines 7 and 8
Accuracy: lines 9 and 10
Speed and Accuracy: lines 11 and 12

CLOSE

Review proper technique and the reach for the 7& key.

RESOURCES

- Lesson Plan: LP36
- Wallchart: Point out reach to the 7& key
- Transparency 1
- CD-ROM: 7& Key; Get the Scoop
- Software: 7& Key

4$ & 7& Review

FOCUS
Review learned keys. Review the 4$ and 7& keys.

BELLRINGER
As soon as their workstations are set up, have students type each **Tune Up** line twice. This reviews alphabetic keys plus the 4$ and 7& keys.

TEACH
Review the importance of proper posture and keying technique. Demonstrate the correct reaches from the home keys to the 4$ and 7& keys.

REVIEW 4$ AND 7& KEYS
Have students complete lines 3–5. Remind them to leave a blank line between each line group. Make sure students are using the proper fingers when typing. Make sure they are using the shift key to type $ and &.

BUILD YOUR SKILL
Have students type lines 6–11 twice. Instruct them to keep their eyes on the text.

Have students build accuracy by typing lines 12–15 in **Special Word Groups.** If more than 5 errors are made on the 4 lines, they should retype the lines.

REVIEW

4$ & 7& Review

Goal:
- Review the 4$ and 7& keys

TUNE UP

Type each line 2 times. Press Return/Enter at the end of each line. Tap the keys lightly and quickly. Keep your eyes on the copy.

1 zest exam much vest brag next time post
2 ;;; ;:; ;/; ;?; 1.1 k,k ;'; ;"; ;-; ;_;

REVIEW

Type each line 2 times. Leave a blank line between line groups.

3 The 4 men paid $444 for the 44 tickets.
4 Buy the 77 pizzas for $777 on Thursday.
5 Did the 47 bathrobes cost $474 or $747?

BUILD YOUR SKILL

Type each line 2 times.

6 Green & Grow charges $47 for lawn care.
7 The 7 boys need to earn $474 by Monday.
8 47 cats, 74 deer, 747 birds, 447 eagles
9 shoes & socks: $47; coats & hats: $477.
10 Ed collected 477 dimes and 744 nickels.
11 Jo paid L&T $7.47 & $4.77 for supplies.

SPECIAL WORD GROUPS

If you do not know where the places are located, look them up in an atlas or other reference book. Then type each line 2 times.

12 Aniakchak, Aztec Ruins, Fort Matanzas
13 Death Valley, Fort Sumter, Ocmulgee

110 Section 6 Number and Symbol Keys

RESOURCES

- Lesson Plan: LP36
- Wallchart: Point out reaches to the 4$ and 7& keys
- Transparency 1
- CD-ROM: Build Skill on the 4$ and 7& Keys; Uncover the Event
- Software: Build Skill on the 4$ and 7& Keys

REVIEW

```
14  Chiricahua, Fossil Butte, Jewel Cave
15  Rainbow Bridge, Statue of Liberty
```

TIME YOURSELF

Take two 1-minute timings on the copy below. If you finish all three lines before time is up, start over again. Press Return/Enter at the end of the paragraph only.

```
16       Please take a $74 check to Rent &
17  Run Videos to get movies and snacks for
18  47 girls who will be here from 4-7 p.m.
    | 1 | 2 | 3 | 4 | 5 | 6 | 7 | 8
```

Language Link

Numbers may be expressed in words or in numerals.

Spell out numbers from one through ten. Use numerals for numbers above ten. Use words for a number that begins a sentence. Study these examples:

> The first stagecoaches traveled **392** miles.
> **Three thousand one hundred** stagecoaches existed in England by 1836.
> Did these stagecoaches carry more than **five** passengers?

✓ Check Your Learning

Correct the number forms if necessary in the following sentences.

1. 200 years ago the United States Congress began mail service by stagecoach.
2. Horse-drawn coaches carried an average of 6 people on a trip.
3. Some stagecoaches covered a distance of six hundred fifty-one kilometers.
4. A trip of three hundred sixty miles meant drivers changed horses several times.
5. Four horses were needed to haul the stagecoaches up the steep hills.

4$ and 7& Review

Teacher's Notes

4$ & 7& Review

Aniakchak is in Alaska; *Aztec Ruins*, in Mexico; *Fort Matanzas*, in Florida. *Death Valley* is in California and Nevada; *Fort Sumter* is in South Carolina; *Ocmulgee* is in Georgia. *Chiricahua* is in Arizona; *Fossil Butte*, in Wyoming; *Jewel Cave*, in South Dakota. *Rainbow Bridge* is in Utah; the *Statue of Liberty* is in the New York harbor.

ASSESS

Using lines 16–18, have students take two 1-minute timings or three 12-second timings. The goal should be to increase the number of words or decrease the number of errors on each attempt.

While students are typing, walk around the class observing and commenting on techniques.

Language Link
ANSWERS
1. Two hundred
2. six
3. 651
4. 360
5. (correct)

CLOSE

Review the **Language Link** section with your class. Have students team up to complete **Check Your Learning** and discuss the correct answers.

1! Key

FOCUS

Review learned keys. Learn the 1! key.

BELLRINGER

Have students type **Tune Up.**

TEACH

Point out the location of the 1! key. Demonstrate the proper reach, showing them how the A finger reaches up and to the left to the 1! key. Remind them that the exclamation point (!) is the shift of the 1 key.

Dictate the line shown under **Learn the 1! Key** and then have the students type it as you observe.

PRACTICE THE 1! KEY

Have students type lines 3–6. Remind them to leave a blank line between each group of lines. Encourage students to keep their eyes on the text, not the keyboard.

ASSESS

While students are typing each line in **Number and Symbol Practice** twice, observe and comment on proper hand position and technique in reaching for the 1! key.

Speed: lines 7 and 8
Accuracy: lines 9 and 10
Speed and Accuracy: lines 11 and 12

CLOSE

Review proper technique at the keyboard and the reach for the 1! key.

Goal:
- Use the 1! key

Space once after an exclamation point—do not space before it.

TUNE UP

Type each line 2 times. Press Return/Enter at the end of each line. Tap the keys lightly and quickly. Keep your eyes on the copy.

1. park down sing hand wind land soap make
2. The 4 students won 7 medals last month.

LEARN THE 1! KEY

The exclamation point (!) is the shift of the 1. Use the A finger to type a 1 or an exclamation point (!). The reach is up and to the left. Reach from A to 1, keeping your F finger at home. Practice the following line.

aaa aqa aq1a a1a aaa a1a aaa

PRACTICE THE 1! KEY

Type each line 2 times. Leave a blank line between each line group.

3. aqa aq1a a1a 111 a1a 1/11 a1a 1.11 aq1a
4. aqa aq1a a1a a1!a a!a a1!a a!a a1!a a!a
5. 11 arms, 11 areas, 11 aunts, 11 animals
6. No! Yes! Wow! Help! Fire! Great! Hurry!

NUMBER AND SYMBOL PRACTICE

Type each line 2 times. Remember to use good technique.

7. I had 1 red, 1 white, and 11 blue pens.
8. There is a cry for help! Hurry to them!
9. 41 quit, 17 quays, 71 quarts, 14 quints
10. Stop! Look! Listen! Hurrah! It's great!
11. I bought 17 erasers and 41 red pencils.
12. Alice won! It can't be true! Wonderful!

112 Section 6 Number and Symbol Keys

RESOURCES

- Lesson Plan: LP37
- Wallchart: Point out reach to the 1! key
- Transparency 1
- CD-ROM: 1! Key; Get the Scoop
- Software: 1! Key

0) Key

Goal:
- Use the 0) key

TUNE UP

Type each line 2 times. Press Return/Enter at the end of each line.

1. fast jump rest plum zest kiln cart link
2. Andy Lucy Doug Jean Walt Mary Thom Nora

LEARN THE 0) KEY

Do This
Space once after a right parenthesis. Do not space before it.

The right parenthesis) is the shift of the zero (0). Use the Sem finger to type a 0 or a)—a right (closing) parenthesis. The reach is up and to the left. Reach from P to 0, keeping your J finger at home. Practice the following line.

   ;;; ;p; ;p0; ;0; ;;; ;0; ;;;

PRACTICE THE 0) KEY

Type each line 2 times. Leave a blank line between each line group.

3. ;p; ;p0; ;0; 000 ;0; 0/00 ;0; 0.00 ;p0;
4. ;p; ;p0; ;0; ;0); ;); ;0); ;); ;0); ;);
5. 10 pots, 100 peas, 400 pins, 700 people
6. 10) 14) 17) 40) 41) 47) 70) 71) 74) 77)

NUMBER AND SYMBOL PRACTICE

Type each line 2 times. Remember to use good technique.

7. Can you add these: 10, 40, 70, and 100?
8. Was the right answer a), b), c), or d)?
9. 10 x 10 equals 100; 10 x 40 equals 400;
10. 10) or 11); 40) or 41); 7), 17), or 70)
11. Divide 7,000 by 10. That answer is 700.
12. I chose Option A); Pat chose Option B).

0) Key **113**

RESOURCES
- Lesson Plan: LP37
- Wallchart: Point out reach to the 0) key
- Transparency 1
- CD-ROM: 0) Key
- Software: 0) Key

---

0) Key

FOCUS
Review learned keys and the 1! key. Learn the 0) key.

BELLRINGER
Have students type **Tune Up**.

TEACH
Show the class the location of the 0) key. Demonstrate the proper reach, showing them how the P finger reaches up and to the left to the 0) key. Remind students that the right parenthesis [)]is the shift of the zero (0) key.

Dictate the line shown, and then have the students type it.

PRACTICE THE 0) KEY
Have students type lines 3–6. Remind them to leave a blank line between each group of lines.

ASSESS
While students are typing each line in **Number and Symbol Practice** twice, observe and comment on proper position and technique.

Speed: lines 7 and 8
Accuracy: lines 9 and 10
Speed and Accuracy: lines 11 and 12

CLOSE
Review proper keyboarding technique and the reach for the 0) key.

1! & 0) Review

FOCUS
Review learned keys. Review the 1! and 0) keys.

BELLRINGER
As soon as their workstations are set up, have students type each **Tune Up** line twice. This reviews alphabetic keys.

TEACH
Review the importance of proper posture and keying technique. Demonstrate the correct reaches from the home keys to the 1! and 0) keys.

REVIEW 1! AND 0) KEYS
Have students complete lines 3–5. Remind them to leave a blank line between each line group. Make sure students use the proper fingers and the shift key to type ! and).

BUILD YOUR SKILL
Have students type lines 6–11 twice. Instruct them to keep their eyes on the text.

Have students build accuracy by typing lines 12–15 in **Special Word Groups.** Because these are long, difficult words, students will have to focus. This should improve their accuracy. If more than 5 errors are made on the 4 lines, they should retype the lines.

REVIEW

1! & 0) Review

Goal:
- Review the 1! and 0) keys

TUNE UP
Type each line 2 times. Press Return/Enter at the end of each line. Tap the keys lightly and quickly. Keep your eyes on the copy.

1. ripe lend also make dusk pale with male
2. Quickly mix up seven jugs of brown dye.

REVIEW
Type each line 2 times. Remember to leave a blank line between line groups.

3. 10 years, 41 months, 70 weeks, 100 days
4. Pick from a), b), or c). No! Do it now!
5. Wow! I didn't answer 10), 14), or 100)!

BUILD YOUR SKILL
Type each line 2 times.

6. 10 vans, 40 autos, 70 bikes, 100 trains
7. I could not choose either 10A) or 10B)!
8. 10 and 47 and 74 and 100 and 140 and 70
9. Go, team, go! Fire! 1), 4), 7), and 10)
10. Get 100 black pens and 100 red pencils.
11. The answers to both A) and B) is 1,010!

SPECIAL WORD GROUPS
If you are not familiar with the words, look them up in a dictionary or other reference book. Then type each line 2 times.

12. alstroemeria begonia calendula daffodil
13. edelweiss forget-me-not gladiolus hosta

114 Section 6 Number and Symbol Keys

RESOURCES
- Lesson Plan: LP38
- Wallchart: Point out reaches to the 1! and 0) keys
- Transparency 1
- CD-ROM: Build Skill on the 1! and 0) Keys; Uncover the Event
- Software: Build Skill on the 1! and 0) Keys

REVIEW

```
14  Bears Bengals Bills Broncos Buccaneers
15  Cardinals Chargers Chiefs Colts Cowboys
```

TIME YOURSELF

Take two 1-minute timings on the copy below. If you finish all three lines before time is up, start over again. Press Return/Enter at the end of the paragraph only.

```
16       Grace said, "Buy a dozen pumpkin
17  pies at $1.74 from the new deli at 1047
18  Quixote Road." They have just 10 left!
    |  1  |  2  |  3  |  4  |  5  |  6  |  7  |  8
```

Language Link

An interjection is a word or group of words that expresses strong feeling.

An interjection may be one word followed by an exclamation point. An interjection may be separated from the rest of the sentence with a comma. Study the examples:

> **Oops!** The paint spilled!
> **Oh,** I am going to be late for class.
> Have you ever seen such images? **Look!**

✓ Check Your Learning

Identify each interjection in the following sentences.

1. Hooray! Our team won the race.
2. Really! He seems old-fashioned by comparison.
3. Sorry, I didn't notice you standing there.
4. Well, I hope he goes with us.
5. Hey, I feel silly about what I said.

1! & 0) Review

Lines 12 and 13 contain flowers; lines 14 and 15, football teams.

ASSESS

Using lines 16–18, have students take two 1-minute timings or three 12-second timings. The goal should be to increase the number of words or decrease the number of errors on each attempt.

While students are typing each line twice, walk around the class observing and commenting on techniques.

Language Link

ANSWERS

1. Hooray!
2. Really!
3. Sorry,
4. Well,
5. Hey,

CLOSE

Review the **Language Link** section with your class. Have students type sentences with correct interjections for **Check Your Learning.** They should exchange papers and check each other's answers.

Teacher's Notes

3# Key

FOCUS

Review learned keys. Learn the 3# key.

BELLRINGER

Have students type **Tune Up**.

TEACH

Point out the location of the 3# key. Demonstrate the proper reach, showing students how the D finger reaches up and to the left to the 3# key. Remind them that # is the shift of the 3 key. The # sign is the *number* sign when it precedes a number. It means *pounds* when it follows a number.

Dictate the line shown under **Learn the 3# Key**; then have students type it.

PRACTICE THE 3# KEY

Have students type lines 3–6. Remind them to leave a blank line between each group of lines. Encourage students to keep their eyes on the text, not the keyboard.

ASSESS

While students are typing each line in **Number and Symbol Practice** twice, observe and comment on proper technique in reaching for the 3# key.

Speed: lines 7 and 8
Accuracy: lines 9 and 10
Speed and Accuracy: lines 11 and 12

CLOSE

Review proper technique at the keyboard and the reach for the 3# key.

116

Goal:
- Use the 3# key

TUNE UP

Type each line 2 times. Press Return/Enter at the end of each line.

1. jump free plum star yolk crab milk brag
2. exit pore zest only gate hump vest kiln

LEARN THE #3 KEY

The number sign (#) is the shift of the 3. The # before a number means *Number*. The # after a number means *pounds*. Use the D finger to type a 3 or the number sign (#). The reach is up and to the left. Reach from D to the 3, keeping your A finger at home. Practice the following line.

   ddd ded de3d d3d ddd d3d ddd

PRACTICE THE #3 KEY

Type each line 2 times. Leave a blank line between each line group.

3. ded de3d d3d 333 d3d 3/33 d3d 3.33 de3d
4. ded de3d d3d d3#d d#d d3#d d#d d3#d d#d
5. 33 days, 33 dates, 33 deeds, 33 details
6. #3 lead, #3 pencils, 3# of nuts, PO #33

NUMBER AND SYMBOL PRACTICE

Type each line 2 times. Remember to use good technique.

7. The 33 dogs ate 333 bones every 3 days.
8. Their Order #1034 is for 37# of butter.
9. 13 pies, 37 cakes, 34 cookies, 30 rolls
10. #3, #13, #43, #73, #303; 34#, 37#, 130#
11. The 3 people caught 37 fish in 13 days.
12. Cartons #13, #34, and #73 belong to me.

Section 6 Number and Symbol Keys

RESOURCES

- Lesson Plan: LP38
- Wallchart: Point out reach to the 3# key
- Transparency 1
- CD-ROM: 3# Key
- Software: 3# Key

8* Key

Goal:
- Use the 8* key

TUNE UP

Type each line 2 times. Press Return/Enter at the end of each line.

1. pet quo out who ink eat urn rid you tan
2. big net van mad cry hop axe job zip get

LEARN THE 8* KEY

The asterisk (*) is the shift of the 8. Do not space between the (*) and the word to which it is related. Use the K finger to type an 8 or an asterisk (*). The reach is up and to the left. Reach from K to 8, keeping your Sem finger at home. Practice the following line.

kkk kik ki8k k8k kkk k8k kkk

PRACTICE THE 8* KEY

Type each line 2 times. Leave a blank line between each line group.

3. kik ki8k k8k 888 k8k 8/88 k8k 8.88 ki8k
4. kik ki8k k8k k8*k k*k k8*k k*k k8*k k*k
5. 88 kids, 88 keys, 88 knives, 88 kittens
6. Note* Robertson* See below* Report 108*

NUMBER AND SYMBOL PRACTICE

Type each line 2 times. Remember to use good technique.

7. I gave 8 people 8 days to build 8 huts.
8. The * symbol is often called a "star"*.
9. 8 inches, 18 feet, 583 yards, 878 miles
10. Source* Title 18* Lesson 83* Reference*
11. That zoo owns 38 zebras and 88 monkeys.
12. The manual* and report* are in my desk.

8* Key **117**

RESOURCES

- Lesson Plan: LP39
- Wallchart: Point out reach to the 8* key
- Transparency 1
- CD-ROM: 8* Key; Get the Scoop
- Software: 8* Key

8* Key

FOCUS

Review learned keys. Learn the 8* key.

BELLRINGER

Have students type **Tune Up**.

TEACH

Show the class the location of the 8* key. Demonstrate the proper reach, showing them how the K finger reaches up and to the left to the 8 key. Add the shift key to type an asterisk (*) sign. This sign is generally used in a document to reference a note in the copy.

Dictate the line shown, and then have the students type it as you observe.

PRACTICE THE 8* KEY

Have students type lines 3–6. Remind them to leave a blank line between each group of lines.

ASSESS

While students are typing each line in **Number and Symbol Practice** twice, observe and comment on proper technique in reaching for the 8* key.

Speed: lines 7 and 8
Accuracy: lines 9 and 10
Speed and Accuracy: lines 11 and 12

CLOSE

Review proper keyboarding technique and the reach for the 8* key.

117

3# & 8* Review

FOCUS
Review learned keys. Review the 3# and 8* keys.

BELLRINGER
As soon as their workstations are set up, have students type each **Tune Up** line twice. This reviews learned keys.

TEACH
Review the importance of proper posture and keying technique. Demonstrate the correct reaches from the home keys to the 3# and 8* keys.

REVIEW 3# AND 8* KEYS
Have students complete lines 3–5. Remind them to leave a blank line between each line group. Make sure students use the proper fingers when typing. Make sure they use the shift key to type # and *.

BUILD YOUR SKILL
Have students type lines 6–11 twice. Instruct them to keep their eyes on the text.

Have students build accuracy by typing lines 12–15 in **Special Word Groups**. If more than 5 errors are made on the 4 lines, they should retype the lines.

Because these words are so unusual, students will have to focus on them. This should help improve accuracy.

REVIEW

3# & 8* Review

Goal:
- Review the 3# and 8* keys

TUNE UP
Type each line 2 times. Press Return/Enter at the end of each line. Tap the keys lightly and quickly. Keep your eyes on the copy.

1. 10 dogs 47 houses 40 plants 71 children
2. Gail Paul Ruth Jack Cora Noah Edie Hank

REVIEW
Type each line 2 times. Remember to leave a blank line between line groups.

3. Asam asked us to order 33# of potatoes.
4. Grace donated 88 first editions* to us.
5. I chose #83 as my lucky sweeps* number.

BUILD YOUR SKILL
6. The 8 clerks sold 1,383 kinds of seeds.
7. That mysterious* sea chest weighed 38#.
8. 38# of #47, Invoice #10, page #83, #308
9. Warning* War & Peace* 1830-1834* Total*
10. The 38 adults* enrolled in 180 classes.
11. I ordered 38 #3 pencils for $8 on 8/30.

SPECIAL WORD GROUPS
If you are not familiar with the words, look them up in a dictionary or other reference book. Then type each line 2 times.

12. iris jonquil kalanchoe lily marigold
13. nasturtium orchid peony aquilegia rose
14. Dolphins Eagles Falcons Giants Jaguars
15. Jets Lions Oilers Packers Panthers

Section 6 Number and Symbol Keys

RESOURCES
- Lesson Plan: LP39
- Wallchart: Point out reaches to the 3# and 8* keys
- Transparency 1
- CD-ROM: Build Skill on the 3# and 8* Keys; Uncover the Event
- Software: Build Skill on the 3# and 8* Keys

REVIEW

TIME YOURSELF

Take two 1-minute timings on the copy below. If you finish all three lines before time is up, start over again. Press Return/Enter at the end of the paragraph only.

```
16      Expo sent Invoice #38 for the sale
17 of my home at 83 Zory Lane; another law
18 firm* charged Jackson quite a bit more.
   | 1 | 2 | 3 | 4 | 5 | 6 | 7 | 8
```

CULTURAL KALEIDOSCOPE

In Brazil, **fútbol**, or soccer, is an important part of everyday life. Most villages have soccer fields, and larger cities have soccer stadiums. Brazilians are extremely devoted soccer fans. They close schools and businesses when the national team plays an important game.

3# and 8* Review **119**

CULTURAL KALEIDOSCOPE

One of the most popular sports in the world, soccer is played throughout South America, Europe, and Asia. The World Cup matches, held every four years, feature competition among national teams from many countries.

3# & 8* Review

ASSESS

Using lines 16–18, have students take two 1-minute timings or three 12-second timings. The goal should be to increase the number of words or decrease the number of errors on each attempt.

While students are typing each line twice, walk around the class observing and commenting on techniques.

CLOSE

Review the **Cultural Kaleidoscope** feature with students. Soccer is becoming more and more popular in the United States. Ask students to name the sports in which they like to participate. Write their answers on the board. Have students type the list.

2@ Key

FOCUS
Review learned keys. Learn the 2@ key.

BELLRINGER
Have students type **Tune Up**.

TEACH
Show the class the location of the 2@ key. Demonstrate the proper reach, showing them how the S finger reaches up and to the left to the 2@ key. Remind students that @ is the shift of the 2 key. The @ sign means "at" and is used to express amounts in invoices (e.g., 2 items @ $1.00 per item).

Dictate the line shown under **Learn the 2@ Key** and then have the students type it.

PRACTICE THE 2@ KEY
Have students type lines 3–6. Remind them to leave a blank line between each group of lines.

ASSESS
While students are typing each line in **Number and Symbol Practice** twice, observe and comment on proper technique.

Speed: lines 7 and 8
Accuracy: lines 9 and 10
Speed and Accuracy: lines 11 and 12

CLOSE
Review proper technique at the keyboard and the reach for the 2@ key. Urge students to practice keyboarding at least 20 minutes a day.

Goal:
- Use the 2@ key

TUNE UP
Type each line 2 times. Press Return/Enter at the end of each line.

1. will apple bubble hummer assess whittle
2. What is the total of 100 and 38 and 47?

LEARN THE 2@ KEY
The "at" sign (@) is the shift of the 2. Space once before and after the @ symbol. Use the S finger to type a 2 or an at sign (@). The reach is up and to the left. Reach from S to 2, keeping the F finger at home. Practice the following line.

   Sss sws sw2s s2s sss s2s sss

PRACTICE THE 2@ KEY
Type each line 2 times. Leave a blank line between each line group.

3. sws sw2s s2s 222 s2s 2/22 s2s 2.22 sw2s
4. sws sw2s s2s s2@s s@s s2@s s@s s2@s s@s
5. 22 skis, 22 sleds, 22 skates, 22 swings
6. 2 @ $22, 12 @ $211, 24 @ $42, 27 @ $727

NUMBER AND SYMBOL PRACTICE
Type each line 2 times. Remember to use good technique.

7. The class used 22 disks and 27 ribbons.
8. Order 122 @ 28 cents and 72 @ 82 cents.
9. 22 cars, 24 trucks, 12 trains, 2 planes
10. 22 @ $22; 28 @ $82; 27 @ $72; 2 @ $1.42
11. Answer questions 21 and 22 on page 221.
12. We sold 2 pens @ $2.40 and 12 @ $22.82.

120 Section 6 Number and Symbol Keys

RESOURCES
- Lesson Plan: LP40
- Wallchart: Point out reach to the 2@ key
- Transparencies 1 and 2
- CD-ROM: 2@ Key
- Software: 2@ Key

9(Key

Goal:
- Use the 9(key

TUNE UP

Type each line 2 times. Press Return/Enter at the end of each line.

1. your tank urge risk isle ends ogre wind
2. Keith Sonya Duncan Ingrid Sergei Tamara

LEARN THE 9(KEY

The left parenthesis (is the shift of the 9. Space once before a left parenthesis. Do not space after it. Use the L finger to type a 9 or a (—the left (opening) parenthesis. The reach is up and to the left. Reach from L to the 9, keeping your J finger at home. Practice the following line.

lll lol lo9l l9l lll l9l lll

PRACTICE THE 9(KEY

Type each line 2 times. Leave a blank line between each line group.

3. lol lo9l l9l 999 l9l 9/99 l9l 9.99 lo9l
4. lol lo9l l9l l9(. 1(1 l9(1 1(1 l9(1 1(1
5. 99 limes, 99 lakes, 99 lives, 99 lemons
6. (99 dogs) (99 cats) (99 pans) (99 rows)

NUMBER AND SYMBOL PRACTICE

Type each line 2 times. Remember to use good technique.

7. I put 29 books on Shelf 9 on August 19.
8. Chris has several (three or four) cats.
9. 1909 1919 1929 1939 1949 1979 1989 1999
10. (1 pound) (9 tons) (19 feet) (99 miles)
11. In 1929, the 299 men lived in 9 lodges.
12. Jan (my sister) and Sue (my aunt) left.

9(Key

FOCUS

Review learned keys. Learn the 9(key.

BELLRINGER

Have students type **Tune Up**.

TEACH

Show the class the location of the 9(key. Demonstrate the proper reach, showing them how the L finger reaches up to the left and over the O key to the 9 key. Add the shift key to type an opening parenthesis [(]. Dictate the line shown, and then have the students type it.

PRACTICE THE 9(KEY

Have students type lines 3–6. Remind them to leave a blank line between each group of lines.

ASSESS

While students are typing each line in **Number and Symbol Practice** twice, observe and comment on proper position and technique in reaching for the 9(key.

Speed: lines 7 and 8
Accuracy: lines 9 and 10
Speed and Accuracy: lines 11 and 12

CLOSE

Review proper keyboarding technique and the reach for the 9(key. Remind students that typing is a skill and must be practiced.

RESOURCES

- Lesson Plan: LP40
- Wallchart: Point out reach to the 9(key
- Transparency 1
- CD-ROM: 9(Key; Get the Scoop
- Software: 9(Key

2@ & 9(Review

FOCUS
Review learned keys. Review the 2@ and 9(keys.

BELLRINGER
As soon as their workstations are set up, have students type each **Tune Up** line twice. This reviews learned keys.

TEACH
Review the importance of proper posture and keying technique. Demonstrate the correct reaches from the home keys to the 2@ and 9(keys.

REVIEW 2@ AND 9(KEYS
Have students complete lines 3–5. Remind them to leave a blank line between each line group. Make sure students use the proper fingers when typing. Make sure they are using the shift key to type @ and (.

BUILD YOUR SKILL
Have students type lines 6–11 twice. Instruct them to keep their eyes on the text.

Have students build accuracy by typing lines 12–15 in **Special Word Groups.** Students should type the paragraph with no more than three errors. They should repeat the exercise until this goal is met.

REVIEW

2@ & 9(Review

Goal:
- Review the 2@ and 9(keys

TUNE UP
Type each line 2 times. Press Return/Enter at the end of each line. Tap the keys lightly and quickly. Keep your eyes on the copy.

1 vest mine cram none zest jump five exam
2 aq1a sw2s de3d fr4f ju7j ki8k lo91 ;p0;

REVIEW
Type each line 2 times. Remember to leave a blank line between line groups.

3 Buy 2 pots @ 12 cents and 22 @ 2 cents.
4 Jack missed questions 9 (a) and 19 (d).
5 I got 2 mugs @ $9 each and 9 @ $2 each.

BUILD YOUR SKILL
Type each line 2 times.

6 Buy 129 boxes of sugar @ 92 cents each.
7 Paul needs both (1) money and (2) time.
8 1 @ 9 cents; 2 @ 9 cents; 9 @ 22 cents;
9 (2 x 9) (23 x 89) (94 x 79) (292 x 929)
10 Get me 29 @ 82 cents and 92 @ 49 cents.
11 I (a) follow rules and (b) do the work.

SPECIAL WORD GROUPS
If you do not know the meanings of the words, look them up in a dictionary. Then type each line 2 times.

12 rhododendron snapdragon tulip uvularia
13 violet wisteria xerophyte yucca zinnia

122 Section 6 Number and Symbol Keys

RESOURCES
- Lesson Plan: LP41
- Wallchart: Point out reaches to the 2@ and 9(keys
- Transparency 1
- CD-ROM: Build Skill on the 2@ and 9(Keys; Uncover the Event
- Software: Build Skill on the 2@ and 9(Keys

REVIEW

```
14  Patriots Raiders Rams Ravens Redskins
15  Saints Seahawks Steelers Vikings 49ers
```

TIME YOURSELF

Take two 1-minute timings on the copy below. If you finish the entire paragraph before time is up, start over again. Press Return/Enter at the end of the paragraph only.

```
16        Zoo tour #29 begins at noon and
17  lasts just 2 hours. If Quint and Dave
18  (Mackin) pay now, the exact cost will
19  be 2 @ $9.
      |  1  |  2  |  3  |  4  |  5  |  6  |  7  |  8
```

Language Link

**Use figures to express the time of day with a.m. or p.m.
Use words to express the time when using o'clock.**

Study the examples:

My computer applications class starts at 8:30 a.m.
The basketball game starts at seven o'clock.

✓ Check Your Learning

Correct the number forms if necessary in the following sentences.

1. We will leave on our trip at seven a.m.
2. Todd and Katsue went to the 1 o'clock matinee.
3. The sun will set after 7 p.m. today.
4. Will the assembly begin at 1 o'clock or at 2 o'clock?
5. My dentist appointment is at three-thirty p.m.

2@ and 9(Review

2@ & 9(Review

Lines 12–13 contain flowers.
Lines 14–15, football teams.

ASSESS

Using lines 16–19, have students take two 1-minute timings or three 12-second timings. The goal should be to increase the number of words or decrease the number of errors on each attempt.

While students are typing each line twice, walk around the class observing and commenting on techniques.

Language Link

ANSWERS

1. 7 a.m.
2. one o'clock
3. 7 p.m.
4. one o'clock, two o'clock
5. 3:30 p.m.

CLOSE

Review the **Language Link** section with your class. Have students type the sentences in **Check Your Learning** using the correct expressions. They should exchange papers and check each other's work.

Teacher's Notes

5% Key

FOCUS

Review learned keys. Learn the 5% key.

BELLRINGER

Have students type **Tune Up.**

TEACH

Point out the location of the 5% key. Demonstrate the proper reach, showing how the F finger reaches up and to the right to the 5% key. Remind students that % is the shift of the 5 key. The % sign is used in statistical data and follows the number. There is no space between the number and the % sign.

Dictate the line shown under **Learn the 5% Key** and then have the students type it as you observe.

PRACTICE THE 5% KEY

Have students type lines 3–6. Remind them to leave a blank line between each group of lines.

ASSESS

While students are typing **Number and Symbol Practice** twice, observe and comment on proper technique.

Speed: lines 7 and 8
Accuracy: lines 9 and 10
Speed and Accuracy: lines 11 and 12

CLOSE

Review proper technique at the keyboard and the reach for the 5% key.

124

Goal:
- Use the 5% key

TUNE UP

Type each line 2 times. Press Return/Enter at the end of each line.

1. equal judge exert pounce zinnia weather
2. Can you add 10 plus 29 plus 38 plus 47?

LEARN THE 5% KEY

Use the F finger to type a 5 or a percent sign (%). Do not space between a number and the % which follows. The reach is up and slightly to the right. Reach from F to 5, keeping your A finger at home. Practice the following line.

```
Fff frf fr5f f5f fff f5f fff
```

PRACTICE THE 5% KEY

Type each line 2 times. Leave a blank line between each line group.

3. frf fr5f f5f 555 f5f 5/55 f5f 5.55 fr5f
4. frf fr5f f5f f5%f f%f f5%f f%f f5%f f%f
5. 55 figs, 55 flies, 55 forts, 55 friends
6. 5% off, 55% fees, 55% finds, 555% fines

NUMBER AND SYMBOL PRACTICE

Type each line 2 times. Remember to use good technique.

7. The zoo had 525 animals from 15 states.
8. The test scores were 75%, 85%, and 95%.
9. May 5, 5/05, May 15, 5/15, May 25, 5/25
10. 5%, 7%, 9%, 10%, 29%, 38%, 47.5%, 34.5%
11. There were 55 parents and 154 children.
12. Adding 15.3% and 35.2% gives you 50.5%.

124 Section 6 Number and Symbol Keys

RESOURCES

- Lesson Plan: LP41
- Wallchart: Point out reach to the 5% key
- Transparency 1
- CD-ROM: 5% Key
- Software: 5% Key

6^ Key

Goal:
- Use the 6^ key

TUNE UP

Type each line 2 times. Press Return/Enter at the end of each line.

1. slam lake panel slant kayak bland ivory
2. Practice these numbers: 10, 29, 38, 47.

LEARN THE 6^ KEY

The caret (^) is the shift of the 6. Do not space before or after the caret (^). Use the J finger to type the 6 and the caret (^). The reach is up and to the left. Reach from J to 6, keeping the Sem finger at home. Practice the following line.

   jjj jyj jy6j j6j jjj j6j jjj

PRACTICE THE 6^ KEY

Type each line 2 times. Leave a blank line between each line group.

3. jyj jy6j j6j 666 j6j 6/66 j6j 6.66 jy6j
4. jyj jy6j j6j j6^j j^j j6^j j^j j6^j j^j
5. 66 jobs, 66 jams, 66 jolts, 666 jungles
6. 6^, 6 jars, 66^, 66 jets, 66^, 66 jumps

NUMBER AND SYMBOL PRACTICE

Type each line 2 times. Remember to use good technique.

7. We need 656 pounds of food for 66 kids.
8. Your test had these problems: 5^2, 3^4.
9. 65 pianos, 6 banjos, 56 horns, 66 drums
10. 66, 92^6, 66, 83^6, 66, 74^6, 66, 65^6,
11. Reports 26 and 61 are due on October 6.
12. You explain how to find 136^5 and 75^6.

6^ Key **125**

RESOURCES

- Lesson Plan: LP42
- Wallchart: Point out reach to the 6^ key
- Transparency 1
- CD-ROM: 6^ Key
- Software: 6^ Key

6^ Key

FOCUS

Review learned keys. Learn the 6^ key.

BELLRINGER

As soon as their workstations are properly set up, students should begin typing the **Tune Up,** which reviews learned keys.

TEACH

Show the class the location of the 6^ key. Demonstrate the proper reach, showing them how the J finger reaches up to the left to the 6 key. Add the shift key to type the caret (^). Dictate the line shown, and then have the students type it as you observe.

PRACTICE THE 6^ KEY

Have students type lines 3–6. Remind them to leave a blank line between each group of lines.

ASSESS

While students are typing each line in **Number and Symbol Practice** twice, observe and comment on proper technique in reaching for the 9(key.

Speed: lines 7 and 8
Accuracy: lines 9 and 10
Speed and Accuracy: lines 11 and 12

CLOSE

Review proper keyboarding technique and the reach for the 6^ key.

125

5% & 6^ Review

FOCUS

Review learned keys. Review the 5% and 6^ keys.

BELLRINGER

As soon as their workstations are set up, have students type each **Tune Up** line twice. This reviews learned keys.

TEACH

Review the importance of proper posture and keying technique. Demonstrate the correct reaches from the home keys to the 5% and 6^ keys.

REVIEW % AND ^ KEYS

Have students complete lines 3–5. Remind them to leave a blank line between each line group. Make sure students are using the proper fingers when typing. Make sure they are using the shift key to type % and ^.

BUILD YOUR SKILL

Have students type lines 6–11 twice. Instruct them to keep their eyes on the text.

Have students build accuracy by typing lines 12–15 in **Special Word Groups.** The goal is to type the lines with no more than 3 errors.

REVIEW

Goal:
- Review the 5% and 6^ keys

TUNE UP

Type each line 2 times. Press Return/Enter at the end of each line. Tap the keys lightly and quickly. Keep your eyes on the copy.

1. joy snow dive zebra fight quick example
2. 10 and 29 and 38 and 47 and 56 and 1029

REVIEW

Type each line 2 times. Remember to leave a blank line between line groups.

3. Pamela rented 56 tables and 562 chairs.
4. Ben said 2^3 and 20% of 40 is the same.
5. Find 15% of 56, 6% of 65, 26^5 and 5^6.

BUILD YOUR SKILL

Type each line 2 times.

6. 10 maps 29 eggs 38 pans 47 tops 56 oaks
7. a1! S2@ d3# f4$ f5% j6^ j7& k8* l9(;0)
8. Save 56% on 29 @ $47 for 3.8# of tiles.
9. A-OK Laundry* (7th & Rte. 109) is gone!
10. I bought 3# @ $42 & got 5% off ($2.10).
11. Wow! Ed ran 10.83 miles* in 47 minutes.

SPECIAL WORD GROUPS

If you do not know the meanings of the words, look them up in a dictionary. Then type each line 2 times.

12. penalize patronize pizzicato puzzling
13. yam balmy jumpy myopic mouldy tympani

126 Section 6 Number and Symbol Keys

RESOURCES

- Lesson Plan: LP42
- Wallchart: Point out reaches to the 5% and 6^ keys
- Transparency 1
- CD-ROM: Build Skill on the 5% and 6^ Keys; Uncover the Event
- Software: Build Skill on the 5% and 6^ Keys

REVIEW

14 ox proxy toxin exotic foxtrot peroxide
15 tuba abut habit rabbit tablet bobtail

TIME YOURSELF

Take two 1-minute timings on the copy below. If you finish the entire paragraph before time is up, start over again. Press Return/Enter at the end of the paragraph only.

16   Vicki ran 20.93 miles and Gwen ran
17 18.83 miles (10% less). They qualified
18 for a 5K run just scheduled by Zeon for
19 next April.
    | 1 | 2 | 3 | 4 | 5 | 6 | 7 | 8

DID YOU KNOW

Tympani, or timpani, is a set of kettledrums. They are different from most drums in that they are tuned to produce a definite note. Most orchestras use timpani of three sizes—small, medium, and large—so that many sounds can be made. Usually, one person plays timpani in the orchestra.

5% and 6^ Review **127**

5% & 6^ Review

ASSESS

Using lines 16–19, have students take two 1-minute timings or three 12-second timings. The goal should be to increase the number of words or decrease the number of errors on each attempt.

While students are typing each line twice, walk around the class observing and commenting on techniques.

CLOSE

Remind students to practice keyboarding every day. They should practice both alphabetic and number and symbol keys.

DID YOU KNOW

A drum beat may be used to establish a rhythm for typing. Bring in music that has a steady drum beat—a tympani drum beat if you can find it! Use this music in class to establish a beat for your next **Tune Up**.

Teacher's Notes

127

=+ Key

FOCUS

Review learned keys. Learn the =+ key.

BELLRINGER

Have students type **Tune Up**. Play some fun music with a steady beat, as they type the **Tune Up** to the beat.

TEACH

Explain that the plus (+) is the shift for the equal (=) key. Demonstrate the correct reach to the =+ key, stretching up and to the right with the Sem finger. Emphasize the importance of keeping the J finger on its home key. Space once before and after an equal or a plus sign.

Dictate the line shown under **Learn the =+ Key;** have students type it as you observe.

PRACTICE THE =+ KEY

Have students type lines 3–6. Remind them to leave a blank line between each group of lines.

ASSESS

While students are typing **Number and Symbol Practice,** observe and comment on proper technique.

Speed: lines 7 and 8
Accuracy: lines 9 and 10
Speed and Accuracy: lines 11 and 12

CLOSE

Review proper technique at the keyboard and the reach for the =+ key.

128

Goal:
- Use the =+ key

TUNE UP

Type each line 2 times. Press Return/Enter at the end of each line.

1. Aaron bubble accept middle beetle puffs
2. Add 10 plus 29 plus 38 plus 47 plus 56.

LEARN THE =+ KEY

The plus (+) is the shift of the equal (=). Space once before and after an equal (=) or a plus (+) sign. Use the Sem finger to type an equal (=) or plus (+) sign. The reach is up and way to the right. Reach from Sem to equal (=), keeping the J finger at home. Practice the following line.

;;; ;p; ;p-= ;=; ;;; ;=; ;;;

PRACTICE THE =+ KEY

Type each line 2 times. Leave a blank line between each line group.

3. ;;; ;-; ;=; === ;=; ;;; ;-; ;=; === ;=;
4. ;=; ;=+; ;+; ;=+; ;+; ;=+; ;+; ;=+; ;+;
5. A = 95, B = 85, C = 75, D = 70, F = 65,
6. 10 + 29 + 38 + 47 + 56 + 74 + 100 = 354

NUMBER AND SYMBOL PRACTICE

Type each line 2 times. Remember to use good technique.

7. Grades: 90 to 100 = A and below 65 = F.
8. Can you add these numbers: 56 + 29 + 8?
9. 56 - 47 = 9, 83 x 10 = 830, 29 - 9 = 20
10. 2 + 12 = 14, 4 + 14 = 18, 8 + 118 = 126
11. I know that 5 + 5 = 10 and 10 + 5 = 15.
12. If 56 + 47 = 103, what is 38 + 29 + 10?

128 Section 6 Number and Symbol Keys

RESOURCES

- Lesson Plan: LP43
- Wallchart: Point out reach to the =+ key
- Transparency 1
- CD-ROM: =+ Key; Get the Scoop
- Software: =+ Key

Goal:
- Use the <>\ keys

TUNE UP
Type each line 2 times. Press Return/Enter at the end of each line.

1. Nikki alley commit annual woolen sloppy
2. We want 29 @ 83 cents or 56 @ 47 cents.

LEARN THE < > \ KEYS

Less than (<) is the shift of the comma. Greater than (>) is the shift of the period. On some keyboards, the backslash (\) is located above the Return/Enter key. On other keyboards, the backslash is located between the =+ key and the backspace key. Use the Sem finger on the backslash wherever it is located. Reach from Sem to \, keeping the J finger at home. Practice the following line.

;;; ;\; ;;; ;\; ;;; ;\; ;;;

PRACTICE THE < > \ KEYS

Type each line 2 times. Leave a blank line between each line group.

3. ;;; ;\; \\\ ;\; c:\main\sub\filename.ex
4. c:\a&b\1998\contract c:\docs\brown\corr
5. 1.>1 >>> 99 > 90 and Y > X and 100 > 99
6. k,<k <<< 90 < 99 and X < Y and 99 < 100

NUMBER AND SYMBOL PRACTICE

Type each line 2 times. Remember to use good technique.

7. A > B; 7 < 8; c:\docs\personal\1998.bno
8. N > M and 92 > 83 and B < C and 56 < 74
9. c:\medical\ronald a:\history\russia.rep
10. I said (X - Y) > 9, but Lea said Y < 9.

<>\ Keys

FOCUS
Review learned keys. Learn the <>\ keys.

BELLRINGER
Have students type **Tune Up**.

TEACH
Point out the location of the <>\ keys. All of these symbols are used with the shift key. Show the proper reaches to the three keys. The backslash key (\) is used in file names. The < and > keys are used in mathematical notations and mean "is less than" and "is greater than," respectively. Do not space before or after a backslash key (\). If possible, show students some computer printouts that have these symbols on them.

Dictate the line shown; then have students type it.

PRACTICE THE < > \ KEYS
Have students type lines 3–6. Remind them to leave a blank line between each group of lines.

ASSESS
While students are typing each line in **Number and Symbol Practice** twice, observe and comment on proper technique in reaching for the <>\ keys.

CLOSE
Review proper keyboarding technique and the reaches for the <>\ keys.

RESOURCES
- Lesson Plan: LP43
- Wallchart: Point out reaches to the <>\ keys
- Transparency 1
- CD-ROM: <>\ Keys
- Software: <>\ Keys

=+ & <>\ Review

FOCUS
Review learned keys. Review the =+ and <>\ keys.

BELLRINGER
As soon as their workstations are set up, have students type each **Tune Up** line twice. This reviews learned keys.

TEACH
Review the importance of proper posture and keying technique. Demonstrate the correct reaches from the home keys to the =+ and <>\ keys.

REVIEW =+ AND <>\ KEYS
Have students complete lines 3–5. Remind them to leave a blank line between each line group. Make sure students use the proper fingers when typing these symbols.

BUILD YOUR SKILL
Have students type lines 6–11 twice. Instruct them to keep their eyes on the text.

Have students build accuracy by typing lines 12–15 in **Special Word Groups**. Students should type the lines with no more than 3 errors. They should repeat the exercise until this goal is met.

Students are learning new meanings for keys they already know. After they have keyed the material in the book, have them compose sentences on their own.

=+ & <>\ Review

Goal:
- Review the =+ and <>\ keys

TUNE UP

Type each line 2 times. Press Return/Enter at the end of each line. Tap the keys lightly and quickly. Keep your eyes on the copy.

1 we 23 up 70 to 59 it 85 wet 235 pot 095
2 row 492 you 697 rip 480 our 974 toy 596

REVIEW

Type each line 2 times. Remember to leave a blank line between line groups.

3 Pat named the file c:\spanish\homework.
4 If X > Y and Y < Z, then is X > or < Z?
5 If A < B and C > D, then is X < or = Z?

BUILD YOUR SKILL

Type each line 2 times.

6 The #8 & #10 sizes are 29% higher here.
7 "Wow!" she exclaimed. "Isn't it great!"
8 Rates went from 5% to 7% and 8% to 10%.
9 Pears @ $.83 and apples @ $.56 = $1.39.
10 How can she (Janice) leave without you?
11 S & L* arrived at 1:47; P&IR,* at 2:10.

SPECIAL SYMBOLS

minutes '
seconds "
feet '
inches "
minus –
times x, ( )
Roman numerals

Study the special symbol meanings in the left margin. Then type each line 2 times.

12 Judd ran the mile in 4' 29" and 4' 38".
13 Measure 2 boards @ 4' 7" and 4 @ 2' 9".

130 Section 6 Number and Symbol Keys

RESOURCES
- Lesson Plan: LP44
- Wallchart: Point out reaches to the =+ and <>\ keys
- Transparency 1
- CD-ROM: Build Skill on the =+ and <>\ Keys; Uncover the Event
- Software: Build Skill on the =+ and <>\ Keys

REVIEW

14 Ling knows that (8 - 3)(7 - 4) = 5 x 3.
15 Read Chapters VIII and IX for homework.

TIME YOURSELF

Take two 2-minute timings on the copy below. If you finish the entire paragraph before time is up, start over again. Press Return/Enter at the end of the paragraph only.

16   Getting up in the morning is quite
17 a job for me. I grab my jacket and run
18 for the yellow bus just in time to miss
19 it. Five extra minutes would have done
20 it. Next time I will not doze so long.
21 Can I still make it on time? Maybe I
22 will beat the bell.
    | 1 | 2 | 3 | 4 | 5 | 6 | 7 | 8

DID YOU KNOW?

In early times, measurements of length were made by comparing distances with available units. People used their fingers, hands, arms, and feet as measuring tools. Now, standard units of measurement are used to measure length.

Similarly, in early times people measured time by watching the sun's movement across the sky. They marked time by comparing the sun's shadow across a sundial. Today, clocks and watches measure time.

=+ and <>\ Review **131**

=+ & <>\ Review

ASSESS

Using lines 16–22, have students take two 1-minute timings or three 12-second timings. The goal should be to increase speed or accuracy on each attempt.

CLOSE

Review proper keyboarding techniques and the reaches for the =+ and <>\ keys. Remind students that typing is a skill and must be practiced. Suggest that they practice timings of 2 and 3 minutes in length.

DID YOU KNOW?

Compare the standard English system of measurement used in the United States to the metric system used in other parts of the world. Ask students if they see advantages in using either system.

Teacher's Notes

131

TEACH

Computers have literally revolutionized the way people perform their jobs. However, today's students may have little appreciation for the way things were done before computers. On the board, write the personal computer applications to be explored in the remaining units of this book (word processing, desktop publishing, spreadsheet, database, telecommunications). Have five students come up to the board and write specific uses for each application. Ask the class to think of how these tasks were done before computers.

Computers can be used to find answers to math problems, to search for information, or to create documents in a very short amount of time. All you need to do is to give the computer the correct information; then, the computer can quickly find the information you need.

Today, many people use computers to help them do their jobs more quickly and more accurately. Where have you seen people using computers to do their work? What kinds of tasks were done using a computer? How did the com-puter help them do their work more easily? Use your computer to compose a few sentences that tell how people use computers to do their jobs.

A clerk uses a computer to process a catalog order.

An operator uses computer-aided drafting to make blueprints.

Warehouse workers use computers to track inventory.

132 Section 6 Number and Symbol Keys

Numeric Keypad

SECTION 7

Focus on Numeric Keypad

The numeric keypad provides another way to enter numbers. Use the keypad when entering mostly numbers rather than words. You will find the keypad very helpful when you complete projects related to math or science that contain many numbers.

OBJECTIVES

- Operate the numeric keypad by touch.
- Type at a minimum rate of 25 words per minute.
- Develop language arts skills.

Words To Know

decimal   digit   num lock

Section 7 Numeric Keypad

SECTION OVERVIEW

This section focuses on the use of the numeric keypad. Each lesson introduces one row of the keypad, which is three numbers. After every two lessons, there is a review lesson.

OPENING ACTIVITY

Discuss the use of the keypad versus the use of the numbers on the keyboard. Have students share their ideas of when you would use the keypad instead of the numeric keys on the keyboard.

Career Exploration Activities: Public Service

The Internal Revenue Service (IRS) is the government agency responsible for collecting tax revenue from businesses and individuals. There are many jobs involved in this process. Have students contact your regional IRS office to inquire about jobs available. Find out which jobs are year-round and which are seasonal. Have students explain why the IRS might hire seasonal workers.

Keypad 4-5-6 and Enter Keys

FOCUS

Review learned keys. Learn the keypad 4-5-6 and enter keys.

BELLRINGER
Have students type **Tune Up.**

TEACH

Point out the location of the 4-5-6 and enter keys on the keypad. Explain that these are the home keys on the numeric keypad. Also point out the location of the Num Lock key, which must be depressed in order to use the numeric keypad. Demonstrate the proper positions of the J, K, and L fingers on the 4, 5, and 6 keys. The Sem finger is used on the keypad enter key.

Dictate the line shown and then have students type it.

PRACTICE THE 4-5-6 AND Enter KEYS

Have students type lines 3–8. If you are not using the correlated software, you may prefer to have students press the + key after each number and the enter key at the end of the line.

ASSESS

While students are typing **Practice the 4-5-6 Keys,** observe and comment on proper technique.

CLOSE

Review proper technique for the numeric keypad.

Goal:
- Use the keypad 4-5-6 and Enter keys

To operate the keypad, the Num Lock key must be depressed. The Num Lock key is located in the upper left corner of the keypad. When the Num Lock key is depressed, an indicator light on the keyboard will be on.

TUNE UP

Type each line 2 times. Press Return/Enter at the end of each line.

1. mumps verse north cringe mizzen exactly
2. alas glad flags shall flash glass flask

LEARN THE 4 5 6 AND Enter KEYS

The home keys for the numeric keypad are 4, 5, and 6. Use your J K L fingers on the 4 5 6. Use your Sem finger on the *keypad* Enter key after each complete number. This will make your numbers appear in a column instead of a line. Practice the following line.

444 555 666 456

PRACTICE THE 4 5 6 KEYS

Type each line 1 time. Press Enter after each 3-digit number. When you finish all lines, repeat them 1 more time.

3. 444 555 666 445 446 554 556 664 665 456
4. 455 466 544 566 644 655 454 545 565 656
5. 464 646 456 465 546 564 645 654 465 546

6. 444 445 446 455 466 456 454 465 464 444
7. 555 554 556 544 566 546 545 564 565 555
8. 666 664 665 644 655 645 646 654 656 666

Section 7 Numeric Keypad

RESOURCES

- Lesson Plan: LP45
- Wallchart: Point out reaches to the keypad 4-5-6 and enter keys
- Transparency 1
- CD-ROM: Keypad 4-5-6 and Enter Keys; Get the Scoop
- Software: Keypad 4-5-6 and Enter Keys

Keypad 7-8-9 Keys

Goal:
- Use the keypad 7-8-9 keys

TUNE UP

Type each line 2 times. Press Enter at the end of each line.

1. span form glen role wisp glut city turn
2. wet 235 you 607 rut 475 pit 085 owe 923

LEARN THE 7 8 9 KEYS

The 7 - 8 - 9 keys are above the 4 - 5- 6 keys on the numeric keypad. Use the J finger on 7, the K finger on 8, and the L finger on 9. Reach from 4 to 7, from 5 to 8, and from 6 to 9. Practice the following line.

444 474 555 585 666 696

PRACTICE THE 7 8 9 KEYS

Type each line 1 time. Press Enter after each complete number. When you finish all lines, repeat them 1 more time.

3. 474 747 477 744 447 774 444 474 585 696
4. 585 858 588 855 558 885 555 585 696 474
5. 696 969 699 966 669 996 666 696 474 585

6. 474 475 476 744 755 766 745 746 547 647
7. 585 584 586 855 844 866 854 856 458 658
8. 696 694 695 966 955 944 964 965 469 569

9. 47 475 7564 47 476 7654 47 567 4567 474
10. 58 584 8465 58 586 8645 58 648 6458 585
11. 69 694 9456 69 695 9654 69 549 5469 696

Keypad 7-8-9 Keys **135**

RESOURCES

- Lesson Plan: LP46
- Wallchart: Point out reaches to the keypad 7-8-9 keys
- Transparency 1
- CD-ROM: Keypad 7-8-9 Keys
- Software: Keypad 7-8-9 Keys

Keypad 7-8-9 Keys

FOCUS

Review learned keys and the keypad home keys. Learn the keypad 7-8-9 keys.

BELLRINGER

Have students type **Tune Up**.

TEACH

Show the class the location of the keypad 7-8-9 keys. Demonstrate the proper reaches, using the J (or 4) finger on 7, K (or 5) finger on 8, and L (or 6) finger on 9.

Dictate the line shown, and then have the students type it.

PRACTICE THE 7 - 8 - 9 KEYS

Have students type lines 3–11. Remind them to leave a blank line between each group of lines.

ASSESS

While students are typing each line in lines 3–11, observe and comment on proper technique.

CLOSE

Review proper keyboarding technique and the reach for the keypad 7-8-9 keys. Encourage students to practice both the alphabetic keyboard and the numeric keypad.

135

Keypad 4-5-6-7-8-9 Review

FOCUS

Review learned keys. Review the keypad 4-5-6-7-8-9 keys.

BELLRINGER

As soon as their workstations are set up, have students type each **Tune Up** line twice. This reviews alphabetic keys.

TEACH

Review the importance of proper posture and keying technique. Demonstrate the correct reaches from the home keys to the 4-5-6-7-8-9 keypad keys.

REVIEW 4 - 5 - 6 - 7 - 8 - 9 KEYS

Have students complete lines 3–5. Students should be able to key these lines rather quickly. Check to make sure that they are using the proper fingers and looking at their books.

BUILD YOUR SKILL

Have students type lines 6–11 twice. Instruct them to keep their eyes on the text.

Have students build accuracy by typing lines 12–15 in **Special Number Groups.**

Remind students of the following: No space before or after a slash in a fraction; in mixed numbers, one space between the number and the fraction; no space before or after a decimal point in a number.

Keypad 4-5-6-7-8-9 Review

Goal:
- Review the keypad 4-5-6-7-8-9 keys

TUNE UP

Type each line 2 times. Press Return/Enter at the end of each line.

1. kayak mambo lapels naught orient pajama
2. rare ploy fret moon wave milk axed jump

REVIEW

Type each line 2 times. Press Enter after each 3-digit number.

3. 444 456 465 555 546 564 666 645 654 456
4. 474 475 476 585 584 586 696 694 695 789
5. 489 579 678 468 549 567 476 584 695 987

BUILD YOUR SKILL

Type each line 2 times. Press Enter after each 3-digit number.

6. 456 546 645 564 654 789 879 978 897 987
7. 744 745 746 855 854 856 966 965 964 759
8. 447 457 467 558 548 568 669 659 649 684

9. 478 479 474 475 476 488 489 494 445 456
10. 587 589 584 585 586 578 589 594 545 556
11. 697 698 694 695 696 678 689 694 645 656

SPECIAL NUMBER GROUPS

Study each line, then type each line 2 times.

12. Type these numbers: 10, 29, 38, 47, 56.
13. Can you type 1/4, 1/3, 3/4, 4/5, & 5/8?
14. I have 1 1/3 pies and 2 3/4 cakes left.
15. The total of 47.10 plus 29.65 is 76.75.

136 Section 7 Numeric Keypad

RESOURCES

Lesson Plan: LP46

CD-ROM: Build Skill on Keypad 4-5-6-7-8-9 Keys; Uncover the Event

Software: Build Skill on Keypad 4-5-6-7-8-9 Keys

Wallchart: Point out reaches to the keypad 4-5-6-7-8-9 keys

Transparency 1

REVIEW

Keypad 4-5-6-7-8-9 Review

TIME YOURSELF

Take two 2-minute timings on the copy below. If you finish the paragraph before time is up, start over again. Press Return/Enter at the end of the paragraph only.

```
16      The end of a term would be just
17 great if it were not for tests. It is a
18 joy to have all the classes done. The
19 only shadow is exams. Some students
20 like tests since they show how much has
21 been learned. What is a puzzle to one
22 is quite clear to others.
   | 1 | 2 | 3 | 4 | 5 | 6 | 7 | 8
```

ASSESS

Students should type the paragraph in lines 16–22 with no more than four errors. Repeat this exercise until they reach this goal.

CLOSE

Remind students to practice daily to maintain the skill level they have now attained. Commend them on the fine work they have done!

Language Link

A comma is often used with a conjunction to make a compound sentence.

When two independent clauses are joined by the conjunction *and, but, or,* or *nor* into one compound sentence, use a comma before the conjunction.

Two independent clauses:
   Philip used a spreadsheet. Paige used a database.

Two independent clauses joined by a conjunction:
   Philip used a spreadsheet, but Paige used a database.

✓ Check Your Learning

Indicate where commas, if any, should be inserted in each of the following sentences.

1. The grass has grown tall and must be cut before the game starts.
2. We can go to the game together or we can meet there.
3. Jonathan cannot go until he finishes his work nor can he play soccer.
4. We provide pencils and calculators and each student brings paper.
5. Alice went to practice but forgot to wear her game shoes.

Teacher's Notes

Keypad 1-2-3 Keys

FOCUS

Review learned keys. Learn the keypad 1-2-3 keys.

BELLRINGER

As soon as their workstations are properly set up, students should begin typing **Tune Up,** which reviews learned keys.

TEACH

Point out the location of the keypad 1-2-3 keys on the numeric keypad. Demonstrate the proper reaches. The J (or 4) finger reaches down to the 1; the K (or 5) finger, to the 2; and the L (or 6) finger, to the 3.

Dictate the line shown and then have the students type it as you observe.

PRACTICE THE 1-2-3 KEYS

Have students type lines 3–11. Encourage them to keep their eyes on the text, not the keyboard.

ASSESS

While students are typing lines 3–11 twice, walk around the room observing and commenting on proper hand position and technique in reaching for the 1-2-3 keys.

CLOSE

Review proper technique for the numeric keypad. Remind them to practice the numeric keypad along with the alphabetic keys.

138

Keypad 1-2-3 Keys

Goal:
- Use the keypad 1-2-3 keys

TUNE UP

Type each line 2 times. Press Return/Enter at the end of each line.

```
1  gowns print quench laughs dismal mantle
2  wire 2843 port 0945 quit 1785 your 6974
```

LEARN THE 1 2 3 KEYS

The 1 - 2 - 3 keys are below the 4 - 5 - 6 on the numeric keypad. Use the J finger on 1, the K finger on 2, and the L finger on 3. Reach from 4 to 1, from 5 to 2, and from 6 to 3. Practice the following line.

```
   444  414  555  525  666  636
```

PRACTICE THE 1 2 3 KEYS

Type each line 2 times. Press Enter after each complete number.

```
3   414  141  411  144  441  114  444  414  525  636
4   525  252  522  255  552  225  555  525  636  414
5   636  363  633  366  663  336  666  636  414  525

6   417  418  419  741  841  941  144  145  146  147
7   527  528  529  752  852  952  254  255  256  258
8   637  638  639  763  863  963  364  365  366  369

9   41  417  4174  41  418  4184  41  419  4194  714
10  52  528  5285  52  529  5295  52  527  5274  825
11  63  639  6396  63  637  6376  63  638  6386  936
```

138 Section 7 Numeric Keypad

RESOURCES

- Lesson Plan: LP47
- Wallchart: Point out reaches to the keypad 1-2-3 keys
- Transparency 1
- CD-ROM: Keypad 1-2-3 Keys; Get the Scoop
- Software: Keypad 1-2-3 Keys

Keypad 0 and Decimal (.) Keys

Goal:
- Use the keypad 0 and decimal (.) keys

TUNE UP

Type each line 2 times. Press Return/Enter at the end of each line.

1 Lia Juan Gila Jesse Reiko Helmut Althea
2 Eli Yuko Ozro Katja Nabil LaRae Cazimer

LEARN THE 0 AND DECIMAL . KEYS

The 0 and decimal (.) keys are below the 4 - 5 - 6 on the numeric keypad. Use the right thumb on 0 and the L finger on the decimal. Reach from 6 to the decimal. Practice the following line.

666 63. 6.6 606 6.06 666

PRACTICE THE 0 AND DECIMAL . KEYS

Type each line 2 times. Press Enter after each complete number.

3   400 401 402 403 501 502 503 601 602 603
4   6.1 6.2 6.3 6.4 6.5 6.6 6.7 6.8 6.9 6.0
5   1.0 2.0 3.0 4.0 5.0 6.0 7.0 8.0 9.0 0.6

6   700 701 702 703 704 1.5 1.6 1.7 1.8 1.9
7   800 801 802 803 804 2.5 2.6 2.7 2.8 2.9
8   900 901 902 903 904 3.5 3.6 3.7 3.8 3.9

9   40 405 4056 50 506 5064 60 604 6045 406
10 .4 4.5 4.56 .5 5.6 5.64 .6 6.4 6.45 4.0
11 .1 .10 1.04 .2 .20 2.05 .3 .30 3.06 8.0

Keypad 0 and Decimal (.) Keys **139**

RESOURCES
- Lesson Plan: LP47
- Wallchart: Point out reaches to the keypad 0 and decimal keys
- Transparency 1
- CD-ROM: Keypad 0 and Decimal Keys
- Software: Keypad 0 and Decimal Keys

Keypad 0 and Decimal (.) Keys

FOCUS

Review learned keys, the keypad Home keys, and the keypad 0 and decimal (.) keys.

BELLRINGER

Have students type **Tune Up**.

TEACH

Show the class the location of the keypad 0 and decimal (.) keys. Demonstrate the proper reaches, using the right thumb on 0 and the L (or 6) finger on the decimal.

Dictate the line shown, and then have the students type it.

PRACTICE THE 0 AND . KEYS

Have students type lines 3–11. Remind them to leave a blank line between each group of lines.

ASSESS

While students are typing lines 3–11 twice, walk around the room observing and commenting on proper position and technique in reaching for the keypad 0 and decimal (.) keys.

CLOSE

Review proper keyboarding technique and the reach for the keypad 0 and decimal (.) keys. Encourage students to practice both the alphabetic keyboard and the numeric keypad.

139

Keypad 1-2-3-0 and Decimal (.) Review

FOCUS

Review learned keys. Review the keypad 1-2-3-0 and decimal (.) keys.

BELLRINGER

As soon as their workstations are set up, have students type each **Tune Up** line twice. This reviews learned keys.

TEACH

Review the importance of proper posture and keying technique. Demonstrate the correct reaches from the home keys to the 1-2-3-0-. keypad keys.

REVIEW KEYPAD 1 - 2 - 3 - 0 AND . KEYS

Have students complete lines 3–5. Students should be able to key these lines rather quickly. Check to make sure that they are using the proper fingers and looking at their books. Remind them to leave a blank line between each line group.

BUILD YOUR SKILL

Have students type lines 6–11 twice. Instruct them to keep their eyes on the text.

Keypad 1-2-3-0-, Review

Goal:
- Review the keypad 1-2-3-0-decimal (.) keys

REVIEW

TUNE UP

Type each line 2 times. Press Return/Enter at the end of each line.

1. $92 & $47; (9 + 10 = 19); 38# @ 56% off
2. "No!" she yelled. "We can't go there*."

REVIEW

Type each line 2 times. Press Enter after each complete number.

3. 4075 5086 6094 7080 1020 8090 2030 4006
4. 1.45 2.56 3.64 47.1 58.2 69.3 40.5 50.6
5. 70.4 50.8 90.6 6.03 2.05 1.04 70.9 8.60

BUILD YOUR SKILL

Type each line 2 times. Press Enter after each complete number.

6. 2.6   7.0   2.8   6.7   3.9   4.9   3.0   5.2   7.7   1.9
7. 7.31 7.51 8.73 5.03 3.21 7.34 5.20 9.62
8. 20.7 55.3 91.0 44.2 40.6 66.2 12.3 45.6

9. 1.21 54.01 4.98 .66   42.05 7.64 .88   9.69
10. .91   92.28 3.37 .48   67.85 5.13 .48   79.80
11. 853.1 6.7   75.5 119.9 9.0   70.4 945.3 2.6

Section 7 Numeric Keypad

RESOURCES

- **Lesson Plan:** LP48
- **CD-ROM:** Build Skill on Keypad 1-2-3 and Decimal Keys; Uncover the Event
- **Software:** Build Skill on Keypad 1-2-3 and Decimal Keys
- **Wallchart:** Point out reaches to the keypad 1-2-3-0 and decimal keys
- **Transparency 1**

REVIEW

SPECIAL WORD GROUPS

Study the common foreign words in the lines below. Then type each line 2 times. Do NOT type the vertical lines—insert a space instead.

```
12  yes|no|please|thank you|house|school
13  si|no|por favor|gracias|casa|escuela
14  ja|nein|bitte|danke|haus|schule
```

TIME YOURSELF

Take two 2-minute timings on the copy below. If you finish the paragraph before time is up, start over again. Press Return/Enter at the end of the paragraph only.

```
15       When you spend time with people
16  every day, you get to know the things
17  that bring them joy. You also find out
18  very quickly what they do not like. A
19  little bit of extra effort in a dozen
20  small ways will make your school a
21  pleasant place in which to be.
    |  1  |  2  |  3  |  4  |  5  |  6  |  7  |  8
```

CULTURAL KALEIDOSCOPE

The Japanese word for yes is hai, *pronounced like the American greeting* hi! *Among the Japanese,* hai *or yes, does not mean* Yes, I agree with you. *Instead,* hai *is used as an acknowledgment, to mean* Yes, I hear you.

Keypad 1-2-3-0-Decimal (.) Review **141**

CULTURAL KALEIDOSCOPE

Just as languages vary among cultures, so, too, does nonverbal communication (or body language). In Japan, for example, eye contact is a sign of disrespect. But in the United States, we do not usually trust people who will not look us in the eye.

Keypad 1-2-3-0 and Decimal (.) Review

Have students build accuracy by typing lines 12–14.

Students should be able to type this **Special Word Groups** very easily, even though there are some foreign words. See if your class notices that the first word in lines 12, 13, and 14 are the English, Spanish and German words for "yes"; the second, "no"' the third, "please"; the fourth, "thank you"; the fifth, "house"; and the last, "school".

ASSESS

Students should type the paragraph (lines 15–21) with no more than four errors. Repeat this exercise until they reach this goal.

CLOSE

Remind students to practice daily to maintain the skill level they have now attained. Commend them on the fine work they have done!

UNIT 3 ORGANIZER

Section	Subsection	Special Features	Projects: Project No., Title, and Page	Projects: Cross-Curricular Connection	Difficulty Level	Student Guide GO TO
8 - Reports	8.1 - One-Page Report	Words to Know, p. 144 Did You Know?, p. 146 Did You Know?, p. 148 Cultural Kaleidoscope, p. 149	Projects 6–8: One-Page Report, MLA Style, pp. 147–149	6–8 Social Studies	6 - L1 7 - L1 8 - L1	p. 146
	8.2 - One-Page Report	Did You Know?, p. 154	Projects 9–11: One-Page Report, pp. 152–154	9–11 Technology	9 - L1 10 - L1 11 - L2	p. 151
	8.3 - Title Page	Cultural Kaleidoscope, p. 157	Projects 12–13: Title Page, pp. 157-158	12–13 Technology	12 - L1 13 - L1	
	8.4 - Journal	Language Link, p. 160	Project 14: Journal, p. 160	14 Technology	14 - L1	p. 159
	8.5 - Multipage Report, MLA Style	Did You Know?, p. 161 Did You Know?, p. 164	Projects 15–17: Multipage Report, MLA Style, pp. 163–165	15–17 Social Studies	15 - L1 16 - L1 17 - L2	p. 162
	8.6 - Multipage Bound Report	In Your Journal, p. 170	Projects 18–20: Multipage Bound Reports with Side Headings, pp. 168–170	18–20 Language Arts	18 - L1 19 - L1 20 - L2	p. 167
	8.7 - Bulleted List	In Your Journal, p. 172	Project 21: Bulleted List, p. 172		21 - L1	p. 171
	8.8 - Numbered List	In Your Journal, p. 173 Language Link, p. 174	Project 22: Numbered List, p. 174	22 Technology	22 - L1	p. 173
			Project 23: Building Your Portfolio, pp. 175–177	23 Science	23 - L2	
9 - Reports with Special Features	9.1 - Reports With Footnotes and Quotations	Words to Know, p. 178 Did You Know?, p. 184 In Your Journal, p. 185	Projects 24–26: Multipage Report with Footnotes and Quotations, pp. 181–185	24–26 Science	24 - L1 25 - L1 26 - L2	p. 180
	9.2 - Reports With Endnotes	Language Link, p. 190	Projects 27–29: Multipage Report With Endnotes, pp. 188–190	27–29 Science	27 - L1 28 - L1 29 - L2	p. 187
	9.3 - Bibliography	Did You Know?, p. 192 In Your Journal, p. 193	Project 30: Bibliography, MLA Style, p. 193	30 Social Studies	30 - L1	p. 192
	9.4 - Bibliography	Did You Know?, p. 195 Did You Know?, p. 199	Project 31: Bibliography, p. 196	31 Social Studies	31 - L1	
			Project 32: Building Your Portfolio, pp. 197–199	32 Math	32 - L2	
	9.5 - Table of Contents	Did You Know?, p. 201 Language Link, p. 204	Projects 33–34: Table of Contents, pp. 202–204	33–34 Language Arts	33 - L1 34 - L2	p. 201
	9.6 - Report Outline	In Your Journal, p. 207	Projects 35–36: Report Outlines, pp. 208–209	35–36 Language Arts	35 - L1 36 - L2	p. 207

UNIT RESOURCES

- Lesson Plans: LP48–LP62
- Transparency Masters: TM4–TM28
- Multicultural Timings: MT1–MT3
- Supplemental Projects: SP1–SP5
- Enrichment Activities
- CD-ROM: Unit 3 Document Templates Reference Guide Cross-curricular Timings
- Software: Unit 3 Document Templates Research Files
- Transparencies: 3–14
- Student Guides: Word Processing
- Student Data Disks

UNIT 3 ORGANIZER

Section	Subsection	Special Features	Projects: Project No., Title, and Page	Projects: Cross-Curricular Connection	Projects: Difficulty Level	Student Guide GO TO
9 - Reports with Special Features (Continued)	9.7 - Multipage Report		Projects 37–39: Multipage Report With Footer, pp. 211–213	37–39 Social Studies	37 - L1 38 - L1 39 - L2	p. 210
			Project 40: Building Your Portfolio, pp. 214–216	40 Science	40 - L2	
10 - Letters and Memos	10.1 - Informal Letter	Words to Know, p. 217 In Your Journal, p. 219 In Your Journal, p. 222	Projects 41–43: Informal Letters, pp. 220–222		41 - L1 42 - L1 43 - L2	p. 219
	10.2 - Formal Letter	In Your Journal, p. 228	Projects 44–46: Formal Letter With Enclosure, pp. 227–229	44–45 Technology	44 - L1 45 - L1 46 - L2	
	10.3 - Memo	Language Link, p. 233	Projects 47–49: Memo, pp. 231–233	47–48 Math	47 - L1 48 - L1 49 - L2	
			Project 50: Building Your Portfolio, pp. 234–235		50 - L2	
11 - Personal Applications	11.1 - Chapter Outline	Words to Know, p. 237 Cultural Kaleidoscope, p. 238	Project 51: Chapter Outline, p. 239	51 Science	51 - L1	
	11.2 - Presentation Outline	In Your Journal, p. 241 In Your Journal, p. 243	Projects 52–53: Presentation Outline, p. 242	52 Science	52 - L1	
	11.3 - Class Notes	In Your Journal, p. 248	Projects 54–56: Class Notes, pp. 246–248	55–56 Language Arts	54 - L1 55 - L1 56 - L2	
		Did You Know?, p. 249	Project 57: Building Your Portfolio, p. 249		57 - L2	

KEY TO DIFFICULTY LEVEL

The following designations will help you decide which activities are appropriate for your students.

L1: Level 1 activities are basic activities and should be within the range of all students.

L2: Level 2 activities are average activities and should be within the range of average and above average students.

L3: Level 3 activities are challenging activities designed for the ability range of above average students.

ASSESSMENT RESOURCES

Check Your Learning

Section 8	Section 9	Section 10
p. 160	p. 190	p. 233
p. 174	p. 204	

Check Your Understanding

Section 8	Section 9	Section 10	Section 11
p. 149	p. 185	p. 222	p. 243
p. 154	p. 190	p. 228	p. 248
p. 165	p. 213	p. 233	
p. 170			

Portfolio Assessment (Building Your Portfolio)

Section 8	Section 9	Section 10	Section 11
pp. 175–7	pp. 214–6	pp. 234–5	p. 249

Unit Tests (Teacher's Resource Binder)
Objective Test
Performance Tests

| Section 8 | Section 9 | Section 10 | Section 11 |

142b

UNIT 3

INTRODUCING THE UNIT

Ask students if they have any experience using a word processing program. Ask them for examples of documents they have created.

Ask if they know the names of the programs they have used. Give examples of popular commercial word processing software and introduce the software they will be using to complete the projects in this unit.

Explain that effective word processing depends on good basic keyboarding skills. Unit 3 is an introduction to basic word processing. The focus is on the most commonly used features of word processing software.

Unit 3
Word Processing

OVERVIEW

Word processing programs make the writing process easier by allowing you to organize your thoughts, edit and revise documents easily, and format documents attractively. Of all the software applications, word processing is the most widely used. In this unit, you will learn word processing features and document formats that will help you communicate more clearly and effectively.

Fun Facts

Author Mark Twain was one of the first American writers to type rather than handwrite his work. His manuscript for **Life on the Mississippi** was the first typed manuscript ever submitted to a publisher. Today handwritten manuscripts are rare in publishing.

UNIT 3

MULTIMEDIA

For this unit, you may use the multimedia CD-ROM to enhance your students' skills in word processing. The CD-ROM contains format guides that serve as models for students to create projects using a word processing software application. These format guides are cross-referenced to the word processing projects in the student text. A Reference Guide links terms to format guides that define and illustrate their use in formatting word processing documents. The Research Files contain cross-curricular typing selections or timings for 1 minute, 2 minutes, and 3- or 5-minutes. The timings, as well as the two games—Get the Scoop and Uncover the Story—reinforce and develop students' typing skills.

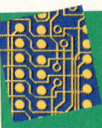

UNIT OBJECTIVES

- Create, edit, and format:
  - Reports in MLA and business styles
  - Journal entries
  - Informal and formal letters
  - Memos
  - Outlines
  - Class notes

Unit Contents

Section 8	Reports
Section 9	Reports With Special Features
Section 10	Letters and Memos
Section 11	Personal Applications

Focus On Careers In Technology

Authors spend many hundreds of hours preparing the manuscript for a book. Between the moment they get their first ideas down on paper and the day they see a printed copy of their book, authors have usually written and rewritten their work countless times. Using a word processing program makes it easy for authors to cut and paste, edit and revise, reorganize, correct spelling errors, and write different versions of their manuscript. Word processing programs allow authors to spend more of their time researching and focusing on their creative writing.

Focus On Careers In Technology

In addition to book authors, many other professional communicators use word processing. Examples of professional communicators include: sports writers, advertising copywriters, magazine editors, and speech writers.

Invite a professional communicator to talk to students about the writing and editing process. Organizations to consider when seeking a speaker include: International Association of Business Communicators (IABC), and the Association for Women in Communications (AWC).

Application: COMPUTERS AT HOME

Divide students into groups of three or four. Ask each group to make a list of ten things you might do with a home computer. Encourage students to include their own experiences along with how they have seen family and friends use home computers.

Items listed might include:
- chat on the Internet
- draw a picture
- keep track of family budget
- make a chart or graph
- play a game
- send e-mail
- write a story

Section 8
Reports

SECTION OVERVIEW

This section focuses on reports—both single and multipage reports. MLA and business styles are introduced.

In Project 14 students are instructed to begin keeping a journal. Journal activities continue throughout the remainder of the text.

CONTENT FOCUS

One-page report
Title page
Journal
Multipage report
Bulleted and numbered lists

CURRICULUM FOCUS

Social Studies
Technology
Language Arts
Science

OPENING ACTIVITY

Create a handout explaining the basic guidelines for using computers in your classroom or lab. Use the same word processing software students will be using. Use some of the word processing features that students will learn in this section. For example, center the title of the handout; use a bulleted or numbered list; and alter the line spacing for a portion of the handout.

Discuss the handout with students. Emphasize the guidelines you have written and at the same time point out some of the word processing features students will learn in this section.

SECTION 8
Reports

OBJECTIVES

- Create, edit, and format:
  - One-page reports in MLA and business styles
  - Report title pages
  - Report headers
  - Journal entries
  - Multipage reports in MLA style
  - Multipage bound reports with side headings
  - Bulleted lists and numbered lists

Focus on Reports

Your teachers have probably asked you to write book reports, research reports, and journals. In this section, you will learn to use your word processing software to create these reports easily. You will also learn acceptable ways to format these reports. You will begin keeping a journal in which you will record your thoughts about the projects you complete and about other topics.

Words To Know

alignment	journal	side heading
body	line spacing	source
bound report	margin	subtitle
bulleted list	MLA report heading	title
byline	navigating	title page
citation	numbered list	window
find and replace	page number	works cited
hanging indent	report in MLA style	zoom
header	selecting	

Career Exploration Activities: Agribusiness

Consider inviting a speaker to talk to your students about agribusiness in your community. Ask the speaker to address the use of technology and computers in agribusiness.

For assistance with this activity, contact your county extension service or a local office of the U.S. Department of Agriculture. The e-mail address for the USDA is http://www.usda.gov/

One-Page Report, MLA Style

FORMATTING A ONE-PAGE REPORT, MLA STYLE

Has your teacher ever asked you to turn in a report that had to be typed and formatted correctly? Reports can be arranged in many acceptable ways. In this lesson, you will learn to type and format a simple, one-page report in a format called MLA style. You will learn another format later in Project 9. Study this illustration. Your finished report may look slightly different.

Goals
- Type and format a simple, one-page report in MLA style
- Practice navigating; selecting text; and changing the zoom, alignment, and line spacing

HEADING. Name of the writer, teacher, class, and date.

TITLE. Subject of the report.

BODY. Text of the report.

Sample report shown (1 inch margins):

Denise Broers
Mr. Rodriguez
Geography 1
9 September 19--

Argentina

Argentina occupies most of the southern part of South America. Uruguay, Brazil, Paraguay, and Bolivia lie on its northern borders. Argentina's eastern coastline is washed by the Atlantic Ocean. Its southern tip reaches almost to the continent of Antarctica. Argentina's varied geography includes the Perito Moreno glacier in the southern Andes. This is one of the few glaciers in the world still advancing.

Argentina has 1,056,640 square miles making it South America's second-largest country, after Brazil. Argentina has a wide variety of landscapes including mountains, forests, plains, and deserts. The Iguacu Falls on Argentina's Brazilian border is one of the scenic wonders of the world. Lowland areas stretch across northern Argentina. To the west, great forests cover the Gran Chaco. To the east, hot, humid grasslands abound. Farmers raise livestock and grow crops in this fertile soil.

The Andes tower over the western part of Argentina. Snow-capped peaks and clear blue lakes draw tourists who come to ski and hike. Mount Aconcagua soars to a height of almost 23,000 feet and is the highest mountain in the Western Hemisphere. East of the Andes is a region of rolling hills and desert valleys. Farmers use mountain stream water to grow sugar cane, corn, cotton, and grapes.

In the center of Argentina are treeless plains known as the Pampa. The Pampa spreads almost 500 miles from the Atlantic coast to the Andes. Argentina's economy depends on this region's fertile soil and mild climate. Most of Argentina's urban areas are here with more than two-thirds of the population living here. Buenos Aires, the capital and largest city, lies in the area where the Pampa meets the Rio de la Plata.

One-Page Report **145**

RESOURCES
- Lesson Plan: LP49
  Supplemental Project: SP1
  Transparency Master: TM4
- CD-ROM: Reference Guide
- Software: Research Files

Lesson Extension

MLA is the abbreviation for Modern Language Association. This association publishes a reference book that is used by many high school and college students as a guide when writing reports and research papers.

8.1 One-Page Report

FOCUS
Type and format a one-page report. Practice navigating and selecting text. Practice changing the zoom, alignment, and line spacing.

BELLRINGER
When students enter the room, direct their attention to the assignment on the board:
   Read pages 145 and 146.

TEACH
Let students know that they will begin using word processing software with Project 6 on page 147. Review basic formatting of a one-page report using MLA style. Use the illustration on page 145 to highlight the heading, title, and body of the report. Also point out the margins and the alignment of the title.

145

One-Page Report

TEACH

Review formatting tips with students. Make sure they understand the concepts presented. Default margins are the margins that exist when you open a new document. Double spacing means that there is a blank line between each printed line. Another term for initial caps is title case. Indenting a paragraph, as used here, refers to indenting the first line of the paragraph.

ASSESS

To assess understanding have students describe the main components of a one-page report using MLA style.

CLOSE

Explain to students that they are now ready to type and format a simple, one-page report in MLA style. Refer to Projects 6, 7, and 8.

DID YOU KNOW? Argentina is a republic in southern South America. Brazil, Bolivia, Chile, Paraguay, and Uruguay share borders with Argentina. The Atlantic Ocean provides approximately 5000 km of coastline.

GO TO Refer students to the appropriate section of the Student Guide.

FORMATTING TIPS

- Use default margins.
- Double-space the entire report.
- Type each item in the heading on a separate line.
- Type the day, month, and year in the heading in that order without commas.
- Center the title and use initial caps (capitalize the first letter of each major word).
- Double-space the paragraphs in the body and indent them 0.5 inch.

DID YOU KNOW? Argentina's name comes from the Latin word *argentum*, which means silver. In the 1500s the first settlers came to Argentina looking for silver and gold. Although the explorers didn't find silver and gold, they found something very valuable. They found rich, fertile soil and other natural resources.

Valley glaciers, such as Perito Moreno in the southern Andes Mountains, shape the land by making deep valleys in the mountains.

GO TO Student Guide, Word Processing
Window	Selecting
Line spacing	Zoom
Navigating	Alignment

146 Section 8 Reports

interNET CONNECTION

Have students use the Internet to learn more about geography. Using a web search engine they might search for sites related to specific countries or geography topics.

Examples of sites might include:

Latin America: http://www.lanic.utexas.edu
Venezuela: http://www.venezuela.mit.edu

146

Project 6

ONE-PAGE REPORT, MLA STYLE

Carefully read and do the following steps to complete a one-page report.

1. In your Student Guide, read and follow the steps for **window** in Unit 3. You will learn some basics about word processing and familiarize yourself with the word processing document window.
2. Open the file WP006 on your data disk.
3. Change the **line spacing** to double.
4. Practice **navigating**, **selecting**, and changing the **zoom** as you follow the steps below to edit the report.
5. Type the heading using your own name, your teacher's name, the name of your geography class, and today's date.
6. Type the title *Argentina* in initial caps. Change the **alignment** to center.
7. Add the paragraph below to the end of the report:

> In the center of Argentina are treeless plains known as the Pampa. The Pampa spreads almost 500 miles from the Atlantic coast to the Andes. Argentina's economy depends on this region's fertile soil and mild climate. Most of Argentina's urban areas are here with more than two-thirds of the population living here. Buenos Aires, the capital and largest city, lies in the area where the Pampa meets the Rio de la Plata.

8. Use the speller. Proofread to check for errors. Preview the document and make corrections as needed.
9. Save the document as STWP006 on your data disk.
10. Print and then close the document.

Note: In the filename STWP006, *ST* stands for student; *WP* stands for the word processing unit; and *006* (zero, zero, 6) stands for Project 6. Be sure to press the zero key and not the letter *O* when typing zeroes.

Project 6
One-Page Report

PRACTICE—LEVEL 1

Purpose
Practice typing and formatting a one-page report.

Time
Thirty minutes

Preparation
Make sure software is loaded, data disks are available, and printers are ready including full paper trays.

Teaching Tip
Have students who finish early reopen the file STWP006 and practice the features learned in this project. For example, change the line spacing or size of the type. Instruct students not to save their work.

Trouble Shooting
Make sure students understand how to save their work to their data disks. Provide individual help to students who are having difficulty.

Wrap Up
Have students review their printed document, mark any errors they see, and turn in their papers.
 If this is the last project for this class period, ask students to return computers and furniture to the appropriate conditions.

Social Studies Connection

To generate interest in social studies, initiate a brief class discussion about Argentina. Discussion questions might include:

- What do you know about the language and culture of Argentina?
- What do you know about the history and government of Argentina?
- Would you like to travel to Argentina?

Project 7
One-Page Report

APPLY—LEVEL 1

Purpose
Apply word processing skills by typing and formatting a one-page report.

Time
Fifteen minutes

Preparation
Make sure software is loaded, data disks are available, and printers are ready including full paper trays.

Teaching Tip
Have students who finish early reopen the file STWP007 and practice some of the features learned in Project 6. Instruct students not to save their work.

Trouble Shooting
Make sure students understand how to save their work to their data disks. Provide individual help to students who are having difficulty.

Wrap Up
Have students review their printed document, mark any errors they see, and turn in their papers.

The first Neanderthal fossils were found near Düsseldorf, Germany, in 1856. They were found by German anthropologists Johann Fuhlrott and Hermann Schaaffhausen. A primitive ancestor of modern humans, Neanderthals lived between 75,000 and 40,000 B.C.

Project 7
Social Studies Connection
ONE-PAGE REPORT, MLA STYLE

Practice using the word processing features you learned in Project 6 by formatting another one-page report in MLA style. Refer to the illustration and information on pages 145 and 146 as often as needed.

1. Open the file WP007 on your data disk.
2. Change the line spacing to double.
3. Practice navigating, selecting, and changing the zoom as you follow the steps below to edit the report.
4. Type the heading using your own name, your teacher's name, the name of your geography class, and today's date.
5. Type the title *The Neanderthals* in initial caps, centered.
6. Add the paragraph below to the end of the report:

> Neanderthals were also builders. In northern areas, for example, they made houses by covering a framework of mammoth bones with animal skins. More bones piled on the bottoms of the skins prevented them from being blown away. As many as 30 people lived in such a house during the cold months of the year. They improved cave dwellings by digging drainage ditches in caves and designing rock protection for entrances.

7. Use the speller. Proofread to check for errors. Preview the document and make corrections as needed.
8. Save the document as STWP007 on your data disk.
9. Print and then close the document.

DID YOU KNOW
Neanderthals are named for the Neander River in Germany. Evidence of Neanderthals has been found throughout Europe and also in Asia and Africa.

148 Section 8 Reports

Social Studies Connection

To generate interest in social studies, initiate a brief class discussion. Discussion questions might include:

What do you know about archeology?
What do you know about anthropology?

interNET CONNECTION

Have students use the Internet to learn more about Germany.

Web site example:
http://www.city.net/countries/germany

Project 8

ONE-PAGE REPORT, MLA STYLE

Practice the word processing features you learned on pages 145–147 by typing an original, one-page report in MLA style. Write your report about any topic in social studies, including civics, geography, economics, or history.

1. Open a new word processing file.
2. Change the line spacing to double.
3. Type the heading using your own name, your teacher's name, the name of your social studies class, and today's date.
4. Type the title in initial caps, centered.
5. Type the body of the report.
6. Practice navigating, selecting, and changing the zoom as you type and revise your report.
7. Use the speller. Proofread to check for errors. Preview the document and make corrections as needed.
8. Save the document as STWP008 on your data disk.
9. Print and then close the document.

✓ Check Your Understanding

1. Did you include your name, your teacher's name, the class name, and the date on separate lines in the heading?
2. Did you format the date with the day, month, and year without commas?
3. Did you center and type the title in initial caps?
4. Did you double-space the entire report?

CULTURAL KALEIDOSCOPE

How people produce goods, what goods they produce, and how they buy and sell those goods are the main factors that affect a country's economy. Under a free enterprise system, such as in the United States, people make their own decisions concerning their businesses.

Canada's economy is also based on free enterprise. People in Canada run productive farms, mines, and businesses. However, the government plays an active role in the country's health care, broadcasting, and transportation systems.

One-Page Report **149**

CULTURAL KALEIDOSCOPE

Countries in the former Soviet Union are moving from a command economy toward a free enterprise system. To achieve free enterprise, these countries must do away with centralized planning and price controls, set up a modern banking system, and instill a sense of entrepreneurship among people.

Social Studies Connection

To generate interest in social studies, show a video related to civics, geography, economics, or history.

Project 8
One-Page Report

ASSESS—LEVEL 1

Purpose
Assess word processing skills by typing and formatting an original one-page report.

Time
One class period

Preparation
Students will need to select and research a social studies topic before they can begin Project 8. Make the following assignment several days before students are expected to complete Project 8:

Select any social studies topic, including civics, geography, economics, or history. Research your topic. Bring your notes to class and be prepared to write a one-page report—approximately 300 words.

Teaching Tip
Students who finish early should review and improve their report.

Trouble Shooting
Make sure students understand how to open a new word processing file. Provide individual help to students who are having difficulty.

Wrap Up
Have students review their printed document using **Check Your Understanding,** make corrections, and turn in their corrected reports.

If this is the last project for this class period, ask students to return computers and furniture to the appropriate conditions.

149

8.2 One-Page Report

FOCUS
Type and format a one-page business report. Practice using find and replace.

BELLRINGER
When students enter the room direct their attention to the assignment on the board:
  Read pages 150 and 151.

TEACH
Point out the differences between standard business format and MLA style for a one-page report. Use the illustration to highlight the margins, line spacing, title, subtitle, byline, and body.

One-Page Report

8.2

Goals
- Type and format a one-page report in standard business format
- Practice using find and replace

FORMATTING A ONE-PAGE REPORT

In this project, you will learn another acceptable format for reports. The report illustrated below is arranged in a standard business format. The biggest difference between this style and the MLA style is in the arrangement of the heading and title. Compare this illustration with the MLA style you learned on page 145.

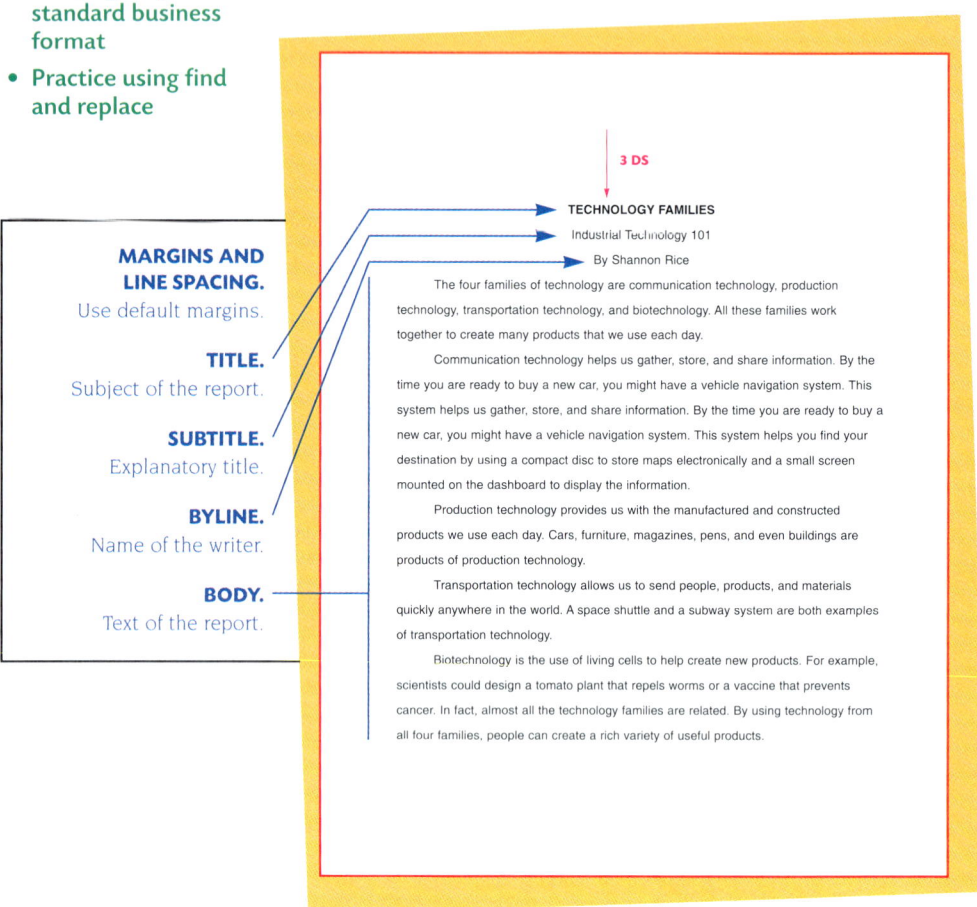

MARGINS AND LINE SPACING. Use default margins.

TITLE. Subject of the report.

SUBTITLE. Explanatory title.

BYLINE. Name of the writer.

BODY. Text of the report.

---

3 DS

TECHNOLOGY FAMILIES
Industrial Technology 101
By Shannon Rice

The four families of technology are communication technology, production technology, transportation technology, and biotechnology. All these families work together to create many products that we use each day.

Communication technology helps us gather, store, and share information. By the time you are ready to buy a new car, you might have a vehicle navigation system. This system helps us gather, store, and share information. By the time you are ready to buy a new car, you might have a vehicle navigation system. This system helps you find your destination by using a compact disc to store maps electronically and a small screen mounted on the dashboard to display the information.

Production technology provides us with the manufactured and constructed products we use each day. Cars, furniture, magazines, pens, and even buildings are products of production technology.

Transportation technology allows us to send people, products, and materials quickly anywhere in the world. A space shuttle and a subway system are both examples of transportation technology.

Biotechnology is the use of living cells to help create new products. For example, scientists could design a tomato plant that repels worms or a vaccine that prevents cancer. In fact, almost all the technology families are related. By using technology from all four families, people can create a rich variety of useful products.

---

150 Section 8 Reports

RESOURCES

Lesson Plan: LP50
Transparency Master: TM5

Transparency 3

CD-ROM: Reference Guide

Software: Research Files

This car has a vehicle navigation system, which displays information on a screen for the driver.

Find and replace is a very useful software feature that allows you to replace a word or group of words with a different word or group of words. In law offices, this feature is often used to replace names or addresses that are used over and over in standard contracts. If you were typing a document that uses the same word repeatedly, you could type an abbreviation for the word to save time. After you finish typing, you could find and replace the abbreviation with the full word. Think about how many different ways you might use find and replace.

Study the illustration on page 150 before beginning. Your finished report may look slightly different.

FORMATTING TIPS

- Double-space the entire report. **Note:** ↓ **3 DS** means change to double spacing, and press Return/Enter 3 times.
- Center the title; use bold and all caps.
- Center the subtitle and use initial caps.
- Center the byline and use initial caps.
- Double-space and indent paragraphs 0.5 inch.

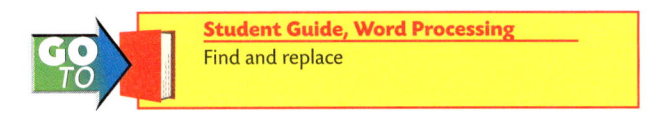

GO TO
Student Guide, Word Processing
Find and replace

One-Page Report **151**

One-Page Report

TEACH

Point out that it is important to include proper spacing. When using the find and replace feature, emphasize the importance of reviewing each change. Suggest that students always save a document before using the find and replace feature. Some examples of find and replace mishaps that can be avoided by matching whole words include:

Find	Replace	Result
her	him	thime
day	afternoon	Monafternoon
his	hers	herstory

Review formatting tips.

ASSESS

To assess understanding have students compare and contrast a one-page report using MLA style and a one-page report in standard business format.

CLOSE

Explain to students that they are now ready to type and format a simple, one-page report in standard business format. Refer to Projects 9, 10, and 11.

GO TO *Refer students to the appropriate section of the Student Guide.*

---

interNET CONNECTION

Have students use the Internet to access an encyclopedia. Using a web search engine, they might search for sites related to encyclopedias or reference books.

Examples of sites might include:

This Day in History   http://www.comptons.com
Cool School Tools   http://www.bham.lib.al.us/cooltools

Project 9
One-Page Report

PRACTICE—LEVEL 1

Purpose
Practice typing and formatting a one-page report and using the find and replace feature.

Time
Fifteen minutes

Preparation
Make sure software is loaded and data disks are available.

Teaching Tip
Have students who finish early open the file STWP009 and practice using the find and replace feature. Instruct students not to save their work.

Trouble Shooting
Make sure students understand how to save their work to their data disks. Provide individual help to students who are having difficulty.

Wrap Up
Have students review their document and make corrections.
  If this is the last project for this class period, ask students to return computers and furniture to the appropriate conditions.

Project 9
ONE-PAGE REPORT

Follow the steps below to complete the one-page report.

1. Open the file WP009 on your data disk.
2. Change the line spacing for the entire report to double.
3. Press Return/Enter 3 times to insert blank lines at the top of the document.
4. Type the title *Technology Families* centered in all caps and bold.
5. Center the subtitle and byline, and change them to initial caps.
6. Use the **find and replace** feature to replace all the occurrences of *tc* with *technology*.
7. Add the paragraph below to the end of the report:

> Biotechnology is the use of living cells to help create new products. For example, scientists could design a tomato plant that repels worms or a vaccine that prevents cancer. In fact, almost all the tc families are related. By using tc from all four families, people can create a rich variety of useful products.

8. Use the find and replace feature again to replace all the occurrences of *tc* with *technology*.
9. Save the document as STWP009 on your data disk.

Note: After each document is finished, always use your speller. Proofread carefully, preview the document, and make corrections as needed before printing. Then print and close the document. These directions will no longer be repeated for the remaining projects in this unit.

152 Section 8 Reports

To encourage interest in technology have students complete the following activities:
1. Read an article about technology in a newspaper or magazine.
2. Write a one-paragraph summary.
3. Discuss key points with classmates.

Project 10

ONE-PAGE REPORT

In this project, you will practice arranging another one-page report in standard business format. Refer to the information on pages 150 and 151 as needed.

1. Open the file WP010 on your data disk.
2. Change the line spacing for the entire report to double.
3. Press Return/Enter 3 times to insert blank lines at the top of the document.
4. Type the title *Global Villages* centered in all caps and bold.
5. Center the subtitle and byline, and change them to initial caps.
6. Use the find and replace feature to replace all the occurrences of *cs* with *computers*.
7. Add the paragraph below to the end of the report:

> While one group watched a video about Hispanic culture, the others were able to send and receive messages on their cs from some students and teachers in Spain. The best thing is that students on both ends learned about each other's countries together as a team. At the end of the class, they really felt like they were all part of a global village working together to make the world a better place.

8. Use the find and replace feature again to replace all the occurrences of *cs* with *computers*.
9. Save the document as STWP010 on your data disk.

Project 10
One-Page Report

APPLY—LEVEL 1

Purpose
Apply word processing skills by typing and formatting a one-page report and using the find and replace feature.

Time
Thirty minutes

Preparation
Make sure software is loaded and data disks are available.

Teaching Tip
Have students who finish early open the file STWP010 and practice the find and replace feature. Instruct students not to save their work.

Trouble Shooting
Make sure students understand how to save their work to their data disks. Provide individual help to students who are having difficulty.

Wrap Up
Have students review their document and make corrections.
   If this is the last project for this class period, ask students to return computers and furniture to the appropriate conditions.

To encourage interest in technology have students complete the following activities:

1. Continue to research the topic selected in the Technology Connection project on page 152. Use a reference book or CD-ROM.
2. Make notes about the selected topic.
3. Think about how to expand the single paragraph and notes to 300 words.

Project 11
One-Page Report

ASSESS—LEVEL 2

Purpose
Assess word processing skills by typing and formatting an original one-page report and using find and replace.

Time
One class period

Preparation
Students will need to select and research a topic related to computer technology before they can begin Project 11. The Technology Connections on pages 152 and 153 can be used as preparation for Project 11. Make the following assignment several days before students are expected to complete Project 11:

Select a topic related to computer technology. Research your topic. Bring your notes to class and be prepared to write a one-page report—approximately 300 words.

Teaching Tip
Students who finish early should review and improve their work.

Trouble Shooting
Make sure students understand how to open a new word processing file. Provide individual help to students who are having difficulty.

Wrap Up
Have students review their document using **Check Your Understanding.** Students should be able to answer "yes" to each question.

154

Project 11
ONE-PAGE REPORT

Practice using the word processing features you learned in Project 9 by typing an original, one-page report. Write your report about any topic related to computer technology.

1. Open a new word processing file.
2. Change the line spacing for the report to double.
3. Press Return/Enter 3 times to insert blank lines at the top of the document.
4. Center the title using all caps and bold.
5. Center the subtitle and byline using initial caps.
6. Identify a word or words you will use repeatedly in this report. Use an abbreviation for that word(s) as you type the report. Use find and replace to change all the occurrences of your abbreviation with the complete word(s).
7. Save the document as STWP011 on your data disk.

✓ Check Your Understanding

1. Did you press Return/Enter 3 times after changing to double spacing?
2. Did you center and type the title in bold and all caps?
3. Did you center the subtitle and byline in initial caps?

DID YOU KNOW?
Computers can be used to program houses to be "smart houses." A smart house is computerized to automatically switch lights on and off, lock and unlock doors, and adjust room temperature. Appliances such as coffee makers and washing machines can be programmed to turn on and off at specific times.

154 Section 8 Reports

Technology Connection

To encourage interest in technology have students present reports on computer technology. See Technology Connections on pages 152 and 153.

8.3 Title Page

Goal
- Type and format a title page

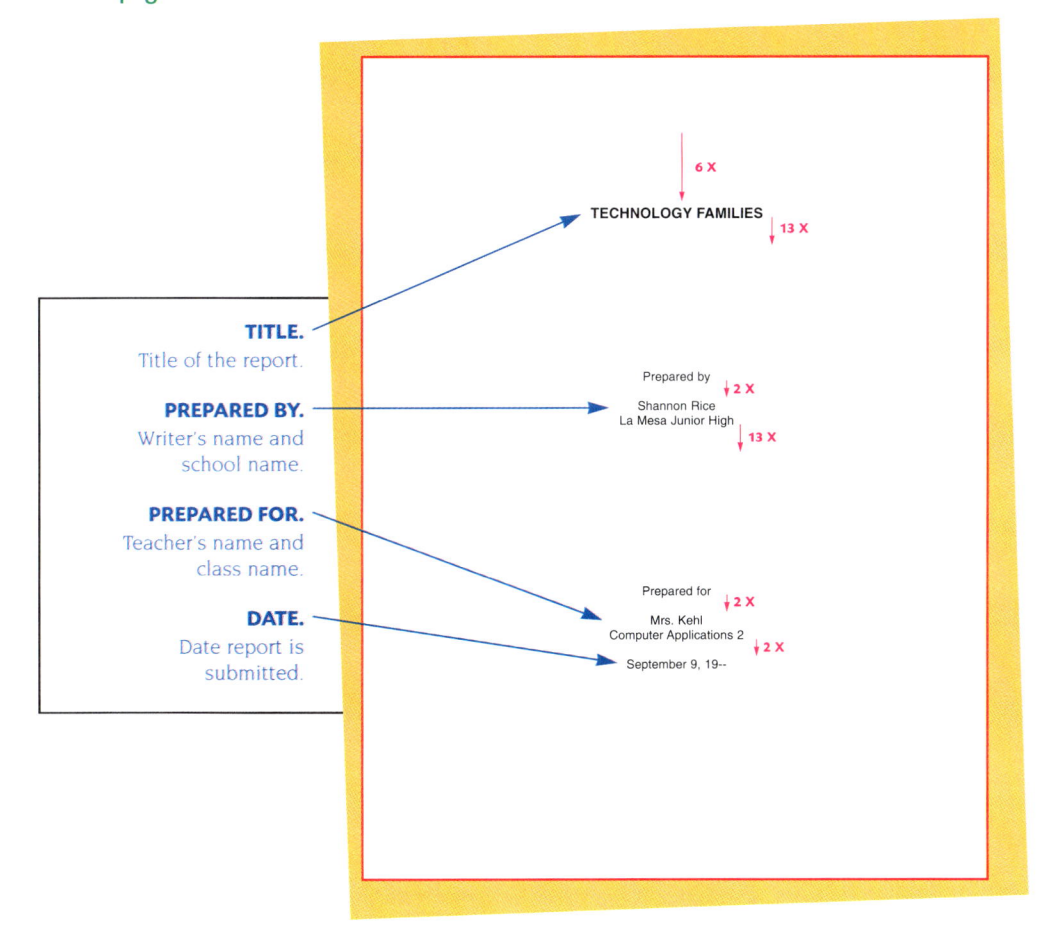

FORMATTING A TITLE PAGE

Title pages are used to give a report a formal, finished look. Title pages identify for the reader something that the report is about. Most title pages for school reports should include the information shown on the following illustration. Often graphics and borders are used to create interest. Your title page may look slightly different.

TITLE.
Title of the report.

PREPARED BY.
Writer's name and school name.

PREPARED FOR.
Teacher's name and class name.

DATE.
Date report is submitted.

Sample title page:

↓ 6 X

TECHNOLOGY FAMILIES

↓ 13 X

Prepared by
Shannon Rice
La Mesa Junior High

↓ 2 X
↓ 13 X

Prepared for
Mrs. Kehl
Computer Applications 2

↓ 2 X
↓ 2 X

September 9, 19--

Title Page **155**

8.3 Title Page

FOCUS
Type and format a title page.

BELLRINGER
When students enter the room, direct their attention to the assignment on the board:
   Read pages 155 and 156.

TEACH
Point out the four elements of a title page. Use the illustration to highlight alignment and line spacing.

RESOURCES
- Lesson Plan: LP50
  Transparency Master: TM6
- Transparency 4
- CD-ROM: Reference Guide
- Software: Research Files

155

Title Page

TEACH

Review formatting tips with students. Point out that borders and graphic images are sometimes used to enhance the appearance of a title page. Students will learn more about borders and graphics in Unit 4.

ASSESS

To assess understanding have students name and describe the four main components of a title page.

CLOSE

Explain to students that they are now ready to type and format a title page. Refer to Projects 12 and 13.

Your title page should include the following information:

- report title
- writer's name
- school name
- teacher's name
- class for which the report was prepared
- date the report was turned in

FORMATTING TIPS

Some important tips to remember include:

- Center the title using bold and all caps. Increase the font size to 2 points greater than the font size used for the body of the report.
- Type each item in the remaining sections on a separate line using initial caps.
- Center and evenly space the information on the page.

Biotechnology involves studying organisms. This process is done in a laboratory under sterile conditions.

Lesson Extension

Prepare several title pages deliberately omitting one or more of the elements shown in the illustration on page 155. Ask students to identify the missing elements.

Project 12

TITLE PAGE

Type and format a title page. Follow the directions.

1. Open a new word processing document.
2. Press Return/Enter 6 times to position the insertion point about 2 inches from the top of the page.

   Note: If your font is Geneva 12 pt., press Return/Enter 5 times.

3. Center the title *Technology Families* in all caps and bold. Increase the font size by 2 points.

   Note: It is easier to type the title page first and then go back, select the title, and apply formatting.

4. Press Return/Enter 13 times.

   Note: If your font is Geneva 12 pt., press Return/Enter 11 times.

5. Center *Prepared by* and press Return/Enter 2 times.
6. Center the writer's name, use your name as the writer, and your school name on separate single-spaced lines.
7. Press Return/Enter 13 times.

   Note: If your font is Geneva 12 pt., press Return/Enter 11 times.

8. Center *Prepared for*. Press Return/Enter 2 times. Center your teacher's name and the class name on separate single-spaced lines.
9. Press Return/Enter 2 times. Center the date, use today's date, of the report.
10. Save the document as STWP012 on your data disk.

Scientists from Russia and the United States are cooperating to share research information and technology. They plan to establish an international space station. American astronaut Shannon Lucid worked with two Russian cosmonauts aboard the Russian spaceship Mir. Together they gathered information about living in space.

Title Page **157**

Project 12
Title Page

PRACTICE—LEVEL 1

Purpose
Practice typing and formatting a title page.

Time
Fifteen minutes

Preparation
Make sure software is loaded and data disks are available.

Teaching Tip
Students who finish early should repeat the project. Provide the following additional instructions:

After completing steps 1–3, increase the font size of the title to 24 pt. Continue with steps 4–10.

Preview the document. After looking at preview, close the document without saving it.

Trouble Shooting
Make sure students are using the centering feature to center text.

Wrap Up
If this is the last project for this class period, ask students to return computers and furniture to the appropriate conditions.

To encourage interest in technology, initiate a class discussion about biotechnology. Sample discussion questions:

What do you know about biotechnology?

What is a vaccine and what kinds of vaccinations have you had?

In 1961 Russia was part of the Soviet Union when Soviet cosmonaut Yury Gagarin became the first man in space. This Soviet accomplishment prompted the United States to set a goal—a man on the moon by the end of the decade. Apollo 11 landed on the moon on July 20, 1969 and U.S. astronaut Neil Armstrong became the first man on the moon.

157

Project 13
Title Page

ASSESS—LEVEL 1

Purpose
Assess word processing skills by typing and formatting a title page.

Time
Fifteen minutes

Preparation
Make sure software is loaded and data disks are available.

Teaching Tip
Students who finish early should repeat the project. Provide the following additional instructions:

After completing steps 1–3, add the subtitle *breaking down barriers and building partnerships* using initial caps. Continue with steps 4–10.

Preview the document. After looking at preview, close the document without saving it.

Trouble Shooting
Provide individual help to students who are having difficulty.

Wrap Up
If this is the last project for this class period, ask students to return computers and furniture to the appropriate conditions.

Project 13
TITLE PAGE

Practice formatting another title page similar to the one for Project 12. Refer to the information on pages 155 and 156 if you need help.

1. Open a new word processing document.
2. Press Return/Enter 6 times to position the insertion point about 2 inches from the top of the page.

   Note: If your font is Geneva 12 pt., press Return/Enter 5 times.

3. Center the title *Global Villages* using all caps and bold. Increase the font size by 2 points.

   Note: It is easier to type the title page first and then go back, select the title, and apply formatting.

4. Press Return/Enter 13 times.

   Note: If your font is Geneva 12 pt., press Return/Enter 11 times.

5. Center *Prepared by* and press Return/Enter 2 times.
6. Center the writer's name, use your name as the writer, and your school name on separate single-spaced lines.
7. Press Return/Enter 13 times.

   Note: If your font is Geneva 12 pt., press Return/Enter 11 times.

8. Center *Prepared for*. Press Return/Enter 2 times. Center your teacher's name and the class name on separate single-spaced lines.
9. Press Return/Enter 2 times. Center the date, use today's date, of the report.
10. Save the document as STWP013 on your data disk.

158 Section 8 Reports

To encourage interest in technology, initiate a class discussion about global villages. Sample discussion questions:

What kinds of technology have made global villages possible?

What kinds of technology will be common in our homes and offices in 20 years?

8.4 Journal

FORMATTING A JOURNAL ENTRY

Occasionally, you will do some journal writing as a part of your projects. In this project, you will create and format a journal report so that you can easily edit and update your journal as you complete other projects. You will begin by creating a header. A **header** is information that appears at the top of each page in a document.

Study the illustration before beginning. Your finished journal report may look slightly different.

Goals
- Create and format a journal entry
- Create a header with a page number

HEADER. Information repeated at the top of each page.

ENTRY. Information related to an assignment.

> Journal of Mark Bardwell, Page 1
>
> Monday, September 2, 19--
> Using Headers
>
> I realize after working with headers that they are very useful. I can see how I might use the header feature in a long report or perhaps in a letter. Anytime I want information to be positioned at the top of a page and repeated on all pages, I will use the header feature.
>
> Tuesday, September 3, 19--

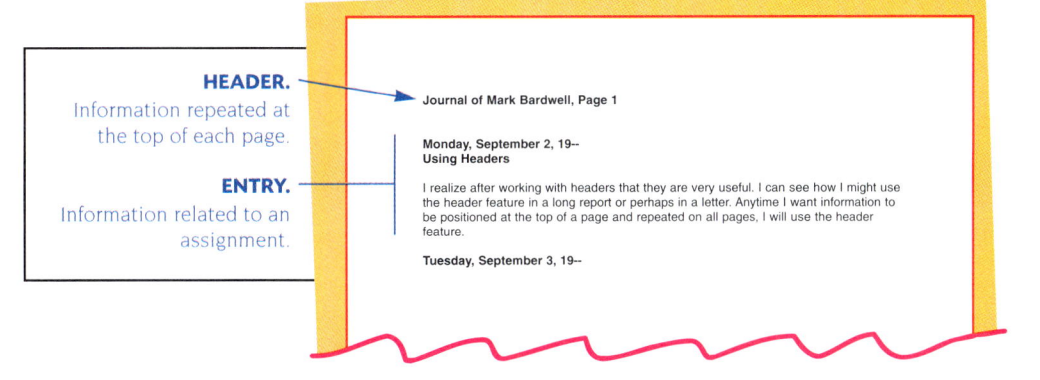

FORMATTING TIPS

- Type the header in bold and increase the font size by 2 points.
- Type the date in bold, and press Return/Enter 1 time.
- Type the subject of the entry in bold, and press Return/Enter 2 times.
- Type the journal entry, and press Return/Enter 2 times to begin the next entry.

GO TO
Student Guide, Word Processing
Header
Page number

Journal **159**

8.4 Journal

FOCUS
Create and format a journal entry. Create a header with a page number.

BELLRINGER
When students enter the room, direct their attention to the assignment on the board:
Read page 159.

TEACH
Explain that writing in a journal will be a continuing activity. Use the illustration on page 159 to highlight the header and the journal entry. Review formatting tips.

Explain the use of the page number command. Make sure students understand that using this command will result in automatic page numbering for the entire document.

ASSESS
To assess understanding have students name and describe the two main components of a journal entry.

CLOSE
Explain to students that they are now ready to create and format a journal entry. Refer to Project 14.

GO TO
Refer students to the appropriate section of the Student Guide.

RESOURCES
- Lesson Plan: LP51
  Multicultural Timing: MT1
  Transparency Master: TM7
- CD-ROM: Reference Guide
- Software: Research Files

159

Project 14
Journal

PRACTICE—LEVEL 1

Purpose
Practice creating a journal entry. New skills include creating a header and using the page number command.

Time
Thirty minutes

Preparation
Make sure software is loaded and data disks are available.

Teaching Tip
Students who finish early should repeat the project.

Trouble Shooting
Review journal entries to be sure students understand the header feature.

Wrap Up
If this is the last project for this class period, ask students to return computers and furniture to the appropriate conditions.

Language Link ANSWERS
1. received
2. Ninety, beginning
3. schedule
4. buses
5. column

Technology Connection

Project 14
JOURNAL

Follow the steps below to create a journal entry. Refer to the illustration on page 159.

1. Open a new word processing document.
2. Create a **header** for your journal.
3. In the header, type *Journal of,* your name, a comma, and *Page.* Use the **page number** command to add page numbering.
4. If necessary, change the alignment to left. Change the header font to bold and increase the font size to 14 points.
5. Insert 2 blank lines between your header and the first journal entry.
6. Type the rest of the journal entry following the formatting tips given on page 159. Use today's date and the subject *Using Headers.*
7. Type a journal entry describing how you might use the header feature in other types of documents.
8. Save the document as STWP014 on your data disk.

Language Link

Learn the correct spelling of frequently misspelled words.

buses	ninety	receive
beginning	schedule	column
access	different	health

✓ Check Your Learning

Correct the spelling of each misspelled word in the following sentences.

1. Ms. Taylor recieved the tickets for her trip to France.
2. Ninty people gathered for the begining of the race.
3. The skedule for last term was full.
4. We were surprised that the busses were still parked in the lot.
5. The final colum of the table is missing from the page.

Section 8 Reports

8.5 Multipage Report, MLA Style

Goals
- Type and format a multipage report, MLA style
- Practice citing sources in reports
- Create a header, MLA style

FORMATTING A MULTIPAGE REPORT, MLA STYLE

Multipage reports that follow the MLA style have a **header** that contains the writer's name and the page number. The format also includes a special way of citing the books, magazines, and other sources used to research a topic. Each **source** is briefly listed in a **citation** in the body of the report. A special reference directs the reader to a section at the end of the report called *Works Cited*. This section includes detailed information on the source. Study the illustration. Your report may look slightly different.

FORMATTING TIPS

- Use right alignment for the header, and position it 0.5 inch from the top of the page.
- Place a citation in parentheses at the end of the sentence before the final period.
- When dividing paragraphs between pages, follow these guidelines:
  - Leave at least 2 lines of the paragraph at the bottom of the page.
  - Carry at least 2 lines of the paragraph to the top of the next page.
  - If necessary, insert extra blank lines at the end of the first page to divide paragraphs correctly between pages.

> **DID YOU KNOW**
> A **widow** is the last line of a paragraph that appears at the top of a new page by itself. An **orphan** is the first line of a new paragraph that appears as the last line on a page. Use the widow and orphan protection feature of your software to avoid these problems.

RESOURCES
- Lesson Plan: LP51
- Transparency Master: TM8
- Transparency 5
- CD-ROM: Reference Guide
- Software: Research Files

8.5 Multipage Report, MLA Style

FOCUS
Type and format a multipage report, MLA style. Practice citing sources in reports. Create a header, MLA style.

BELLRINGER
When students enter the room, direct their attention to the assignment on the board:
Read pages 161–162.

TEACH
Explain that the header will appear on every page in the report even though it is only typed once. Remind students that they should use the page number command in the header so that the pages will be automatically numbered for the whole report. Use the illustration on page 162 to highlight the header and the page number.

Discuss the importance of citing sources in a report. Tell students that they will learn about footnotes and bibliographies later in this unit. Use the illustration on page 162 to point out the citation.

Review formatting tips.

> **DID YOU KNOW**
> Widows and orphans are examples of bad page breaks. Another example is when a subhead falls at the bottom of a page or column. As a general rule, at least two lines of text should follow a subhead. Most word processing software includes a feature that allows you to indicate a block of text that is not to be broken.

Multipage Report, MLA Style

TEACH

Point out the header and the margin associated with it. Also focus on the page numbers as they appear on the two pages illustrated. Point out the citation; note the lack of punctuation.

ASSESS

To assess understanding have students explain the purpose of headers and citations.

CLOSE

Explain to students that they are now ready to type and format a multipage report in MLA style. Refer to Projects 15, 16, and 17.

GO TO — Refer students to the appropriate section of the Student Guide.

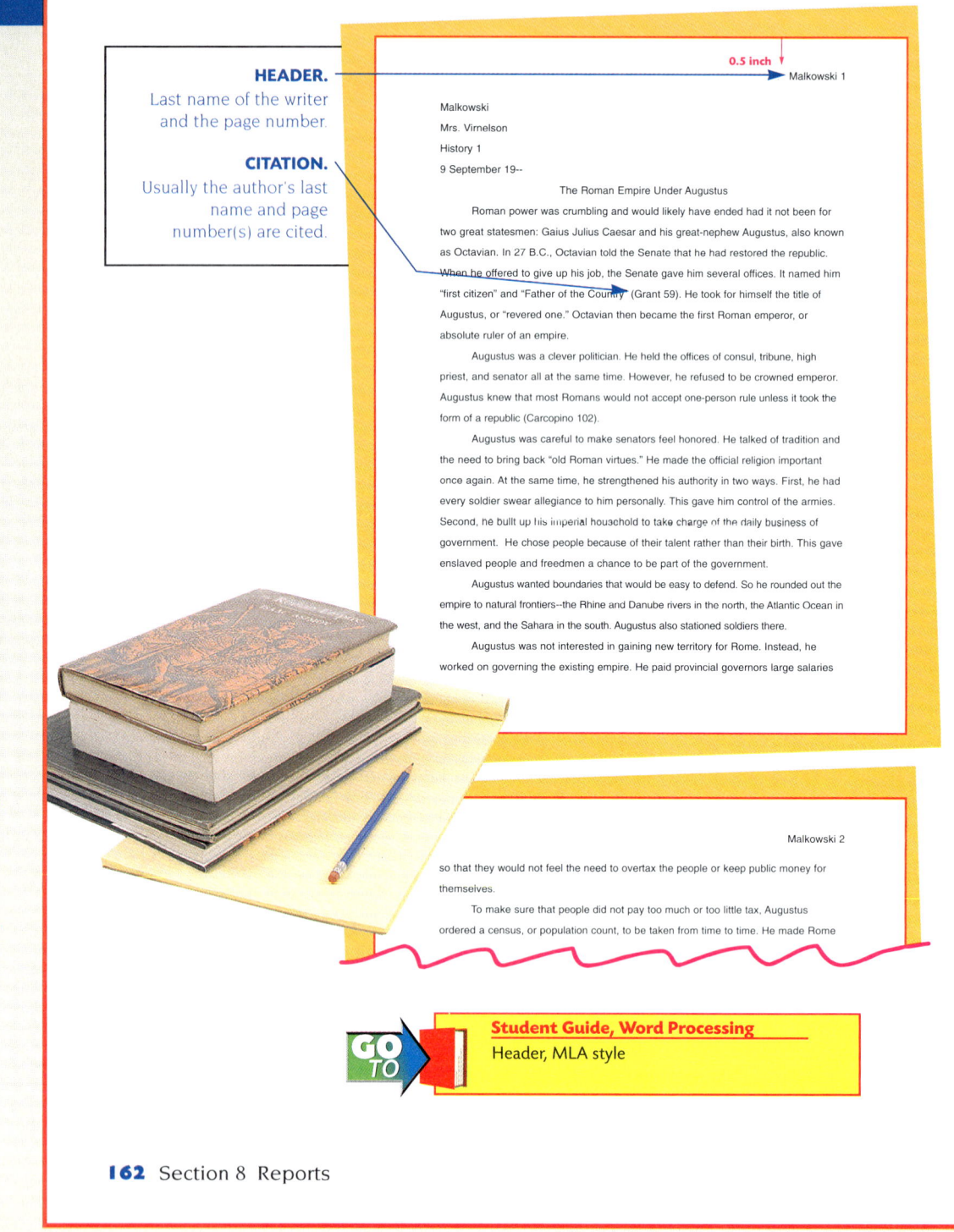

HEADER. Last name of the writer and the page number.

CITATION. Usually the author's last name and page number(s) are cited.

0.5 inch
Malkowski 1

Malkowski
Mrs. Virnelson
History 1
9 September 19--

                    The Roman Empire Under Augustus

    Roman power was crumbling and would likely have ended had it not been for two great statesmen: Gaius Julius Caesar and his great-nephew Augustus, also known as Octavian. In 27 B.C., Octavian told the Senate that he had restored the republic. When he offered to give up his job, the Senate gave him several offices. It named him "first citizen" and "Father of the Country" (Grant 59). He took for himself the title of Augustus, or "revered one." Octavian then became the first Roman emperor, or absolute ruler of an empire.

    Augustus was a clever politician. He held the offices of consul, tribune, high priest, and senator all at the same time. However, he refused to be crowned emperor. Augustus knew that most Romans would not accept one-person rule unless it took the form of a republic (Carcopino 102).

    Augustus was careful to make senators feel honored. He talked of tradition and the need to bring back "old Roman virtues." He made the official religion important once again. At the same time, he strengthened his authority in two ways. First, he had every soldier swear allegiance to him personally. This gave him control of the armies. Second, he built up his imperial household to take charge of the daily business of government. He chose people because of their talent rather than their birth. This gave enslaved people and freedmen a chance to be part of the government.

    Augustus wanted boundaries that would be easy to defend. So he rounded out the empire to natural frontiers--the Rhine and Danube rivers in the north, the Atlantic Ocean in the west, and the Sahara in the south. Augustus also stationed soldiers there.

    Augustus was not interested in gaining new territory for Rome. Instead, he worked on governing the existing empire. He paid provincial governors large salaries

Malkowski 2

so that they would not feel the need to overtax the people or keep public money for themselves.

    To make sure that people did not pay too much or too little tax, Augustus ordered a census, or population count, to be taken from time to time. He made Rome

GO TO — Student Guide, Word Processing
Header, MLA style

162   Section 8   Reports

Lesson Extension

Demonstrate the feature that allows you to keep blocks of text together.

interNET CONNECTION

Have students use the Internet to learn more about Italy. Using a web search engine they might search for sites related to Italy or Rome.

Web site example:
Italy   http://www.mi.cnr.it/woi

Project 15

Social Studies Connection

MULTIPAGE REPORT, MLA STYLE

Follow the steps below to complete a multipage report.

1. Open the file WP015 on your data disk.
2. Change the line spacing for the report to double.
3. Create a **header, MLA style,** for the report.
4. The writer's name is *Malkowski*.
5. Edit the year in the heading to the current year.
6. Add the paragraphs below to the end of the report:

> All kinds of animals were used in the public games. Some animals pulled chariots or performed tricks. Most fought one another or gladiators. Sometimes as many as 5,000 wild animals were killed in a single day. In some cases, whole animal species such as the Mesopotamian lion and the North African elephants were eventually wiped out.
>
> The Pax Romana ended after about 200 years. By 476 A.D., there was no empire left. Instead, much of western Europe was a patchwork of Germanic kingdoms. The Roman Empire fell for many reasons. A large reason was that emperors had no written rule about who was to inherit the throne upon an emperor's death. Economic troubles and foreign enemies also led to its downfall in the end.

7. Save the document as STWP015 on your data disk.

Project 15: Multipage Report, MLA Style

PRACTICE—LEVEL 1

Purpose
Practice creating a multipage report using MLA style.

Time
Thirty minutes

Preparation
Make sure software is loaded and data disks are available.

Teaching Tip
Instruct students to use the preview feature to see the multiple pages of the report including the automatic page numbering.

Encourage students to spell check and proofread their work.

Trouble Shooting
Check to make sure students are using the header feature.

Wrap Up
If this is the last project for this class period, ask students to return computers and furniture to the appropriate conditions.

Social Studies Connection

Initiate a class discussion about what was happening in other parts of the world around the time of Pax Romana. Examples include:

The Temple of the Sun at Teotihuacán, Mexico, was built between A.D. 50 and 200.

The Ajanta caves in east central India, in Maharashtra State (formerly Hyderabad), were painted between 200 B.C. and A.D. 650.

Anastasius I was born in Dyrrhachium (now Durrës, Albania) around the year A.D. 430. He ruled the Byzantine Empire from 491 until his death in 518.

Jutes, an early Germanic tribe of Denmark or northern Germany, conquered southeastern Britain between A.D. 400 and 500.

Source: *Microsoft Encarta 96 Encyclopedia*, Microsoft Corporation, 1993–1995.

Project 16
Multipage Report, MLA Style

APPLY—LEVEL 1

Purpose
Apply word processing skills by creating a multipage report using MLA style.

Time
Thirty minutes

Preparation
Make sure software is loaded and data disks are available.

Teaching Tip
Instruct students to use the preview feature to see the multiple pages of the report including the automatic page numbering.
   Encourage students to spell check and proofread their work.

Trouble Shooting
Provide individual help to students who are having difficulty with widows and orphans.

Wrap Up
Ask students if their report contained a widow or an orphan. Ask students how they corrected the problem.

DID YOU KNOW
A jury that hears evidence and returns a verdict in either a civil or criminal trial is a petit jury, also called a trial jury. A grand jury is impaneled to determine if there is sufficient evidence to warrant a trial of a person accused of a crime. If a grand jury finds sufficient evidence to warrant a trial, they return an indictment or a true bill.

Project 16
Social Studies Connection
MULTIPAGE REPORT, MLA STYLE

Practice arranging another multipage report that follows the MLA style. Refer to the illustration on page 162 as often as needed.

1. Open the file WP016 on your data disk.
2. Change the line spacing for the report to double.
3. Create a header, MLA style, for the report. The writer's name is *Fujimoto*.
4. Edit the year in the heading to the current year.
5. Add the paragraphs below to the end of the report:

> Sometimes a jury cannot agree on a verdict. When that happens, the judge declares a hung jury and rules the trial a mistrial. With a mistrial the prosecution must decide whether to drop the charges or ask for a retrial.
>
> When a defendant is found guilty, the judge sets a court date for sentencing. In some cases a jury recommends a sentence. Most often, however, the judge determines the sentence after considering the defendant's family situation, previous criminal record, employment status, and other relevant information.

DID YOU KNOW
In the United States, people 18 years of age or older are eligible to serve on a jury. Jurors are chosen by random. Your name is selected and you receive a notice to appear in court at a specific time and date. Depending on the number of cases to be heard, you may or may not be needed to serve on a jury.

6. Save the document as STWP016 on your data disk.

164 Section 8 Reports

Social Studies Connection
To encourage interest in social studies, initiate a class discussion about landmark court cases. Examples include:
   Brown v. Board of Education *(1954)*
   Miranda v. Arizona *(1966)*
   Scopes trial *(1925)*

164

Social Studies Connection

Project 17

MULTIPAGE REPORT, MLA STYLE

Practice arranging another multipage report that follows the MLA style by typing an original report. Write your report about any topic related to social studies. Choose a topic based on your own research so that you can cite the sources as needed. When citing your sources, type the author's name followed by the page number(s) in parentheses at the end of the sentence inside the period. Refer to the illustration on page 162 as often as needed.

1. Open a new word processing file.
2. Change the line spacing to double.
3. Create a header, MLA style, for the report.
4. Save the document as STWP017 on your data disk.

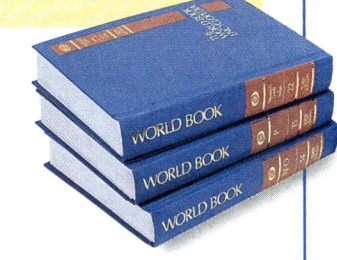

✓ Check Your Understanding

1. Did you include a header with your last name followed by the page number right aligned?
2. Did you use a citation enclosed in parentheses with the author's last name and a page number at the end of the sentence?
3. Did you check to be sure you didn't leave any widows or orphans?

When you research a report, cite the sources of your research. Make careful notes so that your information will be correct.

Multipage Report, MLA Style **165**

Social Studies Connection

Introduce students to reference material they can use in writing a report on a social studies topic. Check your school library and the public library for appropriate material. Examples to consider include:

Geography	Travel magazines and guidebooks
Civics	Government publications
History	Biographies
Economics	Business magazines

Project 17
Multipage Report, MLA Style

ASSESS—LEVEL 2

Purpose
Assess word processing skills by creating a multipage report using MLA style.

Time
One class period

Preparation
Students will need to select and research a social studies topic before they can begin Project 17. They might want to expand the report they completed for Project 8. Make the following assignment several days before students are expected to complete Project 17:

Select any social studies topic, including civics, geography, economics, or history. Research your topic. Bring your notes to class and be prepared to write a multipage report—approximately 500 words. You may expand the report you wrote for Project 8.

Teaching Tip
Instruct students to use the preview feature to see the multiple pages of the report including the automatic page numbering.

Encourage students to spell check and proofread their work.

Trouble Shooting
Provide individual help to students who are having difficulty.

Wrap Up
Have students review their document using **Check Your Understanding.** Have students make corrections.

8.6 Multipage Bound Report

FOCUS
Type and format side headings. Type and format a multipage bound report. Change margins.

BELLRINGER
When students enter the room, direct their attention to the assignment on the board:
　　Read pages 166–167.

TEACH
Demonstrate the use of headings using magazines, newsletters, or newspapers. Point out how the headings focus on key points.
　　Demonstrate the use of a wider left margin by showing students a bound report.

8.6 Multipage Bound Report

FORMATTING A MULTIPAGE BOUND REPORT WITH SIDE HEADINGS

Goals
- Type and format side headings
- Type and format multipage bound reports with side headings
- Practice changing margins

Side headings are the major subdivisions or major topics of a report. Sometimes it is helpful to include side headings in a report so that the main ideas are emphasized.

Side headings are also useful if your report requires a table of contents or an outline. Main points in the outline become side headings in the report. Side headings in the report become entries in the table of contents.

Often a multipage report is bound or stapled on the left side of the pages. You will want to leave a larger left margin to allow room for the binding.

Study the illustration on page 167. Your finished report may look slightly different.

Cecilia is using the computer to locate sources for her report.

166　Section 8　Reports

RESOURCES

- Lesson Plan: LP52
  Transparency Master: TM9
- Transparency 6
- CD-ROM: Reference Guide
- Software: Research Files

Multipage Bound Report

Sample Report Illustration

WRITING A REPORT
Grammar and Composition
By Cecilia Vigil

Expository writing includes writing to compare and contrast, give directions, and give information in a report. The goal of any expository writing is to share knowledge and information with others. Good expository writing follows a series of carefully planned steps. In writing a report, you will have the best chance for success if you will follow a plan of action carefully and consistently.

CHOOSE A TOPIC

You will do a better job of writing and it will be easier for you if you choose a topic that interests you. You also need to choose a topic that is the right size. A topic that is too broad will have too much information for a short report. A topic that is too narrow will not give you enough to write about in a longer report.

GATHER INFORMATION

Reports are built on information--facts, statistics, examples--so you'll need to do some research. A good place to begin looking is the library. There you can find encyclopedias and other reference books to get you started. These materials can help you focus your search for information. They can also help you to ask questions about your topic and lead you to other resources. You may find books, magazine articles, and videos about your topic.

TAKE NOTES

As you read, think about what is important and worth remembering. Take notes, being sure to jot down the title and author of each source. Do not just copy information word for word. Think about what you're reading and write your notes in your own words. If you can use a computer with a word processing program, you will find it is much easier to edit and reorganize your thoughts as

Callouts: 3 DS (top margin); 1.5 inches (left margin); SIDE HEADINGS. Major subdivisions of the report.

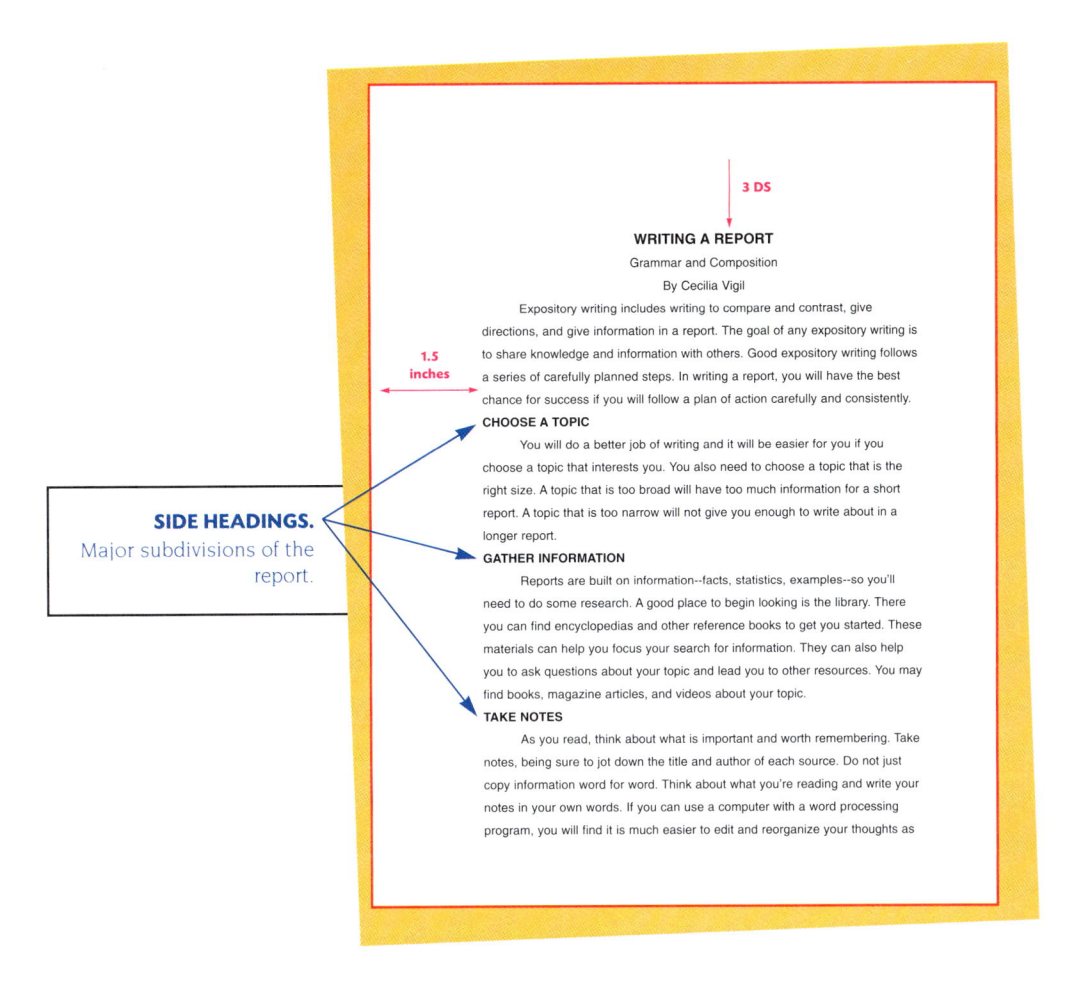

FORMATTING TIPS

- Set the left margin at 1.5 inches. Use the default settings for other margins.
- Type each subheading at the left margin on a line by itself, using bold and all caps.

GO TO: Student Guide, Word Processing — Margin

TEACH
Use the illustration on page 167 to highlight side headings. Review formatting tips.

ASSESS
To assess understanding have students explain the purpose of side headings.

CLOSE
Explain to students that they are now ready to type and format a multipage bound report with side headings. Refer to Projects 18, 19, and 20.

GO TO: Refer students to the appropriate section of the Student Guide.

Project 18
Multipage Bound Report

PRACTICE—LEVEL 1

Purpose
Practice typing and formatting a multipage report. New skills include changing margins and suppressing the header on the first page.

Time
Thirty minutes

Preparation
No special preparation required.

Teaching Tip
Make sure students understand how to suppress the header on the first page. Instruct students to use preview to make sure the header does not appear on the first page.

Encourage students to spell check and proofread their work.

Students who finish early should repeat the project.

Trouble Shooting
Provide individual help to students who are having difficulty suppressing the header on the first page.

Wrap Up
If this is the last project for this class period, ask students to return computers and furniture to the appropriate conditions.

Project 18
Language Arts Connection
MULTIPAGE BOUND REPORTS WITH SIDE HEADINGS

Type and format a multipage bound report by following these steps. Refer to the information on pages 166 and 167 if you need help.

1. Open the file WP018 on your data disk.
2. Change the left **margin** of the document to 1.5 inches.
3. Change the line spacing to double.
4. Position the heading about 2 inches from the top of the page. Center the lines in the heading, and bold the title.
5. Insert a header with a right-aligned page number that will not be seen on the first page.
6. Insert the following side headings typed in bold and all caps in front of the paragraphs that begin with a bold **X**: *choose a topic, gather information, take notes, organize the information, write a draft,* and *revise and edit the draft.*
7. Delete the **X** from the start of the paragraphs after you have inserted the side headings.
8. Add the paragraphs below to the end of the report:

> If you can set your work aside for a day or two, when you return to do the final editing, you will suddenly notice things that you missed before. Check for organization of thoughts first. Finally, check for grammar, punctuation, spelling, and format.
>
> If you follow all these steps, you will find that your final report is thoughtful, well organized, and easy to understand. Evaluate your work and think about what you learned in the process. You will be much better prepared for your next writing assignment because of your hard work on this report.

9. Save the document as STWP018 on your data disk.

Language Arts Connection

To encourage interest in language arts, initiate a discussion about words that sound alike but have different meanings. Ask students for examples. Ask students if they have any tricks for remembering when to use a specific word. Sample tricks include:

principle or principal
The princi**pal** is my **pal**.

right or write
P**e**n, p**e**ncil, and writ**e** all have an **e**.

stationary or stationery
Pap**er** and station**er**y have **er** in them.

Project 19

MULTIPAGE BOUND REPORTS WITH SIDE HEADINGS

Practice arranging another multipage bound report with side headings. Refer to the information and illustration on pages 166 and 167.

1. Open the file WP019 on your data disk.
2. Change the left margin of the document to 1.5 inches.
3. Change the line spacing to double.
4. Position the heading, center the lines, and bold the title.
5. Insert a header with a right-aligned page number that will not be seen on the first page.
6. Insert the following side headings typed in bold and all caps in front of the paragraphs that begin with a bold **X**: *choosing publicity, capturing an audience, using words, using messages and images,* and *planning posters.*
7. Delete the **X** from the start of the paragraphs after you have inserted the side headings.
8. Add the paragraphs below to the end of the report:

> Keeping your purpose in mind will help you decide what information to include on your poster. A poster announcing a lost pet, for example, needs certain information. You will want to have your pet's name, a picture or description, and any other important characteristics, such as whether or not it answers to its name or likes strangers. In addition, be sure to provide your own name and phone number.
>
> Publicity writing can be fun and effective. The next time you see a poster or hear an announcement, think about why it captured your interest or why it didn't. This will help you the next time you are in charge of publicity writing.

9. Save the document as STWP019 on your data disk.

Project 19 Multipage Bound Report

APPLY—LEVEL 1

Purpose
Apply word processing skills by typing and formatting a multipage report. New skills include changing margins and suppressing the header on the first page.

Time
Thirty minutes

Preparation
No special preparation required.

Teaching Tip
Make sure students understand how to suppress the header on the first page. Instruct students to use preview to make sure the header does not appear on the first page.

Encourage students to spell check and proofread their work.

Students who finish early should repeat the project.

Trouble Shooting
Make sure students are using the header feature to insert page numbers.

Wrap Up
If this is the last project for this class period, ask students to return computers and furniture to the appropriate conditions.

Language Arts Connection

To encourage interest in language arts, initiate a discussion about publicity writing and advertising. Point out how publicity writing and advertising do not always follow the standard grammar and punctuation rules. Use printed advertisements from magazines and newspapers to illustrate your point. Some things to look for include: unusual use of capitalization, sentence fragments, and lack of punctuation.

Project 20
Multipage Bound Report

ASSESS—LEVEL 2

Purpose
Assess word processing skills by typing and formatting a multipage report. New skills include changing margins and suppressing the header on the first page.

Time
One class period

Preparation
Students will need to select a topic related to language arts before they can begin Project 20. Refer to the **In Your Journal** box on page 170. Make the following assignment several days before students are expected to complete Project 20:

Select any topic related to language arts. Read the **In Your Journal** box on page 170. Be prepared to write a multipage report including side headings. Your report should be approximately 500 words.

Teaching Tip
Instruct students to use the preview feature to see the multiple pages of the report including the automatic page numbering.

Trouble Shooting
Check to see that students have selected appropriate topics. Help students to expand on the ideas they have written in order to reach 500 words.

Wrap Up
Have students review their document using **Check Your Understanding** and make corrections.

170

Project 20

MULTIPAGE BOUND REPORT WITH SIDE HEADINGS

Practice using the word processing features you learned in Project 18 by typing an original, multipage bound report with side headings. Write your report about any topic related to language arts. Remember to choose a topic that has several clear subtopics so that it will be easier to write the report side headings.

1. Open a new word processing file.
2. Change the left margin of the document to 1.5 inches.
3. Change the line spacing to double.
4. Position the heading. Center the lines in the heading, and bold the title.
5. Insert a header with a right-aligned page number that will not be seen on the first page.
6. Type the body of the report inserting side headings typed in bold and all caps.
7. Save the document as STWP020 on your data disk.

In Your Journal

Explore ideas for a multipage report about a topic related to language arts. Think about a topic you would like to know more about. Do you have a favorite writer? What kinds of stories does this person write? How long has this person been a writer? Ask yourself questions about your topic. Write answers to your questions in your journal. Use your answers as the starting point for your report.

✓ Check Your Understanding

1. Did you set the left margin at 1.5 inches for a bound report?
2. Did you add a header with a right-aligned page number that is not seen on the first page?
3. Did you type side headings at the left margin in bold and all caps?

170 Section 8 Reports

Give students the opportunity to share their reports. Have students exchange papers and read another student's report.

In Your Journal

Help students think of language arts topics. Examples include:

Reading for Fun: Include favorite books and authors.

Everyday Language Arts: Focus on how language arts skills are used.

Careers: Identify careers where language arts skills are important.

Bulleted List

8.7

Goal
- Format a bulleted list

CREATING A BULLETED LIST

When you are making a list of any type, the items in your list will be easier to read if you use bullets or numbers to call attention to each item. Use bullets rather than numbers for the list when the items do not need to be in a specific order.

Each item in a bulleted list begins with a bullet symbol and is followed by an indent. If the item in the list wraps around to a second line, the text in both lines should be indented to the same point. Bullets can be added in either of the two ways described below.

- Issue the software command to insert bullets automatically as you type.
- Type a list at the left margin. Select the text and apply the bullet software feature to your list.

Study the illustration. Your bulleted list may look slightly different.

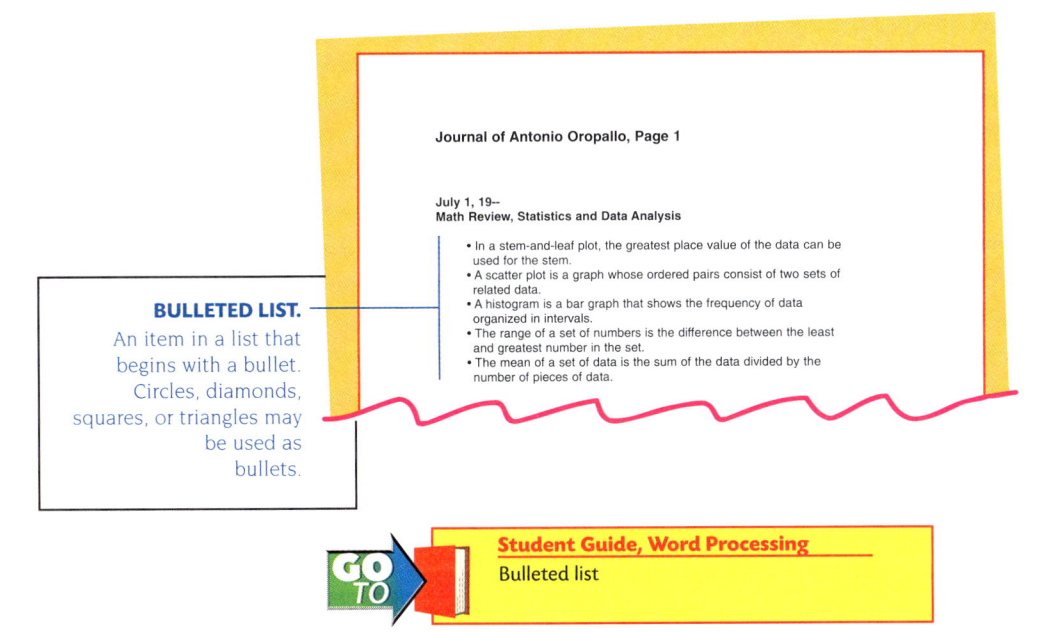

BULLETED LIST. An item in a list that begins with a bullet. Circles, diamonds, squares, or triangles may be used as bullets.

Journal of Antonio Oropallo, Page 1

July 1, 19--
Math Review, Statistics and Data Analysis

- In a stem-and-leaf plot, the greatest place value of the data can be used for the stem.
- A scatter plot is a graph whose ordered pairs consist of two sets of related data.
- A histogram is a bar graph that shows the frequency of data organized in intervals.
- The range of a set of numbers is the difference between the least and greatest number in the set.
- The mean of a set of data is the sum of the data divided by the number of pieces of data.

GO TO
Student Guide, Word Processing
Bulleted list

8.7 Bulleted List

FOCUS
Format a bulleted list.

BELLRINGER
When students enter the room, direct their attention to the assignment on the board:
Read page 171.

TEACH
Use the illustration on page 171 to highlight a bulleted list. Point out the bullets and the hanging indent. Use brochures and advertisements to illustrate bulleted lists using a variety of bullets.

ASSESS
To assess understanding have students provide examples of when they might use a bulleted list.

CLOSE
Explain to students that they are now ready to format a bulleted list. Refer to Projects 21 and 23.

GO TO *Refer students to the appropriate section of the Student Guide.*

RESOURCES

- Lesson Plan: LP52
  Transparency Master: TM10
- CD-ROM: Reference Guide
- Software: Research Files

Project 21
Bulleted List

PRACTICE—LEVEL 1

Purpose
Practice creating a bulleted list.

Time
Thirty minutes

Preparation
No special preparation required.

Teaching Tip
Students who finish early should repeat the project using a different symbol for the bullets.

Trouble Shooting
Provide individual help to students who are having difficulty.

Wrap Up
If this is the last project for this class period, ask students to return computers and furniture to the appropriate conditions.

In Your Journal

Help students think of the kinds of data that can be collected with the instruments listed. Possible responses include:

Calculator
- test grades
- average grade for class
- grade point average

Scales
- weight of vegetables
- weight of letter or package
- weight of patient

Clock
- current time
- length of a speech
- amount of time left in school day

172

Project 21

BULLETED LIST

Create a bulleted list in a journal entry by completing the following steps.

1. Open the file WP021 on your data disk.
2. Change the list in the second journal entry to a **bulleted list.**
3. Practice removing the bullets from the lists and adding them to the lists.
4. Add another journal entry using today's date and the subject *Bulleted List Review.*
5. Type a journal entry as a bulleted list describing what you have learned about creating bulleted lists.
6. Save the document as STWP021 on your data disk.

In Your Journal

You can collect data using many kinds of instruments. Make a list of these categories: calculator, scales, clock. Under each category, list three kinds of data you could collect using each of the instruments. Insert bullets to show each entry.

172 Section 8 Reports

8.8 Numbered List

Goal
- Format a numbered list

CREATING A NUMBERED LIST

When making a list in which the order of information is important, use a numbered list rather than a bulleted list to call attention to each item.

Each item in a numbered list begins with a number and is followed by an indent. If the item in the list wraps around to a second line, the text in both lines should be indented to the same point.

Study the illustration. Your numbered list may look slightly different.

Journal of Your Name, Page 1

January 15, 19--
Database Homework

1. How would you go about creating a good database for a comic book collection?
2. What are the benefits of a computerized database?
3. In what businesses might database be helpful?
4. What are the benefits to both the business and consumer when a business uses a database for records?
5. What kinds of information are available on a database?

NUMBERED LIST. An item in a list that begins with a number.

In Your Journal

Make a numbered list of the ten places that you would most like to visit, the ten people you would most like to meet, or your ten favorite songs. Number your list so that the most important item is number one, followed by the other items in order of their importance.

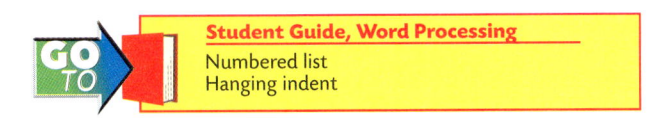

GO TO
Student Guide, Word Processing
Numbered list
Hanging indent

8.8 Numbered List

FOCUS
Format a numbered list.

BELLRINGER
When students enter the room, direct their attention to the assignment on the board:
Read page 173.

TEACH
Use the illustration on page 173 to highlight a numbered list. Point out the numbers and the hanging indent.

Use brochures and advertisements to illustrate numbered lists. Provide examples of how numbers appear in numbered lists.

ASSESS
To assess understanding have students provide examples of when they might use a numbered list.

CLOSE
Explain to students that they are now ready to format a numbered list. Refer to Project 22.

GO TO *Refer students to the appropriate section of the Student Guide.*

RESOURCES

Lesson Plan: LP53
Multicultural Timing: MT2
Transparency Master: TM11

CD-ROM: Reference Guide

Software: Research Files

Project 22
Numbered List

PRACTICE—LEVEL 1

Purpose
Practice creating a numbered list.

Time
Thirty minutes

Preparation
No special preparation required.

Teaching Tip
Students who finish early should repeat the project using Roman numerals.

Trouble Shooting
Provide individual help to students who are having difficulty.

Wrap Up
Have students review their document using **Check Your Understanding.** Have students make corrections.

If this is the last project for this class period, ask students to return computers and furniture to the appropriate conditions.

Language Link

ANSWERS
1. poems appears; appear
2. I reads; read
3. people enjoys; enjoy
4. prize have; has
5. Correct as written.

Project 22

NUMBERED LIST

Follow the steps below to make a numbered list in a journal entry. Refer to the illustration on page 173.

1. Open the file WP022 on your data disk.
2. Change the name in the header to your name.
3. Change the list in the second journal entry to a **numbered list** using either the numbered list feature or the **hanging indent** feature.
4. Add a third journal entry using today's date and the subject *Steps to Create a Numbered List*.
5. Type a journal entry as a numbered list describing what you have learned about creating numbered lists.
6. Save the document as STWP022 on your data disk.

Language Link

A singular subject requires a singular verb.
A plural subject requires a plural verb.

A **scout enjoys** hiking.   **Scouts enjoy** hiking.
(sing sing)   (pl pl)

He reads the book.   **They read** the books.
(sing sing)   (pl pl)

✓ Check Your Learning

For each sentence, first identify the subject and verb. Then, if the subject and verb do not agree, change the verb so that subject and verb agree.

1. Bradstreet's poems appears first in the book.
2. I reads more books than Mary.
3. Many people enjoys her poems.
4. The small prize have the most appeal.
5. The house was destroyed by fire.

174 Section 8 Reports

Technology Connection

To encourage interest in technology provide the following terms:

communications	font	header	point size
database	hanging indent	modem	spreadsheet
desktop publishing	hard drive	mouse	trackball

Instruct students to group terms under the one of the following headings: Computer Hardware, Computer Software, and Word Processing Terms.
Format each group of terms as a numbered or bulleted list.

Project 23
Building Your Portfolio

In this portfolio project, you will review word processing features from Section 8. You will format a multipage report with a title page, header, side headings, and a bulleted list. The title page will be created as a separate document. If you need to review any formatting or software features, refer to previous projects as often as needed.

Study the illustrations. Your finished project may look slightly different.

(continued on next page)

Project 23
Building Your Portfolio

ASSESS—LEVEL 2

Purpose
Assess word processing skills by typing and formatting a multipage report and title page. Specific skills to be assessed include: changing alignment, changing line spacing, inserting a header, using the page numbering feature, inserting side headings, and formatting a bulleted list.

Time
One class period

Preparation
No special preparation required.

Teaching Tip
Remind students to review their work. Do not specify using the speller or proof-reading.

Students who finish early should repeat the project.

Trouble Shooting
Provide individual help to students who are having difficulty with specific formatting or software features.

Wrap Up
Ask students to return computers and furniture to the appropriate conditions.

Science Connection

Computers play an increasingly important role in weather forecasting. Invite a meteorologist to speak to your class. This can be done at school or as part of a field trip. Be sure to let the speaker know that your students are interested in learning about the various computer programs used in forecasting weather and in communicating with the public. Contact the National Weather Service office in your area or a local television station for assistance.

Building Your Portfolio

Project 23 (continued)
Building Your Portfolio

NOW TRY THIS

1. Open a new document.
2. Type the title page following the directions for a title page in Project 8. The title is *Severe Weather*. Use your name as the writer, your school's name, your teacher's name, your science class name, and today's date.
3. Save the document as STWP023A on your data disk.
4. Open the file WP023B on your data disk.
5. Change the line spacing in the report to double.
6. Bold the title and type it in all caps.
7. Center the title, subtitle, and byline—use your name in the byline.
8. Insert a header with a right-aligned page number that will not be seen on the first page.
9. Insert the following side headings in bold and all caps in order in front of the paragraphs that are marked with an **X**: *air masses, thunderstorms, tornadoes,* and *hurricanes*.

(continued on next page)

176 Section 8 Reports

interNET CONNECTION

Have students use the Internet to learn more about weather. Using a web search engine, they might search for sites related to weather, weather forecast, or meteorology.

Example of a Web site:
The Weather Processor
http://wxp.atms.purdue.edu

176

Building Your Portfolio

10. Add the paragraphs below to the end of the report. Use the bullet feature on the 4 items in the list beginning with *thermometers* and ending with *computers*.

> The largest storm that occurs on earth is a hurricane. A hurricane is a very large, swirling, low pressure system that forms over tropical oceans. For a storm to be called a hurricane, it must have winds that blow at least 120 kilometers per hour. Hurricanes may be many kilometers in diameter. Because they form over large bodies of water and have a steady supply of energy, they may go on for many days until they reach land. Hurricanes weaken when they strike land because they no longer receive energy from the warm water.
>
> Hurricanes form over warm, tropical oceans. A low pressure area forms in the middle of the swirl and begins rotating. Warm, moist air is forced up into the middle of the low pressure area; and it begins to condense. The dropping air pressure inside the low pressure area pulls air toward the center, causing even greater winds and lower air pressure.
>
> When people are warned in time that severe weather is approaching, not as many people die or are injured. Scientists have many resources to help forecast the weather:
> thermometers, psychometers, and barometers
> Doppler radar
> satellites
> computers
> Scientists will continue to study severe weather and try to predict the path of these violent storms. In the end, lives and property will be saved.

11. Save the document as STWP023B on your data disk.

Section 9
Reports with Special Features

SECTION OVERVIEW

This section focuses on reports with special features. The special features include quotations, footnotes, and endnotes; table of contents and bibliography pages; and outlines. Footers are also introduced in this section.

CONTENT FOCUS

Reports with footnotes and quotations
Reports with endnotes
Bibliography
Table of contents
Report outline
Multipage report

CURRICULUM FOCUS

Science
Social Studies
Math
Language Arts

OPENING ACTIVITY

Discuss the importance of giving credit when quoting or paraphrasing someone else's work. Introduce the concept of plagiarism. Talk about copyrights.

SECTION 9
Reports With Special Features

OBJECTIVES

- Create, edit, and format:
  - Multipage reports with quotations and footnotes
  - Multipage reports with endnotes
  - Bibliography pages
  - Table of contents pages
  - Report outlines
  - Multipage reports with footers

Focus on Reports With Special Features

In writing reports, you will often need to give credit for ideas that are not your own or for quotes copied from other works. In this section, you will learn ways to cite other works and to format quotations, footnotes, endnotes, and bibliography pages. You will also learn to create and format special elements of reports such as outlines or footers.

Words To Know

bibliography	main heading
dot leaders	outline
endnote	outline style
footer	paragraph indent
footnote	paraphrase
footnote reference number	short quotation
	subheading
hanging indent	tab set
long quotation	table of contents

Career Exploration Activities: Marine Science

Ask students to research a career related to marine science or any science career related to lakes, rivers, or oceans. Have students write a paragraph including the job title and general job description. Suggest references such as the *Occupational Outlook Handbook*, the *Occupational Outlook Quarterly*, and the *Dictionary of Occupational Titles*.

Examples of these careers include:

Marine biologists study organisms that live in salt water.
Limnologists study organisms that live in fresh water.
Oceanographers study oceans and the ocean floor.

9.1 Reports With Footnotes and Quotations

Goals

- Type and format a footnote, a short quotation, a paraphrase, and a long quotation
- Practice the paragraph indent feature
- Practice the footnote feature

FORMATTING A MULTIPAGE REPORT WITH FOOTNOTES AND QUOTATIONS

When you write a report based on research, you must give credit to the sources of information you used in the report. **Footnotes** give credit to the source by telling the reader where the information came from. If you quote from a source word for word, you need to format the information as a direct quotation and include a footnote. When you put someone else's ideas into your own words (paraphrasing), you must also use a footnote to give credit to the source. In Project 24, you will learn how to format a footnote, a short quotation, a paraphrase, and a long quotation.

When you type footnotes, follow these general guidelines:

- The titles of books and magazines are typed in italics with initial caps.
- The titles of articles from magazines are typed in quotation marks with initial caps.
- Periods and commas are always typed inside quotation marks.
- The abbreviation for page is *p*. The abbreviation for pages is *pp*.
- Use *ibid.* meaning *in the same place* when a footnote is identical to the one just before it.
- Use *et al.* meaning *and others* when there are three or more authors.

FORMATTING TIPS

- Type a short direct quote inside quotation marks.
- Type a long quote single spaced without quotation marks. Indent the long quote 0.5 inch from both margins.
- Insert a footnote reference number to indicate the source of your information. The footnote will automatically be inserted at the bottom of the page having the footnote reference number.

Reports With Footnotes and Quotations **179**

9.1 Reports With Footnotes and Quotations

FOCUS

Type and format a footnote. Type and format quotations and paraphrases. Practice paragraph indent feature. Practice the footnote feature.

BELLRINGER

When students enter the room, direct their attention to the assignment on the board:
   Read pages 179 and 180.

TEACH

Review the general guidelines for typing footnotes. Review formatting tips.

RESOURCES

Lesson Plan: LP54
Transparency Master: TM12

CD-ROM: Reference Guide

Software: Research Files

Lesson Extension

Some CD-ROM encyclopedias automatically create a footnote when text or graphic images are copied or printed. Provide a demonstration.

179

Reports With Footnotes and Quotations

TEACH

Use the illustration on page 180 to highlight a paraphrase, a footnote reference number, a short quotation, a long quotation, and a footnote.

ASSESS

To assess understanding have students explain the purpose of a footnote. Have them describe the difference between a quote and a paraphrase.

CLOSE

Explain to students that they are now ready to type and format a footnote, a short quotation, a paraphrase, and a long quotation. Refer to Projects 24, 25, and 26.

GO TO *Refer students to the appropriate section of the Student Guide.*

Study the illustration. Your finished report may look slightly different.

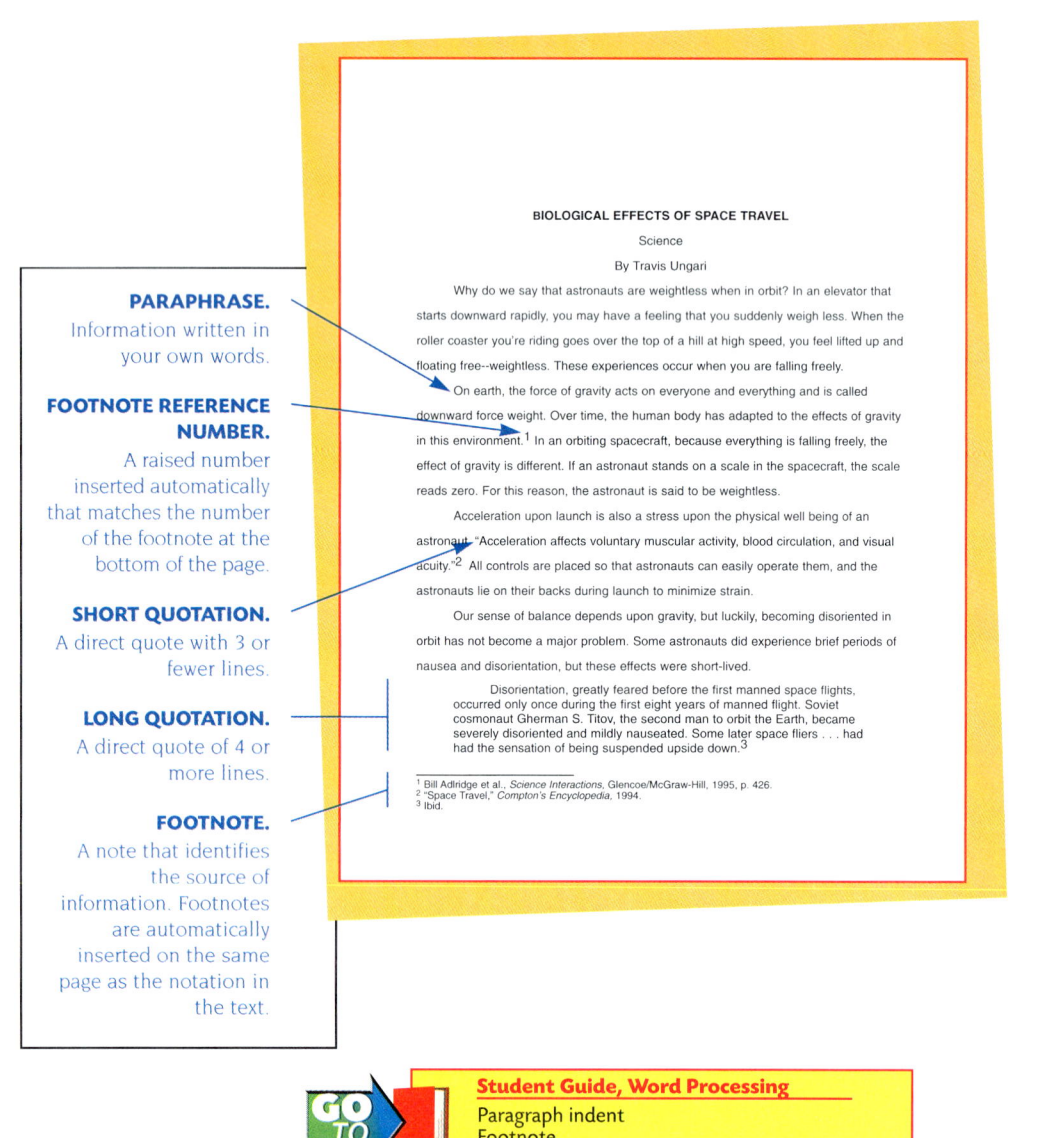

PARAPHRASE. Information written in your own words.

FOOTNOTE REFERENCE NUMBER. A raised number inserted automatically that matches the number of the footnote at the bottom of the page.

SHORT QUOTATION. A direct quote with 3 or fewer lines.

LONG QUOTATION. A direct quote of 4 or more lines.

FOOTNOTE. A note that identifies the source of information. Footnotes are automatically inserted on the same page as the notation in the text.

BIOLOGICAL EFFECTS OF SPACE TRAVEL
Science
By Travis Ungari

Why do we say that astronauts are weightless when in orbit? In an elevator that starts downward rapidly, you may have a feeling that you suddenly weigh less. When the roller coaster you're riding goes over the top of a hill at high speed, you feel lifted up and floating free--weightless. These experiences occur when you are falling freely.

On earth, the force of gravity acts on everyone and everything and is called downward force weight. Over time, the human body has adapted to the effects of gravity in this environment.[1] In an orbiting spacecraft, because everything is falling freely, the effect of gravity is different. If an astronaut stands on a scale in the spacecraft, the scale reads zero. For this reason, the astronaut is said to be weightless.

Acceleration upon launch is also a stress upon the physical well being of an astronaut. "Acceleration affects voluntary muscular activity, blood circulation, and visual acuity."[2] All controls are placed so that astronauts can easily operate them, and the astronauts lie on their backs during launch to minimize strain.

Our sense of balance depends upon gravity, but luckily, becoming disoriented in orbit has not become a major problem. Some astronauts did experience brief periods of nausea and disorientation, but these effects were short-lived.

    Disorientation, greatly feared before the first manned space flights, occurred only once during the first eight years of manned flight. Soviet cosmonaut Gherman S. Titov, the second man to orbit the Earth, became severely disoriented and mildly nauseated. Some later space fliers . . . had had the sensation of being suspended upside down.[3]

[1] Bill Adlridge et al., *Science Interactions*, Glencoe/McGraw-Hill, 1995, p. 426.
[2] "Space Travel," *Compton's Encyclopedia*, 1994.
[3] Ibid.

GO TO **Student Guide, Word Processing**
Paragraph indent
Footnote

180 Section 9 Reports With Special Features

Fun Facts

The first U.S. astronauts, selected in 1959, were pilot astronauts. Some of the requirements for the first astronauts included:
- Less than 40 years old
- Excellent physical condition
- No taller than 5' 11" (180) cm
- Bachelors degree in engineering
- Trained jet pilot with at least 1500 hours of flying time

Project 24

MULTIPAGE REPORT WITH FOOTNOTES AND QUOTATIONS

Follow the steps to format a multipage report with footnotes and quotations.

1. Open the file WP024 on your data disk.
2. Insert quotation marks around the short quotation located in paragraph 3, sentence 2: *Acceleration affects voluntary muscular activity, blood circulation, and visual acuity.*
3. Select the lines of the long quotation in paragraph 5 that begin with *Disorientation, greatly feared* and end with *suspended upside down.*
4. Change the spacing for the long quotation to single. You might have to adjust the spacing above or below the single-spaced paragraph by deleting a line.
5. Use the **paragraph indent** feature to indent the paragraphs of the long quotation 0.5 inch from the left and right margins.
6. Click in front of the first bold **X** that marks the spot where you must insert a footnote.
7. Delete the bold **X** and use the **footnote** feature to insert the following footnote:

> Bill Aldridge et al., *Science Interactions,* Glencoe/McGraw-Hill, 1995, p. 426.

8. Repeat Steps 6 and 7 to insert the following two footnotes:

> "Space Travel," *Compton's Encyclopedia,* 1994.
>
> Ibid.

(continued on next page)

Reports With Footnotes and Quotations **181**

Project 24
Reports With Footnotes and Quotations

PRACTICE—LEVEL 1

Purpose
Practice typing and formatting footnotes and quotations.

Time
Thirty minutes

Preparation
No specific preparation required.

Teaching Tip
Make sure students understand the difference between indenting the first line of a paragraph and using the paragraph indent feature.

Trouble Shooting
Check punctuation in footnotes and provide individual help to students who are having difficulty.

Wrap Up
If this is the last project for this class period, ask students to return computers and furniture to the appropriate conditions.

To generate interest in science, initiate a discussion about the qualifications for becoming an astronaut. Ask students what kinds of skills they think astronauts need to perform their jobs.

interNET CONNECTION

Access the Web site for NASA for additional information about astronauts. See the following address:

NASA   http://www.nasa.gov

181

Reports With Footnotes and Quotations

Project 24 (continued)

9. Add the paragraph below to the end of the report.

> Other observed effects of weightlessness are the loss of calcium in the bones and the loss of body mass. So far, astronauts have quickly regained lost body mass after returning to Earth. With every returning space flight crew, doctors are learning more about how the human body reacts to long periods of weightlessness.

10. Save the document as STWP024 on your data disk.

Astronauts on missions in space gather and send back to Earth valuable scientific data.

Section 9 Reports With Special Features

CULTURAL KALEIDOSCOPE

Space travel has brought different cultures together. U.S. astronauts have traveled to the Russian space station Mir and stayed for longer than 100 days. Russian cosmonauts have traveled aboard U.S. space shuttle missions in order to reach Mir. International crews include:

1985	Patrick Baudry(France) and	
	Prince Sultan Salman al-Saud (Saudi Arabia)	Discovery
1985	Rodolfo Neri (Mexico)	Atlantis
1994	Sergei Kirkalev (Russia)	Discovery

Project 25

MULTIPAGE REPORT WITH FOOTNOTES AND QUOTATIONS

In this project, you will practice arranging another multipage report with footnotes and quotations. Refer to the illustration on page 180 as needed.

1. Open the file WP025 on your data disk.
2. Insert quotation marks around the first sentence in the report: *A volcano is a vent, or opening, in the surface of the Earth through which magma and associated gases and ash erupt.*
3. Select the lines of the long quotation in paragraph 4 that begin with *One of the most spectacular* and end with *in Washington State.*
4. Change the spacing for the long quotation to single. You might have to adjust the spacing above or below the single-spaced paragraph by deleting a line.
5. Use the paragraph indent feature to indent the paragraphs of the long quotation 0.5 inch from the left and right margin.
6. Click in front of the first bold **X** that marks the spot where you must insert a footnote.
7. Delete the bold **X** and use the footnote feature to insert the following footnote:

   > "Volcano," *Compton's Encyclopedia,* 1994.

8. Repeat Steps 6 and 7 to insert the following two footnotes:

   > Bill Aldridge et al., *Science Interactions,* Glencoe/McGraw-Hill, 1995, p. 494.
   >
   > "Volcano," *Compton's Encyclopedia,* 1994.

(continued on next page)

Reports With Footnotes and Quotations **183**

Initiate a discussion about volcanoes. Ask each student to pick a volcano from the list at right to research for a class discussion. For the volcano selected, the student should be able to state when it last erupted and to locate it on a map or globe.

Dates of significant eruptions are in parentheses.

El Chichón	Mexico, 1982
Etna	Sicily, 1995
Krakatau	Indonesia, 1995 (1883)
Mount Pinatubo	Philippines, 1995 (1991)
Mount Saint Helens	Washington, 1991 (1980)
Mount Shasta	California, 1786
Mount Rainier	Washington, 1894
Nevada del Ruiz	Colombia, 1985
Papandayan	Java, 1772
Paricutín	Mexico, 1943

Project 25
Reports With Footnotes and Quotations

APPLY—LEVEL 1

Purpose
Apply word processing skills by typing and formatting footnotes and quotations.

Time
Thirty minutes

Preparation
No specific preparation required.

Teaching Tip
Make sure students understand the difference between indenting the first line of a paragraph and using the paragraph indent feature.

Trouble Shooting
Provide individual help to students who are having difficulty determining the difference between a short quotation, a long quotation, and a paraphrase.

Wrap Up
If this is the last project for this class period, ask students to return computers and furniture to the appropriate conditions.

183

Reports With Footnotes and Quotations

Project 25 (continued)

DID YOU KNOW

Other examples of cinder cone volcanoes include:

Tamboro	Indonesia
Pélee	Martinique
Arenal	Costa Rica

Other examples of shield volcanoes include:

Laki	Iceland
Kilauea Iki	Hawaii

Other examples of strato-volcanos, also called composite volcanoes, include.

Vesuvius	Italy
Lassen	California

Source: Bill Aldridge et al., *Science Interactions*, Glencoe/McGraw Hill, 1995.

---

9. Add the paragraph below to the end of the report.

> Bulging is another indication of a potential volcanic eruption. The bulge that formed on the north flank of Mt. Saint Helens prior to the 1980 eruption was monitored and showed a very slow but steady growth rate of a few meters per day from March until the May eruption. Because the growth rate was slow, geologists were unable to determine when the volcano would erupt. In many cases, if such a bulge changes size abruptly, an eruption usually follows quickly.

DID YOU KNOW

- A volcano is an opening in Earth's surface through which gas or lava escape. Over time, these materials form cone-like structures.
- Cinders from lava that escapes from the earth form cinder cone volcanoes. Mount Paricutín in Mexico was formed in this way.
- Shield volcanoes are gently sloping mountains made from free-flowing lava. Mauna Loa in Hawaii is the largest active volcano of this type on Earth.
- Strato-volcanoes are made of alternating layers of lava and ash. Mt. St. Helens is an example of this type of volcano.

10. Save the document as STWP025 on your data disk.

---

interNET CONNECTION

For more information about volcanoes, visit VolcanoWorld. See the following address:

http://volcano.und.nodak.edu/

Project 26

Science Connection

MULTIPAGE REPORT WITH FOOTNOTES AND QUOTATIONS

Practice arranging another multipage report with footnotes and quotations. Use the word processing features you learned in Project 24 to type an original report. Write your report about any topic related to science. Choose a topic that lends itself to short quotes, long quotes, and paraphrasing. Refer to the illustration on page 180 as needed.

1. Open a new word processing file.
2. Insert quotation marks around any short quotation(s).
3. Change the spacing for any long quotation(s) to single. You might have to adjust the spacing above or below the single-spaced paragraph by deleting a line.
4. Use the paragraph indent feature to indent the paragraphs of the long quotation(s) 0.5 inch from the left and right margins.
5. Save the document as STWP026 on your data disk.

In Your Journal

To gather ideas for your report, ask yourself questions about science-related topics. Some questions you might ask:

- What recent scientific discoveries interest me?
- What science topics would I like to know more about?

Make a list of four or five possible topics. Use the numbered list feature to list your ideas. List the most promising idea as number 1, the next idea as number 2, and so on.

✓ Check Your Understanding

1. Did you add a footnote whenever you paraphrased or quoted directly?
2. Did you type short quotations using quotation marks?
3. Did you indent any long quotations 0.5 inch from both margins and single-space them?

In Your Journal

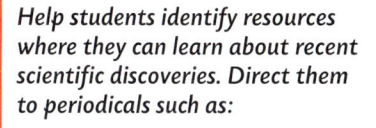

Help students identify resources where they can learn about recent scientific discoveries. Direct them to periodicals such as:

Discover
Newsweek
Popular Science
Scientific American

Science Connection

To generate interest in science, create a collage or bulletin board display with pictures and headlines that focus on recent scientific discoveries. You can initiate the project and ask students to add to it.

Project 26
Reports With Footnotes and Quotations

ASSESS—LEVEL 2

Purpose
Assess word processing skills by typing and formatting a multipage report with footnotes and quotes.

Time
One class period

Preparation
Students will need to select and research a science topic before they can begin Project 26. Make the following assignment several days before students are expected to complete Project 26:

Select any science topic. Research your topic. You must have at least two references. Bring your notes and references to class and be prepared to write a multipage report—approximately 500 words. Be sure to write down or photocopy the information you will need for your footnotes.

Teaching Tip
Help students to select appropriate science topics for this project. Students who finish early should review and improve their report.

Trouble Shooting
Provide individual help to students who are having difficulty.

Wrap Up
Have students review their document using **Check Your Understanding.** Have students make corrections.

Ask students to return computers and furniture to the appropriate conditions.

9.2 Reports With Endnotes

FOCUS

Change footnotes to endnotes. Add endnotes to a report.

BELLRINGER

When students enter the room, direct their attention to the assignment on the board:
> Read pages 186–187.

TEACH

Explain that endnotes and footnotes are both acceptable ways of citing references. Footnotes are convenient for the reader because they appear on the same page as the reference. Endnotes, however, are more convenient for the person typing the report.

Point out that many teachers and professors have a preference for endnotes or footnotes. For each report you need to know the instructor's preference.

9.2 Reports With Endnotes

Goals
- Change footnotes to endnotes
- Add endnotes to a report

FORMATTING A MULTIPAGE REPORT WITH ENDNOTES

Footnotes and endnotes both give credit to the source of information in reports. However, footnotes appear at the foot of the page and endnotes appear at the end of a report. Different software programs position endnotes differently. Sometimes the endnotes are inserted on a page by themselves as the last page in the document. Sometimes endnotes are inserted directly after the last line in the report with or without a separator line.

In Project 27, you will learn how to change footnotes into endnotes and how to add endnotes to a multipage report. Study the illustrations on page 187. Your finished report may look slightly different.

Astronauts in space experience the effects of weightlessness while doing their jobs.

186 Section 9 Reports With Special Features

RESOURCES

Lesson Plan: LP54
Multicultural Timing: MT3
Transparency Master: TM13

CD-ROM: Reference Guide

Software: Research Files

186

Reports With Endnotes

TEACH

Use the illustration on page 187 to highlight the endnote. Remind students that endnotes are not always on a separate page. They sometimes appear on the last page of your report.

ASSESS

To assess understanding have students explain the difference between footnotes and endnotes.

CLOSE

Explain to students that they are now ready to change footnotes to endnotes and add endnotes to a report. Refer to Projects 27, 28, and 29.

Refer students to the appropriate section of the Student Guide.

2

All body functions are carefully monitored during a flight. The only factor that has shown a significant change is the pulse rate, which often increases during lift-off and space walks. In all cases, however, the rate has returned to normal in a very short time. All astronauts have experienced "lazy heart." This is a condition in which the heart loses its normal tone because it is not working as hard as it usually does when it is pumping blood that is weightless. The astronauts have special exercises they can do to try to combat this condition, but the condition can still not be prevented.

Upon return to Earth, some astronauts feel faint when they first stand up. Some Soviet cosmonauts found it difficult to adjust to the effects of gravity on Earth after 17 days in orbit. For several days, their arms, legs, and head felt as if they were very heavy. They also seemed to have less blood and some changes in the walls of their veins. The reasons are not yet clearly understood.

Other observed effects of weightlessness are the loss of calcium in the bones and the loss of body mass. So far, astronauts have quickly regained lost body mass after returning to Earth. With every returning space flight crew, doctors are learning more about how the human body reacts to long periods of weightlessness.

---

[1] Bill Aldridge et al., *Science Interactions*, Glencoe/McGraw-Hill, 1995, p. 426.
[2] "Space Travel," *Compton's Encyclopedia*, 1994.
[3] Ibid.

ENDNOTE. A note that identifies the source of information. Endnotes are automatically inserted at the end of the report.

GO TO — **Student Guide, Word Processing**
Endnote

Reports With Endnotes **187**

---

interNET CONNECTION

Have students use the Internet to learn more about space exploration. Using a web search engine, they might search for sites related to space, astronauts, or NASA.

Examples of sites might include:

Quest   http://quest.arc.nasa.gov
Astronaut Biographies   http://www.jsc.nasa.gov/Bios/astrobio.html

Project 27
Reports With Endnotes

PRACTICE—LEVEL 1

Purpose
Practice typing and formatting a multipage report with endnotes.

Time
Thirty minutes

Preparation
No special preparation required.

Teaching Tip
Students who finish early should repeat the project.

Trouble Shooting
Make sure students understand the proper use of *Ibid* and *et al.* Refer to page 179.

Wrap Up
If this is the last project for this class period, ask students to return computers and furniture to the appropriate conditions.

188

Project 27
Science Connection
MULTIPAGE REPORT WITH ENDNOTES

Follow the steps to format a multipage report with endnotes.

1. Open the file WP027 on your data disk.
2. Change the existing footnote at the end of the long quotation to an **endnote.**
3. Click in front of the first bold **X** that marks the spot where you must insert an endnote.
4. Delete the bold **X** and use the endnote feature to insert the following endnote:

   > Bill Aldridge et al., *Science Interactions,* Glencoe/McGraw-Hill, 1995, p. 426.

5. Click in front of the second bold **X** that marks the spot where you must insert an endnote.
6. Delete the bold **X** and use the **endnote** feature to insert the following endnote:

   > "Space Travel," *Compton's Encyclopedia,* 1994.

7. Insert the paragraph below as the first paragraph of the report.

   > Why do we say that astronauts are weightless when in orbit? In an elevator that starts downward rapidly, you may have a feeling that you suddenly weigh less. When the roller coaster you're riding goes over the top of a hill at high speed, you feel lifted up and floating free--weightless. These experiences occur when you are falling freely.

8. Save the document as STWP027 on your data disk.

188 Section 9 Reports With Special Features

To generate interest in science, show a video about space travel.

Project 28

MULTIPAGE REPORT WITH ENDNOTES

Practice changing footnotes in an existing multipage report into endnotes and then adding endnotes to the report.

1. Open the file WP028 on your data disk.
2. Change the footnote at the end of the long quotation to an endnote.
3. Click in front of the first bold **X** that marks the spot where you must insert an endnote.
4. Delete the bold **X** and use the endnote feature to insert the following endnote:

   > "Volcano," *Compton's Encyclopedia,* 1994.

5. Click in front of the second bold **X** that marks the spot where you must insert an endnote.
6. Delete the bold **X** and use the endnote feature to insert the following endnote:

   > "Where Do Volcanoes Occur?" *Science Interactions,* Glencoe/McGraw-Hill, 1995, p. 494.

7. Add the paragraph below between the first and second paragraphs of the report.

   > Where the plates pull apart, magma is forced upward to Earth's surface and erupts as lava. Lava that flows from underwater rifts cools quickly in the cold ocean water. As eruptions continue over time, layers of cooled lava accumulate. Iceland was formed when the layers of lava accumulated to form an island.

8. Save the document as STWP028 on your data disk.

Reports With Endnotes **189**

Project 28
Reports With Endnotes

APPLY—LEVEL 1

Purpose
Apply word processing skills by typing and formatting a multi-page report with endnotes.

Time
Thirty minutes

Preparation
No special preparation required.

Teaching Tip
Students who finish early should repeat the project.

Trouble Shooting
Provide individual help to students who are having difficulty.

Wrap Up
If this is the last project for this class period, ask students to return computers and furniture to the appropriate conditions.

To generate interest in science, ask students to make a list of natural disasters. Compile the list on the board. Possible responses:

Cyclone	Hurricane
Earthquake	Tidal Wave
Flood	Tornado

Project 29
Reports With Endnotes

ASSESS—LEVEL 2

Purpose
Assess word processing skills by changing footnotes into endnotes and adding endnotes to a multipage report.

Time
Thirty minutes

Preparation
Students need to use the report they created in Project 26 in order to complete Project 29. If students did not complete Project 26, this project should be skipped.

Teaching Tip
Students who finish early should repeat the project

Trouble Shooting
Provide individual help to students who are having difficulty.

Wrap Up
Have students review their document using **Check Your Understanding.** Have students make corrections.

If this is the last project for this class period, ask students to return computers and furniture to the appropriate conditions.

Language Link
ANSWERS
1. *The World Book Encyclopedia*
2. "Learning About Printers,"
3. "Wandering Trails,"
4. "Election '96 Update"
5. *Mona Lisa*

Project 29
Science Connection
MULTIPAGE REPORT WITH ENDNOTES

Practice changing footnotes into endnotes and adding endnotes to a multipage report. Using the word processing features you learned in Project 27, edit the original report you typed in Project 26. If you did not complete Project 26, you should skip this project.

1. Open the file STWP026 on your data disk.
2. Change any existing footnotes to endnotes.
3. Add one endnote to the document.
4. Save the document as STW029 on your data disk.

✓ Check Your Understanding

1. Did you use the endnote feature to change the footnotes into endnotes?
2. Did you add one endnote at the end of your report?

Language Link
Use italics or quotation marks in titles.

Use italics for the title of a book, magazine, newspaper, or work of art. Use quotation marks around the title of a poem, essay, song, newspaper article, or book chapter.

> *Newsweek* is a magazine published each week.
> The poem "Autumn Trees" reminds me of fall colors.

✓ Check Your Learning

In each sentence, indicate which words should be italicized and which words should appear in quotation marks.

1. Delores searched for the information in The World Book Encyclopedia.
2. I read Learning About Printers, the fourth chapter in the book.
3. Her original poem, Wandering Trails, earned high marks.
4. Read the article Election '96 Update in today's newspaper.
5. The painting Mona Lisa is well known throughout the world.

Section 9 Reports With Special Features

Science Connection
To generate interest in science, invite a speaker to talk about the science concepts related to a natural disaster. Contact the science department at a nearby college or university for help locating a speaker.

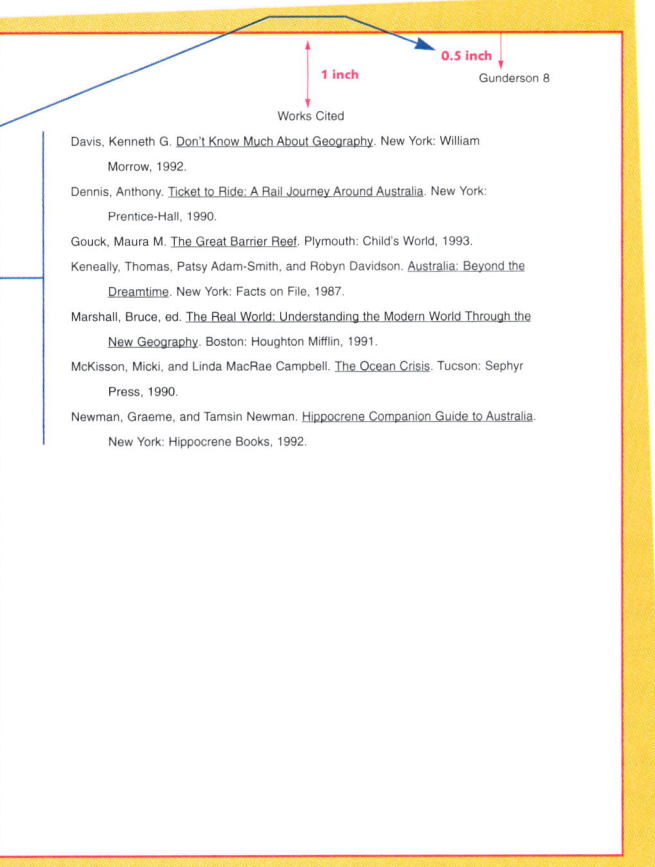

9.3 Bibliography, MLA Style

Goals
- Type and format a bibliography in MLA style
- Practice the hanging indent feature

FORMATTING A BIBLIOGRAPHY, MLA STYLE

Any report you write that is based on research should include a bibliography. A bibliography is placed at the end of the report. It provides complete information about the sources you have used in writing the report. In MLA style, the term *Works Cited* is used rather than the term *Bibliography*. The citation in the bibliography should be complete enough to allow the reader to locate the source in a library.

Study the illustration. Your finished works-cited list may look slightly different.

MLA STYLE HEADER. The author's last name followed by the page number.

WORKS-CITED LIST. An alphabetical list of sources of information.

Gunderson 8

Works Cited

Davis, Kenneth G. *Don't Know Much About Geography*. New York: William Morrow, 1992.

Dennis, Anthony. *Ticket to Ride: A Rail Journey Around Australia*. New York: Prentice-Hall, 1990.

Gouck, Maura M. *The Great Barrier Reef*. Plymouth: Child's World, 1993.

Keneally, Thomas, Patsy Adam-Smith, and Robyn Davidson. *Australia: Beyond the Dreamtime*. New York: Facts on File, 1987.

Marshall, Bruce, ed. *The Real World: Understanding the Modern World Through the New Geography*. Boston: Houghton Mifflin, 1991.

McKisson, Micki, and Linda MacRae Campbell. *The Ocean Crisis*. Tucson: Sephyr Press, 1990.

Newman, Graeme, and Tamsin Newman. *Hippocrene Companion Guide to Australia*. New York: Hippocrene Books, 1992.

Bibliography **191**

9.3 Bibliography

FOCUS
Type and format a bibliography in MLA style. Practice the hanging indent feature.

BELLRINGER
When students enter the room, direct their attention to the assignment on the board:
Read pages 191 and 192.

TEACH
Explain the difference between a bibliography and footnotes or endnotes. Emphasize that a bibliography includes all references used in researching a report. Footnotes or endnotes only provide references for quotations or paraphrases. Point out that a bibliography lists references in alphabetical order by author's last name.

Use the illustration on page 191 to highlight the MLA style header and the works-cited list.

RESOURCES
- Lesson Plan: LP55
- Transparency Master: TM14
- Transparency 8
- CD-ROM: Reference Guide
- Software: Research Files

Bibliography

TEACH
Review the general guidelines and formatting tips.

ASSESS
To assess understanding have students identify the components of a citation for a book.

CLOSE
Explain to students that they are now ready to type and format a bibliography in MLA style. Refer to Project 30.

DID YOU KNOW? The Great Barrier Reef is the largest deposit of coral in the world. It is located off the coast of Australia in the Coral Sea. The reef is approximately 2000 km long. It stretches from Mackay, Queensland, to the strait between Australia and New Guinea, off the northeastern coast of Australia.

Source: *Microsoft Encarta 96 Encyclopedia*, Microsoft Corporation, 1993–1995.

GO TO Refer students to the appropriate section of the Student Guide.

When you prepare a list of works cited, follow these general guidelines:

1. Center and type the title *Works Cited* in initial caps.
2. Double-space the entire list just as you double-spaced the entire report.
3. Begin the first line of each entry at the left margin and use the hanging indent feature to indent any continuing lines by 0.5 inch.
4. List entries in alphabetical order.
5. When citing books, arrange entries in this general order and format: Author's last name, first name. <u>Book title</u>. City of publication: Publishing company, year of publication.

FORMATTING TIPS
- Type the header 0.5 inch from the top of the page.
- Type the works-cited list at the end of the report. Double-space the list and use hanging indents for each entry that has continuing lines.

DID YOU KNOW? Coral is found in warm water near the equator. Coral is made up of tiny animals. These animals build hard, boxlike capsules around their bodies. They build these capsules with calcium they remove from seawater. The coral cement themselves to other capsules to form a colony called a reef.

The Great Barrier Reef is the world's largest coral formation. It is found off the coast of Australia.

GO TO Student Guide, Word Processing — Hanging indent

192 Section 9 Reports With Special Features

Project 30

BIBLIOGRAPHY, MLA STYLE

Follow the steps below to format a bibliography in MLA style.

1. Open the file WP030 on your data disk.
2. Change the works-cited list to double-spacing.
3. Type the title *Works Cited* centered at the top of the list.
4. Add the two entries shown below to the works-cited list. Insert them in alphabetical order by the author's last name. Do not underline the period at the end of the name of the book.

> Dennis, Anthony. <u>Ticket to Ride: A Rail Journey Around Australia</u>. New York: Prentice-Hall, 1990.
>
> Keneally, Thomas, Patsy Adam-Smith, and Robyn Davidson. <u>Australia: Beyond the Dreamtime</u>. New York: Facts On File, 1987.

5. Apply the hanging indent feature to all the listings that have continuing lines.
6. Save the document as STWP030 on your data disk.

In Your Journal

1. Find out new information about Australia by locating several sources in the library.
2. Make a list of five interesting facts to know about Australia.
3. Make a works-cited list to show where you found the interesting facts.

Bibliography **193**

Project 30 Bibliography

PRACTICE—LEVEL 1

Purpose
Practice formatting a bibliography in MLA style.

Time
Fifteen minutes

Preparation
No special preparation required.

Teaching Tip
Students who finish early should repeat the project.

Trouble Shooting
Provide individual help to students who are having difficulty with the hanging indent feature.

Wrap Up
If this is the last project for this class period, ask students to return computers and furniture to the appropriate conditions.

In Your Journal

Guide students to appropriate resource material in the library. Ask your librarian for suggestions.

Social Studies Connection

To generate interest in social studies, ask students what day and what time it is in Sydney, Australia.

Answer: The day and time depend on where you are and the time your class meets. When it is 12:00 noon Eastern Standard Time, it is 3:00 A.M. the following day in Sydney.

CULTURAL KALEIDOSCOPE

December 26 is Boxing Day in Australia. Boxing Day is also celebrated in Canada, England, and Wales. Traditionally, this was a day for land owners to give presents to servants and others of lesser means.

193

9.4 Bibliography

FOCUS

Type and format a bibliography. Practice the hanging indent feature.

BELLRINGER

When students enter the room, direct their attention to the assignment on the board:
  Read pages 194 and 195.

TEACH

Review with students the difference between a bibliography and footnotes or endnotes. Emphasize that a bibliography includes all references used in researching a report. Footnotes or endnotes only provide a reference for quotations or paraphrases. Point out that a bibliography lists references in alphabetical order.

Use the illustration on page 194 to highlight the header and the bibliography. Compare the illustration on page 194 with the one on page 191. Discuss differences between this style and MLA style.

9.4 Bibliography

Goals
- Type and format a bibliography
- Practice the hanging indent feature

FORMATTING A BIBLIOGRAPHY

In this project, you will learn another acceptable format for a bibliography. There are many differences between the MLA works-cited page and this bibliography. Compare the illustration below with the one on page 191. Notice the differences in the header, the title, the position of the title, and the spacing of the entries. Both styles also have similarities. They both list the entries in alphabetical order and use a hanging indent on each entry.

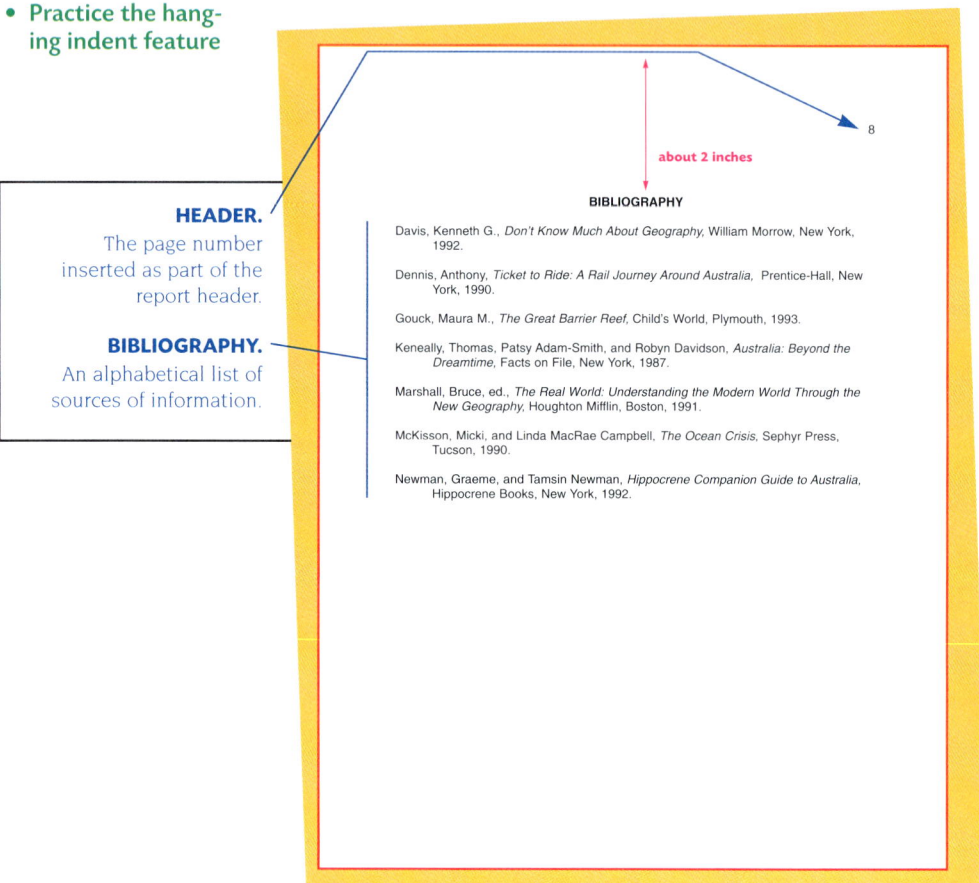

HEADER. The page number inserted as part of the report header.

BIBLIOGRAPHY. An alphabetical list of sources of information.

about 2 inches

BIBLIOGRAPHY

Davis, Kenneth G., *Don't Know Much About Geography*, William Morrow, New York, 1992.

Dennis, Anthony, *Ticket to Ride: A Rail Journey Around Australia*, Prentice-Hall, New York, 1990.

Gouck, Maura M., *The Great Barrier Reef*, Child's World, Plymouth, 1993.

Keneally, Thomas, Patsy Adam-Smith, and Robyn Davidson, *Australia: Beyond the Dreamtime*, Facts on File, New York, 1987.

Marshall, Bruce, ed., *The Real World: Understanding the Modern World Through the New Geography*, Houghton Mifflin, Boston, 1991.

McKisson, Micki, and Linda MacRae Campbell, *The Ocean Crisis*, Sephyr Press, Tucson, 1990.

Newman, Graeme, and Tamsin Newman, *Hippocrene Companion Guide to Australia*, Hippocrene Books, New York, 1992.

194 Section 9 Reports With Special Features

RESOURCES

Lesson Plan: LP55
Transparency Master: TM15

Transparency 9

CD-ROM: Reference Guide

Software: Research Files

When you prepare a bibliography, follow these general guidelines:

1. Center and type the title BIBLIOGRAPHY in all caps and bold about 2 inches from the top of the page.
2. Insert one blank line after *BIBLIOGRAPHY*.
3. Single-space each entry in the bibliography, and insert one blank line after each entry.
4. Begin the first line of each entry at the left margin. Use the hanging indent feature to indent any continuing lines by 0.5 inch.
5. List entries in alphabetical order.
6. When citing books, arrange entries in this general order and format: Author's last name, first name, *book title*, publisher, place of publication, year of publication.

FORMATTING TIPS

- Type the bibliography at the end of the report.
- Use single spacing with hanging indents.
- Insert a blank line between entries.

DID YOU KNOW

Librarians have a system for organizing materials in the library so you can find them easily. One system of classification is the Dewey Decimal System. This system, which was developed by Melvil Dewey, in 1872, is commonly used to organize books by category. Books are shelved according to their classification. Then they are sorted alphabetically by the author's last name.

Books of fiction usually are not given a Dewey Decimal number. Instead, they are given a two-line call number. The first line is usually an F or FIC, for fiction; the second line is the first three letters of the author's last name.

Bibliography **195**

Bibliography

TEACH

Review the general guidelines and formatting tips.

ASSESS

To assess understanding have students compare and contrast the MLA works-cited page with the bibliography presented in this lesson.

CLOSE

Explain to students that they are now ready to type and format a bibliography in MLA style. Refer to Projects 31 and 32.

DID YOU KNOW

Libraries usually include periodicals in their catalogs. The listing in the catalog usually includes the name of the periodical and the dates for which it is available. For information about a specific topic, article, or author, you need to use a periodical reference. Many periodical references are now available on-line.

195

Project 31
Bibliography

PRACTICE—LEVEL 1

Purpose
Practice formatting a bibliography using standard business style.

Time
Fifteen minutes

Preparation
No special preparation required.

Teaching Tip
Students who finish early should repeat the project.

Trouble Shooting
Provide individual help to students who are having difficulty with the hanging indent feature.

Wrap Up
If this is the last project for this class period, ask students to return computers and furniture to the appropriate conditions.

Project 31
Social Studies Connection
BIBLIOGRAPHY

Follow the steps to format a bibliography in a standard business style.

1. Open the file WP031 on your data disk.
2. Move to the top of the document. Type the title BIBLIOGRAPHY centered, in all caps and bold about 2 inches from the top of the page.

   Note: If your default header area begins 1 inch from the top of the page, press Return/Enter 3 times to position the title about 2 inches from the top of the page. If your default header area begins 0.25 inch or 0.5 inch from the top of the page, press Return/Enter 5 times to position the title about 2 inches from the top of the page.

3. Insert one blank line after the title.
4. Add the two entries shown below to the bibliography. Insert them in alphabetical order by the author's last name. Do not italicize the comma at the end of the name of the book.

   > Davis, Kenneth G., *Don't Know Much About Geography*, William Morrow, New York, 1992.
   >
   > McKisson, Micki, and Linda MacRae Campbell, *The Ocean Crisis*, Sephyr Press, Tucson, 1990.

5. Apply the hanging indent feature to all the entries to indent continuing lines 0.5 inch.
6. Insert one blank line after each entry.
7. Save the document as STWP031 on your data disk.

196 Section 9 Reports With Special Features

Social Studies Connection

To generate interest in social studies, ask students to research one aspect of Australian history. Instruct them to make notes and be prepared to share information with their classmates. Examples of topics include:

Australian Aborigines
British interests
Commonwealth of Australia
Dutch interests
Gold Rush
James Cook
Penal colonies
Portuguese interests
Spanish interests
Tasmania

Project 32
Building Your Portfolio

In this portfolio project, you will review some of the formatting and word processing features you learned in this section. You will format a multipage report with footnotes and a bibliography. If you need to review any formatting or software features, refer to previous projects as often as needed. Study the illustrations. Your finished project may look slightly different.

(continued on next page)

Project 32
Building Your Portfolio

ASSESS—LEVEL 2

Purpose
Assess word processing skills by formatting a multipage report with footnotes and a bibliography.

Time
One class period

Preparation
No special preparation required.

Teaching Tip
Students who finish early should review their work.

Trouble Shooting
Provide individual help to students who are having difficulty.

Wrap Up
Ask students to return computers and furniture to the appropriate conditions.

Math Connection

To generate interest in mathematics, have students calculate the answers to the following:

You have been asked to write a 500-word review of a new movie for the school newspaper. The font size you are using is 12 point and the margins are set for a 6-inch line. You estimate that you usually get 18 words on a line. How many lines will you type for 500 words? Round your answer to the nearest whole number.

Answer: Approximately 28 lines are needed for 500 words.
Calculation: 500 ÷ 18 = 27.78

Building Your Portfolio

Project 32 (continued)
Building Your Portfolio

NOW TRY THIS

1. Open the file WP032 on your data disk.
2. Click in front of the bold **X** at the end of the second paragraph that marks the spot where you should insert a footnote. Delete the bold **X** and use the footnote feature to insert the following footnote:

   "Mathematics," *Compton's Encyclopedia,* 1994.

3. Move to the last paragraph of the body of the report, and insert the following paragraphs:

   The puzzle of the tiles did not die with Tan. Instead it grew in popularity as it was passed on from one generation to the next and from one country to another. Legend says that Napoleon used tangrams to help calm himself while he was imprisoned on St. Helena.

   A famous puzzle expert by the name of Sam Loyd wrote about tangrams in the early 1900's. Tangrams can be as simple as shapes cut out of paper or as elaborate as a fancy wood-carved set. Whatever you use, tangrams will open a world of creativity. Perhaps you will understand why tangrams can be a special gift to someone with an imagination.

(continued on next page)

Section 9 Reports With Special Features

interNET CONNECTION

Have students use the Internet to learn trivia or play a game. Using a web search engine, they might search for sites related to trivia or games.

Example of a Web site:

http://www.gene.com/ae/WN/Factoids/factoids.html

> **DID YOU KNOW**
> Sam Loyd was interested in puzzles at an early age. When he was 14, Loyd began inventing chess problems. He also invented several games, including Parcheesi. In 1896 Loyd and his son began publishing a puzzle column that appeared in newspapers and magazines.

Building Your Portfolio

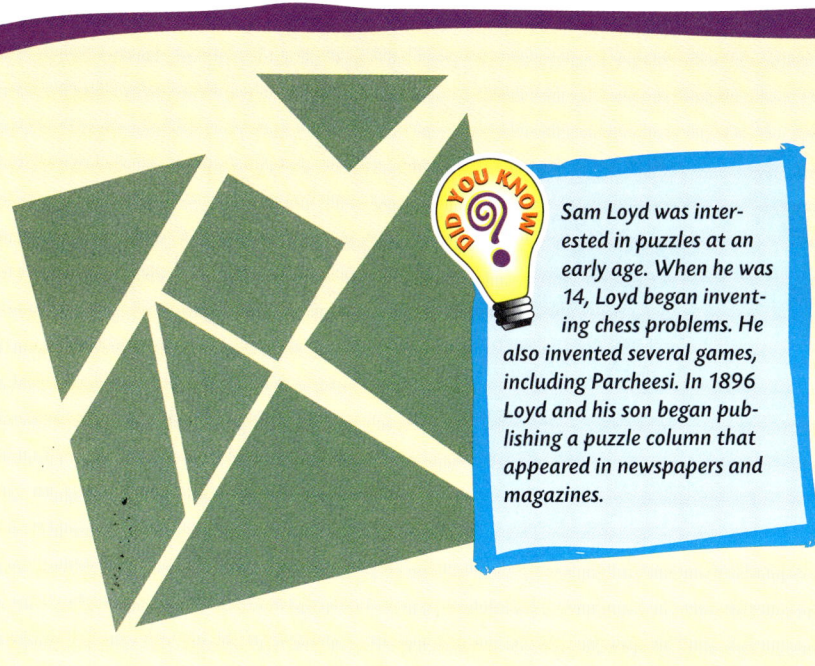

> **DID YOU KNOW**
> In 1995 the top selling computer game was Myst (Brøderbund).

4. Move to the last page of the report, and add the two entries shown below to the bibliography. Insert them in alphabetical order by the author's last name. Do not italicize the comma at the end of the name of the book.

> Schriver, Maria, *Chinese Myths and Legends,* Bradshaw Publishing, Salt Lake City, 1992.
>
> Foster, David, Sandie Gilliam, Jack Price, Kay McClain, Barney Martinez, and Linda Dritsas, *Interactive Mathematics,* Glencoe/McGraw-Hill, Columbus, 1995.

5. Apply the hanging indent feature to all the entries in the bibliography to indent continuing lines by 0.5 inch.
6. Insert one blank line after each entry.
7. Save the document as STWP032 on your data disk.

9.5 Table of Contents

FOCUS
Type and format a table of contents. Create dot leaders. Practice the tab set feature.

BELLRINGER
When students enter the room, direct their attention to the assignment on the board:
  Read pages 200 and 201.

TEACH
Use the illustration on page 200 to highlight contents, main heading, subheadings, page number, and dot leaders.

Table of Contents

9.5

Goals
- Type and format a table of contents
- Create dot leaders
- Practice the tab set feature

FORMATTING A TABLE OF CONTENTS

A **table of contents** is a listing of all the main topic and subtopic headings in a report and their corresponding page numbers. A table of contents is generally used only for long reports. It helps the reader to identify the main ideas in a report. **Dot leaders** (periods) are used to lead the reader's eye from the section headings to the page numbers.

Study the illustration. Your finished table of contents may look slightly different.

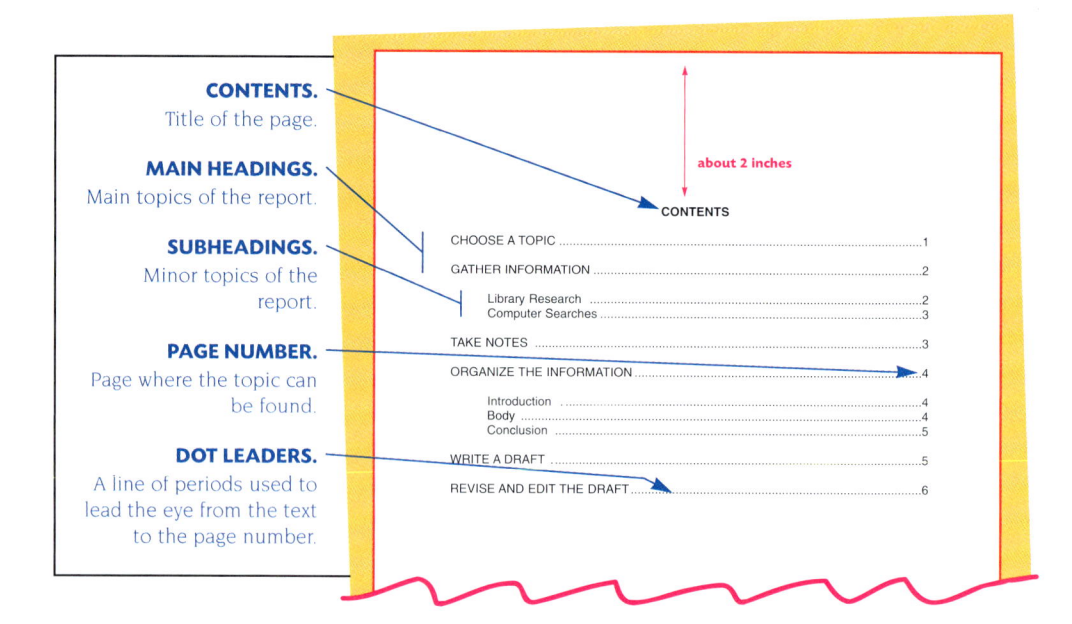

CONTENTS. Title of the page.

MAIN HEADINGS. Main topics of the report.

SUBHEADINGS. Minor topics of the report.

PAGE NUMBER. Page where the topic can be found.

DOT LEADERS. A line of periods used to lead the eye from the text to the page number.

about 2 inches

CONTENTS

CHOOSE A TOPIC 1
GATHER INFORMATION 2
    Library Research 2
    Computer Searches 3
TAKE NOTES 3
ORGANIZE THE INFORMATION 4
    Introduction 4
    Body 4
    Conclusion 5
WRITE A DRAFT 5
REVISE AND EDIT THE DRAFT 6

200 Section 9 Reports With Special Features

RESOURCES

Lesson Plan: LP56
Transparency Master: TM16

Transparency 10

CD-ROM: Reference Guide

Software: Research Files

200

FORMATTING TIPS

- Type the title CONTENTS about 2 inches from the top of the page in bold and all caps.
- Type main headings at the left margin in all caps. Follow with dot leaders and a page number. Insert a blank line above and below each main heading.
- Type subheadings, single spaced, in initial caps. Follow with dot leaders and a page number. Indent side headings 0.5 inch.
- Type the page number at the right margin after the dot leaders.

GO TO
Student Guide, Word Processing
Tab set

DID YOU KNOW
You can research information without going to the library. Some libraries have placed their catalogs on-line. People can search the library catalog using a computer at home or at school. Some libraries allow you to request and check out books on-line.

You can use your computer to search for and locate information for reports.

Table of Contents **201**

Table of Contents

TEACH
Review the formatting tips.

ASSESS
To assess understanding have students identify the main elements of the table of contents of several books and magazines.

CLOSE
Explain to students that they are now ready to type and format a table of contents. Refer to Projects 33 and 34.

GO TO
Refer students to the appropriate section of the Student Guide.

DID YOU KNOW
Because every library cannot afford to own every book, many libraries belong to consortiums. These consortiums provide libraries with the ability to share holdings with other libraries. On-line databases allow the libraries to communicate with each other and make requests for borrowing books from distant cities.

201

Project 33
Table of Contents

PRACTICE—LEVEL 1

Purpose
Practice typing a table of contents.

Time
Fifteen minutes

Preparation
No special preparation required.

Teaching Tip
Students who finish early should repeat the project.

Trouble Shooting
Provide individual help to students who are having difficulty.

Wrap Up
If this is the last project for this class period, ask students to return computers and furniture to the appropriate conditions.

Project 33
Language Arts Connection
TABLE OF CONTENTS

Type a table of contents using the following steps.

1. Open a new word processing document.
2. Use the **tab set** feature to set tabs for a table of contents with dot leaders.
3. Position the insertion point about 2 inches from the top of the page by pressing Return/Enter 6 times.

   Note: If your default font is Geneva 12 pt., press Return/Enter 5 times to position the insertion point at 2 inches.

4. Center the word CONTENTS using all caps and bold. Press Return/Enter 2 times.
5. Type the first main heading CHOOSE A TOPIC in all caps. Insert the dot leaders, and type the page number.
6. Press Enter twice to insert a blank line below the main heading.
7. Press Tab once to indent the subheading. Type the subheading *Narrowing A Topic* in initial caps. Insert the dot leaders, and type the page number at the right margin.
8. Finish typing the table of contents below by repeating the directions in Steps 5-7. Single-space all subheadings.

CHOOSE A TOPIC	1
Narrowing a Topic	1
Broadening a Topic	2
GATHER INFORMATION	2
Library Research	2
Computer Searches	3
TAKE NOTES	3
ORGANIZE THE INFORMATION	4
Introduction	4
Body	4
Conclusion	5
WRITE A DRAFT	5
REVISE AND EDIT THE DRAFT	6

9. Save the document as STWP033 on your data disk.

Language Arts Connection

To generate interest in language arts, ask students what kinds of resources they might use when researching a topic. Make a list of their answers on the board. Possible responses include:

- Books
- Correspondence
- Court records
- Dictionaries
- Encyclopedias
- Interviews
- Magazines and journals
- Newspapers
- Original research
- Television and radio programs
- Videotapes and movies
- Web pages

Project 34

TABLE OF CONTENTS

Practice formatting another table of contents. Refer to the information on pages 200 and 201 as often as needed.

1. Open a new word processing document.
2. Use the tab set feature to set tabs for a table of contents with dot leaders.
3. Position the insertion point about 2 inches from the top of the page by pressing Return/Enter 6 times.

   Note: If your default font is Geneva 12 pt., press Return/Enter 5 times to position the insertion point at 2 inches.

4. Center the words CONTENTS in all caps and bold. Press Return/Enter 2 times.
5. Type the first main heading CHOOSING PUBLICITY in all caps. Insert the dot leaders and type the page number.
6. Press Enter twice to insert a blank line below the main heading.
7. Repeat Step 5 for the next main heading.
8. Press Tab once to indent the subheading. Type the subheading *Print Media* in initial caps. Insert the dot leaders and type the page number at the right margin.
9. Follow the directions given in steps 5–8 to finish typing the table of contents.

CHOOSING PUBLICITY	1
CAPTURING AN AUDIENCE	2
Print Media	2
Electronic Media	3
USING WORDS	3
USING MESSAGES AND IMAGES	4
PLANNING POSTERS	5
Purpose	6
Design	6
Content	6

10. Save the document as STWP034 on your data disk.

(continued on next page)

Table of Contents **203**

Project 34
Table of Contents

ASSESS—LEVEL 2

Purpose
Assess word processing skills by typing a table of contents.

Time
Fifteen minutes

Preparation
No special preparation required.

Teaching Tip
Students who finish early should repeat the project.

Trouble Shooting
Provide individual help to students who are having difficulty.

Language Arts Connection

To create interest in language arts, ask students what skills are needed to produce effective publicity. Write answers on the board. Possible responses include:

Design
Grammar
Interpersonal communication
Music
Organization
Photography
Planning
Public speaking
Research
Vocabulary
Writing

203

Table of Contents

Wrap Up

Have students review their document using **Check Your Understanding.** Have students make corrections.

If this is the last project for this class period, ask students to return computers and furniture to the appropriate conditions.

Language Link

ANSWERS

1. began
2. swam
3. came
4. sang
5. got

Project 34 (continued)

✓ Check Your Understanding

1. Did you type the word CONTENTS about 2 inches from the top of the page in bold and all caps?
2. Did you type the main headings at the left margin in all caps?
3. Did you type the subheadings single spaced, indented, in initial caps?
4. Did you type the page number at the right margin preceded by dot leaders?

Language Link

Irregular Verbs

Use caution when forming the past tense of irregular verbs. Many follow irregular patterns. Study the examples.

Pattern	Present	Past
One vowel changes to form the past tense.	begin	began
	sing	sang
	swim	swam
	come	came
	get	got

✓ Check Your Learning

For each sentence, supply the past tense of the verb in parentheses.

1. (begin) We _____ to research our report.
2. (swim) Sherry _____ the length of the pool.
3. (come) I _____ home after practice.
4. (sing) My mother _____ in the choir.
5. (get) He _____ a puppy for his birthday.

204 Section 9 Reports With Special Features

9.6 Report Outline

Goals
- Type a report outline
- Learn the outline style feature

FORMATTING A REPORT OUTLINE

When you are writing a report, your first step is usually to write an **outline** of your main topics and subtopics. You usually rearrange your topics several times before you are done. If you create your outline using your software, editing your outline is much easier because you can cut, paste, and move items. In general, use roman numerals for your main topics. Use letters and numbers for subtopics and subdivisions.

An outline can be created automatically by applying an **outline style** feature, or it can be created manually using preset tabs.

Outline Created With Outline Style

To create an outline automatically:

1. Type the title as illustrated below.
2. Issue the software command to create an outline style as you type.

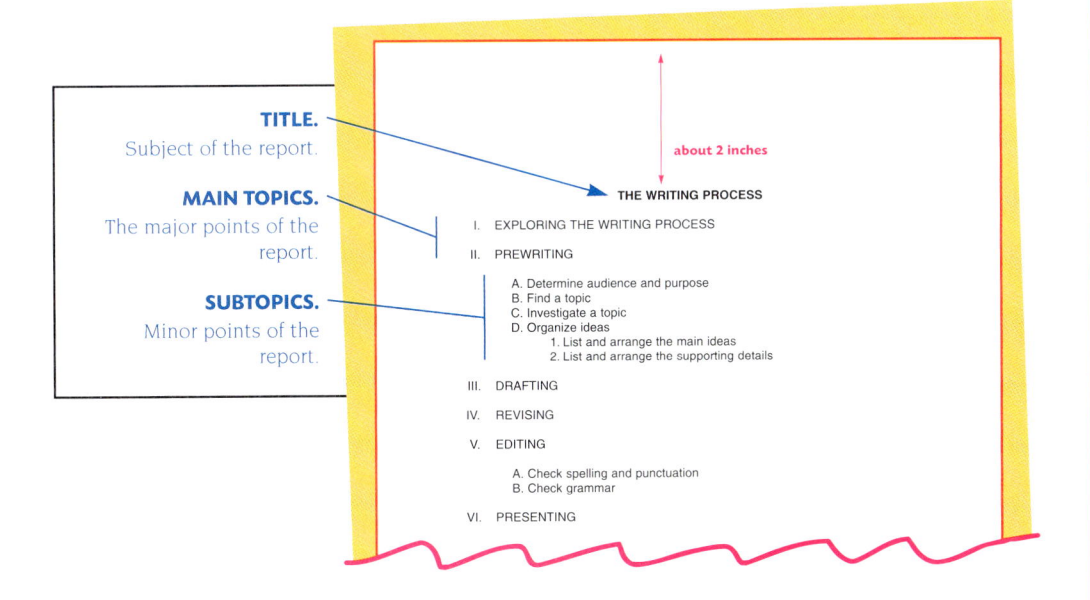

TITLE. Subject of the report.

MAIN TOPICS. The major points of the report.

SUBTOPICS. Minor points of the report.

about 2 inches

THE WRITING PROCESS

I. EXPLORING THE WRITING PROCESS
II. PREWRITING
    A. Determine audience and purpose
    B. Find a topic
    C. Investigate a topic
    D. Organize ideas
        1. List and arrange the main ideas
        2. List and arrange the supporting details
III. DRAFTING
IV. REVISING
V. EDITING
    A. Check spelling and punctuation
    B. Check grammar
VI. PRESENTING

Report Outline **205**

RESOURCES

- Lesson Plan: LP56
  Transparency Masters: TM17, TM18
- Transparency 11
- CD-ROM: Reference Guide
- Software: Research Files

9.6 Report Outline

FOCUS
Type a report outline. Learn the outline feature.

BELLRINGER
When students enter the room, direct their attention to the assignment on the board:
    Read pages 205 to 207.

TEACH
Focus on the usefulness of preparing an outline before writing a report. Review the steps to create an outline using outline style if the software students are using has this feature. If not, explain that students will create outlines manually. Use the illustration on page 205 to highlight the title, main topics, and subtopics.

205

Report Outline

TEACH

Review the steps to create an outline manually if the software students are using does not have an outline style feature. Use the illustration on page 206 to highlight the elements of an outline.

Outline Created Manually

To create an outline manually:

1. Type the title as illustrated below.
2. Type the first outline level (roman numeral I., for example).
3. Press Tab. Type the text for the main heading, and press Return/Enter.
4. Repeat Steps 2 and 3 for all main headings.
5. Type the next outline level (the letter A or the number 1., for example).
6. Press Tab. Type the text for the subheading, and press Return/Enter.
7. Repeat Steps 5 and 6 for all subheadings.

Study the illustrations before beginning. Your finished outline may look slightly different.

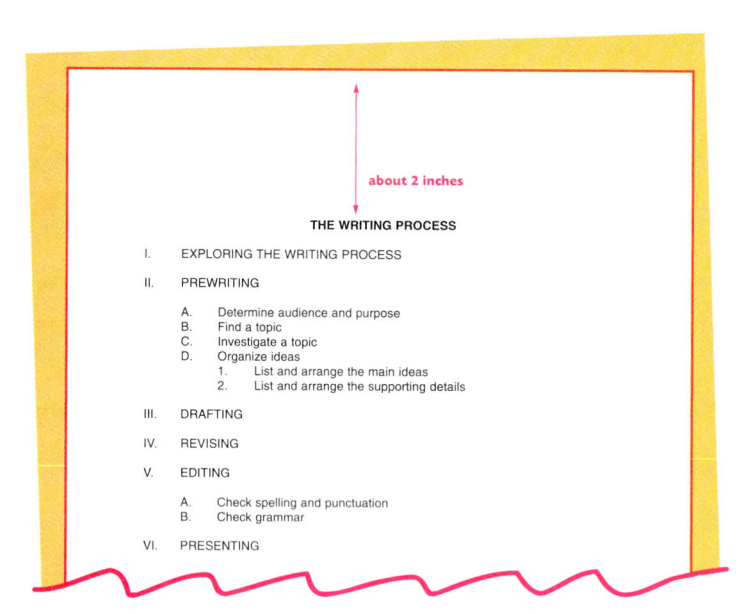

about 2 inches

THE WRITING PROCESS

I. EXPLORING THE WRITING PROCESS

II. PREWRITING
    A. Determine audience and purpose
    B. Find a topic
    C. Investigate a topic
    D. Organize ideas
        1. List and arrange the main ideas
        2. List and arrange the supporting details

III. DRAFTING

IV. REVISING

V. EDITING
    A. Check spelling and punctuation
    B. Check grammar

VI. PRESENTING

Section 9 Reports With Special Features

FORMATTING TIPS

- Type the title about 2 inches from the top of the page in bold and all caps. Insert a blank line after the title.
- Begin main topic lines with a roman numeral typed at the left margin. Use all caps, and leave a blank line above and below main topics.
- Begin a subtopic line with a letter or number. Capitalize the first word in the line. Use single spacing and indent subtopic lines as illustrated.

GO TO
Student Guide, Word Processing
Outline style

In Your Journal

Create an outline of important events in your life. List the most important events as main headings. List details about the events as subheadings.

Using the steps of the writing process will help you present your ideas more effectively.

Report Outline **207**

Report Outline

TEACH
Review formatting tips.

ASSESS
To assess understanding have students describe the main elements of a report outline.

CLOSE
Explain to students that they are now ready to type and format a report outline. Refer to Projects 35 and 36.

GO TO
Refer students to the appropriate section of the Student Guide.

In Your Journal

Offer some suggestions if students are having difficulty thinking of important events in their lives. Suggestions include:
    Your birth
    Birth of your brothers, sisters, cousins, etc.
    Moving into new apartment or house
    Moving from one city to another
    Starting school
    Learning to walk, talk, ride a bike, skate, etc.
    Getting glasses or braces
    Joining a club, scouting, or sports team

Project 35
Report Outline

PRACTICE—LEVEL 1

Purpose
Practice creating a report outline.

Time
Fifteen minutes

Preparation
Review the process for creating an outline for the software your students are using.

Teaching Tip
Students who finish early should repeat the project.

Trouble Shooting
Provide individual help to students who are having difficulty.

Wrap Up
If this is the last project for this class period, ask students to return computers and furniture to the appropriate conditions.

Language Arts Connection

Project 35

REPORT OUTLINE

Type a report outline by following these steps.

1. Open a new word processing document.
2. Position the insertion point about 2 inches from the top of the page by pressing Return/Enter 6 times.

   Note: If your default font is Geneva 12 pt., press Return/Enter 5 times to position the insertion point at 2 inches.

3. Center the title THE WRITING PROCESS using all caps and bold. Press Return/Enter 2 times.
4. Type the outline below either manually or using the **outline style** feature.

   I. EXPLORING THE WRITING PROCESS
   II. PREWRITING
      A. Determine audience and purpose
      B. Find a topic
      C. Investigate a topic
      D. Organize ideas
         1. List and arrange the main ideas
         2. List and arrange the supporting details
   III. DRAFTING
   IV. REVISING
   V. EDITING
      A. Check spelling and punctuation
      B. Check grammar
   VI. PRESENTING

5. Save the document as STWP035 on your data disk.

208 Section 9 Reports With Special Features

Language Arts Connection

To create interest in language arts, demonstrate the use of a thesaurus. Use a printed thesaurus. Ask students for suggestions of words to look up or use words that appear on page 208 including:

audience	main
details	new
feature	purpose
idea	report
investigate	top
list	topic

Project 36

REPORT OUTLINE

Practice formatting another report outline. Refer to the illustrations and steps on pages 205 and 206 as often as needed.

1. Open a new word processing document.
2. Position the insertion point about 2 inches from the top of the page by pressing Return/Enter 6 times.

   Note: If your default font is Geneva 12 pt., press Return/Enter 5 times to position the insertion point at 2 inches.

3. Center the title *EXPOSITORY WRITING* using all caps and bold. Press Return/Enter 2 times.
4. Type the outline below either manually or using the outline style feature.

   I. CONVEYING INFORMATION
   II. STRUCTURING AN EXPLANATION
   III. WRITING TO COMPARE AND CONTRAST
   IV. WRITING ABOUT A PROCESS
       A. Have a clear purpose
       B. Make the order clear
   V. ANSWERING AN ESSAY QUESTION
   VI. WRITING REPORTS
       A. Researching a topic
           1. Books
           2. Magazines
           3. Encyclopedias
           4. Video Materials
       B. Planning and drafting
       C. Revising, editing, and presenting

5. Save the document as STWP036 on your data disk.

Project 36
Report Outline

ASSESS—LEVEL 2

Purpose
Assess word processing skills by creating a report outline.

Time
Fifteen minutes

Preparation
Review the process of creating an outline for the software your students are using.

Teaching Tip
Students who finish early should repeat the project.

Trouble Shooting
Provide individual help to students who are having difficulty.

Wrap Up
If this is the last project for this class period, ask students to return computers and furniture to the appropriate conditions.

To create interest in language arts, plan a trip to the school library or the public library. Arrange for a librarian to speak to students about the resources of the library. If possible, ask for a demonstration of the on-line resources available.

9.7 Multipage Report

FOCUS
Type and format a multipage report with footer. Use the page number feature.

BELLRINGER
When students enter the room, direct their attention to the assignment on the board:
Read page 210.

TEACH
Explain that a footer is information that appears at the bottom of the page. Use the illustration on page 210 to highlight the footer.

ASSESS
To assess understanding have students use their own words to describe a footer.

CLOSE
Explain to students that they are now ready to type and format a multipage report with a footer. Refer to Projects 37, 38, 39, and 40.

Refer students to the appropriate section of the Student Guide.

210

Multipage Report with Footer

9.7

FORMATTING A MULTIPAGE REPORT WITH A FOOTER

A **footer** is information that appears at the bottom of the page in a document. Multipage reports frequently have page numbers at the foot of the page. Study the illustration. Your finished report may look slightly different.

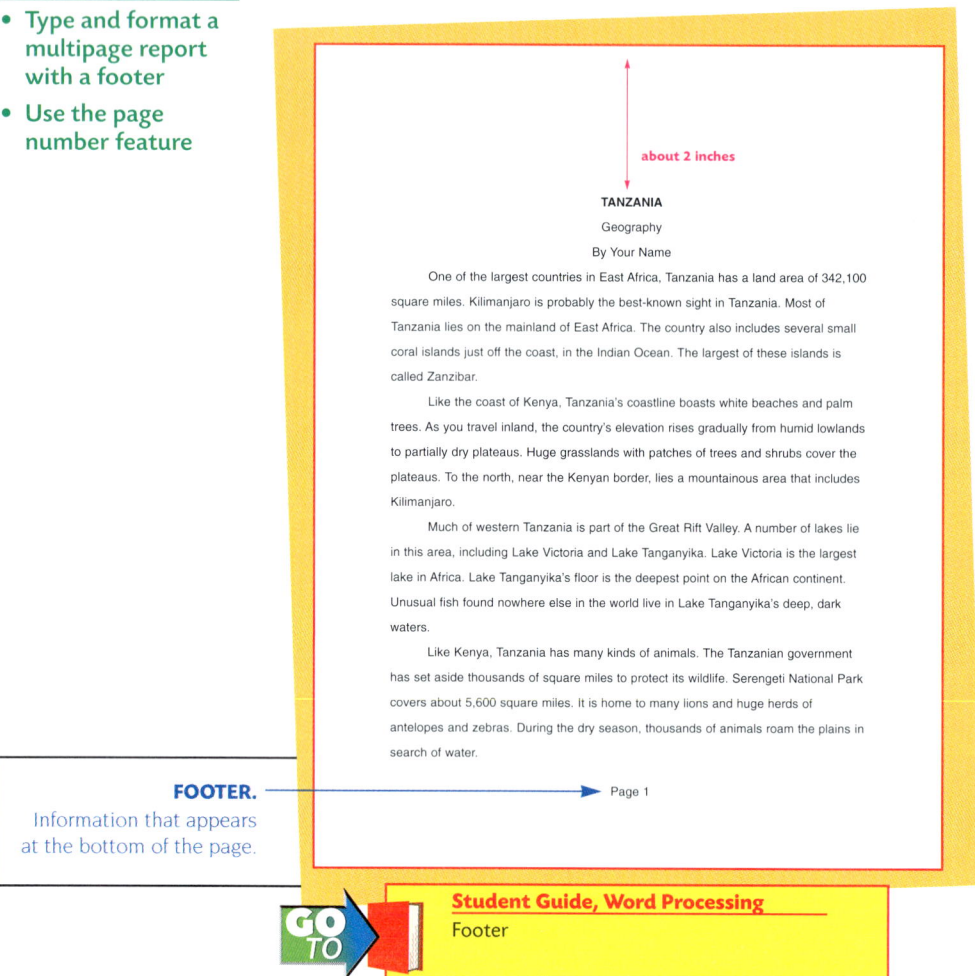

Goals
- Type and format a multipage report with a footer
- Use the page number feature

about 2 inches

TANZANIA
Geography
By Your Name

One of the largest countries in East Africa, Tanzania has a land area of 342,100 square miles. Kilimanjaro is probably the best-known sight in Tanzania. Most of Tanzania lies on the mainland of East Africa. The country also includes several small coral islands just off the coast, in the Indian Ocean. The largest of these islands is called Zanzibar.

Like the coast of Kenya, Tanzania's coastline boasts white beaches and palm trees. As you travel inland, the country's elevation rises gradually from humid lowlands to partially dry plateaus. Huge grasslands with patches of trees and shrubs cover the plateaus. To the north, near the Kenyan border, lies a mountainous area that includes Kilimanjaro.

Much of western Tanzania is part of the Great Rift Valley. A number of lakes lie in this area, including Lake Victoria and Lake Tanganyika. Lake Victoria is the largest lake in Africa. Lake Tanganyika's floor is the deepest point on the African continent. Unusual fish found nowhere else in the world live in Lake Tanganyika's deep, dark waters.

Like Kenya, Tanzania has many kinds of animals. The Tanzanian government has set aside thousands of square miles to protect its wildlife. Serengeti National Park covers about 5,600 square miles. It is home to many lions and huge herds of antelopes and zebras. During the dry season, thousands of animals roam the plains in search of water.

FOOTER. Information that appears at the bottom of the page. → Page 1

GO TO Student Guide, Word Processing
Footer

210 Section 9 Reports With Special Features

RESOURCES
- Lesson Plan: LP57
  Transparency Master: TM19
- Transparency 7
- CD-ROM: Reference Guide
- Software: Research Files

Social Studies Connection

Project 37

MULTIPAGE REPORT WITH FOOTER

Follow these steps to format a multipage report with a footer.

1. Open the file WP037 on your data disk.
2. Change the line spacing for the report to double.
3. Press Return/Enter 3 times to position the insertion point about 2 inches from the top of the page.
4. Center the title of the report *TANZANIA* in bold and all caps.
5. Center the title of the class *Geography* under the report title.
6. Center your name under the class name.
7. Create a **footer.**
8. Center the word *Page* followed by a space and the page number. Use the page number feature to insert the page number.
9. Add the paragraphs below to the end of the report:

> Scientists have found the remains of some of the earliest human settlements in Tanzania. By about A.D. 500, Bantu-speaking peoples had settled in this area. Nearly 600 years later, Arabs from Southwest Asia set up major trading centers on Zanzibar and other islands. The region that is now Tanzania came under European control beginning in the early 1500s. After periods of Portuguese and German rule, the area came under British control following World War I. In the 1960s, the Tanzanians finally won their independence as the United Republic of Tanzania.
>
> Today about 80 percent of Tanzania's people live in rural villages. Dar es Salaam, on the Indian Ocean, is Tanzania's largest city and major port. The central area of Tanzania has few people. In an effort to encourage people to move there, the Tanzanian government has built a new national capital named Dodoma in the area.

10. Save the document as STWP037 on your data disk.

Project 37
Multipage Report

PRACTICE—LEVEL 1

Purpose
Practice formatting a multi-page report with a footer including a page number.

Time
Thirty minutes

Preparation
Review the page number feature for the software your students are using.

Teaching Tip
Make sure that students understand that the page number feature will automatically number the pages of the report.

Students who finish early should repeat the project

Trouble Shooting
Provide individual help to students who are having difficulty.

Wrap Up
If this is the last project for this class period, ask students to return computers and furniture to the appropriate conditions.

Social Studies Connection

Ask students to research an African nation and create a fact sheet that contains the official name of the country, the country's flag, and answer these questions.

- *What are the area and population?*
- *What are the form of government and the title of the head of state?*
- *What year did the country become a nation?*

Lesson Extension

Help students to select an African nation for the activity described in the Social Studies Connection. Following are some lesser-known African nations:

Benin	Guinea-Bissau
Cape Verde	Mali
Comoros	Seychelles
Djibouti	

Project 38
Multipage Report

APPLY—LEVEL 1

Purpose
Apply word processing skills by formatting a multipage report with a footer including a page number.

Time
Thirty minutes

Preparation
Review the page number feature for the software your students are using.

Teaching Tip
Remind students about guidelines for page breaks—no widows or orphans.
   Students who finish early should repeat the project

Trouble Shooting
Provide individual help to students who are having difficulty.

Wrap Up
If this is the last project for this class period, ask students to return computers and furniture to the appropriate conditions.

Project 38
Social Studies Connection
MULTIPAGE REPORT WITH FOOTER

Practice formatting another multipage report with a footer similar to the one in Project 37. Refer to the illustration on page 210 as often as needed.

1. Open the file WP038 on your data disk.
2. Change the line spacing for the report to double.
3. Press Return/Enter 3 times to position the insertion point about 2 inches from the top of the page.
4. Center the title of the report ANTARCTICA in bold and all caps.
5. Center the title of the class *Geography* under the report title.
6. Center your name under the class name.
7. Create a footer.
8. Center the word *Page* followed by a space and the page number. Use the page number feature to insert the page number.
9. Add the paragraphs below to the end of the report:

> A high, flat plateau covers the area east of the Transantarctic Mountains. The earth's southernmost point, the South Pole, lies on the plateau at the center of Antarctica. West of the mountains is a group of low islands buried under layers and layers of ice. On Ross Island rises the peak of Mount Erebus. At 12,220 feet, it is Antarctica's most active volcano.
>
> Scientists believe Antarctica hides a treasure chest of minerals. The mining of resources on this continent is a source of international disagreement, however. Antarctica has major deposits of coal and lesser amounts of copper, gold, iron ore, manganese, and zinc hidden underneath its ice cap. Petroleum may lie offshore. None of Antarctica's mineral resources have been developed. Many people believe that mining these resources would harm Antarctica's fragile environment.

10. Save the document as STWP038 on your data disk.

212 Section 9 Reports With Special Features

Social Studies Connection

Have students name the continents and the largest country (area) and highest mountain on each continent. Correct responses include:

Continents	Largest Country	Highest Mountain
1. Africa	Sudan	Kilimanjaro (Tanzania)
2. Antarctica	(No countries)	Vinson Massif
3. Asia	China	Everest (Nepal-Tibet)
4. Australia	Australia	Kosciusko
5. Europe	Russia	Mont Blanc (France-Italy)
6. N. America	Canada	McKinley (Alaska)
7. S. America	Brazil	Aconcagua (Argentina)

Project 39

MULTIPAGE REPORT WITH FOOTER

Practice formatting another multipage report by typing an original multipage report with a footer. Write your report about any topic related to geography. Refer to the information given on pages 210 and 211 as often as needed.

Animals that are common to a country can be an interesting topic related to geography. This photo shows zebras on the Serengeti Plain in Tanzania.

1. Open a new word processing file.
2. Center the title of your report about 2 inches from the top of the page.
3. Center the title of the class *Geography* under the report title.
4. Center your name under the class name.
5. Create a footer.
6. In the footer, center the word *Page* followed by a space and the page number. Use the page number feature to insert the page number.
7. Type the body of the report.
8. Save the document as STWP039 on your data disk.

✓ Check Your Understanding

1. Did you use the footer feature to insert a page number at the bottom of each page?
2. Did you type the word *Page* followed by a space and the page number?

Multipage Report **213**

Social Studies Connection

To create interest in social studies, ask students to select an animal that is native to Africa. Ask students to research the animal selected and be prepared to share three facts with classmates. Encourage students to bring pictures of the animal selected. African animals include:

camel	jackal
cheetah	jerboa
flamingo	mamba
gazelle	mongoose
giraffe	rhinoceros
hyena	zebra
ibex	

Project 39
Multipage Report

ASSESS—LEVEL 2

Purpose
Assess word processing skills by creating a multipage report with a footer.

Time
One class period

Preparation
Students will need to select and research a geography topic before they can begin Project 39. They might want to expand the fact sheet they created for the Social Studies Connection assignment on page 211. Make the following assignment several days before students are expected to complete Project 39:

Select and research any geography topic. Bring your notes to class and be prepared to write a multipage report—approximately 500 words. You may use the fact sheet you wrote about an African nation.

Teaching Tip
Students who finish early should review their work and make improvements.

Trouble Shooting
Provide individual help to students who are having difficulty.

Wrap Up
Have students review their document using **Check Your Understanding.** Have students make corrections.

If this is the last project for this class period, ask students to return computers and furniture to the appropriate conditions.

Project 40
Building Your Portfolio

ASSESS—LEVEL 2

Purpose
Assess word processing skills by formatting a multipage report including side headings, a footer, and a table of contents.

Time
One class period

Preparation
No special preparation required.

Teaching Tip
Students who finish early should repeat the project.

Trouble Shooting
Provide individual help to students who are having difficulty.

Wrap Up
Ask students to return computers and furniture to the appropriate conditions.

Project 40
Building Your Portfolio

In this project, you will review formatting and word processing features. You will format a multipage report with side headings, a footer, and a table of contents. The table of contents will be created as a separate document. If you need to review any formatting or software features, refer to previous projects as often as needed.

Study the illustration. Your finished project may look slightly different.

(continued on next page)

214 Section 9 Reports With Special Features

Science Connection

To create interest in science, create a bulletin board display about the solar system. Ask students to help with the display.

NOW TRY THIS

1. Open the file WP040A on your data disk.
2. Change the line spacing for the report to double.
3. Insert a footer. In the footer, center the word *Page* followed by the page number.
4. Center your name under the title of the class.
5. Insert the following side headings typed in bold and all caps in front of the paragraphs that begin with a bold **X:** *formation of the solar system, motions of the planets, terrestrial planets, the outer planets, pluto and charon,* and *other objects in the solar system.*

(continued on next page)

Building Your Portfolio

Project 40 *(continued)*
Building Your Portfolio

6. Add the paragraphs below to the end of the report:

> While the space between planets is mostly empty, space does contain millions of solid particles. Most of these particles come from comet nuclei that have broken up or collisions that have caused asteroids to break up. These small pieces of rock moving through space are then called meteorides. Meteorides range in size from grains of sand to huge fragments of rock. If a meteoride enters Earth's gravitational field and is pulled toward Earth's surface, it becomes a meteor. A meteor that strikes Earth's surface is called a meteorite.
>
> As scientists continue to explore our solar system, it is possible that one day an astronaut may be sent as far away as Mars. However, it seems more likely that a space probe could do the same amount of exploration at a much lower cost. Also, lives are not at risk when a space probe rather than a human is used. Whatever the end result is, the solar system is a vast place that holds a wealth of information.

7. Save the document as STWP040A on your data disk.
8. Open a new word processing file.
9. Type the table of contents below. Add the page numbers by referring to the report created earlier:

> FORMATION OF THE SOLAR SYSTEM
> MOTIONS OF THE PLANETS
> TERRESTRIAL PLANETS
> THE OUTER PLANETS
> PLUTO AND CHARON
> OTHER OBJECTS IN THE SOLAR SYSTEM

10. Save the document as STWP040B on your data disk.

Section 9 Reports With Special Features

SECTION 10

Letters and Memos

Focus on Letters and Memos

You can use letters to communicate informally with a friend or relative or to communicate more formally with a business or individual. Memos are used to communicate informally with another member of a group. Your letters and memos are like personal messengers. Your reader will form an impression of you based on the content and appearance of your messages. Follow the formatting guidelines and use the word processing features in this section to make a good impression on your reader.

OBJECTIVES

- Create, format, and edit:
  - Informal letters
  - Formal letters with enclosures
  - Memos from rough draft copy with proofreaders' marks

Words To Know

block style
body
closing
date (command)
enclosure
enclosure notation
envelope
formal letter
greeting
informal letter
inside address
memo
memo heading
return address

Section 10 Letters and Memos

SECTION OVERVIEW

This section focuses on correspondence both formal and informal. Proofreaders' marks are also introduced. Students will use the block style for formal letters.

CONTENT FOCUS

Informal letter
Formal letter
Memo

CURRICULUM FOCUS

Technology
Math

OPENING ACTIVITY

Ask students why people write letters. Make a list on the board. Examples of the reasons to write a letter include:
  Ask someone to purchase something
  Complain about a product or service
  Congratulate someone on an achievement
  Express an opinion
  Introduce a product or service
  Make someone a job offer
  Provide information
  Request information
  Share good news

Career Exploration Activities: Environment

Have students plan to write a formal letter to the Human Resources Manager of a local business, government agency, or organization that deals with environmental issues. Each student will need to locate a mailing address for the entity they select.

Students should request information about careers related to the environment.

Note: Students can write actual letters as part of Project 46.

10.1 Informal Letter

FOCUS
Type and format an informal letter. Practice the date command.

BELLRINGER
When students enter the room, direct their attention to the assignment on the board:
Read pages 218 and 219.

TEACH
Use the illustration on page 118 to highlight the parts of the letter: date, greeting, body, and closing.

10.1 Informal Letter

Goals
- Type and format an informal letter
- Practice the date command

FORMATTING AN INFORMAL LETTER

An **informal letter** is a personal letter you might write to a friend, a family member, or maybe a teacher. It might be a thank-you letter, an invitation, or just a conversational note. Because this is a personal letter, your writing should have a casual tone. You might want to choose a font that looks like handwriting. Study this illustration. Your informal letter may look slightly different.

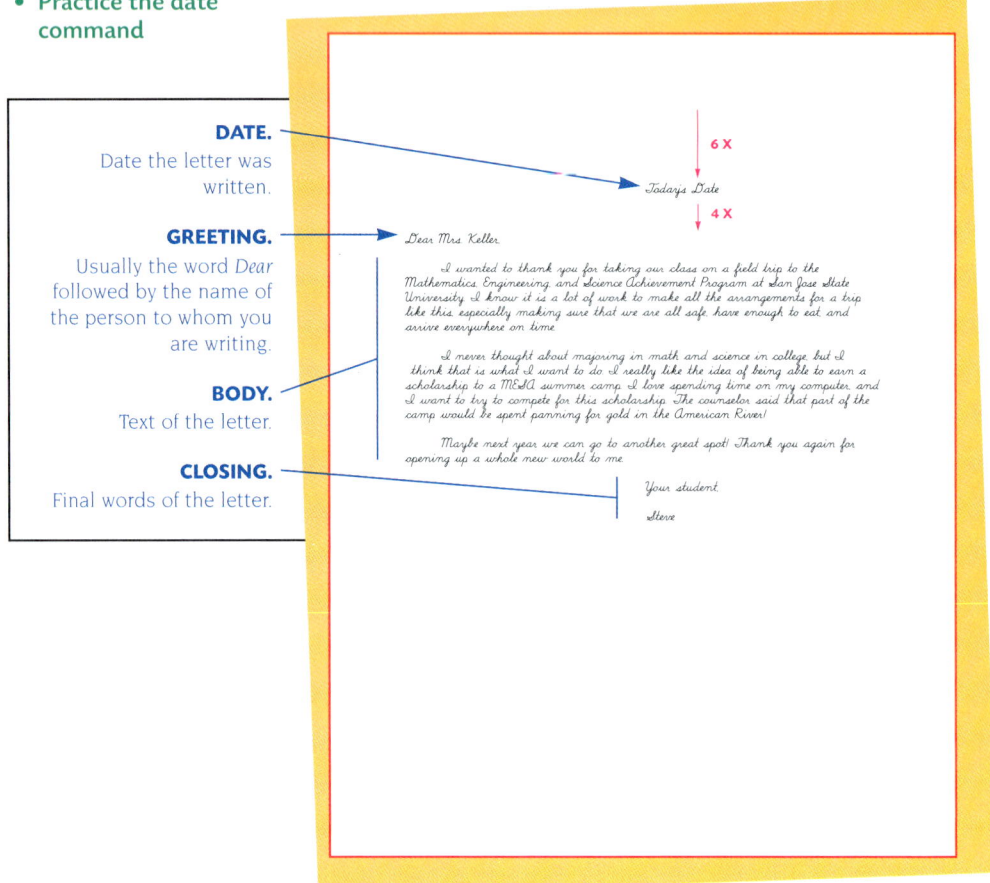

DATE. Date the letter was written.

GREETING. Usually the word *Dear* followed by the name of the person to whom you are writing.

BODY. Text of the letter.

CLOSING. Final words of the letter.

218 Section 10 Letters and Memos

RESOURCES
- Lesson Plan: LP58
- Supplemental Project: SP2
- Transparency Master: TM20
- Transparency 12
- CD-ROM: Reference Guide
- Software: Research Files

FORMATTING TIPS

- Type the date about 2 inches from the top starting at the horizontal center of the page.
- Type the greeting 4 lines below the date followed by a comma.
- Indent the first line of each paragraph 0.5 inch. Use single spacing and leave one blank line between paragraphs.
- Follow the closing with a comma, 1 blank line, and the name of the writer. Type the closing and the writer's name starting at the horizontal center of the page.

GO TO Student Guide, Word Processing
Date

In Your Journal

Write an informal note to a friend describing what kinds of courses you think you might study in college or some other school you might wish to attend.

Colleges, such as San Jose State University, provide opportunities for studies in math and science.

Informal Letter

TEACH

Review formatting tips.

ASSESS

To assess understanding have students identify the components of an informal letter.

CLOSE

Explain to students that they are now ready to type and format an informal letter. Refer to Projects 41, 42, and 43.

GO TO Refer students to the appropriate section of the Student Guide.

In Your Journal

Ask students to include information about the courses they plan to take in high school that will prepare them for additional education.

Informal Letter **219**

Project 41
Informal Letter

PRACTICE—LEVEL 1

Purpose
Practice typing an informal letter using the date command.

Time
Thirty minutes

Preparation
Review the use of date commands for the software your students are using.

Teaching Tip
Explain the difference between the command that inserts today's date and the command that inserts a date field. Whenever you open the file, the current date appears in the field. Also point out that the format of the date can be changed.

Students who finish early should repeat the project. Experiment with various date formats.

Trouble Shooting
Provide individual help to students who are having difficulty with the date command.

Wrap Up
If this is the last project for this class period, ask students to return computers and furniture to the appropriate conditions.

Project 41

INFORMAL LETTER

Type an informal letter using the following steps.

1. Open the file WP041 on your data disk.
2. Change the font to a script (handwriting) font of your choice.
3. Set two left tabs for the document. Set the first tab at 1.5 inches from the left edge of the page (0.5 inch from the 1.25-inch left margin). Set the second tab at 4.25 inches from the left edge of the page (3 inches from the 1.25-inch left margin). Remember to select all text before setting tabs.
4. At the top of the document, press Return/Enter 6 times. Press Tab twice to move to the center of the page. Use the **date** command to insert the current date.
5. If necessary, change the format of the date to one that has the month (spelled out), day of the month, and year.
6. Press Return/Enter 4 times. Type the greeting *Dear Mrs. Keller* followed by a comma.
7. Type the paragraph below immediately after the first paragraph.

> I never thought about majoring in math and science in college, but I think that is what I want to do. I really like the idea of being able to earn a scholarship to a MESA summer camp. I love spending time on my computer, and I want to try to compete for this scholarship. The counselor said that part of the camp would be spent panning for gold in the American River!

8. Press Tab twice. Type the closing *Your student*, followed by a comma. Press Return/Enter 2 times.
9. Press Tab twice, and type your name.
10. Insert blank lines between paragraphs as needed.
11. Save the document as STWP041 on your data disk.

Section 10 Letters and Memos

Project 42

INFORMAL LETTER

Practice using the formatting and word processing features you learned in Project 41 by arranging another informal letter. Refer to the illustration and information on pages 218 and 219 as often as needed.

1. Open the file WP042 on your data disk.
2. Change the font to a script (handwriting) font of your choice.
3. Set two left tabs for the document. Set the first tab at 1.5 inches from the left edge of the page (0.5 inch from the 1-inch left margin). Set the second tab at 4.25 inches from the left edge of the page (3 inches from the 1.25-inch left margin). Remember to select all text before setting tabs.
4. Press Return/Enter 6 times. Press Tab twice to move to the center of the page. Use the date command to insert the current date.
5. If necessary, change the format of the date to one that has the month (spelled out), day of the month, and year.
6. Press Return/Enter 4 times. Type the greeting *Dear Ron* followed by a comma.
7. Type the paragraph below immediately after the first paragraph.

> I am also very interested in competing for the scholarship to the summer camp. Since the counselor said that we could have several people on the team, I was wondering if you would be interested in being on a team that I am organizing. There will be a total of four of us, and I think we would have a great chance at winning the scholarship.

8. Press Tab twice. Type the closing *Your friend*, followed by a comma. Press Return/Enter 2 times.
9. Press Tab twice, and type your name.
10. Insert blank lines between paragraphs as needed.
11. Save the document as STWP042 on your data disk.

Project 42
Informal Letter

APPLY—LEVEL 1

Purpose
Apply word processing skills by formatting an informal letter.

Time
Thirty minutes

Preparation
Review the use of date commands for the software your students are using.

Teaching Tip
Review with students the difference between the command that inserts today's date and the command that inserts a date field. Also point out that the format of the date can be changed.

Students who finish early should repeat the project. Experiment with various date formats.

Trouble Shooting
Provide individual help to students who are having difficulty using the date command.

Wrap Up
If this is the last project for this class period, ask students to return computers and furniture to the appropriate conditions.

Project 43
Informal Letter

ASSESS—LEVEL 2

Purpose
Assess word processing skills by typing and formatting an informal letter.

Time
One class period

Preparation
Have students complete the In Your Journal activity on page 222 before they start Project 43.

Teaching Tip
Students who finish early should repeat the project. Encourage them to write to a different person.

Trouble Shooting
Provide individual help to students who are having difficulty.

Wrap Up
Have students review their document using **Check Your Understanding.** Have students make corrections.

Students who would like to actually send their letters should be encouraged to do so.

In Your Journal
Help students to locate addresses for the persons to whom they want to write.

Project 43
INFORMAL LETTER

Practice using the word processing and formatting features you learned in Project 41 by typing an original informal letter. Write your letter to anyone you wish about anything that interests you.

1. Open a new word processing file.
2. Set two left tabs for the document. Set the first tab at 1.5 inches from the left edge of the page (0.5 inch from the 1-inch left margin). Set the second tab at 4.25 inches from the left edge of the page (3 inches from the 1.25-inch left margin). Remember to set tabs before typing or after selecting all text.
3. Type the letter.
4. Save the document as STWP043 on your data disk.

In Your Journal

Think about a person to whom you would like to write an informal letter. You might write to someone you know about, but have never met, such as a scientist or an athlete. To help you begin writing the letter, ask yourself questions such as:

- *What do I know about this person?*
- *Why do I want to write a letter to this person?*
- *What will I talk about in my letter?*

✓ Check Your Understanding

1. Did you type the date about 2 inches from the top of the page starting at the center?
2. Did you type the greeting 4 lines below the date?
3. Did you type the closing followed by a comma, 1 blank line, and your name starting at the center?

222 Section 10 Letters and Memos

10.2 Formal Letter

FORMATTING A FORMAL LETTER

A **formal letter** is a letter you might write to a person in business or to an organization. It might be a letter asking for information, a letter expressing an opinion, or perhaps a letter of complaint. Your writing for this type of letter should have a formal rather than a casual tone.

Study the illustration. Your formal letter may look slightly different.

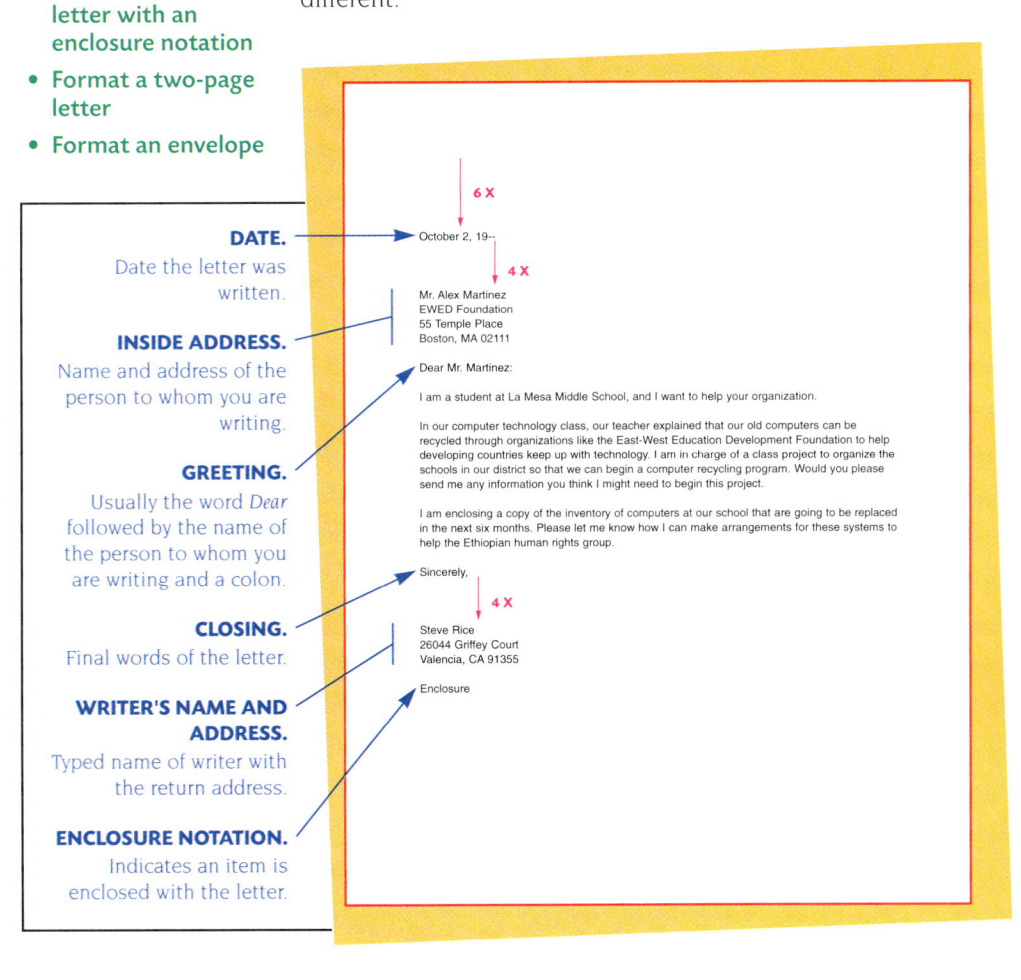

Goal
- Format a formal letter with an enclosure notation
- Format a two-page letter
- Format an envelope

DATE. Date the letter was written.

INSIDE ADDRESS. Name and address of the person to whom you are writing.

GREETING. Usually the word *Dear* followed by the name of the person to whom you are writing and a colon.

CLOSING. Final words of the letter.

WRITER'S NAME AND ADDRESS. Typed name of writer with the return address.

ENCLOSURE NOTATION. Indicates an item is enclosed with the letter.

---

6 X

October 2, 19--

4 X

Mr. Alex Martinez
EWED Foundation
55 Temple Place
Boston, MA 02111

Dear Mr. Martinez:

I am a student at La Mesa Middle School, and I want to help your organization.

In our computer technology class, our teacher explained that our old computers can be recycled through organizations like the East-West Education Development Foundation to help developing countries keep up with technology. I am in charge of a class project to organize the schools in our district so that we can begin a computer recycling program. Would you please send me any information you think I might need to begin this project.

I am enclosing a copy of the inventory of computers at our school that are going to be replaced in the next six months. Please let me know how I can make arrangements for these systems to help the Ethiopian human rights group.

Sincerely,

4 X

Steve Rice
26044 Griffey Court
Valencia, CA 91355

Enclosure

Formal Letter **223**

10.2 Formal Letter

FOCUS
Format a formal letter with an enclosure notation. Format a two-page letter. Format an envelope.

BELLRINGER
When students enter the room, direct their attention to the assignment on the board:
Read pages 223–225.

TEACH
Use the illustration on page 223 to highlight the parts of a formal letter: date; inside address; greeting; body; closing; writer's name and address; and enclosure notation. Use the illustration on page 218 to compare and contrast formal and informal letters.

RESOURCES
Lesson Plan: LP58
Supplemental Project: SP3
Transparency Masters: TM21, TM22, TM23

Transparency 13

CD-ROM: Reference Guide

Software: Research Files

Formal Letter

TEACH

Review the formatting tips. Use the illustration on page 224 to highlight the heading used for a two-page letter.

Because this is a formal letter, it should follow a standard business format. To simplify the letter, you will type all the information at the left margin in what is called **block style**. A **return address** should be included so that the person you are writing to will be able to write back to you easily. If you are including another item with a letter—perhaps a copy of something—that item is called an **enclosure**. You will need to type a special notation at the end of the letter called an **enclosure notation**.

FORMATTING TIPS

- Type the date about 2 inches from the top of the page.
- Type the inside address 4 lines below the date.
- Type the greeting 4 lines below the date.
- Capitalize the first word of the closing and follow it with a comma.
- Type the writer's name and return address 4 lines below the closing on separate lines.
- Type the enclosure notation 2 lines below the writer's address.

Some formal letters are more than one page long. The illustration of a two-page letter shows you information that should be included at the top of the second page.

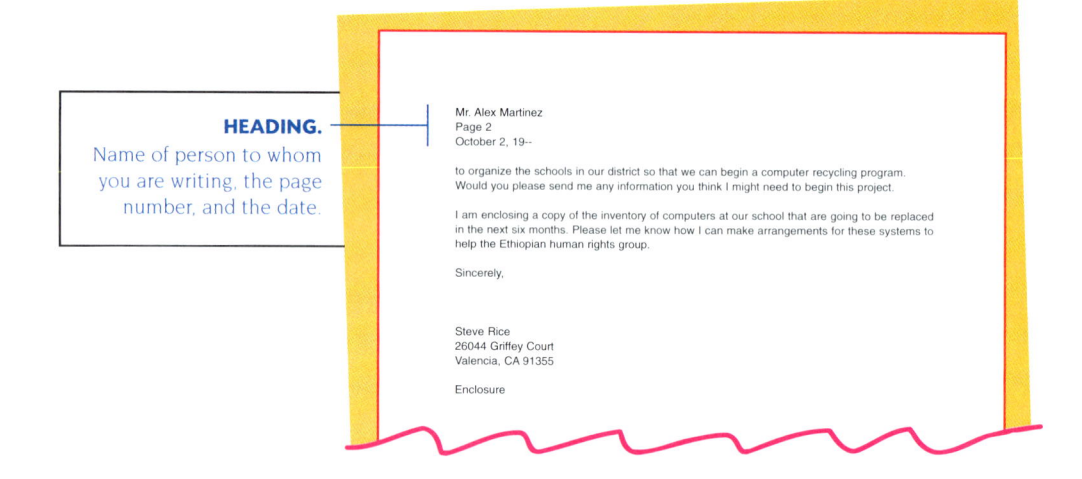

HEADING. Name of person to whom you are writing, the page number, and the date.

Mr. Alex Martinez
Page 2
October 2, 19--

to organize the schools in our district so that we can begin a computer recycling program. Would you please send me any information you think I might need to begin this project.

I am enclosing a copy of the inventory of computers at our school that are going to be replaced in the next six months. Please let me know how I can make arrangements for these systems to help the Ethiopian human rights group.

Sincerely,

Steve Rice
26044 Griffey Court
Valencia, CA 91355

Enclosure

224 Section 10 Letters and Memos

Lesson Extension

Some word processing software programs have an envelope feature. If the software your students are using has it, demonstrate the feature.

FORMATTING TIPS

- Type each item of the second-page heading on a separate line.
- Double-space from the heading to the body of the letter.

A formal letter should be mailed in a standard large envelope with a typed address. Many software programs have an envelope feature that makes creating an envelope easy. The illustration of the large envelope shows you where to type the address information.

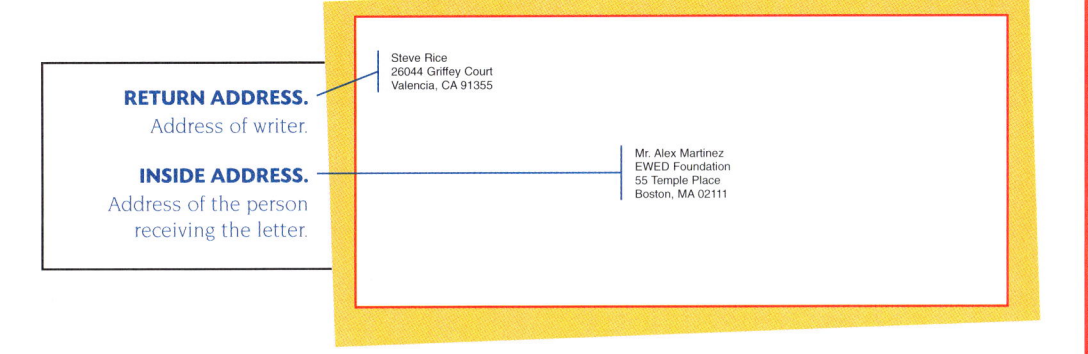

RETURN ADDRESS. Address of writer.

INSIDE ADDRESS. Address of the person receiving the letter.

Steve Rice
26044 Griffey Court
Valencia, CA 91355

Mr. Alex Martinez
EWED Foundation
55 Temple Place
Boston, MA 02111

FORMATTING TIPS

- Type the return address about 0.5 inch from the top of the envelope and about 0.5 inch in from the left edge.
- Type the inside address about 2 inches from the top of the envelope and about 4 inches in from the left edge.

It is important to use the correct formatting style when writing business letters.

Formal Letter

TEACH

Review formatting tips for a two-page letter. Use the illustration on page 225 to highlight the parts of a standard large envelope: return address and inside address. Review formatting tips for an envelope.

ASSESS

To assess understanding have students identify the components of a formal letter.

CLOSE

Explain to students that they are now ready to type and format a formal letter. Refer to Projects 44, 45, 46, and 50.

Project 44
Formal Letter

PRACTICE—LEVEL 1

Purpose
Practice typing and formatting a formal letter including an enclosure notation.

Time
Fifteen minutes

Preparation
No special preparation required.

Teaching Tip
Students who finish early should repeat the project.

Trouble Shooting
Provide individual help to students who are having difficulty formatting a formal letter.

Wrap Up
If this is the last project for this class period, ask students to return computers and furniture to the appropriate conditions.

Project 44
Technology Connection
FORMAL LETTER WITH ENCLOSURE

Follow these steps to create a formal letter with an enclosure notation. Refer to the illustration on page 223.

1. Open the file WP044 on your data disk.
2. Press Return/Enter 6 times and insert the current date.
3. Press Return/Enter 4 times and type the inside address.

> Mr. Alex Martinez
> EWED Foundation
> 55 Temple Place
> Boston, MA 02111

4. Press Return/Enter 2 times. Type the greeting *Dear Mr. Martinez* followed by a colon.
5. Type the closing *Sincerely* followed by a comma. Press Return/Enter 4 times.
6. Type the writer's name and address on separate lines:

> Steve Rice
> 26044 Griffey Court
> Valencia, CA 91355

7. Press Return/Enter 2 times and type *Enclosure*.
8. Insert blank lines between paragraphs as needed.
9. Save the document as STWP044 on your data disk.

226 Section 10 Letters and Memos

Technology Connection

To create interest in technology, check to see if a computer recycling program is available in your area. If one exists, share information with your students.

Project 45

FORMAL LETTER WITH ENCLOSURE

Practice using the formatting and word processing features you learned in Project 44 by arranging another formal letter with an enclosure notation. Refer to the illustration and information on pages 223 and 224 as often as needed.

1. Open the file WP045 on your data disk.
2. From the top of the document, press Return/Enter 6 times and insert today's date.
3. Press Return/Enter 4 times and type the inside address on separate lines:

   > Ms. Patricia Lee
   > Boston Computer Society
   > 101A First Avenue
   > Waltham, MA 02154

4. Press Return/Enter 2 times. Type the greeting *Dear Ms. Lee* followed by a colon.
5. Type the closing *Sincerely* followed by a comma. Press Return/Enter 4 times.
6. Type the writer's name and address on separate lines:

   > Natalie Fisher
   > 39244 La Vita Court
   > Boulder, CO 80323

7. Press Return/Enter 2 times and type *Enclosure*.

   > Enclosure

8. Insert blank lines between paragraphs as needed.
9. Save the document as STWP045 on your data disk.

Formal Letter **227**

Project 45
Formal Letter

APPLY—LEVEL 1

Purpose
Apply word processing skills by typing and formatting a formal letter with an enclosure notation.

Time
Fifteen minutes

Preparation
No special preparation required.

Teaching Tip
Students who finish early should repeat the project.

Trouble Shooting
Provide individual help to students who are having difficulty formatting a formal letter.

Wrap Up
If this is the last project for this class period, ask students to return computers and furniture to the appropriate conditions.

To create interest in technology, have students create tabletop displays about the technology they are learning about in this course. To encourage cooperative learning, divide the class into groups of three or four students. Have each group create a display. Showcase the displays during an open house or parent-teacher conferences.

Project 46
Formal Letter

ASSESS—LEVEL 2

Purpose
Assess word processing skills by typing and formatting an original formal letter with an enclosure.

Time
One class period

Preparation
Direct students to the **In Your Journal** activity on page 228 before they begin writing their letters. If your students completed the **Career Exploration** activity on page 217, they can use the information in that activity to complete this project.

Teaching Tip
Consider having students actually mail their letters. In this case an enclosure notation might not be appropriate. Provide instructions for typing and formatting an envelope.

Trouble Shooting
Provide individual help to students who are having difficulty formatting a formal letter or an envelope.

Wrap Up
Have students review their document using **Check Your Understanding.** Have students make corrections.

In Your Journal
Show students how to copy their journal entry to make it the body of their letter.

Project 46

FORMAL LETTER WITH ENCLOSURE

Practice using the word processing and formatting features you learned in Project 44 by typing an original formal letter with an enclosure notation. Write your letter to anyone you wish about anything that interests you.

1. Open a new word processing file.
2. From the top of the document, press Return/Enter 6 times and insert today's date.
3. Press Return/Enter 4 times. Type the inside address on separate lines.
4. Press Return/Enter 2 times. Type the greeting followed by a colon.
5. Type the body of the letter.
6. Type the closing *Sincerely* followed by a comma. Press Return/Enter 4 times.
7. Type your name and address as the writer.
8. Press Return/Enter 2 times and type *Enclosure*.
9. Insert blank lines between paragraphs as needed.
10. Save the document as STWP046 on your data disk.

In Your Journal
Think about what you will say in your formal letter. Are you asking someone for information? Are you expressing an opinion? Are you complaining about something you would like the person to handle? Pretend you are meeting with the person face to face. Write what you would say to this person. Use your journal entry as the starting point for your letter.

✓ Check Your Understanding

1. Did you begin all your lines at the left margin?
2. Did you type a colon after the greeting and a comma after the closing?
3. Did you include an enclosure with the letter and type the enclosure notation two lines below your address?

228 Section 10 Letters and Memos

10.3 Memo

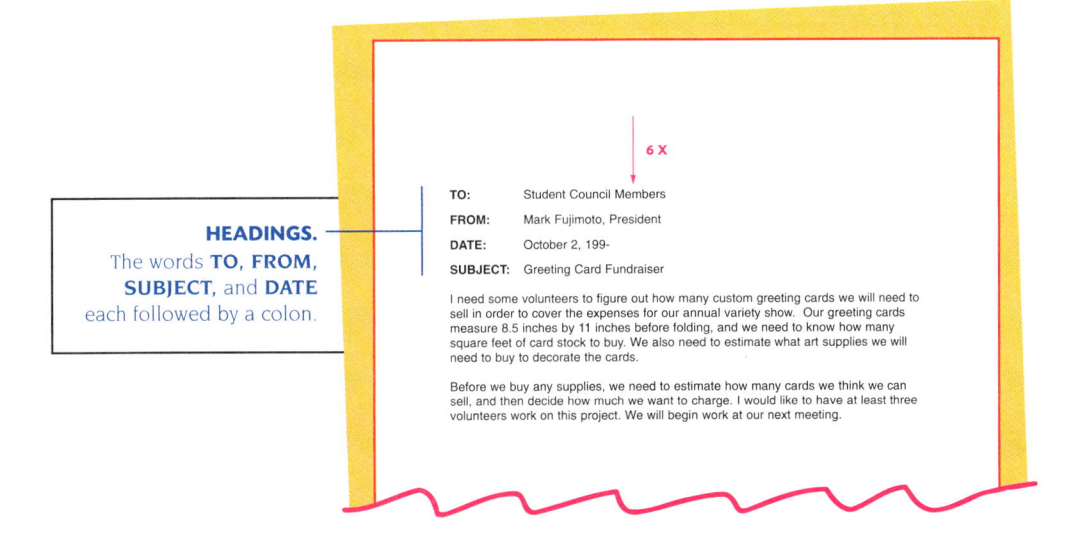

FORMATTING A MEMO

A **memo** is an informal way to exchange information, usually between people within the same group. For example, you might be a member of a student club and need to communicate information to club members, a teacher, or perhaps the principal. A memo would be ideal. Memos have headings that make them easier to read and answer. If a memo is being composed by members of a group, using proofreaders' marks might be helpful if you need to make changes or corrections.

Study the illustration. Your memo may look slightly different.

Goals
- Type and format a memo
- Type from copy with proofreaders' marks

HEADINGS. The words **TO, FROM, SUBJECT,** and **DATE** each followed by a colon.

6 X

TO: Student Council Members
FROM: Mark Fujimoto, President
DATE: October 2, 199-
SUBJECT: Greeting Card Fundraiser

I need some volunteers to figure out how many custom greeting cards we will need to sell in order to cover the expenses for our annual variety show. Our greeting cards measure 8.5 inches by 11 inches before folding, and we need to know how many square feet of card stock to buy. We also need to estimate what art supplies we will need to buy to decorate the cards.

Before we buy any supplies, we need to estimate how many cards we think we can sell, and then decide how much we want to charge. I would like to have at least three volunteers work on this project. We will begin work at our next meeting.

FORMATTING TIPS

- Press Tab once or twice to align the information after the heading words.
- Type headings in bold and all caps followed by a colon.

10.3 Memo

FOCUS
Type and format a memo. Type from copy with proofreaders' marks.

BELLRINGER
When students enter the room, direct their attention to the assignment on the board:
Read pages 229 and 230.

TEACH
Discuss the advantages of using a memo instead of a letter. Use the illustration on page 229 to highlight the headings used in a memo: TO, FROM, DATE, and SUBJECT. Review formatting tips.

RESOURCES
Lesson Plan: LP59
Supplemental Project: SP4
Transparency Master: TM25

Transparency 14

CD-ROM: Reference Guide

Software: Research Files

Memo

TEACH

Review the proofreaders' marks on page 230. Let students know that this list includes only the most commonly used marks.

ASSESS

To assess understanding have students identify the components of a memo.

CLOSE

Explain to students that they are now ready to type and format a memo. Refer to Projects 47, 48, and 49.

PROOFREADERS' MARKS

Symbol	Draft Copy	Final Copy
∧ Insert	the ∧student club	the student club
⸺ Delete	the ~~final~~ estimate	the estimate
∽ Reverse	they find all	they all find
¶ New paragraph	to finish. They want	to finish. They want
⊙ Period	She left⊙ He followed her.	She left. He followed her.
∧ Comma	If I go∧so will he.	If I go, so will he.
≡ Capital letter	president Lincoln	President Lincoln
/ Lower-case letter	our club President	our club president

Creating a memo is a great way to share information with group members.

230 Section 10 Letters and Memos

Lesson Extension

Dictionaries and style manuals can be used as resources for additional proofreaders' marks. Ask students to look up some additional proofreaders' marks. Ask them to find the symbols for the following:

Center
Close up space
Insert space
Spell out
Start new line

Project 47

MEMO

Follow these steps to create a memo. Refer to the proofreaders' marks on page 231 as needed.

1. Open a new word processing document.
2. Type the memo below following the directions in Steps 3–5 and making the changes indicated by the proofreaders' marks.

> TO: Student ^Council^ Members
>
> FROM: Marlene Fujimoto, President
>
> DATE: October 2, 199-
>
> SUBJECT: Variety Show Fund Raiser ~~Activities~~
>
> I need some volunteers to figure out how many greeting ~~custom~~ cards we will need to sell in order to cover the expenses for our annual variety show. Our ~~G~~reeting ~~C~~ards measure 8.5 inches by 11 inches before folding and we need to know how many square feet of card stock to buy. We also need to estimate what art supplies we will need to buy to decorate the cards. Before we buy any supplies, we need to estimate how many cards we think we can sell, and then decide how much we want to charge. I would like to have at least three volunteers work on this project. we will begin work at our next meeting.

3. At the top of the document, press Return/Enter 6 times. Type each heading followed by a colon in bold.
4. Press Tab once or twice as needed to align the information after the headings.
5. Insert one blank line after each heading and between the paragraphs.
6. Save the document as STWP047 on your data disk.

Project 47
Memo

PRACTICE—LEVEL 1

Purpose
Practice typing a memo incorporating the changes indicated by proofreaders' marks.

Time
Fifteen minutes

Preparation
No special preparation required.

Teaching Tip
Students who finish early should repeat the project.

Trouble Shooting
Provide individual help to students who are having difficulty with proofreaders' marks.

Wrap Up
If this is the last project for this class period, ask students to return computers and furniture to the appropriate conditions.

Math Connection: If your word processing software includes a formula or mathematics command, demonstrate the feature to your class. Refer to the reference material for the software for help in explaining this command. When using the help command, search for formula and/or mathematics.

Project 48
Memo

APPLY—LEVEL 1

Purpose
Apply word processing skills by typing and formatting a memo from copy with proofreaders' marks.

Time
Fifteen minutes

Preparation
No special preparation required.

Teaching Tip
Students who finish early should repeat the project.

Trouble Shooting
Provide individual help to students who are having difficulty with proofreaders' marks.

Wrap Up
If this is the last project for this class period, ask students to return computers and furniture to the appropriate conditions.

Project 48
MEMO

Practice creating another memo from copy with proofreaders' marks. Refer to the illustration and information on pages 230 and 231 as often as needed.

1. Open a new word processing document.
2. Type the memo below following the directions in Steps 3–5 and making the changes indicated by the proofreaders' marks.

> TO: Mr. Zanuck
>
> FROM: Kelly McKay
>
> DATE: March 11, 199-
>
> SUBJECT: Survey for math Class
>
> As part of a math assignment my teacher has asked me to survey the students in your class by asking them several questions. After I tally the responses, I will then prepare a bar graph and pie chart of the results of the survey. Would it be possible for me to take ten minutes of your students' time on Tuesday to conduct the survey? I promise to be very quick and organized so that everything will go smoothly. I will also be happy to send your class the results of the survey. Please let me know if you approve of my project. Thank you.

3. Press Return/Enter 6 times. Type each heading followed by a colon in bold.
4. Press Tab once or twice as needed to align the information after the headings.
5. Insert one blank line after each heading and between the paragraphs.
6. Save the document as STWP048 on your data disk.

232 Section 10 Letters and Memos

Math Connection

To create interest in mathematics, demonstrate how to insert a pie chart in a word processing document. For example, you might create a document that explains how you will calculate grades for this course. You can include a pie chart to show the relationship among the various elements used to calculate the grade. See sample data below.

Attendance	5%
Class participation	10%
Homework assignments	10%
Tests	25%
Final Project	50%

Project 49

MEMO

Practice using the formatting features you learned in Project 47 by typing an original memo. Write your memo to anyone about anything you wish.

1. Open a new word processing file.
2. Press Return/Enter 6 times. Type each heading followed by a colon in bold.
3. Press Tab once or twice as needed to align the information after the headings. Insert one blank line after each heading.
4. Type the body of the memo.
5. Save the document as STWP049 on your data disk.

✓ Check Your Understanding

1. Did you type the heading about two inches from the top of the page?
2. Did you type the heading words in bold and all caps followed by a colon?
3. Did you press the tab key to align the information after the heading words?

Language Link

Carefully proofread your document and correct any errors.

The color on the blue ~~pear~~ *pair* of shoes is fading.
He located the ~~from~~ *form* on top ~~the of~~ *of the* desk.
The attendant ~~begun~~ *began* to check the many ~~order~~ *orders*.

✓ Check Your Learning

Proofread each sentence, and identify all errors.

1. The group has write there letter.
2. That sight was marked for the biulding.
3. Your are going to drive the new car.
4. Where our the papers you requested?
5. The dog winced with each breathe.

Memo **233**

Project 49
Memo

ASSESS—LEVEL 2

Purpose
Assess word processing skills by typing and formatting an original memo.

Time
Fifteen minutes

Preparation
No special preparation required.

Teaching Tip
Students who finish early should repeat the project. Instruct them to write a different memo.

Trouble Shooting
Provide individual help to students who are having difficulty deciding on a topic.

Wrap Up
Have students review their document using **Check Your Understanding.** Have students make corrections.

If this is the last project for this class period, ask students to return computers and furniture to the appropriate conditions.

Language Link
ANSWERS

1. *written their*
2. *site, building*
3. *You*
4. *are*
5. *breath*

233

Project 50
Building Your Portfolio

ASSESS

Purpose
Assess word processing skills by formatting and editing a formal letter.

Time
Thirty minutes

Preparation
No special preparation required.

Teaching Tip
Students who finish early should repeat the project.

Trouble Shooting
Provide individual help to students who are having difficulty.

Wrap Up
Ask students to return computers and furniture to the appropriate conditions.

Project 50
Building Your Portfolio

Math Connection 4x=64

In this portfolio project you will review formatting and word processing features you have learned. You will format a formal letter with an enclosure and edit the letter based on rough draft copy. If you need to review any formatting or software features, refer to previous projects as often as needed.

Study the illustration. Your finished formal letter may look slightly different.

[Today's Date]

Mr. Robert Shearson
Academy of Finance
131 Livingston Street
Brooklyn, NY 11201

Dear Mr. Shearson:

I first learned about the Academy of Finance during a career day at our school. I was so encouraged to find out that businesses are willing to work with young students to prepare us for the working world.

A good friend of mine qualified for a job-shadowing arrangement, and I think it would be great to be in a real business and watch everything that goes on firsthand. Would you please send me some information or forms so that I can apply? I am enclosing a copy of my school records so that you can see what classes I am taking and what grades I have earned.

Thank you so much for your help.

Sincerely,

Corey Springer
22825 Lockness Avenue
Queens, NY 11378

Enclosure

NOW TRY THIS

1. Open the file WP050 on your data disk.
2. Press Return/Enter 6 times, and insert the current date.
3. Press Return/Enter 4 times. Type the inside address on separate lines:

   > Mr. Robert Shearson
   > Academy of Finance
   > 131 Livingston Street
   > Brooklyn, NY 11201

4. Press Return/Enter 2 times. Type the greeting *Dear Mr. Shearson* followed by a colon.

(continued on next page)

234 Section 10 Letters and Memos

5. Make the changes in the body of the letter as shown by the proofreaders' marks below.

> I first learned about the academy of finance during a career day at our school. I was so encouraged to find out that Businesses are willing to work with young students to prepare us for the working world.
>
> A very good friend of mine qualified for a job-shadowing arrangement and I think it would be great to be in a real business and watch everything that goes on firsthand. Would you please send me some information or forms so that I can apply? I am enclosing a copy of my school records so that you can see what classes I am taking and what grades have I earned. Thank you so much for your help.

6. Type the closing *Sincerely* followed by a comma. Press Return/Enter 4 times.
7. Type the writer's name and address on separate lines:

> Corey Springer
> 22825 Lockness Avenue
> Queens, NY 11378

8. Press Return/Enter 2 times and type *Enclosure*.
9. Insert blank lines between paragraphs as needed.
10. Save the document as STWP050 on your data disk.

Section 11
Personal Applications

SECTION OVERVIEW

This section focuses on personal applications including outlines and class notes. Students will practice typing from handwritten notes.

CONTENT FOCUS

Chapter Outline
Presentation Outline
Class Notes

CURRICULUM FOCUS

Science
Language Arts

OPENING ACTIVITY

Ask students to brainstorm about personal applications for word processing. Ask them to think of personal applications that they have not yet learned.

SECTION 11
Personal Applications

OBJECTIVES

- Create, format, and edit:
  - Chapter outlines
  - Presentation outlines
  - Class notes

Focus on Personal Applications

You can use your word processing software as a tool to help you learn and study more effectively. In this section, you will practice creating chapter and presentation outlines to organize your thoughts and identify key points and details. You will also type class notes to review and reinforce your learning.

Words To Know

chapter outline
class notes
column feature
heading
main topic
presentation outline
subtopic

---

236 Section 11 Personal Applications

Career Exploration Activities: Personal Service

There are many careers that involve personal service. Some examples include: barber, dog groomer, flight attendant, hair stylist, housekeeper, nail technician, nanny, and personal shopper. Ask students how individuals with careers in personal service might use a personal computer. Possible responses include:

Create a brochure or flyer about services
Develop a database of clients
Generate mailing labels for advertising or promotion
Keep track of appointments
Maintain financial records
Produce invoices and statements
Write a resume and cover letter

11.1 Chapter Outline

FORMATTING A CHAPTER OUTLINE

When you are reviewing for a test or writing a report, it is a good idea to outline the chapter you are studying. Typing an outline of the main topics and subtopics in a chapter makes you an active learner, and it is a good study habit to develop. Outlining helps you organize and clarify your thoughts.

Goals
- Type a chapter outline
- Practice the outline style feature

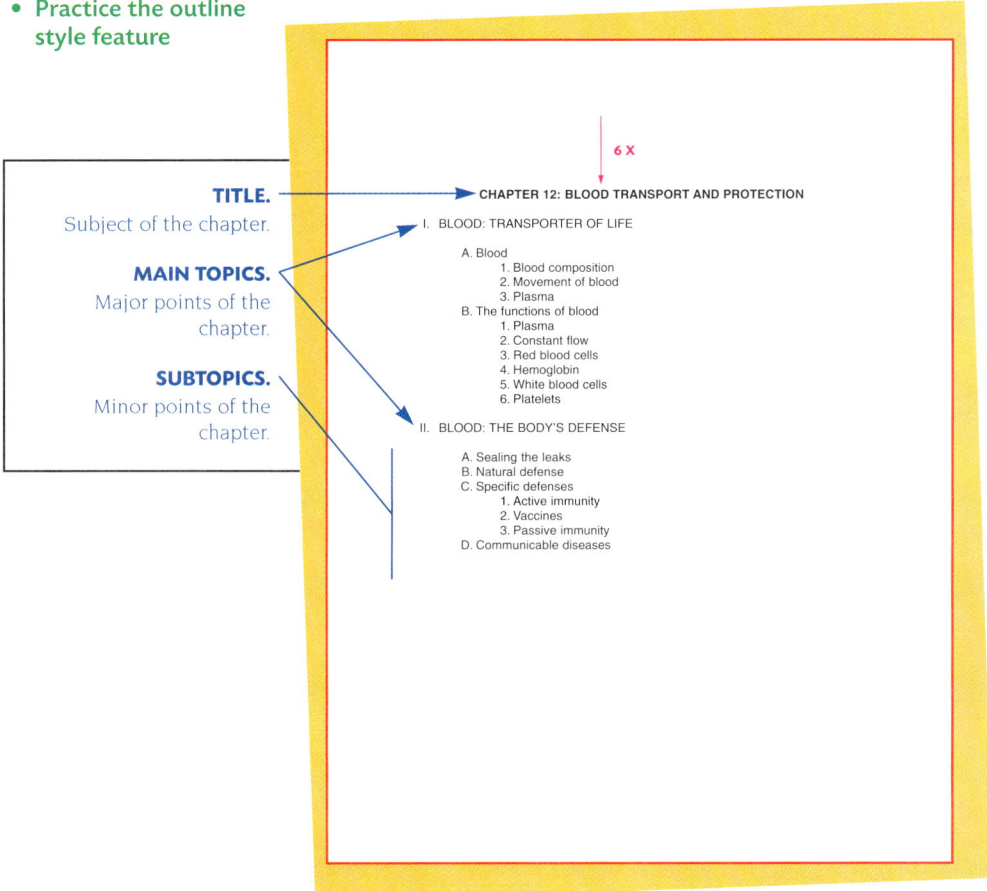

TITLE. Subject of the chapter.

MAIN TOPICS. Major points of the chapter.

SUBTOPICS. Minor points of the chapter.

↓ 6 X

CHAPTER 12: BLOOD TRANSPORT AND PROTECTION

I. BLOOD: TRANSPORTER OF LIFE
  A. Blood
    1. Blood composition
    2. Movement of blood
    3. Plasma
  B. The functions of blood
    1. Plasma
    2. Constant flow
    3. Red blood cells
    4. Hemoglobin
    5. White blood cells
    6. Platelets

II. BLOOD: THE BODY'S DEFENSE
  A. Sealing the leaks
  B. Natural defense
  C. Specific defenses
    1. Active immunity
    2. Vaccines
    3. Passive immunity
  D. Communicable diseases

11.1 Chapter Outline

FOCUS
Type a chapter outline. Practice the outline style feature.

BELLRINGER
When students enter the room direct their attention to the assignment on the board:
Read pages 237 and 238.

TEACH
Use the illustration on page 237 to highlight the elements of an outline: title, main topics, and subtopics.

RESOURCES
- Lesson Plan: LP60
- Transparency Master: TM26
- CD-ROM: Reference Guide
- Software: Research Files

Chapter Outline

TEACH

Remind students that good outline style requires that at least two lower level topics be used when dividing a higher level topic.

ASSESS

To assess understanding have students identify the components of a chapter outline.

CLOSE

Explain to students that they are now ready to type a chapter outline. Refer to Projects 51 and 57.

DID YOU KNOW

In addition to donated blood, modern medicine also depends on tissue and organ donation. The first successful kidney transplant was done in 1951. The first heart transplant was in 1967. While there have been many advances, transplantation medicine still depends on the availability of donor organs and tissue.

Chapter outlines are created in the same way as a report outline. In general, use roman numerals for your main topics. Use letters and numbers for any subtopics and subdivisions.

Look over Project 35 (page 208) if you need to review the steps to create an outline. Study the illustration before beginning. Your finished chapter outline may look slightly different.

FORMATTING TIPS

- Type the title about 2 inches from the top of the page in bold and all caps. Insert a blank line after the title.

- Begin main topic lines with a roman numeral typed at the left margin. Use all caps, and leave a blank line above and below main topics.

- Begin a subtopic line with a letter or number. Capitalize the first word in the line. Use single spacing and indent subtopic lines as illustrated.

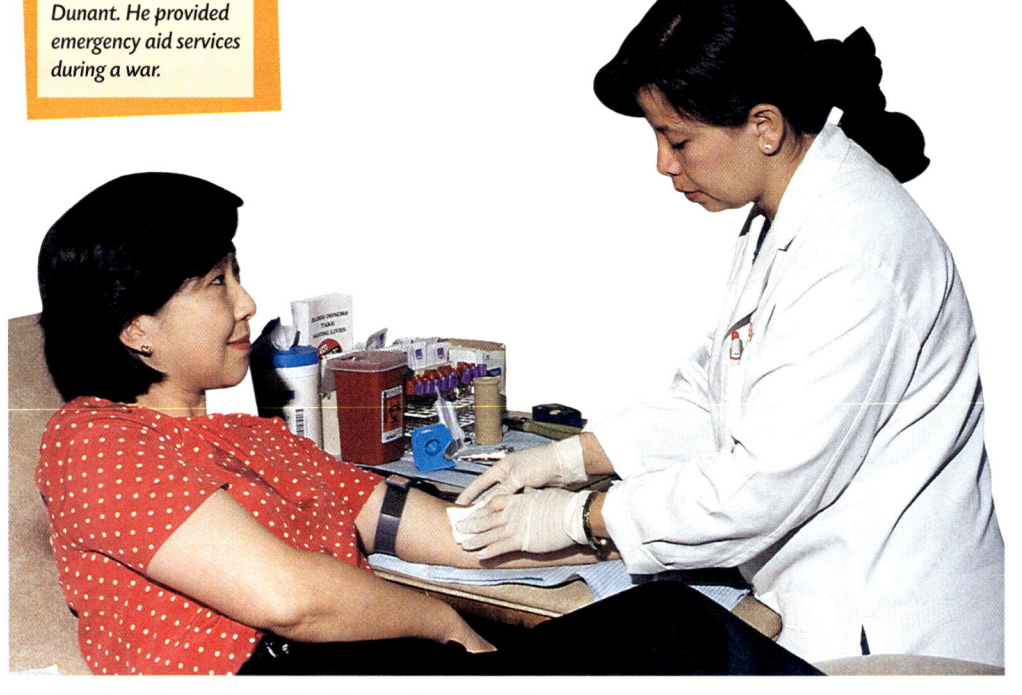

CULTURAL KALEIDOSCOPE

The International Red Cross provides services that benefit people all around the world. This organization maintains blood banks around the world. The idea for the Red Cross came from a Swiss humanitarian, Jean-Henri Dunant. He provided emergency aid services during a war.

Blood banks collect and store blood for use in emergencies.

238 Section 11 Personal Applications

CULTURAL KALEIDOSCOPE

The American Red Cross was founded in 1881 by Clara Barton. The organization's current mission is to provide disaster relief and help people prevent, prepare for, and respond to emergencies. The American Red Cross includes about 2200 local chapters, 44 regional blood centers, and 26 tissue services centers. There are more than 1.5 million volunteers participating in American Red Cross programs.

The American Red Cross is affiliated with the International Red Cross and Red Crescent Movement. In Muslim nations the relief organizations are known as Red Crescent societies.

Source: *Microsoft Encarta 96 Encyclopedia*, Microsoft Corporation, 1993–1995.

Project 51

CHAPTER OUTLINE

Follow these steps to create a chapter outline.

1. Open a new word processing document.
2. Position the insertion point about 2 inches from the top of the page by pressing Return/Enter 6 times.

   Note: If your default font is Geneva 12 pt., press Return/Enter 5 times to position the insertion point at 2 inches.

3. Center the title CHAPTER 12: BLOOD TRANSPORT AND PROTECTION using all caps and bold.
4. Press Return/Enter 2 times.
5. Type the outline below either manually or using the outline style feature.

   I. BLOOD: THE TRANSPORTER OF LIFE
      A. Blood
         1. Blood composition
         2. Movement of blood
         3. Plasma
      B. The functions of blood
         1. Plasma
         2. Constant flow
         3. Red blood cells
         4. Hemoglobin
         5. White blood cells
         6. Platelets
   II. BLOOD: THE BODY'S DEFENSE
      A. Sealing the leaks
      B. Natural defense
      C. Specific defenses
         1. Active immunity
         2. Vaccines
         3. Passive immunity
      D. Communicable diseases

6. Save the document as STWP051 on your data disk.

Project 51 Chapter Outline

PRACTICE—LEVEL 1

Purpose
Practice creating a chapter outline.

Time
Fifteen minutes

Preparation
Review the process for creating an outline for the software your students are using.

Teaching Tip
Students who finish early should repeat the project.

Trouble Shooting
Provide individual help to students who are having difficulty creating an outline.

Wrap Up
If this is the last project for this class period, ask students to return computers and furniture to the appropriate conditions.

Science Connection

To generate interest in science, teach students to measure their heart rate. Provide the following instructions:

1. *Place your fingers on your neck between your ear and your Adam's apple.*
2. *Push gently and move your fingers around until you feel a strong beat.*

What you are feeling is blood as it pulses through the carotid artery.

3. *Count the number of beats you feel for 15 seconds. Then multiply that number by four. This number is your heart rate for one minute.*

Source: Bill Aldridge et al., *Science Interactions*, Glencoe/McGraw Hill, 1995.

11.2 Presentation Outline

FOCUS
Type and format a presentation outline. Practice the outline style feature.

BELLRINGER
When students enter the room, direct their attention to the assignment on the board:
Read pages 240 and 242.

TEACH
Use the illustration on page 240 to highlight the elements of an outline: title, main topics, and subtopics.

11.2 Presentation Outline

FORMATTING A PRESENTATION OUTLINE

When you are preparing to give an oral presentation, you must understand your content, practice your presentation, and maintain your confidence. Creating an outline of the main topics and subtopics in a presentation helps you organize and clarify your thoughts so that you truly understand your content.

Goals
- Type and format a presentation outline
- Practice the outline style feature

TITLE. Subject of the presentation.

MAIN TOPICS. Major points of the presentation.

SUBTOPICS. Minor points of the presentation.

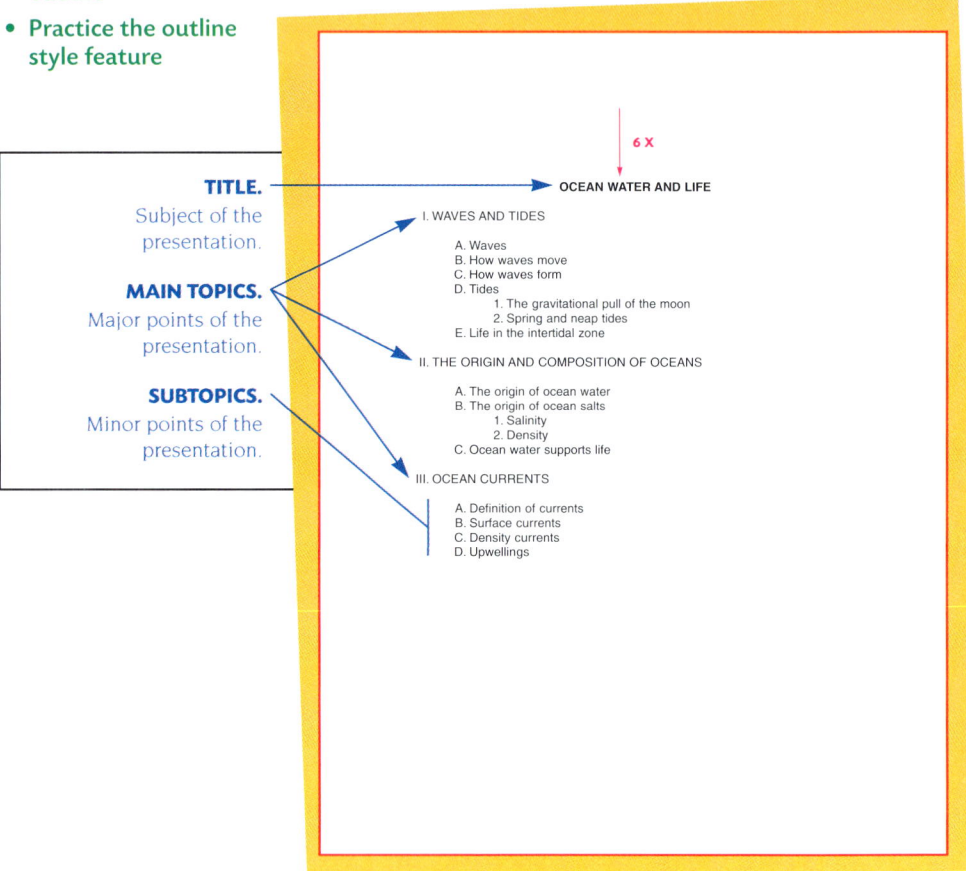

↓ 6 X

OCEAN WATER AND LIFE

I. WAVES AND TIDES
    A. Waves
    B. How waves move
    C. How waves form
    D. Tides
        1. The gravitational pull of the moon
        2. Spring and neap tides
    E. Life in the intertidal zone

II. THE ORIGIN AND COMPOSITION OF OCEANS
    A. The origin of ocean water
    B. The origin of ocean salts
        1. Salinity
        2. Density
    C. Ocean water supports life

III. OCEAN CURRENTS
    A. Definition of currents
    B. Surface currents
    C. Density currents
    D. Upwellings

240 Section 11 Personal Applications

RESOURCES

Lesson Plan: LP61
Supplemental Project: SP5
Transparency Master: TM27

CD-ROM: Reference Guide

Software: Research Files

A **presentation outline** is created in the same way as a report outline. In general, use roman numerals for your main topics. Use letters and numbers for subtopics and subdivisions.

Look over Project 35 (page 208) if you need to review the steps to create an outline. Study the illustration before beginning. Your finished presentation outline may look slightly different.

FORMATTING TIPS

- Type the title about 2 inches from the top of the page in bold and all caps. Insert a blank line after the title.
- Begin main topic lines with a roman numeral typed at the left margin. Use all caps and leave a blank line above and below main topics.
- Begin a subtopic line with a letter or number. Capitalize the first word in the line. Use single spacing and indent subtopic lines as illustrated.

In Your Journal

Think about a subject you could talk about in an oral presentation for your classmates. Write an outline that includes main topics and subtopics about the subject. Include details that you feel would interest your classmates.

Making an outline helps you organize your thoughts and clarify what you heard.

Presentation Outline **241**

Presentation Outline

TEACH
Review the formatting tips.

ASSESS
To assess understanding have students identify the components of a presentation outline.

CLOSE
Explain to students that they are now ready to type a presentation outline. Refer to Projects 52 and 53.

In Your Journal
Encourage students to look at previous journal entries for topic ideas.

CULTURAL KALEIDOSCOPE

Arabic numerals were developed in India around 300 B.C. The system was introduced in the Arab world around A.D. 700. Roman numerals were created more than 2000 years ago. This system uses only seven letters. For larger numbers, a small line is placed over the top of the letter to indicate multiplication by 1000.

Arabic	Roman
1	I
5	V
10	X
50	L
100	C
500	D
1,000	M
5,000	$\overline{V}$

241

Project 52
Presentation Outline

PRACTICE—LEVEL 1

Purpose
Practice creating a presentation outline.

Time
Fifteen minutes

Preparation
Review the process for creating an outline for the software your students are using.

Teaching Tip
Students who finish early should repeat the project.

Trouble Shooting
Provide individual help to students who are having difficulty creating an outline.

Wrap Up
If this is the last project for this class period, ask students to return computers and furniture to the appropriate conditions.

DID YOU KNOW
Offshore wells produce approximately 25 percent of the world's annual oil output. The first offshore drilling was done in shallow water using a platform that was supported by legs that rested on the ocean floor. Currently, floating platforms are used to drill in waters as deep as 1000 m.

Project 52

Science Connection

PRESENTATION OUTLINE

Follow the steps below to create a presentation outline.

1. Open a new word processing document.
2. Position the insertion point about 2 inches from the top of the page by pressing Return/Enter 6 times.

   Note: If your default font is Geneva 12 pt., press Return/Enter 5 times to position the insertion point at 2 inches.

3. Center the title OCEAN WATER AND LIFE using all caps and bold.
4. Press Return/Enter 2 times.
5. Type the outline below either manually or using the outline style feature.

   I. WAVES AND TIDES
      A. Waves
      B. How waves move
      C. How waves form
      D. Tides
         1. The gravitational pull of the moon
         2. Spring and neap tides
      E. Life in the intertidal zone
   II. THE ORIGIN AND COMPOSITION OF OCEANS
      A. The origin of ocean water
      B. The origin of ocean salts
         1. Salinity
         2. Density
      C. Ocean water supports life
   III. OCEAN CURRENTS
      A. Definition of currents
      B. Surface currents
      C. Density currents
      D. Upwellings

6. Save the document as STWP052 on your data disk.

242 Section 11 Personal Applications

Science Connection

To generate interest in science, ask students what resources oceans provide.
Possible answers include:

   Seafood
   Minerals
   Petroleum (oil and gas)
   Thermal energy (potential for conversion to electricity)

Project 53

CHAPTER OR PRESENTATION OUTLINE

Practice using the formatting features you learned in either Project 51 or 52 by typing either an original chapter outline or an original presentation outline. Choose any topic that interests you.

1. Open a new word processing document.
2. Position the insertion point about 2 inches from the top of the page by pressing Return/Enter 6 times.

   Note: If your default font is Geneva 12 pt., press Return/Enter 5 times to position the insertion point at 2 inches.

3. Center the outline title using all caps and bold.
4. Press Return/Enter 2 times.
5. Type the outline either manually or using the outline style feature.
6. Save the document as STWP053 on your data disk.

In Your Journal

Think of a subject you would like to discuss in a presentation. The subject might be something you read about in your science or geography class. List the main topics and subtopics about the subject that you would discuss. Use your list as the starting point for your presentation outline.

✓ Check Your Understanding

1. Did you type the title about 2 inches from the top of the page in bold and all caps?
2. Did you use roman numerals to identify your main topics?
3. Did you use letters and arabic numbers to identify your subtopics?
4. Did you insert one blank line before and after all main topics?

Presentation Outline

Project 53
Presentation Outline

ASSESS—LEVEL 1

Purpose
Assess word processing skills by creating an original chapter or presentation outline.

Time
One class period

Preparation
Review the process for creating an outline for the software your students are using.

Teaching Tip
Students who finish early should repeat the project.

Trouble Shooting
Provide individual help to students who are having difficulty deciding on a topic.

Wrap Up
Have students review their document using **Check Your Understanding.** Have students make corrections.

If this is the last project for this class period, ask students to return computers and furniture to the appropriate conditions.

In Your Journal

Some students may prefer to outline a chapter of a textbook. Encourage students to use the heads in the text as a starting point for their outline.

11.3 Class Notes

FOCUS
Type class notes from handwritten copy.

BELLRINGER
When students enter the room, direct their attention to the assignment on the board:
> Read pages 244 and 245.

TEACH
Emphasize that typing your notes reinforces what you learned in class. It also provides neat, organized notes for studying.

Use the illustration on page 244 to highlight the heading, main topic, and subtopics.

Class Notes

11.3

Goal
- Type class notes from handwritten copy

FORMATTING CLASS NOTES

Is it hard for you to remember what your teacher discussed in class a few days ago? If you took class notes, you can probably remember a great deal. Taking notes, like outlining, helps you organize your thoughts and clarify what you heard. If you get in the habit of typing your class notes when you have access to a computer, you will reinforce what you learned in class.

When you take notes, be brief. Write only the main ideas and key details. Use abbreviations and don't worry about writing in complete sentences. Use numbers or bullets when you need to list points. Use bold to emphasize key words.

Study the illustration before beginning. Your finished class notes may look slightly different.

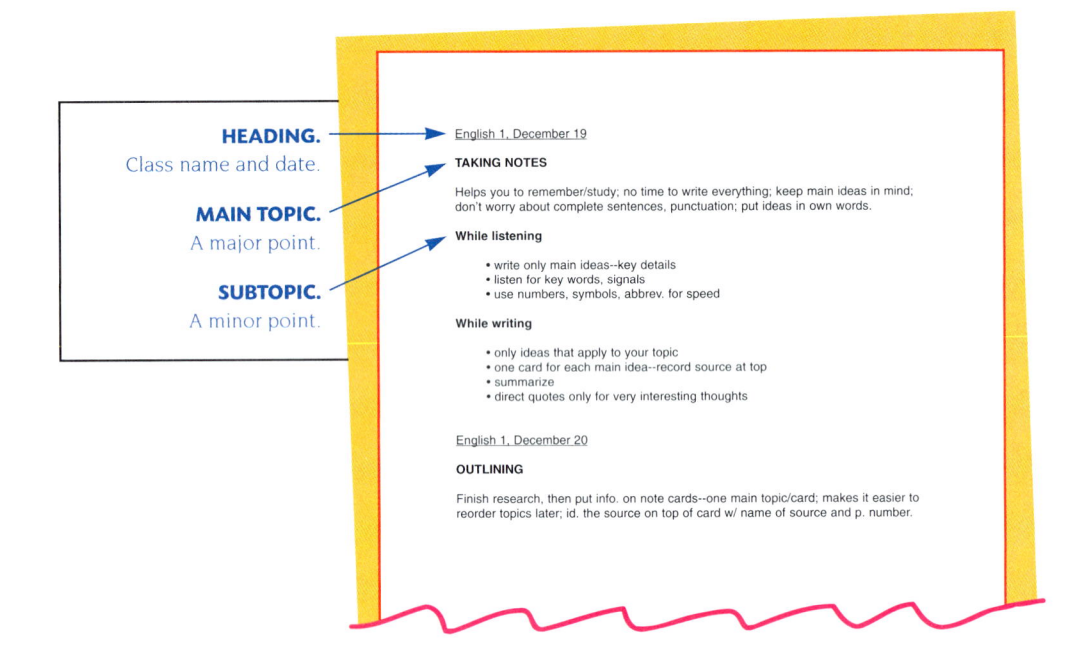

HEADING. Class name and date.

MAIN TOPIC. A major point.

SUBTOPIC. A minor point.

English 1, December 19

TAKING NOTES

Helps you to remember/study; no time to write everything; keep main ideas in mind; don't worry about complete sentences, punctuation; put ideas in own words.

While listening
- write only main ideas--key details
- listen for key words, signals
- use numbers, symbols, abbrev. for speed

While writing
- only ideas that apply to your topic
- one card for each main idea--record source at top
- summarize
- direct quotes only for very interesting thoughts

English 1, December 20

OUTLINING

Finish research, then put info. on note cards--one main topic/card; makes it easier to reorder topics later; id. the source on top of card w/ name of source and p. number.

244 Section 11 Personal Applications

RESOURCES

Lesson Plan: LP61
Transparency Master: TM28

CD-ROM: Reference Guide

Software: Research Files

FORMATTING TIPS

- Underline the class name and date heading, and insert a blank line after it.
- Type a main topic in bold and all caps. Leave a blank line above and below the main topic.
- Type subtopics in bold with the first word capitalized. Leave a blank line above and below subtopics.
- Use bullets or numbers as needed to emphasize key points.

CLASS NOTES, TWO-COLUMN FORMAT

Some software programs have an automatic column feature that makes it convenient to list your key topics in the left column and brief explanations in the right column. This is called a parallel column feature. You can also use a two-column table to get the same results. The illustration below shows you how class notes might appear if they were arranged in columns.

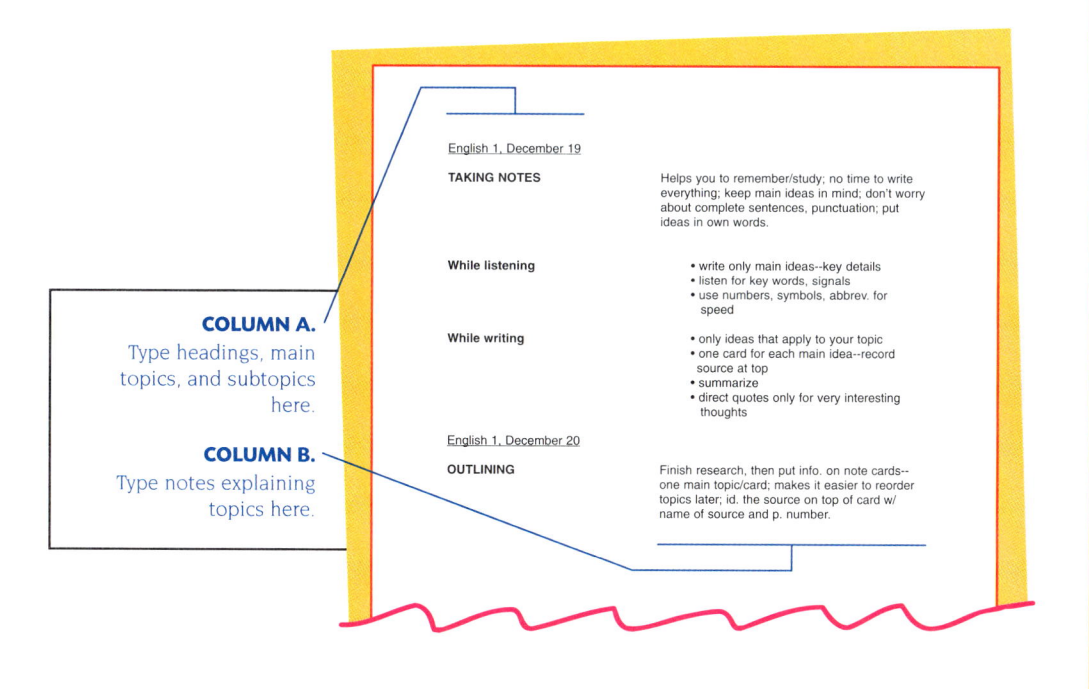

COLUMN A. Type headings, main topics, and subtopics here.

COLUMN B. Type notes explaining topics here.

English 1, December 19

TAKING NOTES — Helps you to remember/study; no time to write everything; keep main ideas in mind; don't worry about complete sentences, punctuation; put ideas in own words.

While listening
- write only main ideas--key details
- listen for key words, signals
- use numbers, symbols, abbrev. for speed

While writing
- only ideas that apply to your topic
- one card for each main idea--record source at top
- summarize
- direct quotes only for very interesting thoughts

English 1, December 20

OUTLINING — Finish research, then put info. on note cards--one main topic/card; makes it easier to reorder topics later; id. the source on top of card w/ name of source and p. number.

Class Notes **245**

Class Notes

TEACH

Review the formatting tips. Explain how to format class notes in parallel columns. Consider demonstrating the process to the class.

Use the illustration on page 245 to highlight the two-column format.

ASSESS

To assess understanding have students name some benefits of typing class notes.

CLOSE

Explain to students that they are now ready to type class notes. Refer to Projects 54, 55, and 56.

Project 54
Class Notes

PRACTICE—LEVEL 1

Purpose
Practice typing and formatting class notes using a one-column format.

Time
Fifteen minutes

Preparation
No special preparation required.

Teaching Tip
Students who finish early should repeat the project.

Trouble Shooting
Provide individual help to students who are having difficulty using the bullet feature.

Wrap Up
If this is the last project for this class period, ask students to return computers and furniture to the appropriate conditions.

Project 54
Language Arts Connection
CLASS NOTES

Type the class notes in one-column format by following the steps below.

1. Open a new word processing document.
2. Type the class notes shown below following the directions in Steps 3–7.

> English 1, December 19
> TAKING NOTES
> Helps you to remember/study; no time to write everything; keep main ideas in mind; don't worry about complete sentences, punctuation; put ideas in own words.
> While listening
> - write only main ideas--key details
> - listen for key words, signals
> - use numbers, symbols, abbrev. for speed
>
> While writing
> - only ideas that apply to your topic
> - one card for each main idea--record source at top
> - summarize
> - direct quotes only for very interesting thoughts
>
> English 1, December 20
> OUTLINING
> Finishing research, then put info. on note cards--one main topic/card; makes it easier to reorder topics later; id. the source on top of card w/name of source and p. number

3. Type the class name and date headings underlined, and insert one blank line below them.
4. Type the main topics TAKING NOTES and OUTLINING in bold and all caps.
5. Type the subtopics *While listening* and *While writing* in bold with the first letter capitalized.
6. Use the bullet feature to type the bulleted lists.
7. Insert two blank lines above the second heading.
8. Save the document as STWP054 on your data disk.

246 Section 11 Personal Applications

Project 55

Language Arts Connection

CLASS NOTES

Practice using the formatting features you learned in Project 54 by typing another set of class notes. Refer to the illustration on page 245 as often as needed.

1. Open a new word processing document.
2. Type the class notes shown below following the directions in Steps 3–7.

English 1, April 14
INFORMAL SPEAKING
Talking w/friends, small groups, class, phone
Using phone
- speak clearly
- leave clear, complete message w/person or ans. machine
- be polite
Giving directions
- be precise
- give steps in order
- give complete steps
- ask for feedback; repeat steps

English 1, April 15
INFORMAL DISCUSSION
Small meeting in class; planning party/vacation; be relaxed, but ready; disagree politely.

---

3. Type the class name and date headings underlined and insert 1 blank line below them.
4. Type the main topics INFORMAL SPEAKING and INFORMAL DISCUSSION in bold and all caps.
5. Type the subtopics Using phone and Giving directions in bold with the first letter capitalized.
6. Use the bullet feature to type the bulleted lists.
7. Insert 2 blank lines above the second heading.
8. Save the document as STWP055 on your data disk.

Project 55
Class Notes

APPLY—LEVEL 1

Purpose
Apply word processing skills by typing and formatting class notes using a one-column format.

Time
Fifteen minutes

Preparation
No special preparation required.

Teaching Tip
Students who finish early should repeat the project.

Trouble Shooting
Provide individual help to students who are having difficulty using the bullet feature.

Wrap Up
If this is the last project for this class period, ask students to return computers and furniture to the appropriate conditions.

Project 56
Class Notes

ASSESS—LEVEL 2

Purpose
Assess word processing skills by typing and formatting class notes.

Time
One class period

Preparation
Review formatting features used in Projects 54 and 55.

Teaching Tip
Students who finish early should repeat the project, using notes from another class.

Trouble Shooting
Provide individual help to students who are having difficulty.

Wrap Up
Have students review their document using **Check Your Understanding.** Have students make corrections.

Ask students to return computers and furniture to the appropriate conditions.

In Your Journal
Each student will list different abbreviations in the journal. Ask the class to share their lists. Have students write abbreviations and their meanings on the board.

Project 56
Language Arts Connection

CLASS NOTES

Practice using the formatting features you learned in Project 54 by typing an original set of class notes. Choose any topic that interests you for your original class notes.

1. Open a new word processing document.
2. Type your class notes following the directions in Steps 3–7.
3. Type the class name and date headings underlined, and insert one blank line below them.
4. Type the main topics in bold and all caps.
5. Type the subtopics in bold with the first letter capitalized.
6. Use the bullet feature to type any bulleted lists.
7. Insert 2 blank lines above additional headings.
8. Save the document as STWP056 on your data disk.

In Your Journal
To help you take class notes, write a list of abbreviations you might use. Some common abbreviations used in taking notes include:

p.	page
info.	information
w/	with
@	at
ch	chapter
&	and

✓ Check Your Understanding

1. Did you type your class name and date underlined and followed by a blank line?
2. Did you type your main topics at the left margin in bold and all caps?
3. Did you type your subtopics in bold with the first word capitalized?

248 Section 11 Personal Applications

Language Arts Connection

To create interest in language arts, initiate a discussion about the use of abbreviations in formal writing. In general abbreviations are not used in formal writing. Ask students to think of some exceptions. Write their ideas on the board. Possible responses include:

A.M. and P.M.
B.C. and A.D.
D.D.S., M.B.A., Ph.D.
Jr. and Sr.
Ms., Mr., and Mrs.

Project 57
Building Your Portfolio

In this portfolio project, you will practice some of the formatting and word processing features you learned in Section 11. Choose any textbook chapter from any class you are taking, and type a chapter outline. If you need to review any formatting or software features, refer to previous projects as often as needed.

NOW TRY THIS

1. Open a new word processing document.
2. Position the insertion point about 2 inches from the top of the page by pressing Return/Enter 6 times.

   Note: If your default font is Geneva 12 pt., press Return/Enter 5 times to position the insertion point at 2 inches.

3. Center the chapter title in all caps and bold.
4. Press Return/Enter 2 times.
5. Type the chapter outline either manually or using the outline style feature.
6. Save the document as STWP057 on your data disk.

DID YOU KNOW?

Many people use portfolios to display examples of their work. Photographers keep portfolios with examples of the best photographs that they have taken. Artists keep portfolios with pictures of paintings, drawings, or sculptures they have created. Writers keep portfolios with examples of their best writing. Portfolios are sometimes used as part of job interviews.

Building Your Portfolio **249**

Project 57
Building Your Portfolio

ASSESS—LEVEL 2

Purpose
Assess word processing skills by typing and formatting a chapter outline.

Time
One class period

Preparation
Review the process for creating an outline for the software your students are using.

Teaching Tip
Students who finish early should repeat the project.

Trouble Shooting
Provide individual help to students who are having difficulty.

Wrap Up
Ask students to return computers and furniture to the appropriate conditions.

DID YOU KNOW?

Artists often use slides of their work as part of their portfolios. It is common practice for fine art galleries to request slides of works that are being considered for exhibit.

UNIT 4 ORGANIZER

Section	Subsection	Special Features	Projects: Project No., Title, and Page	Projects: Cross-Curricular Connection	Difficulty Level	Student Guide GO TO
12 - Document Enhancement	12.1 - Title Page With Borders	Words To Know, p. 252 In Your Journal, p. 255 Cultural Kaleidoscope, p. 256	Projects 58–59: Report With a Border, pp. 255–256		58 - L1 59 - L2	p. 254
	12.2 - Cover Page		Projects 60–61: Cover Page With Drawings, Text, Fills, and Borders, pp. 259 and 262		60 - L1 61 - L2	p. 258
	12.3 - Flyer	Cultural Kaleidoscope, p. 263 In Your Journal, p. 265	Projects 62–63: Flyer With Drawings, Text, Fills, and Borders, pp. 265 and 267		62 - L1 63 - L2	p. 264
			Project 64: Building Your Portfolio, p. 268		64 - L2	
13 - Graphics	13.1 - Flyer With Clip Art	Words To Know, p. 270 Cultural Kaleidoscope, p. 271	Projects 65–66: Flyer With Clip Art, pp. 273 and 275		65 - L1 66 - L2	p. 272
	13.2 - Personal Stationery		Projects 67–68: Stationery With Original Pictures, pp. 278 and 280		67 - L1 68 - L2	p. 277
			Project 69: Building Your Portfolio, p. 281		69 - L2	
14 - Templates	14.1 - Invitation, Greeting Card, or Letterhead	Words To Know, p. 283 Cultural Kaleidoscope, p. 284 Language Links, p. 286	Project 70: Invitation, Greeting Card, or Letterhead, p. 286		70 - L1	p. 285
	14.2 - Certificate	In Your Journal, p. 289	Project 71: Certificate, p. 289		71 - L1	
	14.3 - Newsletter	In Your Journal, p. 291	Project 72: Newsletter, p. 292 Project 73: Building Your Portfolio, p. 293		72 - L1 73 - L2	p. 291

UNIT RESOURCES

- Lesson Plans: LP63–LP76
- Transparency Masters: TM29–TM31
- Supplemental Projects: SP6–SP10
- Enrichment Activities
- CD-ROM: Unit 4 Document Templates Reference Guide Cross-curricular Timings
- Software: Unit 4 Document Templates Research Files
- Transparencies: 15–26
- Student Guides: Desktop Publishing
- Student Data Disks

UNIT 4 ORGANIZER

KEY TO DIFFICULTY LEVEL

The following designations will help you decide which activities are appropriate for your students.

L1: Level 1 activities are basic activities and should be within the range of all students.

L2: Level 2 activities are average activities and should be within the range of average and above average students.

L3: Level 3 activities are challenging activities designed for the ability range of above average students.

ASSESSMENT RESOURCES

Check Your Understanding

Section 12	Section 13	Section 14
p. 256	p. 275	
p. 262	p. 280	
p. 267		

Portfolio Assessment (Building Your Portfolio)

Section 12	Section 13	Section 14
p. 268	p. 281	p. 293

Unit Tests (Teacher's Resource Binder)

Objective Test

Performance Tests

UNIT 4

INTRODUCING THE UNIT

Ask your students what they know about desktop publishing. Introduce examples of desktop publishing that you have seen around your school. Ask students to identify some of the components of a flyer or a newsletter.

Explain that desktop publishing requires good basic keyboarding and word processing skills.

Unit 4 is an introduction to basic desktop publishing. The focus is on the most commonly used features of desktop publishing software including document enhancement, graphics, and templates.

Unit 4
Desktop Publishing

OVERVIEW

Desktop publishing takes you a step beyond word processing to producing documents that are more creative, fun, and effective in communicating your messages. In this unit, you will learn desktop publishing features and design tips that will help you format documents attractively, use art and color to make documents more interesting, and use draw and paint tools to create original artwork for your documents.

Fun Facts

Paper was invented by Ts'ai Lun in China in A.D. 105. Papermaking was introduced to Japan in 610. By the middle of the twelfth century papermaking mills had been established in Europe. The first mill in the United States was built in 1690.

The United States and Canada are the largest producers of paper and paper products. Finland, Japan, and Sweden are leaders in the production of wood pulp and newsprint.

Source: *Microsoft Encarta 96 Encyclopedia*, Microsoft Corporation, 1996.

UNIT 4

MULTIMEDIA

For this unit, you may use the multimedia CD-ROM to enhance your students' skills in desktop publishing. The CD-ROM contains format guides that serve as models for students to create projects using a desktop publishing software application. These format guides are cross-referenced to the desktop publishing projects in the student text. A Reference Guide links terms to format guides that define and illustrate their use in formatting desktop publishing documents. The Research Files contain cross-curricular typing selections or timings for 1 minute, 2 minutes, and 3 or 5 minutes. The timings, as well as the two games—Get the Scoop and Uncover the Story—are great ways to build typing skills.

UNIT OBJECTIVES

- Create documents with:
  - borders
  - original drawings
  - color
  - fills and patterns
  - clip art
  - original paintings
- Use draw and paint tools.
- Apply effective design principles.
- Use software stationery and templates.

Unit Contents

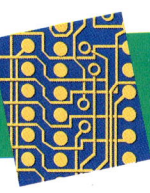

Section 12	Document Enhancement
Section 13	Graphics
Section 14	Templates

Focus On Careers In Technology

Interior designers are often small-business owners. The success of their businesses depends on their ability to advertise and communicate with potential clients and to use technology effectively. Desktop publishing and graphics programs enable interior designers to create attractive advertising brochures, sale announcements, price lists, stationery, and business cards. They can also use draw and paint tools to create several different room designs and layouts for their customers, enhancing each design with colors that highlight its particular theme. Text may be added to incorporate a complete listing of materials and costs.

Focus On Careers In Technology

Interior designers may be employed in design firms, furniture stores, architectural firms, or construction companies. The use of computers in interior design has provided new ways of doing things. For instance, residential designers can use a computer to show a customer how selected fabric will appear on a chair or sofa.

Consider inviting an interior designer to speak to your class. Ask if a software demonstration is possible.

Application: COMPUTERS IN THE COMMUNITY

Divide students into groups of three or four. Assign topics related to community services to each group. Ask each group to make a list of ways computers are used by agencies and services related to their assigned topic. Ask each group to select a representative to write their list on the board.

Topics to consider, along with sample responses, include:

Transportation and Traffic: Traffic lights
Public Safety: Emergency services (911)
Government Records: Tax records
Parks and Recreation: Scheduling
Libraries and Museums: Card catalog

251

Section 12
Document Enhancement

SECTION OVERVIEW

This section focuses on document enhancement. The emphasis is on title pages, cover pages, and flyers. Borders and drawings are emphasized along with changing the appearance of text. The use of color and patterns is introduced along with the concepts of selecting, resizing, and moving.

CONTENT FOCUS

Title Page With Borders
Cover Page
Flyer

OPENING ACTIVITY

Ask students to look at a title page they created for a project in Unit 3. Instruct them to make notes about possible enhancements. They should make their notes directly on the title page. Ask students to share some of their ideas with classmates.

SECTION 12
Document Enhancement

OBJECTIVES

- Create cover pages and flyers with borders, drawings, text, fills, and patterns.
- Apply design tips.

Focus on Document Enhancement

You probably create cover pages for book reports and other class assignments and flyers for school events or personal activities. In this section, you will learn to use the desktop publishing features of your software to make these cover pages and flyers more attractive. You will also learn to apply important document design tips.

Words To Know

border	sans serif font
color spectrum	selecting
draw	serif font
fill	stack
group	text object
moving	tool
resizing	typeface
reverse text	window

252 Section 12 Document Enhancement

Career Exploration Activities: Construction

Computers and technology are important in both residential and commercial construction. Computers are used for a wide range of activities including scheduling, computer-assisted drawing (CAD), and preparation of bids. Invite a construction professional to speak to your class about the use of computers in the construction industry. Organizations to consider when seeking a speaker include: your local home builder's association and the local chapters of the American Institute of Architects, General Contractors of America, and Construction Industry Manufacturers Association.

252

12.1 Title Page With Borders

CREATING A TITLE PAGE WITH A BORDER

Would you like to make your reports look outstanding? It can be as easy as adding a simple border and changing the font used on the title page.

Study the illustration. Your finished title page may look slightly different.

Goals
- Create a page border
- Select, resize, and move objects
- Enhance a border using color and patterns

BORDER. The outline of an object or page.

OBJECT. An item that can be selected, moved, changed, or deleted. Objects can be drawn in a shape such as a rectangle, circle, or straight line. Objects can also hold a picture or text and have a border and fill pattern.

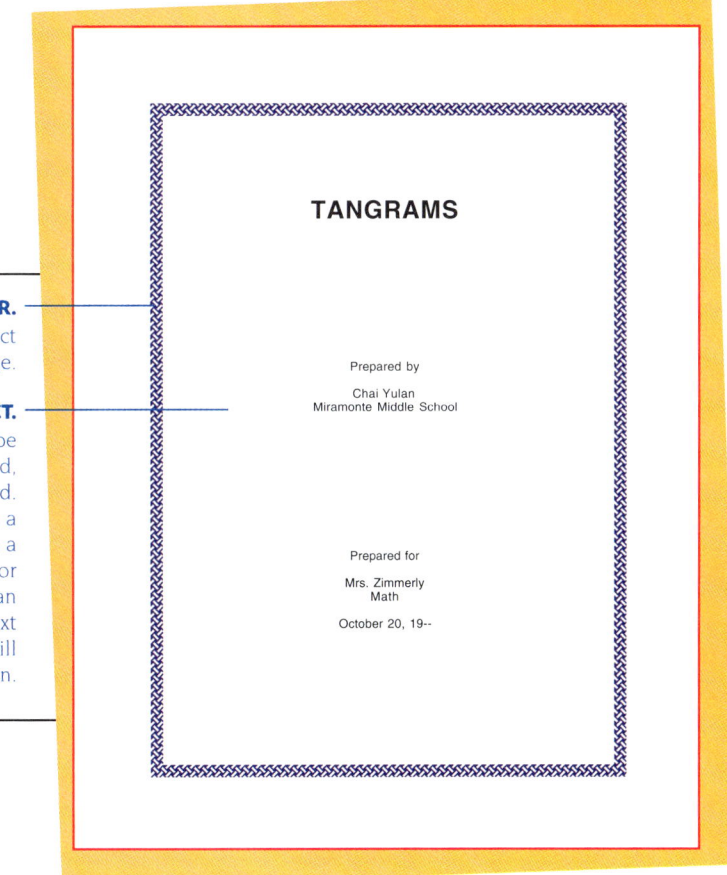

TANGRAMS

Prepared by
Chai Yulan
Miramonte Middle School

Prepared for
Mrs. Zimmerly
Math
October 20, 19--

Title Page With Borders **253**

12.1 Title Page With Borders

FOCUS
Create a page border. Select, resize, and move objects. Enhance a border using color and patterns.

BELLRINGER
When students enter the room, direct their attention to the assignment on the board:
Read pages 253 and 254.

TEACH
Use the illustration on page 253 to highlight the border and the object.

RESOURCES
- Lesson Plan: LP64
- Transparency Master: TM29
- Transparency 15
- CD-ROM: Reference Guide
- Software: Research Files

253

Title Page With Borders

TEACH

Review design tips on page 254.

DID YOU KNOW

The point size of a font is measured from the top of a letter with an ascender to the bottom of a letter with a descender. Letters with ascenders include: b, d, f, h, k, and l. Examples of letters with descenders are: g, j, p, q, and y. A single point is equal to approximately 1/72 of an inch.

GO TO Refer students to the appropriate section of the Student Guide.

ASSESS

To assess students' understanding, have them identify the components of a title page. Have them discuss effective title page design.

CLOSE

Have students create a title page with border. Refer to Projects 58 and 59.

Borders can be added to pages in different ways. One approach is to draw a rectangle just inside the page margins and then change the border of the rectangle. The text is then stacked on top of the rectangle so you can read it. A border feature in which text and blank lines are selected and a border is applied can also be used.

Throughout this unit, you will learn to enhance your documents using borders, pictures, and text changes. It is important to follow some basic rules of design so that your finished product is pleasing to the eye. The first basic rule of a good design is to keep it simple.

DESIGN TIPS

- Keep the design simple—less is more.
- For main headings, use bold and a font size of 18 points or more. The higher the point size, the taller the letter.
- The border design should enhance but not overpower the page.

Chai works on a tangram.

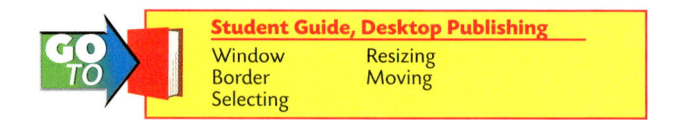

GO TO **Student Guide, Desktop Publishing**
Window   Resizing
Border   Moving
Selecting

254 Section 12 Document Enhancement

Project 58

TITLE PAGE WITH A BORDER

Carefully read and do the following steps to format a title page with a border.

1. In your Student Guide, go to Unit 4, **window.** Find and read the Help topics listed. Next, read the information for this topic in your Student Guide. You will learn about basic desktop publishing features and tools.
2. Open the file DP058 on your data disk.
3. Increase the font size in the title to 24 points and bold the title.
4. Add a **border** just inside the margins. Enhance the border by changing the color, width, and pattern. Experiment and have fun with your changes.
5. If you used a rectangle tool to draw the border, practice **selecting, resizing,** and **moving** the border as you edit it.

   Note: If your software uses a border feature to create a page border rather than using a rectangle tool to draw a border, be sure to read about selecting, resizing, and moving objects in your Student Guide. You will use these features in other projects.

6. Save the document as STDP058 on your data disk.

   Note: In the filename STDP058, ST stands for student; DP stands for desktop publishing; and 58 stands for project 58.

In Your Journal

Write about the font sizes and border styles you prefer to use. Make a note of which ones work best for you. Record your choices in your journal.

Chai solved the tangram puzzle.

Title Page With Borders **255**

Project 58
Title Page With Borders

PRACTICE—LEVEL 1

Purpose
Practice creating a title page with a border.

Time
Thirty minutes

Preparation
Review step 5 in Project 58. Become familiar with the various ways a border can be created with the software your students are using.

Teaching Tip
Students who finish early should repeat the project. Encourage students to experiment.

Trouble Shooting
Provide individual help to students who are having difficulty with using borders.

Wrap Up
Remind students of the naming system for saving documents.

If this is the last project for this class period, ask students to return computers and furniture to the appropriate conditions.

In Your Journal

Encourage students to make additional notes about their personal preferences. Point out that readability and visual interest are always important.

Project 59
Title Page With Borders

ASSESS—LEVEL 2

Purpose
Assess desktop publishing skills by creating a title page with a border.

Time
Thirty minutes

Preparation
If your students completed the Opening Activity described on page 252 of the Teacher's Edition, they might want to use their work as a starting point for this project.

Teaching Tip
Students who finish early should repeat the project. Instruct them to use a different title page the second time they complete Project 59.

Trouble Shooting
Make sure students are experimenting with different colors, line widths, and patterns. Provide individual help to students who are having difficulty.

Wrap Up
Have students review their work using **Check Your Understanding.** They should be able to answer "yes" to each of the questions. If this is the last project for this class period, ask students to return computers and furniture to the appropriate conditions.

Project 59

TITLE PAGE WITH A BORDER

Practice using the desktop publishing features you learned in Project 58 by designing another title page with a border. Change the information on the title page so that you can use it for an actual report in one of your classes. Experiment with different font sizes and border styles. Refer to the illustration and information on pages 255–257 as often as needed.

1. Open the file DP059 on your data disk.
2. Change the title to match any report you have prepared for one of your classes.
3. Increase the font size in the title to 24 points and bold the title.
4. Change the other information on the title page as needed.
5. Add a border just inside the margins. For this step, zoom out to get the best view of the page.
6. Enhance the border by changing the color, width, and pattern. Experiment and have fun with your changes.
7. If you used a rectangle tool to draw the border, practice selecting, resizing, and moving the border as you edit it.
8. Save the document as STDP059 on your data disk.

✓ Check Your Understanding

1. Did you increase the font size for the title to 24 points?
2. Did you remember to bold the title?
3. Did you choose a border that is outstanding but not overpowering?

CULTURAL KALEIDOSCOPE

Ancient Egyptians used hieroglyphics, a form of writing that used picture symbols to represent sounds and ideas. Hieroglyphics were used for inscriptions on temples and stone monuments. These symbols were carved by trained men called scribes.

Section 12 Document Enhancement

CULTURAL KALEIDOSCOPE

Hieroglyphics evolved into typefaces. Many typefaces originally were designed for printing presses and have been in use for centuries. Older typefaces were frequently named after the artisans who designed them. The names of some common typefaces, the designers, and when they were designed include:

Garamond (serif)	Claude **Garamond** (France)	16th century
Caslon (serif)	William **Caslon** (England)	17th century
Bodoni (serif)	Giambattista **Bodoni** (Italy)	18th century
Times Roman (serif)	Commissioned by the **Times** of London	20th century

12.2 Cover Page

Goals
- Design and create a cover page
- Use draw tools
- Add fills and borders
- Create text objects
- Stack objects

DESIGNING A COVER PAGE

In Project 60, you will create the cover page shown in the illustration on page 258. A cover page is used in many ways. It could be used instead of a title page to dress up a report or as an insert in the front jacket of a view binder. The cover page should have a headline to identify the contents.

When you need to move text around freely on a page, you should use a text object. A **text object** is drawn with special tools and the text is typed inside. The object can be freely positioned anywhere on the page.

Study the illustration on page 258. Notice how you can create unusual effects by using drawing tools to add some interesting shapes, borders, and fills that draw attention to the subject. Your finished cover page may look slightly different.

David is creating a cover page.

12.2 Cover Page

FOCUS
Design and create a cover page. Use draw tools. Add fills and borders. Create text objects. Stack objects.

BELLRINGER
When students enter the room, direct their attention to the assignment on the board:
Read pages 257 and 258.

TEACH
Explain the difference between a title page and a cover. Review the meaning of text object.

RESOURCES
- Lesson Plan: LP65
  Transparency Master: TM30
- Transparency 16 and 17
- CD-ROM: Reference Guide
- Software: Research Files

Cover Page

TEACH

Review the design tips on page 258. Use the illustration to highlight typeface, sans serif font, and serif font.

> **Go To:** Refer students to the appropriate section of the Student Guide.

ASSESS

To assess students' understanding, have them identify the components of a cover page. Have them discuss effective cover page design.

CLOSE

Have students design a cover page. Refer to Project 60.

DESIGN TIPS

- Type headlines in all caps in bold or italic in a very large point size.
- Use all caps for headlines only.
- Use only two different typefaces on a page.
- Add variety to the same typeface by changing the point size, adding bold, or adding italic.
- Mix serif and sans serif fonts for contrast.

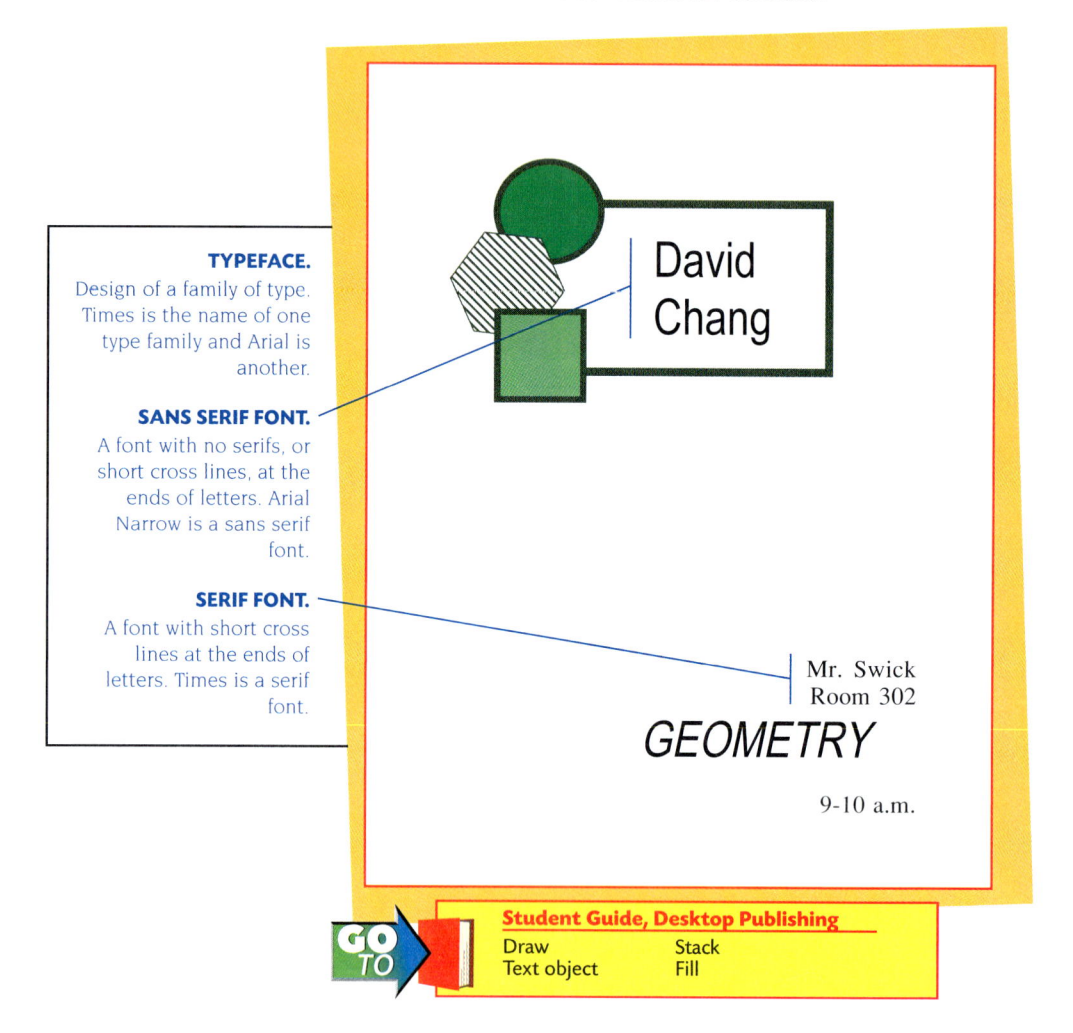

TYPEFACE. Design of a family of type. Times is the name of one type family and Arial is another.

SANS SERIF FONT. A font with no serifs, or short cross lines, at the ends of letters. Arial Narrow is a sans serif font.

SERIF FONT. A font with short cross lines at the ends of letters. Times is a serif font.

David Chang

Mr. Swick
Room 302

GEOMETRY

9–10 a.m.

> **Go To — Student Guide, Desktop Publishing**
> Draw   Stack
> Text object   Fill

258 Section 12 Document Enhancement

Project 60

COVER PAGE WITH DRAWINGS, TEXT, FILLS, AND BORDERS

Create a cover page by following the directions below.

1. Open a new word processing file.
2. In your Student Guide, go to Unit 4, **draw.** Find and read all the Help topics to learn how to use each of the draw tools. Experiment with each tool.
3. Change the zoom setting so that you can see the full page when you draw the text objects. Change the setting back again when you type text.

   Note: This direction will not be repeated.

4. Create a **text object** for *David Chang*. Type the name using Arial Narrow sans serif font, 48 points.
5. Draw a rectangle border around the name. Change the color of the border to any color you wish. **Stack** the rectangle border behind the name.
6. Position the name and border on the page approximately as shown in the illustration.
7. Draw three shapes of your choice to place beside the name. Add **fill** and borders to the shapes as you like.
8. Resize, move, and stack the objects approximately as shown in the illustration.
9. Create another text object for *GEOMETRY*. Type *GEOMETRY* using Arial Narrow sans serif font, 48 points.
10. Create one or more text objects for *Mr. Swick, Room 302,* and *9-10 a.m.* Type the lines using Times or Courier serif font, 24 points. Right align the text.
11. Insert blank lines or space between text objects to allow for the title *GEOMETRY*. Stack *GEOMETRY* over the text object as shown.
12. Save the document as STDP060 on your data disk.

Cover Page **259**

Project 60
Cover Page

PRACTICE—LEVEL 1

Purpose
Create a cover page.

Time
Thirty minutes

Preparation
Review the elements used to create the cover page on page 258.

Teaching Tip
Students who finish early should repeat the project. Instruct them to use a different geometric shape the second time they complete Project 60.

Trouble Shooting
Depending on the drawing program your students are using, some geometric shapes might be difficult or impossible to create. Suggest that students use other geometric shapes that might be appropriate.

Provide individual help to students who are having difficulty.

Wrap Up
If this is the last project for this class period, ask students to return computers and furniture to the appropriate conditions.

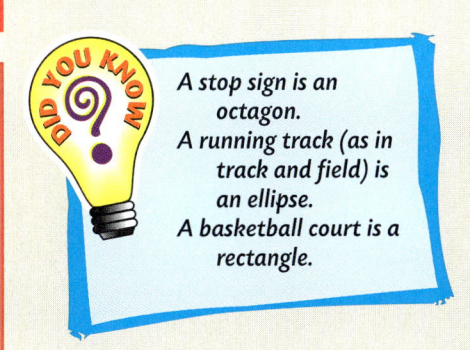

---

interNET CONNECTION

Have students use the Internet to learn more about geometric shapes. Examples of sites might include:

Geometry Center Picture Archive:
http://www.geom.umn.edu/graphics/

Gallery of Interactive On-Line Geometry:
http://www.geom.umn.edu/apps/gallery.html

DID YOU KNOW?
A stop sign is an octagon.
A running track (as in track and field) is an ellipse.
A basketball court is a rectangle.

Cover Page

TEACH

Provide additional examples of how geometric shapes can be combined to create a picture. For example, a square or rectangle can be combined with a triangle to make the outline of a house. Rectangles can be used for the door, windows, and chimney.

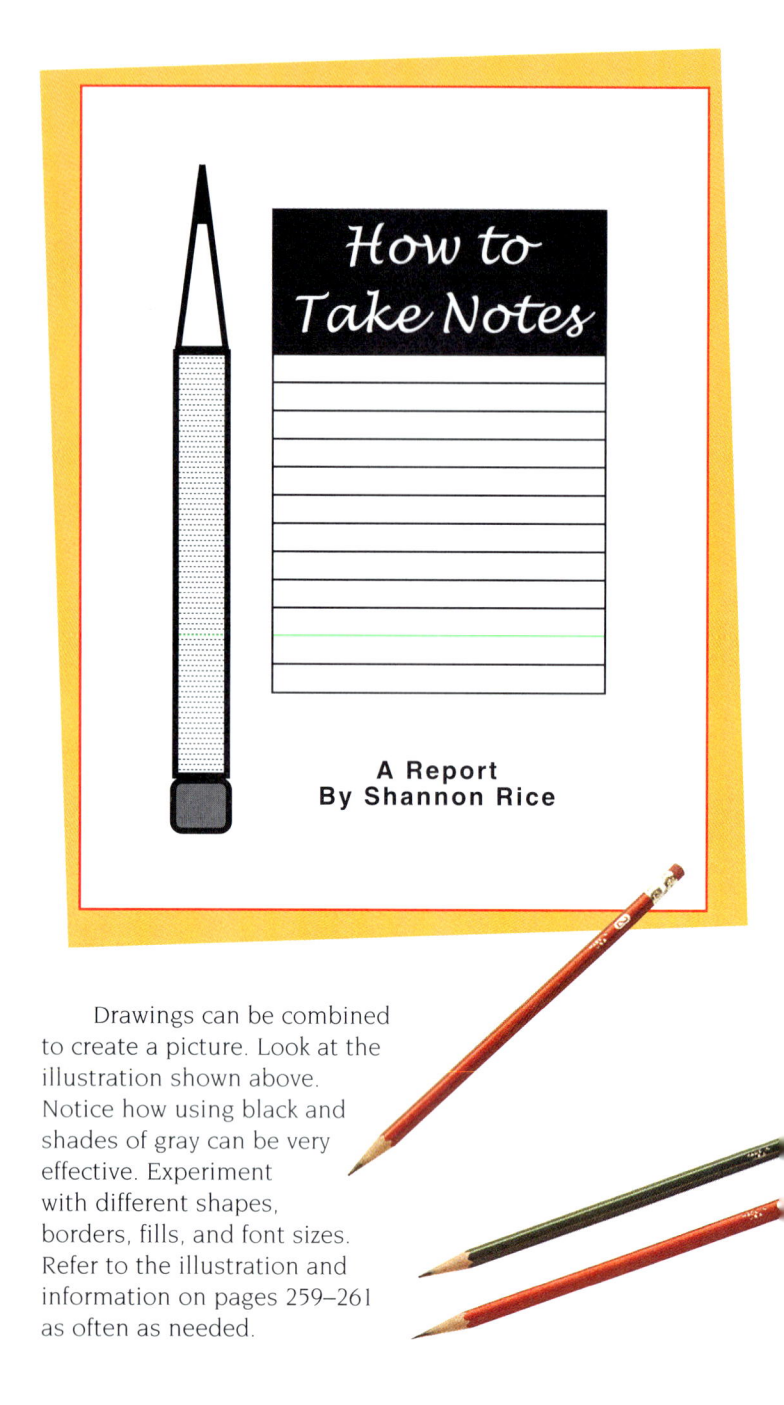

How to Take Notes

A Report
By Shannon Rice

Drawings can be combined to create a picture. Look at the illustration shown above. Notice how using black and shades of gray can be very effective. Experiment with different shapes, borders, fills, and font sizes. Refer to the illustration and information on pages 259–261 as often as needed.

260 Section 12 Document Enhancement

Lesson Extension

Let students know that many other kinds of graphics can be added to a document. Examples include photographs, scanned images, drawings and clip art. Point out that they will learn about clip art in Section 13.

Shannon uses a computer to help her design a cover page.

DESIGN TIPS

- The pencil was created using a combination of triangles, rectangles, rounded rectangles, and various fills.
- The reverse text was created with a combination of a white foreground and a black background. You could also stack a text box that has white letters over a black rectangle.
- The notepad lines were created using a group of slightly stacked rectangles. The first rectangle was copied and pasted several times to keep the sizes even.
- Avoid using all caps with a script font.

Cover Page

TEACH

Review design tips on page 261.

ASSESS

To assess students' understanding, ask them to differentiate between a title page and a cover page. Ask them to explain the importance of using shades of gray, shapes, borders, fills, and font sizes.

CLOSE

Have students design a cover page with drawing, text, fills, and borders. Refer to Project 61.

Project 61
Cover Page

ASSESS—LEVEL 2

Purpose
Assess desktop publishing skills by creating a cover page with original drawings, text, objects, borders, and fills.

Time
Thirty minutes

Preparation
Remind students that they can use a title page they created in Unit 3 as a starting point for this activity.

Teaching Tip
Students who finish early should repeat the project. Instruct students to experiment with all elements of the cover page.

Trouble Shooting
Attempts to use reverse text might cause some confusion. In most cases creating reverse text requires 5 steps. (1) Type the text that is to be reversed. (2) Draw a box around the text. (3) Fill the box using black or another color (not white). (4) Select the box and send to back. (5) Select the text and change the color to white. For additional help, refer to the reference material for the software your students are using.

Wrap Up
Have students review their work using **Check Your Understanding.** Students should be able to answer "yes" to each of the questions.

262

Project 61

COVER PAGE WITH DRAWING, TEXT, FILLS, AND BORDERS

Practice using the desktop publishing features you learned in Project 60 to design an original cover page. This cover page could be for another binder or for a report. You should create an original design using drawings, text objects, borders, and fills.

1. Decide on a theme for a cover page.
2. Open a new word processing file and create text objects as needed.
3. Use a large, bold font for your headline.
4. Use a font with a smaller point size for any details.
5. Draw shapes as desired.
6. Add fills and borders as you like.
7. Stack the objects as you like.
8. Resize and move the objects as you like.
9. Save the document as STDP061 on your data disk.

✓ Check Your Understanding

1. Did you use a combination of serif and sans serif fonts?
2. Did you limit your typefaces on the page to two?
3. Did you change point size, add bold, or add italic to add variety to the typeface?

262 Section 12 Document Enhancement

12.3 Flyer

DESIGNING A FLYER

Flyers are used to publicize activities or special events. The information in a flyer should answer the questions *who*, *what*, *when*, *where*, and *why*. The headline should identify the purpose of the flyer, and the drawings should reflect the theme of the event.

Study the illustration shown below. Your finished flyer may look slightly different.

Goals
- Design and create a flyer
- Group objects
- Enhance a flyer with drawings, borders, and fills

STUDENT COUNCIL CAR WASH

- We need volunteers to sign up for the car wash on Sunday, August 12, from 10 a.m. to 2 p.m.
- The money we raise will be used to buy new volleyball equipment.
- A sign-up sheet will be posted in the cafeteria.

CULTURAL KALEIDOSCOPE

Many Chinese paintings have a verse or poem written in calligraphy, the art of beautiful writing. In Chinese writing, characters represent words or ideas instead of sounds. Chinese writing has over 50,000 characters. The average person can recognize only about 8,000 characters.

Flyer **263**

12.3 Flyer

FOCUS
Design and create a flyer. Group objects. Enhance a flyer with drawings, borders, and fills.

BELLRINGER
When students enter the room direct their attention to the assignment on the board:
Read pages 263 and 264.

TEACH
Use the illustration on page 263 to highlight the answers to the questions who, what, when, where, and why as described in the **In Your Journal** feature.

RESOURCES
- Lesson Plan: LP67
- Transparencies 18, 19, and 20
- CD-ROM: Reference Guide
- Software: Research Files

Flyer

TEACH

Review design tips on page 264.

GO TO — Refer students to the appropriate section of the Student Guide.

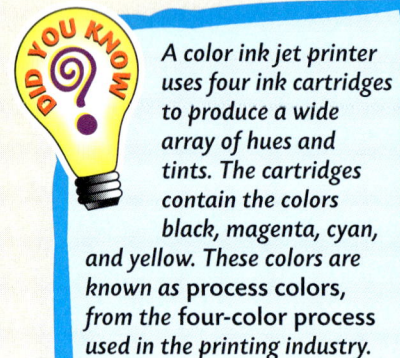

DID YOU KNOW? A color ink jet printer uses four ink cartridges to produce a wide array of hues and tints. The cartridges contain the colors black, magenta, cyan, and yellow. These colors are known as **process colors**, from the four-color process used in the printing industry.

ASSESS

To assess students' understanding, have them identify the five questions to ask when designing a flyer. Have them discuss effective flyer design.

CLOSE

Have students create a flyer. Refer to Project 62.

COLOR SPECTRUM

Cool colors. Use to produce feelings of coolness and calm.

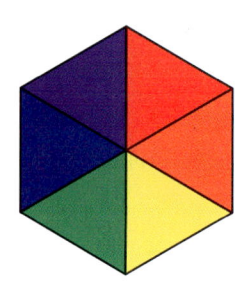

Warm colors. Use to produce feelings of warmth and high energy.

DESIGN TIPS

- The drawing design should reflect the mood of the document—fun, serious, or humorous, for example.
- Add color to emphasize the message of the flyer.
- Choose colors that contrast for good readability. Colors next to each other on the spectrum such as blue and violet do not have good contrast.
- Use no more than four different colors on the page.
- If you don't have a color printer, try printing on colored paper to add interest to the flyer.
- Use the group feature in your software when you need to move several drawings as one unit.

GO TO — Student Guide, Desktop Publishing
Group

264 Section 12 Document Enhancement

Lesson Extension

If a color printer is available, show students the inside of the printer and point out the color sources.

Project 62

FLYER WITH DRAWINGS, TEXT, FILLS, AND BORDERS

Follow these steps to create the flyer as shown in the illustration on page 263.

1. Open a new word processing file.
2. Read and practice the steps under Unit 4, **group** in your Student Guide. Use the group feature to group bubbles or text lines you will create in this project so you can move them easily.
3. Create two text objects: one for the headline and one for the details.
4. Type the headline *STUDENT COUNCIL CAR WASH* with the words right aligned. Use a serif font, such as Times or Courier, 48 points, bold.
5. Type the bulleted list below using a sans serif font, such as Arial, 24 points, bold. If you cannot use the bullet feature inside the text object, draw small circles with black fill as a substitute.

> We need volunteers to sign-up for the car wash on Sunday, August 12, from 10 a.m. to 2 p.m.
>
> The money we raise will be used to buy new volleyball equipment.
>
> A sign-up sheet will be posted in the cafeteria.

6. Draw a rectangle with a border and fill to create the text background.
7. Draw the bubbles using several different sizes of circles. Stack them for variety.
8. Save the document as STDP062 on your data disk.

In Your Journal

Think of an upcoming school event for which you could design a flyer to advertise. In your journal, answer who, what, when, where, *and* why *about the event.*

Flyer **265**

Project 62
Flyer

PRACTICE—LEVEL 1

Purpose
Practice creating a flyer.

Time
One class period

Preparation
No special preparation required.

Teaching Tip
Students who finish early should repeat the project.

Trouble Shooting
Provide individual help to students who are having difficulty with the bullet feature.

Wrap Up
Discuss the **In Your Journal** feature on this page. If this is the last project for this class period, ask students to return computers and furniture to the appropriate conditions.

In Your Journal

Help students think of upcoming events. Examples might include:

*Career day
Dance or social
Field trip
Fund raising activity
Parent-teacher conferences
Play or musical presentation
Science fair
Speech competition
Spelling bee
Tryouts for athletic teams*

Flyer

TEACH

Use the illustration on page 263 to highlight the answers to the questions *who*, *what*, *when*, *where*, and *why*.

ASSESS

To assess students' understanding, have them identify the elements of the flyer shown on page 266. Have them discuss effective flyer design as described on page 267.

CLOSE

Have students design an original flyer using drawings, text objects, borders, and fills. Refer to Project 63.

In Project 63, you will design a flyer to advertise a school event or a special occasion at home like a party or garage sale. The illustration below should help give you some ideas. Experiment with different shapes, borders, fills, and font sizes. Refer to the illustration and information on pages 263–267 as often as needed.

BASEBALL SEASON IS HERE AGAIN!

Sign up for tryouts in the lobby of the gym during school hours.

The last day to sign up is Friday, March 19.

266 Section 12 Document Enhancement

DESIGN TIPS

- Experiment with the freehand/freeform tool to draw cartoon-like figures. Don't try to make the drawings perfect. Their imperfections make them interesting.
- The baseballs were designed with the oval/ellipse and arc tools with freehand/freeform lines for the stitching.
- The color red draws immediate attention. Use it carefully.
- Choose a fill color that is light enough so that the text can be read easily.

Project 63

FLYER WITH DRAWINGS, TEXT, FILLS, AND BORDERS

Practice using the desktop publishing features you learned in Project 62 to design an original flyer using drawings, text objects, borders, and fills.

1. Decide on a theme for the flyer.
2. Open a new word processing file and create text objects as needed.
3. Use a large, bold font for your heading.
4. Use a font with a smaller point size for any details.
5. Draw, move, resize, and stack shapes as needed.
6. Add fills and borders as you like.
7. Save the document as STDP063 on your data disk.

✓ Check Your Understanding

1. Do your drawings fit the mood of your flyer?
2. Did you use colors that contrast well with each other?
3. Did you limit the number of different colors to a maximum of four?

Flyer **267**

Project 63
Flyer

TEACH
Review design tips on page 267.

ASSESS—LEVEL 2

Purpose
Assess desktop publishing skills by creating a flyer including original drawings, text, objects, borders, and fills.

Time
Thirty minutes

Preparation
No special preparation required.

Teaching Tip
Students who finish early should repeat the project.

Trouble Shooting
Make sure students are using a variety of desktop publishing features in their flyers.

Wrap Up
Have students review their work using **Check Your Understanding.** Students' answers will vary. If this is the last project for this class period, ask students to return computers and furniture to the appropriate conditions.

Project 64
Building Your Portfolio

ASSESS—LEVEL 2

Purpose
Assess desktop publishing skills by creating a flyer using drawings, text objects, borders, and fills.

Time
One class period

Preparation
No special preparation required.

Teaching Tip
Review the design tips on page 268.
   Students who finish early should repeat the project.

Trouble Shooting
Provide individual help to students who are having difficulty with this project.

Wrap Up
Ask students if the design tips were helpful to them as they created their flyers. If this is the last project for this class period, ask students to return computers and furniture to the appropriate conditions.

Project 64
Building Your Portfolio

Review the desktop publishing features you learned in Section 12 by creating this flyer using drawings, text objects, borders, and fills. If you need to review any desktop publishing features, refer to previous projects as often as needed. Study the illustration. Your finished project may look slightly different.

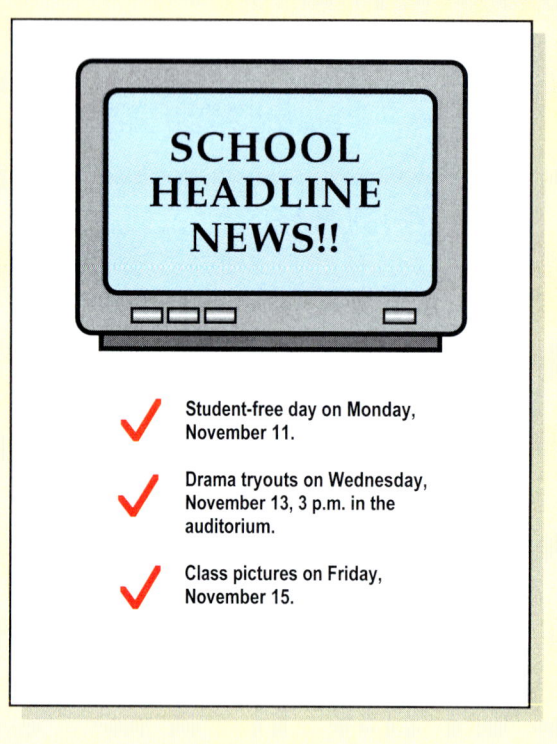

DESIGN TIPS

- The television was created using a combination of rectangles, rounded rectangles, a text object, and fills.
- The check marks were created with the line tool. After one check mark was drawn, it was grouped, copied, and pasted to create the others.
- Red is a powerful color that grabs attention immediately.

(continued on next page)

Section 12 Document Enhancement

Building Your Portfolio

NOW TRY THIS

1. Open a new word processing file.
2. Create text objects as needed.
3. Type the heading *SCHOOL HEADLINE NEWS!!* in all caps. Use a serif font, 48 points, bold.
4. Type the checklist below using a sans-serif font, 24 points, bold:

> Student-free day on Monday, November 11.
>
> Drama tryouts on Wednesday, November 13, 3 p.m. in the auditorium.
>
> Class pictures on Friday, November 15.

5. Draw shapes as needed.
6. Add fills and borders as shown.
7. Group the objects as needed. Stack the objects as shown.
8. Resize and move the objects as shown.
9. Save the document as STDP064 on your data disk.

Section 13
Graphics

SECTION OVERVIEW

This section focuses on the use of graphics including clip art and original pictures.

CONTENT FOCUS

Flyer With Clip Art
Personal Stationery

OPENING ACTIVITY

Ask students to review their work from Projects 58–64. Ask how they would like to enhance their desktop designs.

SECTION 13
Graphics

OBJECTIVES

- Choose and arrange clip art pictures to enhance documents.
- Create original pictures using draw and paint tools.
- Apply design tips.

Focus on Graphics

Pictures add interest to flyers, programs, and report covers making them fun to read. You will choose clip art pictures and create original pictures using draw and paint tools to enhance your documents. You will also continue to learn and apply design tips.

Words To Know

clip art   paint   picture

270 Section 13 Graphics

Career Exploration Activities: Health Care

Ask students how they think computers are used by health care professionals. Use the following list of careers to stimulate discussion:

Dietitian or Nutritionist
Emergency Medical Technician
Medical Records Technician
Medical Technologist

Occupational Therapist
Physician
Registered Nurse

Invite a health care professional to speak to your class about how he or she uses a computer at work. Contact a local hospital, clinic, or health department for help in obtaining a speaker.

270

13.1 Flyer With Clip Art

CREATING A FLYER WITH CLIP ART

In earlier projects, you added simple drawings to your documents to make them more interesting. In this section, you will choose, arrange, and even create pictures that will grab the interest of your reader and make your message more fun to read.

Study the following illustration. Your finished flyer may look slightly different.

Goals
- Choose clip art pictures
- Add clip art to a flyer
- Create a border using clip art

The party is here...

Your Student Council Invites you!

```
Who:    Everyone from Castair Middle School
What:   End-of-Year Party
When:   June 10 from 6 to 9
Where:  The gymnasium
Why:    To say HELLO to summer
```

Be There!

Flyer With Clip Art **271**

CULTURAL KALEIDOSCOPE

Germany was the site of the invention of the printing press. In the early 1400's, Johannes Gutenberg invented a type mold that made it possible to print words in lines that were even. Letters were arranged in rows to make up an entire page. His invention made it easier to print books.

13.1 Flyer With Clip Art

FOCUS
Choose clip art pictures. Add clip art to a flyer. Create a border using clip art.

BELLRINGER
When students enter the room direct their attention to the assignment on the board:
   Read pages 270 and 271.

TEACH
Use the illustration on page 271 to highlight the clip art of balloons.

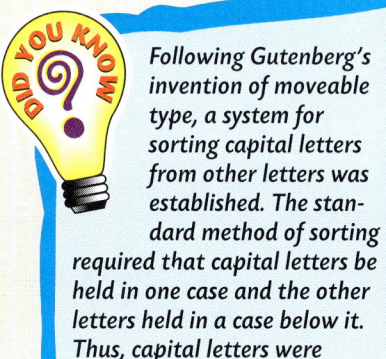

DID YOU KNOW?
Following Gutenberg's invention of moveable type, a system for sorting capital letters from other letters was established. The standard method of sorting required that capital letters be held in one case and the other letters held in a case below it. Thus, capital letters were called uppercase and the other letters, called lowercase.

Source: *Microsoft Encarta 96 Encyclopedia*, Microsoft Corporation, 1996.

RESOURCES

- Lesson Plan: LP69
  Supplemental Project: SP6
- Transparency 21
- CD-ROM: Reference Guide
- Software: Research Files

Flyer With Clip Art

TEACH

Provide some examples of clip art that is available with the software your students are using. Explain that additional clip art can be purchased. Some packages contain a variety of clip art images. Other packages contain images for a single subject area. Examples include: animals, athletics, education, holidays, and safety.

GO TO *Refer students to the appropriate section of the Student Guide.*

ASSESS

To assess students' understanding, have them identify the clip art on the flyer shown on page 271. Have them discuss the effective use of clip art in the flyer.

CLOSE

Have students create a flyer with clip art. Refer to Project 65.

Clip art is another name for a gallery of pictures. Most software packages come with their own clip art. You can often use clip art from other software programs, or buy it separately. Before you buy, read your software user's guide to find out if the clip art can be imported or used by your software.

Before you begin this project, take some time to look through the clip art available in your software. The picture you choose will likely be the focal point or the place your reader will look first. You must choose it carefully. Find a picture that matches your message. For example, if your message is lighthearted and fun, use a picture that brings a smile to your face.

DESIGN TIPS

- The picture you choose should capture the mood of the flyer.
- The fonts and wording should reflect the feeling of the flyer.
- Copy, paste, and rotate or flip the same picture to create a border as shown at the bottom of this flyer.

GO TO **Student Guide, Desktop Publishing** — Picture

272 Section 13 Graphics

Lesson Extension

Demonstrate how to use clip art from a CD-ROM.

Project 65

FLYER WITH CLIP ART

Follow the steps below to create a flyer with clip art.

1. Open a new word processing file.
2. Insert a **picture** with a party theme.
3. Insert another picture with a party theme to be repeated in the border at the bottom of the page.
4. Type the heading *The party is here . . .* using a script font, 48 points, bold.
5. Type the second heading *Your Student Council invites you!* using a sans serif font, 24 points, bold.
6. Type the body text and list below using a sans serif font, 18 points, bold.

> Who: Everyone from Castaic Middle School
>
> What: End-of-Year Party
>
> When: June 10 from 6 to 9
>
> Where: The gymnasium
>
> Why: To say HELLO to summer

7. Type the *Who:*, *What:*, *When:*, *Where:*, and *Why:* words in a separate text object right aligned.
8. Type *Be There!* using the same front as the heading at the top of the flyer.
9. Save the document as STDP065 on your data disk.

Flyer With Clip Art **273**

Project 65
Flyer With Clip Art

PRACTICE—LEVEL 1

Purpose
Practice creating a flyer with clip art.

Time
One class period

Preparation
No special preparation required.

Teaching Tip
Students who finish early should repeat the project.

Trouble Shooting
Provide individual help to students who are having difficulty working with clip art.

Wrap Up
Discuss the significance of using different sizes of fonts in a flyer. If this is the last project for this class period, ask students to return computers and furniture to the appropriate conditions.

Flyer With Clip Art

TEACH

Review design tips on page 274.

ASSESS

To assess students' understanding, have them discuss effective use of colors in a flyer with clip art.

CLOSE

Have students create a flyer with clip art. Refer to Project 66.

In Project 66, you will design a flyer to announce a seasonal school event. A Thanksgiving celebration, winter holiday, or summer vacation theme would be fun. The illustration shows a design for a flyer announcing a seasonal party.

DESIGN TIPS

- If you have a color printer, choose colors that highlight the theme.
- Don't overuse different colors. Using a maximum of three or four colors is a good rule of thumb.
- Faces, children, and animals are designs that always grab attention.

I almost forgot!

Valencia Valley's Fall Harvest party is coming up! We need volunteers for the following committees:

- Decorations
- Refreshments
- Entertainment

See Mr. Antonio in Room 202 between 8:30 and 9:30 a.m. this week to sign up.

274 Section 13 Graphics

CULTURAL KALEIDOSCOPE

Days of thanksgiving are celebrated around the world throughout the year. Thanksgiving is the fourth Thursday of November in the United States. Canadian Thanksgiving is observed on the second Monday in October. In the Virgin Islands, Thanksgiving is celebrated on October 25 and marks the end of hurricane season.

Project 66

FLYER WITH CLIP ART

Practice using the desktop publishing features you learned in Project 65 to design an original flyer using clip art pictures. Experiment with different pictures. Refer to the information on pages 271–274 as often as needed.

1. Open a new word processing file.
2. Insert pictures, drawings, text objects, borders, fills, etc., as needed.
3. Use a large, bold font for your headline.
4. Use a font with a smaller point size for any details.
5. Draw, move, resize, and stack any objects as you like.
6. Save the document as STDP066 on your data disk.

✓ Check Your Understanding

1. Did you choose clip art that captures the mood of your topic?
2. Did you flip or rotate the clip art to add interest?
3. Does the information in your flyer answer the questions *who, what, when, where,* and *why*?

Project 66
Flyer With Clip Art

ASSESS—LEVEL 2

Purpose
Assess desktop publishing skills by designing an original flyer.

Time
One class period

Preparation
No special preparation required.

Teaching Tip
Students who finish early should repeat the project.

Trouble Shooting
Provide individual help to students who are having difficulty working with clip art.

Wrap Up
Have students review their work using **Check Your Understanding.** Students should be able to answer "yes" to each of the questions. Ask students to return computers and furniture to the appropriate conditions.

13.2 Personal Stationery

FOCUS
Create original pictures using draw and paint tools. Create personal stationery with original pictures.

BELLRINGER
When students enter the room, direct their attention to the assignment on the board:
    Read pages 276 and 277.

TEACH
Use the illustration on page 276 to highlight various desktop publishing elements including a border, a drawing, and reversed text.

Personal Stationery

13.2

Goals
- Create original pictures using draw and paint tools
- Create personal stationery with original pictures

DESIGNING PERSONAL STATIONERY

Wouldn't it be fun to be able to create your own personal stationery? You could design some seasonal stationery to use at different times of the year. The paint feature in your software makes designing original pictures easy and fun.

Study the illustration. You can create unusual effects by combining borders, drawings, and paintings to reflect the season or theme. Your finished stationery may look slightly different.

276 Section 13 Graphics

RESOURCES

Lesson Plan: LP70
Supplemental Project: SP7

Transparencies 22 and 23

CD-ROM: Reference Guide

Software: Research Files

276

Before you begin painting, practice using each of the paint tools in your software. You will use tools like a pencil, spray can, brush, paint bucket, and eraser to create paintings that become a part of your document. You can also combine drawing tools with paint tools. Your design is limited only by your imagination.

DESIGN TIPS

- Simple designs are often the best.
- If you don't have confidence in your drawing ability, remember that cartoonlike drawings are interesting and fun to make.
- Look through clip art, magazines, and card shops for design ideas.

GO TO
Student Guide, Desktop Publishing
Paint

Personal Stationery **277**

Personal Stationery

TEACH

Review design tips on page 277.

GO TO *Refer students to the appropriate section of the Student Guide.*

ASSESS

To assess students' understanding, have them discuss painting tools available to design personal stationery.

CLOSE

Have students design stationery with original pictures. Refer to Project 67.

Lesson Extension

Have students look at books, magazines, newsletters, and web pages for desktop publishing design ideas.

277

Project 67
Personal Stationery

PRACTICE—LEVEL 1

Purpose
Create seasonal stationery with original pictures.

Time
Thirty minutes

Preparation
No special preparation required.

Teaching Tip
Students who finish early should repeat the project. Suggest that they select a different season or holiday.

Trouble Shooting
Provide individual help to students who are having difficulty working with paint tools.

Wrap Up
Ask the class what other types of stationery they might like to make. If this is the last project for this class period, ask students to return computers and furniture to the appropriate conditions.

Project 67

STATIONERY WITH ORIGINAL PICTURES

Follow the steps below to create seasonal stationery.

1. Open a new word processing file.
2. In your Student Guide, go to Unit 4, **paint.** Find and read all the Help topics listed to learn to use each of the paint tools.
3. Create a candy cane page border. Use a striped fill with a foreground color of red.
4. Draw a paint frame to hold a drawing of the holly.
5. Draw the holly using a dark green outline and a lighter green fill.
6. Draw round holly berries with red fill.
7. Insert a text object for the heading.

8. Type *Season's Greetings* in a script font, 24 or 36 points.
9. Add fills to the painting as you like.
10. Resize and move the objects approximately as shown in the illustration on page 276.
11. Save the document as STDP067 on your data disk.

278 Section 13 Graphics

CULTURAL KALEIDOSCOPE

Kwanzaa, December 26 through January 1, is a celebration of family, community, and culture. Kwanzaa, which means "first fruits" in Swahili, can be traced back to ancient African harvest celebrations. The modern celebration began in 1966.

As you learn more about using desktop publishing features, you may enjoy designing additional stationery.

Choose a theme for your stationery. For example, your design may reflect your favorite hobby, sport, food, or season of the year. Add a painting to accent your theme. Experiment with different paint tools and colors.

DESIGN TIPS

- Two different flowers were created in individual paintings at a 200% zoom. They were then copied, pasted, and flipped.
- The flower border was stacked over the pink background to add interest.
- A script font was used for a personal touch.

Personal Stationery **279**

Personal Stationery

TEACH

Review design tips on page 279. Use the illustration on this page to highlight components of personal stationery.

ASSESS

To assess students' understanding, have them identify the design elements in "Shannon's Notes" and discuss whether or not they feel it is an effective design for stationery.

CLOSE

Have students create personal stationery using paint and drawing tools. Refer to Project 68.

279

Project 68
Personal Stationery

ASSESS—LEVEL 2

Purpose
Assess desktop publishing skills by creating personal stationery.

Time
One class period

Preparation
No special preparation required.

Teaching Tip
Encourage students to use a theme that relates to an interest or hobby. Students who finish early should repeat the project.

Trouble Shooting
Provide individual help to students who are having difficulty with paint or drawing tools.

Wrap Up
Have students review their work using **Check Your Understanding**. Students' answers will vary. Ask students to return computers and furniture to the appropriate conditions.

Project 68

STATIONERY WITH ORIGINAL PICTURE

Practice using the desktop publishing features you learned in Project 67 to design more personal stationery using paint tools and drawing tools. Refer to the illustration and information on pages 276–279 as often as needed.

1. Open a new word processing file.
2. Create text objects, drawings, and paintings as needed.
3. Draw, move, resize, and stack objects as needed.
4. Add fills and borders as you like.
5. Save the document as STDP068 on your data disk.

✓ Check Your Understanding

1. Did you zoom in to draw and paint small details?
2. Did you zoom out to get a sense of proportion when you resized and moved your objects?

280 Section 13 Graphics

Project 69
Building Your Portfolio

In this project, you will review the desktop publishing features you learned in Section 13 by creating a flyer. Use clip art pictures, original pictures, and any other features you would like to add. The purpose of the flyer is to publicize an awards ceremony for a track team named the Valley Rockets. You might want to paint a rocket for your original picture using a rectangle with a striped fill and a triangle on top. The spray paint tool could be used to paint the rocket exhaust.

If you need to review desktop publishing features, refer to previous projects. Study the illustration as an example only. Your finished project should look very different.

Template

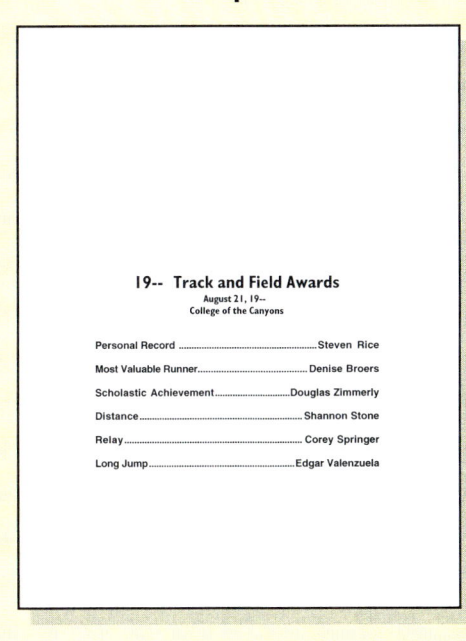

Sample Portfolio Project

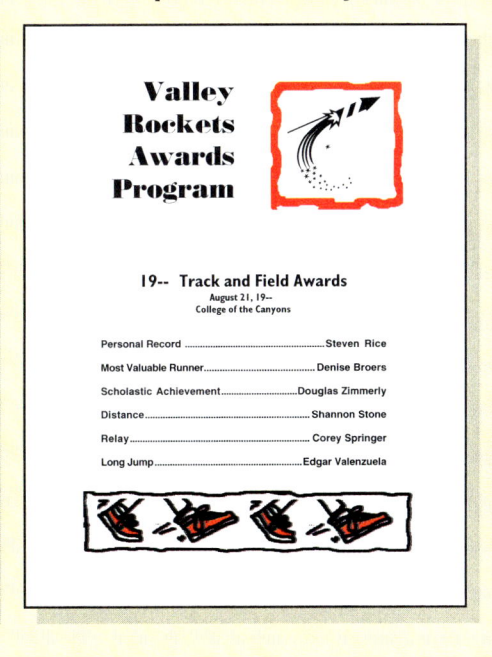

(continued on next page)

Building Your Portfolio **281**

Project 69
Building Your Portfolio

ASSESS—LEVEL 2

Purpose
Assess desktop publishing skills by creating a flyer.

Time
One class period

Preparation
No special preparation required.

Teaching Tip
Students who finish early should repeat the project. Suggest that they use a different piece of clip art.

Trouble Shooting
Make sure students are including a variety of desktop publishing features in their flyers.

Wrap Up
Remind students of the importance of compiling a portfolio of their work. Ask students to return computers and furniture to the appropriate conditions.

281

Building Your Portfolio

DID YOU KNOW?

Track and field events are one of the highlights of the Summer Olympics. The first modern Olympic Games were held in Athens, Greece, in 1896. One hundred years later the United States hosted the 1996 Centennial Olympic Games in Atlanta, Georgia. More than 10,000 Olympic athletes participated in the 1996 games. Approximately 2 million visitors to Atlanta purchased approximately 11 million tickets to attend more than 270 Olympic Events.

Project 69 (continued)
Building Your Portfolio

NOW TRY THIS

1. Open the file DP069 on your data disk.
2. Create a text object for the headline *Valley Rockets Awards Program*. Use a large, bold font of your choice.
3. Paint at least one original picture in the project. The picture could be a freehand border, a rocket, or any design you like.
4. Insert at least one clip art picture that relates to the theme of the flyer.
5. Draw, move, resize, and stack objects as needed.
6. Add fills and borders as you like.
7. Save the document as STDP069 on your data disk.

282 Section 13 Graphics

Templates

SECTION 14

Focus on Templates

Many software programs come with predesigned documents called templates. These templates make creating complicated documents much easier. You will use templates to create invitations, greeting cards, certificates, and other documents. You will use the thesaurus feature to find synonyms for words to make your writing more interesting.

Words To Know

caption
headline
masthead
newspaper columns
switch windows
template
thesaurus

OBJECTIVES

- Create documents using software templates.
- Use the thesaurus.
- Practice switching windows.

Section 14 Templates

SECTION OVERVIEW

This section focuses on using templates including invitations, greeting cards, letterhead, certificates, and newsletters. Using the thesaurus and switching between two open documents are introduced.

CONTENT FOCUS

Invitation, Letterhead, or Greeting Card
Certificate
Newsletter

OPENING ACTIVITY

Provide samples of the items listed below. Ask students to examine some of the samples and ask questions about how certain effects were achieved. As a class, decide if it is possible to replicate the samples using desktop publishing. Samples should include:
Invitations
Greeting cards
Letterhead
Certificates
Newsletters

Career Exploration Activities: Hospitality and Recreation

Hospitality and recreation are growing career fields. List five careers on the board. Ask students which of the careers listed requires good keyboarding skills and basic computer knowledge. The list on the board might include: airline reservationist, catering manager, hotel desk clerk, resort manager, and travel agent.

Invite a professional from the hospitality or recreation industry to speak to your class about how computers are used in the industry.

14.1 Invitation, Greeting Card, or Letterhead

FOCUS
Use a template. Create an invitation, greeting card, or letterhead.

BELLRINGER
When students enter the room, direct their attention to the assignment on the board:
　　Read pages 284 and 285.

TEACH
Use the illustration on page 284 to help explain a template. Point out the template components.

14.1 Invitation, Greeting Card, or Letterhead

Goals
- Use a template
- Create an invitation, greeting card, or letterhead

CREATING AN INVITATION, GREETING CARD, OR LETTERHEAD

Can you think of documents that you might like to use more than once? Examples might include party invitations, greeting cards, or letterheads. Rather than creating these complicated documents each time you want to use them, you could use a special file called a template.

CULTURAL KALEIDOSCOPE

The custom of sending greetings on Valentine's Day may have started with a Frenchman. In 1415, the Duke of Orléans was captured by England during a battle. While in prison in London, he sent his wife a love letter on Valentine's Day. The letter contained a rhyme.

HOLIDAY PARTY

It's that time of year again! Please join us for our annual holiday festivities.

Bring warm clothes. We are planning a moonlight sleigh ride!

December 18th
8:00 p.m.
at the Hollister's

Please RSVP to Becky or Jim by December 2nd

284 Section 14 Templates

RESOURCES
- Lesson Plan: LP73
- Transparency 24
- CD-ROM: Reference Guide
- Software: Research Files

CULTURAL KALEIDOSCOPE

People celebrate their culture with a variety of festivals. Some examples are:

**Bastille Day (France)
Beach Day (Uruguay)
Carnival (Brazil)
Fasching (Germany)
Feast of Nowdurga (India)
Homstrom (Switzerland)**

284

Most word processing packages come with very attractive predesigned templates. A **template** is a ready-made document that may be used many times. It already has a preset design that can include special fonts, drawings, pictures, and other formatting features. Usually you open a template document, personalize it by making changes, and then save it under a new name. The original template is unchanged.

Now, can you imagine opening a beautifully designed template, answering a few questions, and having your finished document magically appear? An automated template can make this happen. Your software will lead you step-by-step through a series of questions. When you finish making your choices, the document is created automatically.

In this project, you will create a document based on a template. Your finished document will look different depending upon the choices and changes you make.

GO TO — **Student Guide, Desktop Publishing** Template

Invitation, Greeting Card, or Letterhead

TEACH

Review the templates that are available for the software your students are using.

GO TO — *Refer students to the appropriate section of the Student Guide.*

ASSESS

To assess students' understanding, have them break up into groups and brainstorm the benefits of using a template to create documents. Have a spokesperson from each group present the list to the class.

CLOSE

Have students create an invitation, greeting card, or letterhead using a template. Refer to Project 70.

Lesson Extension

Explain that in addition to predesigned templates that are included with commercial software packages, it is possible to create your own template.

Project 70
Invitation, Greeting Card, or Letterhead

PRACTICE—LEVEL 1

Purpose
Practice creating a document with a template.

Time
Thirty minutes

Preparation
No special preparation required.

Teaching Tip
Students who finish early should repeat the project.

Trouble Shooting
Provide individual help to students who are having difficulty with the template feature.

Wrap Up
Review the answers to **Check Your Learning** for the **Language Link**. If this is the last project for this class period, ask students to return computers and furniture to the appropriate conditions.

Language Link
ANSWERS
1. it's
2. lose
3. except
4. bear
5. beside

Project 70

INVITATION, GREETING CARD, OR LETTERHEAD

Follow the steps below to create a document using a template.

1. In your Student Guide, go to Unit 4, **template**. Find and read the Help topics listed to learn about the template feature of your software.
2. Choose the template indicated for Project 70. Follow the steps in both the Student Guide and in your software.
3. Save the document as STDP070 on your data disk.

Language Link

Troublesome words require extra thought to avoid confusion.

Some words are confusing because they look and sound somewhat alike.

it's	it is	It's cold in this room.
its	shows possession	The dog lost its bone.
accept	receive	Most stores accept credit cards.
except	leave out	We shipped all items except the lamp.
beside	next to	The shoe store is beside the bank.
besides	in addition to	Besides shoes, it carries socks.
loose	not firmly attached	The little girl's tooth is loose.
lose	come to be without	Soon she will lose the tooth.
bear	an animal	The bear performed in the circus.
bare	empty	The cupboard was bare.

✓ Check Your Learning

Choose the correct word in parentheses to complete each sentence.

1. Tourists agree that (its, it's) a beautiful country.
2. We feared we would (loose, lose) our way.
3. All of the puzzle pieces fit (except, accept) these.
4. The (bear, bare) ate all the berries.
5. Tanya put her books (besides, beside) the table.

286 Section 14 Templates

14.2 Certificate

Certificate

CREATING A CERTIFICATE

A certificate is another document you can create using a template. It could be a certificate of appreciation, a gift certificate, an award, or a diploma to name a few examples. Change the information on the certificate as you like. Explore the choices and have fun experimenting. The illustration shown on page 288 is one example of a certificate you might create.

Goals
- Create a certificate using a template

Certificate **287**

14.2 Certificate

FOCUS
Create a certificate using a template.

BELLRINGER
When students enter the room, direct their attention to the assignment on the board:
 Read page 287 and look at the illustration on page 288.

TEACH
Review the kinds of certificates that can be created using templates.

RESOURCES

Lesson Plan: LP74
Supplemental Project: SP9

Transparency 25

CD-ROM: Reference Guide

Software: Research Files

287

Creating a Certificate

TEACH

Use the illustration on page 288 to highlight the components of the certificate.

ASSESS

To assess students' understanding, have them brainstorm the types of accomplishments for which a certificate would be appropriate.

CLOSE

Have students use a template to create a certificate. Refer to Project 71.

288 Section 14 Templates

Lesson Extension

Show students samples of preprinted certificate paper. Emphasize the importance of using paper that is compatible with the printer you are using.

288

Project 71

CERTIFICATE

Practice using another template to create a certificate.

1. In your Student Guide, go to Unit 4, **template.**
2. Choose the template indicated in the Student Guide for Project 71. Follow the steps in the Student Guide and in your software.
3. Save the document as STDP071 on your data disk.

In Your Journal
Tell about a certificate you have earned or describe a certificate you would like to create for someone.

Certificate **289**

Project 71
Certificate

PRACTICE—LEVEL 1

Purpose
Practice creating a certificate using a template.

Time
Thirty minutes

Preparation
No special preparation required.

Teaching Tip
Students who finish early should repeat the project.

Trouble Shooting
Provide individual help to students who are having difficulty using the template.

Wrap Up
Discuss students' ideas for the **In Your Journal** feature for creating customized certificates. If this is the last project for this class period, ask students to return computers and furniture to the appropriate conditions.

In Your Journal
Encourage students to include details about the content of the certificate.

289

14.3 Newsletter

FOCUS

Create a newsletter. Enhance the newsletter with clip art or original pictures. Use the thesaurus. Switch between two open documents.

BELLRINGER

When students enter the room, direct their attention to the assignment on the board:
Read pages 290 and 291.

TEACH

Share copies of any school newsletters available.
Explain how to use the thesaurus feature.

14.3 Newsletter

Goals

- Create a newsletter using a template
- Enhance the newsletter with clip art or original pictures
- Use the thesaurus
- Switch windows to copy text between two open documents

CREATING A NEWSLETTER

Newsletters are becoming more and more common. In schools, they are used to communicate information about activities, events, and people. Most newsletters have standard features like a masthead, flowing newspaper columns, headlines and captions, text objects and pictures, and sometimes a small table of contents.

Have you ever found yourself searching for the right word to replace another word that just doesn't fit? In this project, you will use the thesaurus feature to replace these difficult words. You will also copy and paste information between two open documents.

290 Section 14 Templates

RESOURCES

Lesson Plan: LP75
Supplemental Project: SP10
Transparency Master: TM31

Transparency 26

CD-ROM: Reference Guide

Software: Research Files

Study the illustration. Your finished newsletter may look different.

MASTHEAD. Title of the newsletter, usually with an issue number and a date.

HEADLINE. Main topic in a newsletter.

NEWSPAPER COLUMNS. Text prints in two columns.

CAPTION. Words or phrases that draw attention or emphasize a graphic.

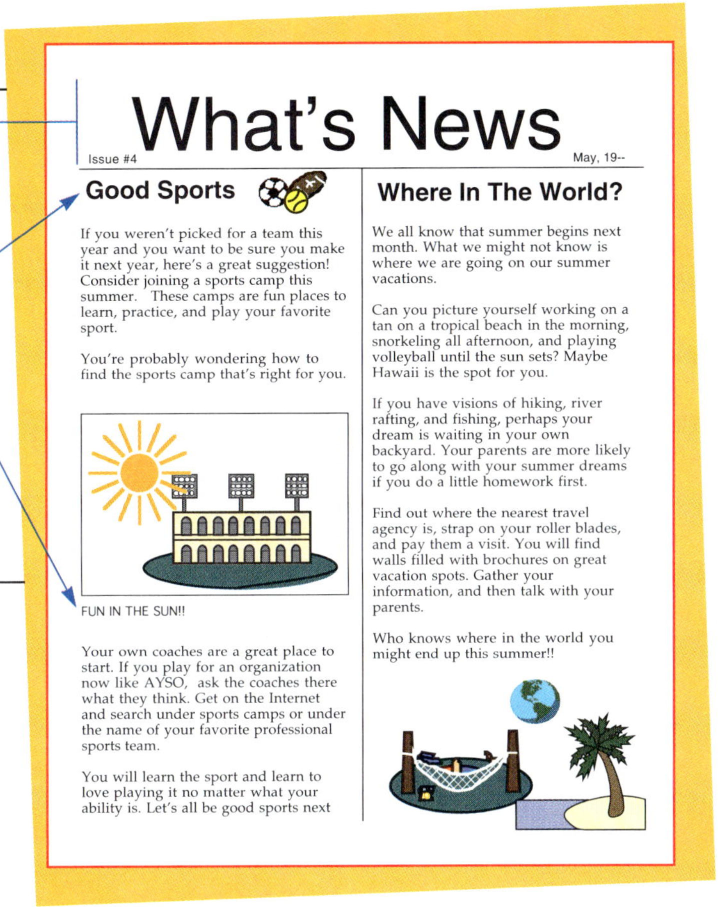

What's News

Issue #4 — May, 19--

Good Sports

If you weren't picked for a team this year and you want to be sure you make it next year, here's a great suggestion! Consider joining a sports camp this summer. These camps are fun places to learn, practice, and play your favorite sport.

You're probably wondering how to find the sports camp that's right for you.

FUN IN THE SUN!!

Your own coaches are a great place to start. If you play for an organization now like AYSO, ask the coaches there what they think. Get on the Internet and search under sports camps or under the name of your favorite professional sports team.

You will learn the sport and learn to love playing it no matter what your ability is. Let's all be good sports next

Where In The World?

We all know that summer begins next month. What we might not know is where we are going on our summer vacations.

Can you picture yourself working on a tan on a tropical beach in the morning, snorkeling all afternoon, and playing volleyball until the sun sets? Maybe Hawaii is the spot for you.

If you have visions of hiking, river rafting, and fishing, perhaps your dream is waiting in your own backyard. Your parents are more likely to go along with your summer dreams if you do a little homework first.

Find out where the nearest travel agency is, strap on your roller blades, and pay them a visit. You will find walls filled with brochures on great vacation spots. Gather your information, and then talk with your parents.

Who knows where in the world you might end up this summer!!

In Your Journal

Write in your journal about three events or activities that would be of interest to your classmates. Use your ideas to develop a newsletter.

GO TO — Student Guide, Desktop Publishing
Switch windows
Thesaurus

Newsletter **291**

interNET CONNECTION

Zines are self-published on-line magazines. Use a search engine to locate a zine that is appropriate to share with your class.

Newsletter

TEACH

Use the illustration on page 291 to highlight the masthead, headline, newspaper columns, and caption.

In Your Journal

For each of the three events or activities selected, ask students to make a bulleted list of the key points they want to include in each article.

GO TO — *Refer students to the appropriate section of the Student Guide.*

ASSESS

To assess students' understanding, have them identify the parts of a newsletter other than the example in the book.

CLOSE

Have students create a newsletter using a template. Refer to Project 72.

Project 72
Newsletter

PRACTICE—LEVEL 1

Purpose
Practice creating a newsletter using a template.

Time
One class period

Preparation
You will need to be familiar with the newsletter template your students will be using.

Teaching Tip
Students who finish early should review their work, correct errors, and make improvements.

Trouble Shooting
Provide individual help to students who are having difficulty with the thesaurus feature.

Wrap Up
Tell students to come prepared to the next class with ideas for a template to use in the **Building Your Portfolio** project. If this is the last project for this class period, ask students to return computers and furniture to the appropriate conditions.

Project 72

NEWSLETTER
Follow the steps below to create a newsletter using a template.

1. Open the file DP072A on your data disk. This file contains the text for the body of your newsletter. Later, you will **switch windows** and copy and paste the text from this file into your newsletter. Leave this file open until your newsletter is finished.
2. Use the **thesaurus** feature in your software to replace *preferred* with a better choice at the end of the first paragraph.
3. Open the file DP072B on your data disk. This file holds special directions for your newsletter. Print these directions and close the file.
4. In your Student Guide, go to Unit 4, **template.**
5. Choose the newsletter template indicated in the Student Guide for Project 72.
6. Create the newsletter by following the directions you printed in Step 3 above.
7. Save the finished newsletter as STDP072 on your data disk.

292 Section 14 Templates

Project 73
Building Your Portfolio

Review the features you learned in Section 14 by creating a document based on a template of your choice. Choose from any of the templates you used earlier in this section or discover a brand new template on your own. The illustration is an example of a new template with information and pictures added. Your choice may look different.

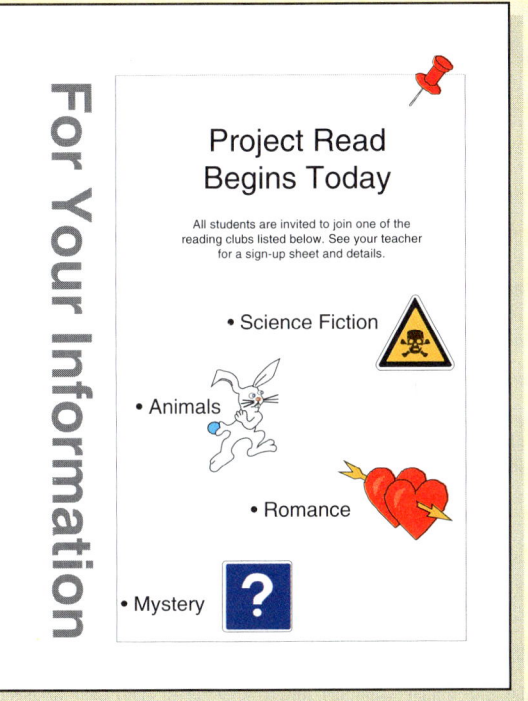

NOW TRY THIS

1. In your Student Guide, go to Unit 4, **template.**
2. Follow the directions to create a regular template or an automated template of your choice.
3. Edit the template as you like and add pictures, drawings, text, and so on.
4. Save the document as STDP073 on your data disk.

Building Your Portfolio **293**

Project 73
Building Your Portfolio

ASSESS—LEVEL 2

Purpose
Assess desktop publishing skills by creating a document using a template.

Time
One class period

Preparation
No special preparation required.

Teaching Tip
Help students select an appropriate template. Offer suggestions for content. Students who finish early should repeat the project.

Trouble Shooting
Provide individual help to students who are having difficulty with their templates.

Wrap Up
Congratulate the class on the fine documents they have prepared while working on this desktop publishing unit. Ask students to return computers and furniture to the appropriate conditions.

293

UNIT 5 ORGANIZER

Section	Subsection	Special Features	Projects: Project No., Title, and Page	Projects: Cross-Curricular Connection	Projects: Difficulty Level	Student Guide GO TO
15 - Spreadsheet Basics	15.1 - Explore a Spreadsheet	Words To Know, p. 296	Project 74: Explore a Spreadsheet, p. 299	74 Math	74 - L1	p. 298
	15.2 - Enter, Format, and Edit Data	In Your Journal, p. 302	Project 75: Enter, Edit, and Format Data, p. 302	75 Math	75 - L1	p. 301
	15.3 - Create a Spreadsheet		Projects 76–78: Create a Spreadsheet, pp. 304–306	76–78 Social Studies	76 - L1 77 - L2 78 - L2	p. 303
	15.4 - Formulas and Print Range	In Your Journal, p. 309 In Your Journal, p. 313 Cultural Kaleidoscope, p. 315	Projects 79–81: Enter Formulas and Print a Range, pp. 310–315	79–81 Social Studies	79 - L1 80 - L1 81 - L2	p. 309
			Project 82: Building Your Portfolio, p. 316		82 - L2	
	15.5 - Functions, Copy, and Move		Projects 83–85: Enter Functions, Copy, and Move Data, pp. 319–322	83–85 Math	83 - L1 84 - L1 85 - L2	p. 318
	15.6 - Fill Right, Fill Down, and Fill Series	Did You Know?, p. 326	Projects 86–88: Fill Right, Fill Down, And Fill Series, pp. 323–327	86–88 Technology	86 - L1 87 - L1 88 - L2	p. 323
	15.7 - Spreadsheet Structure	Did You Know?, p. 329 Did You Know?, p. 332	Projects 89–90: Change the Structure of a Spreadsheet, pp. 330–332	89–90 Science	89 - L1 90 - L2	p. 329
			Project 91: Building Your Portfolio, p. 333	91 Science	91 - L2	
16 - Enhanced Spreadsheets and Charts	16.1 - Borders, Gridlines, and Pictures	Words To Know, p. 334 In Your Journal, p. 336	Projects 92–94: Borders, Gridlines, and Pictures, pp. 337–339	92–93 Language Arts	92 - L1 93 - L1 94 - L2	p. 336
	16.2 - Styles	Cultural Kaleidoscope, p. 341	Projects 95–96: Styles, pp. 341–342	95–96 Technology	95 - L1 96 - L2	p. 340
	16.3 - Bar and Line Charts	Did You Know?, p. 345 Did You Know?, p. 346	Project 97: Bar Chart, p. 345 Project 98: Line Chart, p. 346 Project 99: Bar and Line Charts, p. 347	97 Social Studies 98 Social Studies 99 Social Studies	97 - L1 98 - L1 99 - L2	p. 344
	16.4 - Pie Charts	Cultural Kaleidoscope, p. 350	Projects 100–102: Pie Charts, pp. 350–352	100–102 Science	100 - L1 101 - L1 102 - L2	
			Project 103: Building Your Portfolio, p. 353		103 - L2	

UNIT RESOURCES

- Lesson Plans: LP76–LP94
- Transparency Masters: TM32–TM39
- Multicultural Timings: MT5–MT14
- Supplemental Projects: SP11–SP15
- Enrichment Activities
- CD-ROM: Unit 5 Document Templates, Reference Guide, Cross-curricular Timings
- Software: Unit 5 Document Templates, Research Files
- Transparencies: 27–29
- Student Guides: Spreadsheet
- Student Data Disks

294a

UNIT 5 ORGANIZER

Section	Subsection	Special Features	Projects			Student Guide GO TO
			Project No., Title, and Page	**Cross-Curricular Connection**	**Difficulty Level**	
17 - Analysis and Integration	17.1 - What If Analysis	Words To Know, p. 355 In Your Journal, p. 356 In Your Journal, p. 359	Projects 104–105: What If Analysis, pp. 357–358	104–105 Math	104 - L1 105 - L1	
			Project 106: What If Analysis Using a Template, p. 359	106 Math	106 - L2	p. 359
	17.2 - Integration		Projects 107–108: Integrate Spreadsheets and Word Processing Documents, pp. 361–362	107–108 Science	107 - L1 108 - L2	
		In Your Journal, p. 363 Did You Know?, p. 364	Projects 109–110: Create a Table in a Word Processing Document, pp. 363–364	110 Language Arts	109 - L1 110 - L2	
			Project 111: Building Your Portfolio, p. 365		111 - L2	

KEY TO DIFFICULTY LEVEL

The following designations will help you decide which activities are appropriate for your students.

L1: Level 1 activities are basic activities and should be within the range of all students.

L2: Level 2 activities are average activities and should be within the range of average and above average students.

L3: Level 3 activities are challenging activities designed for the ability range of above average students.

ASSESSMENT RESOURCES

Check Your Understanding

Section 15	Section 16	Section 17
p. 306		
p. 315		
p. 322		

Portfolio Assessment (Building Your Portfolio)

Section 15	Section 16	Section 17
p. 316	p. 353	p. 365
p. 333		

Unit Tests (Teacher's Resource Binder)
Objective Test
Performance Tests

Section 15   Section 16   Section 17

UNIT 5

INTRODUCING THE UNIT

Ask your students if they have ever used a spreadsheet. Draw a spreadsheet grid on the board and ask students to think of applications that might lend themselves to the column and row arrangement. Examples might include a teacher's grade book, sports statistics, or allowance tracking. Choose one of the examples and fill in the grid. If you have a computer with an overhead projection device, use an electronic spreadsheet to build the same application. Make changes to the spreadsheet. Ask students to calculate the changes by hand, while you (or a student) make the changes to the electronic spreadsheet. Point out the speed and accuracy with which the changes can be made on the electronic spreadsheet.

Unit 5
Spreadsheet

OVERVIEW

Have you ever wanted to buy something very badly but haven't had enough money to pay for it? Maybe you weren't sure how long it would take you to save the money. A spreadsheet is an excellent tool to help you answer this type of question. Accountants and others who work with numbers have used worksheets for centuries to find the answers to similar questions. A spreadsheet is an electronic worksheet that can help you manage and organize information. In this unit, you will learn to create and edit spreadsheets, format the information attractively, use formulas and functions, and create charts to display spreadsheet data.

Fun Facts

The first microcomputer-based spreadsheet, VisiCalc, was developed in the late 1970s by Dan Bricklin, who was at the time a Harvard Business School student. **VisiCalc** was originally written for the Apple II computer and is widely credited with spurring the growth in microcomputer use in corporate America.

UNIT 5

UNIT OBJECTIVES

- Identify key parts of a spreadsheet
- Create, edit, and format a spreadsheet
- Calculate in a spreadsheet using formulas and functions
- Print a spreadsheet
- Create and edit a spreadsheet chart
- Answer "what if" questions using a spreadsheet
- Integrate spreadsheet data with other programs

Unit Contents

Section 15 Spreadsheet Basics
Section 16 Enhanced Spreadsheets and Charts
Section 17 Analysis and Integration

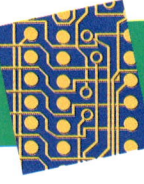

Focus On Careers In Technology

Businesses of all kinds employ accountants to figure the companies' income and expenses. Accountants advise businesses to make sure the companies are operating successfully to make a profit.

A spreadsheet program is the most powerful tool an accountant can use. It can compile data and perform calculations on the inventory or raw materials the business purchases, the expenses paid for employees' wages, and the revenues taken in from sales. If the accountant makes a change to one number, the totals are recalculated automatically.

With the data in a spreadsheet program, an accountant can create professional-looking documents that display eye-catching graphs, charts, and financial reports. These documents help the business analyze its financial position and budget for the future.

MULTIMEDIA

For this unit, you may use the multimedia CD-ROM to enhance your students' skills in creating spreadsheets. The CD-ROM contains format guides that serve as models for students to create projects using a spreadsheet software application. These format guides are cross-referenced to the spreadsheet projects in the student text. A Reference Guide links terms to format guides that define and illustrate their use in formatting spreadsheets. The Research Files contain cross-curricular typing selections or timings for 1 minute, 2 minutes, and 3 or 5 minutes. The timings, as well as the two games—Get the Scoop and Uncover the Story—are great ways to build typing skills.

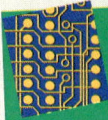

Focus On Careers In Technology

Discuss with students the fact that while spreadsheets can be used to create professional-looking documents, the information provided in them must still be verified for accuracy. Remind them of the GIGO principle—Garbage In, Garbage Out.

Application: COMPUTERS AT WORK

Divide the class into small groups and assign an occupational area to each group. Ask each group to start a list of ways a spreadsheet might be used in their assigned area. As time permits, ask each group to select a spokesperson. Have the spokesperson for each group share the group's list with the class.

Occupational areas to consider include:

Advertising	Library Science
Biochemistry	Recreation
Carpentry	Social Work
Engineering	Teaching
Forestry	Telemarketing
Journalism	Vision Care

295

Section 15
Spreadsheet Basics

SECTION OVERVIEW

This section introduces students to the most commonly used spreadsheet features. Use a computer to show students the spreadsheet they will be using. Identify the parts of the spreadsheet (cell, row, column, and so on). Point out that there are different spreadsheet programs available, but they all have similar capabilities.

CONTENT FOCUS

Explore a spreadsheet
Enter, format, and edit data
Create a spreadsheet
Formulas and print range
Functions, copy, and move
Fill right, fill down, fill series
Spreadsheet structure
Print

CURRICULUM FOCUS

Math
Social Studies
Technology
Science
Language Arts

OPENING ACTIVITY

Ask students to brainstorm advantages of using an electronic spreadsheet instead of handwritten calculations. Possible responses include easier to read, easier to make changes, and more likely to be accurate. Ask them to think about disadvantages. Possible responses include failure to check for accuracy ("the computer is always right" syndrome) and failure to apply human judgment.

296

SECTION 15
Spreadsheet Basics

● OBJECTIVES

- Identify the parts of a spreadsheet
- Use the basic features of a spreadsheet
- Enter, edit, and format text (labels) and numbers (values) in a spreadsheet
- Calculate using formulas and functions in a spreadsheet
- Print a spreadsheet

Focus on Spreadsheet

A spreadsheet is a tool to help you manage and organize numbers and text. Formulas may be used in the spreadsheet to add, subtract, multiply, and divide the numbers in the spreadsheet. In this unit, you will learn the basics of using a spreadsheet. You will also learn to format the spreadsheet and use formulas and functions.

Words To Know

active cell	fill right	MAX function
alignment	fill series	MIN function
AUTOSUM function	find and replace	page orientation
AVERAGE function	format	portrait
bar chart	formula results	print range
cell	formulas	protect cells
cell name or address	functions	relative cell referencing
cell pointer	insert rows and columns	row
cell range	label	sort
column	landscape	spreadsheet
delete rows and columns	line chart	SUM function
entry bar	mathematical operators	value
fill down		

296 Section 15 Spreadsheet Basics

Career Exploration Activities: Construction

Spreadsheets have proven useful in the construction trades. Ask students to research a job related to the construction industry using references such as the *Occupational Outlook Handbook, Occupational Outlook Quarterly* and *Dictionary of Occupational Titles*. Have them write a paragraph including the job title, educational requirements, and average salary. Ask them to discuss ways spreadsheets might prove useful for the position they have chosen. Examples might include using a spreadsheet to calculate the cost of materials for a building project or to calculate hourly labor rates for the project.

15.1 Explore a Spreadsheet

EXPLORING A SPREADSHEET

A **spreadsheet** is a tool used to organize and analyze information. Answering "what if" questions is what spreadsheets do best. For example, suppose you see a pair of in-line skates that cost $150. You have saved $60. You usually spend about $45 a month, and you earn $75 a month between your allowance and odd jobs. You could use a pencil, paper, and calculator to figure out how much you need to save each month to buy the skates and how long it would take. You could also use a spreadsheet for these same calculations. A spreadsheet would automatically calculate how long it would take to save enough money to buy the skates *if* you earned, spent, and saved the same amount each month. Your list of monthly expenses and income might look something like the illustration.

Goals
- Navigate through a spreadsheet
- Select cells, rows, and columns

	D11	× ✓	=D8+D9+D10	
	A	**B**	**C**	**D**
1		September	October	November
2	Monthly Income			
3	Allowance	50	50	50
4	Odd Jobs	25	25	25
5	Total Income	75	75	75
6				
7	Monthly Expenses			
8	Entertainment	25	25	25
9	Food	10	10	10
10	Other	10	10	10
11	Total Expenses	45	45	45

Rows and columns are used to organize information in a spreadsheet. Information in a **column** is arranged vertically and is identified by a letter such as A, B, or C, and so on. Information in a **row** is arranged horizontally and is identified by a number such as 1, 2, or 3, and so on.

15.1 Explore a Spreadsheet

FOCUS
Navigate through a spreadsheet. Select cells, rows, and columns.

BELLRINGER
When students enter the room, direct their attention to the assignment on the board:

Review the parts of a spreadsheet that appear on page 298.

RESOURCES
- Lesson Plan: LP77
- Multicultural Timing: MT5
- Transparency Master: TM32
- Transparency 27
- CD-ROM: Reference Guide
- Software: Research Files

Fun Facts
According to the **Guinness Book of World Records**, *the fastest mathematical computation was completed by Shakuntala Devi in June 1980. She multiplied (in her head!) two randomly selected 13-digit numbers in just 28 seconds. This same feat can be accomplished by a computer in less than one second.*

Explore a Spreadsheet

TEACH

Guide your students through the spreadsheet components shown on this page. Using a computer with an overhead display device, enter some of the labels and values shown in the figure. Show how to navigate through the spreadsheet window and how to select a cell.

ASSESS

To assess students' understanding, have them identify the basic components of a spreadsheet, including active cell, cell, cell address, cell pointer, column, entry bar and, row.

CLOSE

Have students explore a spreadsheet as described in Project 74.

GO TO — Refer students to the appropriate section of the Student Guide.

The point where a column and row meet forms a rectangle called a **cell**. The **cell name** or **address** is a combination of the column letter and the row number. For example, the highlighted cell in the illustration is named D11. When you click a cell, it is displayed as a rectangle with solid black lines surrounding it. The cell name appears at the top of the spreadsheet along with the contents of the selected cell. Study the illustration. Your spreadsheet may look slightly different.

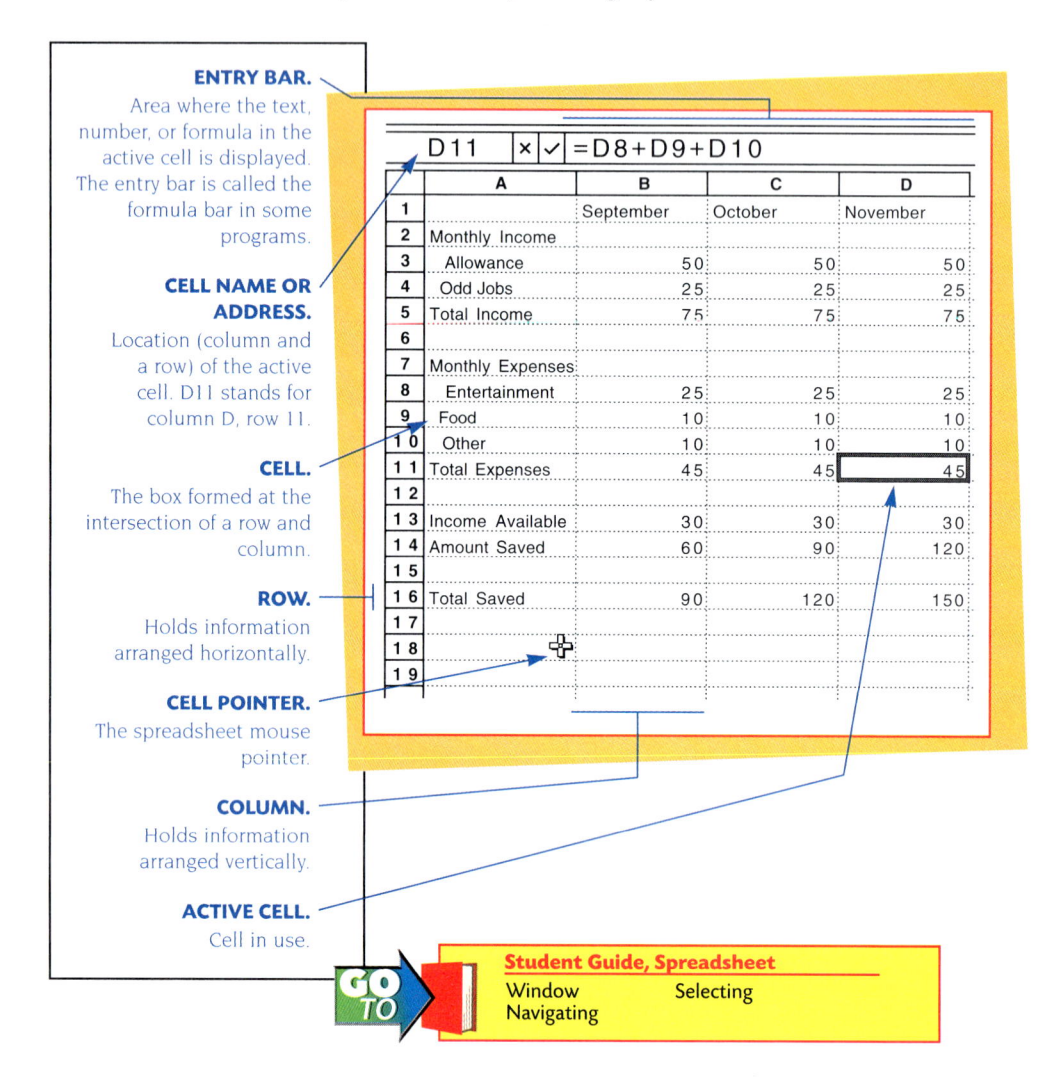

ENTRY BAR. Area where the text, number, or formula in the active cell is displayed. The entry bar is called the formula bar in some programs.

CELL NAME OR ADDRESS. Location (column and a row) of the active cell. D11 stands for column D, row 11.

CELL. The box formed at the intersection of a row and column.

ROW. Holds information arranged horizontally.

CELL POINTER. The spreadsheet mouse pointer.

COLUMN. Holds information arranged vertically.

ACTIVE CELL. Cell in use.

D11	× ✓	=D8+D9+D10	
	A	B	C	D

	A	B	C	D
1		September	October	November
2	Monthly Income			
3	Allowance	50	50	50
4	Odd Jobs	25	25	25
5	Total Income	75	75	75
6				
7	Monthly Expenses			
8	Entertainment	25	25	25
9	Food	10	10	10
10	Other	10	10	10
11	Total Expenses	45	45	45
12				
13	Income Available	30	30	30
14	Amount Saved	60	90	120
15				
16	Total Saved	90	120	150
17				
18				
19				

GO TO — Student Guide, Spreadsheet
Window Navigating   Selecting

Section 15 Spreadsheet Basics

Lesson Extension

Show students what happens when columns are too small to handle the information entered in a cell. If the information is text, it does not matter if the text extends into the next column; as long as the next cell is empty, the text will just flow to the next cell. If values are entered and the column is too small, most spreadsheets display a series of pound signs or error message. Students are taught how to change column width later in the section, but you might want to show them how to do it here as a "sneak preview."

Project 74

EXPLORE A SPREADSHEET

Carefully read and do the following steps to explore a spreadsheet.

1. In your Student Guide, read Unit 5, **window** to learn about the spreadsheet window. Find and read the Help topics listed here to learn some basics about spreadsheets.
2. Open the file SS074.
3. Practice **navigating** by clicking cell A2, *Monthly Income*.
4. Press the down arrow 3 times. You should be on cell A5, *Total Income*. Check the cell reference at the top of the spreadsheet to be sure you are on the correct cell.
5. Use the arrow keys to move the cell pointer to cell A9 containing the word *Food*.
6. Use the arrow keys to move the cell pointer to cell A7 containing the words *Monthly Expenses*.
7. Practice **selecting** by using the mouse to select cells A5 through D5.
8. Move the cell pointer to the top row of the spreadsheet.
9. Move the cell pointer to the bottom row of the spreadsheet.
10. Scroll down until rows 41–50 are visible in the spreadsheet window.
11. Move to cell A1, the beginning of the spreadsheet.
12. Select cell D11 and observe the formula in the entry bar and the results in cell D11.
13. Select row 2.
14. Deselect row 2 by clicking outside the row.
15. Select column E.
16. Deselect column E.
17. Save the document as STSS074 on your data disk.
18. Close the file.

Note: In the filename STSS074, ST stands for student; SS stands for the spreadsheet unit; and 074 stands for Project 074.

To encourage interest in math, have students use paper and pencil to create a simple worksheet. A sample appears below. (Results of calculations appear in italics.)

Rate Sheet	Hourly Rate	1 Hour	2 Hours	3 Hours
Babysitting	1.50	*1.50*	*3.00*	*4.50*
Grass mowing	2.25	*2.25*	*4.50*	*6.75*
Leaf raking	1.75	*1.75*	*3.50*	*5.25*
Snow shoveling	2.00	*2.00*	*4.00*	*6.00*

Project 74
Explore a Spreadsheet

PRACTICE—LEVEL 1

Purpose
Practice navigating through a spreadsheet, selecting cells, and entering labels in the spreadsheet

Time
Fifteen minutes

Preparation
Make sure the spreadsheet software is ready to use. Make sure students have data disks to store their files.

Teaching Tip
Observe students to make sure they are using the proper techniques to select cells and enter data. With some spreadsheets, it is easy to grab the fill handle instead of selecting the desired range of cells; help students identify this problem and show them how to correct it.

Make sure students understand the difference between selecting an entire row or column versus selecting a range of cells within a row or column.

Remind students to save their files to their data disks and not to the hard drive.

Trouble Shooting
Provide individual help to students who are having difficulty.

Wrap Up
Have students return computers and furniture to the appropriate conditions.

15.2 Enter, Format, and Edit Data

FOCUS
Enter labels and values. Format and edit data.

BELLRINGER
When students enter the room direct their attention to the assignment on the board:
Read the text and look at the illustration on page 300.

TEACH
It is difficult for students to understand why they should not include dollar signs, percent signs, and commas when they enter values in a spreadsheet. Instead, they should just type the numbers and then use the format command to change the way the numbers are displayed.

Explain that some spreadsheets interpret formatting symbols (such as dollar signs) as labels; if they are entered as part of a number, the spreadsheet will treat the number as a label and will not include it in mathematical calculations. In addition, it is much easier to type numbers without the special symbols—every time a special symbol is included with the number, the computer user increases the likelihood that he or she will type something incorrectly.

Enter, Format, and Edit Data
15.2

Goals
- Enter labels and values
- Format and edit data

ENTERING, EDITING, AND FORMATTING DATA

When entering data in a spreadsheet, you need to understand how the spreadsheet interprets the data you enter. When you enter words in a cell, the spreadsheet considers this data a **label**. When you enter a number in a cell, the spreadsheet considers this data a **value**. Numbers should be typed without commas or dollar signs. If a number has decimal places, the decimal should be typed. Numbers, dates, and times are all values. When a cell contains mathematical calculations such as the addition of numbers in a group of cells, these calculations are called **formulas**.

Formatting a spreadsheet cell refers to changing the way the information is displayed in a cell. Data can be displayed in bold or italics and in various type faces or point sizes. Look at the illustration. Notice the label January is bold. A cell containing a value can be formatted to display commas, a dollar sign (currency), a percent sign, or decimal places. A date can be formatted as 06/28/97 or June 28, 1997. Notice that the format of the values in the illustration includes dollar signs and two decimal places.

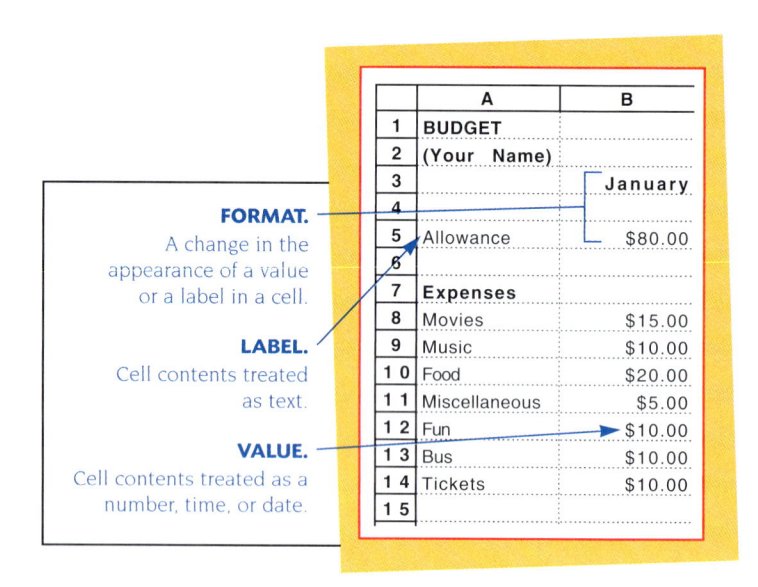

FORMAT. A change in the appearance of a value or a label in a cell.

LABEL. Cell contents treated as text.

VALUE. Cell contents treated as a number, time, or date.

	A	B
1	BUDGET	
2	(Your Name)	
3		January
4		
5	Allowance	$80.00
6		
7	Expenses	
8	Movies	$15.00
9	Music	$10.00
10	Food	$20.00
11	Miscellaneous	$5.00
12	Fun	$10.00
13	Bus	$10.00
14	Tickets	$10.00
15		

300 Section 15 Spreadsheet Basics

RESOURCES
Lesson Plan: LP78
Transparency Master: TM33

CD-ROM: Reference Guide

Software: Research Files

Alicia earns money to use to pay her expenses for movies, music, and food.

Alignment is the placement of information within a cell either at the left edge, right edge, or centered within the cell. By default, labels are aligned at the left and values are aligned at the right. The alignment of data in a cell can be changed. Labels that serve as column heads for values are often right aligned to match the alignment of the values in the same column. Notice the right alignment of the label *January*. Your spreadsheet may look slightly different.

> **Student Guide, Spreadsheet**
> Enter data   Alignment
> Cell, edit   Format

Enter, Format, and Edit Data **301**

Enter, Format, and Edit Data

TEACH

Point out that by default, text is left-aligned in the cell, while values are right-aligned. Proper alignment of labels over columns of numbers can help clarify which column heading goes with which set of numbers.

ASSESS

To assess students' understanding, have them explain the difference between a label and a value. Have them discuss formatting and alignment.

CLOSE

Have students enter data in a spreadsheet. Refer to Project 75.

Refer students to the appropriate section of the Student Guide.

interNET CONNECTION

Have students use the Internet or a commercial on-line service to find a site that discusses the spreadsheet program you are using. The site can be maintained either by the developer of the spreadsheet or by a user of the product. Ask students to write a paragraph that discusses the information they found.

Examples of sites might include:
Lotus: http://www.lotus.com
Glimpse: http://glimpse.cs.arizona.edu:1994

Project 75
Enter, Format, and Edit Data

PRACTICE—LEVEL 1

Purpose
Practice entering, editing, and formatting labels and values.

Time
Fifteen minutes

Preparation
Make sure the spreadsheet software is available and that students have their data disks. Make sure the printers are ready.

Teaching Tip
Observe students closely to make sure they are using the format command or buttons to change the format of the labels and values.

Students who finish early should repeat the project.

Trouble Shooting
Provide individual help to students who are having difficulty formatting data.

Wrap Up
Have students return computers and furniture to the appropriate conditions.

In Your Journal
Have students make a list of a few items for which they would like to save money. Ask them to include estimated prices.

Project 75

Math Connection

ENTER, EDIT, AND FORMAT DATA

Follow the steps below to enter, edit, and format data in a spreadsheet.

1. Open the file SS075 on your data disk.
2. Select cell A2 and **enter data** by typing your first and last name.
3. Follow the steps under **cell, edit** in Unit 5 of your Student Guide to edit cell B3 by changing *October* to *January*.
4. Change the **alignment** of cell B3 to right.
5. Select cell A7 and type *Expenses*.
6. Bold the labels in cells A1, A2, A7, and B3.
7. Select cell B5 and delete the contents.
8. Type the value *80* in cell B5.
9. Type the label *Bus* in cell A13.
10. Type the label *Tickets* in cell A14.
11. Type the value *10* in cell B13.
12. Type the value *10* in cell B14.
13. **Format** all values as currency with two decimal places.
14. Use the speller. Proofread to check for errors. Preview the document and make corrections as needed.
15. Save the spreadsheet as STSS075 on your data disk.
16. Print and then close the spreadsheet.

In Your Journal
Make a list that includes all the money you earned for a week. Then keep a list of all your expenses for a week. Next, compare your two lists. What information can you find out just by looking at your two lists? Write two summary statements that tell what you found after making this comparison.

Math Connection

To encourage interest in math, have students make a list of everyday calculations. The list might include:

Sales tax

Tip for service in a restaurant

Discount on sale merchandise

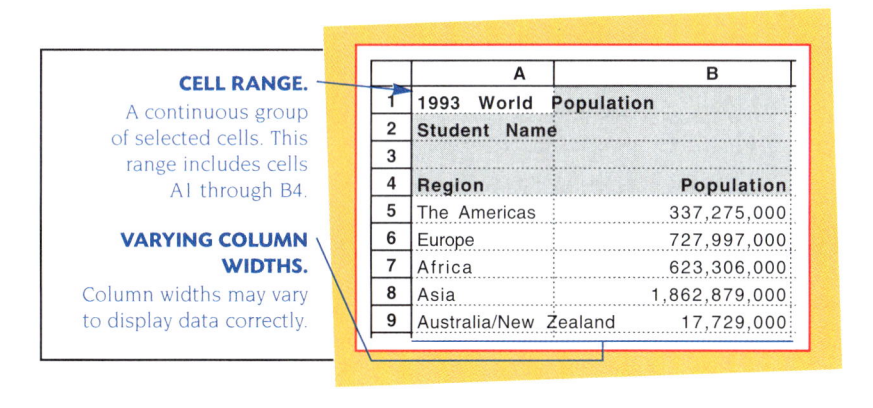

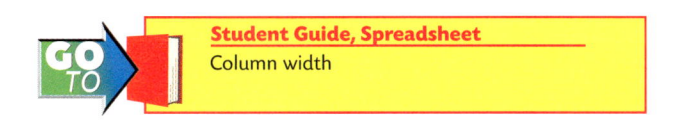

15.3 Create a Spreadsheet

CREATING A SPREADSHEET

To create a new spreadsheet, you will enter and format the spreadsheet title, labels, and values. When you open a new spreadsheet file, you will notice that all the columns have the same width. You may need to widen some of the columns for the data to display correctly. If a value is too wide to fit in a column, the software displays number signs (#####). To remove the number signs and display the value, you must widen the column. If a label is too wide to fit in a column, the label will display over the next cell if that cell is empty. If the next cell is not empty, the word will be cut off. You will need to widen the column for the label or value to display correctly.

In formatting a spreadsheet, it is often helpful to work with a cell range. A **cell range** is a continuous group of selected cells. Once a range is selected, you can apply formatting changes to all the cells at once.

Study the illustration which shows a selected cell range and columns of varying widths. Your spreadsheet may look slightly different.

Goals
- Create a spreadsheet
- Format a cell range
- Change column widths

CELL RANGE. A continuous group of selected cells. This range includes cells A1 through B4.

VARYING COLUMN WIDTHS. Column widths may vary to display data correctly.

	A	B
1	1993 World	Population
2	Student Name	
3		
4	Region	Population
5	The Americas	337,275,000
6	Europe	727,997,000
7	Africa	623,306,000
8	Asia	1,862,879,000
9	Australia/New Zealand	17,729,000

GO TO
Student Guide, Spreadsheet
Column width

Create a Spreadsheet **303**

RESOURCES
- Lesson Plan: LP78
- Transparency Master: TM33
- CD-ROM: Reference Guide
- Software: Research Files

15.3 Create a Spreadsheet

FOCUS
Create a spreadsheet. Format a cell range. Change column widths.

BELLRINGER
Have students read the text and look at the illustration on page 303.

TEACH
Demonstrate what happens when columns are not wide enough for the data. Use both text and numeric data as part of the demonstration. Also, point out that labels that extend into the next column might not print properly unless the print range is expanded to include the adjoining column. When in doubt, make the column wider!

Most spreadsheets provide more than one method to change the column width. A menu-based command is usually available to specify a specific column width. The user can also just drag the column border to make the column smaller or larger.

ASSESS
To assess students' understanding, have them explain why column widths might vary.

CLOSE
Have students create a new spreadsheet. Refer to Projects 76, 77, and 78.

GO TO *Refer students to the appropriate section of the Student Guide.*

303

Project 76
Create a Spreadsheet

PRACTICE—LEVEL 1

Purpose
Practice creating a new spreadsheet and changing column widths

Time
Thirty minutes

Preparation
Make sure the spreadsheet software is available and that students have their data disks. Make sure the printers are ready.

Teaching Tip
Observe students carefully to make sure they understand how to change the column widths and apply the specified formatting characteristics to the cells. Students who finish early can experiment with other formatting techniques, such as changing the cell alignment, using italics, and so on.

Trouble Shooting
Provide additional help to students who are having difficulty with changing column widths.

Wrap Up
Have students return computers and furniture to the appropriate conditions.

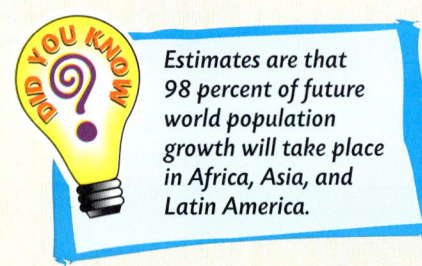

DID YOU KNOW
Estimates are that 98 percent of future world population growth will take place in Africa, Asia, and Latin America.

Project 76
Social Studies Connection
CREATE A SPREADSHEET

Follow the steps below to create a new spreadsheet and change the column widths.

1. Open a new spreadsheet file.
2. Type the label *1993 World Population* in cell A1. Notice that the label flowed over into column B and displays because column B is empty.
3. Type your first and last name in cell A2.
4. Type the labels and values as shown below:

	A	B
4	Region	Population
5	The Americas	337275000
6	Europe	727997000
7	Africa	623306000
8	Asia	1862879000

5. Type the label *Australia/New Zealand* in cell A9. Notice that the label flowed over into column B because column B is now empty.
6. Type the value *17729000* in cell B9. Notice that the label in column A is only partially displayed because column B is no longer empty.
7. Change the **column width** for column A until all text in the longest label, A9, can be seen.
8. Select the cell range A1 through B4 by placing the pointer in cell A1 and dragging across and down to cell B4.
9. Bold the cells in the selected range A1 through B4.
10. Select the cell range B5 through B9. Format the values in the selected range to include commas.
11. Change the column width until all numbers display correctly.
12. Change the label *Population* in B4 to right alignment.
13. Use the speller. Proofread to check for errors. Preview the document and make corrections as needed.
14. Save the spreadsheet as STSS076 on your data disk.
15. Print and then close the spreadsheet.

304 Section 15 Spreadsheet Basics

Social Studies Connection

To generate interest in social studies, create a spreadsheet that includes large city population statistics for three years. Assign a country and year to each student. Compile the results in a spreadsheet similar to the one below:

	1994	1995	1996
Tokyo, Japan	26,518,000	—	—
New York City, U.S.	16,271,000	—	—
São Paulo, Brazil	16,110,000	—	—
Mexico City, Mexico	15,525,000	—	—
Your city or town		—	—

Social Studies Connection

Project 77

CREATE A SPREADSHEET

Practice using the spreadsheet features your learned earlier by formatting a spreadsheet that shows the final medal standings from the 1996 Summer Olympic Games. Refer to the illustration and information on pages 303 and 304 as needed.

1. Open a new spreadsheet file.
2. Type the information in columns A through D as shown below:

	A	B	C	D
1	FINAL MEDAL STANDING			
2	1996 SUMMER OLYMPIC GAMES			
3				
4	Nation	Gold	Silver	Bronze
5	United States	44	32	25
6	Russia	26	21	16
7	Germany	20	18	27
8	China	16	22	12
9	Czech Republic	4	3	0

3. Change the alignment of the labels in B4 through D4 to right.
4. Reduce the width of Columns B, C and D until one or two spaces are left between the longest item in each column.
5. Select and bold the label in cell A1.
6. Select and bold all labels in row 4.
7. Select cell A11 and type your first and last name.
8. Select cell A12 and type the name of this class.
9. Select cell A13 and type the current date.
10. Format cell A13 as a date using this format: Month (spelled out) day (in numbers), year.
11. Use the speller. Proofread to check for errors. Preview the document and make corrections as needed.
12. Save the spreadsheet as STSS077 on your data disk.
13. Print and then close the spreadsheet.

Create a Spreadsheet **305**

Project 77 Create a Spreadsheet

APPLY—LEVEL 1

Purpose
Apply skills learned by creating and formatting a spreadsheet.

Time
Thirty minutes

Preparation
Make sure the spreadsheet software is available and that students have their data disks. Make sure the printers are ready.

Teaching Tip
Observe students carefully to make sure they are using the formatting commands properly. Make sure they understand how to adjust columns so the size is appropriate for the data to be included.

Trouble Shooting
Provide individual help to students who are having difficulty with spreadsheet formatting features.

Wrap Up
Discuss the fact that the summer Olympic Games are held every four years. The next time they will be held is the year 2000.

Have students return computers and furniture to the appropriate conditions.

Social Studies Connection

To generate interest in social studies, discuss the size and population of countries shown in the spreadsheet on page 305. Size and population data is provided below.

	Area (sq. mi.)	Population
United States	3,679,192	263,814,032
Germany	137,823	81,337,541
China	3,696,100	1,203,097,268
Czech Republic	30,450	10,432,774

305

Project 78
Create a Spreadsheet

ASSESS—LEVEL 2

Purpose
Assess skills by creating and formatting a spreadsheet.

Time
Thirty minutes

Preparation
Make sure the spreadsheet software is available and that students have their data disks. Make sure the printers are ready.

Teaching Tip
Students who finish early can apply additional formatting features to the spreadsheet.

Trouble Shooting
Provide individual help to students who are having difficulty formatting their speadsheets.

Wrap Up
Have students review their work using **Check Your Understanding.**

Have students return computers and furniture to the appropriate conditions.

Project 78
Social Studies Connection
CREATE A SPREADSHEET

Create the spreadsheet below as directed. Refer to the illustration and information on pages 303 and 304 as needed.

1. Open a new spreadsheet file.
2. Type the information below into a spreadsheet. Change the column widths as needed to display all the data correctly.

	A	B	C
1	CITY SPENDING FOR 1997		
2	PREPARED BY (YOUR FIRST AND LAST NAME)		
3			
4			
5	EXPENSE	MIDVILLE	MUDVILLE
6	Education	1233544	2544682
7	Police and Fire Dept.	503417	652198
8	Roads and Highways	150000	125000
9	Employees	10256980	2113800
10	Insurance	98000	101000

3. Type the current date in cell A3.
4. Italicize all labels in row 5.
5. Change the alignment in cells B5 and C5 to right.
6. Bold all labels under *Expense* and in rows 1 and 2.
7. Format all values for commas.
8. Save the spreadsheet as STSS078 on your data disk.

Note: After each document is finished, always use your speller. Proofread carefully, preview the document, and make corrections as needed before printing. The last step in a project should always be to print and close the file. These directions will no longer be repeated.

✓ Check Your Understanding

1. Did you widen the columns as needed?
2. Did you align the column headings in columns two and three to the right?
3. Did you change the look of your numbers by adding commas?

---

306 Section 15 Spreadsheet Basics

Social Studies Connection

Explain that a city receives the money it spends through various revenue sources. Share with the class the following spreadsheet that displays the sources of income collected for Midville and Mudville.

Revenue	Midville	Mudville
Property tax	2,448,388	1,107,336
Sales tax	9,958,710	885,869
Personal income tax	1,224,194	553,668
Corporate income tax	612,097	276,834
Federal government contribution	1,836,291	830,502
Other	4,162,261	1,882,471

15.4 Formulas and Print Range

ENTERING FORMULAS AND PRINTING A RANGE

A spreadsheet **formula** is a combination of values or cell references and **mathematical operators** such as addition (+), subtraction(−), multiplication(*), and division(/). The results of a formula display in the cell, and the actual formula displays in the entry bar. Whenever the values in any cell referenced in the formula change, the formula results are automatically recalculated and displayed.

To create a formula, begin by selecting the cell where you want to display the formula results. Type an equal sign (=) and then build the formula, step by step. For example, the formula =B2 + B3 adds the values in cells B2 and B3.

Study the formula displayed in the illustration. The formula in active cell B8 (=B5+B6+B7) adds the contents of the three cells (B5+B6+B7) and displays the answer in cell B8 ($250.75).

ENTRY BAR. Displays the contents of the active cell.

CELL REFERENCE OF ACTIVE CELL.

FORMULA IN ACTIVE CELL B8.

ACTIVE CELL. Displays the data or formula results.

FORMULA RESULTS. A formula is used to add the values in row 5 (=B5+C5) and to total the values in column D (D5+D6+D7).

	A	B	C	D
	B8	× ✓	=B5+B6+B7	
1	STUDENT GOVERNMENT FUND RAISING			
2	PREPARED BY (YOUR FIRST AND LAST NAME)			
3				
4		Room 9	Room 11	Total
5	Car Wash	$23.50	$31.75	$55.25
6	Candy Sales	$125.00	$142.25	$267.25
7	Softball Game	$102.25	$86.50	$188.75
8	Total	$250.75	$260.50	$511.25
9	Today's Date in November 21, 1997 format			

Formulas and Print Range

RESOURCES

Lesson Plan: LP79
Supplemental Project: SP11
Transparency Masters: TM34

CD-ROM: Reference Guide

Software: Research Files

Lesson Extension

Explain that the mathematical order of precedence is the same with spreadsheets as it is with any mathematical equation. Items in parentheses are evaluated first, followed by multiplication and division (in left to right order), and finally addition and subtraction (in left to right order).

15.4 Formulas and Print Range

FOCUS

Enter a formula. Print a cell range. Change the page orientation

BELLRINGER

When students enter the room, direct their attention to the assignment on the board:
  Read the text and look at the illustration on page 307.

TEACH

Formulas are the heart of the spreadsheet. Without them, an electronic spreadsheet would be no more efficient than handwritten calculations. Use the illustration on page 307 to help explain formulas.

Goals
- Enter a formula
- Print a cell range
- Change the page orientation

Formulas and Print Range

TEACH

Remind students that most spreadsheets require that formulas begin with an equal sign (=); otherwise, the spreadsheet will treat the cell entry as text or numbers rather than a formula.

Point out the advantages of using landscape orientation. Use the illustration on page 308 to demonstrate page orientation.

> **DID YOU KNOW?**
>
> Bill Gates, founder and chief executive of Microsoft Corporation, was a billionaire by the time he hit the age of 31. His company, known largely for its Windows operating system, also develops one the most widely used spreadsheets on the market, Microsoft Excel.

Another formula could include multiplying a cell value times a value you supply. For example, the formula =B5*3 multiplies the value in cell B5 by 3. The formula =A5/C2 divides the value in cell C2 into the value in cell A5. Parentheses may be needed in a formula to ensure correct calculation. For example, =(B2*C3)+D1. Remember to begin each formula with an equal sign. If you forget to enter the equal sign as the first character, the data is treated as a label rather than a formula.

Spreadsheets can be printed in different ways on the page. The direction in which the information is printed across the paper is called the **page orientation.** The default page orientation for a spreadsheet is **portrait.** Portrait page orientation means the printing is across the short edge of the paper and looks like the illustration on the left. If a spreadsheet is too wide to print on one page in portrait page orientation, you change the page orientation to landscape. **Landscape** page orientation means printing across the long edge of the paper and looks like the illustration on the right.

Portrait Page Orientation

Landscape Page Orientation

308 Section 15 Spreadsheet Basics

Lesson Extension

Because spreadsheets often are used for annual budgets, it is useful to print them in landscape mode because this makes it easy to fit all twelve months on the same page. Previewing the spreadsheet before printing it is always recommended.

There may be times when you want to print only a selected range of cells rather then the entire spreadsheet. To print a **cell range,** first select the range you want to print. For instance, to print the data in columns A through C in the illustration, you would select the print range of A1 through C9. In some programs, selecting the print range and choosing Print is all you need to do. In other programs, you must also enter the print range in a dialog box.

	B8	× ✓	=B5+B6+B7	
	A	B	C	D
1	STUDENT GOVERNMENT FUND RAISING			
2	PREPARED BY (YOUR FIRST AND LAST NAME)			
3				
4		Room 9	Room 11	Total
5	Car Wash	$23.50	$31.75	$55.25
6	Candy Sales	$125.00	$142.25	$267.25
7	Softball Game	$102.25	$86.50	$188.75
8	Total	$250.75	$260.50	$511.25
9	Today's Date in November 21, 1997 format			

In Your Journal

You are in charge of a fund-raiser for the student council at your school. What are some activities you might consider doing to raise money? Make a list of your ideas. Share your list with members of the student council.

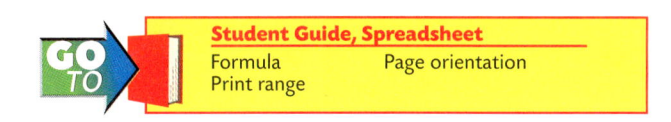

GO TO
Student Guide, Spreadsheet
Formula   Page orientation
Print range

Formulas and Print Range **309**

Formulas and Print Range

TEACH

The process used to print ranges varies from one spreadsheet to another. Demonstrate this process to your students.

GO TO *Refer students to the appropriate section of the Student Guide.*

ASSESS

To assess students' understanding, have students identify a range to be printed.

CLOSE

Have students enter formulas and print a range. Refer to Projects 79, 80, and 81.

In Your Journal

Remind students to include fund-raising activities that have been successful at school in the past.

Lesson Extension

Ask students to list reasons why it might be necessary to print only portions of a spreadsheet. One possible response centers around confidentiality; for example, each student should see only his or her test scores from the teacher's worksheet.

Project 79
Formulas and Print Range

PRACTICE—LEVEL 1

Purpose
Practice entering formulas and printing a range.

Time
Thirty minutes

Preparation
Make sure the spreadsheet software is available and that students have their data disks. Make sure the printers are ready.

Teaching Tip
Observe students carefully to make sure they are entering the formulas properly. Students who finish early should repeat the project. This time, ask them to experiment with different formatting attributes.

Trouble Shooting
Provide individual help to students who are having difficulty changing the page orientation of the spreadsheet.

Project 79

Social Studies Connection

ENTER FORMULAS AND PRINT A RANGE

Follow the steps as given to enter formulas in a spreadsheet, print a cell range, and change the page orientation. Refer to pages 307–309 if you need help.

1. Open the file SS079 on your data disk. The illustration below shows the information in the file. Look at the illustration under the description of formulas in this project as you follow the steps below to complete this spreadsheet.

	A	B	C
1	STUDENT GOVERNMENT FUND RAISING		
2	PREPARED BY (YOUR FIRST AND LAST NAME)		
3			
4		Room 9	Room 11
5	Car Wash	23.5	31.75
6	Candy Sales	125	142.25
7	Softball Game	102.25	86.5

2. Edit cell A2 by typing your name in all caps after the PREPARED BY in row 2.
3. Type the label *Total* in cell D4.
4. Change the alignment of information in row 4 to centered.
5. Bold all labels in row 4.
6. Type the label *Total* in cell A8.
7. Type today's date in cell A9 using the format of mm/dd/yy. For example: 11/21/97.
8. Format cell A9 for a date with the month spelled out. For example: November 21, 1997.

(continued on next page)

310 Section 15 Spreadsheet Basics

Social Studies Connection

To encourage interest in social studies, further explore local government revenue sources. As a class, have students calculate the total revenues for the governments of Midville and Mudville, using the spreadsheet data given in the Social Studies Connection on page 306.

Project 79 (continued)

9. Type the following **formula** in cell B8: =B5+B6+B7. Observe the formula in the entry bar before you press Return/Enter.
10. Type the following formula in cell C8: =C5+C6+C7.
11. Type the following formula in cell D5: =B5+C5.
12. Type the following formula in cell D6: =B6+C6.
13. Type the following formula in cell D7: =B7+C7.
14. Type the following formula in cell D8: =D5+D6+D7.
15. Format all values as currency with two decimals.
16. Print the spreadsheet. Save the spreadsheet as STSS079A on your data disk.
17. Select a **print range** which includes all data in columns A through C.
18. Print this range using landscape **page orientation.**
19. Save the spreadsheet as STSS079B on your data disk.

Formulas and Print Range

Teaching Tip
Students who finish early should print the spreadsheet again, this time using portrait orientation.

Wrap Up
Have students return computers and furniture to the appropriate conditions.

DID YOU KNOW? The largest chocolate model was created in Barcelona in 1991. It was in the shape of a traditional Spanish sailing ship and weighed over four tons. Just think of the fund-raising possibilities!

Project 80
Formulas and Print Range

APPLY—LEVEL 1

Purpose
Apply spreadsheet skills by entering formulas and printing a range.

Time
Thirty minutes

Preparation
Make sure the spreadsheet software is available and that students have their data disks. Make sure the printers are ready.

Teaching Tip
Observe students carefully to make sure they are entering the formulas properly. Students who finish early should repeat the project.

Trouble Shooting
Provide individual help to students who are having difficulty with creating formulas or printing in landscape and portrait page orientation.

Wrap Up
Discuss the journal entries students have made for **In Your Journal.** Ask them to think of ways spreadsheets could be used for school elections.

Have students return computers and furniture to the appropriate conditions.

Project 80
Social Studies Connection
ENTER FORMULAS AND PRINT A RANGE

Practice using the features your learned earlier by creating formulas and printing in landscape and portrait page orientation. Refer to the illustration and information on pages 307–311 if you need help.

1. Open File SS080 on your data disk. The illustration below shows the information in the file.

	A	B	C	D
1	STUDENT BODY ELECTION FOR PRESIDENT			
2	VOTE BY CAMPUS			
3	PREPARED BY (YOUR NAME)			
4				
5	PRESIDENTIAL CANDIDATE	NORTH	WEST	CENTRAL
6	DEBBIE YOUNG	125	189	159
7	LEE QUAN	151	203	189
8	GEORGE SMITH	112	157	188

2. Edit row 3 and type your name after the PREPARED BY in column A.
3. Type *TOTAL* in cell E5.
4. Type *TOTAL VOTES* in cell A9.
5. Type *VOTES AVAILABLE* in cell A11.
6. Type *1612* in cell E11.
7. Bold all labels in row 5.
8. Change the alignment in cells B5, C5, D5 and E5 to right.
9. Type *PERCENT OF VOTES CAST* in cell A13.
10. Format cell A15 for a date. Use the format that shows numbers separated by slashes (/).Type today's date in cell A15.
11. Total the votes for Debbie Young by typing the following formula in cell E6: =B6+C6+D6.
12. Total the votes for Lee Quan by typing the following formula in cell E7: =B7+C7+D7.
13. Total the votes for George Smith by typing the following formula in cell E8: =B8+C8+D8.

(continued on next page)

312 Section 15 Spreadsheet Basics

Social Studies Connection

To create interest in social studies, have students research the party affiliation of the members of the U.S. Senate and House of Representatives for recent years. Sample data is shown below.

Term	Congress	Democratic Senators	Republican Senators	Other Senators	Total Senators
1993–95	103rd	57	43	0	100
1995–97	104th	48	52	0	100
1997–99	105th	–	–	–	–
1999–2001	106th	–	–	–	–

Project 80 (continued)

14. Total all votes by typing the following formula in cell E9: *=E6+E7+E8*.
15. Format cell E13 for percent with 2 decimals.
16. Type the formula in cell E13 to calculate the percentage of votes cast in the election: *=E9/E11*. This formula divides the total votes cast by the total votes available.
17. Save the spreadsheet as STSS080A on your data disk.
18. Print the entire spreadsheet in landscape page orientation.
19. Print the cell range A1 through D8 in portrait page orientation.
20. Save the spreadsheet as STSS080B on your data disk.

In Your Journal

Imagine you are a candidate to be Student Body President at your school. What qualifications would make you the best choice for the position? Write your ideas in a short paragraph.

Formulas and Print Range

In Your Journal

Ask students to write in their journals a few ideas for using spreadsheets during an election. Possibilities include tracking campaign expenses, monitoring contributions, and tabulating election results.

Formulas and Print Range **313**

Social Studies Connection

To create interest in social studies, initiate a discussion about local, state, or federal elections. Ask students to research the dates of upcoming elections. They should determine when the next elections will be held for your state legislators, the U.S. House of Representatives and Senate, and the president.

interNET CONNECTION

Have students use the Internet or a commercial on-line service to find the results of a recent local, state, or federal election. Have them build a spreadsheet similar to the one in this project showing the results of their research.

Project 81
Formulas and Print Range

ASSESS—LEVEL 2

Purpose
Assess spreadsheet skills by entering formulas and printing a range.

Time
Thirty minutes

Preparation
Make sure the spreadsheet software is available and that students have their data disks. Make sure the printers are ready.

Teaching Tip
Observe students carefully to make sure they are entering the formulas properly. Students who finish early should repeat the project.

Trouble Shooting
Provide individual help to students who are having difficulty creating formulas.

Wrap Up
Have students review their work using **Check Your Understanding.** They should be able to answer "yes" to each of the three questions.

Have students return computers and furniture to the appropriate conditions.

Project 81
Social Studies Connection
ENTER FORMULAS AND PRINT A RANGE

Practice using the features your learned earlier by creating formulas and changing page orientation. Refer to the illustrations and information on pages 307–311 if you need help.

1. Open a new spreadsheet file.
2. Create the spreadsheet displayed below by entering all the data *except* the values in row 11 and in column C.

	A	B	C
1	PRESIDENTIAL ELECTION--1996		
2	PREPARED BY (YOUR FIRST AND LAST NAME)		
3			
4		POPULAR	PERCENTAGE
5		VOTE	OF POPULAR VOTE
6	BILL CLINTON	45,628,667	49.16%
7	BOB DOLE	37,869,435	40.80%
8	ROSS PEROT	7,874,283	8.48%
9	OTHER	1,435,025	1.55%
10			
11	TOTAL	92,807,410	
12			
13	TODAY'S DATE		

3. Type a formula in cell B11 to total the popular votes. In cells C6 through C9, enter formulas to divide the popular vote by the total votes. For example, in cell C6 enter: =B6/B11.
4. Enter the current date in cell A13 and format the cell in a date format of your choice.
5. Change the alignment for all labels in rows 4 and 5 to right alignment.
6. Widen columns if necessary to display all information.
7. Format the values in column B for commas.
8. Format the values in column C for percent with two decimals.
9. Bold the labels in cells A1, A2 and A13.

(continued on next page)

314 Section 15 Spreadsheet Basics

---

interNET CONNECTION

Have students use the Internet or a commercial on-line service to find out who else ran in this presidential election. Students who finish early can replace the "Other" category with the names and vote totals of the other candidates.

Social Studies Connection

Initiate a discussion about the state and federal legislators who represent your area. Have students research a legislator and write a one-paragraph report. Examples of the kind of information that should be included:

Legislator's name Year first elected
Party affiliation Beginning/ending
Current position dates of term

314

Project 81 (continued)

10. Save the spreadsheet as STSS081A on your data disk.
11. Print the spreadsheet in landscape page orientation.
12. Print the data in columns A and B in portrait page orientation.
13. Save the spreadsheet as STSS081B on your data disk.

✓ Check Your Understanding

1. Did you start all your formulas with the equal sign?
2. Did you change the page orientation?
3. Did you use the correct slash when creating a formula with the division operator?

Formulas and Print Range

CULTURAL KALEIDOSCOPE

In April 1994, South Africa held its first election in which all citizens, regardless of race, could vote. Before 1994, blacks were not allowed to vote. In the election, Nelson Mandela was elected as South Africa's first black president.

CULTURAL KALEIDOSCOPE

More than 22 million voters cast ballots in South Africa's 1994 election. Nelson Mandela's victory is particularly interesting given the fact that he was imprisoned in 1964, largely because of his campaigns against the South African government; he was released from prison in 1990.

Project 82
Building Your Portfolio

ASSESS—LEVEL 2

Purpose
Assess spreadsheet skills by creating, editing, and formatting a spreadsheet.

Time
One class period

Preparation
Ask students to compile the necessary data before trying to build the spreadsheet. They will need the following information to complete the project: the names of five classmates and the number of brothers and sisters each classmate has.

Make sure the spreadsheet software is available and that students have their data disks. Make sure the printers are ready.

Teaching Tip
Observe students carefully to make sure they are entering the formulas properly. Students who finish early should repeat the project, this time using five different classmates.

Trouble Shooting
Provide individual help to students who are having difficulty formatting their spreadsheets.

Wrap Up
Remind students of the purpose and importance of building a portfolio of projects from this class.

Have students return computers and furniture to the appropriate conditions.

316

Project 82
Building Your Portfolio

Review spreadsheet features learned in earlier projects by creating, editing, and formatting a simple spreadsheet.

NOW TRY THIS

1. Open a new spreadsheet file.
2. In cell A1, type the spreadsheet title *FAMILY SIZE*. Bold the title.
3. In cell A2, type *Prepared By* and your first name and last name.
4. In cell A3, type the name of this class.
5. Type the column headings *Name* in cell A5, *Girls* in cell B5, and *Boys* in cell C5. Bold the headings and right align cells B4 and C4.
6. In cells A6 through A10 type the names of five of your classmates.
7. Edit cell B5 to replace Girls with *Sisters*.
8. Edit cell C5 to replace Boys with *Brothers*.
9. In cells B6 through B10, type the number of sisters each of your classmates has.
10. In cell C6 through C10, type the number of brothers each of your classmates has.
11. In cell A11 type *Total* in bold.
12. In cell A12 type *Average* in bold.
13. In cell B11 enter a formula to calculate the total number of sisters for your classmates.
14. In cell C11 enter a formula to calculate the total number of brothers for your classmates.
15. In cell B12 enter a formula to calculate the average number of sisters for your classmates.
16. In cell C12 enter a formula to calculate the average number of brothers for your classmates.
17. Edit the title in cell A1 to replace FAMILY SIZE with *SISTERS AND BROTHERS*.
18. Type the current date in cell C14 and format the cell using a date format of your choice.
19. Adjust column widths to display all the information attractively.
20. Change the page orientation to landscape and print the spreadsheet.
21. Save the spreadsheet as STSS082 on your data disk.

316 Section 15 Spreadsheet Basics

15.5 Functions, Copy, and Move

Goals
- Use functions in formulas
- Copy data
- Move data

ENTERING FUNCTIONS

Spreadsheets include numerous built-in formulas called **functions**. One of the most frequently used functions is SUM. The **SUM function** adds the values in a range of cells. Like other formulas, formulas that use functions must begin with an equal sign. The equal sign is followed by the function name. Next, the range of cells to be included in the formula is typed in parentheses. For example, the formula =SUM(A1..A2) adds the values in cells A1 and A2. Study the illustration below. Your spreadsheet may look slightly different.

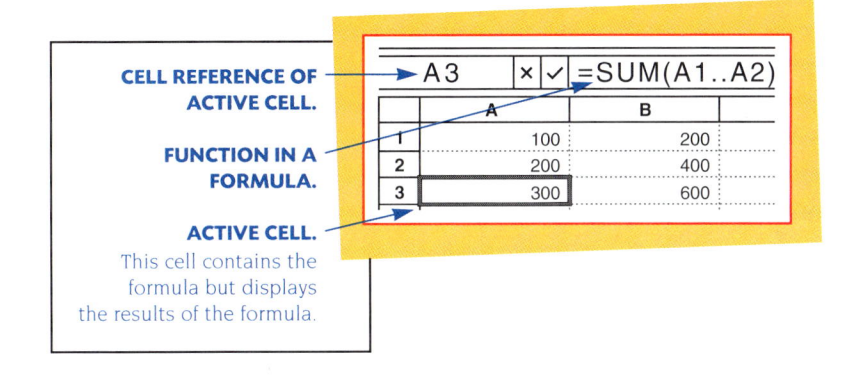

CELL REFERENCE OF ACTIVE CELL.

FUNCTION IN A FORMULA.

ACTIVE CELL. This cell contains the formula but displays the results of the formula.

	A	B
1	100	200
2	200	400
3	300	600

(A3 =SUM(A1..A2))

Since adding values is done so frequently in spreadsheets, a special tool called **AUTOSUM** is included in spreadsheets. The AUTOSUM button quickly creates a formula to add a selected range of cells. The formula created by AUTOSUM looks the same as a SUM formula that has been typed.

Other frequently used functions include AVERAGE, MIN (minimum) and MAX (maximum). The **AVERAGE function** adds the values in a selected range of cells and divides the sum by the number of values in the range. The **MIN function** determines the smallest or minimum number in a cell range. The **MAX function** determines the largest or maximum number in a cell range.

Functions, Copy, and Move **317**

15.5 Functions, Copy, and Move

FOCUS
Use functions in formulas. Copy data. Move data

BELLRINGER
When students enter the room, direct their attention to the assignment on the board:

Read the text and look at the illustration on page 317.

TEACH
Functions are built-in formulas the spreadsheet provides. Functions are convenient to use because they reduce the number of keystrokes that must be entered to produce the calculation; whenever keystrokes are minimized, accuracy tends to increase.

Some spreadsheets use a colon to separate the cells in a range rather than the ellipsis shown in the illustration. Demonstrate the proper way to type ranges with the spreadsheet your students are using.

RESOURCES

Lesson Plan: LP81
Multicultural Timing: MT6
Supplemental Project: SP12
Transparency Master: TM35

CD-ROM: Reference Guide

Software: Research Files

317

Functions, Copy, and Move

TEACH

Demonstrate the copy process. Show how relative cell addresses are automatically updated relative to their new location on the spreadsheet.

ASSESS

Have students draw a spreadsheet grid on a piece of paper and practice "copying" formulas from one cell to another on their grid. For example, assume =B5+B6 appears in cell B7. Ask students to predict how the formula will read if the formula is copied to cell C7. How will it read if it is copied to cell D8? After they have made their predictions, use an actual spreadsheet with a display device to show the results of the copy operation.

CLOSE

Have students enter functions, copy data, and move data. Refer to Projects 83, 84, and 85.

Refer students to the appropriate section of the Student Guide.

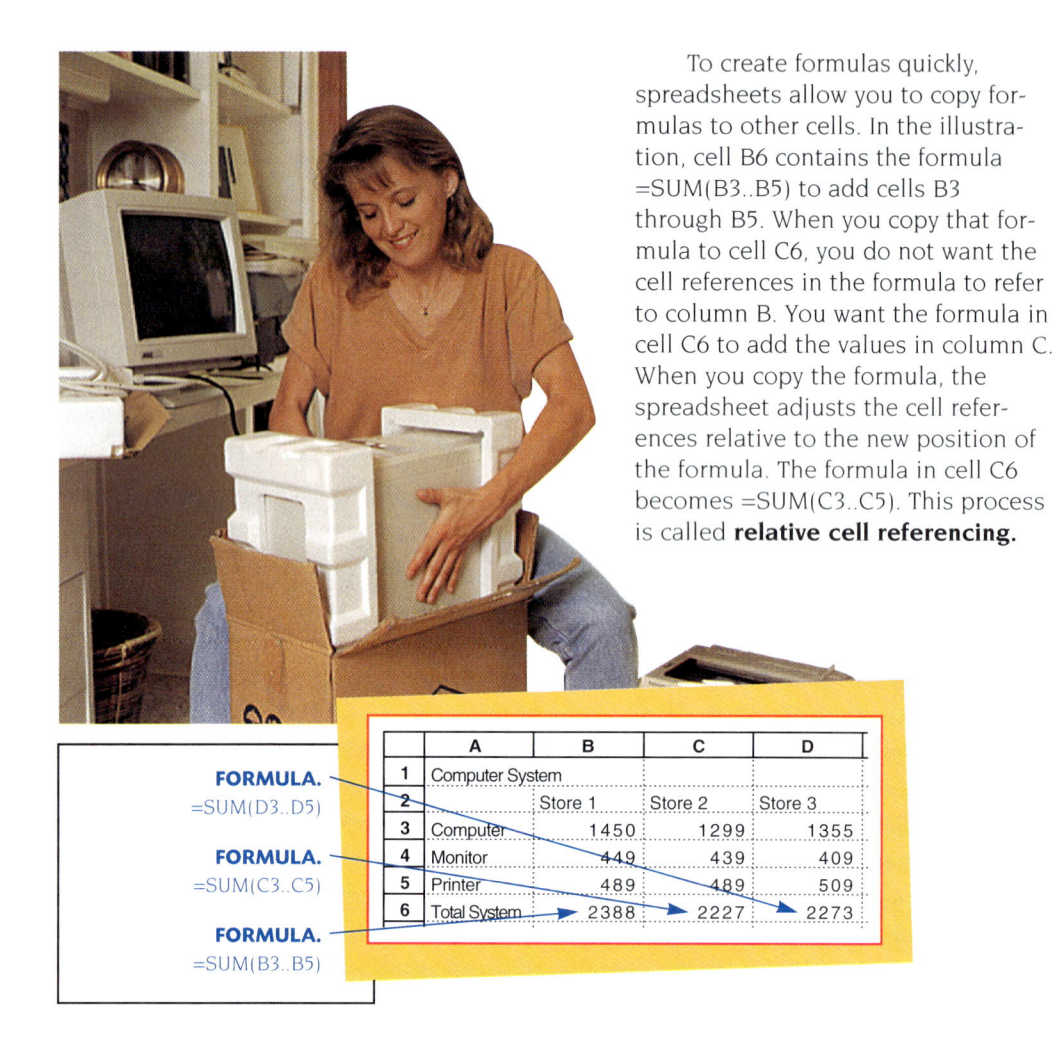

To create formulas quickly, spreadsheets allow you to copy formulas to other cells. In the illustration, cell B6 contains the formula =SUM(B3..B5) to add cells B3 through B5. When you copy that formula to cell C6, you do not want the cell references in the formula to refer to column B. You want the formula in cell C6 to add the values in column C. When you copy the formula, the spreadsheet adjusts the cell references relative to the new position of the formula. The formula in cell C6 becomes =SUM(C3..C5). This process is called **relative cell referencing**.

FORMULA.
=SUM(D3..D5)

FORMULA.
=SUM(C3..C5)

FORMULA.
=SUM(B3..B5)

	A	B	C	D
1	Computer System			
2		Store 1	Store 2	Store 3
3	Computer	1450	1299	1355
4	Monitor	449	439	409
5	Printer	489	489	509
6	Total System	2388	2227	2273

In Project 83 you will use formulas that include functions. You will also edit a spreadsheet by copying and moving the contents of cells.

GO TO Student Guide, Spreadsheet
Move data — Function, AVERAGE
Copy — Function, MIN
Function, AUTOSUM — Function, MAX

318 Section 15 Spreadsheet Basics

interNET CONNECTION

Have students use the Internet to find current prices for the items shown in the illustration. Ask them to record the information they found, including the item name, the vendor, the price, and other relevant information.

Project 83

ENTER FUNCTIONS, COPY, AND MOVE DATA

Follow the steps below to update the spreadsheet with new information about income and costs.

1. Open the file SS083 on your data disk. The illustration below shows the information in the file.

	A	B	C
1	CONCERT FUND RAISERS		
2			
3	Income		
4	Tickets		
5	Snacks		
6	Total Income		
7			
8			
9	Expenses	Fall	Spring
10	Rent Hall	250	250
11	Clean-Up	100	100
12	Advertising	225	
13	Band	450	
14	Security	175	150
15	Total Expenses		
16			
17	Average Expense		
18	Minimum Expense		
19	Maximum Expense		
20			
21	Profit		

2. Type *Prepared By* and your first and last name in cell A2.
3. Follow the steps under **move data** in Unit 5 of your Student Guide. Move the data in cells A3 through A6 to be relocated to cells A4 through A7.
4. Move the label *Fall* from cell B9 to cell B3.
5. Move the label *Spring* from cell C9 to cell C3.
6. In cell B5 type *1150* for tickets income.
7. In cell B6 type *125* for snacks income.

(continued on next page)

Functions, Copy, and Move **319**

Project 83
Functions, Copy, and Move

PRACTICE—LEVEL 1

Purpose
Practice moving data, copying data, and using functions.

Time
One class period

Preparation
Make sure the spreadsheet software is available and that students have their data disks. Make sure the printers are ready.

Teaching Tip
Observe students carefully to make sure they are actually copying data and not just re-typing it. Make sure they use shortcuts, such as the AUTOSUM button. Students who finish early should repeat the project.

Trouble Shooting
Provide individual help to students who are having difficulty with the functions. Make sure they are copying and moving contents of cells correctly.

Wrap Up
Have students return computers and furniture to the appropriate conditions.

Have students expand the spreadsheet they created in Project 82 on page 316 (STSS082). In cell D5, have them type the column heading **Pets**. *In cells D6–D10, have them type the number of pets each classmate has. Have them calculate the total in cell D11 using AUTOSUM and calculate all of the averages in the spreadsheet using the AVERAGE function.*

Functions, Copy, and Move

Project 83 (continued)

8. Read the steps under **copy** in Unit 5 of your Student Guide. Copy the same ticket and snack income from column B into column C.
9. Copy the value *100* for clean-up expense into cell C12 for advertising.
10. Type *300* for band expense for the spring concert.
11. Read the steps under **function, AUTOSUM** in Unit 5 of your Student Guide. In cell B7 total the fall income by using AUTOSUM.
12. In cell C7 total the spring income by using AUTOSUM.
13. In cell B15 total the fall expenses by using AUTOSUM.
14. In cell C15 total the spring expenses by using AUTOSUM.
15. Read the steps under **function, AVERAGE** in Unit 5 of your Student Guide. In cell B17 calculate the average fall expense.
16. Copy the formula in cell B17 to cell C17 to calculate the average spring expense.
17. Read the steps under **function, MIN** in Unit 5 of your Student Guide. In cell B18 type a formula to find the minimum fall expense.
18. Copy the formula in cell B18 to cell C18 to find the minimum spring expense.
19. Read the steps under **function, MAX** in Unit 5 of your Student Guide. In cell B19 type a formula to find the maximum fall expense.
20. Copy the formula in cell B19 to cell C19 to find the maximum spring expense.
21. In cell B21 calculate the fall profit by typing a formula to subtract the total expenses from the total income: *=B7–B15* .
22. Copy the formula in cell B21 to cell C21 to find the spring profit.
23. Format all values as currency with commas and no decimals.
24. Widen columns as needed to display all information.
25. Save the spreadsheet as STSS083 on your data disk. Print the spreadsheet in portrait page orientation.

320 Section 15 Spreadsheet Basics

Fun Facts

The largest band ever to perform was in Oslo, Norway; over 20,000 musicians played at the Ullevaal Stadium in 1964. The largest marching band was also from Norway; this time, over 6,000 people marched at the Stafsberg Airport in Hamar.

Project 84

ENTER FUNCTIONS, COPY, AND MOVE DATA

Practice using functions, moving data, and copying data within a spreadsheet. Refer to the illustration and information on pages 317–320.

1. Open the file SS084 on your data disk. The illustration below shows the information in the file.

	A	B
1	MONTHLY AUTO EXPENSES	
2		
3		
4		
5	Payment	194
6	Insurance	79
7	Gas	35
8	Maintenance	50
9		
10	Total Expenses	
11		
12	Average Expense	
13	Minimum Expense	
14	Maximum Expense	

2. Type *Prepared By* and your first and last name in cell A2.
3. Move the information in the range A5 through B8 to A6 through B9.
4. Type *January, February, March* as column headings in cells B5, C5 and D5.
5. Type *Quarterly* in cell E4 and *Total* in cell E5.
6. Bold and right align the column headings.
7. Copy the value in cell B6 to cells C6 and D6.
8. Copy the value in cell B7 to cells C7 and D7.
9. Type *45* in cell C8, *30* in cell D8, *0* in cell C9, and *80* in cell D9.
10. In column E rows 6 through 9, use AUTOSUM to find the quarterly totals.
11. Using AUTOSUM, find the total expenses for columns B, C, D and E.
12. Find the average expense for each month and for the quarter. Place the results in cells B12, C12, D12, and E12. Find the minimum and maximum expense for each month and quarter. Place the results in row 13 and row 14.
13. Format all values as currency with commas and two decimals.
14. Print the spreadsheet in portrait page orientation.
15. Save the spreadsheet as STSS084 on your data disk.

Functions, Copy, and Move **321**

Project 84 Functions, Copy, and Move

APPLY—LEVEL 1

Purpose
Apply spreadsheet skills by using functions and moving and copying data.

Time
Thirty minutes

Preparation
Make sure the spreadsheet software is available and that students have their data disks. Make sure the printers are ready.

Teaching Tip
Observe students carefully to make sure they are actually copying data and not just re-typing it. Make sure they use shortcuts, such as the AUTOSUM button. Students who finish early should repeat the project.

Trouble Shooting
Provide individual help to students who are having difficulty using the AUTOSUM feature.

Wrap Up
Have students return computers and furniture to the appropriate conditions.

interNET CONNECTION

Have students use the Internet to find information about automobiles. Examples of sites might include:

Ford: http://www.ford.com
Honda: http://www.honda.com
Pontiac: http://www.pontiac.com
Toyota: http://www.toyota.com

To encourage interest in math, have students obtain information about actual expenses their parents or relatives incur in operating their automobiles. Or, share with them the amounts of your actual automobile expenses. As a class, create a spreadsheet using these actual expenses.

Project 85
Functions, Copy, and Move

ASSESS—LEVEL 2

Purpose
Assess spreadsheet skills by using functions and moving and copying data.

Time
Thirty minutes

Preparation
Make sure the spreadsheet software is available and that students have their data disks. Make sure the printers are ready.

Teaching Tip
Observe students carefully to make sure they are actually copying data and not just re-typing it. Make sure they use shortcuts, such as the AUTOSUM button. Students who finish early should repeat the project.

Trouble Shooting
Provide individual help to students who are having difficulty using speadsheet functions.

Wrap Up
Have students review their work using **Check Your Understanding**. They should be able to answer "yes" to each of the three questions.
   Have students return computers and furniture to the appropriate conditions.

Project 85

ENTER FUNCTIONS, COPY, AND MOVE DATA

Practice using functions, moving data, and copying data within a spreadsheet. Refer to the illustration and information on pages 317–320 if you need help.

1. Open a new spreadsheet file. Create the spreadsheet displayed below.

	A	B	C
1	CONCERT TICKET SALES		
2	Prepared by (Your First and Last Name)		
3			
4	SECTION	SPRING	
5	Balcony	111	
6	Mezzanine	64	
7	Main Floor	225	
8	Total		
9	Average		

2. Use appropriate formulas to calculate a total in B8 and an average in B9.
3. Move the contents of B4 through B9 to C4 through C9.
4. Type *FALL* in cell B4.
5. Type *124* in cell B5.
6. Copy cells C6 through C9 to cells B6 through B9.
7. Right align the labels in cells B4 and C4.
8. Format all values as fixed numbers with two decimals.
9. Bold the labels in cells A1, A2, A8, A9.
10. Print the spreadsheet in landscape page orientation.
11. Save the spreadsheet as STSS085 on your data disk.

✓ Check Your Understanding

1. Did you format all values for two decimals?
2. Did you use AUTOSUM to add numbers quickly?
3. Did you print in landscape page orientation?

322 Section 15 Spreadsheet Basics

To create interest in math, have students complete some calculations using paper and pencil. Have them keep track of how long it takes to complete each calculation. Complete the same calculations using a spreadsheet. What is the difference in the times? Sample calculations, including answers, are shown.

Calculate Total	Calculate Average
4,740,566	4,740,566
8,914,878	8,914,878
2,289,675	2,289,675
78,076,789	78,076,789
94,021,908	23,505,477

15.6 Fill Right, Fill Down, and Fill Series

USING FILL RIGHT, FILL DOWN, AND FILL SERIES

Spreadsheets provide commands to help you copy or generate data quickly. The **fill right** command copies cell contents to a range of cells to the right of the active cell. The **fill down** command copies cell contents to a range of cells below the active cell. Study the illustration below.

Some programs also provide a fill series command. The **fill series** command generates a series of values (numbers, dates, or times) based on the value in the active cell. In the illustration, the value *1995* was typed in the active cell B3. Cells B3, C3, and D3 were selected and the fill series command given. The fill series command automatically entered the values *1996* and *1997* to complete the series.

In Project 86 you will learn to copy information using the fill right and fill down commands. You will also use the fill series command to generate values.

Goals
- Copy data using fill right and fill down
- Generate data using fill series

FILL SERIES. Generates values based on the value in the active cell. Cells C3 and D3 filled with fill series.

FILL RIGHT. Cells C4 through D5 filled with fill right.

FILL DOWN. Cells A7 through A9 filled with fill down.

	A	B	C	D
1	COMPUTER CLASS ENROLLMENTS			
2				
3	Teacher	1995	1996	1997
4	Mrs. Perez	15	15	15
5	Mrs. Perez	20	20	20
6	Mr. Roberts	20	15	20
7	Mr. Roberts	12	15	12
8	Mr. Roberts	18	15	17
9	Mr. Roberts	17	15	16

GO TO — Student Guide, Spreadsheet
Fill series   Fill down
Fill right

15.6 Fill Right, Fill Down, and Fill Series

FOCUS
Copy data using fill right and fill down. Generate data using fill series.

BELLRINGER
When students enter the room, direct their attention to the assignment on the board:

Read the text and look at the illustration on page 323.

TEACH
Fill right and fill down should be used whenever possible to save time. Besides facilitating quick data entry, these commands help ensure accuracy, since no additional typing is required with these commands.

The fill series command is also helpful to use, but the user needs to make sure the spreadsheet has filled with the correct data. Just as the search and replace feature in the word processor sometimes makes some unexpected changes, the fill series command can produce unexpected results.

GO TO — Refer students to the appropriate section of the Student Guide.

RESOURCES
- Lesson Plan: LP83
- Transparency Master: TM36
- CD-ROM: Reference Guide
- Software: Research Files

Lesson Extension
In addition to filling values, some spreadsheets extend the fill series command to include labels as well. For example, if the user types January and February in two adjoining columns, the fill series command will know to continue filling with subsequent months. If your spreadsheet has this feature, demonstrate it to your students.

Project 86
Fill Right, Fill Down, and Fill Series

PRACTICE—LEVEL 1

Purpose
Practice using the fill right, fill down, and fill series commands.

Time
Thirty minutes

Preparation
Make sure the spreadsheet software is available and that students have their data disks. Make sure the printers are ready.

Teaching Tip
Observe students carefully to make sure they are using the appropriate fill commands instead of just typing the information. Students who finish early should repeat the project.

Trouble Shooting
Provide individual help to students who are having difficulty with the fill commands.

Wrap Up
Have students return computers and furniture to the appropriate conditions.

Did You Know?
Slightly more than one million users accessed the Internet in 1991. That number has doubled every year since then.

Project 86
Technology Connection
FILL RIGHT, FILL DOWN, AND FILL SERIES

Complete the spreadsheet below using the commands for fill right, fill down, and fill series.

1. Open File SS086 on your data disk. The illustration below shows the information in the file.

	A	B	C	D	E
1	INTERNET USAGE				
2					
3		1995			
4	Hosts	149945	566095	1443800	3590289
5	Domains	7891869	15095885	28876019	

2. Type *Prepared By* and your first and last name in cell A2.
3. Use **fill series** to enter the years 1996, 1997, and 1998 into cells C3, D3, and E3.
4. Type *6110290* in cell E5.
5. In cell A6 type *Total* in bold.
6. In cell B6 calculate the total of cells B4 and B5.
7. Use **fill right** to copy the formula from cell B6 to cells C6 through E6.
8. Type *Total* in cell F3.
9. In cell F4 calculate the total hosts for 1995 through 1998.
10. Use **fill down** to copy the total formula in cell F4 to cell F5 and F6.
11. Bold all the labels in row 3 and right align cell F3.
12. Format the cells B4 through F6 to display commas.
13. Print the spreadsheet with landscape page orientation.
14. Save the spreadsheet as STSS086 on your data disk.

Technology Connection

To create interest in technology, have students research inventions of the 20th century. Have students create a table showing five inventions. Specify information you want them to include about each item. A sample appears below.

Invention	Year	Inventor	Nationality
Electrocardiograph	1903	Einhoven	Dutch
Ballpoint pen	1938	Biro	Hungarian
Tupperware	1945	Tupper	American
Velcro	1948	de Mestral	Swiss
Polaroid camera	1948	Land	American

Project 87

FILL RIGHT, FILL DOWN, AND FILL SERIES

Practice the features your learned earlier by completing a spreadsheet using the commands for fill right, fill down, and fill series. Refer to the illustration and information on pages 323 and 324 if you need help.

1. Open File SS087 on your data disk. The illustration below shows the information in the file.

	A	B	C
1	COMPUTER RENTALS		
2			
3			
4		December	
5	Desktop--100 MHz	245	275
6	Multimedia--200 MHz	455	395
7	Palmtop--75 MHz	195	205
8	Laptop--100 MHz	255	305
9			

2. Type *Prepared By* and your first and last name in cell A2.
3. Use fill series to generate the months *January* and *February* as column titles in cells C4 and D4.
4. Copy the rental price values from cells C5 through C8 into cells D5 through D8 using fill right.
5. Type *Totals* in cell E4 in bold.
6. In cell E5 use AUTOSUM to add the values in row 5.
7. Copy the formula in cell E5 into cells E6 through E8 using fill down.
8. Type *Maximum* in cell A9 in bold.
9. Type *Minimum* in cell A10 in bold.
10. Use the MAX function in cell B9 to calculate the largest monthly price for December.
11. Copy the MAX formula from cell B9 into cells C9 through D9 using fill right.

(continued on next page)

Fill Right, Fill Down, and Fill Series **325**

Project 87
Fill Right, Fill Down, and Fill Series

APPLY—LEVEL 1

Purpose
Apply spreadsheet skills by using the fill right, fill down, and fill series commands.

Time
Thirty minutes

Preparation
Make sure the spreadsheet software is available and that students have their data disks. Make sure the printers are ready.

Teaching Tip
Observe students carefully to make sure they are using the appropriate fill commands instead of just typing the information. Students who finish early should repeat the project.

Trouble Shooting
Provide individual help to students who are having difficulty.

Wrap Up
Have students return computers and furniture to the appropriate conditions.

To create interest in technology, have students find advertisements that show retail sales prices for various computer hardware components. As a class, create a spreadsheet with this information, using a separate column for each student's information. Use the AUTOSUM, Maximum and Minimum spreadsheet features to summarize and compare the data.

325

Fill Right, Fill Down, and Fill Series

Did You Know?

Software developers must be careful when they sell their programs in other countries. Icons that have one meaning in the United States can have a totally different meaning in another country. For example, the open-palm hand gesture that means "stop" in this country may be offensive in other cultures.

Project 87 (continued)

13. Use the MIN function in cell B10 to calculate the smallest monthly price for December.
14. Copy the MIN formula from cell B10 into cells C10 through D10 using fill right.
15. Bold and right align the labels in row 4.
16. Format all values as currency with two decimals.
17. Type today's date in cell A12.
18. Print the spreadsheet using landscape page orientation.
19. Save the spreadsheet as STSS087 on your data disk.

Did You Know?

Most spreadsheet programs used in the United States are done in English. Many of these spreadsheet programs are also popular overseas. Some software companies translate their spreadsheet programs into other languages.

326 Section 15 Spreadsheet Basics

Project 88

FILL RIGHT, FILL DOWN, AND FILL SERIES

Complete a spreadsheet using the commands for fill right, fill down, and fill series. Refer to the illustration and information on pages 323 and 324 if you need help.

1. Open a new spreadsheet file. Create the spreadsheet displayed below.
2. Use fill series for the room numbers in cells A4 through A7 and the months in the column headings.
3. Use fill right to copy the same hours of use for all rooms from the May column into the June column.

	A	B	C	D
1	COMPUTER USAGE IN HOURS			
2				
3	Room	April	May	June
4	101	1545	1258	
5	102	2584	4587	
6	103	2139	2258	
7	104	3298	3587	
8	Total			
9	Average			
10	Minimum			
11	Maximum			

4. Use appropriate formulas in cells B8 through D11 to find the total, average, minimum, and maximum for each month.
5. Type *2nd Quarter* in cell E3 in bold.
6. In E4 calculate the quarter total for Room 101.
7. Use fill down to copy the formula in E4 to E5 through E7.
8. Use fill right to copy the total, average, minimum, and maximum formulas in D8 through D11 to E8 through E11.
9. Right align the labels in cells B3 through E3.
10. Format the numbers in B4 through E11 for commas. Use one decimal in the average row and no decimals in the other rows.
11. In cell A13, type *Prepared By* and your first and last name.
12. Type today's date in cell A14.
13. Print the spreadsheet in landscape page orientation.
14. Save the spreadsheet as STSS088 on your data disk.

Fill Right, Fill Down, and Fill Series **327**

Project 88
Fill Right, Fill Down, and Fill Series

ASSESS—LEVEL 2

Purpose
Assess spreadsheet skills by using the fill right, fill down, and fill series commands.

Time
Thirty minutes

Preparation
Make sure the spreadsheet software is available and that students have their data disks. Make sure the printers are ready.

Teaching Tip
Observe students carefully to make sure they are using the appropriate fill commands instead of just typing the information. Students who finish early should repeat the project.

Trouble Shooting
Provide individual help to students who are having difficulty.

Wrap Up
Discuss computer usage in your school's computer lab—if you have one.
    Have students return computers and furniture to the appropriate conditions.

To encourage interest in technology, gather information about actual computer usage in your school's computer lab. As a class, create a spreadsheet similar to that in Project 88 using the actual usage data. Have them create another spreadsheet that displays the types of computer equipment and software available to students in the lab.

15.7 Spreadsheet Structure

FOCUS

Insert rows and columns. Delete rows and columns. Sort data. Protect cells.

BELLRINGER

When students enter the room, direct their attention to the assignment on the board:

Read the text and be familiar with the terms presented on page 328.

TEACH

The Insert and Delete commands allow the user to easily change the structure of the spreadsheet to accommodate changing conditions. Have students think about changes that would be required to a teacher's grade book when new students enter a class or existing students leave a class. Without the ability to easily change the structure of the spreadsheet, these changes would be time-consuming to make.

The ability to sort data comes in handy when managing lists of data. A teacher could, for example, sort the grade book in alphabetical order by student last name or in descending order by grade.

Cell protection allows spreadsheet designers to "protect" certain cells from unintentional changes. This helps ensure that formulas are not accidentally replaced with values.

15.7 Spreadsheet Structure

CHANGING THE STRUCTURE OF A SPREADSHEET

Goals
- Insert rows and columns
- Delete rows and columns
- Sort data
- Protect cells

Sometimes you need to add or delete rows or columns as you create or edit a spreadsheet. You **insert rows or columns** when you want to insert additional information after some of the spreadsheet has been typed. You **delete rows or columns** when you want to quickly delete a complete row or column of data or remove blank rows from your spreadsheet.

Data in a spreadsheet may be easier to understand or use if the data is sorted into alphabetic or numeric order. For example, in the illustration the fossils are sorted by age. You could sort the fossils in alphabetic order by name instead. To **sort** data, you simply select the range of data to be sorted and give the sort command. In some programs, you may need to select entire rows when sorting to keep labels with their correct values. In other programs, the entire row of data automatically stays together.

Once a spreadsheet has been created, you can **protect cells** in the spreadsheet so they cannot be easily changed. Cell protection is useful when you use a spreadsheet over and over, changing some cells but not others. For example, you might have a monthly budget that shows how much you plan to spend each month for various items. At the end of the month, you could enter the amounts you actually spent and compare them with the amounts in your budget. The budget amounts would stay the same each month while the actual amount spent would vary. You might protect the cells containing the budget amounts to keep them from being changed accidentally.

What kinds of data could you sort pertaining to this fossil?

328 Section 15 Spreadsheet Basics

RESOURCES

Lesson Plan: LP84
Multicultural Timing: MT7

CD-ROM: Reference Guide

Software: Research Files

	A	B
1	TYPES OF FOSSILS	
2		
3	TYPE	YEARS OLD
4	Cenozoic Fish	30,000,000
5	Pterosaurs	150,000,000
6	Dunkleosteus	375,000,000

CELL PROTECTION. Cells B4 through B6 protected from editing.

DID YOU KNOW
One of the earliest zoos was established in Egypt around 1500 B.C. Zoos at that time were used to show how wealthy and powerful rulers were. Today, zoos do more than just exhibit animals. Zoos conduct research and maintain breeding programs for animals that are in danger of becoming extinct.

GO TO
Student Guide, Spreadsheet
Insert row or column   Delete row or column
Sort   Protect cell

Spreadsheet Structure **329**

Spreadsheet Structure

TEACH

Ask students to make a list of the types of cell entries that would most likely be protected. Responses might include budget amounts that don't change, a formula to calculate a student's grade, and so on.

ASSESS

To assess students' understanding, have them explain why it is desirable to be able to insert or delete spreadsheet rows or columns; to sort data; and to protect cells.

CLOSE

Have students change the structure of a spreadsheet. Refer to Projects 89 and 90.

GO TO Refer students to the appropriate section of the Student Guide.

DID YOU KNOW
The oldest zoo in the United States is the Philadelphia Zoo. It received its charter from the state of Pennsylvania in 1859 and opened to the public in 1874.

interNET CONNECTION

Have students use the Internet or a commercial on-line service to find information about animals or zoos.

Examples of sites might include:

ZooNet: http://www.mindspring.com/~zoonet
Birmingham Zoo: http://www.bhm.tis.net/zoo

329

Project 89
Spreadsheet Structure

PRACTICE—LEVEL 1

Purpose
Practice inserting rows and columns, deleting rows and columns, sorting data, and protecting cells.

Time
One class period

Preparation
Make sure the spreadsheet software is available and that students have their data disks. Make sure the printers are ready.

Teaching Tip
Carefully observe students as they insert and delete columns and rows. If just a few cells are selected instead of an entire row or column, the insert or delete command may not work as expected. Students who finish early should repeat the project.

Trouble Shooting
Provide individual help to students who are having difficulty.

Wrap Up
Have students return computers and furniture to the appropriate conditions.

Project 89

SPREADSHEET STRUCTURE

Follow the steps below to insert rows and columns, delete rows and columns, sort data, and protect cells in a spreadsheet.

1. Open the file SS089 on your data disk. The illustration below shows the information in the file.

	A	B	C
1	LIFE SPAN		
2			
3	Animal	Type	Years
4	Chimpanzee	Mammal	45
5	Tiger	Mammal	11
6	Elephant	Mammal	60
7	Lion	Mammal	22

2. Read the steps under **insert row or column** in Unit 5 of your Student Guide. Insert a new row under row 1.
3. Insert a row under row 4.
4. Type *Horse* in cell A5, *Mammal* in B5, and *25* in C5.
5. **Sort** the list of animals so column A will be in alphabetic order.
6. Type *Maximum* in cell A10 and *Minimum* in cell A11 in bold.
7. In cell C10 enter a formula to calculate the maximum number of years.
8. In cell C11 enter a formula to calculate the minimum number of years.
9. Insert a new row under Lion.
10. In row 9 type *Squirrel, Mammal,* and *9* in the appropriate cells.
11. Read the steps under **delete row or column** in Unit 5 of your Student Guide. Delete the row containing the animal with the longest life span.
12. Insert a column before column B.
13. Change the title in A1 to *LIFE SPAN OF MAMMALS*.
14. Delete column C.
15. Right align the column head in C4.
16. **Protect cells** with values in column C.
17. Type *Prepared By* and your first and last name in cell A2.
18. Print the spreadsheet using portrait page orientation.
19. Save the spreadsheet as STSS089 on your data disk.

Section 15 Spreadsheet Basics

Discuss the various careers available to students who like science. Examples include botanist (flowering plants), zoologist (animals), and ornithologist (birds). Have them rank these careers in terms of interest; then make a spreadsheet and sort the spreadsheet (1) in alphabetical order; and (2) by rank.

Project 90

CHANGE THE STRUCTURE OF A SPREADSHEET

Practice using the spreadsheet features your learned earlier to insert rows, delete rows and columns, sort data, and protect cells in a spreadsheet. To make the spreadsheet more readable, you will divide the list into birds and reptiles and amphibians. Refer to the illustration and information on pages 328–330 if you need help.

1. Open the file SS090 on your data disk. The illustration below shows the information in the file.

	A	B	C
1	LENGTH OF LIFE		
2	Blue Jay	4	48
3	Canada Goose	32	384
4	Penguin	26	312
5	Raven	69	828
6	Ostrich	50	600
7	Whale	20	240
8	Alligator	56	672
9	Crocodile	13	156
10	Gila Monster	20	240
11	Bullfrog	15	180
12	Rattlesnake	18	216

2. Insert three rows under row 1.
3. Insert three rows under row 9.
4. Type *BIRDS* in cell A4, *YEARS* in B4, and *MONTHS* in C4.
5. Type *REPTILES AND AMPHIBIANS* in cell A12.
6. Insert one row under row 6.
7. Delete row 7 containing the information about whales.

(continued on next page)

Spreadsheet Structure **331**

Project 90
Spreadsheet Structure

ASSESS—LEVEL 2

Purpose
Assess spreadsheet skills by inserting rows and columns, deleting rows and columns, sorting data, and protecting cells.

Time
One class period

Preparation
Make sure the spreadsheet software is available and that students have their data disks. Make sure the printers are ready.

Teaching Tip
Carefully observe students as they insert and delete columns and rows. If just a few cells are selected instead of an entire row or column, the insert or delete command may not work as expected. Students who finish early should repeat the project.

Trouble Shooting
Provide individual help to students who are having difficulty changing the structure of their spreadsheets.

Wrap Up
Have students return computers and furniture to the appropriate conditions.

To encourage student interest in science, discuss the fact that some species become extinct over time. Have students create a spreadsheet using the following information about the number of vertebrate extinctions since the year 1600. Have students sort the animal classes alphabetically, then total and average the numbers.

Vertebrate Extinctions

Mammals	60
Birds	122
Reptiles	23
Amphibians	2

331

Spreadsheet Structure

DID YOU KNOW

An emperor penguin once dove to a depth of 1,584 feet in the Ross Sea, Antarctica. This dive, which was recorded in 1990, is the deepest dive on record for a bird of any species.

Project 90 (continued)

8. Type *Golden Eagle* in A7, *20* in B7, and *240* in C7.
9. Sort the list of birds so the list will be in alphabetical order.
10. Sort the list of reptiles and amphibians so the list will be in alphabetical order.
11. Right align the column headings in columns B and C.
12. Protect all cells with values in them.
13. Type *Prepared By* and your first and last name in cell A2.
14. Print the spreadsheet using landscape page orientation.
15. Save the spreadsheet as STSS090A on your data disk.
16. Delete column C. You may need to unprotect cells to delete column C.
17. Print the spreadsheet again using portrait page orientation.
18. Save the spreadsheet as STSS090B on your data disk.

DID YOU KNOW

Penguins are flightless birds that are adapted to live in extreme cold. Their wings and feet are modified for swimming. Penguins breed on islands off the coasts of Africa, Australia, New Zealand, and South America.

332 Section 15 Spreadsheet Basics

interNET CONNECTION

Have students use the Internet or a commercial on-line service to find more information about penguins or other birds. Examples of sites might include:

Penguin Page:
   http://pobox.com/~penguins
Bird Cage
   http:/www.thams.com/birdcage.html

332

Project 91
Building Your Portfolio

SCIENCE Connection

In this project you will review the spreadsheet features you have learned. You will copy data, use functions in formulas, insert rows, delete rows and columns, sort data, and protect cells in a spreadsheet. If you need to review any formatting or software features, refer to previous projects as often as needed.

NOW TRY THIS

1. Open the file SS091 on your data disk. The illustration shows the information in the file.
2. Insert one row under row 1.
3. Insert one row under row 6.
4. Type *Golden Eagle* in A7, *120* in B7, and *193* in C7.
5. Sort the list of animals so column A will be in alphabetic order.
6. Type *MAXIMUM* in cell A10 and *MINIMUM* in cell A11.
7. In cell B10 type a formula to calculate the maximum MPH.
8. In cell B11 type a formula to calculate the minimum MPH.
9. Copy the MAX and MIN formulas into column C to find the maximum and minimum KPH.
10. Delete the row containing data for the animal with the greatest speed.
11. Right align the column headings in columns B and C.
12. Insert a row under row 2.
13. Protect the cells with values in columns B and C.
14. Type *Prepared By* and your first and last name in cell A2.
15. Print the spreadsheet using portrait page orientation.
16. Save the spreadsheet as STSS091A on your data disk.
17. Delete column B. You may have to unprotect cells to delete the column.
18. Print the spreadsheet using landscape page orientation.
19. Save the spreadsheet as STSS091B on your data disk.

	A	B	C
1	COMPARATIVE SPEEDS OF ANIMALS		
2	TYPE	MPH	KPH
3	Housefly	5	8
4	Cheetah	70	110
5	Race Horse	45	72
6	Goldfish	4	6
7	Whale	20	32

Fun Facts
The fastest mammal on record is the cheetah, which zips around East Africa, Iran, Turkmenistan, and Afghanistan at speeds of up to 60–70 mph. The three-toed sloth of South America takes honors for being the slowest mammal; it maintains an average speed of 6–8 feet per minute (about 0.07–0.1 mph).

Science Connection
To generate interest in science, have students brainstorm ways in which animals can be compared. Possibilities include size (height, length, weight), taxonomic classification (phylum, class, order, family, genus, species), method of breathing, etc. Have them think of real situations for which spreadsheets would be used to organize such information.

Project 91
Spreadsheet Structure

ASSESS—LEVEL 2

Purpose
Assess spreadsheet skills by copying data, using functions, inserting rows and columns, deleting rows and columns, sorting data, and protecting cells.

Time
One class period

Preparation
Make sure the spreadsheet software is available and that students have their data disks. Make sure the printers are ready.

Teaching Tip
Carefully observe students as they insert and delete columns and rows. If just a few cells are selected instead of an entire row or column, the insert or delete command may not work as expected. Students who finish early should repeat the project.

Trouble Shooting
Provide individual help to students who are having difficulty.

Wrap Up
Have students return computers and furniture to the appropriate conditions.

**Section 16
Enhanced Spreadsheets and Charts**

SECTION OVERVIEW

This section introduces students to the more advanced spreadsheet features, such as borders, gridlines, pictures, and styles. Students are also introduced to the charting feature of their spreadsheet application. Use a computer to show students how easy it is to produce attractive spreadsheets. In addition, with a click of a button, a chart can be produced.

CONTENT FOCUS

Borders, gridlines, and pictures
Styles
Bar and line charts
Pie charts

OPENING ACTIVITY

Ask students to describe and/or bring examples to class of printouts that use some of the advanced formatting features of spreadsheets. They may remember a particularly attractive printout with lots of borders and shading, or perhaps they saw a spreadsheet that included a graphic image. You may want to bring some examples to class to get the discussion started.

SECTION 16
Enhanced Spreadsheets and Charts

OBJECTIVES

- Enhance a spreadsheet with borders, gridlines, pictures, and styles
- Create, format, and edit a spreadsheet chart

Focus on Spreadsheet

Arranging and formatting data effectively in a spreadsheet can make the data easier to read and understand. Creative use of borders, gridlines, and pictures can dress up your spreadsheet and help your eye follow the flow of data across rows or down columns. Charts can be used to show the relationships among the data and provide a "snapshot" view of the information. In this unit you will learn to enhance spreadsheets using borders, gridlines, and pictures and to create charts in spreadsheets.

Words To Know

bar chart
border
chart
clip art
gridlines
legend
line chart
picture
pie chart
style
X axis
Y axis

Career Exploration Activities: Health Care

Spreadsheets are useful in the health care industry. In addition to using them for financial analyses, health care professionals use spreadsheets to track patient care and monitor hospital occupancy. Ask students to research health care jobs using references such as the *Occupational Outlook Handbook* and the *Occupational Outlook Quarterly*. Have them write a paragraph including the job title, educational requirements, and average salary for the position. Ask them to discuss ways spreadsheets might be useful. An example might be to use a spreadsheet to keep track of the number of patients in the hospital emergency room, and then creating a chart to make the data easier to understand.

16.1 Borders, Gridlines, and Pictures

Goals
- Display and print a spreadsheet with and without gridlines
- Display and print a spreadsheet with borders
- Insert a picture in a spreadsheet

USING BORDERS, GRIDLINES, AND PICTURES

The appearance of a spreadsheet can be enhanced by adding borders or changing the settings for gridlines. Some programs also allow you to insert pictures in a spreadsheet.

To draw attention to a cell or group of cells in your spreadsheet, you can use borders. A **border** is a solid line around the cell or range of cells. The illustration below includes a border around the column headings and above the total line.

Gridlines are the lines that appear around each cell in a spreadsheet. Gridlines are automatically displayed on screen to assist you in seeing and entering information in individual cells. Gridlines may or may not automatically be a part of your printed spreadsheet depending upon the software you use. You can change your software settings so the gridlines will not be displayed on screen. You can also determine whether or not the gridlines will be printed as part of your spreadsheet. The illustration shows a spreadsheet with gridlines not displayed. Notice how the borders and picture display more clearly with gridlines off.

BORDER. A solid line on a cell. Borders draw attention to cells. This spreadsheet has borders around cells A5 through C5 and a bottom border on cells A10 through C10.

GRIDLINES. The dotted lines that appear around each cell.

	A	B	C	D
1				
2		SUNSHINE BOOKS		
3		SALES BY STORE		
4				
5	Categories	Westmall	Downtown	
6	Classics	25,648.25	78,541.00	
7	Mystery	14,789.39	55,441.12	
8	Children	9,875.79	12,475.25	
9	Computer	4,562.65	2,789.23	
10	Reference	152.25	1,479.95	
11	Total	55,028.33	150,726.55	
12	Average	11,005.67	30,145.31	
13	Minimum	152.25	1,479.95	
14	Maximum	25,648.25	78,541.00	
15				

16.1 Borders, Gridlines, and Pictures

FOCUS
Display and print a spreadsheet with and without gridlines. Display and print a spreadsheet with borders. Insert a picture in a spreadsheet.

BELLRINGER
When students enter the room, direct their attention to the assignment on the board:
Read the text and look at the illustration on page 335.

TEACH
Remind students that spreadsheets enhanced with borders, gridlines, and charts are much more likely to get attention than those that just include minimal formatting. In today's environment, it's not just what you say, but how you say it that's important.

The border feature lets the user dress up a spreadsheet and call attention to specific cells or cell ranges. Gridlines come in handy when entering data, but they can sometimes distract from the message of the spreadsheet. Sometimes it is preferable to print the spreadsheet without the gridlines.

RESOURCES
Lesson Plan: LP87
Transparency Master: TM37

Transparency 28

CD-ROM: Reference Guide

Software: Research Files

interNET CONNECTION
Have students use the Internet to find an on-line bookstore. Ask them to compare buying books on-line versus going to the bookstore. What are the advantages of on-line browsing? What about the disadvantages?

Borders, Gridlines, and Pictures

TEACH

Use the illustration on page 336 to highlight the use of clip art. Point out the lack of gridlines.

ASSESS

To assess students' understanding, have them identify borders, gridlines, and clip art. Have them explain gridline options.

CLOSE

Have students add borders and a picture to a spreadsheet. Refer to Projects 92, 93, and 94.

In Your Journal

Ask students to think about what it would be like to be an author. Do they think they would like writing books for others to read? Why or why not?

GO TO Refer students to the appropriate section of the Student Guide.

In Your Journal

Do you enjoy reading mysteries, biographies, or adventures? Think of the favorite kind of book you enjoy reading. Describe why you like to read this type of book.

Many programs include a library of pictures, often called **clip art,** which can be added to a document. You may be able to add a picture to a spreadsheet depending upon the software you use. A **picture** has been added to the spreadsheet in the illustration below. Look at the pictures included with your software to see what pictures are available to you.

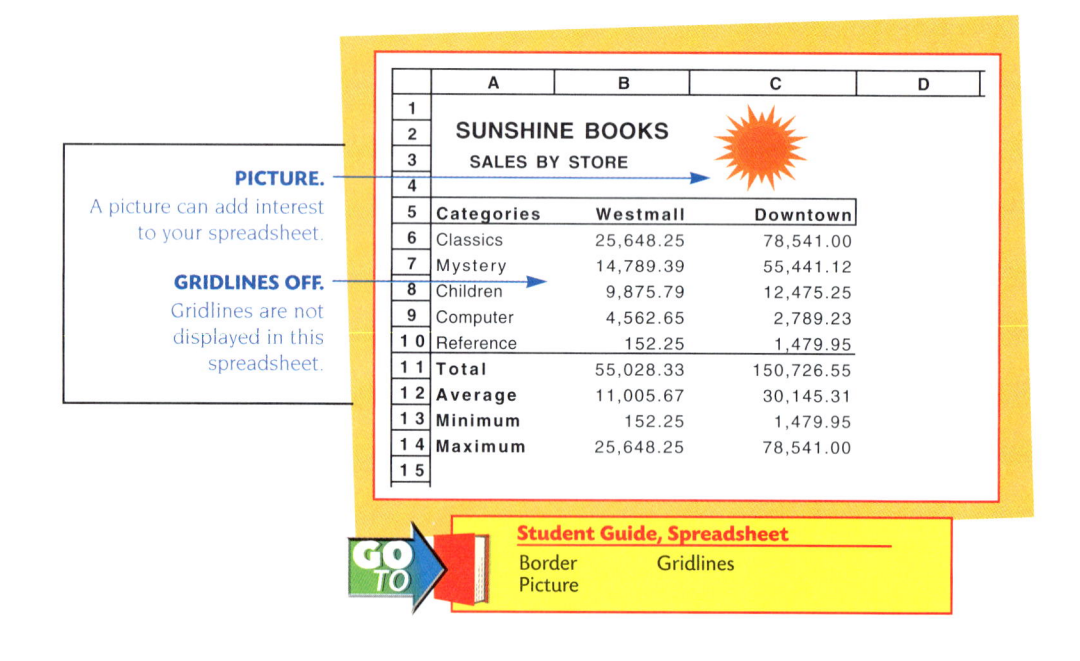

PICTURE. A picture can add interest to your spreadsheet.

GRIDLINES OFF. Gridlines are not displayed in this spreadsheet.

	A	B	C	D
1				
2	SUNSHINE BOOKS			
3	SALES BY STORE			
4				
5	Categories	Westmall	Downtown	
6	Classics	25,648.25	78,541.00	
7	Mystery	14,789.39	55,441.12	
8	Children	9,875.79	12,475.25	
9	Computer	4,562.65	2,789.23	
10	Reference	152.25	1,479.95	
11	Total	55,028.33	150,726.55	
12	Average	11,005.67	30,145.31	
13	Minimum	152.25	1,479.95	
14	Maximum	25,648.25	78,541.00	
15				

GO TO Student Guide, Spreadsheet
Border   Gridlines
Picture

336 Section 16 Enhanced Spreadsheets and Charts

Fun Facts

The most expensive printed book ever sold was the Old Testament Gutenberg Bible, printed in 1455 in Mainz, Germany. It was purchased recently by the Tokyo bookseller Maruzen Co., Ltd., for a whopping $5.39 million.

Lesson Extension

Many of today's applications come with clip art libraries. Additional art can be purchased at a relatively low cost or downloaded from the Internet, sometimes free of charge.

Project 92

BORDERS, GRIDLINES, AND PICTURES

Follow the steps below to add borders and a picture to a spreadsheet and to change the display of gridlines.

1. Open the file SS092 on your data disk. The illustration below shows the information in the file.

	A	B	C	D
1				
2	SUNSHINE BOOKS			
3	SALES BY STORE			
4				
5	Categories	Westmall	Downtown	
6	Classics	25,648.25	78,541.00	
7	Mystery	14,789.39	55,441.12	
8	Children	9,875.79	12,475.25	
9	Computer	4,562.65	2,789.23	
10	Reference	152.25	1,479.95	
11	Total	55,028.33	150,726.55	
12	Average	11,005.67	30,145.31	
13	Minimum	152.25	1,479.95	
14	Maximum	25,648.25	78,541.00	
15				

2. Place a **border** around cells A5 through C5 to outline the cell range.
3. Add a border to the bottom of cells A10 through C10.
4. Place an appropriate **picture** at the top of the spreadsheet near the store name. Resize the picture as needed to fit in the space.
5. Type your first and last name in cell A16.
6. Type today's date in cell A17.
7. Print the spreadsheet with **gridlines** displayed using portrait page orientation. Save the spreadsheet as STSS092A.
8. Change the setting for gridlines so that gridlines are not displayed in your spreadsheet.
9. Print the spreadsheet without gridlines using portrait page orientation.
10. Save the file as STSS092B on your data disk.

Project 92 Borders, Gridlines, and Pictures

PRACTICE—LEVEL 1

Purpose
Practice adding borders and a picture to a spreadsheet and changing the display of gridlines.

Time
Thirty minutes

Preparation
Make sure the spreadsheet software is available and that students have their data disks. Make sure the printers are ready.

Teaching Tip
Carefully observe students as they work with the borders and clip art. Students who finish early should repeat the project, this time using a different picture.

Trouble Shooting
Provide individual help to students who are having difficulty placing their pictures.

Wrap Up
Have students return computers and furniture to the appropriate conditions.

Language Arts Connection

To encourage interest in language arts, ask students to make a list of books they have recently read. Instruct them to include complete titles and authors. Have students include a short comment about the book. Compile the books from all the lists and make the master list available to other students.

Project 93
Borders, Gridlines, and Pictures

APPLY—LEVEL 1

Purpose
Apply spreadsheet skills by adding borders and a picture to a spreadsheet and changing the display of gridlines.

Time
Thirty minutes

Preparation
Make sure the spreadsheet software is available and that students have their data disks. Make sure the printers are ready.

Teaching Tip
Carefully observe students as they work with the borders and clip art. Students who finish early should repeat the project, this time using a different picture.

Trouble Shooting
Provide individual help to students who are having difficulty.

Wrap Up
Have students return computers and furniture to the appropriate conditions.

Language Arts Connection

Project 93
BORDERS, GRIDLINES, AND PICTURES

Practice using the features your learned earlier by formatting a spreadsheet, adding borders, adding a picture, and removing the gridlines. Refer to the illustrations and information on pages 335–337 as needed.

1. Open the file SS093 on your data disk. The illustration below shows the information in the file.

	A	B	C	D	E
1					
2					
3	STAR PERFORMERS				
4	Best-Selling Books By State				
5					
6	Book	Texas	Iowa	Illinois	Total
7	Love of Literature	1,253	3,578	6,321	11,152
8	Math Madness	2,547	5,587	1,427	9,561
9	Bears Tails	3,216	2,431	2,233	7,880
10	Total	7,016	11,596	9,981	28,593
11					
12					

2. Right align cells B6 through E6.
3. Bold cell A10 and the column headings in row 6.
4. Place a top and bottom border on cells A6 through E6.
5. Place a top border on cells A10 through E10.
6. Place a left border on cells E6 through E10.
7. Place a border around cells A1 through E10 to outline the cell range.
8. Place an appropriate picture on the spreadsheet to the right of the spreadsheet title in columns D and E. Resize the picture as needed to fit in the space.
9. Remove the gridlines from the display.
10. Type your first and last name in cell A12.
11. Type today's date in cell A13.
12. Print the spreadsheet without gridlines using portrait page orientation.
13. Save the spreadsheet as STSS093 on your data disk.

Language Arts Connection

To encourage interest in language arts, obtain information on actual best-selling books for a recent month or year from a local bookstore, a trade magazine such as **Publisher's Weekly**, or the Internet. Obtain the information in spreadsheet form, if possible. Share the information with your class.

Fun Facts

Why buy a book at all? Why not just check it out from the library? This is a great idea if you remember to return it. Consider the patron who checked out a book from a university library in 1823; the book was returned by the borrower's great-grandson in 1968. Fortunately, the university agreed to waive the $2,264 fine!

Project 94

BORDERS, GRIDLINES, AND PICTURES

Practice working with borders, pictures, and gridlines as you create an original spreadsheet to show win/loss records for sports teams. Refer to the illustrations and information on pages 335–337 as needed.

1. Open a new spreadsheet file.
2. In cell A2, type TEAM RECORDS in bold.
3. Type *Team* in cell A4, *Wins* in B4, and *Losses* in C4.
4. Bold the column headings in row 4.
5. Right align cells B4 and C4.
6. Type the names of four sports teams in cells A5 through A8. Use school teams or professional teams of your choice.
7. Type the number of wins for each team in cells B5 through B8. Type the number of losses for each team in cells C5 through C8. Use real win/loss data for the current year or guess what the team record will be for the year.
8. Place a border around the column heading cells in row 4 to outline the cell range.
9. Type your first and last name in cell A10.
10. Type today's date in cell A11.
11. Place a picture on the spreadsheet related to the sport, a team logo or mascot, or the season of the year when the sport is played. Insert rows or adjust column widths as needed to place the picture attractively on the page.
12. Display the spreadsheet without gridlines.
13. Print the spreadsheet without gridlines using landscape page orientation.
14. Save the spreadsheet as STSS094 on your data disk.

---

interNET CONNECTION

Have students use the Internet or a commercial on-line service to find statistics for their favorite teams and players.

Examples of sites might include:

Pro Sports Standings: http://wwcd.com/prostand.html
World Wide Web of Sports:
   http://tns-www.lcs.mit.edu/cgi-bin/sports/nba

Project 94
Borders, Gridlines, and Pictures

ASSESS—LEVEL 2

Purpose
Assess spreadsheet skills by adding borders and a picture to a spreadsheet and changing the display of gridlines.

Time
Thirty minutes

Preparation
Students should prepare a list of four sports teams (either school teams or professional teams), along with each team's win/loss record, before they begin this project. Make sure the spreadsheet software is available and that students have their data disks. Make sure the printers are ready.

Teaching Tip
Carefully observe students as they work with the borders and clip art. Students who finish early should repeat the project, this time using different sports teams and a different picture.

Trouble Shooting
Provide individual help to students who are having difficulty.

Wrap Up
Have students return computers and furniture to the appropriate conditions.

16.2 Styles

FOCUS
Format a spreadsheet using styles.

BELLRINGER
When students enter the room, direct their attention to the assignment on the board:
  Read the text and look at the illustration on page 340.

TEACH
Styles help automate the task of formatting spreadsheets. For those who are not artistically inclined, or who just do not want to spend much time with formatting, styles can be a great time-saver.

GO TO: *Refer students to the appropriate section of the Student Guide.*

16.2 Styles

Goal
- Format a spreadsheet using styles

USING STYLES

Some spreadsheet programs allow you to apply many formatting changes at once using the style feature. A **style** is a combination of various shading or colors, borders, cell formatting, and row and column sizes that work together to give the spreadsheet a distinctive look. You may use a style to format a range of cells or the entire spreadsheet. To apply a style, you select the range you wish to format and then select a style from the ones provided. The illustration below shows the results of applying a style.

	A	B
1	Computer Peripheral Prices	
2		
3	Item	Price
4	Modem	199.98
5	Scanner	179.95
6	Joystick	89.25
7	Total	$469.18

STYLE. A style applies many formatting changes at once.

GO TO: Student Guide, Spreadsheet — Style

340 Section 16 Enhanced Spreadsheets and Charts

RESOURCES
- Lesson Plan: LP88
- CD-ROM: Reference Guide
- Software: Research Files

Lesson Extension
Make sure the Num Lock light is on, indicating that the numeric keypad is active. Otherwise, using the keypad will have unintended consequences, such as erratic cursor movement.

Project 95

STYLES

In this project you will enhance a spreadsheet by applying a style. Follow the steps below.

1. Open the file SS095 on your data disk. The illustration below shows the information in the file.

	A	B
1	Computer Peripheral Prices	
2		
3	Item	Price
4	Modem	199.98
5	Scanner	179.95
6	Joystick	89.25

2. Type your first and last name in cell A9.
3. Type the current date in cell A10.
4. Select the range, A1 through B7.
5. Use the **style** feature to change the appearance of the spreadsheet.
6. Print the spreadsheet after applying the style without gridlines in portrait page orientation.
7. Save the spreadsheet as STSS095 on your data disk.

CULTURAL KALEIDOSCOPE

Japan is a leading manufacturer because of its use of high technology, including robots. Robots are used to manufacture automobiles, cameras, and VCRs.

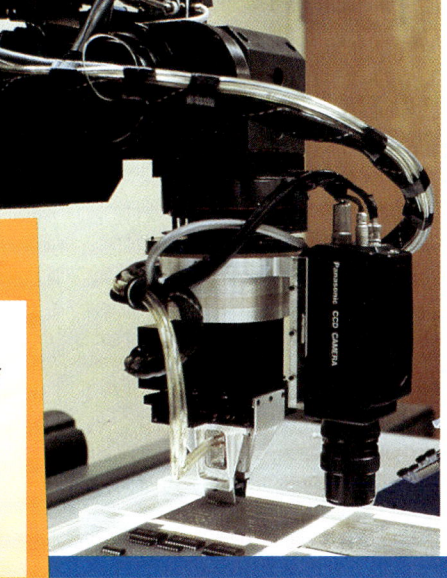

Project 95 Styles

PRACTICE—LEVEL 1

Purpose
Practice applying a style to a spreadsheet.

Time
Fifteen minutes

Preparation
Make sure the spreadsheet software is available and that students have their data disks. Make sure the printers are ready.

Teaching Tip
Carefully observe students as they work with the style feature. If ranges are not selected properly before applying the style, the spreadsheet might not look quite as good as expected. Students who finish early should repeat the project, this time using a different style.

Trouble Shooting
Provide individual help to students who are having difficulty.

Wrap Up
Have students return computers and furniture to the appropriate conditions.

CULTURAL KALEIDOSCOPE

Major industries in Japan are metallurgical and engineering industries, electrical and electronic industries, and textiles. Japanese industries follow strict quality standards for their products. Both Japan and the United States also abide by the ISO 9000 system of international quality standards.

Technology Connection

To generate students' interest in computer technology, have them find advertisements for computer peripherals. As a class, create a spreadsheet using the prices given in the ads.

Project 96
Styles

ASSESS—LEVEL 2

Purpose
Assess spreadsheet skills by applying a style to a spreadsheet.

Time
Fifteen minutes

Preparation
Make sure the spreadsheet software is available and that students have their data disks. Make sure the printers are ready.

Teaching Tip
Carefully observe students as they work with the style feature. If ranges are not selected properly before applying the style, the spreadsheet might not look as expected. Students who finish early should repeat the project, this time using a different style.

Trouble Shooting
Provide individual help to students who are having difficulty.

Wrap Up
Have students return computers and furniture to the appropriate conditions.

Project 96

Technology Connection

STYLES

Practice applying a style in this spreadsheet. Refer to the illustration and information on pages 340 and 341 as needed.

1. Open the file SS096 on your data disk. The illustration below shows the information in the file.

	A	B	C
1	RENTAL PRICES		
2			
3	Equipment	Weekly	Monthly
4	Computer	75	270
5	Color Monitor	55	198
6	Laser Printer	60	216
7	Total	190	684
8			

2. Type your first and last name in cell A9.
3. Type the current date in cell A10.
4. Select the range, A1 through C7.
5. Use the style feature to change the display of the spreadsheet.
6. Print the spreadsheet after applying the style without gridlines in portrait page orientation.
7. Save the spreadsheet as STSS096 on your data disk.

342 Section 16 Enhanced Spreadsheets and Charts

Technology Connection

To stimulate interest in technology, expand the spreadsheet your class created for the Technology Connection on page 325. Have students find newer advertisements from the same store for the same hardware components. Update your spreadsheet with these new components. Use the style feature to change the spreadsheet's look.

16.3 Bar and Line Charts

Goals
- Create and edit a bar chart
- Create and edit a line chart
- Change a chart type

CREATING AND EDITING BAR AND LINE CHARTS

Spreadsheet programs allow you to create charts from data in a spreadsheet. A **chart** uses bars, lines, or other pictures to show the relationships among the values in the spreadsheet. Sometimes data is easier to understand by viewing a chart than by looking just at numbers. Spreadsheets provide many different chart types. You will practice creating and editing bar, line, and pie charts.

A **bar chart** has vertical or horizontal bars representing spreadsheet values. In a vertical bar chart, such as the one shown in the illustration, the vertical, **Y axis** displays a scale showing the range of the values charted. In the illustration, the values range from 0 to 70. The spreadsheet value determines the length of the bar. High values have taller bars than low values. The horizontal, **X axis** displays labels for the bars. In the illustration, the bar labels indicate the grade or total categories. A chart title and a **legend** can be used to describe the data being charted. In the illustration, the legend shows which color bars correspond to the three students.

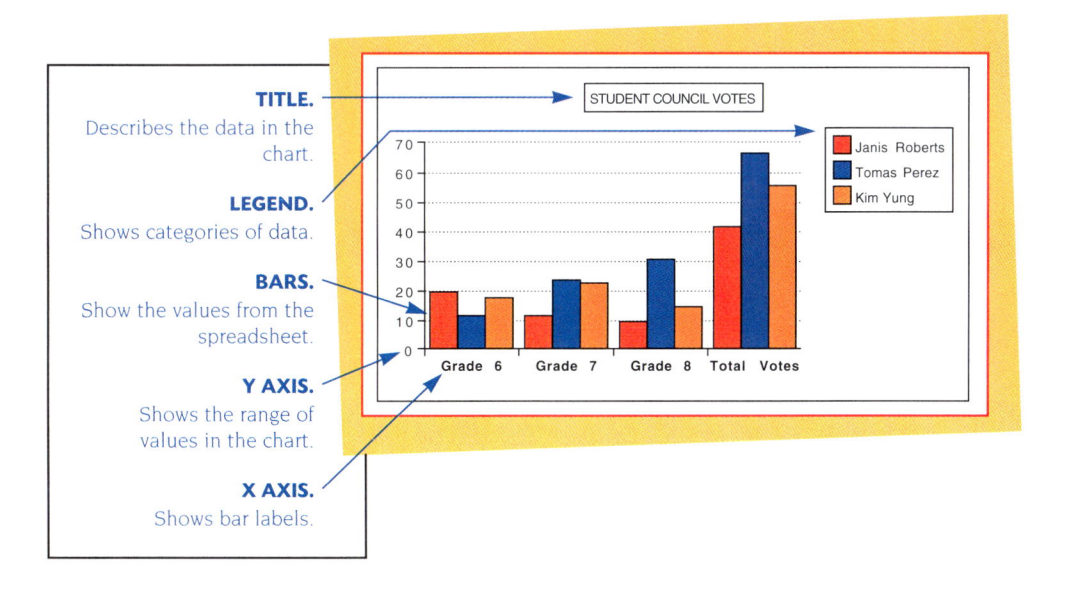

TITLE. Describes the data in the chart.

LEGEND. Shows categories of data.

BARS. Show the values from the spreadsheet.

Y AXIS. Shows the range of values in the chart.

X AXIS. Shows bar labels.

STUDENT COUNCIL VOTES

Janis Roberts
Tomas Perez
Kim Yung

Grade 6   Grade 7   Grade 8   Total Votes

16.3 Bar and Line Charts

FOCUS
Create and edit a bar chart.
Create and edit a line chart.
Change a chart type.

BELLRINGER
When students enter the room, direct their attention to the assignment on the board:
Read the text and look at the illustration on page 343.

TEACH
Charts are useful tools for explaining a table of data. They can help clarify data that might otherwise be difficult to interpret.

Ask students to bring examples of their favorite charts from a newspaper, magazine, or other source to class. Use the charts as a basis for discussion about different chart types.

Caution students that charts are not necessarily appropriate for every situation. In some cases, it might be easier to look at a table of numbers than a chart. Also, remind them that charts must be used ethically. Using a chart with incorrect data or intentionally deceptive data representation is unethical.

Bar charts are good for showing how one data element compares with another data element. Typical uses include showing sales by product category, or candidate votes by grade.

RESOURCES
Lesson Plan: LP89
Multicultural Timing: MT13
Transparency Master: TM38

Transparency 29

CD-ROM: Reference Guide

Software: Research Files

Lesson Extension
If you have access to a color printer, show students the impact color can make on a chart. Also, caution them about using colors together that do not contrast well with one another, making the chart hard to read.

Bar and Line Charts

TEACH

Line charts are useful for showing trends or values over time. For example, a chart might come in handy when showing temperature fluctuations over a month or year, or stock prices over a period of days, months, or years.

ASSESS

To assess students' understanding, have them identify the components of a bar chart and a line chart.

CLOSE

Have students create bar and line charts. Refer to Projects 97, 98, and 99.

GO TO *Refer students to the appropriate section of the Student Guide.*

Many women represent their districts in the United States congress.

A **line chart** uses points on a grid connected by lines to represent the spreadsheet values. A line chart is often the best choice for showing trends or changes in values over time. The chart in the illustration shows the growing number of women in the United States Congress.

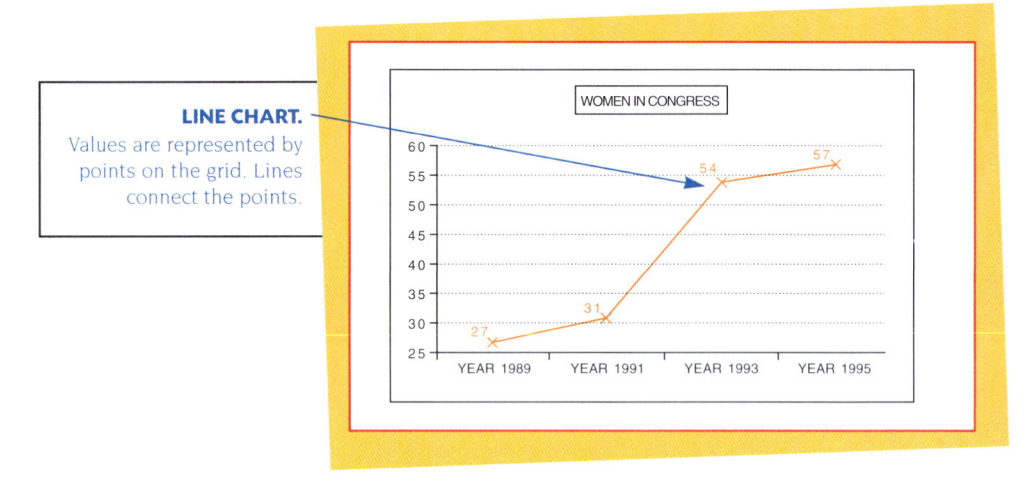

LINE CHART. Values are represented by points on the grid. Lines connect the points.

WOMEN IN CONGRESS

- YEAR 1989: 27
- YEAR 1991: 31
- YEAR 1993: 54
- YEAR 1995: 57

GO TO **Student Guide, Spreadsheet** Chart, create

344 Section 16 Enhanced Spreadsheets and Charts

interNET CONNECTION

Have students use the Internet or a commercial on-line service to find out how many women now serve in the House and the Senate. Ask students to keep track of the each representative's name, district, political party, and years served. This information could be entered into a spreadsheet and used as a basis for a graphing activity.

Project 97

BAR CHART

Practice creating a bar chart. Follow the steps below to create a bar chart with a title and a legend.

1. Open the file SS097 on your data disk. The illustration below shows the information in the spreadsheet.

	A	B	C	D
1	STUDENT COUNCIL ELECTION			
2	Votes Received			
3				
4		Grade 6	Grade 7	Grade 8
5	Janis Roberts	20	12	10
6	Tomas Perez	12	24	31
7	Kim Yung	18	23	15

2. Type *Total Votes* in cell E4 in bold. Right align the cell.
3. Calculate the total votes for each student in cells E5 though E7.
4. Follow the steps under **chart, create** in your Student Guide. Create a bar chart from the spreadsheet data. Include cells A4 through E7 in the range selected for the chart.
5. Type STUDENT COUNCIL VOTES for the chart title.
6. If your chart appears on the same page with the spreadsheet, position the chart under the spreadsheet data. Resize the chart as needed so that all the information displays clearly.
7. Print the spreadsheet and the bar chart without gridlines using landscape page orientation.
8. Save the spreadsheet as STSS097 on your data disk.

Did You Know? The President of the United States is officially elected by the electoral college and not by popular vote. The electoral college is a group of representatives chosen by the voters in each state. This group meets in the December following the election to cast ballots for President and Vice President. The presidential candidate who gets the majority of electoral votes is declared President.

Bar and Line Charts **345**

To encourage interest in social studies, initiate a discussion about the electoral college. Discussion points include:

How many members does the electoral college have?

How is the number of members calculated?

What day and where does the electoral college meet?

What are the qualifications for being a member of the electoral college?

Project 97
Bar and Line Charts

PRACTICE—LEVEL 1

Purpose
Practice creating a bar chart.

Time
Thirty minutes

Preparation
Make sure the spreadsheet software is available and that students have their data disks. Make sure the printers are ready.

Teaching Tip
Carefully observe students as they create the chart. If your spreadsheet has a chart wizard or assistant feature, help students use it as they create their charts. Students who finish early should repeat the project.

Trouble Shooting
Provide individual help to students who are having difficulty.

Wrap Up
Have students return computers and furniture to the appropriate conditions.

Did You Know? In Mexico the president is popularly elected. This means that the candidate who receives the most votes wins. Mexican citizens old enough to vote are legally required to do so. Usually more than 80 percent of eligible voters participate in presidential elections.

345

Project 98
Bar and Line Charts

APPLY—LEVEL 1

Purpose
Apply spreadsheet skills by creating a line chart.

Time
Fifteen minutes

Preparation
Make sure the spreadsheet software is available and that students have their data disks. Make sure the printers are ready.

Teaching Tip
Carefully observe students as they create the chart. If your spreadsheet has a chart wizard or assistant feature, help students use it as they create their charts. Students who finish early should repeat the project.

Trouble Shooting
Provide individual help to students who are having difficulty.

Wrap Up
Have students return computers and furniture to the appropriate conditions.

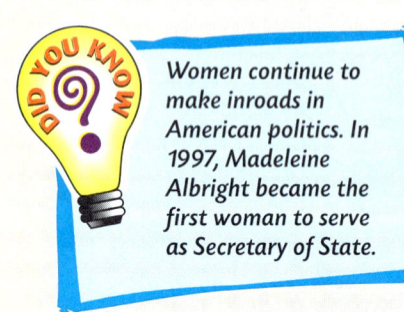

> **DID YOU KNOW**
> Women continue to make inroads in American politics. In 1997, Madeleine Albright became the first woman to serve as Secretary of State.

346

Project 98
Social Studies Connection
LINE CHART

Practice the features you learned earlier to create a line chart with a title and a legend. This chart shows the growing number of women in the United States Congress. Refer to the illustrations and instructions on pages 344 and 345 as needed.

1. Open a new spreadsheet file. Type the data as shown in the illustration below.

	A	B
1	WOMEN IN CONGRESS	
2		
3		Number
4	YEAR 1989	27
5	YEAR 1991	31
6	YEAR 1993	54
7	YEAR 1995	57

2. Create a line chart using the spreadsheet data. Include cells A3 through B7 in the range selected for the chart.
3. Type WOMEN IN CONGRESS for the chart title. If your chart appears on the same page with the spreadsheet, position the chart under the spreadsheet data. Resize the chart as needed so that all the information displays clearly.
4. Print the spreadsheet and the line chart without gridlines using landscape page orientation.
5. Save the spreadsheet as STSS098 on your data disk.

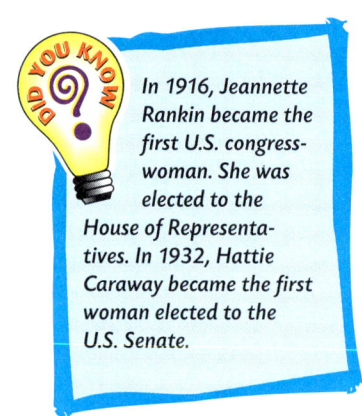

> **DID YOU KNOW**
> In 1916, Jeannette Rankin became the first U.S. congresswoman. She was elected to the House of Representatives. In 1932, Hattie Caraway became the first woman elected to the U.S. Senate.

346 Section 16 Enhanced Spreadsheets and Charts

Social Studies Connection

To generate interest in social studies, lead a discussion about how spreadsheets can be used to organize information about elected officials. Possibilities include tracking information about individual officials' voting records on specific issues (i.e., environmental protection or gun control), number of years in current office, or party affiliation.

Project 99

BAR AND LINE CHARTS

Practice the features you learned earlier to create bar and line charts. Refer to the illustrations and instructions on pages 343–346 as needed.

1. Open the file SS099 on your data disk. The illustration below shows the information in the spreadsheet.

	A	B	C
1	SCHOOL FUNDING SOURCES		
2	Elementary and Secondary Education		
3			
4		$ Billions	
5	State	108.2	
6	Local	100.9	
7	Federal	14.2	
8	Other	5.6	
9	Total	228.9	

2. Create a bar chart using the data in cells A4 through B8.
3. Type *SCHOOL FUNDING SOURCES* for the title.
4. If your chart appears on the same page with the spreadsheet, position the chart to the right of the spreadsheet data. Resize the chart as needed so that all the information displays clearly.
5. Print the spreadsheet and the bar chart without gridlines using landscape page orientation.
6. Save the spreadsheet as STSS099A on your data disk.
7. Copy the data in cells A5 through A8 to cells A12 through A15.
8. In cell B11, type *Percent of Total*.
9. In cells B12 through B15, type formulas to calculate the percent of total funds that comes from each source. For example, in cell B12, type =B5/B9.
10. Format cells B12 through B15 to show percents with two decimal places.
11. Create a bar chart using the data in cells A11 through B15 to show the percent data.

(continued on next page)

Bar and Line Charts **347**

Project 99
Bar and Line Charts

ASSESS—LEVEL 2

Purpose
Assess spreadsheet skills by creating bar and line charts.

Time
Thirty minutes

Preparation
Make sure the spreadsheet software is available and that students have their data disks. Make sure the printers are ready.

Teaching Tip
Carefully observe students as they create the charts. If your spreadsheet has a chart wizard or assistant feature, help students to use it as they create their charts. Students who finish early should repeat the project.

Trouble Shooting
Provide individual help to students who are having difficulty creating their charts.

Wrap Up
Have students return computers and furniture to the appropriate conditions.

Social Studies Connection

To spur interest in social studies, have students brainstorm the ways in which school systems spend the revenue they collect through state, local, and federal taxation. Discuss the funding situation in your school district. Ask students why some voters might vote for school tax levies while others might vote against them.

347

Bar and Line Charts

Project 99 (continued)

12. Type *SCHOOL FUNDING SOURCES* for the title.
13. If your chart appears on the same page with the spreadsheet, position the chart to the right of the spreadsheet data under the first chart. Resize the chart as needed so that all the information displays clearly.
14. Change the first chart showing dollar amounts to a line chart.
15. Print the spreadsheet and both charts without gridlines using landscape page orientation.
16. Save the spreadsheet again as STSS099B on your data disk.

348 Section 16 Enhanced Spreadsheets and Charts

interNET CONNECTION

Have students use the Internet or a commercial on-line service to find out how much their local district or state spends on education. Web sites to research might include those of your local school district or state government.

16.4 Pie Charts

CREATING AND EDITING PIE CHARTS

As with bar and line charts, **pie charts** show the relationships among the values in a spreadsheet. The pie chart displays a circle shown in "slices." Each slice corresponds to a spreadsheet value with all the values making up the entire circle or "pie." A pie chart is often the best way to show values as a part or percentage of a whole. In the illustration, each slice of the pie chart represents a percentage of the total rainfall. The labels from the spreadsheet and the percentage for each slice are displayed in the legend making the chart easier to understand.

Goals
- Create and edit a pie chart
- Change a chart type and title

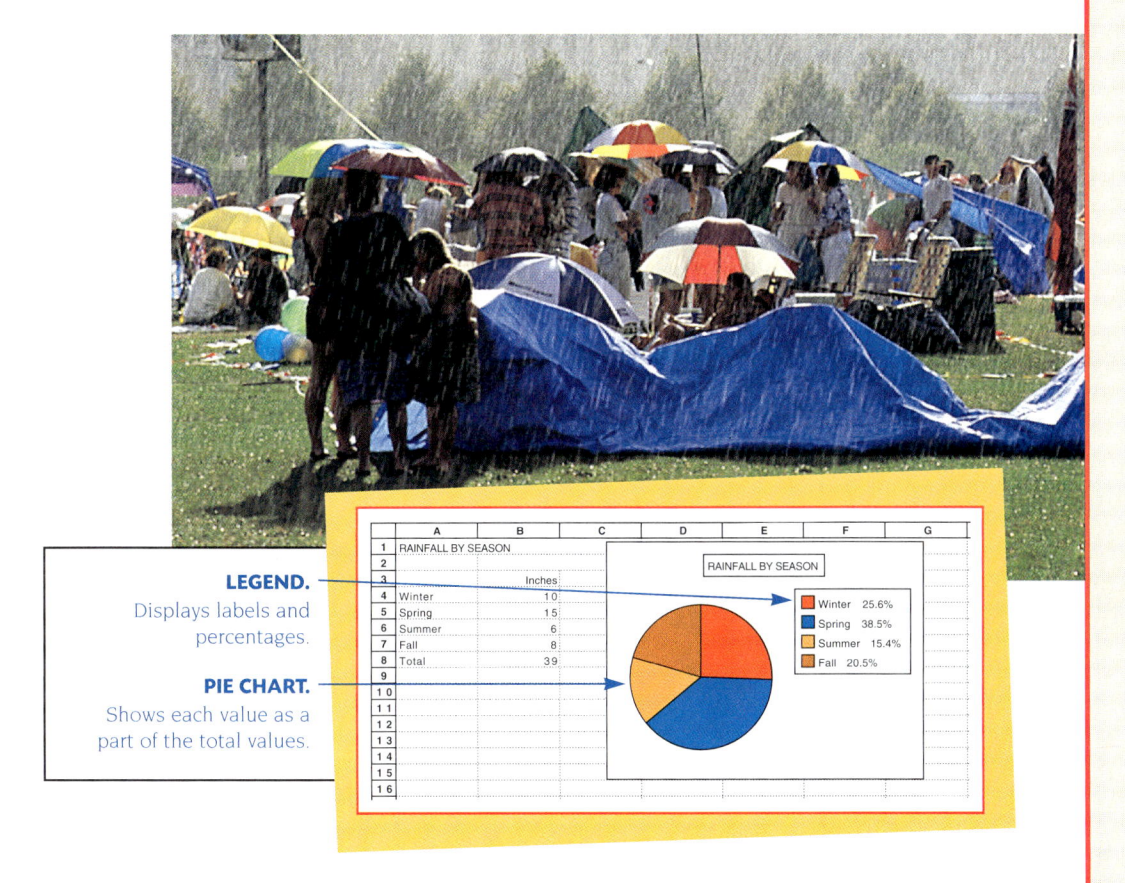

LEGEND. Displays labels and percentages.

PIE CHART. Shows each value as a part of the total values.

Pie Charts **349**

16.4 Pie Charts

FOCUS
Create and edit a pie chart. Change a chart type and title.

BELLRINGER
When students enter the room, direct their attention to the assignment on the board:
Read the text and look at the illustration on page 349.

TEACH
Pie charts help show values as a part or percentage of a whole. Ask students to bring examples of pie charts to class. Discuss the charts in terms of clarity, emphasis, balance, and attractiveness. Demonstrate the impact that an "exploding" pie chart can have.

ASSESS
To assess students' understanding, have them give examples of the appropriate use of pie charts.

CLOSE
Have students create a pie chart. Refer to Projects 100, 101, and 102.

RESOURCES
- Lesson Plan: LP90
- Supplemental Project: SP13
- Transparency Master: TM38
- Transparency 29
- CD-ROM: Reference Guide
- Software: Research Files

DID YOU KNOW? The United States record for rainfall in a 24-hour period belongs to Alvin, Texas. Forty-three inches of rain poured on the town on July 25–26, 1979.

349

Project 100
Pie Charts

PRACTICE—LEVEL 1

Purpose
Practice creating a pie chart.

Time
Thirty minutes

Preparation
Make sure the spreadsheet software is available and that students have their data disks. Make sure the printers are ready.

Teaching Tip
Carefully observe students as they create the chart. If your spreadsheet has a chart wizard or assistant feature, help students use it as they create their charts. Students who finish early should repeat the project.

Trouble Shooting
Provide individual help to students who are having difficulty with their pie charts.

Wrap Up
Have students return computers and furniture to the appropriate conditions.

Project 100

PIE CHART

Follow the steps below to create a pie chart. Review the information under chart in Unit 5 of your Student Guide as needed.

1. Open a new spreadsheet. Type the data as shown in the illustration below.

	A	B
1	RAINFALL BY SEASON	
2		
3		Inches
4	Winter	10
5	Spring	15
6	Summer	6
7	Fall	8
8	Total	39

2. Create a pie chart using the data in cells A4 through B7.
3. Type RAINFALL BY SEASON for the title.
4. Display the percentage numbers for each season on your chart.
5. If your chart appears on the same page with the spreadsheet, position the chart to the right of the spreadsheet data. Resize the chart as needed so that all the information displays clearly.
6. Print the spreadsheet and the pie chart without gridlines using landscape page orientation.
7. Save the spreadsheet as STSS100 on your data disk.

CULTURAL KALEIDOSCOPE
One of the wettest places in the world is Cherrapunji, India. On average, this place receives 457 inches of rain a year. India receives much of its rain from monsoons, or seasonal winds. The monsoon season lasts from November through February.

350 Section 16 Enhanced Spreadsheets and Charts

CULTURAL KALEIDOSCOPE
Cherrapunji, Meghalaya, India holds the world record rainfall for a one-month period; more than 361 inches of rain fell in July, 1861. The 12-month record also goes to Cherrapunji, where more than 1,040 inches of rain fell between August 1, 1860, and July 31, 1861.

Science Connection
To generate interest in science, initiate a class project related to weather. Compile weather data for your community for one or two weeks. As a class, design a spreadsheet and enter the data. Create graphs with the information. Kinds of data to include are temperature highs and lows; precipitation; river level; humidity

Project 101

PIE CHART

Practice using the features your learned earlier to create a pie chart. Refer to the illustration and information on pages 349 and 350 as needed.

1. Open the file SS101 on your data disk. The illustration below shows the information in the file.

	A	B	C
1	BACKYARD BIRD SIGHTINGS		
2			
3			
4			
5	Scientific Name	Common Name	Number
6	Cyanocitta cristata	Blue Jay	7
7	Carduelis tristis	American Goldfinch	5
8	Progue subis	Purple Martin	4
9	Cardinalis cardinalis	Cardinal	2
10	Dryocopus pileatus	Woodpecker	1
11	Melospiza melodia	Song Sparrow	1

2. Type your first and last name in cell A2.
3. Type the current date in cell A3.
4. Create a pie chart using the data in cells B6 through C11.
5. Use BIRD SIGHTINGS for the chart title.
6. Display the percentage numbers for each bird on your chart.
7. If your chart appears on the same page with the spreadsheet, position the chart below or beside the spreadsheet data. Resize the chart as needed so that all the information displays clearly.
8. Print the spreadsheet and the pie chart without gridlines using landscape page orientation.
9. Save the spreadsheet as STSS101A on your data disk.
10. Delete row 11 that contains data about the song sparrow.
11. Change the number of cardinals to 3. Notice how the chart automatically adjusts to show the new data.
12. Print the spreadsheet and the pie chart without gridlines using landscape page orientation.
13. Save the spreadsheet as STSS101B on your data disk.

Project 101 Pie Charts

APPLY—LEVEL 2

Purpose
Apply spreadsheet skills by creating a pie chart.

Time
Fifteen minutes

Preparation
Make sure the spreadsheet software is available and that students have their data disks. Make sure the printers are ready.

Teaching Tip
Carefully observe students as they create the chart. If your spreadsheet has a chart wizard or assistant feature, help students use it as they create their charts. Students who finish early should repeat the project.

Trouble Shooting
Provide individual help to students who are having difficulty.

Wrap Up
Have students return computers and furniture to the appropriate conditions.

Phoebe Snetsinger of Webster Groves, Missouri, is an avid bird watcher. Since 1965 she has spotted more than 8,000 different bird species.

To generate interest in science, ask students to select a species of animal. Have them select three animals within the species and collect some data about the species. Spreadsheets can be used to graph information about the animals. A sample appears below:

	Average Wingspan	Average Weight	Average Length
Robin			
Sparrow			
Crow			

Project 102
Pie Charts

ASSESS—LEVEL 2

Purpose
Assess spreadsheet skills by creating a pie chart.

Time
Fifteen minutes

Preparation
Make sure the spreadsheet software is available and that students have their data disks. Make sure the printers are ready.

Teaching Tip
Carefully observe students as they create the chart. If your spreadsheet has a chart wizard or assistant feature, help students use it as they create their charts. Students who finish early should repeat the project.

Trouble Shooting
Provide individual help to students who are having difficulty creating their pie charts.

Wrap Up
Have students return computers and furniture to the appropriate conditions.

Project 102

PIE CHART

In this project you will use the features your learned earlier to create a pie chart. You will also edit the chart title and chart type. Refer to the illustration and information on pages 349–351 as needed.

1. Open a new spreadsheet file. Type the data as shown in the illustration below.

	A	B
1	ANIMALS IN ZOO	
2		
3		Number
4	Birds	125
5	Reptiles	56
6	Amphibians	145
7	Herd Animals	91
8	Predators	43
9		
10		

2. Type your first and last name in cell A10.
3. Type the current date in cell A11.
4. Create a pie chart from the data in cells A4 through B8.
5. Type ZOO ANIMALS as the title of the pie chart.
6. Display the percentage numbers for each animal type on your chart.
7. If your chart appears on the same page with the spreadsheet, position the chart below or beside the spreadsheet data. Resize the chart as needed so that all the information displays clearly.
8. Print the spreadsheet and the pie chart without gridlines using landscape page orientation.
9. Save the spreadsheet as STSS102A on your data disk.
10. Change the pie chart to a bar chart.
11. Change the title to COMPARISON OF ZOO ANIMALS.
12. Print the bar chart without gridlines using landscape page orientation.
13. Save the spreadsheet as STSS102B on your data disk.

352 Section 16 Enhanced Spreadsheets and Charts

To generate interest in science, obtain information from the zoo closest to your area regarding the types and number of animals it houses. Share the information with your class. Have them brainstorm ways in which spreadsheets can be used to organize the information.

Project 103
Building Your Portfolio

In this portfolio project you will review the spreadsheet features you learned in this section. You will format and enhance a spreadsheet using borders, a picture, and a style. You will create a chart from the spreadsheet data and change the settings for gridlines. If you need to review any formatting or software features, refer to previous projects as often as needed.

NOW TRY THIS

1. Open a new spreadsheet file. Create the spreadsheet displayed below.

	A	B	C	D
1	PARNELL AIR CARGO			
2	Packing Department			
3	Salary Report			
4		Hours	Hourly	Total
5	Employee	Worked	Salary	Salary
6	Lee, June	24	6.25	150.00
7	Diaz, Ina	16	5.50	88.00
8	Sythe, Tom	40	5.80	232.00
9	Total Salary			470.00

2. Enter formulas to calculate the total salary for each employee by multiplying the hours worked by the hourly salary.
3. Enter a formula in cell D9 to add the total salary numbers.

(continued on next page)

Project 103
Building Your Portfolio

ASSESS—LEVEL 2

Purpose
Assess spreadsheet skills by applying features learned in this section.

Time
One class period

Preparation
Make sure the spreadsheet software is available and that students have their data disks. Make sure the printers are ready.

Teaching Tip
Carefully observe students as they work through this assignment. Students who finish early should repeat the project.

Trouble Shooting
Provide individual help to students who are having difficulty.

Wrap Up
Have students return computers and furniture to the appropriate conditions.

Building Your Portfolio

Did You Know? The United States has the world's largest mail service. In 1994 the U.S. population mailed 177.1 billion letters and packages.

Project 103 (continued)
Building Your Portfolio

4. Add a top border to cell D9.
5. In the row under Diaz, Ina, insert a row for another employee.
6. Type *Green, Ann* in cell A8, *25* in B8, and *6.00* in C8.
7. Copy a formula into cell D8 to calculate the total salary.
8. Sort rows 6 through 9 alphabetically by employee name.
9. Create a bar chart showing the employees and their hours worked using the data in cells A6 through B9.
10. Type HOURS WORKED as the title of the chart.
11. If your chart appears on the same page with the spreadsheet, position the chart below or beside the spreadsheet data. Resize the chart as needed so that all the information displays clearly.
12. Place an appropriate picture at the top of the spreadsheet near the company name. If you need to make room for the picture, insert rows.
13. Format the spreadsheet data area, including the picture, using a style. Adjust column widths, if needed, to display all data clearly.
14. Change the number format, if needed, to show the hours worked in column B as fixed numbers with no decimal places. Show the salary numbers in columns C and D as currency with two decimal places. Make other adjustments, as desired, for an attractive overall format.
15. Print the spreadsheet and the chart without gridlines using landscape page orientation.
16. Save the spreadsheet as STSS103 on your data disk.

Section 16 Enhanced Spreadsheets and Charts

interNET CONNECTION

Have students use the Internet or a commercial on-line service to find information about companies that provide air cargo services. Ask them to write down the company name, number of employees, and the type of cargo the company transports.

Analysis and Integration

SECTION 17

Focus on Spreadsheet

A spreadsheet can help you analyze data and answer questions to make better decisions. You can enter various sets of data into the spreadsheet and compare the results. This process is often called a "What If" analysis because the questions may begin "What if the value changes to . . . ?" Spreadsheet data and charts can be integrated with word processing documents to provide details or illustrations of data discussed in those documents. In this unit you will complete a **"what if" analysis** and integrate spreadsheet and word processing documents using a template.

OBJECTIVES

- Perform a "what if" analysis using a spreadsheet
- Create a spreadsheet using a template
- Integrate spreadsheet data and a chart into a word processing document

Words To Know

"what if" analysis
integrate
switch windows
spreadsheet frame
template

Section 17 Analysis and Integration

SECTION OVERVIEW

This section introduces students to "what if" analysis, thus unleashing the true power of a spreadsheet. Students are also introduced to spreadsheet templates, as well as integration of spreadsheet information with other applications.

CONTENT FOCUS

"What if " analysis
Integration

OPENING ACTIVITY

The ability to perform "what if" analysis is a major benefit of spreadsheet usage. Changes in data can now be evaluated with a few keystrokes rather than time-consuming recalculations. To illustrate, show students a hypothetical situation in which a student is approaching a test. Show the impact of getting an A on the test versus a lower grade. By playing "what if," the student can easily see the impact each test grade will have on the course grade.

Data integration is also important. It eliminates the need to re-type columns of numbers in order to incorporate them in a memo, for example. Instead, it is possible to cut and paste or link the data from one application to another. Ask students to find examples of documents in which data was probably shared between applications. Likely candidates include corporate annual reports and fund-raising letters.

Career Exploration Activities: Health Care

Spreadsheets can be useful in fine arts and humanities careers. Managers of fine arts organizations can use spreadsheets to track the financial condition of the organization. When it is time to raise funds, financial numbers can be linked to a fund-raising letter and sent to possible contributors. Ask students to research fine arts and humanities jobs using references such as the *Occupational Outlook Handbook*, the *Occupational Outlook Quarterly*, and the *Dictionary of Occupational Titles*. Have them write a paragraph including job title, educational requirements, and average salary for the position. Ask them to discuss ways in which spreadsheets might prove useful for the position they have chosen.

17.1 What If Analysis

FOCUS

Perform a "what if" analysis using a spreadsheet. Create a spreadsheet using a template.

BELLRINGER

Have students read the text and look at the illustration on page 356.

TEACH

Use the example on page 356 to illustrate the advantages of "what if" analysis. Using a spreadsheet with an overhead display device, build the model shown. Show what happens to the average score if the score for one of the tests changes.

ASSESS

To assess students' understanding, have them explain "what if" analysis in their own words.

CLOSE

Have students perform "what if" analysis. Refer to Projects 104, 105, and 106.

In Your Journal

Help students think of "what if" questions. Examples include:

How many hits do you need to improve a batting average?

How much profit will you make if you sell a baseball card?

How much money will you make if you increase your fees for lawn mowing?

356

What If Analysis

17.1

Goals
- Perform a "what if" analysis using a spreadsheet
- Create a spreadsheet using a template

PERFORMING A "WHAT IF" ANALYSIS

A spreadsheet can help you **analyze** data by allowing you to change numbers easily, quickly recalculate formulas, and display the new results. You can answer questions such as "What if we each sell 12 boxes of candy instead of 10? How will this affect the amount of money we make?" or "What if I make a score of 80 percent on my final test? What will my grade average be? What if I make a score of 90 percent instead? How will my grade average change?" Answering these "what if" questions is one of the best uses of a spreadsheet.

To answer "what if" questions and consider various options, first create a spreadsheet using one set of data. Next, enter or change the numbers that relate to your question and observe the new results. In the example below, the spreadsheet shows a student's current scores on Tests 1 and 2 received during the grading period. The student can find an average score by viewing the results of various possible scores on Test 3.

If the student wants an 89% average, the data in column B shows that a 90% score is needed on Test 3. What if the student only scores 85% on Test 3? The data in column C shows that this score will result in an 87% average.

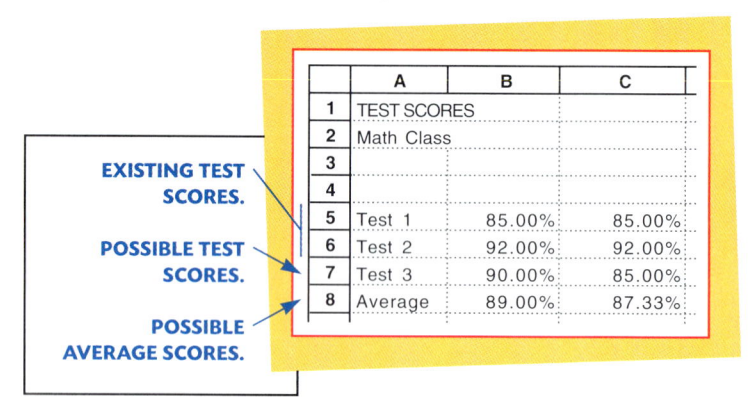

In Your Journal

Think of a "What if" question you would like to answer by using a spreadsheet. Your question might deal with a hobby, a sport, or another activity involving numbers. Make a list of the data you would like to analyze.

	A	B	C
1	TEST SCORES		
2	Math Class		
3			
4			
5	Test 1	85.00%	85.00%
6	Test 2	92.00%	92.00%
7	Test 3	90.00%	85.00%
8	Average	89.00%	87.33%

EXISTING TEST SCORES. (rows 5–6)
POSSIBLE TEST SCORES. (row 7)
POSSIBLE AVERAGE SCORES. (row 8)

356 Section 17 Analysis and Integration

RESOURCES

Lesson Plan: LP92
Multicultural Timing: MT14
Supplemental Project: SP14
Transparency Master: TM39

CD-ROM: Reference Guide

Software: Research Files

Project 104

"WHAT IF" ANALYSIS

In this project you will create a spreadsheet to find the average of three test scores. The first two tests have been completed so the scores will not change. You will enter possible scores for the third test to project possible test averages.

1. Open a new spreadsheet file. Type the data as shown in the illustration below.

	A	B
1	TEST SCORES	
2	Math Class	
3		
4		
5	Test 1	85.00%
6	Test 2	92.00%
7	Test 3	
8	Average	
9		

2. Format cells B5 through B8 for percents with two decimal places.
3. In cell B7 type 90% for the first possible score for Test 3.
4. In cell B8 type a formula to find the average of the three test scores.
5. Copy cells B5 through B8 to cells C5 through C8.
6. Edit cell C7 to see how the average will change if the third test score is 85%.
7. Copy cells C5 through C8 to cells D5 through D8.
8. Edit cell D7 to see how the average will change if the third test score is 76%.
9. Copy cells D5 through D8 to cells E5 through E8.
10. In cell E7 type the score the student must make to have a test average of 90%. Experiment with different numbers until you find the correct number. Print the spreadsheet using portrait page orientation.
11. Save the spreadsheet as STSS104 on your data disk.

Project 104
What If Analysis

PRACTICE—LEVEL 1

Purpose
Practice using "what if" analysis.

Time
Thirty minutes

Preparation
Make sure the spreadsheet software is available and that students have their data disks. Make sure the printers are ready.

Teaching Tip
Carefully observe students as they manipulate the data. Students who finish early should repeat the project.

Trouble Shooting
Provide individual help to students who are having difficulty with "what if" analysis.

Wrap Up
Have students return computers and furniture to the appropriate conditions.

To stimulate students' interest in math, have them create personal spreadsheets with actual grades they have earned so far in your class. Have them perform "what if" analysis, supplying their own hypothetical figures for grades yet to be earned. This should help provide motivation to improve performance, if necessary.

Project 105
What If Analysis

APPLY—LEVEL 1

Purpose
Apply spreadsheet skills by using "what if" analysis.

Time
Thirty minutes

Preparation
Make sure the spreadsheet software is available and that students have their data disks. Make sure the printers are ready.

Teaching Tip
Carefully observe students as they manipulate the data. Students who finish early should repeat the project.

Trouble Shooting
Provide individual help to students who are having difficulty.

Wrap Up
Have students return computers and furniture to the appropriate conditions.

The fastest tennis serve ever recorded was 138 mph. This sizzler was hit by Steve Denton in Beaver Creek, Colorado, on July 29, 1984.

Project 105
"WHAT IF" ANALYSIS

In this project you will analyze different price options for tennis balls at the sporting goods store. The store buys a can of tennis balls for $2.97. This is the wholesale price. Use a spreadsheet to determine the profit if the store sells the can of tennis balls for $3.99, or for $4.29. Refer to the illustration and information in Project 104 as needed.

1. Open a new spreadsheet file. Type the data as shown in the illustration below.

	A	B
1	TENNIS BALL SALE	
2		
3	Retail Sale Price	
4	Wholesale Price	$2.97
5	Profit	
6	Percentage Profit	

2. Format cells B3 through B5 for currency with two decimal places.
3. In cell B3 enter $3.99 for the first possible retail sale price.
4. Calculate the profit in cell B5 by subtracting the wholesale price from the retail sale price.
5. Calculate the profit percentage in cell B6 by dividing the profit by the wholesale price.
6. Format cell B6 for percent with two decimal places.
7. Copy cells B3 through B6 to cells C3 through C6.
8. Edit cell C3 to see how the profit will change if the retail sale price is $4.29.
9. Copy cells C3 through C6 to cells D3 through D6.
10. In cell D3 type the retail sale price the store must use to have a profit of 25.25%. Experiment with different numbers until you find the correct number. Print the spreadsheet using portrait page orientation.
11. Save the spreadsheet as STSS105 on your data disk.

358 Section 17 Analysis and Integration

To generate interest in math, have students find advertisements for sporting goods. As a class, create a spreadsheet using the prices in the ads and calculate the amount of profit earned, given different profit percentages (i.e., 15%, 20%, 25%, 30%).

Project 106

"WHAT IF" ANALYSIS USING A TEMPLATE

In this project, you will use a template file provided with your software program to analyze the monthly payments for various home mortgages or other loans. While it may be several years before you are ready to buy a home, you can share this information with your parents now. Take a sample of this project home and ask your parents if they would like to have any particular home mortgage loans calculated for them. Refer to the illustration and information on pages 356 and 357 as needed.

GO TO
Student Guide, Spreadsheet
Template

1. Read and follow the steps under **template** in Unit 5 of your Student Guide to open and complete the template file.
2. Enter data as prompted for a $100,000 mortgage principal with an interest rate of 10% to be paid back over 30 years.
3. Edit the mortgage principal amount to find out what amount can be borrowed that will result in monthly payments of approximately $1,200. Use even thousands such as $125,000 or $133,000.
4. Print the spreadsheet.
5. Save the spreadsheet file as STSS106 on your data disk.
6. Think of an item you would like to purchase such as motor bike, a musical instrument, or a home entertainment system.
7. In the cell where $100,000 was entered for the mortgage, edit the spreadsheet to enter the approximate cost of the item.
8. Change the time for the loan to be repaid to 3 years.
9. Observe the results of the changes you made in your spreadsheet. What would the monthly payments be for this loan?
10. Print your revised spreadsheet if you wish to keep it.
11. Close the file without saving.

In Your Journal
Find out the cost of a new car, home, or a similar item. Research the current interest rates for a loan on the item you selected. Using this information, create a spreadsheet to calculate the monthly payments on the item.

"What If" Analysis **359**

Students may be interested to know that there are many different types of home-mortgage loans available. Some of the categories include (1) 30-year fixed mortgage, (2) 15-year fixed mortgage, and (3) adjustable rate mortgages. Have students gather information about these rates from the business section of a local newspaper.

Project 106
What If Analysis

ASSESS—LEVEL 2

Purpose
Assess spreadsheet skills by performing "what if" analysis using a template.

Time
Thirty minutes

Preparation
Make sure the spreadsheet software is available and that students have their data disks. Make sure the printers are ready.

Teaching Tip
Carefully observe students as they manipulate the data. Students who finish early should repeat the project using a different item.

Trouble Shooting
Provide individual help to students who are having difficulty using the template for "what if" analysis.

Wrap Up
Have students return computers and furniture to the appropriate conditions.

In Your Journal
Ask students to play "what if" by using several different interest rates and purchase prices. They should record the different payment amounts in their journal.

GO TO
Refer students to the appropriate section of the Student Guide.

359

17.2 Integration

FOCUS

Integrate spreadsheet data into a word processing document. Integrate a spreadsheet chart into a word processing document. Create a new spreadsheet table within a word processing document.

BELLRINGER

When students enter the room, direct their attention to the assignment on the board:

Read the text and look at the illustration on page 360.

TEACH

Data integration saves time because the user does not need to enter the same information over and over again.

Spreadsheets also can be created in a spreadsheet window or frame within a word processing document. This way, the spreadsheet can be integrated into the word processing document as it is created.

ASSESS

To assess students' understanding, have them explain how to integrate a spreadsheet into another document.

CLOSE

Have students integrate a spreadsheet into another document. Refer to Projects 107, 108, 109, and 110.

360

17.2 Integration

Goals

- Integrate spreadsheet data into a word processing document
- Integrate a spreadsheet chart into a word processing document
- Create a new spreadsheet table within a word processing document

INTEGRATING SPREADSHEET AND WORD PROCESSING DOCUMENTS

Information in a spreadsheet can be used in many different ways. As you have learned in the projects you have completed, you can organize, calculate, format, and chart spreadsheet data. Sometimes you may want to include the data or chart from a spreadsheet file in a word processing document. To save time and eliminate the need to retype information, the software programs include tools and features that let you integrate data among programs easily. In the illustration, a chart created in a spreadsheet has been integrated into a report.

You can also create tables within word processing documents using a **spreadsheet frame.** When you create a spreadsheet frame, you open a window within the word processing document. When you select the spreadsheet frame, you have all the same menu options and tools available as you do in the spreadsheet program. When you deselect the spreadsheet frame, you are back to your word processing document with the word processing menus and tools available.

INTEGRATED DOCUMENT. A spreadsheet chart has been integrated into this word processing document.

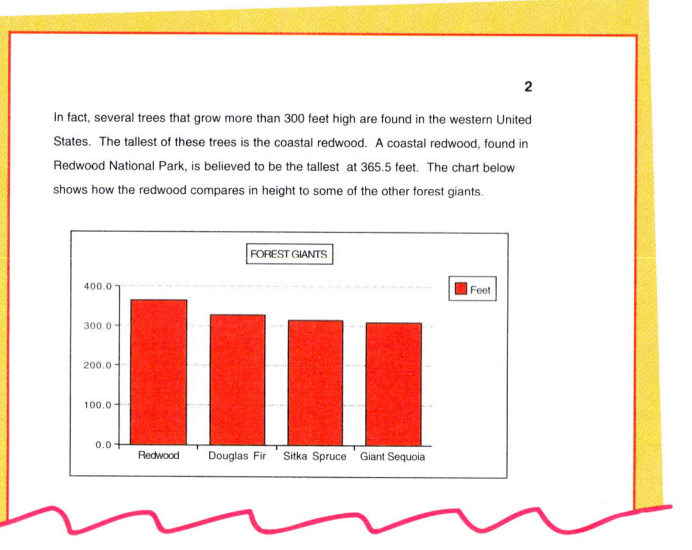

In fact, several trees that grow more than 300 feet high are found in the western United States. The tallest of these trees is the coastal redwood. A coastal redwood, found in Redwood National Park, is believed to be the tallest at 365.5 feet. The chart below shows how the redwood compares in height to some of the other forest giants.

FOREST GIANTS

360 Section 17 Analysis and Integration

RESOURCES

Lesson Plan: LP93
Supplemental Project: SP15

CD-ROM: Reference Guide

Software: Research Files

Project 107

INTEGRATE SPREADSHEET DATA, CHART, AND WORD PROCESSING DOCUMENTS

In this project you will learn to integrate spreadsheet data and a chart into a word processing document. Follow the steps below.

1. Open the spreadsheet file SS107 from your data disk in your spreadsheet program.
2. Open the file WP107 in your word processor. This document contains a report titled SPREADSHEET FRAMES.
3. Edit the line under the title of the report to include your first and last name.
4. Print the report.
5. Read the report which explains how to integrate spreadsheet data and charts into a word processing document.
6. In the report, place the insertion point at the beginning of the line: PLACE SPREADSHEET TABLE HERE.
7. Following the steps in the report, create a spreadsheet frame and copy the spreadsheet data into the frame. Review the steps to **switch windows** in Unit 4 of your Student Guide if needed.
8. Resize and position the spreadsheet frame as described in the report.
9. Delete the words: PLACE SPREADSHEET TABLE HERE.
10. In the report, place the insertion point at the beginning of the line: PLACE CHART HERE.
11. Following the steps in the report, place the spreadsheet chart in the report.
12. Resize and position the chart as described in the report.
13. Delete the words: PLACE CHART HERE.
14. Print the report with the integrated spreadsheet data and chart.
15. Save the word processing document as STWP107 on your data disk.
16. Close the spreadsheet file without saving it.

Project 107 Integration

PRACTICE—LEVEL 1

Purpose
Practice integrating a spreadsheet with a word processing document.

Time
Thirty minutes

Preparation
Make sure the appropriate software is available and that students have their data disks. Make sure the printers are ready.

Teaching Tip
Carefully observe students as they integrate the data. Students who finish early should repeat the project.

Trouble Shooting
Provide individual help to students who are having difficulty.

Wrap Up
Have students return computers and furniture to the appropriate conditions.

To generate interest in science, ask students to research arthropods. Each student should write a one-paragraph report about one of the following arthropods:

ants	shrimp
bees	spiders
crabs	termites
crickets	wasps
lobsters	

Project 108
Integration

ASSESS—LEVEL 2

Purpose
Assess spreadsheet skills by integrating a spreadsheet with a word processing document.

Time
Thirty minutes

Preparation
Make sure the appropriate software is available and that students have their data disks. Make sure the printers are ready.

Teaching Tip
Carefully observe students as they integrate the data. Students who finish early should repeat the project.

Trouble Shooting
Provide individual help to students who are having difficulty.

Wrap Up
Have students return computers and furniture to the appropriate conditions.

Project 108
Science Connection
INTEGRATE SPREADSHEET AND WORD PROCESSING DOCUMENTS

Practice the procedure you learned earlier to integrate spreadsheet and word processing documents. Refer to the steps in the report SPREADSHEET FRAMES from Project 107 as needed.

1. Open the spreadsheet file SS108 from your data disk in your spreadsheet program.
2. Open the file WP108 in your word processor.
3. Edit the line under the title of the report to include your first and last name.
4. In the report, place the insertion point at the beginning of the line: PLACE SPREADSHEET TABLE HERE.
5. Create a spreadsheet frame. Copy the spreadsheet data into the frame.
6. Resize and position the spreadsheet frame as needed.
7. Delete the words: PLACE SPREADSHEET TABLE HERE.
8. In the report, place the insertion point at the beginning of the line: PLACE CHART HERE.
9. Place the spreadsheet chart in the report.
10. Resize and position the chart as needed.
11. Delete the words: PLACE CHART HERE.
12. Print the report with the integrated spreadsheet data and chart.
13. Save the word processing document as STWP108 on your data disk.
14. Close the spreadsheet file without saving it.

Section 17 Analysis and Integration

Science Connection

To generate interest in science, ask students to research one of the topics below. Students should prepare a two-minute oral presentation about the their topics.

Arbor Day	Julius Sterling
Forest fires	Morton
Forestry	Rain forest
Lumber Industry	Sierra Club
John Muir	

Project 109

CREATE A TABLE IN A WORD PROCESSING DOCUMENT

Information in table form which could be created in a spreadsheet file can also be created in a word processing file using a spreadsheet frame. In this project you will learn to create a spreadsheet table in a word processing document.

1. Open the file WP109 in your word processor.
2. Print the report.
3. Read the contents of the report to learn how to create and format a table in a word processing document using a spreadsheet frame.
4. Place the insertion point at the beginning of the line: PLACE TABLE HERE.
5. Following the steps in the report, create the table shown below.

Organization	Members
Science Club	31
Garden Club	20
Backyard Bird Watchers	15
Net Surfers	18
Community Helpers	23

6. Resize and position the table as described in the report.
7. Delete the words: PLACE TABLE HERE.
8. Save the report as STWP109 on your data disk.

In Your Journal

Find out the names of clubs and organizations at your school. Make a list of these clubs and the numbers of members who belong to each one. Use this information to develop a spreadsheet.

Integration **363**

Project 109 Integration

PRACTICE—LEVEL 1

Purpose
Practice creating a spreadsheet table in a word processing document.

Time
Thirty minutes

Preparation
Make sure the appropriate software is available and that students have their data disks. Make sure the printers are ready.

Teaching Tip
Carefully observe students as they create the table. Students who finish early should repeat the project.

Trouble Shooting
Provide individual help to students who are having difficulty.

Wrap Up
Have students return computers and furniture to the appropriate conditions.

In Your Journal

Ask students to identify a club or organization that they might like to join. Ask them to write a paragraph in their journal explaining why the club appeals to them.

interNET CONNECTION

Have students use the Internet or a commercial on-line service to find information from another school about the clubs available there. Have students add this new information to their spreadsheet.

363

Project 110
Integration

ASSESS—LEVEL 2

Purpose
Assess spreadsheet skills by creating a spreadsheet table in a word processing document.

Time
Thirty minutes

Preparation
Students should come prepared with a list of four of their favorite books. Make sure the appropriate software is available and that students have their data disks. Make sure the printers are ready.

Teaching Tip
Carefully observe students as they create the table. Students who finish early should repeat the project.

Trouble Shooting
Provide individual help to students who are having difficulty.

Wrap Up
Have students return computers and furniture to the appropriate conditions.

Did You Know? Many libraries have computerized card catalogs. In many cases you can reach the card catalog via the Internet.

Language Arts Connection

Project 110

CREATE A TABLE IN A WORD PROCESSING DOCUMENT

Practice the procedure you learned earlier to create a spreadsheet table in a word processing document. Refer to the information from Project 109 as needed.

1. Open the file WP110 in your word processor.
2. Place the insertion point at the beginning of the line: PLACE TABLE HERE.
3. Create a table with two columns and six rows.
4. In cell A1, type *Title*.
5. In cell B1, type *Author*.
6. Bold the column headings in cells A1 and B1.
7. In cells A3 through A6, type the titles of four of your favorite books.
8. In cells B3 through B6, type the author's last name for each book.
9. Delete the words: PLACE TABLE HERE.
10. Resize the table, as needed, to display the data clearly.
11. Position the table so that it is approximately centered between the left and right margins.
12. Insert your first name as the writer at the end of the document.
13. Save the report as STWP110 on your data disk.

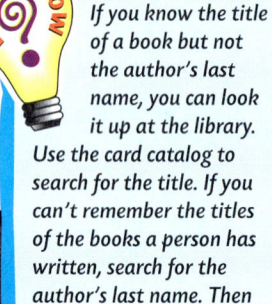

Did You Know? If you know the title of a book but not the author's last name, you can look it up at the library. Use the card catalog to search for the title. If you can't remember the titles of the books a person has written, search for the author's last name. Then look at the list of books this person has written.

364 Section 17 Analysis and Integration

Language Arts Connection

To generate interest in language arts, have students brainstorm ways in which your school library might use spreadsheets. Try to obtain actual spreadsheets used by your library administrator to share with the class. If your school does not have a library, contact the librarian of your local library.

Project 111
Building Your Portfolio

In this portfolio project you will practice the integration procedures you learned in this section. You will create an original report that includes a spreadsheet table. Refer to previous projects as needed.

NOW TRY THIS

1. Open a new word processing file.
2. Create a one-page report in standard business style. Refer to page 150 of this text for a sample report and formatting tips.
3. Write the report about an interesting topic you have learned recently in one of your classes.
4. Use an appropriate main title and your name as a subtitle.
5. At the end of the report, create a spreadsheet table with two columns. In the first column, briefly list three important points or facts about the topic of the report. In the second column, type either the date the points were discussed in class or page numbers where the points are discussed in your textbook.
6. Save the file as SSWP111 on your data disk.

Project 111
Building Your Portfolio

ASSESS—LEVEL 2

Purpose
Assess spreadsheet skills by using the integration features learned earlier in this section.

Time
One class period

Preparation
Students should come prepared with an outline for their report and all relevant data. Make sure the appropriate software is available and that students have their data disks. Make sure the printers are ready.

Teaching Tip
Carefully observe students as they create the report.

Trouble Shooting
Provide individual help to students who are having difficulty.

Wrap Up
Have students return computers and furniture to the appropriate conditions.

UNIT 6 ORGANIZER

Section	Subsection	Special Features	Projects: Project No., Title, and Page	Projects: Cross-Curricular Connection	Difficulty Level	Student Guide GO TO
18 - Database Basics	18.1 - Use a Database	Words To Know, p. 368	Project 112: Explore a Database, p. 371	112 Science	112 - L1	p. 370
	18.2 - Update a Database	Did You Know?, p. 373 In Your Journal, p. 373	Projects 113–114: Update and Print a Database, pp. 372–374	113–114 Science	113 - L1 114 - L2	p. 372
	18.3 - Create a New Database	In Your Journal, p. 375	Project 115: Create a Database, p. 376	115 Language Arts	115 - L1	p. 375
	18.4 - Design a Database	Bits & Bytes, p. 377	Projects 116–117: Design and Create a Database, pp. 378–380	116–117 Language Arts	116 - L1 117 - L2	p. 377 p. 380
	18.5 - Sort Records	In Your Journal, p. 381 Language Link, p. 383	Project 118: Sort a Database, p. 383		118 - L1	p. 382
	18.6 - Find Records	In Your Journal, p. 384 Did You Know?, p. 385 In Your Journal, p. 386 Did You Know?, p. 387	Projects 119–120: Find Records in a Database, pp. 386–387	119 Social Studies 120 Science	119 - L1 120 - L2	p. 385
			Project 121: Building Your Portfolio, p. 388	121 Technology	121 - L2	
19 - Enhanced Databases and Reports	19.1 - Database Structure	Words To Know, p. 389 In Your Journal, p. 390	Project 122: Change Database Structure, p. 391	122 Math	122 - L1	p. 390
	19.2 - Formula Field		Projects 123–124: Change Structure of a Database, pp. 393–394	123 Math 124 Technology	123 - L1 124 - L2	p. 392
	19.3 - Search a Database	Cultural Kaleidoscope, p. 395 Did You Know?, p. 396	Projects 125–127: Search a Database, pp. 396–398	125 Social Studies 127 Technology	125 - L1 126 - L1 127 - L2	p. 395
			Project 128: Building Your Portfolio, p. 399		128 - L2	
	19.4 - Enhance a Form	In Your Journal, p. 403	Projects 129–131: Enhance a Form, pp. 401–404	129–131 Language Arts	129 - L1 130 - L1 131 - L2	p. 400

UNIT RESOURCES

- Lesson Plans: LP94–LP111
- Transparency Masters: TM40–TM46
- Multicultural Timings: MT21–MT26
- Supplemental Projects: SP16–SP21
- Enrichment Activities
- CD-ROM: Unit 6 Document Templates Reference Guide Cross-curricular Timings
- Software: Unit 6 Document Templates Research Files
- Transparencies: 30–32
- Student Guides: Database
- Student Data Disks

UNIT 6 ORGANIZER

Section	Subsection	Special Features	Projects: Project No., Title, and Page	Cross-Curricular Connection	Difficulty Level	Student Guide GO TO
19 - Enhanced Databases and Reports (continued)	19.5 - Create a Report	In Your Journal, p. 405 Did You Know?, p. 406 In Your Journal, p. 407	Projects 132–133: Create a Report, pp. 407–408	132 Science 133 Technology	132 - L1 133 - L2	p. 406
	19.6 - Database Template	Did You Know?, p. 410 Did You Know?, p. 412	Projects 134–135: Create a Database With a Template, pp. 411–412	134–135 Technology	134 - L1 135 - L2	p. 410
			Project 136: Building Your Portfolio, p. 413		136 - L2	
	19.7 - Database Integration	In Your Journal, p. 415 Bits & Bytes, p. 416 Did You Know?, p. 417 In Your Journal, p. 419	Project 137: Integrate a Database and Spreadsheet, p. 418	137 Social Studies	137 - L1	
			Project 138: Integrate a Spreadsheet and Database, p. 419	138 Technology	138 - L1	
			Project 139: Integrate a Database and Report, p. 420	139 Science	139 - L2	
			Project 140: Building Your Portfolio, p. 421		140 - L2	

KEY TO DIFFICULTY LEVEL

The following designations will help you decide which activities are appropriate for your students.

- **L1:** Level 1 activities are basic activities and should be within the range of all students.
- **L2:** Level 2 activities are average activities and should be within the range of average and above average students.
- **L3:** Level 3 activities are challenging activities designed for the ability range of above average students.

ASSESSMENT RESOURCES

Check Your Understanding

Section 18	Section 19
p. 380	p. 398
p. 388	p. 399
	p. 404
	p. 413
	p. 421

Portfolio Assessment (Building Your Portfolio)

Section 18	Section 19
p. 388	p. 399
	p. 413
	p. 421

Unit Tests (Teacher's Resource Binder)

Objective Test

Performance Tests

Section 18	Section 19

366b

UNIT 6

INTRODUCING THE UNIT

Ask students to make a list of the databases they have used in the past week. Examples might include the telephone book, the library card catalog, or a kiosk at a CD store that lists CDs available in the store. Ask students to classify each database in terms of whether it is electronic or manual, how the data is organized, how the data is used, and who compiles the data.

Discuss with students the advantages of using an electronic database over the manual variety. Sample advantages include quick data access, easy data editing, sophisticated searches, and the ability to change the order in which data appears on the screen or in reports.

Unit 6
Database

OVERVIEW

A database is an organized collection of information. You probably use databases every day. For example, every time you look up a friend's phone number in the school directory, you are using a database. When you look up a topic in an encyclopedia, you are using a database. Even the TV guide you use to find your favorite program is a database.

In this unit, you will explore databases using the computer. You will learn how to create, edit, sort, and find information using an electronic database. You will also learn how to enter and display the information stored in a database by creating and printing forms and reports.

Fun Facts

The first computer input was in the form of punched cards. In 1890 this new "card-punch" system was used to tally data for the U.S. Census. The new system compiled population statistics for 1890 in six weeks. The previous census of 1880 had taken seven years to tally!

UNIT 6

UNIT OBJECTIVES

- Define database and list common uses of a database.
- Identify key parts of a database.
- Design, create, edit, sort, and save a database.
- Type information in a database using different views.
- Search and find specific information.
- Display or print database information in forms and reports you create.

Unit Contents

Section 18 Database Basics
Section 19 Enhanced Databases and Reports

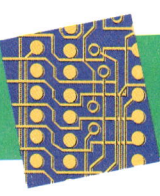

MULTIMEDIA

For this unit, you may use the multimedia CD-ROM to enhance your students' skills in creating a database. The CD-ROM contains format guides which are cross-referenced to the text. These format guides serve as models for creating projects using a database software applications. A Reference Guide links terms to format guides that define and illustrate their use in formatting a database. The Research Files contain cross-curricular typing selections or timings for 1 minute, 2 minutes, and 3 or 5 minutes. The timings, as well as the two games—Get the Scoop and Uncover the Story—are great ways to build typing skills.

Focus On Careers In Technology

Inventory trackers are responsible for maintaining up-to-date information about the supplies of merchandise (inventory) a business has in stock. A database program can make this job much easier to do. Stores keep many kinds of records in their inventory databases: lists of stock items, model numbers, stock identification numbers, quantities of items on hand, quantities sold, prices of items, locations of items in their warehouse, the names and addresses of manufacturers and suppliers, and the dates on which they place orders for new merchandise. The database can organize and sort all this information in many different ways to compile reports and predict future sales.

Focus On Careers In Technology

Many inventory systems use scanners, which makes the process even faster and more accurate. For example, scanners used at most grocery and retail stores ring up the sale on the cash register, provide the customer with a detailed receipt, and update the store's inventory database.

If possible, invite an inventory manager or manager of a local retail store to talk with the class about how the inventory system works and how the technology has improved the store operations.

Application: COMPUTERS IN THE COMMUNITY

Local election offices often make use of databases to help with record keeping and data analysis. For example, a database might be used to keep information about all registered voters in the county or precinct. Invite a local election official to speak to the class about ways in which the election office uses databases.

367

Section 18
Database Basics

SECTION OVERVIEW

This section introduces students to the most common features of databases—designing, creating, updating, and sorting. Students are taught how to navigate through the database and are introduced to the common database views (list view and form view).

CONTENT FOCUS

Use a Database
Update a Database
Create a Database
Design a Database
Sort Records
Find Records

CURRICULUM FOCUS

Science
Language Arts
Social Studies

OPENING ACTIVITY

Ask students how many of them have used a database. Point out that if they have ever used a telephone directory or even a TV Guide, they have used a database. With the help of the class, make a list of the type of information included in a telephone book. Students should come up with categories such as name, address, and telephone number. Point out that the key advantage of a database is that it is organized in a specific order.

SECTION 18
Database Basics

OBJECTIVES

- Identify various types of databases.
- Identify key parts of a database.
- Design, create, edit, save, sort, and print a database.

Focus on Database

An electronic database helps you organize information so it is easy to find and use. You can keep track of names and addresses, sort a video list by topic, or organize information for a class project using a database. In this section, you will learn how to design and create a database. You will also learn how to update, edit, find, sort, and print the data.

Words To Know

database	form view	record
field	forms	search
field name	header	selecting
field type	list view	single-field sort
find	multiple-field sort	sort
footer	navigating	view

Career Exploration Activities: Fine Arts and Humanities

Databases can be useful in the fine arts field. Musicians, for example, might use a database to keep track of performance locations and dates, customers, and a list of the music performed at a particular concert (this helps ensure that the same audience doesn't hear the same music over and over again).

If possible, invite a professional musician to speak to the class about the "business" side of being a performer. Students often lose site of the fact that software tools can play a role in nearly any profession.

18.1 Use a Database

Goals
- Change views
- Navigate through a database
- Select records and fields
- Change field size

EXPLORING A DATABASE

Have you ever been asked to perform an experiment as part of a science class? A database can help you organize the results of such an experiment in a clear and effective way. A **database** is any organized collection of information on a given subject or topic. In this project, you will explore an electronic database that was created to summarize the results of a science class experiment. In this experiment, each student was told to listen to music while doing homework and again while doing household chores. They had to determine whether or not they actually "heard" the music while doing these other things or whether they "tuned out" the music. When they finished, they organized the results of the experiment using a database as a tool.

In a database, one category of information is called a **field**. A field is given a name that describes in a general way the main subject or idea of the field. Some of the field names used to summarize the results of the science class experiment are *Artist*, *Title of CD*, *Song Title*, and *Activity*. A field entry is the specific information for each field. In the field named Activity, for example, the field entries are *chores* and *homework*.

A **record** is a group of fields that are all related to the same topic or idea. Together, all the records make up the database. In a database, the information can be displayed in different ways. The information itself doesn't change even though the way it is displayed may change. These different ways of displaying information are called **views**.

Two commonly used database views are *list view (Datasheet View)* and *form view*. List view looks much like a spreadsheet displaying the fields in columns and the records in rows. This view is used to enter information into the records and to display several records at once. Form view looks more like a form document and may include pictures, borders, or special formatting to make it attractive or easy to use. Form view is used to display one or a few records at a time, to change the design of the form, or to enter information into the database.

Use a Database **369**

RESOURCES

Lesson Plan: LP95
Supplemental Project: SP16
Transparency Master: TM40

Transparency 30

CD-ROM: Reference Guide

Software: Research Files

18.1 Use a Database

FOCUS
Change views. Navigate through a database. Select records and fields. Change field size.

BELLRINGER
When students enter the room, direct their attention to the assignment on the board:
Read pages 369–370 to become familiar with database terms.

TEACH
This lesson introduces students to the basic database elements—fields and records. Use a computer with an overhead display device to show students how fields and records are related. A field is a category of information, while a record is a group of related fields.

369

Use a Database

TEACH

Use the illustrations on page 370 to point out fields and records and to show students the different views available in the database. Point out that the information remains the same even when the view changes. Note the use of graphic elements in the form view. While the elements do not change the information in the database, they make it more interesting to view!

ASSESS

To assess students' understanding, have them identify the different database elements (fields and records) and describe the different database views (list view and form view).

CLOSE

Have students explore a database as described in Project 112.

Refer students to the appropriate section of the Student Guide.

DID YOU KNOW? The compact disc was first available for consumer purchase in 1983. In that year, only 100,000 CDs were sold. By 1988 sales of CDs topped those of LPs, and by 1992, CD sales exceeded cassette tape sales. Today, approximately two-thirds of all music sold is produced on CDs.

The database for this project is shown in the illustrations in list view and then in form view. Notice the differences between the two views.

LIST VIEW.
(Datasheet View)
Displays data in columns and rows.
FIELD.
RECORD.

Artist	Title of CD	Song Title	Activity	Heard
Sophie B. Hawkins	Whaler	Right Beside You	Chores	Yes
Sophie B. Hawkins	Whaler	Did We Not Choose Each Other	Homework	No
Billy Best	America's Songs	The Golden Wheat	Homework	No
Purple	Studying History	The American Dream	Chores	Yes
Bing Crosby	Winter Songs	Winter Wonderland	Chores	No
Neil Diamond	Beautiful Noise	Street Sounds	Chores	Yes
J. S. Bach	Classical Hits	Fugue in D Minor	Homework	No
Andrew Weber	Great Themes	Memories	Chores	Yes
Billy Best	America's Songs	Star Spangled Times	Homework	Yes
Grace Evonne	Winter Songs	Jingle Bells	Homework	Yes
James Gallway	Flute Concertos	Flute in D Minor	Homework	No
Carl Orff	Carmina Burana	Swan Song	Chores	No

FORM VIEW.
Displays data in document form.
FIELD.
RECORD.

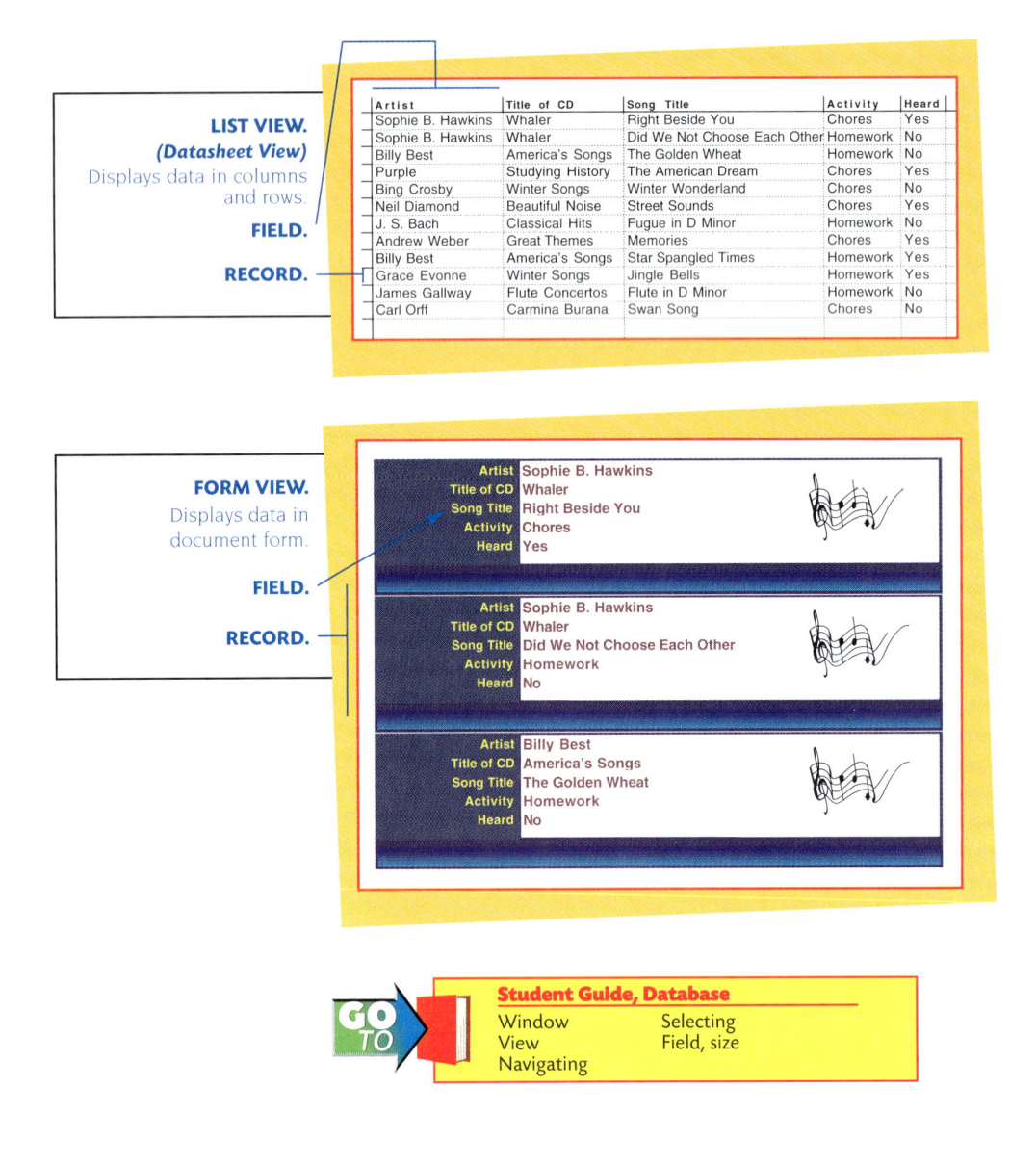

Artist: Sophie B. Hawkins
Title of CD: Whaler
Song Title: Right Beside You
Activity: Chores
Heard: Yes

Artist: Sophie B. Hawkins
Title of CD: Whaler
Song Title: Did We Not Choose Each Other
Activity: Homework
Heard: No

Artist: Billy Best
Title of CD: America's Songs
Song Title: The Golden Wheat
Activity: Homework
Heard: No

GO TO **Student Guide, Database**
Window — Selecting
View — Field, size
Navigating

370 Section 18 Database Basics

Project 112

EXPLORE A DATABASE

Carefully read and do the following steps to explore a database.

1. In your Student Guide, read Unit 6, **window** to learn about the database window. Find and read the Help topics listed here to learn about fields, records, and creating databases.
2. Open the file DB112 on your data disk.
3. Practice changing the **view** of the database.
4. Practice **navigating** through each of the database views.
5. Practice **selecting** fields and records in each of the database views.
6. In list view, enlarge the **field size** under the field name *Artist* until all the words in the longest field entry *Sophie B. Hawkins* can be seen.
7. In list view, reduce the field size under the field name *Heard* until one or two spaces are left between fields.
8. Enlarge or reduce the field size of the rest of the fields as needed.
9. Save the database file as STDB112 on your data disk.
10. Close the database file.

Note: In the filename STDB112, *ST* stands for student; *DB* stands for the database unit; and *112* stands for Project 112.

Use a Database **371**

Project 112
Explore a Database

PRACTICE—LEVEL 1

Purpose
Practice exploring a database.

Time
Fifteen minutes.

Preparation
Make sure the database software is available and that students have their data disks.

Teaching Tips
Observe students carefully to make sure they are navigating through the database and using different database views. Students who finish early should repeat the project.

Trouble Shooting
Provide individual help to students who are having difficulty navigating through the database views.

Wrap Up
If this is the last project for this class period, ask students to return computers and furniture to the appropriate conditions.

Many CDs have been made with various nature-oriented themes and sounds. To generate interest in science, ask students to visit a local music store or library and find at least two CDs that are related to nature. Ask them to keep a list of the relevant information about the CD—title, artist, and so on. The CD information can be added to the database after students learn how to add records.

371

18.2 Update a Database

FOCUS
Enter data. Delete, edit, duplicate, and add records. Print data.

BELLRINGER
When students enter the room, direct their attention to the assignment on the board:
Read page 372 to learn about updating a database.

TEACH
Demonstrate to students how to use their database software to enter data, modify records, add new records, and print data.

ASSESS
To assess students' understanding, have them describe how to add, modify, delete, and print records.

CLOSE
Have students update and print a database as described in Project 113.

GO TO *Refer students to the appropriate section of the Student Guide.*

PRACTICE-LEVEL 1

Purpose
Practice updating and printing a database.

Time
Thirty minutes.

18.2 Update a Database

UPDATING A DATABASE
As information changes, you need to be able to delete old records and add new ones to a database. Sometimes you may add records where a number of fields are the same. If so, duplicating a record may save editing time.

Goals
- Enter data
- Delete, edit, duplicate, and add records
- Print data

GO TO Student Guide, Database
Record, delete	Record, add
Record, edit	Enter data
Record, duplicate	Print

Project 113
UPDATE AND PRINT A DATABASE
Follow these steps to update and print a database in list view.

1. Open the file DB113 on your data disk.
2. The database has two identical records for Liverwort. Follow the steps under **record, delete** in Unit 6 of your Student Guide to delete the second duplicate record for Liverwort.
3. Follow the steps under **record, edit** in Unit 6 of your Student Guide to edit the record for Jellyfish. Change the field entry under Kingdom from *Kingdom* to *Animal*.
4. Follow the steps under **record, duplicate** in Unit 6 of your Student Guide to duplicate the record for Peninsula turtles.
5. Change the field entry in the duplicate record from *Peninsula turtles* to *Seahorse*.
6. Follow the steps under **record, add** in Unit 6 of your Student Guide to add a record at the end of your database.

(continued on next page)

372 Section 18 Database Basics

RESOURCES
- Lesson Plan: LP96
- Supplemental Project: SP17
- CD-ROM: Reference Guide
- Software: Research Files

Science Connection
To encourage interest in science, ask students to make a list of the fields they think would be useful in a database about animals. Ask them to explain why each field should be included.

Project 113 (continued)

7. **Enter data** in the new record using the following information:

   | Swallowtail butterfly | Animal | Phylum Arthropoda |

8. Use the speller. Proofread to check for accuracy. Preview the database and make corrections as needed.
9. Save the database as file STDB113 on your data disk.
10. **Print** the database while in list view. Then close the database. Remember that a database is printed in the view you are using when you give the command to print.

DID YOU KNOW? The word *butterfly* comes from an Old English word meaning *butter* and *flying creature*. Swallowtail butterflies are found all over the world, though most live in the tropics. The swallowtail butterfly gets its name from the long extension on each hind wing. These extensions resemble the tails of certain swallows.

In Your Journal

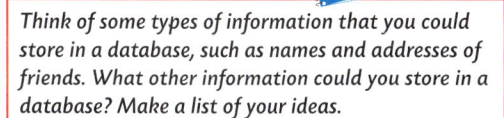

Think of some types of information that you could store in a database, such as names and addresses of friends. What other information could you store in a database? Make a list of your ideas.

Update a Database **373**

Project 113
Update a Database

Preparation
Make sure the database software is available and that students have their data disks. Make sure the printers are ready.

Teaching Tip
Observe students carefully to make sure they are entering the new data. Students who finish early should repeat the project; they might want to add new records of their own choosing.

Trouble Shooting
Provide individual help to students who are having difficulty updating the database.

Wrap Up
If this is the last project for this class period, ask students to return computers and furniture to the appropriate conditions.

DID YOU KNOW? At 300 beats per minute, the swallowtail butterfly has the slowest wing-beat of any insect.

In Your Journal

Put students with similar database interests together in groups and ask them to decide what fields their database should include.

373

Project 114
Update and Print a Database

ASSESS—LEVEL 2

Purpose
Assess skills by updating and printing a database.

Time
Class period.

Preparation
Make sure the database software is available and that students have their data disks. Make sure the printers are ready.

Teaching Tip
Observe students carefully to make sure they are deleting, editing, and printing records as instructed. Students who finish early should repeat the project.

Trouble Shooting
Provide individual help to students who are having difficulty using the database features.

Wrap Up
If this is the last project for this class period, ask students to return computers and furniture to the appropriate conditions.

Project 114
UPDATE AND PRINT A DATABASE

Practice using the database features you learned in Projects 112 and 113 by updating and printing a database. Refer to the previous projects as often as needed.

1. Open the file DB114 on your data disk.
2. Look over the database in list view. Two records are identical.
3. Delete one of the duplicate records for Jamie Burns.
4. Delete one of the duplicate records for Sally Jones.
5. Jamie Burns did a test on the mineral sphalerite. Add a new record with the following information.

Tester:	Jamie Burns
Phone:	344-9948
Email Address:	none
Mineral:	sphalerite
Color:	brown
Crystal System:	cubic

6. Jamie also tested the mineral olivine. Duplicate the record you just entered. Then edit the following fields with the new information.

Mineral:	olivine
Color:	olive green
Crystal System:	orthorhombic

7. Sally Jones' phone number is 457-9960. Edit this field entry where it is incorrect.
8. Lindsay Tracey's phone number is 459-9987. Edit this field entry where it is incorrect.
9. Adjust the field size so all information is visible in each field.
10. Use the speller. Proofread to check for accuracy. Preview the database and make corrections as needed.
11. Save the database file as STDB114 on your data disk.
12. Print the database while in list view. Then close the database.

Section 18 Database Basics

To generate interest in science, ask students to make a list of different minerals. Ask them to include the mineral name, the color, and the crystal system.

---

interNET CONNECTION

For more information about minerals, check out this Web site:

http://mineral.galleries.com/

18.3 Create a New Database

CREATING A DATABASE

The first step in creating a database is to define and name the fields. Fields are defined according to the type of information they hold. For example, a field that holds names (letters) is a text field. A field that holds numbers, such as age or weight, is a number field. A field that holds numbers could also be defined as a text field if the field will not be used for a calculation. For example, a phone number would never be used in a formula. However, a person's age or birth date might be. If the numbers in a field are to be used in a formula, then the field must be defined as a number field. Most database software offers a choice of text, number, date, and time fields.

You must also consider whether or not the category for which you have created a field can be broken into smaller units of information. For example, a name is a category for which you might create a field. However, the name can be divided into the smaller units of first name and last name. You will find using these smaller units helpful when you want to organize the information in your database.

Goals
- Create a new database
- Name and define a field
- Move a field

In Your Journal
List at least 10 ideas for a database. For each idea, suggest three or more fields to use in organizing the information. Identify each field as a text, number, date, or time field.

GO TO
Student Guide, Database
- Create database
- Field, name
- Field, move
- Field, type

Create a New Database **375**

18.3 Create a New Database

FOCUS
Create a new database. Name and define a field. Move a field.

BELLRINGER
When students enter the room, direct their attention to the assignment on the board:
Read page 375 to learn more about database fields.

TEACH
To help students understand about more about fields, ask the class to help you define the fields required for a class database.

ASSESS
To assess students' understanding, have them describe the different field types available with their database software.

CLOSE
Have students create a database as described in Project 115.

In Your Journal
Group students with similar database ideas together to discuss their databases. Ask them to combine the best ideas to present to the class.

GO TO *Refer students to the appropriate section of the Student Guide.*

RESOURCES
- Lesson Plan: LP97
- Supplemental Project: SP18
- CD-ROM: Reference Guide
- Software: Research Files

Project 115
Create a Database

PRACTICE—LEVEL 1

Purpose
Practice creating a database.

Time
Class period.

Preparation
Make sure the database software is available and that students have their data disks. Make sure the printers are ready.

Teaching Tip
Observe students as they create the specified database. Students who finish early should repeat the project, this time creating a different database of your choosing.

Trouble Shooting
Provide individual help to students who are having difficulty creating the database.

Wrap Up
If this is the last project for this class period, ask students to return computers and furniture to the appropriate conditions.

Language Arts Connection

Project 115
CREATE A DATABASE

Follow the steps below to create a new database. The database will contain a listing of names, addresses, and phone numbers that could be used like an address book.

1. Follow the steps under **create database** in Unit 6 of your Student Guide to create a new database file.
2. Follow the steps under **field, name** and **field, type** to create these fields:

Field Name	Field Type
First Name	Text
Last Name	Text
Email Address	Text
Phone	Text
Age	Number

3. Save the database file as STDB115 on your data disk.
4. Add the following records into your database:

First Name	Last Name	Address	Phone	Age
John	Johnson	jjohnson221@aol.com	287-4873	12
Adam	Smith	SmithA@aol.com	366-9987	11
Katie	Crane	1217cranek@ee.net	857-4434	11
Your first name	Your last name	Your email address	Your phone	Your age

5. Save the database again.
6. Change field size as needed so that all information in each field is visible.
7. Follow the steps under **field, move** in Unit 6 of your Student Guide to move the field Last Name to the left of the field First Name.
8. Use the speller. Proofread to check for accuracy. Preview the database and make corrections as needed. Save the database again.
9. Print the database while in list view.

Note: After each database is created or updated, always use your speller, proofread, and preview the database before printing. Then close the file. These directions will no longer be repeated.

376 Section 18 Database Basics

Language Arts Connection

To generate interest in language arts, ask students to list make a list of their favorite books. Ask them to plan a database to store information about the books. Which fields should the database include? What type of data will each field hold?

18.4 Design a Database

DESIGNING A DATABASE

Before creating a database, you must think very carefully about how you will use the information. Well organized information is the easiest to find and use. Answer the following questions as you plan a design for the database.

DESIGN TIPS

- What categories of information are needed?
- Should any of the categories you identified be divided into smaller units of information?
- Will the information in the fields be defined as text, number, or other field types?
- Will any numbers be used for any type of calculation?
- What field names will best describe the information contained in each field?
- In what order should the fields appear?

Goals
- Design a database
- Delete a field
- Change the font for a field entry

Bits & Bytes
A database can be used with a word processing program to "personalize" form letters to many people. The form letter includes special codes. Each code represents information that changes in each letter, such as the name, address, and greeting. Then a list of names, addresses, and other information is typed in a database. Each item in the database is coded to match one of the codes in the form letter. The database is then merged with the form letter to produce personalized letters.

GO TO Student Guide, Database
Field, delete
Font

18.4 Design a Database

FOCUS
Design a database. Delete a field. Change the font for a field entry.

BELLRINGER
When students enter the room, direct their attention to the assignment on the board:
Read page 377 for database design tips.

TEACH
The most critical aspect of creating a database is the design—determining the fields required, field sizes, field types, and so on. Work with students to design a sample database on the board. As the students design the database, ask them to consider the tips on page 377.

ASSESS
To assess students' understanding, have them describe issues to consider when designing a database.

CLOSE
Have students design and create a database as described in Project 116.

GO TO Refer students to the appropriate section of the Student Guide.

RESOURCES
Lesson Plan: LP97
Supplemental Project: SP19

CD-ROM: Reference Guide

Software: Research Files

Lesson Extension
Ask students to evaluate an existing database in terms of the design issues identified on page 377. Ask them to identify the changes they would make and to provide a rationale for each change.

Project 116
Design and Create a Database

PRACTICE—LEVEL 1

Purpose
Practice designing and creating a database.

Time
Class period.

Preparation
Make sure the database software is available and that students have their data disks. Make sure the printers are ready.

Teaching Tip
Observe students as they design and create the specified database. Students who finish early should repeat the project, this time designing and creating a different database of your choosing.

Trouble Shooting
Provide individual help to students who are having difficulty designing the database.

Wrap Up
If this is the last project for this class period, ask students to return computers and furniture to the appropriate conditions.

Language Arts Connection — Project 116

DESIGN AND CREATE A DATABASE

In this project, you will design a database for your teacher. She has asked you to help her keep track of the books in her classroom that students check out. Follow the steps below.

1. Open a new database file.
2. Study the information for the books shown in the box below. Plan a database design for this information using the design questions on page 377.

> The Boxcar Children, *The Mystery of the Lost Mine*, #52, Gertrude Chandler Warner, 120 pages, Copyright 1996.
>
> The Boxcar Children, *Mike's Mystery*, #5, Gertrude Chandler Warner, 128 pages, Copyright 1992.
>
> Valley Farm Mysteries, *The Calico Cat*, #10, J.T. Perez, 96 pages, Copyright 1996.

3. Compare your database design plan to the one shown below. Even though the copyright year is a number, it should still be defined as a text field since you would not use a copyright year in a formula in this database. The page number might be used in a formula. Your teacher might want to track the total number of pages read or to find the average length of the books in class.

Field Name	Field Type
Series	Text
Title	Text
Number	Text
Author	Text
Pages	Number
Copyright	Text

(continued on next page)

378 Section 18 Database Basics

Language Arts Connection

To generate interest in language arts, students can add the records for their favorite books (using the list from Project 115).

Project 116
(continued)

4. Create the database following the design plan. Save the database file as STDB116 on your data disk.
5. Add these records. Type only the numbers under the fields for Number, Pages, and Copyright. In the Author field, type the last name, a comma, the first name or initial, and the middle name or initial.

> The Boxcar Children, *The Mystery of the Lost Mine,* #52, Gertrude Chandler Warner, 120 pages, Copyright 1996.
> The Boxcar Children, *Mike's Mystery,* #5, Gertrude Chandler Warner, 128 pages, Copyright 1992.
> Valley Farm Mysteries, *The Calico Cat,* #10, J.T. Perez, 96 pages, Copyright 1996.

6. Edit any field entries as needed.
7. Follow the steps under **field, delete** in Unit 6 of your Student Guide to delete the Copyright field.
8. Adjust the field sizes so that all information is visible. Save the database file again.
9. Change the window to display the form view.
10. Change the **font** for all the field entries to Arial, 14-point. Change the text color to blue.
11. Adjust the field sizes so that all information is visible. Save the database file again. Print your database in form view.

Design and Create a Database

DID YOU KNOW?
The oldest mechanically printed work is the Dharani scroll (or sutra). Created from wooden printing blocks, it was found in South Korea in 1966. It is believed that this work was created no later than A.D. 704.

interNET CONNECTION

For a terrific on-line bookstore, check out this Web site:
http://www.amazon.com

Project 117
Design and Create a Database

ASSESS—LEVEL 2

Purpose
Assess skills by designing and creating a database.

Time
Class period.

Preparation
Make sure the database software is available and that students have their data disks. Make sure the printers are ready.

Teaching Tip
Observe students as they design and create the specified database. Students who finish early should repeat the project, this time designing and creating a different database of your choosing.

Trouble Shooting
Provide individual help to students who are having difficulty changing the page orientation.

Wrap Up
Have students review their work using **Check Your Understanding.** Students' answers will vary.
If this is the last project for this class period, ask students to return computers and furniture to the appropriate conditions.

Project 117

Language Arts Connection

DESIGN AND CREATE A DATABASE

Follow the steps below to design and create an original database to organize your CD, tape, or video collection. In planning the design for your database, consider the information you may want to include about each item. For example, you might wish to identify videos by category such as drama, comedy, or musical in addition to including the title of the video. You might also want to record the names of the actors who star in the film or the year the film was released. What other information might you find helpful to include in your database?

GO TO Student Guide, Database
Page orientation

1. Plan the design for your database. Decide on an appropriate field name and field type for each field.
2. Open a new database file.
3. Create your database.
4. Type information for at least three records in your database.
5. Save the database file as STDB117.
6. Format the text in the fields choosing a different font.
7. Change the size of the text in the fields.
8. Change the color of the text to a color of your choice.
9. Adjust the field sizes so all information in each field is visible.
10. Change the **page orientation** to landscape orientation.
11. Save your database file again.
12. Print your database in a view of your choice.

✓ Check Your Understanding

1. Did you create a field for each category of information divided into smaller units as appropriate?
2. Did you choose field names that describe the contents of each field?
3. Did you define the field types correctly?
4. Did you adjust the field sizes so all information is visible when it is printed?

380 Section 18 Database Basics

Language Arts Connection

Have students research famous novels that were turned into movies. Ask them how a database entry for the book might differ from an entry for the movie. For example, a database that lists the movies probably has fields for actors and actresses, director, screen writer, and so on; the book entry will not have those fields.

18.5 Sort Records

Goals
- Sort records based on a single field
- Sort records based on multiple fields

SORTING RECORDS

Sorting is a process of arranging information in a certain order. Has your teacher ever asked you to alphabetize a list? When you completed this task, you were sorting the information in ascending order from A to Z. If you have ever rearranged pages of a report by page number, you were also sorting information in ascending order. When you sort in descending order, you start your sort with Z and work backwards to A. In a numeric sort, you start with the highest number and sort backwards to the lowest number. A database sorts records easily and quickly. When information is sorted, it is easier to find and use.

In this project, you will use the sort feature to arrange records in a certain order. This database contains fields for the first names, last names, addresses, and ages of a group of students. If you were trying to find a friend's address quickly, you probably would like to see the names sorted in alphabetical order by last name. In your first sort, you will sort the list by the Last Name field in ascending order. This is an example of a sort based on a single field only. If you wanted to arrange your list by the ages of your friends with the oldest ones first, you would sort the records by the Age field in descending order. This is also an example of a single sort.

In Your Journal

Listings in phone books are arranged alphabetically. So are indexes in books. Think of some other examples of sorting information alphabetically. Describe how this type of sorting is helpful.

Sort Records **381**

RESOURCES

- Lesson Plan: LP98
  Transparency Master: TM41
- CD-ROM: Reference Guide
- Software: Research Files

18.5 Sort Records

FOCUS

Sort records based on a single field. Sort records based on multiple fields.

BELLRINGER

When students enter the room, direct their attention to the assignment on the board:

Read pages 381–382 to learn about sorting records.

TEACH

One of the big advantages of an electronic database is the ability to quickly and accurately sort records. To drive home this point, build a database of students in the class. It can contain a minimal number of fields—first name, last name, and birth date of each student should be sufficient. Put the same information on index cards, using one card per student. Shuffle the cards, and ask a volunteer to sort the cards in alphabetical order. Give the student a good head start, and then do the same sort using the computerized version of the database. Finally, show students how easy it is to sort on different fields.

In Your Journal

Ask students to think about other arrangements of data that might be useful. For example, student lists could be arranged in alphabetical order according to hobby, so clubs can be formed by students with similar hobbies.

381

Sort Records

TEACH

Point out that it is sometimes necessary to sort on more than one field. Ask students to look at a common name, such as Green or Smith, in the telephone book or in the illustration on page 382. What happens when more than one person has the same last name?

ASSESS

To assess students' understanding, ask them to explain the sort process.

CLOSE

Have students sort a database as described in Project 118.

DID YOU KNOW? If your last name is Smith, you have lots of company; an estimated 2,382,509 Smiths live in the United States.

GO TO: Refer students to the appropriate section of the Student Guide.

Another type of sort combines the results of sorting several fields in a certain order. This is called a **multiple-field sort.** The last sort in this project is a multiple-field sort. The order in which you choose to sort fields is very important. In this project, the fields will be sorted in ascending order as follows: Last Name, First Name, and Age. In the first sort step, the records will be arranged in alphabetical order by last name. If any last names are identical, the second sort step will look at the next field, First Name, and arrange the records in alphabetic order. If both the last name and the first name are identical, the third sort step moves to the third field, Age, to arrange the records in descending numeric order (oldest first). The result of all three sort steps is that the records are now in alphabetic order by last name, by first name for those with the same last names, and then by age for those with the same last names and first names.

Study the illustration which shows the database after a multiple-field sort. Your printed database may look slightly different than the one shown.

MULTIPLE-FIELD SORT. Records sorted by Last Name, First Name, and Age.

Last Name	First Name	Age	Email Address
Chang	Maya	12	ChangM@aol.com
Chang	Mike	12	none
Green	Alana	13	none
Green	Alana	12	green@0123@peak.net
Green	Alice	11	1216agrn@sync.net
Green	Paulina	13	none
Greene	Candace	13	none
Jones	Adam	12	none
Jones	Erin	11	ejones63@kih.net
Jones	Tommy	12	none
Jones	Tony	13	543352@compuserv.com
Kitsche	Jenny	11	kitsche@peak.net
Martinez	Jose	11	JoseM@efn.com
Thoms	Lindsay	13	ThomsL@aol.com

GO TO: Student Guide, Database — Sort

Section 18 Database Basics

Project 118

SORT A DATABASE

Follow the steps below to practice sorting a database.

1. Open the file DB118 on your data disk.
2. **Sort** the records by Last Name in ascending order. Notice how the order of the records changes after the sort.
3. Sort the records by Age in descending order. Notice how the order of the records changes after the sort.
4. Use a multiple-field sort to sort the records based on three fields in this order: Last Name and First Name in ascending order and Age in descending order. Notice how the order of the records changes after the sort.
5. Save the sorted database file as STDB118 on your data disk.
6. Print the sorted database using the list view.

Language Link

To alphabetize names, consider each part of the person's name as a separate unit.

Compare each name in this order: last name, first name or initial, and any other names or initials.

L. Sanders	Sanders, L.
Lance J. Sanders	Sanders, Lance J.
Paul Sanderson	Sanderson, Paul
Steven Sanderson	Sanderson, Steven
Steven L. Sanderson	Sanderson, Steven L.

✓ Check Your Learning

Alphabetize the following names beginning with the last name.

- Allen P. Roberts
- David P. Robertson
- Arlene Roberts
- Barbara Robertson
- C. D. Roberts

Sort Records **383**

Project 118
Sort a Database

PRACTICE—LEVEL 1

Purpose
Practice sorting a database.

Time
Thirty minutes.

Preparation
Make sure the database software is available and that students have their data disks. Make sure the printers are ready.

Teaching Tip
Observe students as they sort the database. Students who finish early should repeat the project, this time sorting on different fields.

Trouble Shooting
Provide individual help to students who are having difficulty.

Wrap Up
Review students' answers to the **Check Your Learning** activity in **Language Link.**

If this is the last project for this class period, ask students to return computers and furniture to the appropriate conditions.

Language Link
ANSWERS

1. Roberts, Allen P.
2. Roberts, Arlene
3. Roberts, C. D.
4. Robertson, Barbara
5. Robertson, David P.

18.6 Find Records

FOCUS

Find records in a database. Create a header. Create a footer.

BELLRINGER

When students enter the room, direct their attention to the assignment on the board:
Read pages 384–385 to learn how to find records.

TEACH

Most databases provide a Find command. The Find command is typically used to find and display a character string. Matching records are usually displayed only once and not saved for later use.

In Your Journal

Ask students to make a list of fields that would be required for a database about state capitals. They can compare their list to the database they will use in Project 119.

Find Records

18.6

Goals
- Find records in a database
- Create a header
- Create a footer

FINDING RECORDS IN A DATABASE

You can quickly find and display a record or group of records from your database by using the find feature. Using a **search** or **find** request you will state exactly which text or numbers you want the database to find. Only those records containing that text or numbers will be found and displayed. The other records are temporarily hidden from view, but they have not disappeared from the original database.

The database for this project includes fields for States, Admitted, Population, and Capital. In your first find request, you will search for states admitted to the Union in 1788. After the records that match the find request are displayed, you will use a feature called *show all records* to redisplay any records that were hidden.

Headers and footers include information helpful to the reader when database information is printed. A **header** is information that is printed at the top of each page. A header might contain the name of the person who created the database, a name describing the records displayed as a result of using the find feature, or the name of the database. A **footer** is information that is printed at the bottom of each page. A footer might contain a date, a page number or other related information. In Project 119, you will also add a header and footer to the database.

In Your Journal

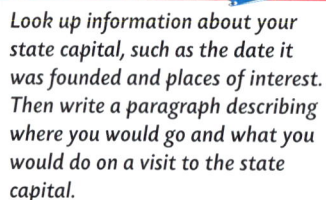

Look up information about your state capital, such as the date it was founded and places of interest. Then write a paragraph describing where you would go and what you would do on a visit to the state capital.

384 Section 18 Database Basics

RESOURCES

- Lesson Plan: LP99
  Multicultural Timing: MT21
- CD-ROM: Reference Guide
- Software: Research Files

interNET CONNECTION

Most states have Web pages that provide a variety of information about the state. Have students search for information about their state.

Study the illustration before beginning your work. Your printed database may look slightly different than the one shown.

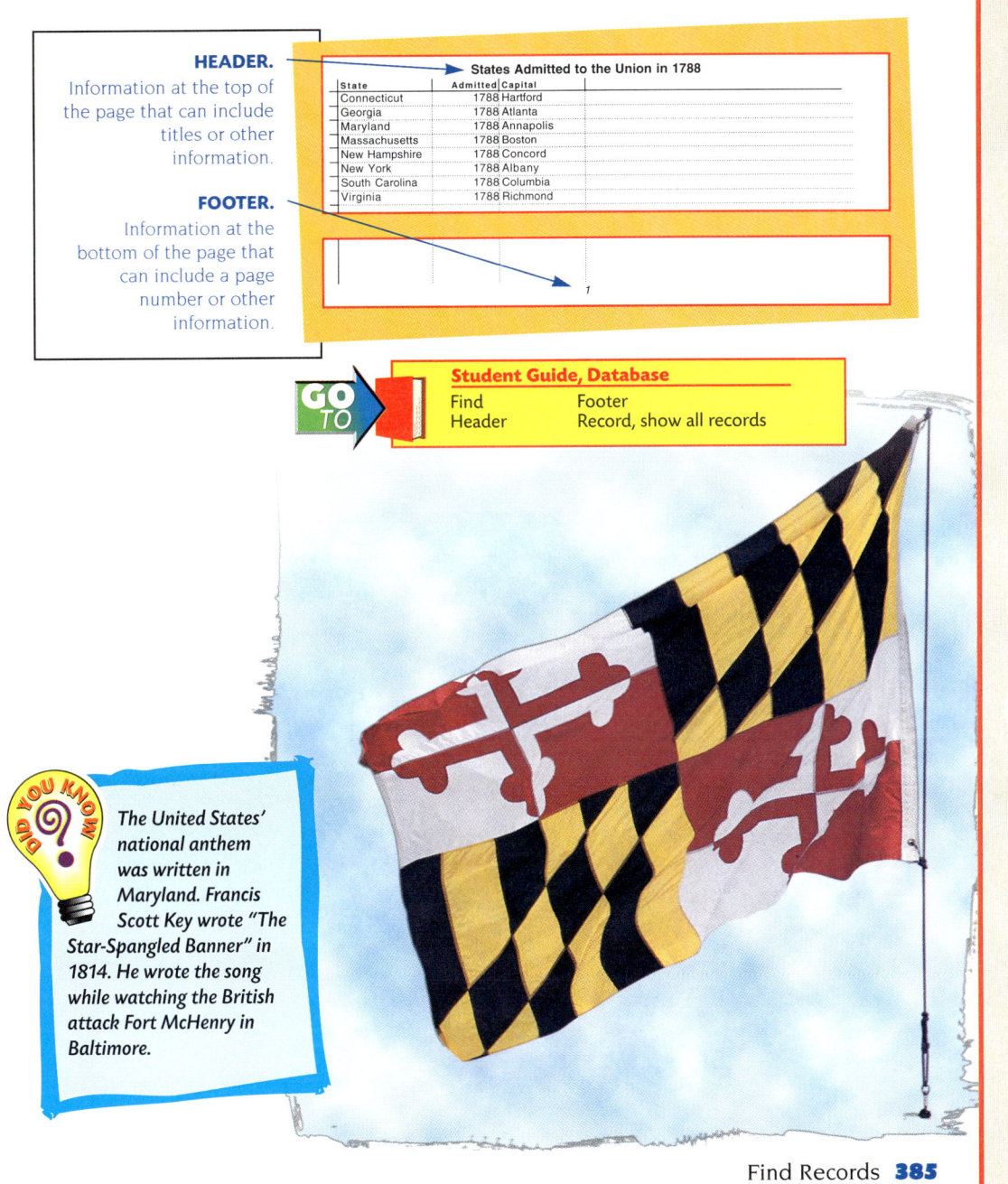

HEADER. Information at the top of the page that can include titles or other information.

FOOTER. Information at the bottom of the page that can include a page number or other information.

States Admitted to the Union in 1788

State	Admitted	Capital
Connecticut	1788	Hartford
Georgia	1788	Atlanta
Maryland	1788	Annapolis
Massachusetts	1788	Boston
New Hampshire	1788	Concord
New York	1788	Albany
South Carolina	1788	Columbia
Virginia	1788	Richmond

GO TO **Student Guide, Database**
Find   Footer
Header Record, show all records

DID YOU KNOW? The United States' national anthem was written in Maryland. Francis Scott Key wrote "The Star-Spangled Banner" in 1814. He wrote the song while watching the British attack Fort McHenry in Baltimore.

Find Records

Find Records

TEACH
Remind students that headers and footers in a database are similar to those in a word processor.

ASSESS
To assess students' understanding, ask them to explain how to use the find or search command.

CLOSE
Have students find records in a database as described in Project 119.

DID YOU KNOW? Because "The Star-Spangled Banner" is so difficult for most people to sing, there has been a push to make "America, the Beautiful" the United States' national anthem.

GO TO Refer students to the appropriate section of the Student Guide.

Project 119
Find Records in a Database

PRACTICE—LEVEL 1

Purpose
Practice finding records in a database.

Time
Thirty minutes.

Preparation
Make sure the database software is available and that students have their data disks. Make sure the printers are ready.

Teaching Tip
Observe students as they search the database. Students who finish early should repeat the project, this time searching for different information.

Trouble Shooting
Provide individual help to students who are having difficulty with the header and footer features.

Wrap Up
If this is the last project for this class period, ask students to return computers and furniture to the appropriate conditions.

In Your Journal
Ask students to find the state flag, bird, motto, song, tree, and flower for the state in which they live.

Project 119
Social Studies Connection
FIND RECORDS IN A DATABASE

In this project you will find a group of related records in a database. You will also add a header and a footer to identify the printed information for these records. Follow the steps below.

1. Open the file DB119 on your data disk.
2. **Find** all the states that were admitted to the Union in 1788.
3. Add a **header** that will serve as the title for the results of using the find feature. Center and type *States Admitted to the Union in 1788* in the header.
4. Add a **footer** to the database that contains a centered page number.
5. Print the database in list view.
6. Follow the steps under **record, show all records** of Unit 6 in your Student Guide to redisplay all the records.
7. Save the database file as STDB119 on your data disk.

In Your Journal
Pick a state you would like to know more about. Then look up information about the state flag, bird, motto, song, tree, flower, and other information. Use the information to write a paragraph about the state.

386 Section 18 Database Basics

Social Studies Connection
To encourage interest in social studies, ask students to research the history behind their state's official bird and flower. Ask them to find out when and why the designations were made.

Project 120

FIND RECORDS IN A DATABASE

Practice using the features you learned in Project 119 to find records and add a header to a database. Refer to Project 119 as needed.

1. Open the file DB120 on your data disk.
2. Find and display all records with a Cubic Crystal System.
3. Add a header. Center and type *Minerals with Cubic Crystal Systems* in the header.
4. Print the results of the find request in list view.
5. Redisplay any hidden records using the record, show all records feature.
6. Save the file as STDB120 on your data disk.

DID YOU KNOW

You probably use minerals every day without realizing it. A mineral is a nonliving substance that has a definite volume and shape. The graphite in a pencil and rock salt are minerals. A crystal is a solid that is shaped in a repeating pattern. This crystal structure may or may not show up on the outside of a mineral.

Find Records **387**

Project 120
Find Records in a Database

ASSESS—LEVEL 2

Purpose
Assess skills by finding information in a database.

Time
Thirty minutes.

Preparation
Make sure the database software is available and that students have their data disks. Make sure the printers are ready.

Teaching Tip
Observe students as they sort the database. Students who finish early should repeat the project, this time sorting on different fields.

Trouble Shooting
Provide individual help to students who are having difficulty.

Wrap Up
If this is the last project for this class period, ask students to return computers and furniture to the appropriate conditions.

DID YOU KNOW

Zircon crystals dating back 4.276 billion years have been found in Western Australia.

Social Studies Connection

To generate interest in science, ask students to find information about the Mineral Management Service (MMS), which assesses the nature, extent, and value of minerals on the outer continental shelf.

Project 121
Building Your Portfolio

ASSESS—LEVEL 2

Purpose
Assess skills by creating, sorting, and printing a database.

Time
Class period.

Preparation
Students should come to class prepared with the information they want to use to create their database. Make sure the database software is available and that students have their data disks. Make sure the printers are ready.

Teaching Tip
Observe students as they complete the assignment.

Trouble Shooting
Provide individual help to students who are having difficulty with database features.

Wrap Up
Have students review their work using **Check Your Understanding.** Students' answers will vary.

If this is the last project for this class period, ask students to return computers and furniture to the appropriate conditions.

Project 121
Building Your Portfolio

In this portfolio project, you will review the database features you learned in Section 18. You will create an original database, sort the records, and add a header and footer to the database. You will also want to make sure that all information in each field is fully visible by adjusting field sizes as needed. If you need to review any of the software features, refer to previous projects as often as needed.

NOW TRY THIS

1. Open a new database.
2. Use any information related to technology for the records in your database. You might include information you have acquired from the Internet, information related to computers or software that you would like to organize, communication information including your friends' phone numbers and/or email addresses, and so on.
3. Create at least three fields in your database.
4. Add information in at least five records to your database.
5. Save the database file as STDB121 on your data disk.
6. Add a header that includes a name describing the information your database contains.
7. Add a footer that contains a centered page number.
8. Adjust the field sizes to ensure that all information in each field is visible.
9. Determine in what order the fields in your database should be sorted to be most useful. Then sort the records.
10. Save your database file again.
11. Print all the sorted records in list view.

✓ Check Your Understanding

1. Did you design your database with the right types of fields for the information in the records?
2. Did you add the header and footer?
3. Did you sort the records before you printed your database in list view?

388 Section 18 Database Basics

Technology Connection

To encourage interest in technology, ask students to bring a current computer magazine to class. They can use the advertisements in the magazine to build a database about hardware products and vendors, software products and developers, and so on.

interNET CONNECTION

Many hardware and software companies have Web sites that provide information about their products. Ask students to find the site for a hardware or software company and report their findings.

Enhanced Databases and Reports

SECTION 19

Focus on Database

Databases allow you to arrange, format, and share information in various ways. You can create a database report to show selected information from your database. You can enhance the appearance of forms using pictures and font styles. You can also bring information into your database from another program such as a spreadsheet. In this section, you will learn to enhance databases, create reports, and integrate data among programs.

OBJECTIVES

- Modify the structure of a database.
- Create a saved search.
- Modify forms by inserting objects and reformatting.
- Create reports with key features.
- Create original databases using stationery and templates.
- Integrate information from other programs into a database.
- Integrate information from a database into other programs.

Words To Know

alignment	formula field	saved search
clip art	integration	structure
column layout	number field	template
draw	picture	text field
drawing	report	

Section 19 Enhanced Databases and Reports **389**

Career Exploration Activities: Marine Science

Ask students to research careers in Marine Science using references such as the *Occupational Outlook Handbook*, *Occupational Outlook Quarterly* and *Dictionary of Occupational Titles*. Have them write a paragraph including the job title, educational requirements, and average salary.

Ask them to discuss ways databases might prove useful for the position they have chosen. Examples might include using a database to keep track of endangered species or to track sources of funding for projects.

Section 19 Enhanced Databases and Reports

SECTION OVERVIEW

This section introduces students to more advanced features of databases, such as changing the database structure, including formulas in fields, enhancing forms, and generating reports. In this section, students begin to see the true power of a database.

CONTENT FOCUS

Database Structure
Formula Field
Search a Database
Enhance a Form
Create a Report
Database Template
Database Integration

CURRICULUM FOCUS

Language Arts
Math
Science
Social Studies
Technology

OPENING ACTIVITY

Ask students to think about the telephone directory. In today's environment, wouldn't it be nice to include an e-mail address for those individuals who wish to list them? To do this, an extra field must be added to the database. When new fields are added or deleted, the structure of the database is modified. Ask students to review one or more of the databases that were created in the previous section and make suggestions for modifications (either additions to or deletions from the database).

389

19.1 Database Structure

FOCUS
Change field types. Delete fields.

BELLRINGER
Have students read page 390.

TEACH
Making changes to the database structure is one advantage of electronic databases. Demonstrate to students how fields can be added or deleted in a matter of seconds.

ASSESS
To assess students' understanding, have them describe the process of changing the database structure.

CLOSE
Have students change a database structure as described in Project 122.

GO TO: Refer students to the appropriate section of the Student Guide.

In Your Journal
Ask students to describe how they think information about fruits and vegetables is monitored in a grocery store. Large stores probably use an electronic cash register to automatically keep track of how many of each item is sold. Smaller stores may use manual methods.

390

19.1 Database Structure

Goals
- Change field types
- Delete fields

CHANGING THE DATABASE STRUCTURE

The way your database is set up (the field names and field types it includes) is called the database structure. As you work with a database, there will be times when you need to add new information or change a field name or field type. When changing fields types, it is important to read the messages carefully that appear on the screen. Some changes of field types may cause data you have entered in that field to be lost. Other changes will not cause any problems with data already in that field.

Before changing the structure of your database in any way, always save your database. It is also a good idea to create a back-up copy of your database just in case a change made to the structure loses valuable information.

In Your Journal
Pretend you work as a stocker in a grocery store. In your journal, make a list of fruits and vegetables to be sorted in the produce department. Sort the items according to color.

GO TO: Student Guide, Database
Field, add

390   Section 19   Enhanced Databases and Reports

RESOURCES
- Lesson Plan: LP101
- Multicultural Timing: MT22
- CD-ROM: Reference Guide
- Software: Research Files

CULTURAL KALEIDOSCOPE
The famous artist Paul Cézanne produced major works of art that focused on fruit. Paintings of this nature are called still lifes.

Project 122

CHANGE THE DATABASE STRUCTURE

In this lesson you will change the database structure by changing field types, adding new fields, and changing the names of existing fields. Follow the steps below.

1. Open the file DB122 on your data disk.
2. Change the field name for Name 1 to *First Name*.
3. Change the field name for Name 2 to *Last Name*.
4. Change the field name for Worked to *Hours Worked*.
5. Resize the fields as needed to display all information in the fields.
6. Save the file as STDB122 on your data disk.
7. Change the field type and format of the field Hourly Wage to number. Choose a currency format with the comma separators and two decimal places.
8. Change the field type and format of the field Hours Worked to number. Choose a general format with comma separators and no decimal places.
9. Follow the steps under **field, add** in Unit 6 in your Student Guide to add a field named *Job Title*.
10. Type the following information in the Job Title field for each of the records.

Last Name	Job Title
Greene	Clerk
Johnson	Cashier
Tapier	Stocker
Harrison	Clerk
Chang	Cashier

11. Sort the records based on two fields in this order: Hourly Wage, ascending order; and then by Last Name, ascending order.
12. Print the sorted database in the view where the numbers are displayed in correct format.
13. Save the database file again.

Project 122 Change the Database Structure

PRACTICE—LEVEL 1

Purpose
Practice changing the database structure.

Time
Class period.

Preparation
Make sure the database software is available and that students have their data disks. Make sure the printers are ready.

Teaching Tip
Observe students as they complete the assignment.

Trouble Shooting
Provide individual help to students who are having difficulty changing the database structure.

Wrap Up
If this is the last project for this class period, ask students to return computers and furniture to the appropriate conditions.

To generate interest in math, ask students to research wages for typical after-school jobs, such as babysitting, lawn care, and newspaper delivery.

19.2 Formula Field

FOCUS
Create formula fields.

BELLRINGER
When students enter the room, direct their attention to the assignment on the board:
   Read page 392 and study the illustration to learn about formula fields.

TEACH
As with spreadsheets, databases can include fields with formulas to automatically perform calculations. Explain that field names may be used in database formulas similar to the way cell references may be used in spreadsheet formulas.
   Show students how to enter a formula field with their database.

ASSESS
Have students write a sample formula field.

CLOSE
Have students change a database structure and insert a formula field as described in Project 123.

Refer students to the appropriate section of the Student Guide.

19.2 Formula Field

Goal
- Create formula fields

USING FORMULA FIELDS

A field that performs a calculation is called a **formula field**. The formula used in a formula field is very similar to formulas you have used many times in your math classes. For example, in this project you will create a formula to calculate the total wages earned in a year. The field for the number of hours will be multiplied by the field for the hourly rate of pay. Both of these fields were previously defined as number types. An **operator** is a symbol used in a formula to define the action to be performed. You will use operators such as an * for multiplication and a / for division. Usually, the name of a numeric field is used to represent an actual number in the formula. In this way, you do not have to type in individual numbers for each record. This is where the power of the database formula field makes your job easy.

Study the illustration below before you begin your work. Your printed database may look slightly different than the one shown.

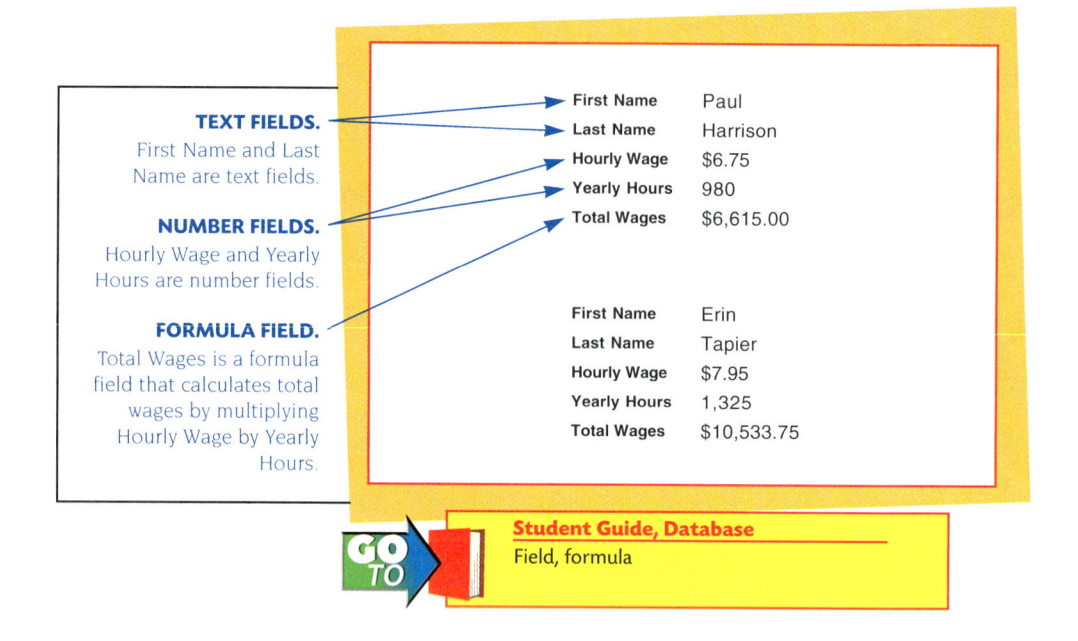

TEXT FIELDS. First Name and Last Name are text fields.

NUMBER FIELDS. Hourly Wage and Yearly Hours are number fields.

FORMULA FIELD. Total Wages is a formula field that calculates total wages by multiplying Hourly Wage by Yearly Hours.

First Name	Paul
Last Name	Harrison
Hourly Wage	$6.75
Yearly Hours	980
Total Wages	$6,615.00

First Name	Erin
Last Name	Tapier
Hourly Wage	$7.95
Yearly Hours	1,325
Total Wages	$10,533.75

Student Guide, Database
Field, formula

392 Section 19 Enhanced Databases and Reports

RESOURCES
Lesson Plan: LP101
Supplemental Project: SP20
Transparency Master: TM42

CD-ROM: Reference Guide

Software: Research Files

Project 123

CHANGE THE STRUCTURE OF A DATABASE

In this project, you will review the features learned in Project 122 by making additional changes to the database. You will also add a formula field.

1. Open the file DB123 on your data disk.
2. Follow the steps under **field, delete** in Unit 6 in your Student Guide to delete the Soc Sec No and the Job Title fields.
3. Change the name of the Hours Worked field to *Yearly Hours*.
4. Follow the steps under **field, formula** of Unit 6 in your Student Guide to add a formula field named Total Wages at the end of the database.
5. Create a formula that multiplies Hourly Wage times Yearly Hours. As a check to ensure that your formula was correct, look at Susan Johnson's Total Wages. Her Total Wages should be $9,250.
6. If your software does not format your numbers automatically, format the Total Wages field for currency with comma separators and 2 decimal places.
7. Save the database file as STDB123 on your data disk.
8. If necessary, change views until you find a view where all the numbers are shown in the correct format.
9. Print the database in this view.

Formula Field **393**

Project 123
Change the Structure of a Database

PRACTICE—LEVEL 1

Purpose
Practice inserting a formula field.

Time
Thirty minutes.

Preparation
Make sure the database software is available and that students have their data disks. Make sure the printers are ready.

Teaching Tip
Observe students as they complete the assignment. Make sure they create a formula field; they may be tempted to just enter the results of the calculation in the field. Students who finish early should repeat the assignment.

Trouble Shooting
Provide individual help to students who are having difficulty making changes and adding the formula field.

Wrap Up
If this is the last project for this class period, ask students to return computers and furniture to the appropriate conditions.

Math Connection: To encourage interest in math, ask students to research the starting wage for several different types of jobs: fast-food restaurant employee, retail clerk, and grocery bagger. Ask them to calculate how much money could be earned in each job if the employee worked five hours per week. What about seven hours per week?

CULTURAL KALEIDOSCOPE: Many countries do not enjoy the high standard of living that we enjoy in the United States. Jobs for which we expect to be paid several dollars per hour are often undertaken by employees in other countries for just dollars a day. Ask students to research wage rates in other countries for the jobs identified in the Math Connection box.

393

Project 124
Change the Structure of a Database

ASSESS—LEVEL 2

Purpose
Assess skills by changing the structure of a database.

Time
Fifteen minutes.

Preparation
Make sure the database software is available and that students have their data disks. Make sure the printers are ready.

Teaching Tip
Observe students as they complete the assignment. Make sure they create a formula field; they may be tempted to just enter the results of the calculation in the field. Students who finish early should repeat the assignment.

Trouble Shooting
Provide individual help to students who are having difficulty.

Wrap Up
If this is the last project for this class period, ask students to return computers and furniture to the appropriate conditions.

394

Project 124

CHANGE THE STRUCTURE OF A DATABASE

Review the features you learned in Projects 122 and 123 by changing the structure of a database and creating a formula field.

1. Open the file DB124 on your data disk.
2. Check to be sure that all fields are the correct field type for the information they contain.
3. Add a formula field named *Inventory Value* as the last field in each record in your database. Enter a formula that multiplies Value times In Inventory.
4. If your software does not format your numbers automatically, format the Inventory Value field for currency with comma separators and 2 decimal places.
5. Adjust field sizes as needed to correctly display all information.
6. Sort the database to show the software in alphabetic order.
7. Save the database file as STDB124 on your data disk.
8. Print the database in a view that shows numbers correctly formatted.

394 Section 19 Enhanced Databases and Reports

Technology Connection

To generate interest in technology, ask students to visit a local computer store. Ask them to make a note of at least five different items stocked in the store. For each item, students should note the item description, price, and approximate quantity. Ask them how this information might be stored in a database. Ask them to write the formula that could be used to calculate the inventory value.

19.3 Search a Database

SEARCHING A DATABASE

In earlier projects when you used the find feature, the results of the find were not saved. As soon as you closed the database or used the show all records feature, the results of the find request were gone. In this project, you will learn how to search a database and save the search results as a part of the database file. This process is called a **saved search**. Saved searches remain as a part of the database until they are deleted. You can view saved searches anytime the database is open.

Study the illustration below before you begin your work. Your printed saved search results may look slightly different than the one shown.

Goals
- Create a saved search
- Sort search results
- Print search results

SAVED SEARCH. Results of the saved search named Highest Mountains displaying mountains equal to or greater than 20,000 feet in elevation.

Mountain	Country	World Location	Elevation
Mt. McKinley	USA	North America	20000
Mt. Aconcaqua	Chile	Latin America	22834
Mt. Chimborazo	Ecuador	Latin America	20561

CULTURAL KALEIDOSCOPE

Ecuador got its name from the Spanish word for equator, *which runs through Ecuador. The equator is an imaginary line that circles the earth midway between the North and South Poles. Quito, the capital of Ecuador, lies almost exactly on the equator.*

GO TO Student Guide, Database — Saved search

RESOURCES
- Lesson Plan: LP102
- Multicultural Timing: MT23
- CD-ROM: Reference Guide
- Software: Research Files

CULTURAL KALEIDOSCOPE

There is a wide range of climates in Ecuador due to differing regional elevations. The Sierra region averages annual temperatures between 45° and 78°F (7° to 21°C); the Costa region, about 78°F (26°C); the Oriente region, about 100°F (37.8°C); and Quito, about 55°F (12.8°C).

19.3 Search a Database

FOCUS
Create a saved search. Sort search results. Print search results.

BELLRINGER
When students enter the room, direct their attention to the assignment on the board:
Read page 395 and review the illustration to learn more about a saved search.

TEACH
Some databases refer to a saved search as a query. Show students how this feature works with their database. Ask students to come up with advantages to saving their searches.

ASSESS
Have students define the term *saved search*.

CLOSE
Have students create a saved search as described in Project 125.

GO TO *Refer students to the appropriate section of the Student Guide.*

Project 125
Search a Database

PRACTICE—LEVEL 1

Purpose
Practice creating saved searches and printing the results.

Time
Thirty minutes.

Preparation
Make sure the database software is available and that students have their data disks. Make sure the printers are ready.

Teaching Tip
Observe students as they complete the assignment. Students who finish early should repeat the assignment.

Trouble Shooting
Provide individual help to students who are having difficulty creating a saved search.

Wrap Up
If this is the last project for this class period, ask students to return computers and furniture to the appropriate conditions.

DID YOU KNOW — The highest mountain in the contiguous 48 states is Mt. Whitney. Located in California, its highest point is 14,494 feet.

Project 125
SEARCH A DATABASE

In this project, you will create three different saved searches and print the search results. Follow the steps below.

1. Open the file DB125 on your data disk.
2. Using the find feature, find all the mountains located in North America.
3. Redisplay all records by using the record, show all records feature.
4. Create a **saved search** named *Highest Mountains*. Search for all elevations equal to or greater than 20,000 feet.
5. Print the search results in list view.
6. Redisplay all records by using the record, show all records feature.
7. Create a saved search named *Lower Than 3 Miles*. Search for all elevations less than 15,780 feet.
8. Print the search results in list view.
9. Redisplay all records by using the record, show all records feature.
10. Create a saved search named *High European Mountains*. Search for all the mountains in Europe with elevations greater than 12,000 feet.
11. Print the search results in list view.
12. Redisplay all records by using the record, show all records feature.
13. Save this file as STDB125 on your data disk.

DID YOU KNOW — Mt. McKinley is the highest mountain in North America. The mountain was named for William McKinley, the twenty-fifth President of the United States. Another name for Mt. McKinley is Denali. This word comes from the Athabaskan Indians in Alaska and means "The Great One."

396 Section 19 Enhanced Databases and Reports

Social Studies Connection
To generate interest in social studies, ask students to research the people who have successfully climbed Mt. McKinley or one of the other mountains listed in the database for this project.

interNET CONNECTION
For more information on climbing (including indoor climbing for those of us who are a bit less bold!), take a look at this Web site:
http://www.cmc.org/cmc/rocklist.html

Project 126

SEARCH A DATABASE

The Student Council in your school wants a list of all the students in the district who are in the 8th grade whose GPA is 3.0 (B) or better. Once they find such a group, they are going to begin a tutoring program in which these students can help other students after school. In this project, you will create a saved search to find this information. You will then sort the results of the saved search to show the information first in numeric order by GPA, then in alphabetic order by Last Name, and finally by First Name. Follow the steps below.

1. Open file DB126 on your data disk.
2. Create a saved search named *Potential New Tutors*.
3. Select those students with a GPA of 3.0 or higher.
4. Sort the results of the search first by GPA in descending (highest to lowest) order, then by Last Name in ascending order, and finally by First Name in ascending order.
5. Print the results of this sorted search in list view.
6. Redisplay all records by using the show all records feature.
7. Save this file as STDB126 on your data disk.
8. Create a saved search named *Honors Tutors*.
9. Select only those students with a GPA greater than 3.5 who are seniors.
10. Sort by Last Name in ascending order; then by First Name in ascending order.
11. Save this file again.
12. Print the sorted results of this search in list view.

Search a Database **397**

Project 126
Search a Database

APPLY—LEVEL 1

Purpose
Apply database skills by searching a database.

Time
Class period.

Preparation
Make sure the database software is available and that students have their data disks. Make sure the printers are ready.

Teaching Tip
Observe students as they complete the assignment. Students who finish early should repeat the assignment.

Trouble Shooting
Provide individual help to students who are having difficulty creating a saved search.

Wrap Up
If this is the last project for this class period, ask students to return computers and furniture to the appropriate conditions.

397

Project 127
Search a Database

ASSESS—LEVEL 2

Purpose
Assess database skills by creating a database with a formula field.

Time
Class period.

Preparation
Students should prepare a list of the information they want to include in their database. Make sure the database software is available and that students have their data disks. Make sure the printers are ready.

Teaching Tip
Observe students as they complete the assignment. Students who finish early should repeat the assignment.

Trouble Shooting
Provide individual help to students who are having difficulty with formula fields and saved searches.

Wrap Up
Have students review their work using **Check Your Understanding.** Students' answers will vary.

If this is the last project for this class period, ask students to return computers and furniture to the appropriate conditions.

Project 127

SEARCH A DATABASE

In this project, you create an original database with formula fields and saved searches. Refer to previous projects as often as needed.

1. Create a database to keep an equipment inventory. This equipment could be:
   - The computers, printers, and other input devices in your classroom
   - The computer games you have at home
   - Another computer-related database of your choice
2. Include at least two number fields in your database. These number fields could be:
   - A count of the number of items
   - The price of the software
   - The amount of storage space or memory required by the software
   - The amount of memory available on the computer
3. Create a formula field in your database. Be sure to format it correctly for the type of information displayed.
4. Save this file as STDB127 on your data disk.
5. Sort your database in ascending alphabetic or numeric order choosing the order in which to sort the fields.
6. Create a saved search choosing an appropriate name. Base the search on at least two fields. Remember that you can use the search operators such as greater than or less than in creating your search.
7. Save the file again.
8. Print the results of this search in list view.
9. Redisplay all records by using the show all records feature.
10. Save the file again.

✓ Check Your Understanding

1. Did you sort the records in alphabetic or numeric order?
2. Did you create a saved search using at least two fields?

398 Section 19 Enhanced Databases and Reports

To generate interest in technology, ask students to complete an inventory of the hardware and software in the school's computer lab.

Project 128
Building Your Portfolio

In this portfolio project, you will review database features learned in Projects 122 to 127. You will change the structure of a database by editing field names and types and adding a formula field. You will then sort the information and search the database for a group of records. If you need to review any software features, refer to previous projects as often as needed.

NOW TRY THIS

1. Open the file DB128 on your data disk.
2. In list view, enter new, more descriptive names for Field 1 and Field 2.
3. Add a formula field named *Total Sales* to create a formula that calculates Total Sales for the months listed.
4. Format the numbers in Total Sales correctly to match the other number fields.
5. Sort the records based on three fields in an order appropriate to the information they contain.
6. Create a saved search that selects a group of records, for example, all records for one state.
7. Add a centered header that contains a name describing the records displayed as a result of the search.
8. Create a footer that contains the page number.
9. Save the database file as STDB128 on your data disk.
10. Print the sorted search results in list view.

✓ Check Your Understanding

1. Did you rename fields so the name describes the content of the fields?
2. Did your formula perform the desired calculation correctly?
3. Did you sort the database before you created your saved search?

Project 128
Building Your Portfolio

ASSESS—LEVEL 2

Purpose
Assess database skills by changing a database structure, editing field names, adding a formula field, sorting the database, and searching for specific information.

Time
Class period.

Preparation
Make sure the database software is available and that students have their data disks. Make sure the printers are ready.

Teaching Tip
Observe students as they complete the assignment. Students who finish early should repeat the assignment.

Trouble Shooting
Provide individual help to students who are having difficulty.

Wrap Up
Have students review their work using **Check Your Understanding.** Students' answers will vary.

If this is the last project for this class period, ask students to return computers and furniture to the appropriate conditions.

19.4 Enhance a Form

FOCUS

Enhance a form with clip art and drawings. Change alignment, style, and text color of a field of entries.

BELLRINGER

Have students read page 400 to learn more about database forms.

TEACH

Demonstrate to students how easy it is to import a clip art image into a form. Once it has been imported into the form design, all of the records include the image. Show students that font and alignment changes are also easy to make, and that the skills they used to change fonts and alignment in the database and word processing units are also relevant with databases.

ASSESS

To assess students' understanding, have students describe how to change the appearance of a database form.

CLOSE

Have students enhance a form with clip art and drawings, as described in Project 129.

Refer students to the appropriate section of the Student Guide.

Enhance a Form

19.4

Goals
- Enhance a form with clip art and drawings
- Change alignment, style, and text color of a field of entries

ENHANCING A FORM

Any database form can be dramatically enhanced by adding a simple picture or drawing. Compare the list view and the form view of the database in the illustrations. Which view do you think is more appealing? The form view is usually preferred for:

- Browsing through records
- Viewing one record in more detail
- Entering information into one record at a time with all fields visible on the page

In this project you will add clip art and drawings to enhance a database form. Clip art is another name for a gallery of pictures. Most software programs come with their own clip art. If you are interested in learning more about adding pictures and drawings, read about these features and others in the Desktop Publishing unit. When you have completed this project, your final form should look similar to the one in the illustration.

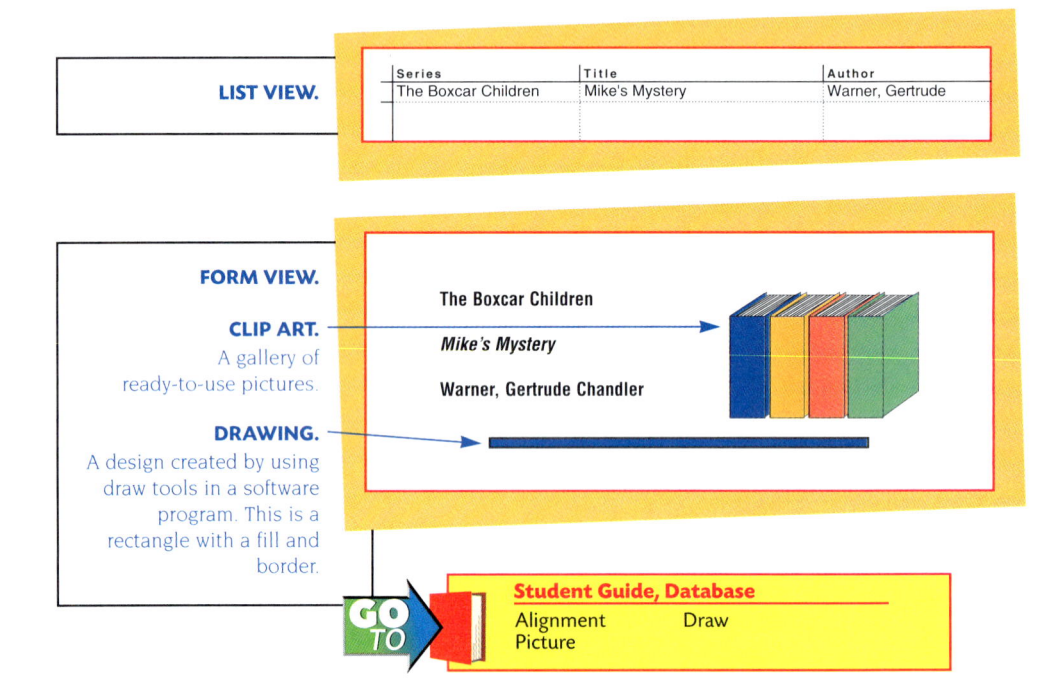

LIST VIEW.

Series	Title	Author
The Boxcar Children	Mike's Mystery	Warner, Gertrude

FORM VIEW.

CLIP ART. A gallery of ready-to-use pictures.

The Boxcar Children
Mike's Mystery
Warner, Gertrude Chandler

DRAWING. A design created by using draw tools in a software program. This is a rectangle with a fill and border.

GO TO *Student Guide, Database*
Alignment   Draw
Picture

400 Section 19 Enhanced Databases and Reports

RESOURCES

Lesson Plan: LP104
Transparency Master: TM43

CD-ROM: Reference Guide

Software: Research Files

Project 129

ENHANCE A FORM WITH CLIP ART AND DRAWINGS

Follow the steps below to enhance a form with clip art and drawings.

1. Open the file DB129 on your data disk.
2. Change to the form view that allows you to design a form.

   Note: Your software may have one view that is used to design a form and another view that is used to see and print the finished design. For more details, see your Student Guide, Unit 6, **view** and **window**.

3. Select, move, and resize the fields so they appear on the form as shown. Your positions do not have to be identical to the example shown here.

   | Series |
   | Title |
   | Author |

   Note: For help with selecting, moving and resizing, see your Student Guide, Unit 4, Desktop Publishing.

4. Adjust the field sizes so the information in the longest field entry is visible.
5. Change the **alignment** in all the fields to left.
6. Change the font for all fields to Arial 18 points bold. If your software has more than one Arial font, choose the one that fits best with your design.
7. Change the font style for the Title field to italic.
8. Add a **picture** of books, a notebook, or any picture related to the theme of the database.
9. **Draw** a rectangle under the fields and clip art as shown in the illustration.
10. Add a border and fill color that looks attractive with the clip art.

    Note: If you need help with adding a border and fill, see your Student Guide, Unit 4, Desktop Publishing.

11. Change the text color for all fields to a color that looks attractive with the picture and drawing.
12. Save your database file as STDB129 on your data disk.
13. Preview your document before printing and make any adjustments to the design as needed.
14. Print one record in form view.

Project 129
Enhance a Form

PRACTICE—LEVEL 1

Purpose
Practice enhancing a form with clip art and drawings.

Time
Class period.

Preparation
Make sure the database and clip art software are available and that students have their data disks. Make sure the printers are ready.

Teaching Tip
Observe students as they complete the assignment. Students who finish early should repeat the assignment.

Trouble Shooting
Provide individual help to students who are having difficulty with clip art.

Wrap Up
If this is the last project for this class period, ask students to return computers and furniture to the appropriate conditions.

Language Arts Connection

To generate interest in language arts, arrange a trip to the school or public library. Ask students to browse through the books and find five books that interest them. Ask students to set a goal to read a specified number of the books in a certain time period. For example, one student might agree to read one book within two weeks, while another student might decide to read all five books by the end of the quarter. Students can build a database of the books they have read.

Project 130
Enhance a Form

APPLY—LEVEL 1

Purpose
Apply database skills by enhancing a form with clip art and drawings.

Time
Class period.

Preparation
Make sure the database and clip art software are available and that students have their data disks. Make sure the printers are ready.

Teaching Tip
Observe students as they complete the assignment. Students who finish early should repeat the assignment.

Trouble Shooting
Provide individual help to students who are having difficulty with clip art.

Wrap Up
If this is the last project for this class period, ask students to return computers and furniture to the appropriate conditions.

Language Arts Connection

Project 130

ENHANCE A FORM WITH CLIP ART AND DRAWINGS

In this project, you will practice using the features you learned in Project 129 to enhance another form. Refer to Project 129 and the illustration as often as needed.

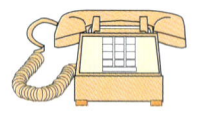

1. Open the file DB130 on your data disk.
2. Change to the form view that allows you to modify the form.

   Note: Your software may have one view that is used to design a form and another view that is used to see and print the finished design. For more details, see your Student Guide, Unit 6, **view** and **window**.

3. Select, move, and resize the fields so they appear on the form as shown in the illustration. Your positions do not have to be identical to the example shown here.

   Note: For help with selecting, moving and resizing, see your Student Guide, Unit 4, Desktop Publishing.

4. Adjust the field sizes so the information in the longest field entry is visible.
5. Change the alignment in all the fields to right or left as you wish.

(continued on next page)

402 Section 19 Enhanced Databases and Reports

Language Arts Connection

To generate interest in language arts, ask students to add clip art to the form they used with the "Books Read" database created in the Language Arts Connection exercise in Project 129.

Project 130 (continued)

Enhance a Form

6. Change the font for the Last Name and First Name fields to Arial 24 points bold. If your software has more than one Arial font, choose the one that fits best with your design.
7. Change the font for Phone and Email Address fields to Arial 14 points. If your software has more than one Arial font, choose the one that fits best with your design.
8. Add a picture of a telephone, or any picture related to the theme of the database.
9. Draw a rounded rectangle under the picture as shown in the illustration.
10. Add a border and fill color that looks attractive with the clip art.

    Note: If you need help with adding a border and fill, see your Student Guide, Unit 4, Desktop Publishing.

11. Change the text color for all fields to a color that looks attractive with the picture and drawing.
12. Save your database file as STDB130 on your data disk.
13. Preview your document before printing and make any adjustments to the design as needed.
14. Print one record in form view.

In Your Journal

If you could design a piece of clip art to use as a personal logo, what would it be? Brainstorm a list of ideas. Then use your software to design the logo.

In Your Journal

Work with students to build a bulletin board or poster using their personal logos.

Enhance a Form **403**

interNET CONNECTION

Some books are available on-line. For an example, check this Web site:

http://www.literature.org/Works/

While many of the classics listed here may not be suitable for the students in your class, you might find one or two works that students will enjoy. Ask them to visit the site. Ask them to discuss whether they prefer reading books on-line or using the printed version.

403

Project 131
Enhance a Form

ASSESS—LEVEL 2

Purpose
Assess database skills by enhancing a form with clip art and drawings.

Time
Class period.

Preparation
Make sure the database and clip art software are available and that students have their data disks. Make sure the printers are ready.

Teaching Tip
Observe students as they complete the assignment. Students who finish early should repeat the assignment.

Trouble Shooting
Provide individual help to students who are having difficulty.

Wrap Up
Have students review their work using **Check Your Understanding.** Students' answers will vary.
   If this is the last project for this class period, ask students to return computers and furniture to the appropriate conditions.

DID YOU KNOW? The Moon has its high points, too. The highlands north of the Korolev Basin reach an elevation of 26,000 feet.

Project 131

Language Arts Connection

ENHANCE A FORM WITH CLIP ART AND DRAWINGS

In this project you will practice using the features you learned in Project 129 to enhance another form. This time, you will choose the layout of the fields on the form, the appearance of the fonts in the fields, and the pictures and drawings you want to add. The illustration below is just an example. Feel free to create whatever design you like. This is your opportunity to be creative. Refer to Project 129 as often as needed.

> Mt. Whitney
> USA
> North America
> 14,494

1. Open the file DB131 on your data disk.
2. Change to the form view that allows you to modify the form.
3. Change the field positions as you choose.
4. Adjust the field sizes and position to be sure all information is visible.
5. Change the fonts in the fields to different sizes, styles, and colors.
6. Change the alignment of at least one field.
7. Insert a picture and a drawing of your choice.
8. Save your database as STDB131 on your data disk.
9. Preview your document before printing and make any adjustments to the design as needed.
10. Print one record in form view with the record information visible.

✓ Check Your Understanding

1. Is all the information in the fields visible with the new form design?
2. Do the pictures and drawings you added enhance the appearance of the form?

404 Section 19 Enhanced Databases and Reports

Language Arts Connection

To generate interest in language arts, ask students to find more information about mountains. Help them build a Mountain Trivia game based on the information they find. The information might come from books, magazines, newsletters, or on-line sources.

19.5 Create a Report

Goals
- Create a report containing all records
- Create a report containing selected fields

CREATING A REPORT

Reports are used when you want to print information from the database in an organized, easily understandable format. The **report** may contain all the records and fields in the database or just selected records or fields. For example, a database of living organisms might contain many different kinds of fields. Your science teacher may ask you to print a report showing only the organism, kingdom, and classification fields for each record as shown in the illustration. When you create the report, you choose only the fields of information that are needed at that time.

Reports can be designed with different layouts in much the same way that a form can be designed. Fonts, text alignment, field sizes, and positions can be changed on a report. You can also add pictures and drawings to a report. However, you cannot change the content of a field or add a record when viewing a report. Reports only display information that has been entered into the database.

Reports are named when they are created. They are saved as part of the database file. Once a report is created, you can view it anytime the database file is open. Reports can be printed when you need that specific information. As you update and add records to your database, the report is also updated. For example, in our living organisms database, you might create the report when you have entered just a few records. When you enter additional records, the report will be updated to include the new information.

The illustration shows a simple report using a column format. The field information is displayed below the field names. This report looks similar to a list view but does not contain the grid lines. Study the illustration on page 406 before beginning your work. Your printed database may look slightly different than the one shown.

In Your Journal
Think of ways you and your classmates could use a database to help your community. You could make a database of recreation areas or parks. Contact the parks or recreation department to find out the names, addresses, and operating hours for these places. Then create a database with this information.

Create a Report **405**

19.5 Create a Report

FOCUS
Create a report containing all records. Create a report containing selected fields.

BELLRINGER
When students enter the room, direct their attention to the assignment on the board:
Read pages 405–406 to learn more about database reports.

TEACH
Point out to students that it is not always necessary or desirable to view all records (and all fields of those records) in a database. The Report feature of most database software allows the user to specify exactly what information should be included. Demonstrate how to use the Report feature of the database software the students are using.

In Your Journal
Assign each student or group of students to research individual facilities away from class. Then have students bring in their information and compile the database as a class.

RESOURCES
- Lesson Plan: LP106
- CD-ROM: Reference Guide
- Software: Research Files

405

Create a Report

TEACH

Show students the different types of report layouts available, such as column layouts and tabular layouts.

ASSESS

To assess students' understanding, have students describe how to create a database report.

CLOSE

Have students create a report, as described in Project 132.

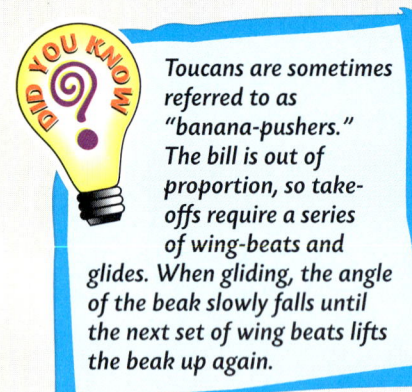

Refer students to the appropriate section of the Student Guide.

DID YOU KNOW
Toucans are sometimes referred to as "banana-pushers." The bill is out of proportion, so take-offs require a series of wing-beats and glides. When gliding, the angle of the beak slowly falls until the next set of wing beats lifts the beak up again.

COLUMN LAYOUT. Report displaying information in columns.

Organism	Kingdom	Classification
Blackberries	Plant	Division Anthophyta
Fairyslipper	Plant	Division Anthophyta
Liverwort	Plant	Division Bryophyta
Peninsula turtles	Animal	Phylum Chordata
Toucan	Animal	Phylum Chordata
Jellyfish	Animal	Phylum Cnidaria

DID YOU KNOW
Toucans are birds with large, colorful bills. Some scientists think toucans use their bills to attract mates. Others think the bright colors of the bill scare birds such as hawks. Toucans live in tropical forests in Central and South America.

Student Guide, Database
Report, create

406 Section 19 Enhanced Databases and Reports

RESOURCES

Lesson Plan: LP106
Multicultural Timing: MT24

CD-ROM: Reference Guide

Software: Research Files

interNET CONNECTION

The Science Learning Network is an educational and entertaining site:
http://www.sln.org/sln.html

Project 132

CREATE A REPORT

For this project, you will sort records in the database and create a simple report using a column format.

1. Open the file DB132 on your data disk.
2. Sort the database. Sort first by Classification in ascending order and then by Organism in ascending order.
3. Follow the steps under **report, create** in Unit 6 of your Student Guide to create a new report titled *Living Organisms*.
4. Add all the fields to the report in the order they appear in the database.
5. Resize fields as necessary on the report layout to ensure that all field information is visible.
6. Save the database as STDB132 on your data disk.
7. Print the report.

In Your Journal

List the names of plants, birds, and animals that are native to where you live. Using an encyclopedia, identify the classification for each organism. Then sort the information by classification and by organism.

Create a Report **407**

Project 132
Create a Report

PRACTICE—LEVEL 1

Purpose
Practice database skills by creating a report.

Time
Class period.

Preparation
Make sure the database software is available and that students have their data disks. Make sure the printers are ready.

Teaching Tip
Observe students as they complete the assignment. Students who finish early should repeat the assignment.

Trouble Shooting
Provide individual help to students who are having difficulty creating the report.

Wrap Up
If this is the last project for this class period, ask students to return computers and furniture to the appropriate conditions.

In Your Journal

Ask students to build an electronic database based on the information listed in their journal.

To encourage interest in science, ask students to design a report for the items they listed in their journal.

407

Project 133
Create a Report

ASSESS—LEVEL 2

Purpose
Assess database skills by creating a report.

Time
Thirty minutes.

Preparation
Make sure the database software is available and that students have their data disks. Make sure the printers are ready.

Teaching Tip
Observe students as they complete the assignment. Students who finish early should repeat the assignment.

Trouble Shooting
Provide individual help to students who are having difficulty creating a report.

Wrap Up
If this is the last project for this class period, ask students to return computers and furniture to the appropriate conditions.

Project 133
CREATE A REPORT

In this project, you will practice creating another report in column layout. First you will sort the database. Then you will select three fields for the report.

1. Open the file DB133 on your data disk.
2. Sort the database by Category in ascending order, then by Software in ascending order.
3. Create a new report titled *Computer Software Inventory*.
4. Add only the following fields to the report in this order: *Software*, *Category*, and *Value*.
5. Preview your report. Make any changes to the field sizes as needed to display all information.
6. Save the database file as STDB133.
7. Print the report.

408 Section 19 Enhanced Databases and Reports

Technology Connection

To generate interest in technology, have students research different software available in today's market. They should find information about two products in each of the following categories: word processing, database, spreadsheet, graphics, desktop publishing, and communications. For each product, ask students to find the following information: product name, category, price, hardware requirements, and vendor.

19.6 Database Template

USING A DATABASE TEMPLATE

As you have discovered, creating and designing a database takes some thought and planning. Because there are certain types of databases that many people use, software packages often include database templates. A template is a model document that may be used many times. A database template usually includes predefined fields and an attractive design.

An address book is an example of a template almost anyone could use. It usually includes fields for names, addresses, birthdays, anniversaries, and so on. Other common database templates include music and video catalogs and household inventories. Many templates are automated. They lead you step by step through the creation of the database.

Goals
- Create a database using a template
- Edit field entries
- Enter new data

19.6 Database Template

FOCUS
Create a database using a template. Edit field entries. Enter new data.

BELLRINGER
When students enter the room, direct their attention to the assignment on the board:
   Read pages 409–410 to learn more about database templates.

TEACH
By now, students should realize that there are several useful applications for a database—address book, CD collection information, home inventory, and so on. Database templates help provide a starting point for common applications. For example, a template for a CD database might include the fields most people want in this type of database, along with a nice form design and report layout. This way, the user only needs to enter the data from his or her CD collection rather than designing and building the database structure.

RESOURCES

Lesson Plan: LP107
Multicultural Timing: MT26
Transparency Master: TM44

CD-ROM: Reference Guide

Software: Research Files

Database Template

TEACH

Ask students to identify applications for which a database template might be useful. Choose one of the applications and ask students to work in teams to design (using pencil and paper) a template for that application.

ASSESS

To assess students' understanding, ask them to describe the uses for a database template.

CLOSE

Have students create a database with a template as described in Project 134.

Did You Know? Many software packages include professionally developed ready-to-use templates.

GO TO Refer students to the appropriate section of the Student Guide.

This illustration shows an address database created using a template. Your finished database may look different than the illustration.

TEMPLATE. A model document. This is an example of an address template.

FIELDS. Fields are created in the template automatically by the software.

GRAPHICS. Pictures and other enhancements are added to make the form attractive.

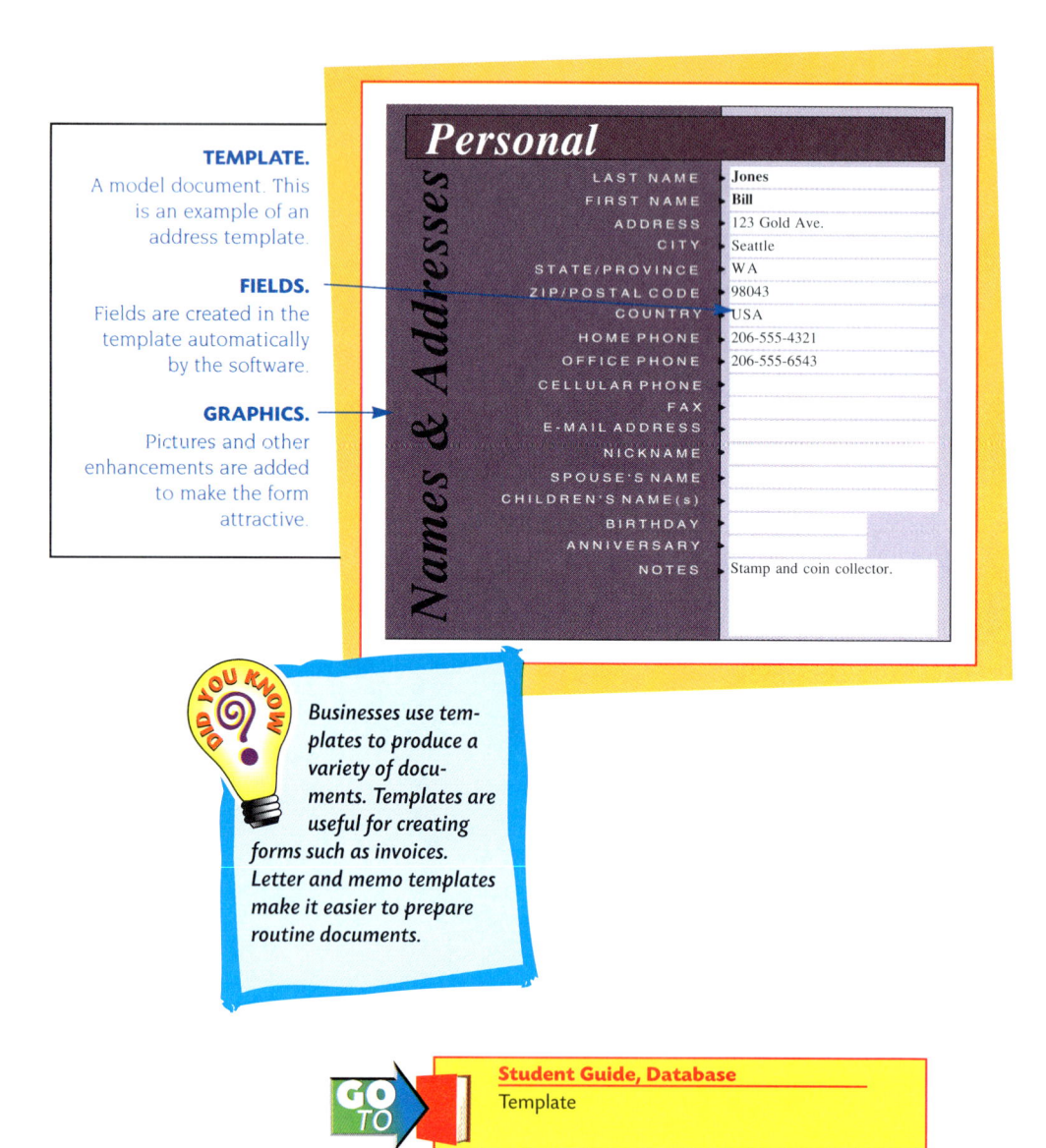

Personal

Names & Addresses

LAST NAME	Jones
FIRST NAME	Bill
ADDRESS	123 Gold Ave.
CITY	Seattle
STATE/PROVINCE	WA
ZIP/POSTAL CODE	98043
COUNTRY	USA
HOME PHONE	206-555-4321
OFFICE PHONE	206-555-6543
CELLULAR PHONE	
FAX	
E-MAIL ADDRESS	
NICKNAME	
SPOUSE'S NAME	
CHILDREN'S NAME(s)	
BIRTHDAY	
ANNIVERSARY	
NOTES	Stamp and coin collector.

Did You Know? Businesses use templates to produce a variety of documents. Templates are useful for creating forms such as invoices. Letter and memo templates make it easier to prepare routine documents.

GO TO Student Guide, Database Template

410 Section 19 Enhanced Databases and Reports

Project 134

CREATE A DATABASE WITH A TEMPLATE

Follow the steps below and in your Student Guide to create an address database using a template.

1. In your Student Guide, go to Unit 6, **template.** Find and read the help topics listed here to learn about this feature for your software.
2. Choose the template indicated in the Student Guide for this project and follow the steps in both the Student Guide and the software.
3. Once the completed database appears on your screen, enter information in the fields for a record for yourself and a record for one of your friends. If one or more of the fields do not apply to you, skip the field.
4. Save this database file as STDB134 on your data disk.
5. Print one record using the form created by the template.

Database Template

Project 134
Create a Database with a Template

PRACTICE—LEVEL 1

Purpose
Practice creating a database with a template.

Time
Thirty minutes.

Preparation
Students should come prepared with the data required to build the database. Make sure the database software is available and that students have their data disks. Make sure the printers are ready.

Teaching Tip
Observe students as they complete the assignment. Students who finish early should repeat the assignment.

Trouble Shooting
Provide individual help to students who are having difficulty with the database template.

Wrap Up
If this is the last project for this class period, ask students to return computers and furniture to the appropriate conditions.

To generate interest in technology, ask students to research the database templates available with their database software. They should find out how many templates are available, and for which applications they are used.

Project 135
Create a Database with a Template

ASSESS—LEVEL 2

Purpose
Assess database skills by creating a database with a template.

Time
Thirty minutes.

Preparation
Make sure the database software is available and that students have their data disks. Make sure the printers are ready.

Teaching Tip
Observe students as they complete the assignment. Students who finish early should repeat the assignment.

Trouble Shooting
Provide individual help to students who are having difficulty with the database template.

Wrap Up
If this is the last project for this class period, ask students to return computers and furniture to the appropriate conditions.

Software Publishing Corporation later merged with Allegro New Media, Inc.

Project 135
Technology Connection
CREATE A DATABASE WITH A TEMPLATE

In this project, you will use a template to create a database that will organize information about a videotape collection. As you enter information into the records, be sure the information is appropriate for that field. If a field does not apply to you, leave it blank. You may want to go back later and add this information.

1. Refer to your Student Guide, Unit 6, **template** for the template to select and the steps to follow to create this database.
2. Once the database form appears on your screen, enter the following information about video tapes:

	Record 1	Record 2	Record 3
Title:	E.T.	Toy Story	Mike Mulligan
Category:	Drama	Comedy	Children
Director/Artist:	Steven Spielberg	John Lasseter	Michael Sporn
Comments:	Science fiction	Great animation!	Cartoon

3. Save this database file as STDB135 on your data disk.
4. Print one record of this database using the form created by the template.

DID YOU KNOW
In 1980, John Page developed the first easy data-management system in his garage. His invention, called Personal Filing System, ran on Apple II computers. Along with two friends, Page tried to find a company to market the program. When that didn't work, the three formed their own company called Software Publishing Corporation. The company later became a multimillion dollar corporation.

Section 19 Enhanced Databases and Reports

Technology Connection
To generate interest in technology, ask students to find information about the products developed by Software Publishing Corporation. Students should investigate the product names, uses, prices, and other information they can find about the company.

interNET CONNECTION
Software Publishing Corporation's Web site address is:
http://www.spco.com/INDEX.HTM

Project 136
Building Your Portfolio

In this portfolio project, you will practice changing the structure of a database, enhancing a form, and creating a report. Refer to your Student Guide and previous projects as often as needed.

NOW TRY THIS

1. Open any database you have created in a previous project.
2. Add one field to the database and type appropriate information for each record into that field.
3. Save the database as STDB136 on your data disk.
4. Enhance the database form by adding a picture or drawing.
5. Change the font and type style in at least two fields.
6. Change the position of at least two fields on the form.
7. Print one record in form view.
8. Save your database again.
9. Sort the records based on one or two fields as appropriate.
10. Create a report that shows three or four fields for all records.
11. Make any needed format changes to the report to enhance its appearance.
12. Save your database again.
13. Print the report.

✓ Check Your Understanding

1. Did you enhance the form by the text and format changes you made?
2. Did you insert a drawing or picture that related to the subject of the information in the database?
3. Is all the information in the fields visible on the printed report?
4. Is the font large enough to read easily?

Project 136
Building Your Portfolio

ASSESS—LEVEL 2

Purpose
Assess database skills by changing the structure of a database, enhancing a form, and creating a report.

Time
Class period.

Preparation
Make sure the database and clip art software are available and that students have their data disks. Make sure the printers are ready.

Teaching Tip
Observe students as they complete the assignment. Students who finish early should repeat the assignment.

Trouble Shooting
Provide individual help to students who are having difficulty.

Wrap Up
Have students review their work using **Check Your Understanding.** Students' answers will vary.

If this is the last project for this class period, ask students to return computers and furniture to the appropriate conditions.

19.7 Database Integration

FOCUS

Integrate database records into a spreadsheet. Integrate spreadsheet data into a database. Integrate database records into a word processing document.

BELLRINGER

When students enter the room, direct their attention to the assignment on the board:

Read pages 414–417 to learn how to integrate data from one application to another.

TEACH

Data integration saves time and helps minimize the chances of making an error—because information does not need to be re-typed from one application to the next, there is less chance that inaccurate information will be generated.

Most applications share data in one of two ways:

1. *Copy and paste. Data in one application is copied and then pasted into the other application. If the data in the source application changes, it must be copied and pasted again in the destination application.*
2. *Linking. Data in one application is linked to a document in the other application. When the source data changes, the destination document is automatically updated. Not all applications support this type of data integration.*

Database Integration

19.7

Goals

- Integrate database records into a spreadsheet
- Integrate spreadsheet data into a database
- Integrate database records into a word processing document

INTEGRATING DATA AMONG PROGRAMS

The process of exchanging data among software applications is known as **integration.** Integration allows you to take advantage of the best features of each program. For example, the power of a database lies in its ability to sort and organize records. A spreadsheet is used to do lengthy calculations, create charts, and graphs, and answer "what if" types of questions. A word processor takes advantage of desktop publishing features to format documents easily and attractively. When you learn to combine the power of all programs, you are using the full power of your software package.

In these integration projects, you will learn to exchange data among software applications.

What data could you gather from looking at this photo?

414 Section 19 Enhanced Databases and Reports

RESOURCES

Lesson Plan: LP109
Multicultural Timing: MT26
Transparency Masters: TM45/,TM46

Transparencies 31 and 32

CD-ROM: Reference Guide

Software: Research Files

In the first integration project, you will move database information into a spreadsheet file and create a simple bar chart.

INTEGRATING DATA

From a database . . .

State	Population	Capital
AK	599000	Juneau
ND	635000	Bismarck
DE	700000	Dover
MT	839000	Helena
NB	1607000	Lincoln
OR	3032000	Salem
KY	3789000	Frankfort
AL	4187000	Montgomery
MN	4517000	St. Paul

to a spreadsheet . . .

	A	B	C
1	AK	599,000	Juneau
2	ND	635,000	Bismarck
3	DE	700,000	Dover
4	MT	839,000	Helena
5	NB	1,607,000	Lincoln
6	OR	3,032,000	Salem
7	KY	3,789,000	Frankfort
8	AL	4,187,000	Montgomery
9	MN	4,517,000	St. Paul
10			

to a chart.

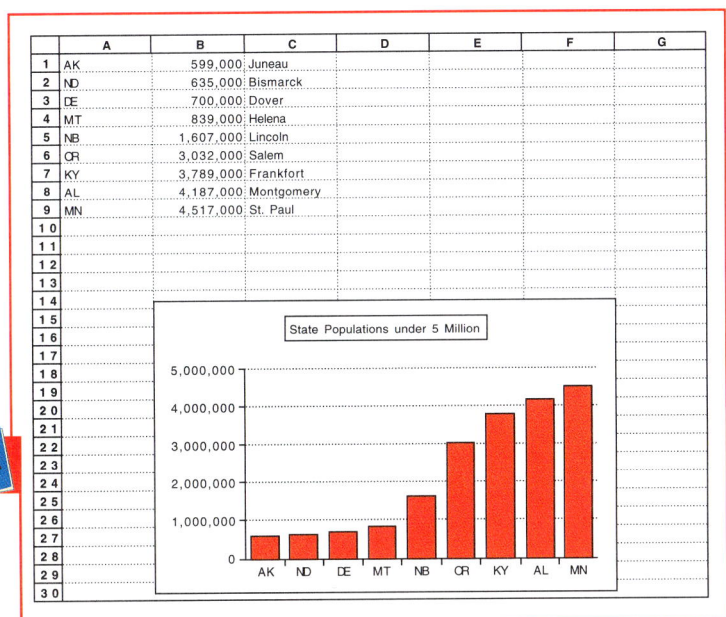

[Spreadsheet with bar chart titled "State Populations under 5 Million" showing populations of AK, ND, DE, MT, NB, OR, KY, AL, MN ranging from 0 to 5,000,000.]

In Your Journal

Identify the ten cities in your state that have the largest populations. List your findings in a database, a spreadsheet, and a chart.

Database Integration **415**

Database Integration

TEACH

When data is shared from a database to a spreadsheet, records become rows in the spreadsheet.

In Your Journal

Work with students to link the data from one application to another; make sure they do not re-type the information each time.

DID YOU KNOW

The U.S. city with the largest population is New York City, with more than 18,000,000 residents.

CULTURAL KALEIDOSCOPE

With more than 26,500,000 residents, Tokyo, Japan, is the most populous city in the world. The most populous country is China, which boasts more than 1,206,600,000 residents. China's population today is larger than the population of the entire world was 150 years ago.

415

Database Integration

TEACH

Once data has been integrated into a different application, it can be edited from within that application.

In the second project, you will learn to copy information from a spreadsheet in a database. Once the information is in the database, you can continue to add new records, edit those already in the database, prepare reports, create searches, and use all the other database features you have learned.

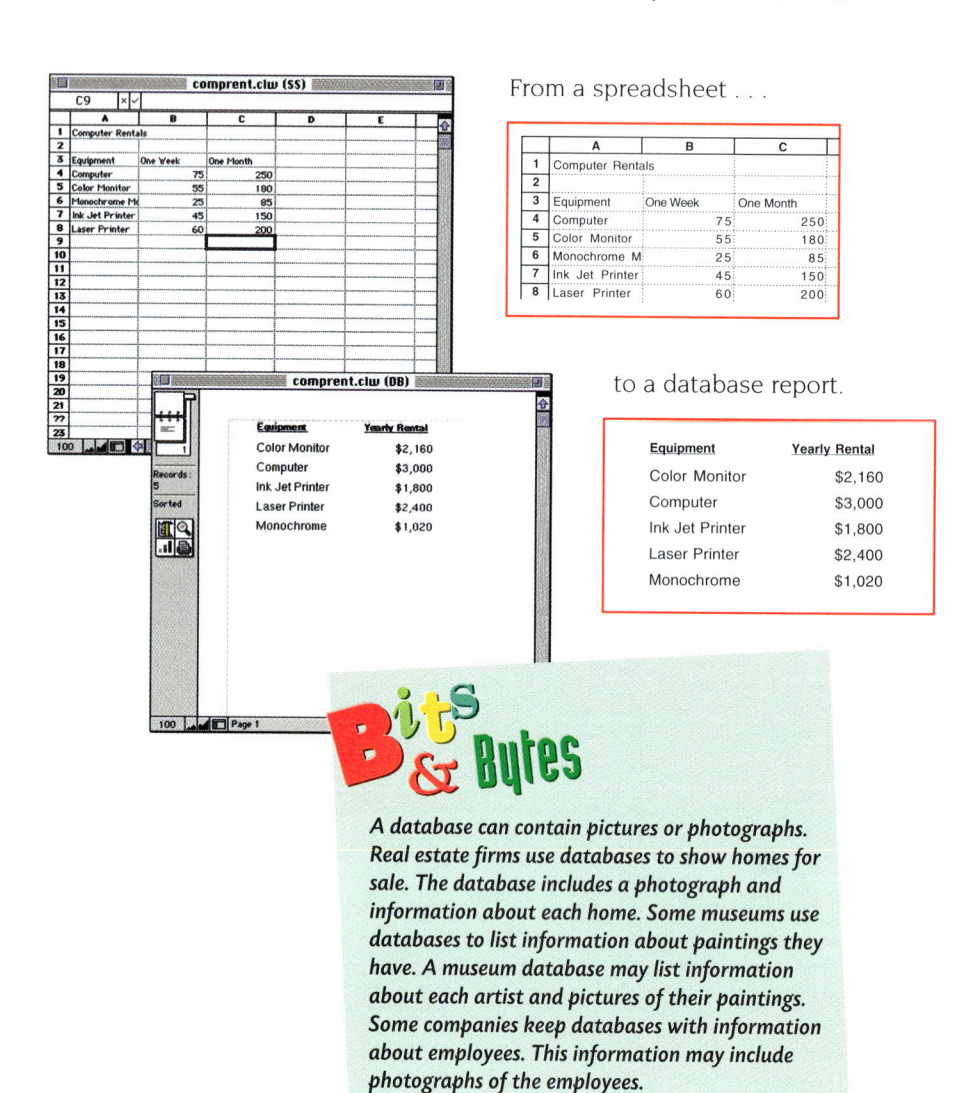

From a spreadsheet . . .

to a database report.

Bits & Bytes

A database can contain pictures or photographs. Real estate firms use databases to show homes for sale. The database includes a photograph and information about each home. Some museums use databases to list information about paintings they have. A museum database may list information about each artist and pictures of their paintings. Some companies keep databases with information about employees. This information may include photographs of the employees.

416 Section 19 Enhanced Databases and Reports

In the final project, you will copy database information into a word processing document and format it as a table.

Database Integration

TEACH

Demonstrate the integration process to students.

ASSESS

To assess students' understanding, ask them to describe the integration process and to identify several advantages of data integration.

CLOSE

Have students integrate data as described in Projects 137–140.

RESULTS OF THE RAS TEST
Science
By Melanie Stone

There is an area in our brains that is called the reticular activating system (RAS). Its purpose is to sort out all the information provided by our senses. It is the RAS that helps to focus our attention and "hear" specific sounds and also lets us "tune out" other sounds. The RAS regulates our level of awareness by screening the messages from our senses and passing on only what seems important or unusual.

In my experiment, I played music while doing homework or chores. I heard some songs but not others. The table below shows the results of my experiment. It lists the song's artist and title, the activity I was doing while the song was playing, and whether or not I heard it. One possible conclusion is that I was able to hear more songs while doing chores than while doing homework.

Artist	Song Title	Activity	Heard
Bing Crosby	Winter Wonderland	Chores	No
J. S. Bach	Fugue in D Minor	Homework	No
James Gallway	Flute in D Minor	Homework	No
Billy Best	The Golden Wheat	Homework	No
Neil Diamond	Street Sounds	Chores	Yes
Sophie B. Hawkins	Right Beside you	Chores	Yes
Purple	The American Dream	Chores	Yes
Andrew Weber	Memories	Chores	Yes
Grace Evonne	Jingle Bells	Homework	Yes
Billy Best	Star Spangled Times	Homework	Yes

INTEGRATED DATA. Data from a sorted database copied to a word processing document.

DID YOU KNOW

Sounds are caused by vibrations in the air. These vibrations are called sound waves. Sound waves enter the ear and are changed into nerve signals. These signals travel to the brain and are interpreted as sounds.

Some animals use hearing to find their way in the dark. Bats and whales make sounds and listen for the echoes made when objects reflect the sounds. These echoes help the animals figure out how far away an object is and the direction in which it lies.

DID YOU KNOW

The human ear can detect three characteristics of sound: volume, pitch, and tone. Volume depends on the intensity of the sound wave. Pitch relates to the number, or frequency, of sound waves per time unit. Tone, a more complex characteristic, depends on the combinations of the sound wave frequencies.

Project 137
Integrate a Database and a Spreadsheet

PRACTICE—LEVEL 1

Purpose
Practice integrating data from a database to a spreadsheet.

Time
Class period.

Preparation
Make sure the database and spreadsheet software are available and that students have their data disks. Make sure the printers are ready.

Teaching Tip
Observe students as they complete the assignment. Students who finish early should repeat the assignment.

Trouble Shooting
Provide individual help to students who are having difficulty.

Wrap Up
If this is the last project for this class period, ask students to return computers and furniture to the appropriate conditions.

Social Studies Connection

Project 137
INTEGRATE A DATABASE AND A SPREADSHEET

In this project, you will integrate database and spreadsheet files.

1. Open the database file DB137 on your data disk.
2. In list view, select all the records in your database. Do not include the field names or blank records in your selection.
3. Copy the records by clicking the Copy button.
4. Create a new spreadsheet file.
5. Place the insertion point in cell A1.
6. Paste the records from the clipboard into your spreadsheet by clicking the Paste button.
7. Select the data in columns A and B, the State and Population fields on the spreadsheet.
8. Create a new bar chart using this information.

   Note: For help in creating a bar chart, see your Student Guide, Unit 5, Spreadsheet, **chart, create.**

9. Enter a title for the chart: *State Population Under 5 Million*.
10. The numbers on your chart should have commas. Change the format for the numbers, if necessary, to show commas.
11. Close the database file.

    Note: To go back to the open database file, switch windows. Refer to your Student Guide, Unit 3, Word Processing for help with the **switch windows** feature.

12. Print a copy of the chart using landscape page orientation.
13. Save your spreadsheet file as STSS137.

418 Section 19 Enhanced Databases and Reports

Social Studies Connection

To generate interest in social studies, ask students to research state populations over the past fifty years. Ask them to look for trends in the data. Did the same state always have the highest population, or has that honor changed from year to year? What about the state with the lowest population? Ask them to list reasons why a state's population might grow or decline over a period of years. For example, Florida has experienced population growth because more people are reaching retirement age and want to live in a warmer climate.

Project 138

INTEGRATE A SPREADSHEET AND DATABASE

In this project, you will copy information already entered and calculated in a spreadsheet into a database.

1. Open the spreadsheet file SS138 on your data disk.
2. Select all of the information in the range A4 to C8.
3. Copy it to the clipboard by clicking the Copy button.
4. Create a new database file.
5. Create the fields and define the field types as indicated: *Equipment* as a text type; *One Week* as a number type; *One Month* as a number type.
6. Switch to list view and position the insertion point to paste the data.

   Note: In ClarisWorks, click the row heading beside the first field. In Microsoft Works, click in the first field of the first record.

7. Paste the information from the spreadsheet into the database file by clicking the Paste button.
8. Delete any blank records.
9. Insert a formula field as the last field in each record. Name it *Yearly Rental*.
10. Format the Yearly Rental field as currency with no decimals. Right align the numbers in this field. This field calculates One Month times 12.
11. Adjust the field sizes to ensure that all information can be seen.
12. Create a report called *Computer Rentals*.
13. Include only the Equipment and Yearly Rental fields in the report.
14. Add a footer to the report that contains your name and the page number.
15. Close the spreadsheet file.
16. Print a copy of the report.
17. Save this database file as STDB138.

In Your Journal

Look in a newspaper or in store advertisements for information about personal computers for sale. Collect information from several stores. Put your information in a database so you can compare prices.

Database Integration **419**

To generate interest in technology, ask students to research computer rental (leasing) opportunities. Ask them to find out how much it costs to rent or lease a computer. Is it better to lease a computer or to buy one? Ask students to list advantages and disadvantages of each approach.

Project 138
Integrate a Spreadsheet and Database

APPLY—LEVEL 1

Purpose
Apply integration skills by integrating a spreadsheet with a database.

Time
Class period.

Preparation
Make sure the database and spreadsheet software are available and that students have their data disks. Make sure the printers are ready.

Teaching Tip
Observe students as they complete the assignment. Students who finish early should repeat the assignment.

Trouble Shooting
Provide individual help to students who are having difficulty.

Wrap Up
If this is the last project for this class period, ask students to return computers and furniture to the appropriate conditions.

In Your Journal

Have students bring in the information they find on personal computers. Compile the database as a class.

Project 139
Integrate a Database and a Report

ASSESS—LEVEL 2

Purpose
Assess database skills by integrating information from a database with a word processing document.

Time
Class period.

Preparation
Make sure the database and word processing software are available and that students have their data disks. Make sure the printers are ready.

Teaching Tip
Observe students as they complete the assignment. Students who finish early should repeat the assignment.

Trouble Shooting
Provide individual help to students who are having difficulty.

Wrap Up
If this is the last project for this class period, ask students to return computers and furniture to the appropriate conditions.

Project 139
INTEGRATE A DATABASE AND A REPORT

In this project, you will select and sort records from your database and use the information to create a table in a word processing document.

1. Open the database file DB139A on your data disk.
2. Sort the records first by Heard in ascending order; then by Activity in ascending order.
3. Select all of the records (but not blank records or field names).
4. Copy them to the clipboard by clicking the Copy button.
5. Open the word processing file WP139B on your data disk.
6. Place the insertion point at the end of the document.
7. Press the Enter/Return key once to insert a blank line.
8. Paste the records into the document at this position by clicking the Paste button.
9. The pasted text should be single spaced. Change the spacing, if necessary, to single spacing.
10. Select the text that you just pasted into the document.
11. Use the tab set feature to adjust the tabs so that the columns of information line up correctly and the space between columns is approximately even. Suggested tabs are .5 inch from the left margin, 2.5 inches from the left margin, 4.5 inches from the left margin, and 5.5 inches from the left margin.

   Note: Refer to your Student Guide, Unit 3, Word Processing for help with the tab set feature.

12. If your software did not automatically copy the field names with the records, insert a blank line above the data and key these column heads: *Artist, Song Title, Activity, Heard*.
13. Close the database file.
14. Print a copy of the report.
15. Save this file as STWP139 on your data disk.

420 Section 19 Enhanced Databases and Reports

To generate interest in science, ask students to read an article about a science project or experiment; the article should include a table or chart. Ask students to speculate about what type of application was used to originally create the data, and discuss how the data was integrated into the word-processed article.

Project 140
Building Your Portfolio

In this portfolio project, you will review integration features you learned in Projects 137 to 139. Choose a project for integrating data. You may choose to:

- Integrate database information into a spreadsheet to do additional calculations or chart information
- Integrate information from a spreadsheet into a database to prepare saved searches, sorts, or reports
- Integrate database information into a word processing document

If you have projects for other classes where you can integrate data, that would be ideal. Otherwise, choose which type of integration you would like to do and create an original project on a topic of your choice.

Refer to your Student Guide and previous projects as needed.

NOW TRY THIS

1. Make a back-up copy of each of the files you will use in the project.
2. Open or create the files you will integrate.
3. Select and copy the information to the clipboard.
4. Switch to the file in which the copied information will be pasted.
5. Position the insertion point in the location where the information will be pasted. Paste the information.
6. Review the pasted information to be sure that it is formatted correctly for the document in which it now appears. Make any adjustments necessary.
7. Print the integrated document.
8. Save the file as STDB140, STWP140, or STSS140, as appropriate.

✓ Check Your Understanding

1. Did you select the right information for the integration activity?
2. Did you format the pasted information correctly?
3. Did you save your work?

Project 140
Building Your Portfolio

ASSESS—LEVEL 2

Purpose
Assess database skills by integrating data from one application to another.

Time
Class period.

Preparation
Students need to have a project idea in mind and should bring all relevant data to class. Make sure the word processing, database, and spreadsheet software are available and that students have their data disks. Make sure the printers are ready.

Teaching Tip
Observe students as they complete the assignment. Students who finish early should repeat the assignment.

Trouble Shooting
Provide individual help to students who are having difficulty.

Wrap Up
Have students review their work using **Check Your Understanding.** Students' answers will vary.

If this is the last project for this class period, ask students to return computers and furniture to the appropriate conditions.

UNIT 7 ORGANIZER

Section	Subsection	Special Features	Projects - Project No., Title, and Page	Projects - Cross-Curricular Connection	Difficulty Level	Student Guide GO TO
20 - Communications Basics	20.1 - Network Connections 20.2 - Communications Software	Words To Know, p. 424 Internet Connection, p. 426 In Your Journal, p. 427	Project 141: Explore Communications Software, p. 428	141 Technology	141 - L1	p. 427
21 - E-Mail Basics	21.1 - Introduction to E-Mail 21.2 - E-Mail Messages 21.3 - Communicating Using E-Mail	Words To Know, p. 429 Did You Know?, p. 431 Internet Connection, p. 432 Internet Connection, p. 434 In Your Journal, p. 438	Project 142: Send E-Mail, p. 436 Project 143: Receive and Forward E-Mail, p. 437 Project 144: Manage E-Mail, p. 438 Project 145: Building Your Portfolio, p. 439	142 Social Studies 143 Language Arts 144 Language Arts 145 Social Studies	142 - L1 143 - L1 144 - L1 145 - L2	
19 - Internet Basics	22.1 - Newsgroups 22.2 - Internet Sites 22.3 - Browser 22.4 - Integration	Words To Know, p. 440 Did You Know?, p. 442 In Your Journal, p. 443 Internet Connection, p. 447	Project 146: Explore Internet Sites, p. 445 Project 147: Use Browser, p. 448 Project 148: Building Your Portfolio, p. 449 Projects 149–150: Integration Project, pp. 451–453	146 Social Studies 147 Science 148 Science 149 Science 150 Social Studies	146 - L1 147 - L1 148 - L1 149 - L1 150 - L2	

UNIT RESOURCES

- Lesson Plans: LP111–LP120
- Multicultural Timings: MT27–MT28
- Supplemental Projects: SP21–SP26
- Enrichment Activities

- CD-ROM: Unit 7 Document Templates Reference Guide
- Cross-curricular Timings
- Software: Unit 7 Document Templates Research Files

- Student Guides: Communications
- Student Data Disks

UNIT 7 ORGANIZER

KEY TO DIFFICULTY LEVEL
The following designations will help you decide which activities are appropriate for your students.

L1: Level 1 activities are basic activities and should be within the range of all students.

L2: Level 2 activities are average activities and should be within the range of average and above average students.

L3: Level 3 activities are challenging activities designed for the ability range of above average students.

ASSESSMENT RESOURCES

Check Your Understanding

Section 20	Section 21	Section 22
	p. 439	p. 449

Portfolio Assessment (Building Your Portfolio)

Section 20	Section 21	Section 22
	p. 439	p. 449

Unit Tests (Teacher's Resource Binder)
Objective Test

422b

UNIT 7

INTRODUCING THE UNIT

Telecommunications is one of the most exciting areas of computer literacy for students to explore. World Wide Web addresses have become a standard part of consumer advertising. As a result, students are anxious to get on-line to find information about their favorite gym shoes, star sports figures, toys—you name it!

This unit gives students the opportunity to learn about and explore electronic mail, bulletin board systems, the World Wide Web, and other telecommunications topics. To make the most of this unit, students should have access to a computer and a method of connecting to the Internet (either a modem or a network connection). Students also should have access to an electronic mail account.

Working with the World Wide Web can be a daunting task; the resources are vast, and the search tools sometimes turn up less than optimal results. For a list of popular search engines on the Web see page 446.

Keep in mind that most of the content on the Internet is uncensored. Students should be closely supervised when accessing Web pages. A seemingly benign link can lead the unsuspecting user to unsuitable material for students.

Unit 7
Communications

OVERVIEW

Telecommunications, in simple terms, means communicating electronically over far distances. To communicate electronically, you must have communications software and a computer with a modem connected to a phone line. The modem helps your computer send information over the phone line. Your phone line is used to connect you to a service provider. A service provider is a company that links your computer to the Internet. All of these pieces work together as a part of a complete telecommunications system. This unit will focus on communications basics, e-mail, and some other popular Internet features.

Fun Facts

Want still more search engines? There are sites available that just list search engines. Common ones include:

http://metasearch.com/   http://www.search.com/   http://nln.com/

If you want information about how to use search engines, check out:
http://www.monash.com/spidap.html and http://issfw.palomar.edu/Library/TGSEARCH.HTM

UNIT 7

MULTIMEDIA

For this unit, you may use the multimedia CD-ROM to enhance your students' skills in learning to use communications tools. The CD-ROM contains format guides that serve as on-line communications examples for students. These examples are cross-referenced to the communications projects in the student text. The appearance of the communications tools will vary depending on the access to e-mail software applications and Internet browsers that students have. The Research Files contain cross-curricular typing selections or timings for 1 minute, 2 minutes, and 3 or 5 minutes. The timings, as well as the two games—Get the Scoop and Uncover the Story—are great ways to build typing skills.

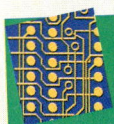

UNIT OBJECTIVES

- Practice communications basics by using a bulletin board system.
- Practice e-mail basics by sending and receiving e-mail.
- Practice Internet basics by finding and retrieving information using the Internet.

Unit Contents

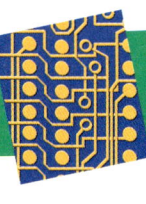

Section 20 — Communications Basics
Section 21 — E-Mail Basics
Section 22 — Internet Basics

Focus On Careers In Technology

Powerful satellites, sophisticated Doppler radar, forecasting models, and automated ground-observing systems make weather forecasting much more accurate today than ever before. It is the job of meteorologists at the National Weather Service to make forecasts and issue severe weather warnings. They make sure that the public is aware of weather conditions.

One way the National Weather Service publicizes this information is over the Internet. When a meteorologist at a regional office uses a computer to type a forecast for the local area, the information is transmitted to the National Weather Service's Web site. This site also presents weather maps, bulletins, current weather conditions, and climate statistics.

Focus On Careers In Technology

Arrange for a field trip to the local news station to look at the weather forecasting equipment available. If a field trip is not possible, ask the local meteorologist to speak at the school about how computers and the Internet are used to update the daily weather forecast.

Application: COMPUTERS IN THE HOME

Divide students into small groups. Ask them to list ways telecommunications might be used at home. Examples might include exchanging e-mail, using the Web for homework research, or shopping on-line. Ask a representative from each group to write a list on the board. Talk about the pros and cons of the items on the list. For example, on-line shopping gives consumers 24-hour access to their favorite stores. But for some people, shopping is a social activity; shopping on-line takes away the human interaction. Also, poor on-line security can make shopping on-line risky.

Section 20
Communications Basics

SECTION OVERVIEW

This section introduces students to some of the most common aspects of telecommunications, including the Internet, e-mail, bulletin boards, and commercial on-line services. Although the World Wide Web gets most of the attention these days, other aspects of the Internet are equally interesting. Bulletin board systems, for example, are often a great place to find inexpensive or even free software applications; these are often "niche" products that might otherwise not be available (teacher gradebook software, for example).

CONTENT FOCUS
Network Connections
Communications Software

CURRICULUM FOCUS
Technology

OPENING ACTIVITY

Ask students how many of them have used a modem to connect to another computer. Ask individual students to describe the process. What happened when the modem dialed the number? Was the connection successful, or did they have to try again? What did they like about being on-line? Was there anything they didn't like?

SECTION 20
Communications Basics

OBJECTIVES

- Identify and describe a bulletin board system, Internet service provider, and commercial on-line service.
- Use communications software to connect to a bulletin board system.

Words To Know

bulletin board system (BBS)
commercial on-line service
communications session
download
Internet
Internet service provider (ISP)
log off
log on
telecommunication
window

Focus on Communications

Communications software, a modem, and a phone line provide the link between your computer and other computers or networks. The **Internet,** sometimes called the information superhighway, is a huge network connecting millions of computers from around the world. The Internet gives you access to information on any subject you can name. You can browse through newspapers, magazines, and even television scripts. You can receive free software, buy tickets to a concert, order pizza, listen to music, and review movies. The Internet is the ultimate telecommunications tool.

424 Section 20 Communications Basics

Career Exploration Activities: Transportation

Computers are becoming an important part of today's automobiles. Besides the typical uses such as monitoring fuel and electrical systems, some cars use computers to help navigate. These computers use the Global Positioning System (GPS) network to show you exactly where you are at any given point in your trip.

Check with local automobile dealers to see if such a system is available on any of the cars currently on their lot. If so, ask for a class demonstration. Ask students to research careers that involve the use of computers in transportation systems. Examples include airline pilots and navigators, mapping software developers, and engineering careers.

Network Connections

20.1

You can use your communications software to connect to bulletin board systems, Internet service providers, and commercial on-line services. These are a few of the popular choices for network connections.

BULLETIN BOARD SYSTEMS

A **bulletin board system,** or BBS, is usually a small computer system managed by one person or maybe by a business. Some BBSs let you use their service for free, and others will charge a fee. For example, many printer manufacturers manage their own bulletin boards where you can go to **download** their latest newsletter or free trial software. Download is the process of transferring programs or information from one computer to another. Other BBSs might post community events and school calendars.

Your communications software should have a feature that allows you to connect to a BBS. Connecting is usually as easy as typing a bulletin board phone number and waiting for a connection. The modem and phone line work together to connect to the bulletin board. When the connection is made, you read and follow the directions on the screen until you find your way to the information you want. Directions appear as typed lines of text without any pictures. When you are finished, you must **log-off** (disconnect) from the bulletin board and electronically hang up using your communications software to end the phone call. This entire process is known as a **communications session.**

Goals

- Identify and describe a bulletin board system
- Identify and describe an Internet service provider
- Identify and describe a commercial on-line service

Network Connections **425**

20.1 Network Connections

FOCUS
Identify and describe a bulletin board system. Identify and describe an Internet service provider. Identify and describe a commercial on-line service.

BELLRINGER
When students enter the room, direct their attention to the assignment on the board:

Read pages 425–426 to become familiar with common communications terms.

TEACH
Discuss the terms included on this page: bulletin board system, download, and log-off. Emphasize the importance of using virus-checking software when downloading software, especially when downloading from sites that do not scan software before it is posted for downloading.

The following rules may help keep your system safe from computer viruses:

- Use only reputable sites when downloading software.
- Use anti-virus software to scan all downloaded data for viruses.
- Whenever possible, download files to floppy disks rather than to your hard drive.
- Be faithful about updating your anti-virus software. New viruses are introduced every day; your anti-virus software will be useless if it is not current.

RESOURCES

Lesson Plan: LP112
Multicultural Timing: MT27
Supplemental Project: SP21

CD-ROM: Reference Guide

Software: Research Files

425

Network Connections

TEACH

Discuss the difference between Internet service providers (ISPs) and commercial on-line services. Although many commercial on-line services provide Internet access, most ISPs do not have their own content areas. As a result, ISPs are often more cost-efficient for users who only want e-mail and Web access. For users who want a sense of "community," commercial on-line services are a better alternative. In addition, the commercial on-line services may offer easier software setup and telephone technical support.

ASSESS

To assess students' understanding, have them define the key terms introduced in this lesson: bulletin board system, download, log-off, Internet service provider, and commercial on-line service.

CLOSE

Have students explore communications software as described in Project 141.

DID YOU KNOW? The smallest modem on the market is manufactured by RAD Data Communications Ltd. of Tel Aviv, Israel. It weighs only 1.1 ounces; its dimensions are 2.4"l x 1.2"w x 0.08"h.

---

interNET CONNECTION

To get connected to the Internet, you need:
- A computer
- A modem
- A phone line
- An Internet service provider (ISP)
- Software (Internet browser and e-mail)

INTERNET SERVICE PROVIDERS

An **Internet service provider,** or ISP, is a company that charges a fee to provide you with easy access to the **Internet.** Most of these providers offer you free communications software to access and search the Internet and use e-mail easily. They usually charge a flat rate monthly fee. You must also pay for the cost of the phone call to connect to the ISP. This is why you should always shop for a provider that has a local phone number. You will be amazed how long these phone calls can last when you start to surf the Net!

COMMERCIAL ON-LINE SERVICES

Commercial on-line services like America Online, Prodigy, or CompuServe also provide you with access to the Internet. However, they are often more expensive than ISPs. They usually charge an hourly fee for time spent on the Internet in addition to a monthly fee for their services. Often people choose commercial on-line services because setup is usually simple; customer support is excellent; and there is usually easy access to the Internet, e-mail, and other topics such as news, weather, stocks, and travel information.

426 Section 20 Communications Basics

Many modems today operate at speeds of 28.8kps, but faster ones are entering the market every day. Ask students to research different types of modems. Ask them to write a short report that identifies the modem manufacturer, the price, and the speed of the modem.

interNET CONNECTION

Many schools have a network connection to the Internet. If this is the case in your school, explain the advantages of this type of setup—no busy signals, faster access, ability to simultaneously access multiple on-line sites, and so on.

426

Communications Software

20.2

Goals
- Use communications software in a communications session
- Connect to a bulletin board system

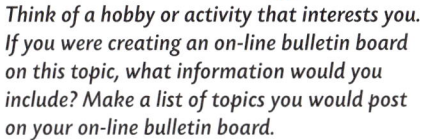

EXPLORING COMMUNICATIONS SOFTWARE

Are you ready to use your communications software to connect to a BBS? Many different steps are involved. Because some of them are very technical, you will just read about the steps in the related Help topics rather than trying them.

The computers in your classroom may or may not be equipped with modems and phone lines. If they are not, you will be able to complete only a few of the steps in the projects. However, you should still read the related Help topics in your Student Guide and complete as many of the steps as possible.

In Your Journal
Think of a hobby or activity that interests you. If you were creating an on-line bulletin board on this topic, what information would you include? Make a list of topics you would post on your on-line bulletin board.

GO TO — Student Guide, Communications
Window
Communications session

Communications Software **427**

RESOURCES
- Lesson Plan: LP113
- CD-ROM: Reference Guide
- Software: Research Files

20.2 Communications Software

FOCUS
Use communications software in a communications session. Connect to a bulletin board system.

BELLRINGER
Have students make a list of the information they would like to find on a bulletin board system.

TEACH
Using a computer with a modem, show students how communications software works.

ASSESS
To assess understanding, have students describe the basic steps to follow when initiating a communications session.

CLOSE
Have students explore communications software as described in Project 141.

GO TO — Refer students to the appropriate section of the Student Guide.

In Your Journal
In addition to topics that would be posted on the bulletin board, ask students to come up with ideas for software that might be useful for other users of the bulletin board to access. How would the software be acquired? Would there be a fee for the software, or would it be free?

427

Project 141
Communications Software

PRACTICE—LEVEL 1

Purpose
Practice connecting to a bulletin board system.

Time
Thirty minutes

Preparation
Make sure the communication software is ready to use. Make sure the modem is connected to the computer and the telephone line is available.

Teaching Tip
If necessary, students can practice this activity in groups rather than individually. This way, they can all experience the project even if modems and phone lines are limited.

Trouble Shooting
Some schools require that you include a special number at the beginning of the dialing sequence to access an outside line. Make sure to include this number at the beginning of the BBS number.
 Provide individual help to students who are having difficulty.

Wrap Up
If this is the last project for this class period, ask students to return computers and furniture to the appropriate conditions.

Project 141

EXPLORE COMMUNICATIONS SOFTWARE

In this project, you will connect to a bulletin board system during a communications session.

1. In your Student Guide, read Unit 7, **window.** Find and read the Help topics next to window to learn about the basic features of communications software and about the communications document window.
2. In your Student Guide, read Unit 7, **communications session,** to learn how to begin and end a communications session.
3. If you have the proper hardware and software, begin a communications session to **log-on** (connect) to the following bulletin board system or to a BBS of your choice:

    Corel WordPerfect BBS at 1-801-225-4414.

   Note: Steps 3-5 should only be taken under the direct supervision of a teacher.
4. Log-off (disconnect from) the bulletin board system.
5. Hang up to end the phone call.

428 Section 20 Communications Basics

Technology Connection

To generate interest in bulletin board systems, ask students who have used a BBS to demonstrate or describe favorites.

interNET CONNECTION

Interested in looking at more bulletin board systems? Check out this Web site that provides a comprehensive list of Internet BBSs:

http://dkeep.com/sbi.html

E-Mail Basics

SECTION 21

Focus on E-Mail Basics

Electronic mail or e-mail is a popular use of the Internet. Using **e-mail** allows you to send and receive electronic mail messages. E-mail is changing the way people think about communicating. Why use paper and pen to send a message when a computer can deliver your message immediately 24 hours a day? Why spend $20 to $30 to have a document delivered by a mail service when you can send it using e-mail for the price of a local phone call? You will come to think of your computer as a substitute for paper, a pen, and a post office. In this section, you will learn about the basic concepts and features of e-mail.

OBJECTIVES

- Identify and explain common e-mail terms.
- Identify and explain basic e-mail features.
- Format, send, and receive e-mail.
- Manage e-mail, including saving, deleting, and printing messages.

Words To Know

address book	forwarding
attachment	in box
bounced message	managing e-mail
CC notation	messages
domain name	netiquette
dots	out box
e-mail	shouting
e-mail address	signature
e-mail message	smiley
flame	user name

Section 21 E-Mail Basics

SECTION OVERVIEW

In this section, students become acquainted with one of the most popular telecommunications applications, electronic mail (e-mail). E-mail can be a very powerful tool allowing messages to be sent and received within seconds.

CONTENT FOCUS
Introduction to e-mail
E-mail messages
Communicate with e-mail

CURRICULUM FOCUS
Language Arts
Social Studies

OPENING ACTIVITY

Ask how many students have used e-mail. Ask the students who have used e-mail what they liked and disliked about it. Did people respond to their messages? Was e-mail used to communicate with a friend, get more information about a product, or communicate with a government official? Make a list on the board of the ways students have used e-mail.

Section 21 E-Mail Basics **429**

Career Exploration Activities:
Marketing and Distribution

Many consumer companies provide e-mail addresses for customers to use when corresponding with the company. Have students research common products to find out which ones provide e-mail addresses on the package.

If possible, invite a marketing representative from a local company to speak to the class about how e-mail and other on-line technology has impacted his or her job. Ask the representative to discuss the computer skills necessary in the marketing profession.

21.1 Introduction To E-Mail

FOCUS
Explain basic e-mail features.
Explain basic e-mail terms.

BELLRINGER
When students enter the room direct their attention to the assignment on the board:
  Read pages 430–432 to become familiar with e-mail features and terms.

TEACH
Emphasize the importance of addressing e-mail correctly. If a message is addressed incorrectly, two things can happen:

1. *The message will be returned to the sender with some sort of (usually) cryptic error message.*
2. *The message is delivered, but not to the person you had hoped would receive it. This might happen if you use an incorrect address, but it just so happens that someone in the world actually uses the address. This can be very embarrassing!*

Addresses should be checked carefully before the mail is sent.

Introduction To E-Mail

21.1

Goals
- Explain basic e-mail features
- Explain basic e-mail terms

Powerful, easy-to-use e-mail software is widely available. Most Internet service providers and commercial on-line services provide their own e-mail software to you as a part of their service. Some e-mail programs, like Eudora, are free and can be **downloaded** from the Internet. Icons, pictures, and other graphics make the software easy to use.

SENDING AND RECEIVING MESSAGES

To send or receive a message, you must first start your communications or e-mail software. Most e-mail software allows you to write your messages off-line, without being connected to the Internet. This saves money on your phone bill. However, to send or receive e-mail, you must be connected to the Internet through your e-mail software. Once you are connected, your messages are usually sent automatically. Any messages waiting for you are automatically downloaded to your computer. When other people send you e-mail, the message waits on your service provider's computer until you connect in a communications session.

E-MAIL ADDRESSES

In the same way that the post office needs to know your mailing address to deliver your mail, your e-mail software needs to know your electronic address. Currently, there is no complete "phone book" for private e-mail addresses. You must ask each person for an address. When you receive e-mail, the sender's address is on the message. You can usually add it to your electronic address book at that time. Most e-mail software includes an **address book** feature for storing **e-mail addresses**.

430 Section 21 E-Mail Basics

RESOURCES

📁 Lesson Plan: LP114
   Multicultural Timing: MT28

💿 CD-ROM: Reference Guide

💾 Software: Research Files

Fun Facts

Other common abbreviations in domain names are **mil** for military address, **org** for nonprofit organizations, and **net** for networking companies. Because it is getting difficult to come up with unique domain names, there is a push in the Internet community to include even more of these abbreviations.

USER NAME. The name of the person's account. A real name, an assigned name, or a nickname.

DOMAIN NAME. The location of the person's account.

To: president@whitehouse.gov
From: yourname@school.edu

Introduction To E-Mail

TEACH

Some institutions assign user names, while others let the user pick his or her own user name. For example, most businesses assign user names based on the user's real name. Commercial services, such as America Online, often let users pick their own user name. This way, the user can participate in on-line activities without revealing their gender or identity.

An address has two parts separated by the @ (at) symbol. There are never any blank spaces in an e-mail address. The first part of the address is called a **user name.** This is usually a real name or a given name. The second part of the address is called the **domain name.** It identifies the Internet service provider's address. Periods called *dots* separate the different parts of the domain name. The last few letters in a domain name give you a clue as to the type of address. *Gov* is a government address. *Edu* is an educational institution address. *Com* is a commercial address. Most commercial on-line services end with *com*.

E-MAIL TERMS

Some commonly used e-mail terms include smileys, flames, bounced message, and shouting. A **smiley** is a group of characters typed in such a way that they look like a human face. The smiley **:-)** looks like a smiling face turned sideways. They are used to help express emotions in a message. A **flame** is an angry message to someone. A **bounced message** is one that has been returned to you because of an error of some kind. **Shouting** is expressed by typing in all caps.

E-MAIL FEATURES

Because e-mail addresses are long and hard to remember, electronic address books are a common feature of communications programs. Rather than typing an e-mail address each time you send mail, you usually type a person's real name in the *To* box. An e-mail address usually pops into place after the first few letters if you have set up an address book.

DID YOU KNOW

There are a variety of smileys you can use when sending e-mail. Here are some examples:

:-(I'm sad
:-D I'm laughing
:-+ I'm exhausted
:-O I'm surprised
:-& I'm tongue-tied

DID YOU KNOW

Entire books of smileys are available. In general, it is a good idea to stick with the common ones that are easy to identify. Otherwise, the recipient of the message will have no idea what the smiley represents.

Introduction to E-Mail **431**

interNET CONNECTION

Some users have access to e-mail but not to other parts of the Internet. If this is the case at your school, your might want to check out the resources available to you through your e-mail account.

CULTURAL KALEIDOSCOPE

Be careful when using smileys in messages sent to friends in other countries. As with gestures and other customs, smileys may not mean the same thing in all cultures.

431

Introduction To E-Mail

TEACH

Address books are essential for most users—they save time, and help minimize the chances of typing an address incorrectly. Demonstrate how to use the address book feature of your e-mail software.

ASSESS

To assess students' understanding, have them describe the basic functions and features of e-mail software.

CLOSE

Have students explore e-mail software as described in Project 142.

ADDRESS BOOK. Records names and e-mail addresses for easy access.

An example of an America Online address book screen.

In boxes and out boxes are another common feature of e-mail programs. Incoming messages are placed in your **in box** and outgoing messages are placed in your **out box.** You can save, delete, or move mail from these boxes as you like. Attachments can be sent with e-mail. An **attachment** is usually a document or file you want to send with an e-mail message. Think of e-mail attachments just like enclosures in a letter.

interNET CONNECTION

When you e-mail someone for the first time, add the e-mail address to your address book at the same time. An easy way to add an e-mail address to your address book is to:
- Highlight and copy the address.
- Go to the dialog box that allows you to add a new user in your address book.
- Paste the address into the appropriate text box.

432 Section 21 E-Mail Basics

interNET CONNECTION

Many e-mail address books let the user set up "nicknames" that they can use to refer to entries in the address book. For example, Aunt Hildegarde might have a long e-mail address (hildegardeis@her-witzend.com, for example). Your address book might let you set up a nickname that associates the address "Aunt Hildegarde" with her long address. This way, you only need to enter Aunt Hildegarde in the To field; the e-mail software automatically enters the long version of her address.

432

21.2 E-Mail Messages

Goals
- Identify the basic parts of an e-mail message
- Describe proper e-mail netiquette

Communicating with e-mail is very different from communicating either face to face or through a letter. You cannot use your voice or body language to communicate in an e-mail message. Therefore, the words in your message must be chosen carefully and thoughtfully. Also, while it may take several days for a letter to be delivered, an e-mail message is delivered almost immediately. This can be a disadvantage if you have sent a message you wish you could take back.

E-MAIL NETIQUETTE

Netiquette is a word used to describe some basic rules to guide you when you compose a proper e-mail message. If you will follow these simple rules, your message will be more effective.

- Write when you are calm and thoughtful, not angry or impulsive.
- Write carefully and clearly.
- Include a subject line that describes your message clearly.
- Check for spelling and grammar errors.
- Do not type in ALL CAPS. Using all-capital letters is like shouting.
- Avoid sarcasm. Remember that your message will be taken literally since the recipient of your message cannot see or hear you.
- Change any words that might be misunderstood.

21.2 E-Mail Messages

FOCUS
Identify the basic parts of an e-mail message. Describe proper e-mail netiquette.

BELLRINGER
When students enter the room, direct their attention to the assignment on the board:
Read page 433 to learn about e-mail netiquette.

TEACH
Discuss with students the importance of using proper "netiquette" when communicating on-line. Much of our face-to-face communication takes place through body language. Make sure students understand how easy it is to misunderstand a message when the other person cannot see your facial expressions.

RESOURCES
- Lesson Plan: LP114
- Supplemental Project: SP22
- CD-ROM: Reference Guide
- Software: Research Files

Fun Facts
Some e-mail systems have an "unsend" feature. This way, if you send something that you regret a moment after hitting the send button, you can get it back (provided, of course, the recipient has not yet read the message).

E-Mail Messages

TEACH

Discuss the importance of concise and well-written e-mail messages.

Point out that although formal closings are not usually used, it is a good idea to include your name at the end of the message. This makes the communication a bit more personal and ensures that the recipient knows who sent it.

ASSESS

To assess students' understanding, have them describe basic netiquette rules for writing e-mail. In addition, have them identify and describe the common components of an e-mail message.

CLOSE

Have students explore e-mail software as described in Project 142.

DID YOU KNOW? Most e-mail packages allow you to attach files as part of the message. This way, you can include more information without writing a wordy e-mail message.

---

interNET CONNECTION
You should keep your e-mail messages short. An e-mail message should be no longer than 25 lines. This is the number of lines that will fit on one screen.

COMPOSING AND FORMATTING A MESSAGE

E-mail messages are written in an informal, conversational style. Greetings and closings are usually not used. A descriptive, short subject line is always used. Paragraphs should be typed single spaced with a blank line between paragraphs. Paragraphs are not indented.

PARTS OF A MESSAGE

Most messages include a heading, body, and signature. The heading includes the captions *To*, *From*, *Date*, and *Subject* similar to a memo. A **CC notation** in the **CC box** is used when you want to send a copy of your message to one or more persons. The headings *From* and *Date* are usually filled in automatically and may not appear on the screen where you compose the message. The body is the text of your message. The **signature,** which usually includes your name and perhaps an address, is at the end of the body. It may be added by the software when the message is sent or perhaps by clicking a button. In the illustration, the *from*, *date*, and *signature* information are added automatically when the message is sent.

E-MAIL MESSAGE. The user enters the e-mail address, subject line, and body of the message. The date and signature information are added automatically by the program.

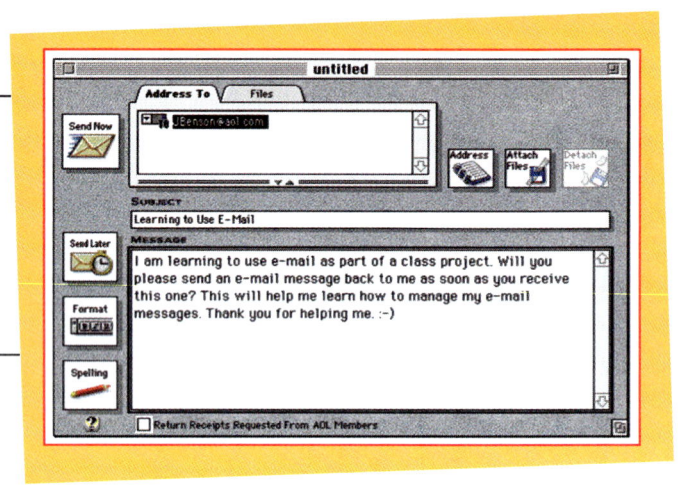

An example of an America Online composed e-mail screen.

434 Section 21 E-Mail Basics

21.3 Communicate Using E-Mail

COMMUNICATING WITH E-MAIL

In this section, you will practice communicating using e-mail. Remember to use clear, direct language that will be easily understood when you write an e-mail message. Check the e-mail address carefully to be sure you have entered it correctly so that your message can be delivered. You will also practice receiving and replying to e-mail messages and forwarding messages to others. **Forwarding** a message is when you send a copy of a message you have written or received to another person. Forwarding is a common feature in most e-mail software.

Once you begin communicating using e-mail, the number of messages you send and receive can grow rapidly. Some messages should be stored for later reference. Others can be deleted right away to free valuable space in your mailbox or on your hard drive. **Managing e-mail messages** involves deleting messages and storing, filing, or printing other messages. You will practice managing e-mail messages in this section.

Because you will most likely use an Internet service provider or a commercial on-line service to send and receive e-mail, the projects will not give exact directions to make this connection. If the computers in your class are networked, you could try to complete the e-mail projects using your local network connections.

If you do not have access to e-mail software and the Internet or a local area network, you should skip Projects 142 through 145.

Goals
- Send an e-mail message
- Receive and reply to an e-mail message
- Manage e-mail messages

RESOURCES
- Lesson Plan: LP115
- Supplemental Project: SP23
- CD-ROM: Reference Guide
- Software: Research Files

21.3 Communicate Using E-Mail

FOCUS
Send an e-mail message. Receive and reply to an e-mail message. Manage e-mail messages

BELLRINGER
When students enter the room, direct their attention to the assignment on the board:

Read page 435 to learn more about e-mail.

TEACH
Point out that one big advantage of e-mail is the ability to forward a message to other e-mail users without having to retype the message.

Proper file management is essential with e-mail. It is tempting to keep every message ever received. Encourage students to resist this temptation! Otherwise, e-mail messages will take up valuable disk space. In addition, the messages you really need will be mixed in with other messages.

Most software allows you to use e-mail off-line, thereby reducing the amount of on-line time. Demonstrate this feature to your students.

ASSESS
Lead a discussion on effective ways to use e-mail, including forwarding and managing messages.

CLOSE
Have students practice using e-mail as described in Projects 142, 143, and 144.

Project 142
Communicate Using E-Mail

PRACTICE—LEVEL 1

Purpose
Practice sending e-mail.

Time
Class period

Preparation
Ask students to bring the e-mail address of one or two friends to class. If they cannot get access to the addresses, tell them to send the messages to you instead. Make sure the communication and e-mail software is ready to use, and the ISP or commercial service provider is available.

Teaching Tip
Observe students carefully to make sure they use the correct e-mail address. Students who finish early can repeat the project, this time sending messages to different recipients.

Trouble Shooting
Provide individual help to students who are having difficulty.

Wrap Up
Make sure students disconnect from the ISP or commercial service provider. If this is the last project for this class period, ask students to return computers and furniture to the appropriate conditions.

Project 142
Social Studies Connection
SEND E-MAIL

In this project, you will send two e-mail messages. Use the Help feature of your e-mail software to guide you through the steps below.

Note: Skip this project if you do not have access to e-mail software and the Internet.

1. Connect to your Internet service provider or your commercial on-line service.
2. Start the e-mail software.
3. Send the e-mail message below to a friend, perhaps someone in class, who will reply to you by tomorrow. The subject is *Learning to Use E-Mail*.

> I am learning to use e-mail as a part of a class project. Will you please send an e-mail message back to me as soon as you receive this one? This will help me learn how to manage my e-mail messages. Thank you for helping me. :-)

4. Send another e-mail message as shown below to the President of the United States at the following address: *president@whitehouse.gov*. The subject is *Funding for Technology in Middle Schools*. Send a copy of this message to a friend.

> I am a middle school student and am enrolled in a class to learn how to use e-mail and the Internet. I want to thank you, Mr. President, for making it possible for me to send you an e-mail message. I know you support education.
>
> Our schools are struggling to buy the hardware and software we need to keep up with technology. I would like to know if you are trying to help our middle schools get money for new computers, software, and so on. Thank you for taking time to read my message.

5. Send an e-mail message to yourself if your software allows.
6. Disconnect from your software and hang up.

Section 21 E-Mail Basics

Social Studies Connection

To generate interest in social studies, ask students to compile a list of the e-mail addresses of all of the local representatives to your city, state, and federal government.

Project 143

RECEIVE AND FORWARD E-MAIL

In this project, you will practice replying to an e-mail message and forwarding a message to another person. Use the Help feature of your e-mail software to guide you through the steps below.

Note: Skip this project if you do not have access to e-mail software and the Internet.

1. Connect to your Internet service provider or your commercial on-line service.
2. Start the e-mail software.
3. Check to see if you have received any e-mail.
4. Compose an answer and reply to any messages you have received.
5. If you have not received any e-mail, forward the message you sent to the President in Project 142 to a classmate or friend.
6. Disconnect from your software and hang up.

Good Afternoon

Welcome to the White House

Communicate Using E-Mail

To generate interest in language arts, work with students to proofread their e-mail messages before they send them.

Project 143
Communicate Using E-Mail

PRACTICE—LEVEL 1

Purpose
Practice receiving and forwarding e-mail.

Time
Thirty minutes

Preparation
Make sure each student has at least one message to reply to (this may mean that you send a message to every student in the class). Make sure the communication and e-mail software is ready to use, and the ISP or commercial service provider is available.

Teaching Tip
Observe students carefully to make sure they understand how to use the reply and forward features of their software.

Trouble Shooting
If students did not address messages properly in Project 142, they may receive error messages instead of actual messages from individuals. Help them correct the mistake before sending the message again.

Provide individual help to students who are having difficulty.

Wrap Up
Make sure students disconnect from the ISP or commercial service provider. If this is the last project for this class period, ask students to return computers and furniture to the appropriate conditions.

Project 144
Communicate Using E-Mail

PRACTICE—LEVEL 1

Purpose
Practice managing e-mail, including deleting, storing, filing, and printing e-mail messages.

Time
Thirty minutes

Preparation
Make sure the communication and e-mail software is ready to use, and the ISP or commercial service provider is available.

Teaching Tip
Discourage students from printing every message. Just as they do not need a printed transcript of every phone conversation they have, they do not need a printed record of every e-mail message.

Trouble Shooting
Provide individual help to students who are having difficulty.

Wrap Up
Make sure students disconnect from the ISP or commercial service provider.

In Your Journal
Discuss with students the added complexities of exchanging mail with someone from another country. For example, slang expressions that we take for granted here might not be understood by someone in Japan.

Project 144
Language Arts Connection
MANAGE E-MAIL

Managing messages includes deleting messages and storing, filing, or printing other messages. Use the Help feature of your e-mail software to guide you through the steps below.

Note: Skip this project if you do not have access to e-mail software and the Internet.

1. Connect to your Internet service provider or your commercial on-line service.
2. Start the e-mail software.
3. Check to see if you have received any e-mail.
4. Compose an answer and reply to any messages you have received.
5. Save or delete any messages you have received.
6. File or delete any old messages.
7. Print any messages as you like.
8. Disconnect from your software and hang up.

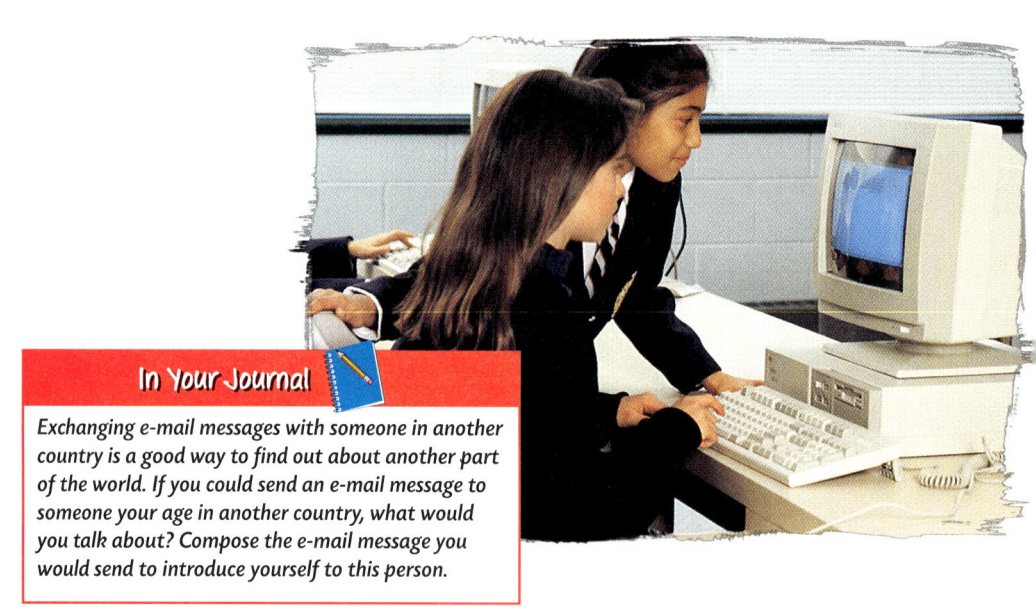

In Your Journal
Exchanging e-mail messages with someone in another country is a good way to find out about another part of the world. If you could send an e-mail message to someone your age in another country, what would you talk about? Compose the e-mail message you would send to introduce yourself to this person.

438 Section 21 E-Mail Basics

Cultural Kaleidoscope
For a good source of electronic pen pals, check out Kidlink at http://www.kidlink.org/ This organization is dedicated to facilitating on-line communication among students from all cultures. You might also find some useful "teacher" information while you are there!

Language Arts Connection
To generate interest in language arts, ask students to write an e-mail message that describes their favorite short story or poem. They can send their message to a friend. Encourage students to ask their friends to respond with a similar message. Discuss the stories and poems in class.

Project 145
Building Your Portfolio

Social Studies Connection

In this portfolio project, you will review the e-mail basics you learned in this section. Use the Help feature of your e-mail software to guide you through the steps below.

Note: Skip this project if you do not have access to e-mail software and the Internet.

NOW TRY THIS

1. Connect to your Internet service provider or your commercial on-line service.
2. Start the e-mail software.
3. Check to see if you have received any e-mail.
4. Reply to any messages you have received.
5. Save or delete any old messages.
6. Compose and send an e-mail message to one of your U.S. senators or anyone as desired. The front pages of your phone book may have listings for government officials that include an e-mail address if one is available.
7. Print a copy of this e-mail message.
8. Disconnect from your software and hang up.

✓ Check Your Understanding

1. Did you use the correct e-mail address for the recipient?
2. Did you proofread your message and follow proper e-mail netiquette?
3. Did you use the Help feature in your e-mail software to guide you through the steps?

Building Your Portfolio **439**

Social Studies Connection

To generate interest in social studies, invite a local, state, or federal elected official to speak with the class. Among other topics, ask him or her to discuss how technology has changed his/her work, any new legislation regarding communications technology, and the role technology plays in education.

Project 145
Building Your Portfolio

ASSESS—LEVEL 2

Purpose
Assess e-mail skills by sending, receiving, and deleting e-mail messages.

Time
Class period

Preparation
Students should bring the e-mail addresses of the message recipients with them to class. Make sure the communication and e-mail software is ready to use, and the ISP or commercial service provider is available.

Teaching Tip
Observe students carefully to make sure they address the messages properly.

Trouble Shooting
Provide individual help to students who are having difficulty.

Wrap Up
Make sure students disconnect from the ISP or commercial service provider.

Have students review their work using **Check Your Understanding.**

If this is the last project for this class period, ask students to return computers and furniture to the appropriate conditions.

439

Section 22
Internet Basics

SECTION OVERVIEW

In this section, students venture onto that vast information highway, the World Wide Web. Monitor students as they use the Internet and instruct them to exit inappropriate sites immediately. Proper supervision is essential to ensure that students have a positive Internet session.

CONTENT FOCUS

Newsgroups
Internet sites
Browser
Integration

CURRICULUM FOCUS

Science
Social Studies

OPENING ACTIVITY

Ask how many students have used the World Wide Web. Ask them to discuss how they used it, what they liked, and what they didn't like.

Ask students to look through magazine advertisements to find Web addresses for their favorite products. Using a computer with an overhead display and a modem, access the Web and take a look at some of the sites provided by the students. Show how easy it is to jump from one site to another.

SECTION 22
Internet Basics

OBJECTIVES

- Explain and define basic Internet features and terms.
- Use proper Internet netiquette.
- Use a browser to find and download information.

Words To Know

bookmark
browser
disclaimer statement
downloading
frequently asked questions (FAQ)
home page
hypertext words
Internet
keywords
net search
Netscape Navigator
newsgroup
search
search engine
search results
Uniform Resource Locator (URL)
Web page
Web site

Focus on Internet Basics

The **Internet** is a huge network of computers around the world that are linked together. If you look at the word Internet, "inter" is a prefix for between: "net" is a suffix for network. So the word Internet means between networks. Some people use the terms information superhighway or cyberspace to refer to the Internet. One way to find your way through this maze of computer networks is to browse or search for information. In this section, you will learn how to use navigation tools to help you explore the Internet.

Career Exploration Activities: Media and Communications

The Internet has dramatically changed the way we receive news. Late-breaking news stories that used to wait for the 6:00 P.M. newscast are now available nearly instantaneously via various on-line news sources. Ask students to explore careers available in on-line news services. They can use on-line research sources, printed materials, or interviews with local media personalities to learn about the opportunities available in this exciting aspect of the media.

22.1 Newsgroups

Goals
- Describe a newsgroup
- Explain FAQs and netiquette
- Identify privacy and safety issues on the Internet

A **newsgroup** is a discussion group that is formed to exchange ideas. There are newsgroups about every subject imaginable. Newsgroups are the second most popular use of the Internet. To join a newsgroup, you subscribe to it similar to the way you subscribe to a magazine. A newsreader program keeps track of articles you have read.

FAQS (FREQUENTLY ASKED QUESTIONS)

If you join an on-line newsgroup, begin by reading the **frequently asked questions (FAQs)** about the newsgroup. The FAQs are documents that list the common questions and answers related to a specific newsgroup. Reading the FAQs first rather than asking the same questions others have already asked is considered good netiquette. If you still have questions, you could send an e-mail message to the newsgroup administrator. Most mail is answered within a few days or sooner.

PRIVACY AND SAFETY ISSUES

Because you are essentially among strangers when you join newsgroups or other public forums, you must be concerned about your privacy and safety. An on-line service provides a monitoring function. You might call this your e-mail police. The monitors try to protect you from harassment, abuse, or tasteless messages. There are also "standards of conduct" posted with each newsgroup and mailing list. On-line service providers forbid users to talk about illegal activities or to use offensive language on-line.

If you receive an inappropriate message, let your on-line service provider know, and the sender may be banned from using the service. If you follow netiquette guidelines, most privacy and safety concerns will be handled.

INTERNET NETIQUETTE

Communicating electronically is not always private. For example, if you send mail to public groups on the Internet,

Newsgroups **441**

22.1 Newsgroups

FOCUS
Describe a newsgroup. Explain FAQs and netiquette. Identify privacy and safety issues on the Internet.

BELLRINGER
When students enter the room, direct their attention to the assignment on the board:
Read pages 441–442 to learn more about newsgroups.

TEACH
When participating in a newsgroup, it is essential that users follow the rules prescribed by the group. Some groups are very informal and invite questions even remotely related to the topic at hand, while others are much more focused and specific. The best way to learn the protocols to follow when participating in a newsgroup is to read the FAQ file. It also helps to listen for a while before becoming an active participant in the group.

DID YOU KNOW
Newsgroups are available for nearly every hobby, occupation, or general interest topic imaginable.

RESOURCES
Lesson Plan: LP117
Supplemental Project: SP24

CD-ROM: Reference Guide

Software: Research Files

441

Newsgroups

TEACH

Discuss with students the importance of using proper netiquette when communicating on the Internet. In addition, remind them that they cannot always trust the person with whom they are communicating. It is not a good idea to reveal too much information (especially personal information, such as a home address or telephone number) until you know more about who you are communicating with.

ASSESS

To assess students' understanding, have them describe the features of a newsgroup, as well as proper netiquette to follow when participating in a newsgroup.

CLOSE

Have students find information about various newsgroups.

DID YOU KNOW
A group of major universities, corporations, and government agencies is currently developing the next Internet, which is currently referred to as Internet 2.

strangers can read and respond to your message. You must be cautious and courteous in such situations.

Follow these simple rules to promote courtesy and safety on-line:

- Others are watching! Be polite and send messages that are in good taste.
- If a message might be considered rude or offensive, rewrite it.
- If you receive a rude or inappropriate message, do not reply. Tell your teacher, parent, or on-line service provider. Let one of those adults handle the problem.
- Do not give out personal information to anyone you meet on-line.

DID YOU KNOW
The Internet began in the United States in the 1960s. Scientists at the U.S. Department of Defense developed a computer network called ARPAnet. They used this network to share information with researchers at universities. ARPAnet was connected to other networks in the 1980s. This network was the basis for the Internet.

442 Section 22 Internet Basics

22.2 Internet Sites

EXPLORING INTERNET SITES

Learning to explore Web sites for information on the Internet is an essential skill. A **Web site** can be a university, a government agency, or a company that maintains Web pages for you to explore. A **Web page** looks a lot like a page in a magazine except it might have sound clips, or video clips, or hypertext words. Hypertext words are words you can click on to link or jump to other Web pages. A **home page** is a Web page that functions like the table of contents in a book. It is a good starting point to search for information.

A Web **browser** is software that helps you move through Web pages. **Netscape Navigator** is a very popular browser and can be downloaded for free. A browser is often part of the package provided by an Internet service provider. When you first connect to the Internet, you will usually have a box where you can type the address of a Web page you want to visit. This address is called a **Uniform Resource Locator (URL).** All URLs start with the abbreviation *http://*. The *www* that follows tells the browser to look through the World Wide Web for the information. URLs are case sensitive. You must type capital and lowercase letters carefully as shown in the source of the address. Also the / (slash) symbol must be typed correctly. Be careful to use the slash (/) rather than the backslash (\ ).

Goals
- Explain Web sites and Web pages
- Locate a Web page using a browser and the URL address

In Your Journal
If you could help design a Web page for your school, what would it look like? What information would you include? Write a letter to the principal with suggestions on starting a Web page for your school. If your school already has a Web page, make suggestions for how to improve it.

RESOURCES
- Lesson Plan: LP117
  Supplemental Project: SP25
- CD-ROM: Reference Guide
- Software: Research Files

22.2 Internet Sites

FOCUS
Explain Web sites and Web pages. Locate a Web page using a browser and the URL address.

BELLRINGER
Have students read pages 443–444 to learn more about the World Wide Web.

TEACH
The World Wide Web is where most of the Internet action is today. Web sites exist for nearly every topic imaginable (and probably a few topics most of us have never imagined!)

The beauty of the Web is that jumping from one site to another is as simple as a mouse click. Use a computer with an overhead projection device and a modem to demonstrate the Web. Show how easy it is to jump from one location to another. Show how to use a search engine to find specific information.

Show students how to enter the Web addresses. Point out that in most cases it is not necessary to type the *http://* part of the address; just start typing with the www portion of the URL.

In Your Journal
Ask students to share their Web page ideas with the rest of the class. Work with the class to decide on the best ideas, and then help students with the preliminary design of the page.

Internet Sites

TEACH
Demonstrate the bookmark feature to the class.

ASSESS
To assess students' understanding, have them define and describe the features of the World Wide Web, including browser, Web site, Web page, home page, URL, and bookmark.

CLOSE
Have students explore the World Wide Web as described in Project 146.

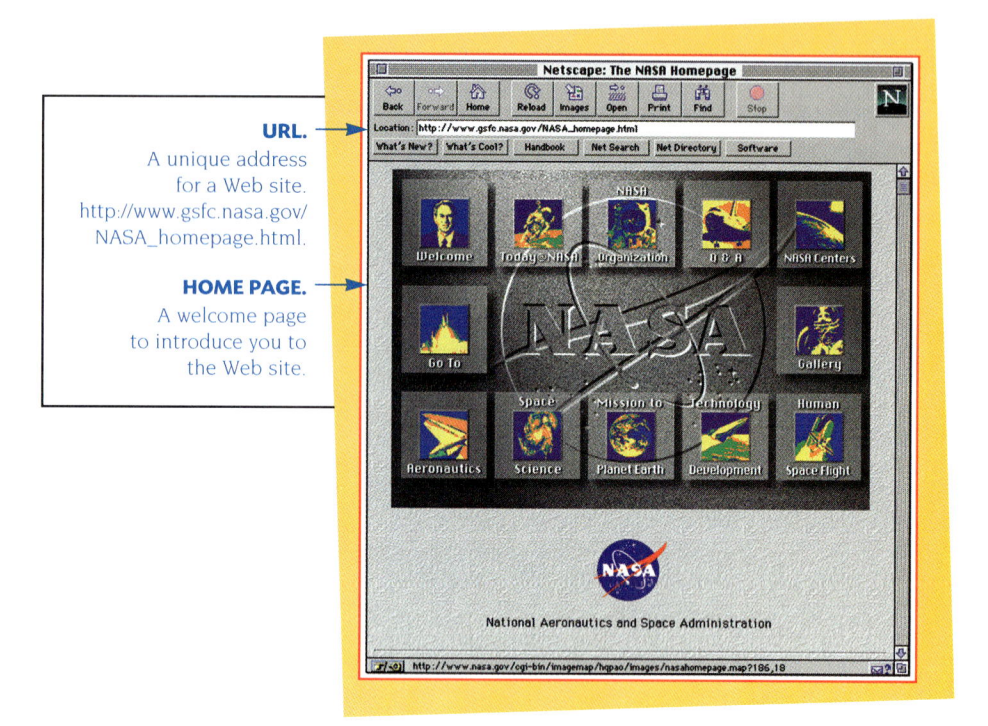

DID YOU KNOW? With over 60 million users in more than 80 countries, the Internet is the largest computer network in the world. Projections call for more than 5 billion people worldwide to be on the Internet by the year 2003.

URL. A unique address for a Web site. http://www.gsfc.nasa.gov/NASA_homepage.html.

HOME PAGE. A welcome page to introduce you to the Web site.

When you find a home page that you would like to revisit later, you can place an electronic bookmark on that page using a simple menu command. To revisit the site, you just click on the **bookmark.** Bookmarks make it easy to revisit your favorite places.

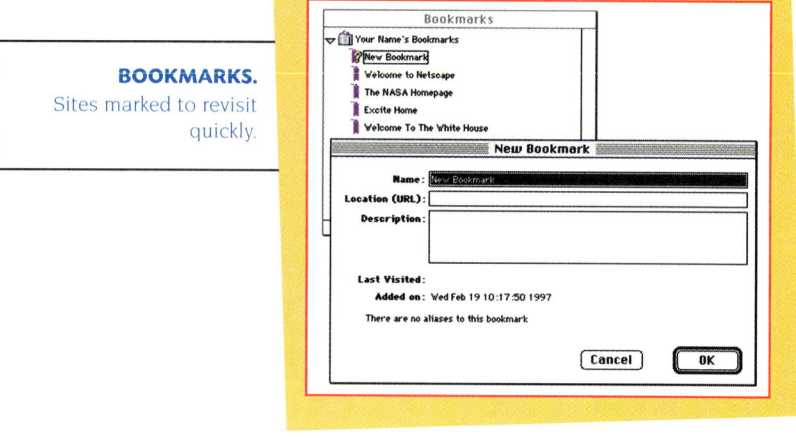

BOOKMARKS. Sites marked to revisit quickly.

Copyright 1996 Netscape Communications Corp. Used with permission. All Rights Reserved. This page may not be reprinted or copied without the express written permission of Netscape.

444 Section 22 Internet Basics

interNET CONNECTION

Many schools or school systems have developed Web pages. Using your browser and a search engine, search for Web pages of other schools. Show the most engaging ones to your students to help them as they brainstorm about ideas for your school's Web page.

444

Social Studies Connection

Project 146

EXPLORE INTERNET SITES

In this project, you will visit and bookmark the White House home page using your browser software. Use the Help feature of your software to guide you through the steps below.

Note: Skip this project if you do not have communications software with access to the Internet.

1. Connect to your Internet service provider or your commercial on-line service.
2. Start your communications software program.
3. Start your Internet browser software.
4. Select the browser search tool or command.
5. In the search window or the URL address line, type: *http://www.whitehouse.gov*
6. Start the search and wait for a response from your Internet service.
7. The home page of the White House should appear.
8. Browse through the information you see on the screen.
9. Once you find something of interest, click the icon to receive the information on your screen.
10. Print a copy of this screen of information.
11. Place a bookmark on the home page of the White House and exit this screen.
12. Quit your Internet browser software.
13. Disconnect (hang up) from the Internet service.

Internet Sites **445**

Social Studies Connection

To generate interest in social studies, have students make a list of the information they think should be available on a White House home page. Ask them to compare their preliminary list with the actual page.

Project 146
Internet Sites

PRACTICE—LEVEL 1

Purpose
Practice using browser software to explore the Internet.

Time
Thirty minutes

Preparation
Make sure the communication and browser software is ready to use, and the ISP or commercial service provider is available.

Teaching Tip
Observe students carefully as they access the Web site. Students who finish early should explore some of the links available on the White House home page.

Trouble Shooting
Provide individual help to students who are having difficulty.

Wrap Up
Make sure students disconnect from the ISP or commercial service provider.
   If this is the last project for this class period, ask students to return computers and furniture to the appropriate conditions.

22.3 Browser

FOCUS
Use a browser to search for information on the Internet. Download and print Internet information.

BELLRINGER
When students enter the room, direct their attention to the assignment on the board:
Read pages 446–447 to learn about browsers.

TEACH
Use a computer and overhead display device to show students how to use a Web search engine. Point out that many of the pages listed as being a potential "match" may in reality have little to do with the topic at hand.

Some search engines list only Web pages, while others search Usenet as well.

Popular search engines on the Web include the following:

Excite (http://www.excite.com/). Another Web/Usenet search engine, this site also lets you access travel and reference information, as well as read the news.

Infoseek (http://www.infoseek.com). Infoseek is a general-purpose search engine.

Yahoo (http://www.yahoo.com/). The granddaddy of today's Web searching tools, Yahoo allows the user to search by words and phrases or by selecting a category. Yahoo also provides instant access to the day's news.

446

22.3 Browser

USING A BROWSER

As you have discovered, an on-line browser search tool is an easy way to navigate through the Internet. There are many different commercial search engines on the Internet. A **search engine** is a software program that acts as your information detective when you don't know a specific address. It looks for word matches based on keywords you type in the search window. **Keywords** can be one or more words that help the search engine find the most appropriate matches.

Search engines look through many electronic files on the World Wide Web (WWW). When a search is complete, a list of matching Web sites appears. You can then browse the list to see which sites you are most interested in visiting. When you click on the site you want to visit, you are usually taken there almost immediately. If there is a lot of traffic on the network where the site is located, it may take a few seconds or even minutes to reach the site. Click the Stop button if you want to cancel movement to a site. If you want to move back to previous sites you have visited during this session, use the Back button to retrace your steps.

Goals
- Use a browser to search for information on the Internet
- Download and print Internet information

NET SEARCH. Click to open the search page.

BROWSER. A program to view and explore the Internet. This is the Netscape Navigator icon.

SEARCH ENGINE. A software feature that looks for word matches based on keyword(s).

Copyright 1996 Netscape Communications Corp. Used with permission. All Rights Reserved. This page may not be reprinted or copied without the express written permission of Netscape.

446 Section 22 Internet Basics

RESOURCES

Lesson Plan: LP118
Supplemental Project: SP26

CD-ROM: Reference Guide

Software: Research Files

SEARCH RESULTS.
Result of a keyword Web search match. The window displaying match results will differ depending on the type of search engine you use.

Note: This search found 261,537 matches. Try to use specific keywords to narrow the search results.

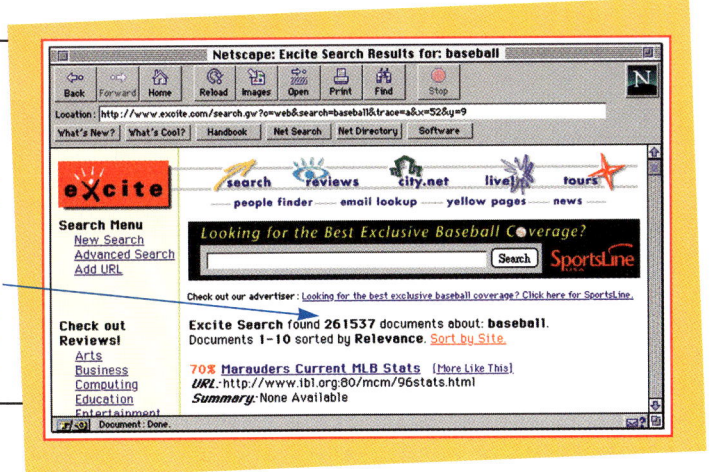

Once you find the information you want, you can print or download the file to your computer. When you download from the Internet, you copy information from a Web site file to another location. You download a file by using the File menu and Save command. If any of the hypertext words say *download*, you can download by simply clicking on these words.

HYPERTEXT.
Words that link you to other Web pages or perhaps a different section of the same Web site. This link will download a file automatically.

interNET CONNECTION
Hypertext links on the World Wide Web work like cross-references in a encyclopedia. For example, an encyclopedia entry on space exploration might have cross-references, or links, to NASA, satellites, and the space shuttle.

Copyright 1996 Netscape Communications Corp. Used with permission. All Rights Reserved. This page may not be reprinted or copied without the express written permission of Netscape.

Browser **447**

Browser

TEACH
Demonstrate how easy it is to access Web pages after a search. If more than one screen of matches is generated after a search, show how to access the next screen of possible matches.

ASSESS
To assess students' understanding, have them describe how to use a browser and how to search for information on the Web.

CLOSE
Have students explore a browser as described in Project 147.

DID YOU KNOW?
Sometimes links move from one location to another. When this happens, a new address is usually provided on the original site.

CULTURAL KALEIDOSCOPE
Point out to students that links will often connect them to sites around the world. In fact, it is possible that they could end up on a page that is not written in English.

447

Project 147
Browser

PRACTICE—LEVEL 1

Purpose
Practice using browser software to search for information and then download the needed information to a local computer.

Time
Class period

Preparation
Make sure the communication and browser software is ready to use, and the ISP or commercial service provider is available. Students need a data disk to receive the downloaded files.

Teaching Tip
Observe students carefully as they access the Web site. Make sure students download the required files to their data disks and not the hard drive.

Students who finish early should explore some of the links available on the NASA home page.

Trouble Shooting
Provide individual help to students who are having difficulty.

Wrap Up
Make sure students disconnect from the ISP or commercial service provider.

If this is the last project for this class period, ask students to return computers and furniture to the appropriate conditions.

Project 147

Science Connection

USE A BROWSER

In this project, you will use your browser software to search a Web site to locate information. Then you will download information to your computer. Use the Help feature of your browser software to guide you through the steps below.

Note: Skip this project if you do not have communications software with access to the Internet.

1. Connect to your Internet service provider or your commercial on-line service.
2. Start your Internet browser software.
3. Select the browser search tool or command.
4. In the search window, type: NASA.
5. Wait a few minutes to see the search results.
6. Once the search is complete, browse the list of results to find information specific to NASA.
7. Click on one of the choices in the list and search for two new interesting science-related topics.
8. Once you have found the information, download the files to your data disk.
9. Save the files as STCM147A and STCM147B.
10. Exit the search engine and disconnect from the on-line service.
11. Print a copy of the files you downloaded.

448 Section 22 Internet Basics

CULTURAL KALEIDOSCOPE

Students might be interested in exploring space programs in other countries. Point them to http://www.esrin.esa.it/ for information about the European Space Agency.

Science Connection

To generate interest in science, ask students to research the training required to be an astronaut. They can do their research on the Web or through printed publications.

Project 148
Building Your Portfolio

SCIENCE Connection

In this portfolio project, you will use a browser search tool to locate information to answer a list of questions for your science class. Use the Help feature of your browser software to guide you through the steps below.

Note: Skip this project if you do not have communications software with access to the Internet.

NOW TRY THIS

1. Connect to your Internet service provider or your commercial on-line service. Start your Internet browser software.
2. Using the browser search tool or command, go to the CNN Weather home page or a similar page that provides weather information.
3. Research the weather in Washington, D.C., to find answers to the following questions:
   - What is the current temperature?
   - What is the current humidity?
   - What is tomorrow's weather forecast?
   - What is the forecast for the next few days?
4. Download the information from the Internet to your data disk.
5. Save the file as STCM148A.
6. Research the weather for your city or area to find answers to the questions in Step 3 for your area.
7. Download the information from the Internet to your data disk.
8. Save the file as STCM148B.
9. Bookmark this site for future use.
10. Quit your Internet browser software and disconnect from the on-line service.
11. Print the weather information you downloaded for Washington, D.C. and for your area.

✓ Check Your Understanding

1. Did you try several keywords to search for information?
2. Did you download information to your data disk?
3. Did you add a bookmark to the weather site?

To encourage interest in science, have students write to the local news station to find out how the Internet is used in the preparation of the daily weather forecast. Or, have them check out and compare weather information found on the Web pages of various local television stations.

Project 148
Building Your Portfolio

PRACTICE—LEVEL 1

Purpose
Practice using a browser search tool to locate information on the World Wide Web.

Time
Class period

Preparation
Make sure the communication and browser software is ready to use, and the ISP or commercial service provider is available. Students need a data disk to receive the downloaded files.

Teaching Tip
Observe students carefully as they access the Web site. Make sure students download the required files to their data disks and not the hard drive.

Students who finish early should explore some of the links available on the page.

Trouble Shooting
Provide individual help to students who are having difficulty.

Wrap Up
Make sure students disconnect from the ISP or commercial service provider.

Have students review their work using **Check Your Understanding.**

If this is the last project for this class period, ask students to return computers and furniture to the appropriate conditions.

22.4 Integration

FOCUS
Integrate information downloaded from the Internet into a document.

BELLRINGER
When students enter the room, direct their attention to the assignment on the board:
Read page 450 to learn about copyrighted information.

TEACH
In this age of easy information access, we sometimes forget that most of the material available is subject to copyright laws. Point out to students that by honoring the copyright laws, they support an environment that encourages the future development and exchange of ideas and other intellectual properties.

ASSESS
To assess students' understanding, have them discuss when it is acceptable to use information and when appropriate credit must be given to the information source.

CLOSE
Have students explore data integration as described in Project 149.

Integration

22.4

Goal
- Integrate information downloaded from the Internet into a document

INTEGRATING DOWNLOADED INFORMATION

After you download information from the Internet, you can integrate facts, direct quotes, pictures, or other information into other documents you create. Carefully read the on-line credits or copyright information provided with any information or images that you wish to download and use in your documents to avoid violating copyright rules.

Facts cannot be copyrighted so you do not have to worry about using facts that you download. For example, if you download information that shows the current yearly rainfall in Cincinnati as 39 inches, you may use that information freely. However, if you download a lengthy article about rainfall in various cities around the country, you need to treat this article as you would an article you find in print. Give credit for the information you quote from the article and observe fair use copyright rules.

Many images (pictures, clip art, drawings, cartoons) on the Internet are copyrighted and should not be used without the owner's permission. However, with a little patient searching, you can find may images on the Internet that you may use freely. A search using the term "free clip art" is a good place to start. To be safe, assume that images are copyrighted unless the credits clearly state that they may be used freely. The illustration shows a sample disclaimer statement for free clip art.

DISCLAIMER STATEMENT.
Details acceptable use of the clip art found on this Web site.

it's the... disclaimer!
Everyone is welcome to grab any of the images that are listed on the "free web art" page.

Please keep in mind that these images are for personal use only, and are not intended to be used for commercial endeavors. If you would like to have an image uniquely created for yourself or an organization, please feel free to contact me.

450 Section 22 Internet Basics

RESOURCES
Lesson Plan: LP119
Supplemental Project: SP26

CD-ROM: Reference Guide

Software: Research Files

Project 149

INTEGRATION

Your science teacher has asked you to search for information on severe weather. You will use keywords and search engines to locate information on thunderstorms, tornadoes, or hurricanes. You will use the information to add sentences to a report you prepared earlier entitled *Severe Weather*. Use the Help feature of your software to guide you through the steps below.

Note: Skip this project if you do not have communications software with access to the Internet.

1. Open the file CM149 on your data disk.
2. Print the report on Severe Weather and then close the file.
3. Connect to your Internet service provider or your commercial on-line service.
4. Start your Internet browser software.
5. Select the browser search tool or command.
6. Search the Internet for information on thunderstorms, tornadoes, or hurricanes.
7. Browse the search results until you find at least three new facts to add to your report.
8. Place a bookmark on one page you would like to revisit later.
9. Download the information you find on severe weather to your data disk.
10. Save the information as STCM149A.
11. Quit your Internet browser software and disconnect from the on-line service.
12. Open the file CM149.
13. Compose a few sentences to add the new facts you found regarding severe weather to an appropriate section(s) in the report.
14. Print the revised report.
15. Save the revised report as STCM149B.

Integration 451

To encourage interest in science, ask students to investigate the impact of a recent snowstorm, flood, wind storm, or other severe weather occurrence on the local community. For example, was the power disrupted? For how long? Students should generate their own list of questions to explore.

Project 149
Integration

PRACTICE—LEVEL 1

Purpose
Practice integrating downloaded information

Time
Class period

Preparation
Make sure the communication and browser software is ready to use, and the ISP or commercial service provider is available. Students need a data disk to receive the downloaded files.

Teaching Tip
Observe students carefully as they access the Web site. Make sure students download the required files to their data disks and not the hard drive.

Students who finish early should explore some of the links available on the page.

Trouble Shooting
Provide individual help to students who are having difficulty.

Wrap Up
Make sure students disconnect from the ISP or commercial service provider.

If this is the last project for this class period, ask students to return computers and furniture to the appropriate conditions.

DID YOU KNOW? Sever weather may result in excessive property damage. The great Midwest flood of 1993 caused nearly $12 billion in property and agricultural damage.

451

Project 150
Integration

ASSESS—LEVEL 2

Purpose
Assess integration skills by gathering information from the Internet and using it to produce a flyer.

Time
Class period

Preparation
Make sure the communication and browser software is ready to use, and the ISP or commercial service provider is available. Students need a data disk to receive the downloaded files.

Teaching Tip
Observe students carefully as they access the Web site. Make sure students download the required files to their data disks and not the hard drive.

Trouble Shooting
Provide individual help to students who are having difficulty.

Wrap Up
Make sure students disconnect from the ISP or commercial service provider.

If this is the last project for this class period, ask students to return computers and furniture to the appropriate conditions.

Project 150

Social Studies Connection

INTEGRATION

Your swim coach has asked you to help design a flyer for the Swim Club to attract young people to competitive swimming. You agree to search the Internet, gather data, and design a flyer. Review the illustration. Your finished project may look a bit different. Use the Help feature of your software to guide you through the steps below.

Note: Skip this project if you do not have communications software with access to the Internet.

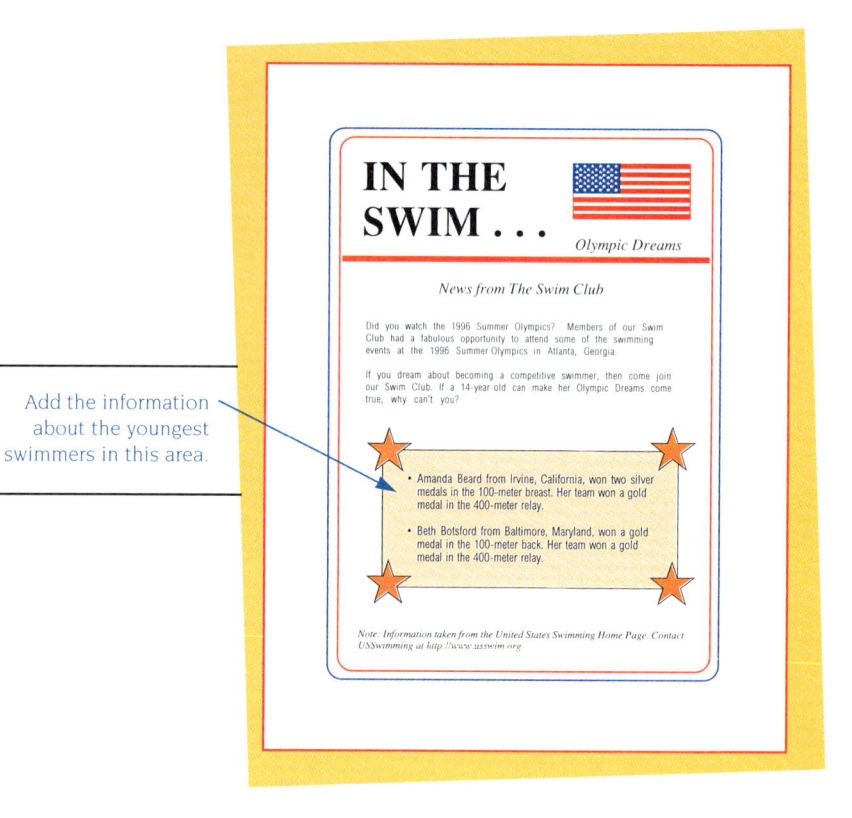

IN THE SWIM . . .
Olympic Dreams

News from The Swim Club

Did you watch the 1996 Summer Olympics? Members of our Swim Club had a fabulous opportunity to attend some of the swimming events at the 1996 Summer Olympics in Atlanta, Georgia.

If you dream about becoming a competitive swimmer, then come join our Swim Club. If a 14-year-old can make her Olympic Dreams come true, why can't you?

Add the information about the youngest swimmers in this area.

- Amanda Beard from Irvine, California, won two silver medals in the 100-meter breast. Her team won a gold medal in the 400-meter relay.
- Beth Botsford from Baltimore, Maryland, won a gold medal in the 100-meter back. Her team won a gold medal in the 400-meter relay.

Note: Information taken from the United States Swimming Home Page. Contact USSwimming at http://www.usswim.org

(continued on next page)

452 Section 22 Internet Basics

Social Studies Connection

Generate interest in social studies by asking students to collect and review flyers from local public agencies, such as the Red Cross or a local food bank. How do the flyers help generate interest in the organization? Ask students to make suggestions for improving the flyers.

Project 150 (continued)

1. Open the file CM150 on your data disk.
2. Print this file to use as a reference when you are researching the Olympics on the Internet.
3. Close the file CM150.
4. Connect to your Internet service provider or your commercial on-line service.
5. Start your Internet browser software.
6. Select the browser search tool or command.
7. Search the Internet for information using the keywords *swimming Olympics*.
8. Review the search results.
9. Find the US Swimming home page at their URL address: *www.usswim.org*.
10. Find the following facts for the two youngest swimmers:
    - Name
    - Home town
    - Age
    - Olympic events
    - Medals won
    - Other information you think would be interesting for use in the flyer
11. Download the information to your data disk and save it as STCM150A.
12. Quit your Internet browser software and disconnect from the on-line service.
13. Open the file CM150.
14. Add a text box containing a bulleted list of information about the two youngest swimmers.
15. Use your desktop publishing skills to highlight this new information and enhance the flyer.
16. Print the revised flyer.
17. Save the flyer as STCM150B.

Integration

Glossary

A

active cell: the cell in use in a spreadsheet. (Sect. 15)

alignment: a software feature you use to change the horizontal position of text such as left, centered, or right. (Sect. 8, 15)

application software: a software program that helps you use the computer to do specific activities like word processing or spreadsheets. (Sect. 2)

arrow keys: keys with arrows on them you use to move the insertion point up, down, left, or right. (Sect. 5)

attachment: an e-mail software feature you use to send a document or file with an e-mail message. (Sect. 21)

AUTOSUM function: a built-in formula in a spreadsheet that adds the values in a cell range. (Sect. 15)

AVERAGE function: a built-in formula in a spreadsheet that adds the values in a cell range and divides the sum by the number of values in the range. (Sect. 15)

B

bibliography: an alphabetical list of the sources of information you used in writing a report. (Sect. 9)

block style: a letter style that has all lines typed at the left margin. (Sect. 10)

border: a software feature you use to add an outline around an object, page, or spreadsheet cells. (Sect. 12, 16)

bookmark: an Internet software feature that allows you to place an electronic bookmark on a page so you can easily revisit the page. (Sect. 22)

bounced message: an e-mail message that has been returned to the sender because of an error of some kind. (Sect. 21)

bound report: a report with extra space added at the left margin to allow for pages to be placed in a notebook. (Sect. 8)

browser: Internet software that helps you view and explore the Internet Web pages. (Sect. 22)

bulleted list: a software feature you use to create a list in which each item begins with a bullet such as a circle, diamond, square, or triangle. (Sect. 8)

byline: the name of the writer in a report. (Sect. 8)

C

caps lock: a key you use to type all characters in uppercase. (Sect. 5)

caption: the words or phrases that draw attention or emphasize a graphic. (Sect. 14)

cc notation: an e-mail software feature you use to send a copy of your message to one or more persons. (Sect. 21)

cell: the box formed at the point where a column and row meet in a spreadsheet or table. (Sect. 15)

cell name or address: the location (column letter and row number) of the active cell in a spreadsheet. (Sect. 15)

cell pointer: the spreadsheet mouse pointer. (Sect. 15)

cell protection: the process of "freezing" cell contents in a spreadsheet so that they cannot be accidentally changed. (Sect. 15)

cell range: a continuous group of selected cells in a spreadsheet. (Sect. 15)

chart: a graphic that uses bars, lines, or other pictures to show the relationships among the values in a spreadsheet. (Sect. 16)

citation: usually the author's last name and page number in an MLA style report; used to give credit to the source of information. (Sect. 8)

454 Glossary

clip art: a gallery or collection of graphic images or pictures that you can add to documents. (Sect. 2, 13, 16)

close: a software feature you use to end or close a document. (Sect. 4)

color spectrum: a range of colors from cool to warm. (Sect. 12)

column: information arranged vertically on a page; in a spreadsheet, columns are identified by letters such as A, B, C. (Sect. 11, 15)

column layout: a database report displaying information in columns. (Sect. 19)

communications: a software program one computer uses to communicate with another. (Sect. 2)

communications session: the process of connecting to a bulletin board system, exchanging programs or messages, and disconnecting from the bulletin board system. (Sect. 20)

computer case: a case that holds the major parts of the computer such as the CPU, hard drive, and disk drives. (Sect. 1)

D

database: a software program you use to organize, find, and display information in many different ways; any organized collection of information on a given subject or topic. (Sect. 2, 18)

date (command): a software feature you use to add the date to a document automatically. (Sect. 10)

desktop computer: a computer designed for you to use on a desktop. (Sect. 1)

desktop publishing: a software program you use to enhance and create documents like newsletters, flyers, and brochures. (Sect. 2)

disclaimer: information that details acceptable use of data found on the Internet. (Sect. 22)

disk drive: hardware that holds, reads from, and writes to computer disks. (Sect. 1)

domain name: the second part of an e-mail address that identifies the Internet service provider's address; periods (dots) separate the different parts of a domain name. (Sect. 21)

dot leaders: a line of periods you use to lead the eye from the text to the page number in a table of contents. (Sect. 9)

dot matrix printer: an inexpensive, durable printer that uses a pattern of tiny ink dots to produce an image. (Sect. 1)

download: the process of transferring programs or information from one computer to another. (Sect. 20, 22)

draw: a software feature you use to draw objects like lines and shapes in a document. (Sect. 12)

E

editing: changing a document in some way such as deleting, moving, or adding characters. (Sect. 4)

e-mail address: an electronic address that has two parts (user name and domain name) separated by the @ (at) symbol. (Sect. 21)

e-mail message: an electronic message that usually includes the e-mail address, subject line, and body of the message. (Sect. 21)

enclosure notation: a special notation at the end of a letter (usually the word *Enclosure*); indicates that an item(s) is included with the letter. (Sect. 10)

endnote: a software feature you use to create endnotes; notes at the end of a report that identify the source of information in a report. (Sect. 9)

Entry bar: area on a spreadsheet where the text, number, or formula in the active cell is displayed; also called the Formula bar in some programs. (Sect. 15)

ethics: the standards of honesty, morality, and fairness as related to using computers. (Sect. 3)

F

fax: short for facsimile which means copy or duplicate; used to produce a copy of a document similar to a photocopy. (Sect. 1)

field: one category of information in a database. (Sect. 18)

field type: a software feature you use to choose a field type such as number in a database. (Sect. 18)

fill: a software feature you use to change the color or shading inside an object. (Sect. 12)

fill down: a spreadsheet feature you use to copy cell contents to a range of cells below the active cell. (Sect. 15)

fill right: a spreadsheet feature you use to copy cell contents to a range of cells to the right of the active cell. (Sect. 15)

fill series: a spreadsheet feature you use to generate a series of values (numbers, dates, or times) based on the value in the active cell. (Sect. 15)

find: a software feature you use to find a record or group of records in a database. (Sect. 18)

find and replace: a software feature you use to replace a word or group of words with a different word or group of words. (Sect. 8)

flame: an angry e-mail message. (Sect. 21)

floppy disk: a removable storage device, usually one flat disk enclosed in a case; used to store small amounts of information. (Sect. 1)

font: a software feature you use to change the style of the text in a document. (Sect. 4)

footer: a software feature you use to add information at the bottom of a page. (Sect. 9, 18)

footnote: a software feature you use to add a note that identifies the source of information in a report. (Sect. 9)

form view: a database view you use to design a form by arranging fields and adding pictures or drawings or other enhancements. (Sect. 18)

format: the appearance of information such as bold or italics; in a spreadsheet displaying commas, dollar signs, percent signs, or decimal places. (Sect. 15)

forms: a graphical representation of a record in a database. (Sect. 18, 19)

formula field: a database field used to create a mathematical formula. (Sect. 19)

formula results: the end product or action of a formula. (Sect. 15)

formula: a combination of values or cell references and mathematical operators (addition, subtraction, multiplication, and division). (Sect. 15)

forwarding: an e-mail software feature you use to send a copy of a message you have written or received to another person. (Sect. 21)

frequently asked question (FAQ): Internet documents that list the common questions and answers related to a specific newsgroup or site. (Sect. 22)

functions: built-in formulas in a spreadsheet. (Sect. 15)

G

graphics: a software program you use to enhance documents with pictures and images. (Sect. 2)

greeting: usually the word *Dear* followed by the name of the person to whom you are writing. (Sect. 10)

gridlines: the dotted or solid lines that appear around cells in a spreadsheet. (Sect. 16)

group: a software feature you use to arrange several items in a drawing into one group. (Sect. 12)

GUI: graphical user interface; uses pictures and symbols to represent files and commands. (Sect. 2)

H

hacking: the unauthorized use of a computer system or program. (Sect. 3)

hanging indent: a software feature you use to indent wraparound lines about 0.5 inch; used in formatting a bibliography. (Sect. 9)

456 Glossary

hard disk: a storage device, usually a stack of disks enclosed in a case; used to store large amounts of information. (Sect. 1)

hardware: the physical parts of a computer system such as the monitor, the keyboard, and the hard drive. (Sect. 1)

header: a software feature you use to add information at the top of the page in a document. (Sect. 8, 19)

headline: the main topic in a newsletter (Sect. 14)

home page: a Web page that functions like the table of contents in a book to introduce you to a Web site. (Sect. 22)

hypertext words: words on an Internet page that you can click on to jump or link to information on another page. (Sect. 22)

I

icon: pictures and symbols in software that represent files or commands. (Sect. 2)

in box: an e-mail software feature you use to store incoming messages. (Sect. 21)

inkjet printer: a medium quality printer that uses an ink cartridge to produce an image. (Sect. 1)

input device: hardware that allows you to communicate with your computer such as a keyboard. (Sect. 1)

insertion point: a mark that blinks on the screen to show the place where text will be inserted. (Sect. 5)

integrated software: software packages that combine several software applications programs into one group. (Sect. 2)

integration: the process of exchanging data among software applications; for example, a drawing created in a paint program or a spreadsheet chart could be copied into a word processing document. (Sect. 17, 19, 22)

interactive: the ability of software to help you react and make choices as you use a software program. (Sect. 2)

Internet: a huge network of computers that connects smaller networks of computers (Sect. 1, 20)

Internet service provider (ISP): a company that charges a fee to provide you with easy access to the Internet. (Sect. 20)

K

keyboard: a common input device that allows you to communicate to a computer; includes letters, numbers, symbols, function keys, etc. (Sect. 1)

keyword: one or more words typed in a search box in order to search for matches on the Internet. (Sect. 22)

L

label: words entered in a spreadsheet cell; cell contents are treated as text by the spreadsheet. (Sect. 15)

landscape: the printing of information across the long edge of a paper so that the page layout is wide. (Sect. 15)

laptop computer: a very small portable computer designed to be small enough and light enough to use on your lap. (Sect. 1)

laser printer: a high-quality printer that uses a laser beam and ink toner cartridge to produce an image. (Sect. 1)

legend: a guide on a chart that explains the symbols, colors, etc., used to represent categories of data. (Sect. 16)

light pen: a hand-held input device that looks like a pen. (Sect. 1)

line chart: a chart type that uses points on a grid connected by lines to represent values in a spreadsheet. (Sect. 16)

line spacing: a software feature you use to adjust the blank space between lines of type. (Sect. 8)

list view: a database view you use to see many records at once in a grid of rows and columns like a spreadsheet. (Sect. 18)

log off: the process of electronically disconnecting one computer from another over a phone line. (Sect. 20)

Glossary **457**

log on: the process of electronically connecting one computer to another over a phone line to exchange data. (Sect. 20)

M

magnetic tape: a storage device, usually stored in a cartridge, reel, or cassette; used to store large amounts of information for a long time. (Sect. 1)

main topic: the major ideas in a chapter or presentation; usually preceded by Roman numerals in a chapter outline. (Sect. 11)

mainframe: a large computer used to process massive amounts of information (Sect. 1)

managing e-mail messages: the process of deleting, storing, filing, and/or printing e-mail messages. (Sect. 21)

margin: a software feature you use to adjust the blank space surrounding a document on all sides. (Sect. 8)

masthead: the title of a newsletter, usually with an issue number and a date. (Sect. 14)

mathematical operators: a mathematical function or symbol such as addition (+), subtraction (−), multiplication (*), and division (/). (Sect. 15)

MAX function: a built-in formula in a spreadsheet that determines the largest or maximum number in a cell range. (Sect. 15)

memo: a document with the headings To, From, Date, and Subject; used to communicate informally usually among people within the same group or organization. (Sect. 10)

memory: hardware that stores computer processing instructions and information. (Sect. 1)

microphone: a device that allows you to record sounds as input to your computer. (Sect. 1)

MIN function: a built-in formula in a spreadsheet that determines the smallest or minimum number in a cell range. (Sect. 15)

minicomputer: a midsize computer used to process large amounts of information. (Sect. 1)

MLA report heading: a special format for the heading of a report that includes the name of the writer, teachers, class, and date. (Sect. 8)

modem: hardware that allows your computer to communicate with other computers over phone lines. (Sect. 1)

monitor: a screen similar to a TV screen you use to view information. (Sect. 1)

mouse: a hand-held input device; you use by rolling it over a flat surface, pointing, clicking, and dragging. (Sect. 1)

moving: a software feature you use to change the position of text or objects. (Sect. 12)

N

navigating: a software feature you use to move around in a document electronically. (Sect. 4, 8)

netiquette: a word used to describe some basic rules to guide you when composing a proper e-mail message. (Sect. 21)

network: a system of computers linked together to share information and hardware. (Sect. 1)

new document: a software feature you use to create a new, blank document. (Sect. 4)

newsgroup: an Internet discussion group that is formed to exchange ideas. (Sect. 22)

notebook computer: a small portable computer designed to unfold like an open notebook. (Sect. 1)

num lock: the key with *num lock* on it; used to operate the numeric keypad. (Sect. 7)

number field: a format you assign to a database field when it will contain a number to be used in a mathematical formula. (Sect. 19)

numbered list: a software feature you use to create a list in which each item begins with a number. (Sect. 8)

O

open: a software feature you use to open a computer file such as a letter or spreadsheet. (Sect. 4)

458 Glossary

operating system software: computer programs that direct all the activities and set all the rules for how the hardware and software work together. (Sect. 2)

optical disc: a storage device, usually called laser disks or compact disks (CDs); used to hold very large amounts of information permanently. (Sect. 1)

out box: an e-mail software feature you use to store outgoing messages. (Sect. 21)

outline style: a software feature that automatically changes the style of the lines in an outline. (Sect. 9)

output device: hardware that allows your computer to communicate with you such as a monitor or printer. (Sect. 1)

P

page number: a software feature you use to add a page number to a document. (Sect. 8)

page orientation: the direction (portrait or landscape) in which information is printed across the paper. (Sect. 15)

paint: a software feature you use to create an original graphic such as a drawing or picture. (Sect. 13)

paragraph indent: a software feature you use to indent a paragraph from both the left and the right margins. (Sect. 9)

personal computer: a smaller, less powerful computer used to perform many of the same tasks as minicomputers but on a smaller scale. (Sect. 1)

picture: a software feature you use to add a graphic or picture to a document. (Sect. 13, 16, 19)

portrait orientation: the printing of information across the short edge of a paper so that the page layout is tall. (Sect. 15)

presentation outline: an outline or listing of the main topics and subtopics in an oral report. (Sect. 11)

preview: a software feature you use to view an entire document, including margins, page numbers, and so on. (Sect. 4)

print: a software feature you use to print copies of documents. (Sect. 4)

print range: a group of selected cells in a spreadsheet used to print selected cells only. (Sect. 15)

printer: an output device that gives you information from the computer in printed form. (Sect. 1)

private data: information that is personal such as credit card numbers and security passwords. (Sect. 3)

public data: information that is either not personal or that carries the owner's permission for use. (Sect. 3)

Q

quit: a software feature you use to close a software program. (Sect. 4)

R

record: a group of fields that are all related to the same topic or idea in a database. (Sect. 18)

reference number: a raised number inserted automatically by the footnote feature in word processing software; matches the footnote number at the bottom of the page. (Sect. 9)

relative cell referencing: an automatic process in a spreadsheet of copying formulas to other cells and adjusting the cell references so that they reflect their new addresses. (Sect. 15)

report: a summary of information in a database you arrange in an attractive, organized, easily understandable format. (Sect. 19)

resizing: a software feature you use to change the size of an object like a drawing, picture, or text box. (Sect. 12)

reverse text: white text on a black background. (Sect. 12)

row: information arranged horizontally on a page; in a spreadsheet, rows are identified by numbers such as 1, 2, or 3. (Sect. 15)

S

sabotage: a deliberate act that causes the damage or destruction of computer hardware or software. (Sect. 3)

sans serif font: a font with no serifs, or short cross lines, at the ends of letters. (Sect. 12)

save: a software feature you use to save data on a hard drive or floppy disk. (Sect. 4)

save as: a software feature you use to save a file under a different name. (Sect. 4)

saved search: a software feature you use to save the results of database search in a database file. (Sect. 19)

scanner: an input device; used to turn pictures or documents into groups of dots or pixels using a light source. (Sect. 1)

scrolling: the movement of text up, down, left, or right on a computer screen. (Sect. 5)

search engine: a software program on the Internet that looks for word matches based on keywords you type in the search window. (Sect. 22)

search results: the findings of a keyword Web search match. (Sect. 22)

selecting: a software feature you use to highlight text in order to change it in some way. (Sect. 4, 8, 12)

serif font: a font with short cross lines at the ends of letters. (Sect. 12)

shouting: an e-mail message typed in all caps. (Sect. 21)

side heading: the major subdivisions or major topics of a report. (Sect. 8)

signature: an e-mail software feature you use to include your name and perhaps an address automatically at the end of your message. (Sect. 21)

smiley: a group of characters used in an e-mail message that look like a human face turned sideways. (Sect. 21)

software: computer programs that tell the computer what to do. (Sect. 2)

software piracy: the unauthorized use or duplication of a software program. (Sect. 3)

sort: a software feature you use to sort or arrange information in a certain order such as alphabetic or numeric. (Sect. 15,18)

speaker: an output device that allows you to hear voice, music, and other sounds from your computer. (Sect. 1)

speller: a software feature you use to check the spelling in a document. (Sect. 4)

spreadsheet: a software program you use to process financial or mathematical information. (Sect. 2)

stack: a software feature you use to place one object on top of or behind another object. (Sect. 12)

start: a software feature you use to launch a computer program. (Sect. 4)

storage device: hardware that allows you to store information such as a hard drive or a floppy disk. (Sect. 1)

structure: the way a database is set up including the field names and field types. (Sect. 19)

style: a group of automatic formatting changes used to enhance the appearance of a document or spreadsheet. (Sect. 16)

subtitle: the explanatory title in a report (Sect. 8)

subtopic: a minor point idea in a chapter or presentation; usually preceded by letters and numbers in a chapter outline. (Sect. 11)

SUM function: a built-in formula in a spreadsheet that adds the values in a cell range. (Sect. 15)

supercomputer: the most powerful type of computer; often used to forecast weather, navigate satellites, etc. (Sect. 1)

switch windows: a software feature you use to move from one open document or program to another. (Sect. 14, 17)

T

tab: a key you use to move the insertion point to a preset position. (Sect. 5)

tab set: a software feature you use to move text to a predefined position on a line. (Sect. 9)

460 Glossary

telecommunication: communicating electronically over distance. (Sect. 3, 7)

telecomputing: the blending of telecommunication and computer technology in things like the telephone system and satellites. (Sect. 3)

template: a software feature you use to create a ready-made document with a preset design. (Sect. 14, 17, 19)

text object: a software feature you use to create a box that holds text so that you can move the text around freely on a page. (Sect. 12)

text field: a format you assign to a database field when it will contain text rather than numbers. (Sect. 19)

thesaurus: a software feature you use to replace one word with another similar word. (Sect. 14)

tool: usually a button on a toolbar in a graphics program; used to draw shapes like rectangles and circles or text boxes. (Sect. 12)

touch screen: an input device; used by touching the computer screen. (Sect. 1)

touchpad: a pressure-sensitive and motion-sensitive input device; used by moving the finger over the touchpad. (Sect. 1)

trackball: a hand-held input device similar to a mouse turned upside down; used by rolling the trackball with the fingers. (Sect. 1)

typeface: the design of a family of type. (Sect. 12)

U

Uniform Resource Locator (URL): the address of a Web site that starts with the abbreviation http://. (Sect. 22)

user name: the first part of an e-mail address that is usually a person's real name or a given name. (Sect. 21)

V

value: numbers entered in a spreadsheet cell; cell contents are treated as number, time, or date by the spreadsheet. (Sect. 15)

view: a software feature you use to look at a document in different ways or to display or hide software features on the screen. (Sect. 4)

W

Web page: An electronic page on the Internet that looks a lot like a page in a magazine except it might have sound clips, video clips, or hypertext words. (Sect. 22)

"what if" analysis: the process of entering various sets of data into a spreadsheet to compare the results in order to analyze data and answer a question. (Sect. 17)

window: a portion of the screen displayed while you are working in a software program or document. (Sect. 4, 8, 12, 20)

word processing: a software program you use to create, edit, and print documents. (Sect. 2)

word wrap: the automatic wrapping of text from the end of one line to the beginning of the next line. (Sect. 5)

workstation: the place where you use a computer such as a desk (Sect. 1)

X

x axis: the horizontal scale on a bar chart that displays the bar labels in a bar chart. (Sect. 16)

Y

y axis: the vertical scale on a bar chart that displays the range of values in a bar chart. (Sect. 16)

Z

zoom: a software feature you use to enlarge or reduce the image on the screen. (Sect. 8)

Glossary **461**

Index

A

a.m., 123
Abbreviation
    for class notes, 248
    for page, 179
    spacing after, 59
Active cell, 298, 307
Address
    book, 409–410, 430, 432
    e-mail, 430–432
    inside, 223
    Internet, 443
    return, 224–225
    spreadsheet, 298
Adjective, 89
Adverbs, 93
Alignment
    changing, 147
    in spreadsheet cell, 301
Alphabetical order, 381–383
Alphabetic keys, 36–105
Ampersand (&), 109–111
Analysis, what if, 356–359
Antivirus software, 62
Apostrophe ('), 94, 96–97, 101
Applications
    communications, 422–453
    database, 366–421
    personal, 236–249
    spreadsheet, 294–365
    word processing, 142–249
Application software, 13–17
Arrow keys, 37
At (@) key, 120, 122–123
Attachment, 432
AUTOSUM, 317
AVERAGE function, 317

B

Backslash (/) key, 129
Bar chart, 343–345, 347–348
Bar code reader, 7
Base ten system, 30
BBS. See Bulletin board system
Bibliography, 191–199
B key, 82, 84–85
Block style, 224
Body
    informal letter, 218
    one-page report, 145, 150
Bold, 27
Bookmark, 444

Border
    design tips, 254
    sample, 253
    spreadsheet, 335–339
    title page, 253–256
Bounced message, 431
Browser, 443, 446–449
Building Your Portfolio
    communications, 439, 449
    database, 388, 399, 413
    desktop publishing, 268–269, 281, 282, 293
    integration, 365, 421
    spreadsheet, 316, 333, 353–354
    word processing, 175–177, 197–199, 214–216, 234–235, 249
Bulleted list, 171–172
Bulletin board system (BBS), 425, 427–428
Business software, 13
Byline, 150

C

Capitalization, 57, 65
Caps lock key, 91–93
Career, 20. See also Focus on Careers in Technology; Job
Caret (^) key, 125–127
cc box, 434
CC notation, 434
CDs. See Compact discs
Cell
    protect, 328–329
    range, 303, 309
    spreadsheet, 298
Central processing unit (CPU), 4
Certificate, 287–289
Changing text, 27–28
Chapter outline, 237–239
Chart, 343–352, 415
Citation, 161–162, 191
C key, 47–49
Class notes, 244–249
Clip art, 15
    in database form, 400
    flyer with, 271–275
    for spreadsheet document, 336
Closing
    document, 152
    file, 28
    formal letter, 223

    informal letter, 218
Colon (:), 63
Color spectrum, 264
Column
    database report, 406
    newspaper, 291
    spreadsheet, 297–298, 303, 328
    word processing, 245
Comma (,)
    after introductory clause, 81
    key, 67–69
    for phrases and clauses, 67
    as separator, 77
    for series, 67
    special uses, 69
    in titles, 179
Commands, 4, 26
Commercial on-line services, 426
Communications, 422–453
    basics, 424–428
    e-mail, 429–439
    Internet, 440–453
    network connections, 425–426
    software, 14, 427–428
Compact discs (CDs), 10
Composing at keyboard, 106
Computer case, 4
Computers
    booting, 46
    cleaning, 90
    ethical use of, 21–24
    hardware, 2–10
    input devices, 6–7
    Macintosh vs. IBM, 12
    output devices, 6, 8–9
    software, 11–17
    storage devices, 6, 9–10
    technology issues, 18–24
    types of, 3–5
    use of, 132
Computer viruses, 23
Contractions, 101
Copy, 31–32, 320
Copyright, 21–22, 450
Cover page, 257–262
CPU. See Central processing unit
Cursor. See Insertion point

D

Data
    integrated, 414–421
    sort, 328
    spreadsheet, 300–302, 356–350

462 Index

Database
- applications, 366–421
- basics, 368–388
- creating, 375–376
- designing, 377–380
- enhanced, 389–421
- exploring, 369–371
- form enhancement, 400–404
- formula field, 392–394
- integration, 414–421
- program, 13
- report, 389–421
- saving, 390
- searching, 369–370, 395–399
- records, 381–387
- structure, 390–391
- template, 409–412
- updating, 372–374

Date
- on formal letter, 223
- on informal letter, 218
- on title page, 155

Decimal system, 30
Desktop computer, 4. *See also* Computers
Desktop publishing
- applications, 250–293
- document enhancement, 252–269
- graphics, 270–282
- software, 15
- templates, 283–293

Disclaimer statement, 450
Disk
- floppy, 9–10
- hard, 9
- removing, 58

Disk drive, 4
Diskette, 9. *See also* Disk
Disk Operating System. *See* DOS
Document
- closing, 152
- enhancement, 252–269
- integrated, 360–365
- new, 26
- previewing, 29–31
- printing, 29–31, 152
- saving, 31–32

Dollar sign ($), 108, 110–111
Domain name, 430–431
DOS, 12
Dot leaders, 200
Dot matrix printer, 8
Downloading, 425, 447
Drawings, 259–261. *See also* Clip art; Graphics; Pictures
Draw tools, 259

E

Editing
- database records, 372
- files, 31–32
- spreadsheet cells, 300–302
- *See also* Proofreading

Education software, 15
E key, 42, 44–45
Electronic-mail message, 9, 19. *See also* E-mail
E-mail
- addresses, 430–431
- basics, 429–432
- commercial on-line services for, 426
- communicating with, 435–439
- features, 431–432
- messages, 433–434
- netiquette, 433
- sending and receiving, 430
- terms, 431
- *See also* Electronic-mail message

Enclosure, 223–224
Encoding, 22
Encyclopedia programs, 15
Endnotes, 186–187
Enter key. *See* Return key
Entertainment and leisure software, 16
Entry, journal, 159
Entry bar, spreadsheet, 298, 307
Envelope, 225
Equal sign (=), 128, 130–131, 307
Et al., 179
Ethics, 21
Exclamation point (!), 112, 114–115

F

Facsimile/fax, 9
FAQs, 441
Fax/modem, 9, 14
Feet (') symbol, 130
Field, database, 369–370, 375, 410
File
- editing, 31–32
- naming, 28, 50
- opening, 28
- safety of, 66
- saving, 31–32, 42

Fill borders, 259
Fill commands, 323–327
Find and replace, 151–152
Find request, database, 384
Flame, 431
Floppy disk, 9–10, 86

Flyer, 263–269, 271–275
Focus on Careers in Technology
- accountants, 295
- authors, 143
- health care, 43
- interior designers, 251
- inventory trackers, 367
- meteorologist, 423
- video game designer, 1

Font style, 28, 258
Footer
- in database record, 384–386
- multipage report with, 210–216

Footnotes, 179–185
Formal letter, 223–228, 234–235
Formatting
- bibliography, 191–199
- chapter outline, 237–238
- class notes, 244–249
- formal letter, 223–225
- informal letter, 218–219
- journal entry, 159
- memo, 229
- multipage report, 161–162, 166–167, 179–190, 210–216
- one-page report, 145–146, 150–154
- presentation outline, 240–243
- report outline, 205–207
- spreadsheet cell, 300
- table of contents, 200–201
- title page, 155–156

Formula
- spreadsheet, 300, 307
- field, 392–394

Form view, 369, 400
Forwarding e-mail message, 435
Fractions, 83, 131
Freeware, 22
Frequently asked questions. *See* FAQs
Frequently misspelled words, 160
Functions, spreadsheet, 317–322

G

G key, 66, 68–69
Global village, 19
Grammar. *See* Language Link
Graphical user interface. *See* GUI design
Graphics, 270–282, 410. *See also* Clip art; Drawings; Pictures
Graphics software, 15
Greater than (>) symbol, 129
Greeting
- on formal letter, 223
- on informal letter, 218

Greeting card, 284–286
Gridlines, 335–339
Group feature, 265
GUI design, 12

H

Hacking, 22
Hanging indent, 174, 193
Hard disk, 9, 42
Hardware, 2–10
Header
    bibliography, 194–199
    database record, 384–386
    journal entry, 159
    MLA style, 161–162, 191
    multipage report, 161–162, 175
Heading
    class notes, 244
    formal letter, 224
    memo, 229
    one-page report, 145
    table of contents, 200
Help feature, 33, 74
H key, 43–45
Home keys, 37–41
Home page, 443–444
Hypertext, 443, 447
Hyphen (-) key, 90, 92–93

I

Ibid., 179
IBM-compatible computers, 12
Icons, 12
I key, 51–53
In box, e-mail, 432
Inches (") symbol, 130
Informal letter, 218–222
Inkjet printer, 8
Input devices, 6–7
Insertion point, 27, 37, 96
Insert rows or columns, 328
Inside address
    on envelope, 225
    on formal letter, 223
Integrated software, 17
Integration, 360–365, 414–421, 450–453
Intellectual property, 21–22
Interactive books, 16
Interjection, 115
Internet, 5, 424
    accessing, 426
    basics, 440–453
    browser, 446–449
    integrating information from, 450–453

    netiquette, 441–442
    newsgroups, 441–442
    sites, 443–445
Internet service provider (ISP), 426
Invitation, 284–286
ISP. *See* Internet service provider
Italic, 27, 190

J

Job, 20. *See also* Career
Journal, 159–160. *See also* In Your Journal

K

Keyboard, 4
    composing at, 106
    as input device, 6–7
Keyboarding, 34–141
Keys
    alphabetic, 36–105
    home, 37–41
    number and symbol, 107–131
    numeric keypad, 133–141
    See also specific keys
Keywords, 446

L

Label, 300
Landscape page orientation, 308
Language Arts Connection projects
    communications, 437–438
    database, 376, 378–380, 401–404
    spreadsheet, 337–338, 364
    word processing, 168–170, 202–204, 208–209, 247–248
Laptop computer, 5
Laser discs, 10
Laser printer, 8
Leaders. *See* Dot leaders
Left shift key, 63–65
Legend
    bar and line charts, 343
    pie chart, 349
Less than (<) symbol, 129
Letter
    formal, 223–228
    informal, 218–222
    memos and, 217–235
    personalizing form, 377
Letterhead, 284–286
Light pen, 7
Line chart, 343–344, 346–348
Line spacing, 147, 150
List
    bulleted, 171–172

    numbered, 173–174
List view, 369–370, 400
Log-off, 425

M

Macintosh computers, 12
Magnetic tape, 10
Mainframes, 3
Main topic
    chapter outline, 237
    class notes, 244
    presentation outline, 240
    report outline, 205
Managing e-mail messages, 435
Margin, 150, 168
Math Connection projects
    database, 391, 393
    spreadsheet, 299, 302, 319–322, 357–359
    word processing, 197–199, 231–233
Mathematical operators, 307
MAX function, 317
Measurement, 131
Memo, 229–235
Memory, 4
Microphone, 7
MIN function, 317
Minicomputers, 3
Minus sign (–), 130
Minutes (') symbol, 130
M key, 62, 64–65
MLA style, 161–165, 191–193
Modem, 9
Monitor, 4, 8–9, 46, 82
Mouse, 4, 6
Move, 31
    data, 318–319
Multipage report
    bound, 166–170
    in Building Your Portfolio project, 175–177
    with endnotes, 186–190
    with footer, 210–216
    with footnotes and quotations, 179–185
MLA style, 161–165
    outline, 205–209
    table of contents, 200–204
    See also Report
Multiple-field sort, 381–382

N

Navigating, 27–28, 147

Netiquette
    e-mail, 433
    Internet, 441–442
Netscape Navigator, 443
Network, 5
Network connections, 425–426
Newsgroup, 441–442
Newsletter, 290–293
Newspaper columns, 291
N key, 75–77
Normal text, 27
Notebook computer, 5
Nouns, 41
Number
    field, 392
    key (#), 116, 118–119
    as word or numeral, 111
    signs (#) in spreadsheet, 303
Numbered list, 173–174
Number and symbol keys, 107–131.
    See also specific keys
Numeric keypad, 133–141, 340
Num Lock key, 134

O

Object, 253, 257, 259
O'clock, 123
O key, 46, 48–49
One-page report, 145–154
On-line services, 426, 441
On-screen help, 33
Operating system software, 12
Operator, 307, 392–394
Optical discs, 10
Orphan, 161
Out box, e-mail, 432
Outline
    chapter, 237–239
    manually created, 206
    presentation, 240–243
    report, 205–209
    style feature, 205, 208
Output devices, 6, 8–9

P

p.m., 123
Page
    abbreviation for, 179
    orientation, 308
Paint feature, 278
Paragraph, 96
    indent feature, 181
    widows and orphans, 161
Paraphrasing, 179–180
Parenthesis

    left, 121–122
    right, 113
    in spreadsheet formula, 308
Password, 23–24, 54
Percent (%) key, 124, 126–127
Period
    in titles, 179
    key (.), 59–61
Personal applications, 236–249
Personal computers, 3
Personal stationery, 276–282
Pictures, 335–339. See also Clip art;
    Drawings; Graphics
Pie charts, 349–352
P key, 79–81
Plus sign (+), 128, 130–131
Pointing stick, 7
Portfolio, 249. See also Building Your
    Portfolio
Portrait page orientation, 308
Presentation outline, 240–243
Previewing documents, 29–31
Printer, 8–9
Printing, 29–31, 152
Print range, spreadsheet, 307–315
Privacy Act of 1974, 24
Private data, 23–24
Program. See Applications; Software
Pronouns, 41
Proofreaders' marks, 230
Proofreading, 147, 152, 233
Protect cells, 328–329
Public data, 23–24

Q

Q key, 74, 76–77
Question mark, 83
Quitting program, 26
Quotation marks
    in footnotes, 179
    in titles, 190
Quotations
    reports with, 179–185
    short and long, 180

R

Record, database, 369–370, 381–387
Reference software, 15
Relative cell referencing, 318
Report, 144–177
    database, 389–421
    folder, 42
    outline, 205–209
    with special features, 178–216
    title page, 155–158

    See also Multipage report
Return/Enter key. See Return key
Return address, 224–225
Return key, 38
Right shift key, 55–57
R key, 50, 52–53
Roman numerals, 130
Row, spreadsheet, 297–298, 328

S

Sabotage, 23
Sans serif font, 258
Satellites, 19
Save as command, 28
Saved search, 395–396
Saving
    database, 390
    files, 31–32
Scanner, 7
Science Connection projects
    database, 371–374, 387, 407
    integration, 361–362, 420
    Internet, 448–449, 451
    spreadsheet, 330–333, 350–352
    word processing, 175–177,
        181–185, 188–190, 214–216,
        239, 242–243
Screen, 8–9. See also Monitor
Scrolling, 37
Search, database, 384, 395–399
Search engine, 446
Seconds (") symbol, 130
Security passwords, 23–24
Selecting text, 31–32, 147
Sentence, 45, 59
Serif font, 258
Shareware, 22
Shouting, 431, 433
Side headings, 166–170, 175
Slash (/)
    with fractions, 131
    in Internet address, 443
    key, 83–85
Smiley, 431
Social Studies Connection projects
    database, 386, 396
    communications, 436, 439, 445,
        452–453
    integration, 418
    spreadsheet, 304–306, 310–315,
        345–348
    word processing, 147–149,
        163–165, 193, 196, 211–216
Software, 11–17

Index **465**

application, 13–17. *See also* Applications
   basics, 25–33
   unlicensed copies, 94
   virus-protection, 23, 62
Software piracy, 21
Software suites, 17
Sorting data, 328, 381–383
Source, MLA style, 161
Space bar, 38
Spacing
   after abbreviation, 59
   after colon, 63
   after exclamation point, 112
   after right parenthesis, 113
   after sentence, 59
   after word, 63
   for slashes, 83
Speakers, 4, 9
Speller, 32, 152
Spreadsheet, 13
   applications, 294–365
   charts, 343–352
   creating, 303–306
   enhancements, 334–354
   entering, editing, and formatting data on, 300–302
   exploring, 297–299
   fill commands, 323–327
   formulas and print range, 307–315
   frame, 360
   functions, copy, and move, 317–322
   integration, 360–365, 415–416
   structure, 328–333
   styles, 340–342
   what if analysis, 356–359
Stacking, 259
Standard business format, 150–154, 194–199
Star (*) key, 117–119
Starting software, 26
Stationery. *See* Personal stationery
Storage devices, 6, 9–10
Subject/verb agreement, 174
Subtitle, report, 150
Subtopics, 170
   chapter outline, 237
   class notes, 244
   presentation outline, 240
   report outline, 205
SUM function, 317
Supercomputer, 3
Switching windows, 292

Symbol keys, 107–131. *See also* specific keys
Symbols, special, 130

T

Tab key, 95–97
Table, 363, 417
Table of contents, 200–204
Tab set feature, 202
Technology
   issues, 18–24
   society and, 19
   See also Focus on Careers in Technology; Technology Connection project
Technology Connection projects
   communications, 428
   database, 388, 394, 398, 408, 411–412
   integration, 419
   spreadsheet, 324–327, 341–342
   word processing, 152–154, 157–158, 160, 174, 226v228
Telecommunication, 19. *See also* Communications
Telecomputing, 19
Telephone system, 19
Template
   certificate, 287–289
   database, 409–412
   defined, 285
   invitation, greeting card, or letterhead, 284–286
   newsletter, 290–293
Text field, 392
Text object, 257, 259
Thesaurus feature, 292
Title
   article, 179
   book, 179
   chapter outline, 237
   italics or quotation marks in, 190
   magazine, 179
   presentation outline, 240
   report, 145, 150, 155
   report outline, 205
   spreadsheet chart, 343
   table of contents, 200
Title page, 155–158, 175, 253–256
T key, 58, 60–61
Touchpad, 7
Touch screen, 7
Touch system, 36
Trackball, 6
Troublesome words, 204, 286

Typeface, 258

U

U key, 71–73
Underline, 27
Uniform Resource Locator (URL), 443–444
URL. *See* Uniform Resource Locator
User name, 430–431

V

Video game, 16
View display, 26
Views, database, 369–370
Viruses. *See* Computer viruses
V key, 78, 80–81

W

WAN. *See* Wide-area network
Web page, 443
Web site, 443
What if analysis, 356–359
Wide-area network, 5
Widow, 161
Windows software, 12
W key, 54, 56–57
Word processing
   applications, 142–249
   integration, 360–365, 417
   program, 13
   reports, 144–177
Words
   spacing after, 63
   troublesome, 204, 286
Word wrap, 37, 96
Works-cited list, 191
Worksheet. *See* Spreadsheet
Workstation, 4, 5
World Wide Web (WWW), 443, 446–447
Write-protect tabs, 23

X

X axis, 343
X key, 70, 72–73

Y

Y axis, 343
Y key, 87–89

Z

Z key, 86, 88–89
Zoom, 147

Photo Credits

Cover (t)John Henley, (l)Crown Studios, (r)Roger Ball/all of The Stock Market (b)Terra Forma™ copyright 1995, Andromeda Interactive Ltd., (bkgrd) file photo; **0** (l)Scott Cunningham, (r)Mark Burnett; **3** (tl)Intel, Inc., (bl)David Young/Tony Stone Images, (tr,br)courtesy IBM Corp.; **4** Aaron Haupt Photography; **5** Apple Computer Inc.; **6** (l)Aaron Haupt Photography, (r)KS Studios; **7** John Coletti/Stock Boston; **8** Rick Becker; **9** KS Studios; **10** (t)courtesy 3M Corp., (b)KS Studios; **12** Aaron Haupt Photography; **14** Michael M. Yamashita/Westlight; **15** Scott Cunningham; **16** Art Tilley/FPG Intl.; **19** Jim Cummins/FPG Intl.; **20** Stacy Pick/Stock Boston; **24** Steve Neidorf/The Image Bank; **30** Vikki Hart/The Image Bank; **32** Jon Feingersh/The Stock Market; **34** (c)Crown Studios, (others)Scott Cunningham; **49** Lynn M. Stone; **53** R. Pleasant/FPG Intl.; **61** Lawrence Migdale; **73** Elaine Shay; **85** Peter Menzel/Stock Boston; **99** John Coletti/Stock Boston; **103** Owen Franken/Stock Boston; **105** Michael Reagan/FPG Intl.; **106** Chuck Savage/The Stock Market; **119** Robert Fried/Stock Boston; **127** Richard Pasley/Stock Boston; **131** (l)Aaron Haupt Photography, (r)John Lund/Tony Stone Images; **132** (t)Chuck Savage/The Stock Market, (bl)John Henley/The Stock Market, (br)Charles Gupton/The Stock Market; **141** Peter Beck/The Stock Market; **142** (tl)Scott Cunningham, (bl,r)Crown Studios; **146** Michael Dwyer/Stock Boston; **151** Yvonne Hemsey/Gamma Liaison; **154** Aaron Haupt Photography; **156** (t)Doug Martin, (b)Steve Chen/Westlight; **163** (l)Robert Fried/Stock Boston, (r)Mark Burnett; **165** (l)Aaron Haupt Photography; (r)Paul Brown; **166** Rod Joslin; **172** Mark Burnett; **182, 186** NASA; **192** Franklin Viola/Comstock, Inc.; **201** Rhoda Sidney/Stock Boston; **207** (l) Paul Brown, (r)L. Schulman; **213** Michele Burgess/Stock Boston; **219** Lawrence Manning/Westlight; **225** Ariel Skelly/The Stock Market; **230** Scott Cunningham; **238** Rhoda Sidney/Stock Boston; **241** Bob Daemmrich/Stock Boston; **250** (t)Aaron Haupt Photography, (l,r)Scott Cunningham; **254** Life Images; **255** Mark Steinmentz; **257** Doug Martin; **260** Studiohio; **261** Ron Watts/Westlight; **262** Comstock Inc.; **264** Michael Heron/The Stock Market; **266** Brent Turner/BLT Productions; **267** Mark Burnett; **269** Doug Martin; **272** (l)Studiohio, (r)Aaron Haupt Photography; **273** Mark Burnett; **275** (l)David Frazier Photolibrary, (r)Aaron Haupt Photography; **276 through 280** Aaron Haupt Photography; **282** Diamond Rose Photography; **285** Charles Krebs/The Stock Market; **287 through 292** Doug Martin; **294** (l)Mark Burnett, (r)Scott Cunningham; **301** MAK-1; **302** Tim Davis/Photo Researchers; **311** (l)Bob Daemmrich/Stock Boston, (r)Stephen Webster; **313** MAK-1; **315** Skip Comer; **318** Stephen Frisch/Stock Boston; **320** MAK-1; **324** Andrew M. Levine/Photo Researchers; **326** James Wilson/Woodfin Camp & Assoc.; **328** Brent Turner; **329** Cosmo Condina/Tony Stone Images; **331** (t)Breck Kent, (b)David Dennis; **332** Johnny Johnson; **336** Young/Hoffhines; **339** MAK-1; **340** Peter Beck/The Stock Market; **341** David R. Frazier Photolibrary; **342** Harry Sieplinga, HMS Images/The Image Bank; **344** Corbis-Bettmann; **348** Life Images; **349** Peter Pearson/Tony Stone Images; **350** Gavin Hellier/Tony Stone Images; **353** Robert Isear/Photo Researchers; **362** Billy E. Barnes/Stock Boston; **363** Brent Turner; **364** Doug Martin; **365** Jon Feingersh/The Stock Market; **366** (l)Scott Cunningham, (r)Mark Burnett, (b)Crown Studios; **371** Michael Heron/The Stock Market; **373** Roger Ball/The Stock Market; **379** Randy Ury/The Stock Market; **381** Brent Turner/BLT Productions; **384, 385** Mark Burnett; **386** (l)A. Steffan, (r)Gregory K. Scott/Photo Researchers; **387** Doug Martin; **390** Elaine Shay; **393** Matt Meadows; **394** Doug Martin; **396** Mark Burnett; **397** Gabe Palmer/The Stock Market; **406** (l)Schaefer & Hill/Tony Stone Images, (r)Roger K. Burnard; **407** (l)Mark Steinmetz, (r)Neil G. McDaniel/Photo Researchers; **408** Mike Venables/The Stock Market; **409** Crown Studios; **411** Harry Sieplinga, HMS Images/The Image Bank; **412** Crown Studios; **414** Aaron Haupt Photography; **422** (t)Mark Burnett, (b)NASA; **425** David Young Wolff/Tony Stone Images; **426** Harry Sieplinga, HMS Images/The Image Bank; **427** Lawrence Migdale; **428** Ian Shaw/Tony Stone Images; **431** Elaine Shay; **432** (t)courtesy America Online Inc., (b)Rob Lewine/The Stock Market; **433** Rod Joslin; **434** Copyright 1997/America Online Inc. used with permission; **435** Peter Steiner/The Stock Market; **437** courtesy The White House; **438** Bernard Fuchs/Westlight; **439** Matt Meadows; **442** Chuck Savage/The Stock Market; **443** NASA; **445** Corbis-Bettmann; **448** NASA; **451** Frederick Myers/Tony Stone Images.

446, 447 Netscape Communications Corporation has not authorized, sponsored, or endorsed, or approved this publication and is not responsible for its content. Netscape and the Netscape Communications Corporation logos are trademarks and trade names of the Netscape Communications Corporation. All other product names and/or logos are trademarks of their respective owners.